CREATIVE COMMUNICATION

TEACHING THE LANGUAGE ARTS

CREATIVE COMMUNICATION
TEACHING THE LANGUAGE ARTS

Lillian M. Logan
and
Virgil G. Logan
Brandon University, Manitoba
Leona Paterson
Mount Royal College
Calgary, Alberta

McGRAW-HILL RYERSON LIMITED
Toronto
Montreal New York London Sydney Johannesburg
Mexico Panama Düsseldorf Singapore
Rio de Janeiro Kuala Lumpur New Delhi

CREATIVE COMMUNICATION: TEACHING THE LANGUAGE ARTS

ISBN 0-07-092672-7

Library of Congress Catalog Card Number: 74-39337

4 5 6 7 8 9 10 D-72 10 9 8 7 6 5 4

Printed and bound in Canada

To
Dr. Gladys Borchers
A great teacher
of
Creative Communication

Foreword

This textbook—*Creative Communication: Teaching the Language Arts*—paints with broad strokes the various components of an effective language arts program for today's elementary school child who is destined to be tomorrow's leader.

The ability to talk over problems, to sit around a conference table and discuss varied points of view, to settle difficulties by means of tongue and pen, not by bombs and guns, is the hallmark of civilized man. As the ability to communicate becomes increasingly significant in this technocratic, global age, schools must assume greater responsibility for releasing the child's language potential. It must cultivate his talents and improve his skills so that language becomes the vehicle for creative communication and self-realization.

An understanding of language arts as the dynamic central core of the child's experiences motivates the teacher to capitalize on the child's innate need for creative communication and makes it a powerful ally in teaching the language arts.

Key concepts in each specific discipline of listening, speaking, reading, and writing; their interrelatedness; the organization of relevant and meaningful learning experiences; and innovative strategies of teaching based on the findings of research and empirical evidence are explored with the reader.

Throughout the text the key role of the teacher in selecting, planning, organizing, developing, and evaluating learning experiences is measured against the aim of creative communication.

This text will have achieved its aim to the extent that the reader brings children and language together into a life-long relationship which has creativity as its means, involvement as its method, and creative communication as its goal.

Preface

The program in the language arts should provide more than a means of sharing experiences and influencing those with whom children come in contact. It should fulfill the need of the child to experiment, to create, to invent, and to communicate. The use of language, both as a tool for communication and as a medium for creative expression, should be a paramount concern to the teacher as he guides children in their learning experiences in listening, speaking, reading, and writing.

The teacher of tomorrow's adults must recognize the need for today's child to listen both creatively and critically, to speak both fluently and logically, to read both appreciatively and analytically, and to write both expressively and concisely.

Central to this book is the concept that creative communication, the goal of the language arts, is attained best through the nurture of each child's creative potential melded with the linguistic skills essential to his purpose. The aim of the book is to guide the prospective teacher and the experienced teacher alike in teaching the skills of communication and the arts of language. Although the elementary school cannot anticipate all the information and skills needed for coping with an uncertain future, it must provide the basic skills of communication and avenues for creative thinking and expression.

Out of the combined experience of some fifty years working in the language arts areas in the public schools and in colleges, the authors deal with principles and teaching strategies essential to success in teaching the arts of listening, speaking, reading, and writing. While guiding children through learning experiences in the discrete areas, emphasis is placed on the interrelatedness of the language arts. In harmony with the child's mode of learning language, his need of freedom to experiment, the necessity of guidance as he develops the disciplines of the language arts and encouragement as he uses the tools to develop his unique mode of creativity, this book is written. Literature assumes the role of the catalyst that moves the child to further creativity and esthetic experiences. The problem of evaluation as a continuing thread consistent with the concept of teaching the language arts in an environment in which the child is motivated to think, to experience, to create, to communicate, to express is examined from the developmental viewpoint of children's growth in language expression.

The authors have kept in mind the individual differences of children at each developmental level and have suggested a variety of activities from which the teacher can help the children choose in order to meet the needs, interests and abilities of each child.

In an environment which is language-oriented, the arts and skills of language merge and meet in creative communication.

Contents

Part Three: The Curriculum — Written Expression

Part Four: Reading and Literature

PART ONE
Toward Creative Communication

1

From Signals to Symbols

Creative communication—the task of the school and the right of the child—involves creativity in each of the language arts. As the child listens to learn, speaks to communicate, reads to discover, writes to share ideas, he is engaging in creative communication.

Logan and Logan

The ability to communicate creatively develops through utilizing both non-verbal and verbal forms of expression.

Every child has a right to an environment rich with language experiences, an environment designed to help him discover both the power of language and an avenue to creative expression. He has a right to experience the feeling of exhilaration and joy that comes when he has created an expression of his own—a poem, a story, an essay, the solution of a problem, an idea—and he is ready to share it with at least one other person. Although the child can complete a creative product, can think through and solve a problem, can come up with a new idea, the joy of creating is not complete until the product is shared, the idea communicated.

A seven-year-old expressed it this way. "I hear a voice. I have to say it to find out if that is what I want to write. If it is I can write it down or tell it to someone who listens." This is similar to the concept held by McLuhan that the content of writing is speech, just as the written word is the content of print. Speech involves thought—non-verbal language—as well as the verbal mode of expression. If one is asked, "What is the content of speech?" it is necessary to say, asserts McLuhan, "It is an actual process of thought, which is in itself non-verbal."[1]

Observe the delight of the ten-year-old when he discovers the precise word in the dictionary that expresses his exact meaning. His expression changes from puzzlement to elation. He is delighted by the creative effect he has achieved, but he is not satisfied until he has communicated the expression of his ideas.

From the earliest tentative efforts of creative communication this need to share is evident. After listening to the story "Karl's Wooden Horse," Jimmie went to the easel and painted a picture. When he finished he hurried over to his teacher. "Come and see Karl's wooden horse—his beautiful magic horse." His teacher came and looked and said with a smile, "You are an artist." Jimmie was content. He had communicated his idea to one who was ready to receive it. Later that day he was not quite so fortunate. Remembering the exhilarating experience of sharing his product with his teacher, he showed it to his mother who was waiting for him at the close of school. He held the picture up proudly. Mother looked at the picture and asked in bewilderment, "What in the world is *that*?" "It's Karl's wooden horse." His mother looked at him blankly. Jimmie crumpled the paper. His creative expression in non-verbal language had communicated to the teacher, but not to the mother.

Fortunately, the teacher understood that when a child is encouraged to share his communicative efforts he is motivated to continue in such endeavors. The child not only must *want* to communicate, but he must have someone to receive his communication. He will be willing to come out of his emotional shell and express his ideas spontaneously when he knows that they will be understood and appreciated.

The goal is to make it possible for each child to create through language just as surely as the artist creates with brush and palette, the sculptor with stone and chisel, the dancer through movement and rhythm, and the musician through harmony and tonal combinations. "Just as Michelangelo looked at a slab of marble and saw within it a figure to be released through his ability to chip away at the bonds which confined it, so the creative teacher looks at a child and comprehends the kinds of experiences needed to enable the child to release his capacity for learning what he needs to make . . . the language come alive for him."[2]

Non-verbal Communication

If the hypothetical "average person" is asked what is meant by communication, he will usually respond by telling you that it means talking to someone or reading what someone has written. If he probes a bit further, he will recall that he knew that his friend was despondent even though he hadn't talked to him, because of the way he walked into the office and sat at his desk. An investigation of how we learn about people and things reveals that a considerable share of our knowledge comes to us through non-verbal communication. We "read" a person's posture, we interpret the tone of his voice. We understand the slight shrug of the shoulders or the lift of an eyebrow. In other words, his actions often speak louder than his words and give us a clue to situations which mere words cannot express.

Non-verbal communication is not limited to the familiar use of the body as cues to meaning and mood. The musician is "sent" by his favorite performer; the lover of art finds his soul refreshed after a day in the museum; the mathematician and scientist read symbols that are incomprehensible to the layman, and understand what they mean.

We are becoming more fully aware of the variety and significance of non-verbal communication: gestures, facial expression, tactile contacts, and the immense range of signs, symbols, and signals by which messages are conveyed, ideas transmitted, and communication understood. Non-verbal communication may reinforce, weaken, or contradict the verbal mesage, just as the tone of voice may distort or negate what is being said. "What you are speaks so loudly that I can't hear what you say."

The extent to which gestures are useful in communicating is vividly brought to mind when one attempts to communicate in a foreign tongue via the telephone. Without the use of non-verbal cues, communication is well-nigh impossible—unless one is expert in the foreign language.

In dealing with those in the lower academic achievement ranks, it is especially important to provide for experiences in non-verbal behavior, giving students opportunity to "learn by observing, imitating, and behaving physically rather than verbally. The process of their language maturation may have to take its natural, if slower, course. In other words, we may have to let these [students] communicate in the classrooms in the most meaningful way they know for right now, with their bodies, and let the refinement of their verbal skills come in its own good time."[3] For other children, too, it is important to keep the channels of non-verbal communication open.

Most of the new programs use non-verbal experiences through physical expression and involvement, or through art, sculpture, or music. For the most part this involvement with the *non*-verbal is not *anti*-verbal or *anti*-intellectual. Non-verbal educational techniques are based on the obvious but little utilized fact that "a child learns most of his emotional response patterns at a very young age—before he can talk."[4] The child has learned to read non-verbal behavior long before he learns to read words. His knowledge of love, rejection, anger, and need comes not through the verbal mode but through the non-verbal manifestations—the flushed face, the tight mouth, the tense posture. When he begins to talk the words are "Mamma", "doggie", "see", words for things and actions, not feelings. It remains for the non-verbal experiences in kindergarten and the elementary school—dramatic play, pantomime, games, rhythms, and role playing—to provide a legitimate outlet for his feelings and his creativity.

Types of Non-verbal Communication

Visible or Sign Language

The only avenue through which the very young child expresses his creativity is in non-verbal communication. He is not bound by conformity to previous patterns of speech. He makes use of the tools he has to express himself. He communicates spontaneously with gestures long before he knows what words mean. At times he continues to use gestures as his sole means of communication, much to the disgust or dismay of the impatient parents. "Visible or sign language is older than the spoken word. It is more uniform. It is written more deeply into our organisms, and carries more basic meanings. We use spoken words for refined thought, but for broad, deep, basic meanings we use action. We are civilized, yes; but the eye is still quicker than the ear."[5]

Empathy: A Form of Non-verbal Communication

Empathy is the physical and emotional response to situations and ideas. It implies a "feeling in with". This feeling of empathy is the basis of the phenominal success of spectator sports. It explains the exhilaration experienced by the spectators as they empathize with muscles tensed, bodies forward, and hands clenched while they play the game with the team on the hockey rink, the football field, or the tennis court. Empathy is involved not only in sports but also in the arts. One is exhilerated by a hilarious comedy or exhausted by a tense tragedy.

Dance: A Refined Form of Non-verbal Communication

Dance is an imaginative, non-verbal language in which feelings and ideas are communicated through the organization of rhythm, movement, color, space, shape, form, and level. The ability of the dancer to transform subjective experiences into non-verbal, creative, visual language is often more effective in communicating thoughts and emotions than the more familiar verbal types of communication. The dancer interprets life as he views it. "For life is not an occasional affair, but a constant balance on the point of intercession where past and future meet."[6]

The core of the creative process lies in the ability to mold experience into creative forms that communicate the experience to another, to translate an idea, an impression into imaginative and at times non-verbal language. Communication of creative ideas in whatever form they take or whatever medium is used for the communication has a spiritual significance in that it releases within us forces that are universal.

An experiment was carried out by Hawkins which integrated dance and art with speech. Students were asked to interpret non-verbally poems selected by the instructor. Following the silent reading of the poems, they were encouraged to communicate the felt meanings through the use of drums, sticks, etc. Finally they were asked to communicate their interpretations through oral reading of the poems.

Many of the students, especially the academically poorer, seemed more interested in communicating through non-verbal physical activity such as striking sticks, beating drums, etc. than through the spoken word (verbal communication). "For many of them, *behaving* expressively seemed more fulfilling than *speaking* expressively."[7]

Verbal Communication

Human beings are difficult to understand merely through non-verbal forms of communication. What is needed for clearer understanding of the refinements of social behavior is verbal communication. It is the highest form of the meeting of minds. "We see, feel, and sense those aspects of the cosmos which our language habits predispose us to interpret. . . . The verbal symbol itself does not tell us what this behavior should be, but it has alerted us to observe both the verbal and nonverbal behavior of the individual. . . ."[8]

Verbal communication is the most refined means for stimulating thoughts, ideas, and concepts. The highest purpose of language is meaningful communication. When we listen we respond in terms of our experience. When we speak or write we share our ideas and experiences with others. We are communicating through verbal media. "Communication is the key that unlocks the mind and puts it in the service of society."[9]

"The ability to . . . express ideas clearly and succinctly, to listen courteously but critically, and to evaluate introspectively yet objectively is important in a democratic society. In fact it is to people who develop such skills, and who are able to get along with others, that we look for leadership."[10] The world in which we live is a verbal one. "Without words our imagination cannot retain distinct objects and their relations, but out of sight is out of mind. . . . The transformation of experience into concepts, . . . not the elaboration of symbols and signs, is the motive for language."[11]

By the time the child enters school, language is his most important activity. "He reaches out for language with a hunger that often exceeds his physical desire for food. Food he eats occasionally; speech is his ceaseless activity in waking moments."[12] We are not blessed with a birthright of vocabularies and syntaxes. Children must be provided with an environment in which they are stimulated and helped to communicate.

Stages in Child Language Development

Before a child speaks his first word—produces a verbal signal with an intended meaning—he normally goes through a series of stages in language acquisition. These stages overlap; the child enters into higher stages well before he has completed earlier stages. Each stage represents a degree of maturity in the cycle of development.

The Random Stage

The random stage is characterized as a pre-linguistic phase. Initially the child babbles and experiments with sounds, but the sounds are not language until he is able to communicate his needs and get the response he desires. He cries when he is left alone, or hungry, or wet, or just "because". Soon he learns the pleasure of making sounds other than those of crying. Near the sixth month he enters the stage of babbling. He now uses a variety of vowels and consonants that will lead to the development of language. During this stage, he utters a wide variety of sounds, many of which only a linguist can identify. Those that he finds most pleasant and which bring a satisfying response he keeps. The infant should be encouraged in this pre-lingual phase of development of speech. He is forming patterns for true speech. Other factors being equal, the happy child has a better opportunity for developing speech skills than the protesting, crying one.

The Jargon Stage

About six months later the child enters the next stage of speech development. He has apparently become entranced with the sounds that he hears and with the pure pleasure of making sounds. He repeats sounds that are pleasurable to him and imitates the melodic patterns of those who talk to him. He gains skill in making chosen sounds at will.

The Echolalia Stage

In the echolalia stage the child imitates the sounds he really hears. He tries consciously to repeat the sounds made by his mother and other adults. This is the true beginning of the child's native speech. Sounds that he has been making that are not given to him by adults tend to disappear. He retains only the sounds that bring response from the people on whom he depends.

The Stage of Expansion

By the time the child is two years of age he should be talking. He will have learned the names of people who are near him and of objects and actions that most concern him. The jargon that he uses to imitate adults' speech in his effort to capture their fluency is rapidly vanishing. Instead, he has become more concerned with communication with the adult world. This means that he must use the oral symbols that are meaningful to them. At first he uses mostly nouns, because these are usually the names of things he can see, feel, and hear. Sixty-five percent of the words used between thirteen and twenty-seven months are nouns. By the time he is three to four years of age, only twenty percent are nouns. At three years of age some children are using all varieties of complete English sentences. At four some children use word order and inflextional suffixes of adult speech.

The Stage of Structural Awareness

As the child develops his powers of perception and observation, he becomes interested in playing with words and making his own sentences. He uses groups of word, phrases, and sentences he hears others saying. He forms his own rules about putting words together, and acquires more precise meanings of words and phrases. He enjoys creating original utterances which he tries out on his friends and family. Because children at this stage tend to think more rapidly than they can speak, they must at times grope for words. Children need time to express their ideas; otherwise, they may resort to meaningless sounds, or prolong the initial sound until they are sure of the word. If pressured to hurry with their utterances, they may develop into stutterers.

The Stage of Automatic Response

By the time the child reaches the automatic stage of language development, his ability to think is greatly increased. This, in turn, provides him with greater language power. He tends to move from his individualistic attempts at communication to the communication patterns he finds in his community. Whatever his dialect, when he has reached the point of automatic control over it, it serves him as a means of communicating his ideas to the people in his environment and responding to children of his own age. The average child has reached the automatic stage of language by the time he begins kindergarten. He has internalized the basic grammar and usage of his home, neighborhood, and community.

It is well for adults to be aware of the sequence in which children develop sounds lest they expect them to perform beyond their capacity and maturity. The visibly-made sounds are the first to be found in the child's meaningful speech. The labials (lip sounds) p, b, m, and w are used in conjunction with the vowels that have been practiced during the jargon and echolalia stages. The next to appear are the front tongue consonants t, d, and n, followed by the back of the tongue consonants k, g, ng. The l and r sounds, which are more difficult, are comparatively late in developing. S, z, and sh are usually the last to appear.

The Creative Stage

The tendency of children to play with words, to create their own mode of communication is to be fostered in the elementary school. As they are encouraged to extend their boundaries and to reach beyond the given, as they push language beyond its conventional limits, they are in the stage of creative communication. Here they increase their skill in thinking both critically and creatively, their power in the use of metaphors and abstractions, their enjoyment in the self-expression afforded by the spoken and written word.

Initially, children are creative in language. However, not all retain this creativity. With encouragement many of the children in today's schools can become writers, storytellers, and oral interpreters of literature. Encouraging children to be original, spontaneous, vivid, and expressive in their communication, and rewarding them for their efforts requires that the teacher have an understanding of creative as well as critical thinking, intuitive as well as analytical thought, and creative problem solving as well as the scientific method. Emphasis on conformity in language in school or at home stifles not only expression but also thought. Language is more than a tool for communication; it is an avenue for creative expression. The acquisition of speech, the development of language, is a continuous process throughout the life of the individual.

The Parent's Role in the Child's Speech Development

The parent sets the stage for verbal communication in the early experiences with words. He helps the child to learn who he is and what he is; he helps him to see the difference between human beings and animals or insects, between the familiar and the strange, between things that are living and things that are not, between what is up and what is down, what is above and what is below. It takes time to help the child sort out things in his physical and social world, but it is through taking the time that the parent teaches the child to move from signals to symbols, from sounds to words, and from words to communication. As he discovers things in the world around him, the child needs helps from his parents to be sure the clues are right.[13]

Children have an inner drive as well as an inner disposition for discovering how the language works. This is indicated by the fact that no one consciously sets out to teach the rules of language to the young child. The child learning to speak requires the opportunity to play with language, to examine a large sample of language in his own way. He must be given the chance to be amazed at the vagaries of the language and to seek and find for himself the framework which words hold for him.

Armstrong points out, "Sometime in the second six months of his life the child says his first word, and from that time on, from a linguistic point of view, he never looks back. He listens and tries to imitate what he hears. He receives responses in the form of warm milk, dry diapers, and approval. He modifies his speech, listens again, adds words and structures, and when success seems obvious, a pattern of language becomes habitual."[14]

To the observer, the child's learning of language proceeds at the outset at an amazing rate. Three-year-olds are able to use an intuitive knowledge of the parts of speech as a first step in determining meaning. Preschool children are able to distinguish words which function as verbs and as particular and mass nouns. By the time they come to kindergarten and the first grade, they know how to use plural, tense, possessive, comparative, and superlative endings.

Brown and Bellugi[15] concluded that some children are so advanced in the language construction process that by three years of age they can produce all the major varieties of English simple sentences up to the length of eleven words.

Loban[16] found that by the time children come to school they know all the basic sentence patterns. O'Donnell[17] found that in first grade speech there were numerous increments in structures and functions that may reasonably be supposed to reflect syntactic control.

Motivating Language Development

Despite the child's natural capacity for language and his remarkable progress in this area in a few years time, the school still must assume considerable responsibility for language development. Children need help in making words serve their communication needs and do what they want them to do—namely, to express ideas clearly. In the attempt to move from sounds to words to communication, to express ideas clearly, children find that ideas lose some of their fuzziness and become clearer, more logical, and more concise. Thought and language are interrelated; language is "the handmaiden of thought".[18] Thought, however, also serves language. Every thought moves, grows and develops, fulfills a function, solves a problem. Verbalizing ideas is a way of refining them so that they become clearer and more precise.

Of interest to teachers in early childhood education is the research by Ursula Bellugi[19, 20] who studied the emergence of negation in the speech of the young child. First it appears that the child negates by beginning sentences with *no*, as in "No can do it" or No get jelly." Next the child positions *no, not, don't,* or *can't* in a sentence, but not always grammatically, as in "He not waking up." A new development is the appearance of multiple negation, with the child sprinkling several negations in one sentence, such as "No one didn't took it." Still later the questions appear. In the sentence "You understand, don't you?" "don't you" is a tag. Tag questions are quite involved, for here the child must make a decision about the affirmative and the negative forms. If the sentence is negative, the tag is affirmative; "He isn't here, is he?" If the sentence is affirmative, the tag is negative; "He's here, isn't he?"

Considering the vagaries of the English language, it is miraculous that children learn it even in the face of dramatic handicaps. "The grammar that they may acquire may not be the King's English, but even children from impoverished, disorganized homes know and use all parts of speech by the time they enter kindergarten. When a child says 'footses' for 'feet' he is revealing a knowledge of one of our rules for forming plurals. He is simply not aware of all the exceptions."[21]

Impressive as the child's language repertoire is when he comes to school, his language development is far from complete. Limited by experience, his understanding of the world around him is in need of clarification. Words are meaningless to him unless they represent aspects of real or vicarious experiences. He seeks and needs opportunities to verbalize, discuss, hypothesize, synthesize. Discussion, charts, creative stories, films, recordings, excursions, and every other possible means at the teacher's disposal must be enlisted to enlarge the child's linguistic frame of reference. Thus he will be able to bring meaning from his own experience in the real world to a wider variety of linguistic symbols when he confronts them in his progression up the educational ladder.

Keeping in mind the concept of the interrelatedness, the unity of the language arts, the responsible teacher will create a learning environment dedicated to the proposition that language competence is the basis for success in creative communication, and creative communication is the basis for success in living.

What is of utmost concern to the parent and teacher alike is the motivation that spurs the child to activity with words. Parents and teachers must realize that in order for the child to communicate effectively in a variety of communication situations he must use a variety of communication patterns.

> Even a very small child speaks differently to his friends than to his parents. He speaks in still other manners when addressing his baby brother, his teddy bear, his imaginary playmate. He also speaks differently to the same person under different circumstances. How he addresses his mother, for instance, is different during a meal than when they are playing together—and either of these situations can be varied still further by such factors as the child's immediate need to go to the bathroom, or his guilt over having recently stolen from the cookie jar.[22]

We are not blessed with a birthright of vocabularies and syntaxes. Children must be stimulated and helped to communicate. Without such help, without skill in verbal communication, today's children will be unprepared to meet the demands of living in tomorrow's world. The role of the various media of communication, international conferences, and world planning in modern society points up the need for developing communication skills and the arts of language in the classroom. Without ability to express himself creatively through language, the individual loses one avenue for attaining self-realization, an essential of every human being.

Unfortunately, "when a child comes to school he is too often told to sit down and to be quiet at a time when the right kind of talking is the key to successful learning. In the first place, . . . learning in school . . . is a social process; that is, children learn in the company of others."[23]

Interrelatedness of the Language Arts

The classic study of Loban[24] shows the interrelatedness of the language arts. He found that the group of children who were high in general language ability were also high in reading ability, while those who were low in general language ability were also low in reading ability, and that children who were proficient in oral language were also proficient in written language.

Burrows[25] also found that a close relationship exists between written and oral language, and that when writing was preceded by oral activities all forms of written communication improved.

Providing for Individual Differences

Children bring with them a wide range in their language equipment when they enter school. Linda, a five-year-old, was being interviewed by the school psychologist. The first part of the interview proceeded without incident. Cooperative, interested, and capable, she talked freely. When asked the question, "Why is it better to use brick than wood as a building material?" she answered, "We haven't yet established that it is better in terms of purpose, locality, and availability of materials."

A father reported reading *Mother Goose* to his four-year-old son.

> I started with "Tom, Tom, The Piper's Son." Right away he started interrupting. "Was Tom about my age? What is a piper? Was Tom's father poor? Is that why Tom stole the pig? If he was my age how did he carry a pig? If the pig was so small, how did it kill a goose? What's a calaboose?"
>
> Another father told of answering as best he could his seven-year-old son's questions about what things are made of. The next day he had a call from the second-grade teacher, complaining of Tommy's disruptive behavior. "I'm afraid he is being over-stimulated at home," she said. "When he came into class today he said, 'You're nothing but a bunch of molecules.' "[26]

In sharp contrast is the child who tugs at the teacher's dress and says plaintively. "Widy div me da wed waddon to pay wi" or calls for "Dwamma Doody" when he is upset. The teacher must be able to decipher the first plea as "Will you give me the red wagon to play with?" and the second as "Grandma Coodry".

Some children have had a stimulating environment and many experiences. They speak fluently and distinctly. Others have had a meager background, and know and speak only a few words. There are great individual differences in both the rate of learning and the level of language development. Children from language-oriented environments are definitely at an advantage when they enter school. Their language develops as a result of their interaction with their social and physical world. An only child who tends to associate largely with adults develops language faster than a child with brothers and sisters. Slowest of all are twins who tend to identify, associate with, and imitate each other and, therefore, have a minimum of linguistic contact with others. They may well have a language of their own which is difficult to decipher.

The physical world also has an impact on children's language development as they respond to the sensory experiences of looking, listening, tasting, smelling, and touching. The adult should keep in mind the words of Rachel Carson. "If a child is to keep alive his inborn sense of wonder without any such gift from the fairies, he needs the companionship of at least one adult who can share it, rediscovering with him the joy, excitement, and mystery of the world we live in."[27]

The amount of time and effort the teacher devotes to developing these skills of listening and speaking must be greatly increased if children are to be prepared to meet the challenges of communicating effectively and creatively. They will require many and varied guided learning experiences in listening, conversation, group discussion, reporting, storytelling, practicing the conventions of spoken English, and other speech activities. "Early neglect of oral language, overemphasis or premature emphasis on reading and writing, lack of experiences . . . interfere with the natural growth and development of language power and threaten success in reading and writing."[28]

Every teacher should be familiar with the variation in language development in a typical classroom. The following chart will serve as clues for the teacher as he seeks to provide for these differences.

The Child	*The Teacher*
Uses a dialect which is difficult for the teacher and peers to understand.	Accepts each child's language. Lets the child know he is interested in carrying on a conversation with him.
Is unable to communicate with classmates or teacher because of shyness or articulatory problems.	Helps each child to express his ideas orally. Plans opportunities for share and tell, planning, newstime, discussion and other opportunities for speaker-audience situations.
Has inadequate vocabulary.	Plans activities for concept development. Observes the child for special interests which may stimulate vocabulary development.
Is excellent at non-verbal communication. Uses actions, gestures, facial expressions and noises to communicate.	Plans opportunities which emphasize non-v e r b a l activities—pantomime, dramatization, rhythmic activity—to help the child gain confidence in something he does well.
Lacks confidence in ability to use oral communication.	Develops child's assurance by providing stimulating activities and exercises that ensure success in oral communication.
Learns and works at a slower pace than do others in the group.	Adapts instruction to individual and group needs. Builds self-chosen activities, flexibility, and individualization into the program.
Shows inability to listen to the teacher or other adults.	Encourages dialogue. Listens when the child talks to him. Intersperses verbal and non-verbal language. Provides child with interesting events to discuss. Gives direct instruction in listening.

Listens actively when *physical* response is required, a creative element is present, or when there is a visual aid as a focal point.	Plans listening games that require action rather than verbal response. Involves listeners in pantomime, refrains, rhythms. Makes provision for conversations, interaction between teacher-pupil and pupil-pupil.
Expresses himself more readily through dramatization because he becomes totally involved.	Encourages child to dramatize, improvise, use puppets for oral expression. Uses realia, pictures, stories, filmstrips and first-hand experiences to stimulate conversation and discussions.
Is hesitant about revealing personal fantasies and imaginative feelings and ideas.	Stimulates creative response to music, stories, poems. Involves child in creating dramatizations of familiar stories or of television characters and incidents.
Pursues individual interests which reveal his personal goals.	Challenges child to extend his interests. Helps him to plan ways of sharing his hobbies with the class.
Approaches problem solving creatively and uses materials and equipment imaginatively.	Rewards original ideas and solutions. Provides activities, equipment, and materials with which to work out solutions to problems. Allows time to share findings with group.
Learns language skills rapidly. Speaks fluently, reads at levels considerably above the other members of the group. Writes with skill and sensitivity.	Provides time for special activities which enable him to work at a chosen activity in depth.
Is happiest and most confident when permitted to engage in movement and physical activities.	Provides ample opportunity and time for pre-speech activities—running, jumping, skipping, dancing, balancing.
Has a background of self-initiated activities. Is ingenious in organizing play and dramatic activities.	Praises independence of thought, speech, action. Encourages creative use of time, ideas, and equipment.
Tells stories well, but is unable to converse about something that has happened to him.	Asks him to dictate a story about his *alter ego* and read it to the group. Invites him to tell it to the children at another time.

Can handle abstract ideas. Is able to see relationships, make classifications, draw inferences, hazard guesses, predict outcomes, formulate conclusions, make hypotheses and generalizations.	Poses problems and questions which trigger creative communication. Sets up situations which require the child to select, relate, explain, evaluate ideas and to make generalizations.
Has problems with articulation, sound substitutions, sound omissions, nonfluency, etc.	Accepts the child's problem. Provides a classroom free from tensions. Encourages him to excel in things he can do well. Makes use of speech improvement games for the whole class.
Has a foreign language background. Learns to speak English as a second language.	Praises the child for his added accomplishment. Helps him take pride in his heritage. Helps him understand the differences in sentence structure, stress, melody pattern, and idoms of English.

Within every classroom there are wide differences in children's development in language abilities, as in every other phase of their development. The influence of environment is a powerful one; so is the influence of heredity. The teacher's responsibility is to provide a program that takes the child where he is, recognizes his potential, capitalizes on his strengths, and stimulates his creative communication skills at a pace consistent with his potential. He recognizes individual differences in such linguistically-oriented areas as:

ability to comprehend and speak English

ability to listen

ability to use both non-verbal and verbal communication

desire and skill in verbalizing experiences and imaginings

size and richness of vocabulary

ability to deal with concepts

accuracy of concepts acquired

ability to use problem solving at a level appropriate for him

joy and satisfaction in expressing his ideas effectively and creatively

Because children develop and learn at different rates, they require different individualized as well as group instructional strategies, experiences, materials, and equipment. From the numerous learning experiences and activities the teacher provides to aid each child in achieving his maximum potential through language, the child will select those activities which have meaning for him. The response of thirty children to a single group experience often surprises a teacher with its rich possibilities for creative communication. The teacher who is sensitive to differences among children will adapt instruction, material, and motivation.

Concluding Statement

Both the acquisition and mastery of language are developmental processes. Children learn language first by articulating the meaningful bits of sounds linguists call phonemes, next by linking these phonemes into words, then by making whole sentences, and finally by expressing ideas in creative communication.

Children learn language by using it. They develop power in language through interacting both non-verbally and verbally with more mature speakers in their social environment. These mature speakers may be members of the family, teachers, or other adults. Interacting is more than listening to mature speakers. It means living in an environment in which there are exciting experiences as well as interested people who will listen to and converse with the children. The environment becomes an instrument or generator of change. The development of language is not automatic. It relies on experiences and opportunities for expression of ideas. There must be time for frequent, varied, and spontaneous talk, as well as planned and guided experiences in the daily program of the school. Through experiences in the social-physical environment the child learns to communicate in both non-verbal and verbal modes.

Growth in language is a developmental process. It depends not on motivation alone. Some form of interaction with the social and physical environment must occur. The teacher can become the catalyst who creates the environment that stimulates growth in every phase of the child's development in a language-oriented environment.

References

1. Marshall McLuhan, "The Medium Is the Message," in Joseph A. Devito (ed.), *Communication: Concepts and Processes,* Prentice-Hall, Inc., Englewood Cliffs, N.J., 1971, pp. 75-76.
2. Muriel Crosby, "Discovering the Art of the Language Arts," in *The Promise of English, 1970 Distinguished Lectures,* National Council of Teachers of English, Champaign, Ill., 1970, p. 31.
3. Robert B. Hawkins, "A Speech Program in an Experimental College for the Disadvantaged," *The Speech Teacher,* 18:118, March, 1969.
4. Terry Borton, "Reach, Touch, and Teach," *Saturday Review,* 52: 69, January 18, 1969.
5. William N. Brigance, *Speech: Its Techniques and Disciplines in a Free World,* 2nd ed., copyright 1961 by Appleton-Century-Crofts, Educational Division of Meredith Corporation, New York, p. 324.
6. C. W. Ceram, *Gods, Graves, and Scholars,* translated by E. B. Garside, Alfred A. Knopf, New York, 1952, p. 20.
7. Hawkins, *op. cit.*, pp. 115-9.
8. Emma Marie Birkmaier, "Modern Languages: Vehicle for the Humanities," *Educational Leadership,* 20:239, January, 1963.
9. Louis A. Fiegler, *Curriculum Planning for the Gifted,* Prentice-Hall, Inc., Englewood Cliffs, N.J., 1961, p. 43.

10. By permission from Lillian M. Logan and Virgil G. Logan, *Teaching the Elementary School Child,* Houghton Mifflin Company, Boston, 1961, p. 226.
11. Susanne K. Langer, *Philosophy in a New Key,* rev., The New American Library, New York, 1958, p. 113.
12. Harry R. Warfel, "Structural Linguistics and Composition," *College English,* 20:209, February, 1959.
13. See Margaret Mead, *Creative Life for Your Children,* Department of Health, Education, and Welfare, Office of Child Development, Washington, D.C., Children's Bureau Headliner Series, No. 1, 1970.
14. By permission of Robert D. Armstrong and W. J. Gage Limited, from *Education 6,* p. 57. Published by W. J. Gage Limited, reprinted by permission of Gage Educational Publishing Limited.
15. Roger W. Brown and Ursula Bellugi, "Three Processes in the Child's Acquisition of Syntax," *Harvard Educational Review,* 34:133, Spring, 1964.
16. Walter D. Loban, *The Language of Elementary School Children,* National Council of Teachers of English, Champaign, Ill. Research Report No. 1, 1963.
17. Roy C. O'Donnell, William J. Griffin, and Raymond C. Norris, *Syntax of Kindergarten and Elementary School Children: A Transformational Analysis,* National Council of Teachers of English, Champaign, Ill., Research Report No. 8, 1967, p. 93.
18. S. L. Vygotsky, *Thought and Language,* edited and translated by Eugenia Kaufman and Gertrude Vakar, The M.I.T. Press, Cambridge, Mass., 1962, p. 119.
19. Ursula Bellugi, "The Acquisition of the System of Negation in Children's Speech," unpublished doctoral dissertation, Harvard University, 1967.
20. Ursula Bellugi. See comprehension tests of linguistic competence; ERIC Center, National Laboratory for Early Childhood Education, Urbana, Ill.
21. Celia Stendler Lavatelli, "An Approach to Language Learning," in *Young Children,* National Association for the Education of Young Children, 24:368, September, 1969.
22. Robert W. Hopper, "Expanding the Notion of Competence: Implications for Elementary Speech Programs," *The Speech Teacher,* 20:30, January, 1971.
23. Armstrong, *op. cit.,* p. 9.
24. Loban, *op. cit.*
25. Alvina Burrows, quoted in Helen K. Mackintosh, *Children and Oral Language,* joint publication of ACEI, ASCD, IRA, and NCTE, 1964.
26. By permission, from "How We Discourage Creative Children," by John Kord Lagemann, *Redbook Magazine,* March, 1963. Copyright © 1963 by The McCall Publishing Company.
27. Rachel Carson, *The Sense of Wonder,* Harper and Row, New York, 1965, p. 44.
28. Miriam E. Wilt, "Using the Implications of Linguistics to Improve Teaching of the English Language in the Elementary School," in *Source Book on English Institutes for Elementary Teachers,* National Council of Teachers of English, Champaign, Ill., 1965, p. 93.

2

Creating the Environment for Communication

In each child there is a mind that can grow, an imagination that can stretch, and a spirit that can flower.

Muriel Crosby

Language and learning are synonymous. However, it is difficult for the child to learn language as creative communication unless the teacher deliberately organizes an environment which is language-oriented. To create such a climate it is essential to give opportunity for developing not only the cognitive, verbal, and technical powers of the child, but also the affective and creative powers as well. Learning experiences which contribute to the child's growing awareness, sense perception, imagination, emotional sensitivity, and bodily poise are essential.

The teacher who would provide a curriculum which is language-oriented must be fully aware of the need of the child to discover, to explore, to imagine, to create *and* to communicate in an environment in which communication is valued. In setting the stage for learning, the teacher will develop a curriculum which emphasizes the developmental nature of language as children naturally learn and utilize it. In other words, the teacher will provide a setting in which children are encouraged to listen, to speak, to use oral language to communicate ideas and feelings as a matrix for developing the written aspects of language, i.e., reading and writing.

The processes of discovering, exploring, creating, and communicating will be the core around which the content of the curriculum is developed. It is through language that the child sorts out and expresses his ideas about life. It is through language that he draws upon other curriculum areas or subjects to grow in self-knowledge, knowledge of others, and knowledge of his world.

Creating a setting for language acquisition requires the intelligent guidance of an insightful, knowledgeable, creative teacher. Such a teacher understands the importance of providing an environment in which listening, speaking, and communicating with children is an integral part of daily living and learning. To perceive clues from the environment, to know each child's background and needs, to understand relationships among the various communication skills, and yet to appreciate the specific, individual nature of the development of each child, and to look upon the goal of language development as creative communication is the responsibility of the teacher. The teacher should organize an environment in which a sound oral language program is the basis of the curriculum.

Activities should be provided which demand independent re-

search, self-initiated and self-directed projects, experimentation, and creative discovery. In such a setting the child is not being continuously evaluated by some external standard of which he has little understanding. Rather, he is guided in developing through discussion, problem solving, and creative thinking to assess increasingly his own work as he moves up the educational ladder.

As children develop competency in the skills essential to express their ideas, they will come to the place where the evaluation by another—peer or teacher—is merely an opportunity to share ideas and to evaluate one's self on the basis of one's best work. At what point an individual reaches this stage of maturity can be judged only on the basis of understanding the child himself. The effective teacher places a premium upon helping each child to build a healthy self-concept of his ability to communicate, and avoids use of denigrating labels and insistence upon one standard of English for all occasions.

What Research Tells Us About Environment and Oral Language Development

Some time ago Margaret Mead narrated a film that has become a classic for beginning students of anthropology. The film, *Four Families,* depicts four average, rural families, one in Japan, one in India, one in France, and one in Canada. Mead asserts that at birth children are capable of becoming one kind of person or another. The viewers are then guided through such daily family routines as bathing, eating, and evening recreation. She suggests that family patterns account for different life styles and character traits in each society.

We will consider here the two families in our Western civilization. In France, for example, she demonstrates that by the time infants have progressed through the oral and anal stages of development they will have become silent and stoic members of the household. They will become responsible for specific tasks assigned to do each day, as well as for the behavior parents expect of them. They are continually admonished by parents to be at their tasks and to follow orders.

In Canada, a Saskatchewan family is depicted as working as a much closer unit and participating in group activity much of the time. Children are rewarded when they assert themselves. The boy, in particular, is encouraged to assert himself, although the parents set the limits of how far the children can go. In the evening the living room becomes a "glorified play pen". The father gets involved only insofar as he introduces the small baby into the games of the older children. He picks up the toys after the children are in bed, while the mother completes the kitchen chores. Although the parents are still the dominant element in the family, vitally concerned about their children's care and welfare, the film narration makes it clear that this is a child-centered home where children are active and independent. Children express their feelings and interests through physical movement and manipulation of objects. They are taught to respect one another's rights, to exercise fair play, and not to show pain.

In relation to the effects of the school environment on oral language development, five aspects will be considered: (1) the influence of the speech and leadership habits of teachers on oral language growth, (2) the effect of language habits of peers on the development of children's language, (3) the effect of administrative organization on the social climate as a factor in oral language development, (4) the curricular and instructional practices conducive to oral language development, and (5) the effect of biological rhythms on communicative behavior.

The Teacher and Oral Language Development

A recent controversy in the field of child language acquisition has focused on the various effects of environmental language upon children's understanding and speech production.

> On the one side, psycholinguists have argued that the degree of complexity involved in children's comprehension and production depends primarily on biological/maturational processes; that is, a child's skill in comprehending and producing complex speech is a function of his age. The opposite view is that it is the syntactic complexity of environmental language (what the child hears) that has the greatest effect on the accuracy of his comprehending and on the complexity of his own speech production.[1]

In a study designed to further investigate the role of the syntactic complexity of environmental language in determining children's comprehending and producing ability, Hynes focused on the effects of certain conjoining rules on children's language skills. Among the findings which have implications for the elementary school teacher are the following.

1. Both increased age level *and* exposure to complex stimulus messages increased the complexity of the children's utterances.
2. The largest number of complex utterances occurred when age level was highest and when complex stimulus messages were used. Both the two variables (age and stimulus conditions) did not appear to interact.
3. Age is a crucial factor in children's language ability.
4. Factors related to psychological maturation appear more important than message-structure factors in determining the child's level of comprehension.
5. The main factor of comprehension lies within the child himself. As he grows, the child's attention span, memory capacity, vocabulary size, grammatical competence, and general sophistication in language use all increase.
6. Giving children complex structured messages, while not improving their comprehension performance, did not hinder their understanding to a significant extent.
7. Environmental language, however, seems to play a crucial role in production behavior. When given messages of some syntactic complexity, the children in the study—except the three-year-olds—produced messages that were relatively complex. Giving children complex structured messages actually increased the amount of complexity in their own produced utterances.

The implications for teachers, parents, and authors of children's books are clear. Apparently, it does little harm to speak to young children in relatively complex sentences. They comprehend or do not comprehend irrespective of message structure which involves constituent sentence connectives. In fact, speaking to children in adult-like structures may stimulate a preschool child to produce complex, adult-like structures himself. It seems of no benefit to simplify the language addressed to a child beyond the age of three by maintaining only kernal structures or simple sentences.

Not only does the teacher's speech pattern influence children's oral language development, the leadership pattern may have an even greater impact. Lippitt and White[2] in their classic study found that democratic leadership in the classroom encouraged discussion of personal matters, sharing of opinions, suggestions for group policy, and joking. On the other hand, the authoritarian pattern of leadership resulted in either apathetic withdrawal which hindered communication or aggressive resistance which inhibited the free flow of communication.

Flanders[3], Perkins[4], Polansky[5], and Whitehall[6] all indicate a relationship between the teacher's role of leadership and children's language development. Teachers who make use of such behaviors as praising, accepting, explaining, clarifying, and supporting will encourage children in expressing their ideas freely.

Randolph and Howe[7] describe an experimental elementary school program in California where the role of the teacher is away from that of an authority figure to that of a "helping person". There is a change in the classroom environment from competition to mutual support, and a change in the learner's self-concept that leads him to contribute instead of remaining quiet and fearing to express his ideas.

Certain types of leadership or teaching styles encourage oral communication; certain types inhibit it. Research is giving continued evidence of the significance of teacher behavior in the development of oral language.

School Peers' Effect on Language Development

At certain ages in a child's life, particularly around pre-puberty and adolescence, a child's peers assume a major role of importance in his behavior and development. The older the school child, the more influential his peers become and the less influential the role both teachers and parents play. McCarthy[8] suggests that little improvement in articulation can be expected if the peers of the adolescent are inarticulate. The peer influence is generally too strong for adults to have much lasting impact. Goldberg[9] points out that Puerto Rican children in metropolitan areas often prefer to speak Spanish instead of English to avoid being mistaken for Negroes by their peers.

The wise teacher will accept the child's language and linguistic development, and at the same time help him toward an understanding of the use of language appropriate to a specific situation or occasion. He will recognize the fact that children develop defensive behaviors in communication and perception. They defend themselves against communication stimuli by not listening, inadequate speech patterns, reading failure, or a combination of these. Children who are talked at by adults instead of being communicated with often refuse to listen. Some children do not speak clearly because they feel that what they say is unimportant, particularly if the adults in their environment ignore what they say. Rejecting a child's language is akin to rejecting the child. "If she [the teacher] communicates rejection, she can expect to have little if any impact on the child's desire to communicate in her presence."[10]

Diebold[11] lists as potential interference phenomena the language loyalty sentiments of the individuals and the acculturation pressures being applied.

Ervin-Tripp[12] lists possible areas of interference as beliefs about the appropriateness or ease of becoming bilingual and feelings of social identity. She reports Labov's observation that working-class boys in New York may have trouble learning speech features of their women teachers because of their hesitancy to identify with a teacher rather than with peers.

Wilson's[13] study shows the peer influence further, suggesting that even socio-economic status may be less important than standards set by peer groups. He found that ninety-three percent of the sons of professional men in predominantly upper-class schools reported that they wanted to go to college, while only sixty-four percent of the professional men's sons in lower-class schools wanted to go to college. Obviously, peer values have a strong influence on aspirations. It is likely that oral language will be affected by school peer values as much as other areas of development, particularly for the older child.

To perceive cues which will aid the teacher in understanding the effect of peer influence on the development of language in the child, the teacher should become aware of implications of socio-linguistic research. Labov[14] maintains, "The social situation is the most powerful determinant of verbal behavior." Evidence to support the hypothesis that linguistic variations are linked to social stratification, peer culture, ethnic, and situational differences in speech continues to mount and become available to those interested in the factors that influence oral language development.[15]

Administrative Organization

The effect of administrative organization limits or encourages language development. Studies of organization structures and practices such as non-grading, team teaching, open area, integrated day, ability grouping, and multi-age grouping shed some light on the relationship between administrative organization of the school and oral language growth.

Non-grading. Research on non-grading continues to be fraught with difficulties in delineation of specific instructional factors and specific achievement results. Carbone[16] compared 122 intermediate grade pupils who had attended non-graded primary with 122 pupils who had attended graded primary. Achievement test results showed that graded pupils scored slightly higher on language tests and other tests. However, further investigation showed that non-grading had not resulted in any major instructional changes, suggesting that teachers of non-graded groups were teaching as they had always taught, but less effectively.

Willajean Williams,[17] in a study to determine the relationship between organizational structure and pupil achievement, also concluded that there is little relationship between graded and non-graded school organization and pupil achievement; nor do the slower pupils profit more from the non-graded structure. However, it must be added that the ratio of pupil-teacher in the graded school was twenty-seven pupils per teacher and in the non-graded school, forty-five per teacher. Obviously, opportunity for oral language development was limited in the non-graded situation.

Multi-age grouping. Research on multi-age grouping has also resulted in inconclusive findings. Foshay[18] found that academic achievement of those who were grouped with children of various ages was not as high as that of those who were grouped in the usual way of children of the same age. However, Chase, Rewoldt, and Hamilton[19] reported that multi-age grouping resulted in a slightly higher achievement. Oral language achievement was not specifically measured in these investigations.

In a study by Holmes and Harvey,[20] the researchers came to the conclusion that an effective teacher, sensitive to children's individuality, influenced achievement more than any type of grouping arrangement.

Team teaching. Team teaching is the subject of a number of studies. Adams[21] reported especially favorable achievement for a fourth grade team. Perhaps the most important factor in team teaching as it relates to oral language development is the opportunity given the child to interact with a number of teachers, one of whom might well be able to stimulate his innate desire for communicating, thus developing his language skills.

Grannis[22] proposed an approach—the family model—in which a community school is characterized by free communication between adults and the young in the vicinity of the school. This would provide for a community seminar in which various age groups deal with all kinds of problems, an excellent means of encouraging oral language development. In this model, he sees both team teaching and non-grading as integral parts of the organization.

Hunter[23] makes it clear that the organizational plan of non-grading does not guarantee quality education. Rather, it is a plan that takes three important considerations into account: the teaching style that most successfully motivates, the peer group that most successfully stimulates, and the educational opportunities that most successfully advance the learning of each child.

In an attempt to organize a language arts curriculum guide for a non-graded system in terms of individual needs, a non-graded developmental approach was used. In this approach, the specific language skills, understandings, and activities proceeded from simple to complex in a spiral organization.[24]

Ability grouping. Research emphasizing oral language development in ability grouping is scarce. There is some evidence, in a study by Drews,[25] to show that "slow" students participated more actively when placed in homogenous groups than when placed in heterogenous groups, thus suggesting the possibility of greater oral language development in such an organization.

Torrance[26] found that "high creatives" grouped together for problem-solving sessions produced more ideas than those who were grouped with less creative peers.

Logan[27] reported similar findings. "High creative" students who were grouped together for problem-solving sessions produced more ideas, generated more creative ideas, and participated more freely than those who were grouped with less creative students.

The open area. Research of the open area schools gives clear evidence of the decisive influence of environment on human behavior. Eckhardt[28], in discussing the open plan of the Bryant Woods Neighborhood School in Columbia, Maryland, attributes the positive effect of such a plan to a number of factors: (1) bright color and light, (2) quiet effect of carpeting, (3) children's choice of independent or group study, and (4) total or partial open space. The open plan is still controversial and "is already undergoing a transformation away from total openness to an understanding that children also need some privacy. So the latest trend in school design, while retaining the open plan, seeks to give children secluded places to hide and retreat as well as to mingle."

Some 900 students attend the junior high school in North Kildonan, Manitoba. The school, which occupies about two acres of land, is built in concentric rings around a resource center and features team teacher preparation rooms, seminar rooms, large group theaters, and individual study areas. By withdrawing folding doors, it is possible to convert three large group instruction centers into a 350 seat theater-auditorium complete with stage and projection control center. The control center also serves as an instructional television center for the school division. Other facilities which the school provides include space for industrial arts, home economics, science, physical education, music, and art. It is possible for these and other areas to be isolated for public use.[29]

The open area or "Open-Space-Plan" reflects an attitude rather than mere physical arrangement, an approach to teaching rather than a facility, a restructuring of the curriculum and of teaching. It is a learning environment rather than an educational fad or frill.[30]

Openness assumes that the classroom is characterized by ease of communication, mutual supportiveness between teacher and student, relaxed and informal control, approachability, and a stimulating learning environment. Merely providing additional "space" will not of itself assure improved learning and creative communication. This approach implies the utilization of "space" in terms of commitment to provide optimal learning conditions for each child.

Whenever one finds such an environment, he is struck by the sense of industry, the free but mostly task-oriented verbal interaction between children, the changed role of the teacher who works with a small group or with an individual. Oral communication is an integral part of almost every activity. First and foremost, the teacher and other adults who create the environment listen actively and intently to the child, so that they really *hear* him, read him, respond to him, and communicate with him.

The integrated day. Although the integrated day is beginning to attract attention in this country, it has been the underlying concept of primary education in England for the last decade. A distinctive feature is the changed role of the teacher who moves from the central figure of responsibility for control to a facilitator of learning. This requires that the teacher must (1) become familiar with the various media of creative expression, (2) use the child's immediate interests and experiences as the starting point of the learning experiences, and (3) view creative communication as the core of the integrated day. Inherent within the concept is the expectation that children will communicate orally and in writing daily about their real experiences.

The teacher in the integrated day classroom capitalizes on his own sense of wonder, and urge to explore, discover, and create. Teachers see children's creative involvement as a means of communicating, extending self, and working out feelings.[31, 32, 33]

Pederson[34] reports on the integrated day experiment in North Dakota's schools. She terms the integrated day program a seamless curriculum organization. She states, "Children change their work at a time most convenient for them. Rigid division of the curriculum into subject matter areas has been eliminated by some teachers because it tends to interrupt the child's train of thought and may interfere with his solution to a problem."

In the final analysis, it must be remembered that for every one of the many possible forms of administrative organization, there is conclusive evidence to show that language growth and language performance "is directly related to the child's language environment, including the available language model, parent and/or teacher, and opportunity for language interaction, his comprehension strategies and objectives, and possibly maturation of his latent language structures."[35]

Curriculum and Instruction

Although administrative organization of the school influences to some degree the opportunities for the development of oral language, research indicates that curricular and instructional practices are considerably more influential. Teachers are becoming more and more aware of their role in oral language development, not merely to aid the child in his beginning reading, but to help him develop the skills that are the foundation of all linguistic skills—skills in oral language. These skills do not develop simply because the teacher wills them to, or even because he provides time for oral communication as a basis for the development of other linguistic skills.

There is evidence that a good curricular design provides for training in speech as an integrated part of the language growth of the student. Speech, when distinguished from oral English, is concerned with more than the specific goals of the English teacher. Speech is concerned with the development of significant skills and techniques. It has its own liberal content and its own responsibility to the total language development of students.

Speech growth is fostered through a well designed program involving: bodily movement, pantomime, dramatization, readers' theater, talks and speeches, group discussions, debate, parliamentary procedure, voice improvement exercises, oral interpretation, and choral reading in harmony with the developmental level of the students. The purpose of speech is to advance these skills to the end that each child develops them to serve him effectively as both a skill and an art in communication.

Pooley recommends that "teachers of English be strongly urged to secure additional training in speech . . . that they may work cooperatively with teachers of speech to develop integrated courses, or to develop parallel, coordinated speech courses which complement but do not duplicate the oral English activities."[36]

Lane[37] explored the use of the student congress as a means of improving the oral language skill of students. They were involved in researching, writing, and discussing bills to be presented in the speech classes. Such activity aids the student in developing a basic understanding of the need for discussion, evaluation, and analysis.

Communication and Biological Rhythms

Studies have shown a direct influence of biological rhythms upon communicative behavior as they affect the individual's ability to respond to stimuli. Some studies found that efficiency and the ability to manage stressful situations vary with time of day.[38]

The individual not only responds to rhythmic stimuli in the environment, he actively seeks out such stimuli so that he can record, select, sort, and amplify useful signals to be utilized for synchronization of his own biological rhythms.[39]

Speech patterns may reveal man's adaptation to an environment that he perceives as constantly alternating, rhythmic. Since some studies found that efficiency and the ability to manage stressful situations vary with the time of day, implications for the teacher of children who are developing in the language arts are that "any attempt to shape or modify communication behavior should take into consideration the influence of the individual's biological rhythms as they limit perception capacity."[40]

Communication is enhanced by presenting the message to the individual at the proper physiologic time, i.e., to structure stimuli to coincide with periods conducive to alertness. Every teacher has learned to recognize the signs that tell him that an individual or class is no longer listening. He must either make use of periods of time characterized by high efficiency potential or make compensational adaptation to periods lacking such potential. That one may examine the probability of the "internal clocks" which govern biological activity recurring in periods of about twenty-four hours is of significance. Research, investigating a possible oral drive cycle in man, shows a relationship between degrees of alertness and oral activity.[41]

Blake[42] reported that personality, body temperature, and time of day have been correlated experimentally. Introverts were found to perform better than extroverts in the early morning, and extroverts surpassed introverts in the afternoon. Such findings suggest that the time of day influences the effectiveness of communicative behavior.

Based on research Lane[43] concludes that "a knowledge of the relationship between endogenous rhythms and communication will provide a better understanding of how man's responses are initiated and sustained, from the point of view of both the speaker and the listener. Futher, the study of rhythmically-occurring phenomena may suggest new principles for analyzing environmental effects on communication, and new techniques and strategies for developing adaptive processes of speech."

Concluding Statement

The task of the modern educator is to nurture communication skills and arts of language in order to help each child reach his potential. In a culture that has tended to reward conformity and to convert the individual into a cog in a machine, it becomes the responsibility of the school to take the child where he is in his development of the communication skills. Through motivation, guidance, and direct teaching in a creative environment which is geared to the needs of each child, creative communication is nurtured. By placing high value on self-expression, independent thinking, the spirit of inquiry, learning through discovery, the school can, through its curriculum and creative teaching, fulfill its task.

The elementary school of the seventies is a new school for a new time. In an age when man first stepped on the moon and communicated with earthlings below, a new role for the teacher of the language arts and the skills of creative communication came into being.

The image of the silent, passive, compliant child as the ideal learner is being replaced by the image of the child who works and talks with others, who uses language creatively as the situation demands, who improves his self-image as he gains competency in thought and communication skills. An environment in which there are opportunities for expressing ideas is an essential part of the learning process.

References

1. Geraldine E. Hynes, "Effects of Complexity of Environmental Language on Children's Sentence Production and Understanding," *The Speech Teacher,* 20:121, March, 1971.
2. Ronald Lippitt and Ralph K. White, "An Experimental Study of Leadership and Group Life," in Eleanor E. Maccoby et al. (ed.), *Readings in Social Psychology,* Henry Holt, New York, 1958.
3. N. A. Flanders, "Teacher Influence, Pupil Attitudes, and Achievement," Manuscript of Research Monograph, University of Michigan, Ann Arbor, 1962.
4. H. V. Perkins, "The Effects of Social-Emotional Climate and Curriculum on Learning of Inservice Teachers," unpublished doctoral dissertation, University of Chicago, Chicago, 1949.
5. Lucy Polansky, "Group Social Climate and the Teacher's Supportiveness of Group Status Systems," *Journal of Educational Sociology,* 1954.
6. John Whitehall, "Mental Health, Teacher Education Research Project," *Journal of Teacher Education,* September, 1963. See also, John Whitehall, "The Development of a Technique for the Measurement of Social-Emotional Climate in the Classroom," *Journal of Experimental Education,* September, 1963.
7. N. Randolph and W. Howe, *Self-enhancing Education,* Stanford University Press, Palo Alto, Calif., 1966.
8. Dorothea McCarthy, "Language Disorder and Parent-Child Relationships," *Journal of Speech and Hearing Disorders,* 19:514-52, December, 1954.
9. Miriam Goldberg, "Factors Affecting Educational Attainment in Depressed Urban Areas," in A. Harry Passow (ed.), *Education in Depressed Areas,* Bureau of Publications Teachers College, Columbia University, New York, 1963.
10. Aaron Lipton, "Classroom Behavior: Messages from Children," *Elementary School Journal,* 71:224-261, February, 1971.
11. Richard A. Diebold, Jr., "The Consequences of Early Bilingualism in Cognitive Development and Personality Formation," paper prepared for symposium on "The Study of Personality," Rice University, Houston, Texas, 1966.
12. Susan Ervin-Tripp, "An Issei Learns English," *The Journal of Social Issues,* 23:78-90, April, 1967.

13. Alan B. Wilson, "Residential Segregation of Social Classes and Aspirations of High School Boys," *American Sociological Review*, 836-845, December, 1959.
14. William Labov, "The Logic of Nonstandard English," in Frederick Williams (ed.), *Language and Poverty: Perspectives on a Theme*, Markham Publishing Company, Chicago, 1970, p. 163.
15. David P. Butts, "Content and Teachers in Oral Language Acquisition: Means or Ends?", *Elementary English*, 48:295, March, 1971.
16. Robert F. Carbone, "A Comparison of Graded and Non-graded Elementary Schools," *Elementary School Journal*, 62:82-88, November, 1961.
17. Willajean Williams, "Academic Achievement in a Graded School and a Non-graded School," *Elementary School Journal*, 67:139, December, 1966.
18. Arthur W. Foshay, "Interage Grouping in the Elementary School," unpublished doctoral dissertation, Columbia University, New York, 1948.
19. E. Stanley Chase et al., "An Analysis of Some Effects of Multiple-Grade Grouping in an Elementary School," unpublished doctoral dissertation, University of Southern California, 1956.
20. D. Holmes and L. F. Harvey, "An Evaluation of Two Methods of Grouping," *Educational Research Bulletin*, 35:213-22, November, 1956.
21. A. S. Adams, "Operation Co-Teaching, Dateline: Oceano, California," *Elementary School Journal*, 62:203-212, January, 1962.
22. Joseph C. Grannis, "The School as Model of Society," in Paul W. F. Witt (ed.), *Technology and the Curriculum*, Teachers College Press, New York, 1968, pp. 103-22.
23. Madeline Hunter, "The Dimensions of Nongrading," *Elementary School Journal*, 65:25, 1964.
24. Helen D. Wolff et al., *Language Arts Curriculum Guide for the Model Developmental Reading School*, Report No. 3 DPSC-67-3407, 1967.
25. Elizabeth D. Drews, *The Effectiveness of Homogenous and Heterogenous Ability Grouping in Ninth Grade English Classes with Slow, Average, and Superior Students*, U.S. Department of Health, Education, and Welfare, Office of Education, Cooperative Research Program, Project No. 608, Government Printing Office, Washington, D.C., 1959.
26. E. Paul Torrance, *Guiding Creative Talent*, Prentice-Hall, Inc., Englewood Cliffs, N.J., 1962.
27. Lillian M. Logan, "Cross-National Research Proposals in Education," paper presented at Canadian Association of Professors of Education, University of Manitoba, May, 1970.
28. Wolf Von Eckhardt, "Life-style Education," *Saturday Review*, 54:64, April, 1971.
29. "The School in the Round," *Winnipeg Free Press*, October 30, 1968, p. 3.
30. Ezra Staples, "The Open-Space-Plan in Education," *Educational Leadership*, 28:458, February, 1971.
31. Allan Muskoff and Joy Moss, "An Integrated Day Workshop," *The Elementary School Journal* 71:319, March, 1971.
32. *Children and Their Primary Schools*, A Report on the Central Advisory Council for Education, vol. 1 and 2, Her Majesty's Stationery Office, London, 1967.
33. John Blackie, *Inside the Primary School*, Her Majesty's Stationery Office, London, 1967.
34. Clara A. Pederson, "New Day in North Dakota: Changing Teachers and Changing Schools," *Childhood Education*, 47:248, February, 1971.
35. Robert B. Rudell, "Language Acquisition and the Reading Process," paper presented at the International Reading Association Conference, Kansas City, Missouri, 1969. Published in Carole Masley Kirkton, NCTE ERIC Report, *Elementary English*, 48:410, March, 1971.
36. Robert C. Pooley, "Oral Communication in the English Curriculum," in Roger L. Cayer et al. (eds.), *Listening and Speaking in the English Classroom: A Book of Readings*, The Macmillan Company, New York, 1971, p. 20.

37. Gloria J. Lane, "The Use of the Student Congress as Valuable Classroom Activity," *The Speech Teacher,* 19:316, November, 1970.
38. J. Aschoff, "Human Circadian Rhythms in Activity, Body Temperature and Other Functions," A. H. Brown and F. G. Favorite (eds.), *Life Science and Space Research V,* Amsterdam, 1967, p. 172.
39. Marcel Monnier, *Functions of the Nervous Systems,* vol. 1, *General Physiology Autonomic Functions,* Amsterdam, 1968, p. 624.
40. Aschoff, *op. cit.,* p. 172.
41. Stanley Friedman and Charles Fisher, "On the Presence of Rhythmic, Diurnal, Oral Instinctual Drive Cycle in Man," *Journal of the American Psychoanalytic Association,* 15:341, 1967.
42. M. F. Blake, "Relationship Between Circadian Rhythm of Body Temperature and Introversion-Extroversion," *Nature,* 215:896, 1967.
43. LeRoy Lane, "Communicative Behavior and Biological Rhythms," *The Speech Teacher,* 20:29, January, 1971.

PART TWO

The Curriculum—Oral Communication

Prologue to the Creative Communications Curriculum

A creative communications curriculum is based on a three-pronged approach: (1) the fostering of creative ideas, (2) the development of the skills essential for the expression of those ideas, and (3) the integration of ideas and skills which results in creative communication.

In Part One creative communication was defined, non-verbal and verbal communication discussed, and the stage was set for creating an environment in which creative communication could flourish.

In Part Two the oral aspects of the language arts—listening and speaking—will be explored, with emphasis on planning, organizing, developing, and evaluating activities which motivate creative communication. The oral aspects of the language program will be seen as the foundation of all creative communication.

In Part Three the authors will build upon the oral foundation to develop the written aspects of language as creative communication.

In Part Four developmental reading will be viewed, not only as a process but as a key to the appreciation and enjoyment of literature in its various forms.

In planning, organizing, and developing activities which stimulate the child to creative expression and effective communication, basic principles are needed. Creative teachers are constantly on the alert to try new ways of teaching when information and knowledge point toward an improved curriculum. Curriculum decisions should be made on the basis of research findings as well as promising practices developed from experience and empirical evidence. The teacher who fails to use these sources effectively may be enticed to climb aboard an inappropriate bandwagon. There are those who always follow along like the folk song which says:

> Come along, children, come along,
> While de moon's shinin' bright, shinin' bright,
> Git on board, down de river float.

Fortunately, most teachers are looking for guidance in deciding which bandwagon to climb aboard. The following principles will serve as a basis for wise decision making in the creative communications program.

Principles Underlying the Language Arts Program

The development of the creative potential of every child should be the paramount concern in the language arts program. The development of the skills in various areas of the language are a necessary prologue to the maximum creative expression.

Language development is dependent upon experiences. An environment rich in both first hand and vicarious experiences contributes to language growth. Children will express their ideas freely and welcome suggestions for improving their skills when they have something interesting to express.

Language arts are an integral part of the daily curriculum, and must be given priority. Provision should be made for (1) integrating the language arts with other curriculum areas, (2) teaching each as a separate discipline, and (3) correlating them with other curriculum areas. The concepts of integration and correlation will be examined in the succeeding chapters. Language learning increases a child's competency in all areas of the curriculum. In turn, these areas provide motivation and content for language activities.

The language arts program should stimulate an increasing understanding of the forms, function, and structure of the English language. As children grow in their understanding of the structure of language, they will discover the relationships of linguistics to spelling, reading, and composition. The "wonder of words" which so intrigues the young child will not be lost as he progresses in the educational program. The fluid nature of the language, the varied ways of experimenting with words will open new doors.

Freedom in bodily movement leads to freedom in speech. A controlled body is essential to effective speech. Bodily movement, gestures, pantomime, and dramatic play afford a natural introduction to oral language. Not only does creative movement and dramatic play promote freedom in bodily action, it enhances the spoken word and reduces the inhibitions children feel in speech activities.

Oral language development is fundamental to the other language arts. Children who express themselves effectively in speech, whose oral language is above average, tend to exceed other children in reading ability as they progress through the elementary school. Written communication, too, is enhanced when it comes as the outgrowth of rich and frequent opportunities for speech activities. "As a child speaks, so shall he read" is no longer merely a truism.

Linguistic skills develop more effectively through a spiral curriculum design. The spiral curriculum affords opportunity to develop increasingly complex skills in language growth through recurring confrontation with language arts activities in harmony with the child's needs, abilities, interests, and educational level. It provides, too, for individual differences which must be met in every classroom.

The mechanics of expression—grammar, punctuation, spelling, and form—are most readily mastered in connection with the need at a specific time in the educational growth of the child. The close relationships of interest, need, and learning should guide the teacher in understanding motivation for learning certain skills. Skills should be taught in the context of meaningful and

purposeful activity applied to significant experiences. They sh(
when they can be put to immediate use in the learning activitie:
day. The spiral organization of the curriculum provides for the re
for language skills among the children at different educational lev
lenge to the teacher is to see that the skills are both refined and l
the child progresses along the educational ladder.

Standards for proficiency at each educational level should be determined. Levels of proficiency of skills should be determined by the staff of a particular school on the basis of the linguistic and cultural needs of the community. To demand the same level of proficiency in all sectors is out of harmony with what is known about child development, language learning, and social morés. To demand the same level of proficiency for each child within a classroom is also questionable in the light of child development and linguistic research.

Continuous evaluation is essential for growth in the skills of communication. Self-evaluation and teacher-evaluation are essential to growth in creative expression. The child must become skillful in evaluating his growth in terms of objectives and purposes cooperatively planned. Through guided experiences and participation in individual and group enterprises, the child will grow in his ability to evaluate his progress in terms of the objectives.

Language learning is imitative. The teacher must be a model for the child by speaking effectively and communicating clearly. The child tends to follow the model provided for him. However, the teacher must be aware that

> . . . in the daily linguistic experience of, say, the child of twelve, the interplay of language which goes on within the school during the five hours of formal instruction is by no means as extensive or as natural as the communication which takes place in the eight or nine hours which he spends on the playground and in the home. In some situations the classroom teacher, representing the principal cultured or quasi-cultured contact which the child encounters, may exercise a linguistic influence of considerable proportions.[1]

The content of language is culturally determined. Language acquisition is related to such factors as socio-economic background, amount and quality of spoken language in the models the child observes, the quantity and quality of parent-child dialogue, and opportunities provided for the expression of ideas. The home and school environments either enhance or hamper language growth.

Language facility is a developmental process. The acquisition of all aspects of language, oral and written, is developmental. Growth in effective communication rather than perfection is the goal of the creative communications program.

Guidelines for Language Arts Teachers[2]

In planning a language curriculum which meets the needs of today's child, one might well keep in mind the five basic concepts presented by James Squire at the International Conference on the English Language at York University, England, July, 1971.

1. Integration of learning experience within the individual learner is fundamental.

2. Defining the degree of classroom freedom required for optimum learning remains an urgent priority.

3. The complexity of the learning process suggests that the teacher's interaction with the learner should vary with the nature of the learning task.

4. Ways of satisfying individual needs of learners require continued experimentation with alternate patterns and approaches.

5. An educational system must both reflect and influence the society which it serves, and in a rapidly changing society education must be prepared for radical changes.

References

1. Albert Marckwardt, "Research Methods of the Linguist Which May Be Useful in Educational Research," *Research Design and the Teaching of English*, Proceedings of the San Francisco Conference, National Council of Teachers of English, Champaign, Ill., 1964, p. 50.

2. From address by James Squire, "Freedom and Control—The Scylla and Charybdis of Language Learning," York University, England, July 18, 1971. Dr. Squire was formerly the Executive Secretary of the National Council of Teachers of English.

3

Perceptive Listening

Nature gave us two ears and only one mouth so that we could listen twice as much as we speak.

Proverb

"To the school is assigned the task of releasing the individual's language potential, of cultivating his talents, of correcting his imperfections, and of developing in him an attitude favorable for future growth. Such an obligation carries with it the responsibility for developing effective communication." "Effective communication at home and abroad is the chief means by which men will find a way of living together around the world in harmony with our belief in the inherent dignity of man and the worth of the individual."[1]

There is no deeper craving of the human heart than the hunger for understanding. Prime Ministers, statesmen, teenagers, and children all suffer from a common complaint. They say, "No one understands me." To a great extent they are right. The cliché, "No man is an island" is in part true; each man is at least a peninsula connected to the mainland of humanity by the common bonds of education and communication.

Sojourner Truth was born in slavery. Because she was an alert child, she was sent to the plantation school to learn the rudiments of reading and writing so she could be a house slave. Many statesmen, the rich and the famous visited her owners. As she unobtrusively went about her duties she *listened*, observed, and learned. She was proud of her heritage as the descendent of a great African chief. She determined to gain her freedom and work for her people.

In the confusion of the Civil War she escaped to Washington. Here her untiring work among the escaping and freed slaves brought her into contact with President Lincoln. He recognized her great compassion and encouraged her to devote her life to bringing about a greater understanding between her race and those who had been their captors.

It was in the 1880's that she visited a university campus. By now Sojourner Truth had become a national figure. The students were eager to hear this former slave who had become the friend of statesmen. She was introduced, then stepped forward. She was a commanding figure as she stood before the students in her simple gray gown.

The notebooks snapped open and pencils were poised, ready to record every word that this great—but simple—woman uttered. She smiled, looked at them for a moment, then said, "Young men and ladies, will you put away your notebooks and pencils? If you listen with your pencils you will not remember what I have to say. If you will listen with your ears and hearts you will always remember Sojourner and what she told you about her people."

"That day," said one of the students who heard her, "was one of the most significant of my life. I learned the true importance of listening to understand and remember. After fifty years I can still recall much of her speech."

As pupils learn to listen to speeches, stories, poems, plays, or music, the teacher should be aware that their understanding is in direct proportion to the background that they bring to the experience and the concentration with which they listen. As they learn to listen, they will come to look upon listening as the other side of the coin of speaking. By early becoming aware of listening and speaking as related aspects of one process, children will simultaneously develop skills of listening and speaking. In developing listening skills in an environment where listening takes its place as a significant language art, the child learns not only to listen for enjoyment and for ideas, but also to observe the speaker's use of his voice, his articulation, and his poise. As he participates in meaningful listening-speaking activities, he becomes a creator of ideas, an appreciative listener, a more effective learner, and a discriminating critic. In a classroom in which the listening climate is structured for language learning as a creative process which requires mastery of skills, the teacher gives evidence that listening is the dominant means of sensory comprehension. Today's children listen much more than they read as a means of acquiring information, ideas, and attitudes. "For every fact which a student can trace to a book, there are many more that can be traced to the spoken word."[2]

In an era in which the spoken word is so vital, in which its significance is no longer questioned, the teacher of the language arts must give specific and systematic instruction in listening. Teaching of effective listening is based on:

an understanding of the nature of listening

a knowledge of formulating of objectives based on the concept of listening as a tool for learning

ability to apply the findings of research which have impiications for teaching children to listen

recognition of the factors which influence listening effectiveness

acquaintance with guides to effective listening

establishing purposes for listening

organization of activities which develop skills in listening for a specific purpose

ensuring balance in the listening program

self-evaluation techniques for the teacher

The Nature of Listening

Before we can formulate objectives for the teaching of perceptive listening, it is essential to get a clear understanding of the nature of listening as a tool, as a skill, as an art, as a process, as a response, and as a creative experience.

Listening as a Tool

"In listening," asserts Jacobs, "the individual hears familiar sound combinations to which, in terms of his experience, he brings meaning and from which he simultaneously takes meaning, and acquires, thereby, sources for reaction, interpretation, and knowing."[3]

Listening as a Communication Skill

Listening as a communication skill involving both aural and oral skills is defined by Nichols as a dual-phased phenoma. "Obviously hearing and listening are not identical. They are most clearly perceived as two distinguishable phases, the hearing of sound and the interpreting of sound, of a total process usually called aural assimilation. If the first phase, hearing, is identified as the perception of sound only, then it is the second phase of the process—the attachment of meaning to the aural symbols perceived—which has come to be largely accepted as the definition of listening."[4]

Listening as an Art

Barbara views the qualities involved in listening as an art when he states: "If we are to learn how to listen well, we must proceed as we would in learning any other art such as music, painting, architecture or acting. The art of listening requires discipline, concentration, active participation, comprehension and evaluation."[5]

Neville also holds the view that "listening is an art, and must be practiced as an art; therefore, the techniques and skills of the art must be understood and practiced before the speaker-listener experience can be fully realized."[6]

Listening as a Process

Listening is a process of complex skills which must be taught in such a way that the end result appears to be a discreet skill. Irwin and Rosenberger delineate four steps in the listening process: (1) hearing, (2) understanding, (3) evaluating, and (4) responding. According to these authorities, ". . . first you *hear* a series of sounds which you call words. Second, you *understand* the meaning of those words in the context in which you hear them. Third, you *evaluate* . . . the meaning to decide whether you accept or reject the idea expressed. Fourth, you *respond*—that is, you convey your reaction to the meaning by bodily movement, facial expression, or audible response to a great or small degree, as the occasion warrants."[7]

Listening as Response

Fest and Cobin stress the response element as a major factor in listening. "Most frequently the speaker's purpose is to secure a response from the listener, ... For the listener to respond effectively he must have a sensory adequacy, interest that goes beyond the most elementary attention, some capacity for interpretation of the message, and both a willingness and a capacity to change relationships."[8]

Irwin and Rosenberger suggest that perceptive listening requires that the individual receive a message intact, understand its full meaning, bounce it back and forth in his mind before deciding whether to hold on to it or throw it away, and convey to the speaker some suggestion of his response.[9]

Listening as Creative Experience

Listening as creative experience goes beyond the other types of listening. Such listening assumes total involvement in an experience that is tinged with pleasure, delight, and satisfaction. Alice Duer Miller held that one could listen ". . . like a blank wall or like a splendid auditorium where every sound comes back fuller and richer. The best listener I ever knew," she states, "was the late Clarence Day, author of *Life with Father*. He laughed, he groaned, he roared; his eyes shone with surprise and delight."[10]

From this cursory examination of the nature of listening, it is evident that listening is a complex process in itself which must be taught as a discrete skill. Underlying the objectives of listening is the concept that the all-important, central contribution to be made by effective listening to the child's growth and development is that of making learning easier, more pleasant, and more economic.

As the child listens to learn, listens to enjoy, listens to evaluate, listens to discriminate sounds, he will be perfecting skills which will enable him to use listening not only as a tool for effective communication, but as an avenue for creative expression and self-fulfillment.

Objectives for Teaching Listening

Creative communication requires the cooperation of at least two individuals: a speaker and a listener, or a writer and a reader. Expressing so that another understands what one feels, believes, or observes is the core of communication. A well organized program will be evaluated on the quality of the objectives to be achieved and the extent to which the objectives are realized in terms of progress toward the predetermined goals.

Basically, educators concern themselves with three levels of definition of objectives: (1) over-all school objectives, (2) content area objectives, and (3) specific objectives for the teacher and specific behavioral objectives for the child. Objectives are goals which provide direction, define scope, and provide the base for evaluation of the instructional program.

Over-all school objectives. Over-all school objectives involve the development of:

- concerned citizenship
- ability to communicate
- sound physical and mental health
- intellectual excellence
- creative potential
- self-fulfillment of the individual

Content area objectives. Content area objectives are concerned with the major aims to be achieved in each of the content areas. For example, in the content area of the language arts the objectives could center around:

knowledge and history of the language

development of skill in listening, speaking, reading, writing, problem-solving processes, appreciation of literature

Specific instructional objectives. Specific instructional objectives are the purposes which guide the selection and development of learning activities (teacher selected). They reflect the *teacher's* ability to identify, select, and interpret the over-all objectives of the school as well as the content area objectives.

Specific behavioral objectives. Specific behavioral objectives are stated in terms of the specific behavior to be demonstrated by the *students,* the learning to be achieved, and the conditions under which they are to be realized.

Using listening as an example these objectives could be delineated as follows.

Over-all Objective: To increase language competency in order to become a more literate and effective citizen.

Content Area Objective: To understand the interrelationships among language, listening, speaking, thought, and behavior.

Specific Instructional Objective: To guide the child through direct instruction to develop respect for listening as a medium of learning.

Specific Behavioral Objective: To listen for the purpose of evaluating a speaker in terms of his ability to hold to a topic.

Specific Instructional Objectives

Because teachers are closely involved in the development of specific instructional objectives, these will be examined in greater detail. Minimal specific instructional objectives the teacher keeps in mind in planning and developing learning activities for listening are to help the student:

gain an appreciation of the significance of listening in the communication process

develop a respect for listening as a medium of learning

develop basic skills, concepts, and attitudes which contribute to perceptive listening

progress toward improvement of listening habits

select the appropriate purpose for listening in a specific situation

distinguish between hearing and listening

develop an awareness of and ability to evaluate propaganda devices used to influence the listener

Specific Behavioral Objectives

Specific behavioral objectives are the other side of the coin of specific instructional objectives. They focus on the child and his behavior in a given situation.

They provide meaningful activities in which children are directed to listen for specific purposes. Among these purposes are to:

listen to learn

listen to enjoy

listen to evaluate

listen to appreciate

listen to communicate ideas and/or feelings

listen to discriminate sounds

listen to solve problems creatively or analytically

In the diagram below the reader is presented with examples demonstrating the relationship between specific instructional (teacher) objectives and specific behavioral (child) objectives.

Specific Instructional Objective	*Specific Behavioral Objective*
To help the child listen to learn to: follow directions, give explanations, understand information presented by the teacher or resource person.	Given a set of directions concerning the day's activities, children should be able to recall directions given for their safety standards for playground behavior, fire drill, and/or cafeteria rules. They will be expected to explain to another student basic rules which govern these procedures. Given an opportunity to listen to the teacher read a story or excerpt from an article, the children should be able to answer questions pertaining to the story. These may be placed on the chalkboard. Evaluation will be based on the extent to which the children are able to answer the questions. After listening to a guest speaker, the children will be asked to formulate questions which they will put to the speaker at the conclusion of the talk. Evaluation will be based on the relevancy of the questions to the topic presented.
To help the child listen for enjoyment.	Given an opportunity to listen to a story read by the teacher, each child will select the episode which most appeals to him and illustrate it in an art medium of his choice. Any child who creates, regardless of the quality of the finished product, will be considered as achieving the objective.
To help the child listen to evaluate.	After listening to a guest speaker, the child will be asked to evaluate the presentation in terms of previously selected criteria.
To help the child listen to appreciate.	Given a poem for choral speaking, half the class will participate actively in the speaking, while the other half will be asked to listen and make suggestions for improving the passage or a particular line. At the conclusion of the reading the group reverses roles. A suggestion for improvement of the choral reading constitutes succesful achievement.

Specific Instructional Objective	*Specific Behaviora.*
To help the child listen to communicate ideas.	Given an opportunity to take a field trip port, or nature safari, the child will cor and/or findings to the other members of th time or listening-speaking time. To engage logue concerning the activity will be conside ...ieve-ment. To give a formal summary of the reacti ...e class at a later time will be considered exceptional behavi .
To help the child listen to communicate feelings.	After listening to a recording of Debussey's *Claire de Lune* or Grieg's "In the Hall of the Mountain King" from the *Peer Gynt Suite*, the student will communicate his feelings with a creative art media —drama, music, movement, poetry, and/or a visual art form. Evaluation is based on his willingness to communicate feelings via a creative medium.
To help the child listen to discriminate and to improve perception of speech sounds.	Given the opportunity to play "Banking", the child listens to discriminate a specific sound or sounds dictated by the teacher. The evaluation is based on the ability of the child to identify *and* pronounce the sound, syllable or word beginning with a specific sound selected. Play money, colored discs, or chips may be used to reward the child who is able to identify and pronounce the sound correctly in isolation, nonsense syllable, or in initial, medial, or terminal position. If he fails to identify the sound (but not necessarily make it), he forfeits his turn, or pays the teacher from the "roll" or "stack" he has.
To help the child listen to solve problems creatively or analytically.	Given a situation which requires an analytical or creative solution, the child will strive to find a solution in his unique way. For example, the teacher may present the following problem: "Can you with one symbol turn IX into the number 6?" Solution: The first assumption is that this is a problem in Roman numerals. Not so. After several attempts some child should come up with the simple answer—IX become SIX. Given the following story by the teacher, the child will be asked to answer a question at the end of the story. "A man went for a walk one day and met a friend he had not seen or heard from in ten years. Following a brief exchange of greetings the man inquired, "Is this your little girl? The friend replied, "Yes, I was married about six years ago." The man asked the child, "What is your name?" She replied, "Same as my Mommy's." "Oh," said the man, "then it must be Margaret." Question: If the man didn't know whom his friend had married, how could he know the child's name? Solution: The friend in the story is the mother of the child. The creative listening motivates the listener to discard the obvious and select the unusual solution.

.r examination of levels of definition of types of objectives in ogram points to the need for establishing criteria for writing and . ese guides in the program. Objectives will serve the teacher and .ıke as facilitators of learning if certain questions are kept in mind.

1. Did I limit the number of objectives to be achieved?
2. Did I provide for both maximum and minimum achievement in order to make successful attainment possible?
3. Did I establish objectives on the basis of abilities of the students in the class?
4. Did I see that objectives are relevant to the area of learning?
5. Did I allow enough time for the achievement of the objectives?
6. Did I base the evaluation on the objectives identified and selected?
7. Did I ask myself this question, "Is this objective worth achieving?"
8. Have I stated the objective behaviorally so that every student knows what he is expected to do?
9. Do I see the relationship between my instructional objectives and the behavioral objectives stated for the children?

If the answer is yes to the majority of the above questions, the objectives as identified, selected, and implemented through activities should have value for the student and should contain within the statement the specific learning to be achieved, the basis for the evaluation, and the promise of successful attainment.

What Research Tells Us About Listening

What we know and what we practice in education do not always go hand in hand. What we know about listening can be of great value to the classroom teacher. However, until the research is taken off the library shelves and made available to the elementary teachers, it will be as valueless as it has been in the past. One earmark of the effective teacher is the interest he takes in research findings.

As early as 1928, Rankin found that the amount of time devoted to the language arts is inversely related to their social utility in human affairs. He found that our daily communication time is divided in this manner: 70 percent of our waking day is spent in verbal communication. Of this communication time, 45 percent is spent listening, 30 percent in speaking, 16 percent in reading, and 9 percent in writing.[11]

In spite of this finding, schools went on teaching children to read, teaching children to write, and occasionally teaching children to speak. Instruction in listening was limited to the admonition, "Put your feet on the floor, fold your hands, sit up straight, and listen."

The last thirty years have brought an increased interest in listening as one of the language arts. Goldstein[12] in 1940 completed a significant study from which two important observations emerged. First, that a person can listen to speech at a rate of more than three times that at which he normally hears it, without loss of comprehension, and second, that schools have overlooked a very important phase of the child's educational development—that of teaching youngsters how to listen. Shortly thereafter Hubbel published a book in which he stated "without equivocation 98 percent of all man learns in a lifetime he learns through his eyes or through his ears."[13]

As recently as 1948 Nichols discovered that only three experimental scientific researches had been published in the area of listening comprehension as compared with over 3,000 scientific studies in the parallel learning medium of reading comprehension.

However, the decade between 1950 and 1960 saw a dramatic increase in interest in listening. Today leading universities not only teach listening, they are at last carrying on graduate research in this field. Training in listening in the schools receives steady support from the National Council of Teachers of English and the Speech Association of America. Their help in preparing language arts guides is considerable. "Typically, these guides give equal emphasis to the four communication skills of reading, writing, speaking and listening."[14]

In 1950 Wilt made a significant study of the listening time of elementary school children and found that they were expected to listen 57.5 percent of the time they were in the classroom, but were given no systematic listening instruction. The following chart shows that out of a five-hour day children were listening more than two and one half hours. The distribution of listening time has implications for the classroom teacher.

Distribution of Listening Time[15]
(Children listening to)

		%
a.	Teacher-talk	33.0
b.	Teacher-read	3.5
c.	Teacher-child conversation	6.0
d.	Questions-answers	14.5
e.	Child-talk	6.0
f.	Child-read	9.5
g.	Child-child conversation	6.5
h.	Group discussion	6.0
i.	Dramatization	—
j.	Radio talk	7.0
k.	Sound film	—
l.	Choric activities	1.0
m.	Public address system	—
n.	Singing	7.0

Most significant in the implications for the classroom teacher is the recommendation that "a wide variety of listening experiences should be introduced into classrooms if children are to learn to adapt the kind of listening they do to that type which will best serve the purpose of the activity."[16]

Hogan[17] reported superior gains made by an experimental group over a six-week period of listening to readings, radio programs, sound motion pictures, individual and group reports, discussions of standards of listening, and differentiating between fact and opinion in radio advertising.

Edgar[18] used two matched groups of fourth, fifth, and sixth grade children in which the experimental group used ten half-hour recorded lessons and the control group read the same material and answered the same questions. Analogy, exposition, vocabulary practice, and the "story" approach were used.

On a post-test eight weeks after the pre-test Edgar found that significant gains were evident in listening in all methods, but that the analogies seemed to be the most effective of the devices used.

Devine[19] used two matched groups of ninth graders in an effort to improve critical listening abilities. He found a significant gain by the experimental group in recognizing the bias of a speaker, determining the competence of a speaker, distinguishing between opinion and fact, and discriminating between report and emotive language.

Lundsteen[20], in a study involving 263 fifth and sixth grade students, found that they gave evidence of the existence of critical listening abilities as distinct from general listening ability and verbal fluency. Through factor analysis the following four components of critical listening ability were revealed: (1) general analysis and inference, (2) reasons for fallacies in arguments, (3) value judgments regarding propaganda, and (4) factual judgments of arguments.

On the assumption that there may be a constellation of interrelated listening abilities and that critical listening may be included in the constellation, Lundsteen later carried on an experiment in critical listening designed to identify, define, teach, and test certain abilities in critical listening. Working again with fifth and sixth grade students from families of middle to high socioeconomic levels, the pupils in the experimental group were taught two lessons a week of forty minutes each. During the first lesson of the week they developed concepts in critical listening; the second lesson enriched the learnings and provided further practice. The content included three major areas or abilities: identification of the speaker's purpose, analysis and judgment of propaganda, and analysis and judgment of arguments. Applications of the study suggest that "the content, the concepts, the processes, and the abilities in critical listening appear to be amenable to empirical analysis and can be improved by practice."[21]

In a study involving fifth grade students, Trivette[22] reports that when specific training was given in listening for main ideas, details, and inferences, not only were gains in these skills significant, but other skills, such as getting word meaning and following directions, also showed improvement.

In another study involving fifth graders, Canfield[23] compared three groups. One experimental group received direct instruction and practice in listening for main ideas, important details, opinions, relevant and irrelevant details, and transitional phrases; a second experimental group received indirect instruction by listening to selections and discussing their content; the third group, a control group, received only the usual language arts program. The direct instruction group made the most significant gains, and the control group showed no significant gains.

In a study involving eighth grade students, a series of taped lessons designed to improve both listening and reading skills was used. The experimental group showed a significant gain in listening, reading, and English skills as measured by standardized tests. Especially outstanding gains were made in following directions in both listening and reading.[24]

In a study at the secondary level which failed to reveal any significant difference in results in listening scores after direct listening instruction, Meyer suggested that "something is amiss with the way we teach listening improvement or with the way we purport to measure it. . . . We may be on the wrong track in both efforts, teaching as well as measurement."[25]

In an attempt to discover the relationship between personality and listening, Kelley[26] found that selected personality traits, notably emotional stability, were characteristic of the good listener. Jackson[27] concurred with the relationship between listening and personality, suggesting that the ability to use listening skills (perceptive listening) may be directly affected by an individual's adjustment. Ross,[28] in a similar study, concluded that good listeners are better adjusted personally and socially than poor listeners.

Winter[29] found significant relationships between such language skills as spelling, usage, word study skills, and mechanics of punctuation and capitalization. These findings further suggest the importance of listening skills as they affect such learnings to an appreciable degree.

Norwich[30] reported improvement in listening skills of children in grades four to six as a result of a career development program which emphasized walking tours, bus trips, visits to business establishments, guest speakers, and many physically-oriented activities. The role of the guest speakers was highly significant in listening improvement. Winter explained this factor by pointing out that "since the speaker is not a teacher but an unfamiliar figure, the children listen to him. Since the teacher has primed the children for the visit with vocabulary and discussion, they ask questions."[31]

Brooks and Wulftange[32] found that interest in the materials presented and the personality of the speaker affected listening comprehension. Furbay[33] learned that the scattered seating of an audience would lead people to be more logically persuaded and influenced by listening to a speech than if they sat together in a compact group.

Relationship between rate of presentation and comprehension is the area of concern of a number of researchers. Increased speaking rates can be achieved through several techniques. Recent developments in technology have made it possible to process an original tape recording and increase the speaking rate without significant distortions of the pitch, intonation, or stress patterns in the speech.[34]

Compressed speech, by eliminating the normal silences between sounds in recorded speech and thus increasing the rate, enables the listener to increase his comprehension to a marked degree. The normal presentation rate for accurate comprehension is considered to be between 150 and 175 words per minute. In working with elementary students, Wood[35] found that they could exceed 90 percent comprehension at presentation rates as high as 350 words per minute. Miller[36] found that comprehension abilities can be increased by practice and that within a short time one can adjust satisfactorily to a rate of 380 wpm. Ernest[37] emphasized the need to consider the type of material as an important variable in employing compressed speech techniques. Earlier, Spicker[38] had found a speaking rate of 125 wpm most effective for the mentally retarded and 175 wpm best for the intellectually normal student.

Implications and Recommendations for the Teacher

Based upon the studies surveyed and similar studies, the following implications and recommendations are presented.

Teachers should become aware of the fact that listening is an important area of the language arts and a skill that can and should be taught.

Students who receive instructions in listening give evidence of significant improvement in listening ability, whereas those who do not receive such instruction do not.

Listening is a skill which can be improved through specific directed instruction.

Reading comprehension is significantly related to listening ability.

Listening ability is significantly related to the entire curriculum.

The language arts curriculum should provide challenging activities which motivate all types of listening experience. At every educational level the teacher should provide listening activities, materials, and instruction which will be meaningful and rewarding to each child.

The content of textbooks in the language arts should be based on the findings of research so as to contribute toward the listening needs of children.

Greater emphasis should be placed on improvement of listening skills in teacher education programs so that future and current teachers are well informed about the significance of teaching listening skills and the importance of keeping up-to-date on the findings of research.

Materials (other than text books) should aid the teacher in implementing the integration of listening instruction with the other areas of language arts and the social studies.

An increased awareness of the interrelatedness of listening comprehension and reading comprehension skills should be fostered in the classroom. The development of these skills should be the responsibility of each teacher.

Listening bears a close relationship to personality development and social adjustment.

Techniques such as compressed speech can aid in eliminating the time discrepancy between speech rate and ability to comprehend.

Listening is more than a unitary skill; it involves a complex of activities.

In the final analysis, the teacher is responsible for becoming aware of the importance of listening. He must utilize the findings of research as well as the available materials for teaching listening.

Particularly useful to the classroom teacher is the information contained in *The Speech Teacher, Speech Monographs,* and *Elementary English,* as well as reproductions of documents from NCTE/ERIC on listening and the monthly announcement of documents available from ERIC in issues of *Research in Education.*[39]

Factors Which Influence Listening

Listening requires a mind set in order to get the most out of a given situation. If we want to become good listeners, we must assume the role of the good listener. We must be conscious of the extent to which environmental, physical, psychological, and experiential factors affect the quality of listening.

Environmental Factors

The teacher should be aware of both the physical environment of the classroom and the social climate of the class. Each is important. Each is essential to a satisfying situation for learning.

Physical environment. In considering the physical environment of the classroom as a factor in motivating listening, it is essential that the acoustics are such that the child is able to hear without strain. The teacher should arrange the tables or desks in a manner that affords every child the same opportunity to hear and be heard. Placing work areas close together so children can communicate when necessary encourages good listening. Too great a distance between speaker and listener impedes communication. The teacher should use a pleasant voice, give clear, concise directions, and be a good listener himself.

The teacher should provide activities which motivate children to shift easily between the roles of listener and speaker. Through such activities as working on committees of various sizes; engaging in panel discussions, symposiums, and role playing; being members of audiences and speakers for groups, the children may alternate between the roles of leader and follower, of listener and speaker.

Social environment. Children readily sense an atmosphere in which they are encouraged to express their ideas, knowing that their contributions will be respected. Children who have an opportunity to be heard will more readily listen when someone else has the floor. An atmosphere which encourages children to experience, to express, and to evaluate ideas is imperative if the communication skills and the arts of language are to develop. This must be the basis for planned experiences and informal activities which require communication.

Obviously, the climate in which the teacher plans experiences through which children will be able to utilize the classroom situation to improve their communication skills is of significance in the total curriculum planning. The teacher should set an example for listening as well as provide opportunities for teaching listening and plan specific activities to promote it.

Physical Factors

Physical conditions within the listener may impede his listening. If he is fatigued, hungry, worried, or ill he will find listening extremely difficult. It is not only the hard-of-hearing who present problems in listening. It is also the undernourished, the disadvantaged, the chronically ill child. The child who is in excellent physical condition is potentially a better listener than one in poor physical condition. Frequently the class before lunch or the class that is held late in the afternoon suffers because children are physically not up to par and find it well-nigh impossible to listen. A mid-morning snack, especially for young children, helps bring the class up to a higher level of listening skill. It takes energy to listen, and it takes food to provide the energy.

Psychological Factors

Psychological factors involving personality traits, attitudes, and biases may also contribute to poor listening. Among psychological "deaf-spots" are areas of sensitivity when the listener is caught up in the emotion-laden words used by the speaker. These cause him to react emotionally, and listening comprehension deteriorates. Poor listeners, on the whole, are more biased than good listeners. The poor listener has less emotional control, broods about what the speaker is doing to destroy his pet theory, stops listening to the speaker, and concentrates on organizing a rebuttal of his own. On the other hand, the good listener tends to listen with an open mind, weighs all the evidence before making a judgment, and gives the speaker courteous attention until he has heard him out before making up his mind. In other words, the good listener tends to use the problem-solving technique and scientific attitude in his listening.

Experiential Factors

We listen with our experience. Observe a group of people in the midst of a conversation. Notice how the eyes light up, the body becomes alive, and the expression of the listener changes when the topic shifts to personal interests. Knowing the interests of all the children is helpful in planning the listening program. The child who has had varied and rich experiences is interested in many facets of living when he comes to school. Others whose experiences are limited will need to find in the curriculum itself broadening experiences and new horizons. It is only as the child broadens his experiences that he is interested enough in a specific subject or area of the curriculum to gain the most in listening to learn. As he enjoys new experiences, he will become not only a better listener, a better conversationalist, but a more effective student.

Guides to Effective Listening

In recent years, research has emphasized the positive approach to negative listening factors and has concentrated on replacing poor listening habits with effective skills as the central concern of the listening programs. Of significance to the elementary school teacher as an individual and as a teacher of children are the following guides to effective listening based on research carried on at the University of Minnesota and reported by Nichols.[40]

Find areas of interest. Whereas poor listeners after the first few sentences declare the subject dry and stop listening, good listeners who find the subject dry, instead of getting up and walking out, look for something in the speech they can put to use. Chesterton summarized this philosophy when he stated, "There is no such thing as an uninteresting subject; there are only uninterested people." Use is the key to the matter of interest in a topic.

Judge content, not delivery. Essentially, we listen with our experience. If this is true, the fact that the speaker may be inept in his delivery should not rob us of the message he has to give us. True, the speaker may have his faults, but we can get something out of the talk if we are interested in finding out what it is he knows that we need to know. We might not like the way he says it, but we *can* learn from what he says.

Hold your view. We must learn not to get too emotional about a speaker's point until we are certain we thoroughly understand it. This calls for withholding evaluation until our comprehension is complete. Over-stimulation either in support of the speaker's point or in opposition reflects a desire to enter into the argument immediately instead of following the development of the speaker's ideas.

Listen for ideas. We are all familiar with the situation of being asked about a speech or sermon we have heard and replying, "It was very good" or "I was really impressed" or some such comment. Upon further questioning we have been embarrassed by our failure to answer, "What was it about?"

Good listeners focus on central ideas; they are able to remember the main idea of the speech and to distinguish between fact and opinion, idea and example, evidence and argument. It is a significant fact that only about twenty-five percent of the people listening to a formal speech are able to grasp the speaker's central idea. "To develop these skills," says Nichols, "requires an ability to recognize conventional organizational patterns, transitional language, and the speaker's use of recapitulation. Fortunately, all of these items can be readily mastered with a bit of effort."[41]

Be flexible. Some of the best listeners never take notes. Instead, they concentrate on listening and later attempt to recall or reconstruct the speech they heard. With programmed material, taped lectures, and other audio aids, it is possible to check on the progress one makes in this type of skill development.

There is, interestingly enough, some evidence to indicate that the volume of notes taken and their value to the taker are inversely related. In any event, it is the ability to take meaningful notes that is important. The old chestnut about the notes going from the notebook of the professor to the notebook of the student without going through the minds of either is an exaggerated statement indicative of the need for flexibility in notetaking in terms of the organizational pattern of the speech to which the students listen.

Work at listening. Poor listeners refuse to spend any energy in listening. "College students, by their own testimony, frequently enter classes all worn out physically, assume postures which only seem to give attention to the speaker, and then proceed to catch up on needed rest or to reflect upon purely personal matters."[42]

As a courtesy to the speaker as well as a favor to ourselves, it is important to give the speaker our conscious attention. Not only does such behavior help the speaker in expressing his ideas more clearly, but we gain by better understanding the improved communication we have helped the speaker to achieve. The mere act of behaving as though we were listening is not enough. It is necessary to establish eye contact and maintain it, to indicate by posture and facial expression that the speaker's efforts are a matter of concern to us, and that we are listening at a high level of comprehension.

Resist distractions. The good listener tends to adjust quickly to adverse situations. He instinctively fights distractions. It is the courteous listener who closes the door, turns off the radio, shuts the window, puts his hand to his ear indicating the need for more projection on the part of the speaker, changes his seat, and if all else fails, concentrates more deeply on the topic at hand.

Exercise your mind. The poor listener is inexperienced in listening to anything that requires more effort on his part than a "soap opera" or light, recreational material. Listening to anything that requires response to technical, expository, difficult material is too much for such an individual. He may recognize that listening is hard work—but hard work is not for him. Such an individual is using only a limited amount of his mental capacity and his listening skill. He is a poor risk in the classroom, the office, or the factory. Good listeners are challenged by material that requires mental effort.

Keep your mind open. Closely related to the blind spots which impair our sight are the psychological deaf spots which impair our ability to perceive or understand. Effective listeners make an effort to identify the "red flag" words or phrases which tend to upset them emotionally, and try to rationalize those which are most upsetting to them. Words which cause communication to drop to zero are well known and vary with the region, the socio-economic level, and the cultural background of the individual.

Capitalize on thought speed. The rate at which a person speaks and the rate at which he thinks differ considerably. There is evidence to show that if thought were measured in words per minute, most of us think easily about four times as fast as we speak. This lag is responsible for much of the "day-dreaming" that goes on in the classroom, as well as for the embarrassing moment when the conversation is turned in our direction and we have been "woolgathering" and can't pick up the conversational thread.

Nichols suggests capitalizing on thought speed by developing the following pattern.

> A. Try to anticipate what a person is going to talk about. On the basis of what he had already said, ask yourself: "What's he trying to get at? What point is he going to make?"
>
> B. Mentally summarize what the person has been saying. What point has he made already, if any?
>
> C. Weigh the speaker's evidence by mentally questioning it. As he presents facts, illustrative stories and statistics, continually ask yourself: "Are they accurate? Do they come from an unprejudiced source? Am I getting the full picture, or is he telling me only what will prove his point?"
>
> D. Listen between the lines. The speaker doesn't always put everything that's important into words. The changing tones and volume of his voice may have a meaning. So may his facial expressions, the gestures he makes with his hands, the movement of his body.[43]

Planning the Listening Program

Any attempt to help children develop skills in listening must take into account the various levels, types, and purposes for listening. Although objectives for developing skills will be in the mind of the teacher, he must recognize that children move from the tentative and early skills of listening in the preschool stage to the higher levels only if there is continual guidance throughout the elementary school years. An outline of the development of listening skills and behavior follows.

Levels of Listening

1. Little conscious listening on the part of the child and then only when he is the center of interest; easily distracted by people and things.

2. Half-listening; the child more interested in his own ideas, waiting to "break in".

3. Passive listening; the child just sitting there, with little or no reaction.

4. Sporadic listening; the child showing interest if the conversation is closely related to his own experience, but shutting off the current when the conversation turns away from him.

5. Listening; some reaction shown through comments or questions.

6. Listening; indication of sincere emotional and intellectual response.

7. Highest level of listening; complete understanding of what is being said.[44]

Children listen at one or more of these levels throughout the day. They need guidance if they are to acquire the highest levels of listening skills.

Purposes for Listening

Just as there are different levels of listening, so there are different purposes for listening. There are numerous classifications of the purposes of listening. Through research and empirical evidence in working with children and teachers in elementary classrooms the following purposes for listening have been established.

- Listening to follow directions
- Listening for information
- Listening for enjoyment
- Listening to evaluate
- Listening to appreciate
- Listening to communicate
- Listening to discriminate sounds
- Listening to solve problems

There is an art to teaching listening just as there is to teaching any other area of the language arts curriculum. There is skill in selecting, organizing, directing, and evaluating learning experiences which will help children achieve skills needed for each purpose for listening. It is as necessary to develop skills in listening for specific purposes as it is to develop skills in reading for specific purposes. It is essential for the teacher to realize that these skills will be used at every level of education according to the situation and the demands of the moment.

Children will not automatically learn the listening skills. They will respond, however, to different types of activities. While the teacher keeps in mind the purposes for listening, the children must be motivated to *want* to listen. Since there are different purposes for listening, teachers may organize the program around purposes for which listening skills are essential. An overview of such an organization for the listening program appears below.

Purposes	*Instructions*
To follow directions.	Listen to the directions the first time they are given. Listen carefully to each detail. Picture each detail in your mind. Jot down the main ideas. Ask questions about doubtful points. Repeat the directions, explanations, or instructions aloud when possible. Repeat the directions, or think them through as you carry them out.
To record information.	Be prepared to take notes when the speaker begins. Be selective in deciding which words, phrases, and/or figures will aid you in recalling the most significant phrases. Be on the alert for points which the speaker emphasizes. Listen for the transition sentences which lead into the following points. Develop your own shorthand system.
For enjoyment.	Listen to enjoy sounds, words, apt phrases, rhythm, and melody of poetry. Listen to enjoy the character portrayals in drama. Listen to enjoy the sounds of nature—bird calls, waterfalls, wind, thunder, etc. In readers' theater productions, listen to identify characterizations through inflectional differences.
To evaluate.	Listen for the main points. Analyze the points made. Note contradictions. Check the authenticity of the information presented. Ascertain the bias of the speaker. Weigh documentation presented. Evaluate supporting evidence.
To appreciate.	Listen to identify the main and subordinate themes in music. Listen to appreciate characterization and plot in stories and dramas. Listen for the style of the author or composer. Listen to radio, television and/or films for the skill of the production. Listen to choral speaking to appreciate the beauty of the spoken language.

Purposes	Instructions
To communicate.	Discover the interests of the person with whom you are communicating. Improve your social relationships through careful listening and appropriate reactions. Expand your vocabulary and ability to make yourself understood. Develop sensitivity to the feelings of others by being aware of the nuances in their speech.
To discriminate speech sounds.	Listen to identify specific speech sounds (phonemes). Imitate speech sounds (phonemes) made by the teacher or on a recording. Listen to the sounds of ones own speech. Recognize the elements of voice quality, force, rate, and pitch. Tune out the noises and elements not involved in a specific exercise.
To solve problems.	Listen for specific ideas and clues. Keep the sequence of ideas in mind. Listen "between the lines". Take the "given" and reorganize it. Add elements that help to see the problem in a new light. Leap from an expressed idea to an idea related to it. Translate, interpolate, and extrapolate from oral problems presented in the form of situations, conflicts, and open-ended incidents.

An Outline of a Listening Program for an Elementary School

In planning a listening program, it is essential to keep in mind the interrelationship among purposes, techniques, activities, and evaluation. These elements appear in the outlines that follow.

Listening to Follow Directions

Successful teachers use a wide variety of techniques, activities, and materials to help children listen with increased attention and perception in following directions. The children develop a "set" for listening with comprehension.

A. Objectives.

To help children develop a "set" for listening by:

1. Putting away distracting materials.
2. Listening from the beginning.
3. Listening actively for who-what-when-where-why.

C. Activities (designed to achieve objectives).

1. Listening to directions and announcements.
2. Playing such games as "Simon Says".
3. Following instructions for cutting and folding paper, drawing pictures, or writing according to oral directions.

B. Techniques of the teacher.

1. Waiting until everyone is attentive.
2. Speaking simply, with clearcut, simple phrases.
3. Checking to see that the children understand.
4. Working toward giving the directions only once.
5. Organizing material so that it is systematic, explicit, brief.
6. Making use of visual aids to support the auditory.
7. Varying the procedure to stimulate children's curiosity.
8. Using non-verbal communication to get children's attention.
9. Utilizing the world of sounds, movement, motion, and language to create interest in listening.
10. Involving the children in the evaluation of activities from the initial listening experiences.

D. Evaluation (cooperative endeavor by teacher and pupils).

1. Did the speaker wait until the children were ready to listen before giving directions?
2. Did everyone in the room listen courteously as well as attentively?
3. Did the children remember the directions and demonstrate their ability to recall?
4. Did they listen for the clues who-what-when-where-why?
5. Did they distinguish specific signals and respond to them quickly and enthusiastically?
6. Did they show enthusiasm and interest in the activity?
7. Did their listening for directions give evidence of increasing efficiency as the year progressed?
8. Did they create new listening games which centered around giving directions?
9. Did they make maps showing directions to places of interest to the group?
10. Did they follow non-verbal as well as verbal directions with ease?

C. Activities, cont.

4. Listening to and repeating directions that might be given to a traveller on a journey to an imaginary place.
5. Listening to and repeating directions that might be given to a traveller on a journey to a specific, real place.
6. Following directions on a prepared worksheet, such as "Put an X . . ," "Circle . . ," "Cross out . . ," "Underline . . ".
7. Playing "Do As I Say". Give three or more directions in sequence and choose a child to carry them out. For example: "Go to the back of the room, turn around three times, pick up a book from the library table, give it to John, walk over to the pencil sharpener, count to ten, and take your seat." In the early experiences the game must be simple. Increase the complexity as the year progresses—or as the individual is able to accomplish it. When a child makes an error another child is chosen.
8. Listening to a list of action words. At a signal perform the designated actions.
9. Responding automatically to signals for fire drills, change of classes, dismissal, gymnasium signals, and so forth.
10. Playing "Follow the Leader". Pantomime action, and describe it, e.g. "I am eating an ice-cream cone." The second player repeats the first action and then adds a new action of his own. The third player repeats the actions of the other two and adds one of his own. If a child forgets an action, puts it in the wrong sequence, or identifies it incorrectly, he is out of the game. The last one to stay in is the winner.
11. Playing "Do This". Give several taps on a toy drum or table and ask the children to imitate you. The child who is able to imitate a pattern set by the teacher is then chosen to create his own pattern. For variation, the patterns of sound may be made by clapping or with percussion instruments.
12. Playing "Traffic Cop". Place pictures of community buildings in various locations around the room. Select a child to be traffic cop. He invites children to come up to ask him the directions to one of the buildings pictured. He must give correct directions, such as "Go past the school, turn right, go down two blocks." If he fails to give correct directions, he loses his post.

C. Activities, cont.

The child receiving the directions must follow them closely or lose his turn. The winner is the traffic cop who keeps his post the longest.

Listening for Information

Before children learn to read, they are entirely dependent on listening for information, both in and out of the classroom. Even after reading skills are developed, they must still depend upon listening for much of their information. Listening to learn is one of the vital purposes for listening.

A. Objectives.

To help children listen to recall facts, ideas, and principles by:

1. Developing an interest in the subject or project.
2. Listening actively to what is said.
3. Noting sequence of ideas.
4. Holding the thread of the discourse in mind.
5. Watching for transitional phrases and change of subject.
6. Reserving judgment until the speech is concluded.
7. Listening for the main idea.
8. Recalling supporting ideas.
9. Relating ideas and distilling and assimilating information.
10. Making mental summaries periodically.
11. Analyzing what is heard.

B. Techniques of the teacher.

1. Establishing a specific purpose for listening.
2. Telling students beforehand what to listen for.
3. Teaching children how to take notes efficiently.
4. Training in listening for points which the speaker emphasizes as important.
5. Emphasizing the organization of the talk heard.
6. Showing how to extract the main ideas.
7. Demonstrating how to distinguish the significant idea from the unimportant.
8. Guiding children to reserve judgment when various points of view are presented.
9. Having children listen to share what was heard.
10. Making intelligent and pertinent observations at the conclusion of the talk

C. Activities.

These can be accomplished through:

1. Sharing period, show and tell, conversations.
2. Carrying on dialogues between teacher-child and child-child.
3. Discussing, planning, and evaluating projects.
4. Answering the telephone and delivering the message accurately.
5. Listening to a short selection and suggesting a title.
6. Reading a short story to the group and asking the students to tell what happened in a one-sentence summary statement.
7. Reading three statements, one containing the main idea and the other two containing subordinate ideas. Have the students select the one that contains the main idea. Example:

    All life on earth is dependent on the sun.

    The sun provides us with heat during the day.

    Ocean plants get their energy from the sun.

8. Reading a series of paragraphs and having students select the main idea from a number of choices. Have them discuss their choice in terms of specificity, relevancy, and accuracy.
9. Having students listen to a description of an object, a place, or a person, knowing that they will complete an outline based on this description. The description should be read again, one sentence at a time. After each sentence, the students should enter information in appropriate places on the partially structured outline form.
10. Having students listen to a selection

B. Techniques of the teacher, cont.
after hearing the observations of the children.
11. Using originality in setting the stage for listening.
12. Involving the children in evaluation procedures.

D. Evaluation (cooperative endeavor by teacher and pupils).
1. Did the children understand the purpose for listening?
2. Did they recall the information?
3. Did they act on the information?
4. Did they work independently as they listened? As they recalled the information?
5. Did they discuss and evaluate what they heard in an increasingly mature level?
6. Did they find original, creative ways of using the information obtained?

C. Activities, cont.
that contains information that could be categorized. After listening to the selection, the students should be given a prepared worksheet containing the basic structure. Reread the selection again, sentence by sentence, allowing time for the students to fill in the chart.
11. Having students listen to a story and asking them to write an original story based on a similar personal experience.
12. Giving the students prepared worksheets containing an outline form with at least one topic and subtopic filled in as a guide. After listening to a simple selection, the students are to fill in the information that they remember.
13. Having pupils listen as announcements are being read over the school's public address system. Compare what they remember. Finally, check with the copy which the announcer read.
14. Reading a description, then asking the children to draw the landscape, animal, person, or building from their memories of what was read.
15. Having children listen to a television program without viewing it and picture imaginatively what they remember.
16. Exchanging a tape recording with another class. Send a copy of the script with the tape. After listening to the tape, have the children recall interesting facts. Check back with the tape.

Listening for Enjoyment

Among the high moments for children in the elementary school are those in which they listen for sheer enjoyment, be it listening to poetry with its flowing rhythm and rhyme, television with its variety of programs, prose with its sequence of happenings, or drama with its exciting climax. Here the teacher can share his enthusiasm with the children and motivate the spark for listening for enjoyment.

A. Objectives.
To act as a catalyst for stimulating listening for enjoyment which may develop into listening for appreciation by:
1. Providing a wealth of listening experiences which pave the way for appreciative listening.
2. Helping children listen to enjoy music, drama, poetry and prose.
3. Helping children find pleasure in listening to sounds of nature.

C. Activities (to motivate listening for enjoyment).
1. Listening to good vocal and instrumental music, drama, poetry, and prose.
2. Responding rhythmically to music.
3. Planning original ending to a story read by the teacher.
4. Arranging instrumentation for the class orchestra.
5. Listening to selected radio and television programs.

A. Objectives, cont.

4. Developing in children a growing sense of the esthetic.

B. Techniques of the teacher.

1. Creating an environment conducive to listening for enjoyment.
2. Providing equipment needed for listening to recordings, transcriptions, radio, television, sound films, etc.
3. Providing time for listening to music, drama, speech programs, both live and recorded.
4. Showing by his own behavior that listening can be fun!

D. Evaluation.

1. Did the children enjoy their listening experience?
2. Did they extend their base for listening for enjoyment?
3. Did they make an effort to listen to music, drama, stories, poems with increasing frequency as the year progressed?
4. Did they grow in their interest in listening for enjoyment as evidenced by such activities as: polling the class members for television listening preferences, personal "hit parades" of stories or poems listened to during the preceding month, greater selection of music, poetry, drama recordings during the self-chosen period, request for stories the teacher read to the group, and number of books checked out from the library, read, and enjoyed?
5. Did they spend more time in listening to programs other members of the class enjoyed and recommended?
6. Did they spend some of their allowances on recordings, books and share them with the class?
7. Did they give evidence of enjoyment of literature read to them by the teacher?

C. Activities, cont.

6. Listening to music for relaxation and during self-chosen activities.
7. Sketching an original cartoon of a character or situation portrayed in a story the teacher reads to the group.
8. Using puppets, or pantomiming, or dramatizing as an outgrowth of a story just listened to.
9. Creating sound effects with such instruments as finger cymbals, bells, triangles, etc. as an accompaniment to a story or poem read by the teacher.
10. Creating sound effects to accompany a "radio" play read into the tape recorder.
11. Composing the "developing story" in which each participant carries on from the point at which the preceding speaker stopped.
12. Making up the second act of a play which the children have seen presented by a committee. In creative dramatics the acts will differ with each group as will the interpretation of the story.
13. Reading from the great literature of the ages as well as from contemporary literature that meets high standards.
14. Listening to contemporary ballads which reflect the childrens' interests.
15. Listening to and dramatizing a favorite story.
16. Listening to a recording while creating a composition in art with finger paint.
17. Listening to the rhythm of raindrops on the window pane and responding in a creative medium—dance, poetry, a story, a picture, or a musical composition.
18. Listening for the rhythm of working machinery—bulldozer, steam shovel, vacuum cleaner, washing machine, hair dryer, motor idling, etc.
19. Listening with "rabbit ears" on a bus or street car. Write a story based on what you hear.
20. Participating in readers' theater. Discuss the reasons for enjoying one group's presentation above another's. Tell why you enjoyed listening to a particular selection.

Through listening to stories, drama, poetry, and music, both live and recorded, children will grow in listening enjoyment. It is the responsibility of the teacher to provide both a literary and a cultural environment for his classroom.

Listening to Evaluate

Critical listening is listening in which the listener analyzes the ideas presented by the speaker and makes critical judgments about the ideas presented. Among the skills involved are distinguishing between fact and opinion, emotionally charged and logical arguments, fallacious and verifiable data; evaluating the arguments of the speaker; drawing inferences and making judgments; recognizing propaganda and rumor; and evaluating sales pitches and "gimmicks".

A. Objectives.

To help children to develop skill and criteria for screening information in terms of source, value, evidence presented by:

1. Providing experiences in analyzing what they hear and judging the material on the basis of pre-determined criteria.
2. Gaining experience in making inferences and arriving at conclusions via critical listening.
3. Developing a questioning attitude in listening to speakers.
4. Developing strategies of listening with an open but skeptical ear.

B. Techniques of the teacher.

1. Evaluating literature by having children distinguish between truth and fancy, fact and fiction, myth and reality.
2. Demonstrating awareness of and ability to evaluate propaganda.
3. Presenting reading material of varying levels of difficulty which calls for critical evaluation.
4. Demonstrating critical listening abilities.
5. Utilizing technological resources such as radio, television, recordings, tapes to provide children with opportunities for critical listening.
6. Setting standards for listening to lectures, speeches, discussions in which strong opinions or views are presented.

D. Evaluation (cooperative endeavor by teacher and children).

1. Did the children distinguish between fact and fancy in literature read to them?
2. Did the children screen information presented as to plausibility, evidence given, source and values?
3. Did the children develop an awareness of and ability to detect devices used to influence acceptance and belief in advertising, sales pitches, political speeches, propaganda, personal relationships?

C. Activities (to develop strategies for critical listening).

1. Listening to discriminate between fact and fancy in "Tall Tales".
2. Role playing "off the cuff" press conferences, then getting facts to prove the oral statements.
3. Listening to panel discussion in which there are conflicting opinions. If possible, get scripts and tape recordings of radio or television programs. Have a before and after opinion poll. Use script to refer to disputed points for evidence.
4. Listening to radio and television commercials and noting techniques of propaganda. Classify the appeals used.
5. Reading statements of personal opinion aloud. Reinforce them by gathering concrete evidence, e.g. "I think the cost of living has gone up rapidly this year." Gather comparative costs of selected items.
6. Listening to a speech with a single purpose in mind (to judge the intent of the speaker).
7. Listening to speeches for evidence of such techniques of propaganda as name calling, glittering generalities, card stacking, testimonial, band wagon, plain folk, and transfer.[45]
8. Comparing the news report and commentaries on radio and television in terms of party affiliations. Do the same with newspaper stories and editorials.
9. Analyzing the sales psychology that underlies advertisements on television, radio or bill boards, and in newspapers or magazines. Watch for sensory appeal, status appeal, physical prowess or well-being.
10. Clipping a statement in which fact and opinion are intertwined. Listen first for opinions and then for facts which are indisputable.
11. Playing "Frog Jump". The teacher describes a jumping animal or object; if the statement is true (e.g. "frogs jump"), the

C. Activities, cont.
children respond by waving their arms. If the statement is false (e.g. "desks jump"), the pupils keep their hands at their sides. The last one to stay in the game becomes the next leader.

Listening to Appreciate (Making Esthetic Judgments)

When does listening for enjoyment become listening for appreciation? Listening, like poetry, begins in wonder and ends in appreciation *if* it is built upon a foundation of listening for enjoyment. The more we know about what we are listening to, the more capable we are of listening to appreciate in the sense of making an esthetic judgment.

A. Objectives.
1. Helping children grow from listening for enjoyment to listening to make an esthetic judgment. This can be achieved by helping children move from a purely emotional response to both an emotional and intellectual response.

B. Techniques of the teacher.
1. Creating an environment in which the creative arts are valued.
2. Providing equipment and time for listening experiences at the levels of listening appreciation of the children in the class.
3. Providing listening experiences which challenge children to grow in appreciation of the beauties of poetry, drama, speech, and music. These activities will be explored in later chapters.
4. Evidencing interest through attending performances of drama, opera, music, ballet.
5. Informing pupils of forthcoming radio and television programs of special value for esthetic growth.
6. Informing and urging attendance at live performances of esthetic value locally and in nearby communities.
7. Being on the alert and searching for new esthetic experiences and expression.

D. Evaluation (cooperative endeavor by teacher and children).
1. Did the children grow in their ability to make esthetic judgments?
2. Did the children give evidence of expanding criteria of taste and preference in listening to drama, radio, television, film, cartoon, live theater?

C. Activities (to stimulate appreciative listening).
1. Having children listen to skillfully interpreted poems, plays, readings, and speeches by gifted professionals.
2. Reading for the children from some of the literary classics for them to observe at first hand the interrelationships of movement, gesture, voice, inflection, cadence, and emphasis.
3. Having children listen to a specific recording with a view to making esthetic judgments about the material and performance.
4. Reading to the students stories, poems, plays, or essays that are high in sensory impact. Ask the children to prepare a selection of their own choice to read to the group.
5. Organizing a readers' theater and having children develop a program centering around their favorite poems, excerpts from plays, or prose they have enjoyed.
6. Inviting another class in and trying to determine the level of listening which the other class evidenced.
7. Having students listen to a recording of a drama they are studying, noting the personal style of delivery of a selected actor.
8. Listening to the same recording, this time noting characteristics of theme, plot, setting.
9. Obtaining different recording of the same play and comparing the two.
10. Having students listen to a poem read by the teacher or a record by an artist and listening for such details as:
  a. voice qualities
  b. inflectional patterns

D. Evaluation, cont.

3. Did the children give evidence of increased appreciation of form, meter, poetic devices in poetry read to them?
4. Did children grow in appreciation of form and medium, dramatic devices in drama and music?
5. Did the children listen in self-chosen periods to programs which offered an opportunity to listen for appreciation?
6. Did the children show an increased attendance at programs offering opportunities for dramatic, literary and musical appreciation?
7. Did the children request the teacher to read favorite poems on days in which they were free to choose activities?
8. Did the children participate freely in readers' theater and request time for evaluation of the degree of artistry achieved by the total group?

C. Activities, cont.

c. imagery
d. emotional level

11. Listening to a dramatization of a favorite story to develop a sense of dramatic devices.
12. Listening to a favorite television program to observe the role of form and medium.
13. Listening to a group of favorite poems and discovering the poetic devices used to communicate emotions and motivate reader and listener response.
14. Creating a group drama and inviting an audience in to listen to the refined product.
15. Listening to various types of sounds from different sizes of bells, then listening to a musical composition in which bells play an important role to appreciate the artistry with which the composer blends them into the composition.
16. Appointing a committee to give advance notice of programs to be presented in a local or nearby concert hall, theater, auditorium, or on radio or television.
17. Discussing the program in class, and forming esthetic judgments.

Listening to Communicate

The good listener inspires lively conversation. Conversation is a two-way affair. The good conversationalist is the good listener. He responds in an animated and involved manner. In turn the speaker, warmed by such wholehearted response, proceeds to return the favor and communicates with a creative response he hardly thought possible.

A. Objectives.

1. Developing listening skills for effective communication.
2. Holding the thread of conversation in mind.
3. Watching for transitional phrases and change of subject.
4. Being courteous, especially when one disagrees.
5. Listening actively to what is being said.
6. Refraining from monopolizing the conversation.
7. Entering the conversation at appropriate times. Avoiding rude interruptions.

B. Techniques of the teacher.

1. Creating an atmosphere where conversation is valued.

C. Activities (to promote communication as a two-way process).

1. Having a designated time each day for "share and tell", conversation, and/or discussion.
2. Providing time in the daily schedule for dialogue or conversations for teacher and child.
3. Discussing, planning, and evaluating classroom activities.
4. Working in groups and committee assignments.
5. Telephoning.
6. Role playing situations in which conversation is significant.
7. Engaging in conversations on specific topics.

B. Techniques of the teacher, cont.

2. Listening courteously to a child when he speaks.
3. Providing time for conversation as well as for formal speaking activities.
4. Reading interesting conversations from literature.
5. Using scenes from plays to analyze good conversation (or bad).
6. Taking time to carry on dialogue with students.
7. Dramatizing favorite stories which have exciting dialogue.
8. Asking children to "put on your listening ears".
9. Asking questions which trigger listening to communicate.
10. Demonstrating good listening in situations outside the classroom, e.g. on the playground, at lunch, etc.

D. Evaluation.

1. Did the children give evidence of courteous listening in everyday activities?
2. Did the children set standards for courteous listening?
3. Did the children take responsibility for participating in both phases of conversation—speaking and listening?
4. Did the children act on the information gained through conversations?
5. Did they converse on an increasingly mature basis?
6. Did they broaden their interests and extend their horizons by engaging in conversations with older students and adults?
7. Did they grow in their discussion and evaluation abilities as a result of their improved skills in conversation and courteous listening?
8. Did children develop habits of listening to communicate to replace habits of interrupting when someone else has "the floor"?
9. Did the children sense the responsibility they have to the listener to talk about things that are interesting to him?
10. Did children refrain from monopolizing the attention of the teacher and allow others to converse with the teacher?
11. Did children listen courteously when speakers were invited to come to the school?
12. Did children listen to communicate on field trips, safaris, and other trips beyond the school?

C. Activities, cont.

8. Writing conversation in stories and reading them to the group.
9. Creating conversation in creative dramatics.
10. Selecting interesting passages from books which illustrate creative communication. Reading them to a group.
11. Inviting children to act as host and/or hostess when visitors come to the school. Discuss elements of courteous listening in a conversational setting.
12. Playing games to stimulate communication, such as "I Am Packing My Suitcase". Children may be at their tables. A child is chosen who says, "I am packing my suitcase and will put something in it that begins with the same letter as my name." The other children think of a word which fits and show that they are ready to supply it. If the child chosen is able to supply an article that fits the situation, he is "IT" for the next playing. He chooses the next and different sound. Children may give a clue by telling the place where they are planning to go.
13. Playing "I am Going to the Moon". Similar to the preceding game, the first child says, "I am going to the Moon. I am taking my .... and some ...." Each succeeding child must repeat all the items mentioned previously in the proper sequence. A variation of this game, which is a prelude to conversational situations, involves saying, "I am going to Italy, France, Germany, Spain, England, etc." Names of cities, rivers, mountains, resorts or tourist attractions stimulate conversational situations.
14. Pantomiming situations in which listening is an integral part.
15. Playing the game "Gossip". The leader whispers a sentence to the child at his right, who in turn whispers it to the child at his right. When it finally reaches the last child, he tells what he has heard. Compare this with the original sentence.

Listening to Discriminate Speech Sounds

Listening to discriminate speech sounds is involved in listening for oral improvement. Even though the child's hearing may be normal, he may not perceive all the speech sounds accurately. Thus he reproduces the sound as he perceives it —not necessarily as he hears it. To help this child improve his speech he must first be helped to perceive and reproduce accurately, in isolation, sounds with which he has difficulty.

A. Objectives.

To help children improve perception by:

1. Helping children learn acceptable pronunciation through listening carefully to the way words are sounded.
2. Helping children to listen to individual speech sounds with discrimination and understanding.
3. Teaching children to listen to the way educated people in the community talk.
4. Helping children with errors of pronunciation previously acquired through poor listening habits.
5. Training the child to produce a sound properly after learning to perceive it correctly.

B. Techniques of the teacher.

1. Setting an example of accurate pronunciation, clear enunciation, and precise articulation.
2. Providing a classroom environment in which listening to discriminate sounds is habitual.
3. Making use of the tape recorder so that children are aware of the sounds they make.
4. Being aware of mispronunciations in one's own speech. (Teachers who pronounce pen "pin" cannot expect children to pronounce it correctly.)
5. Analyzing problems children have in listening accurately to speech sounds and providing exercises and listening games to alleviate the faults.
6. Referring the child who has severe or persistent problems to a speech therapist or to the speech clinic.
7. Providing sensory experiences, group activities and games which make each child feel a part of the group.

C. Activities.

1. Giving direct practice to develop an awareness of sounds as an aid to discriminating listening:
   a. Having students concentrate on everyday sounds around them until they can describe them in detail. Imitate sounds of animals, machines.
   b. Having students listen to contrasting sounds, e.g., noise and music, loud and soft, and note their effect on the listener.
   c. Having students analyze sounds according to pitch, rhythm, timbre, loudness in order to learn to distinguish among these various characteristics.
   d. Having them listen to voices of others and study elements that make them pleasant or unpleasant to the listener.
2. Developing an awareness of pleasing voices by listening critically to those of announcers, actors, professional speakers.
3. Recording the pupils' voices and listening analytically to them played back to help them become conscious of their own needs for improvement.
4. Developing specific procedures for improving the voices through group speech games, poems, and varied speech activities.
5. Playing speech games to develop listening skills, for example, "What Is This Sound?"
6. Listing all the aural impressions that they can identify during a specified period (traffic sounds, birds, machinery, movements).
7. Listening to a series of sounds recorded on tape and identifying them (rain, clatter of dishes, starting a car, paper rattling, etc.).
8. Identifying designated sounds from material read by the teacher.
9. Giving the children a specific speech

D. Evaluation (cooperative endeavor by teacher, speech therapist and children).

1. Did the children develop auditory dis-

D. Evaluation, cont.

crimination through the exercises and games?

2. Did the children learn to discriminate in listening to sounds placed in different positions in a word?

3. Did the children make a sincere effort to make their sounds correctly after the teacher called attention to mistakes and gave concrete suggestions for improvement?

4. Did the children look forward with anticipation to the speech improvement activities? Were they fun?

5. Did the classroom atmosphere contribute toward listening with discrimination?

6. Did the children improve in aural perception?

7. Did children develop sensitivity to speech sounds?

8. Did the children expand their comprehension of dialects?

C. Activities, cont.

sound and having them respond with words in which the sound comes in an initial position, then medial, and then final. Have the words put on the board (g as in girl, figure, fog. Remember—the emphasis is on sound, NOT spelling).

10. Playing "Silent Movie". Select a scorekeeper. The teacher gives out a word like "skip" to the first circle which is expected to think of a rhyming word that can be pantomimed. The first circle now can *skip* around the other circles and score a point; or they could pantomime "flip", "sip" or "whip". The group with the largest number of correct words and well pantomimed actions wins the "Silent Movie".

11. Playing "Add a Word". The teacher names two or three words that begin with the same sound, such as fish, fowl, farmer, fair. The child chosen must add a word beginning with the same sound, for example, family. The game continues as long as children who are successful in adding a word remain in the game in the circle.

Listening to Solve Problems

What makes this type of listening exciting is that the student either can solve problems analytically or he can break out of the mold, go beyond the stereotype, by-pass the usual order of procedure and find solutions in a different way.

A. Objectives.

To help children increase ability to select the key elements that form the most unusual or most useful cues in listening to solve a problem, create a composition, write a story, poem, or drama by:

1. Helping the learner draw inferences, seeing cause and effect relationships.

2. Helping children toy with ideas that offer unique possibilities for coming to a conclusion.

3. Helping children translate, interpret, and extrapolate from oral problems presented in forms of situations, conflicts, critical incidents and "Just Imagine . . . . .".

4. Utilizing creative listening as a means of coping with problems as well as responding esthetically to a given situation.

5. Presenting children with numerous opportunities to project thinking beyond the given situation.

6. Demonstrating both analytical and cre-

C. Activities (to spark listening creatively).

1. Listening to jingles, riddles, unfinished stories, "Just Suppose" and responding with creative interpretation.

2. Role playing problem situations requiring creative, innovative solutions.

3. Listening creatively to legends, myths and folklore and discussing methods used by the writer to solve problems in analytical and creative ways.

4. Selecting from problem situations and incidents read by the teacher the clues that are significant in the solution of the dilemma, and tuning out extraneous elements.

5. Creating problem situations (hypothetical) and presenting them to the class for solutions.

6. Playing "Adding to Tall Tales". Several groups of five or six organize to tell tall tales of the cumulative type. The story teller of the group introduces the tale with an incident to which each member listens and

A. Objectives, cont.
ative listening in the solutions of problems.
7. Inviting children to formulate oral problems which they can present to the group.

B. Techniques of the teacher.
1. Setting up an environment conducive to creative listening.
2. Rewarding children who solve problems creatively by listening to their solutions.
3. Providing experiences in which creative listening is demanded for problem solutions.
4. Identifying relationships between ideas, problems and solutions.

D. Evaluation (cooperative endeavor by teacher and children).
1. Did children enjoy listening to solve problems?
2. Did children give evidence of creative listening in daily activities?
3. Did children identify the need for solving some problem creatively *after* listening to the presentation?
4. Did the children shift gears in critical listening and creative listening for clues which might lead to innovative solutions?
5. Did children act out solutions to problems through role playing?

C. Activities, cont.
in turn adds a new incident. At the close the leader asks a student in the audience to repeat the incidents in a sequence. The more imaginative, the more fantastic, the more entangled the plot, the more the audience will enjoy an unusual solution and imaginative items.
7. Playing "What Would You Have Done?" Present a situation which calls for divergent thinking. Invite different members of the class to present their solution.
8. Listening to the teacher read a play in which the solution is not presented, but is left to the class. Divide into groups and plan how you would end the play. Present it so that the solution is clearly revealed using pantomime, creative drama, or readers' theater.

Ensuring Balance in the Listening Program

In the Nursery School

For the first five years of his life, a child's ears are busy receptors of sounds, words, information, meanings, and concepts. Experiences help him clarify the elements of the world around him. He learns that listening helps him in imitating speech, in forming concepts, and in increasing his store of knowledge. He has learned to listen *without* formal instruction. When he enters school he should be challenged to improve his listening skills by listening to stories, discussion, conversations, directions, explanations, and listening games. The insightful teacher knows when to give direct guidance and when to let the children initiate their own listening experiences.

> When four-year-old Lisa sat down to finger paint she announced, 'I want to make black.' The teacher asked what finger paint colors she wanted. Lisa used red and blue paint to make her first picture. For her second picture she chose blue and green paint. As she mixed these colors she repeated her statement, 'I want to make black.' The teacher repeated her statement, 'Lisa wants to make black.' Then she added, 'Does Lisa want another color?' Lisa took yellow and mixed it over her

picture. When Lisa finished her second picture, the teacher asked if she wanted to make another picture. Lisa took her third paper and took red and green paint repeating her original statement. After she mixed the colors, the teacher added green paint to the picture. Lisa's eyes sparkled when it turned black. She exclaimed, 'I made black.' The teacher said, 'You can tell Mommy and Daddy when you go home. How did you make black, Lisa?' Lisa replied, 'Red and blue make purple. Green makes black. Let's tell all the children.' The teacher got the attention of the class and Lisa told them about her discovery. 'I made black paint. Red and blue make purple. Green made black.' At snack time one of the preschoolers repeated the story of Lisa's discovery using her exact words.[46]

In the Kindergarten

The five-year-old is ready for listening experiences which are an integral part of everyday living. He enjoys listening games such as, "Guess Who Is Here", "Listen and Tell", "What Did I Do?", "Mother Cat and Kittens", and "What Am I?". As he progresses through the year he becomes interested in more sophisticated listening games such as "What Object Is Missing?", "What Is This?", "Bouncing Ball", and "Rub-A-Dub-Dub". He is also ready for guided listening: conversations, directions, explanations, discussions, stories, and music. He also likes to invent his own listening projects and experiments with various materials. He discovers that paper crackles, water swishes, musical instruments make a variety of sounds, tacks sound like rain dripping on the eaves or pattering on the roof. He creates new listening games. He identifies the sounds around him—whistles, bells, trains, wind, rain, thunder, airplanes, etc. Planned listening helps to open an entirely new world for the kindergarten child.

In the Primary Grades

The primary grade teacher will build upon the listening experiences of the preschool years. He will plan stimulating experiences such as:

- conversing
- telephoning
- sharing experiences
- discussing, planning, evaluating
- storytelling
- dramatizing, improvising
- listening to poetry and choral speaking
- listening to music
- reporting on excursions, science experiments, social studies units, and interviews

The primary grade teacher will give specific instruction to aid the children in listening to directions, announcements, sound films, recordings, television programs, assembly programs, concerts, guests who visit the school. He also will help the child to listen creatively for imaginary sensory experiences.

A balance should be maintained between individual and group listening.

Individual listening. Listening to carry out messages, to relay messages; listening to a telephone conversation, to one's own voice from a tape recording. Listening courteously when someone is speaking, either to the individual or to a group.

Group listening. Listening in a group planning activity, listening to instructions and discussion for a new game, listening as a member of a committee, cooperating as a participant in a teacher-pupil planning session, listening to contribute to the conversation of a group of which one is a member, listening to respond as a member of a group.

Listening in a primary class. In a primary grade, the teacher brought to class a large woven basket she had purchased in Mexico to use as a motivation for listening. After examining the basket and admiring its color and designs, one child asked: "What is in the basket?"

> *Miss Helm:* It's a Magic Basket and it has something in it that will take you where ever you want to go. Where shall we go today, boys and girls?
>
> *Jimmy:* I want to go to the moon. Why don't we all go to the moon?
>
> *Miss Helm:* What will you hear on the moon?
>
> *Jimmy:* I don't know.
>
> *Miss Helm:* Reach in the basket and see what you can find that will give you a clue.

Jimmy thrust his hand into the basket and brought out a bag of rocks.

> *Miss Helm:* As soon as you are reminded of sounds that you might hear on the moon, Jimmy, you can write them down and we'll talk about them later. In the meantime, let's look at some of the other objects in the Magic Basket which might suggest where the rest of you want to travel.

The children came up one at a time and drew the following objects from the Magic Basket: a Hallowe'en noisemaker, a small broom, a toy snapping turtle, chop sticks, a music box, a rattle, a pair of scissors, an egg beater, and castanets.

> *Miss Helm:* Now close your eyes while I make a sound with each of these objects. When you hear a sound that makes you think about the place where you would like to travel, take out some paper and write a story or poem, or draw a picture that tells us what you saw when you arrived, what you did, and how you came back.

One by one the children came up with ideas and began expressing them. The time for listening was over; the time for creating had begun. Some twenty minutes later the children were ready for sharing ideas. The products were placed in individual folders for a time later in the week when those who wished would share by reading what they had written or showing what they had drawn. In a quick summary of where they went, the following were represented together with the stimulus which promoted the idea.

Location	*Stimulus*
Moon	Collection of rocks
Egypt	Noisemaker
China	Chopsticks
Switzerland	Music box
Arabia	Egg beater
Spain	Castanets
Barber shop	Scissors
Mexico	Rattle
Holland	Broom

In the Intermediate Grades

The teaching of listening must continue throughout the elementary school as an integral part of the curriculum. Listening for specific purposes must become habitual and automatic if the student is to meet the increased demands and pressures of life in and out of the school. The demands of the intermediate and upper grades require more complex and refined skills in listening. One sixth grade teacher who was having difficulty getting children to listen attentively motivated them to devise the following code for listening.

We identify the specific purpose for which we are listening.

We listen actively and attentively.

We listen with respect.

We evaluate the speeches we hear—radio, television, student rallies.

We listen analytically to oral reports by members of the class.

We listen respectfully to all points of view—even those with which we are in direct opposition.

We listen appreciatively to literature read orally.

Typical activities which develop listening skills include the following.

Listening to speeches

Participating in discussions

Interviewing people

Role-playing situations

Symposiums followed by open forums

Creative dramatics and improvisations

Storytelling

Choral speaking

Oral interpretation of poetry and prose

Readers' theater

Listening to music and drama (recorded)

Playing such games as "Twenty Questions" and "UTELLIT"

Twenty questions. A person is chosen to be IT. He selects an object or person from inside or outside the classroom and whispers the name of his selection to the teacher. IT begins by saying, "I am thinking of someone—or something—I found in the super market—or saw on television—or met in the street." The class is allowed twenty questions which will help identify or describe the person or object. IT must answer truthfully each question asked. Attentive listening is required for the clues as they develop. Finally a student is allowed to ask, "Are you thinking of . . . ?" Until IT's choice is identified, the game goes on. The one who identifies it is IT for the next round.

UTELLIT. A volunteer is chosen to follow directions given by the leader in a rapid-fire sequence which demands careful listening to perform several actions. The directions might relate to some area of the curriculum such as social studies. The leader might say, "Draw a map of Canada. Locate Ottawa. Locate the capital of your province. Label the Ice Fields of Alberta (or any place that has been studied)." Involve the group in deciding whether or not the directions have been followed properly.

In the Junior High

As junior high students continue to develop listening skills, they focus on new situations with which to refine these skills. Personal communication becomes even more important as they participate in such activities as conversation, religious activities, social gatherings, club meetings, panel discussions, role playing, lectures, music, and drama. Radio and television programs can be used effectively for listening learning as students study how to listen to news commentators, documentaries, panel discussions, dramatic productions, and inspirational or religious broadcasts.

At this level emphasis on critical listening in terms of evaluating evidence, propaganda, and high-powered salesmanship gimmicks becomes increasingly important. Fact versus fiction, myth versus reality, and propaganda versus truth are important purposes for listening.

Listening games. Many of the games used at the elementary level are just as effective in the junior high school when the content is varied to correspond to the greater maturity of the students.

Control the speaker. This game involves influencing the verbal and non-verbal behavior of the speaker by altering the type of listener response the class gives during a speech. If the speaker's voice is too soft, the class might refuse to look at him until he projects his voice. A variation is to give rapt attention to the speech for sections and then fail to show attention during another part. Note the difference in the speaker's reaction to good attention and his feeling of inadequacy when the attention shifts. Observe the non-verbal behavior of the speaker as a result of good and poor listening.

Pantomime listening behavior. Pantomime both good and poor listening behavior by listening to a classical music concert, a hockey game, a lecture on nuclear physics, a "bear pit" session on a subject of vital interest to the class, a news broadcast on radio or on television.

Listening retention game. This involves one person reading a passage, word by word, to a group of players. The first player must repeat the first word accurately, the second player must repeat the first plus the second word, and so on. When everyone has had a turn, the first player takes up where the last player left off. The player who successfully repeats the most words of the passage without missing or transposing a word is the winner.

The rumor game. This game involves one person reading a paragraph containing several critical facts to another person while the rest of the players (from four to seven in a group) cover their ears (or carry on a lively conversation among themselves). Now the person to whom the passage was read relates it to one of the persons who had his ears covered. This individual relates it to another, and so on, until all have had an opportunity to relate what he remembers of what was told him. If possible, tape each person's version of the facts, then play back the entire tape. Notice how the version may vary from person to person.

Keep talking and listening. Five students are provided with a written phrase. At a given signal from the instructor, the first student begins telling a story. He tries to include the phrase in the story without "giving it away" to the rest of the group. The teacher taps a bell every thirty seconds and the next student begins the story where the former student left off, trying to include *his* phrase in the story. This continues until each has had an opportunity. The first player picks up the story and includes his phrase. If at any time a player correctly guesses another's phrase, that person drops out of the game.[47]

Self-evaluation for the Teacher

Miss Blake, a fifth grade teacher, was seated at her desk finishing up the cumulative record of one of her students when Brad came up and said, "Miss Blake, you can't guess what happened at home before I came to school this morning."

Miss Blake, trying desperately to complete the report for the office before the first class, looked up briefly and said, "I haven't time to listen now, Brad. Mr. Harris wants this record before he leaves for Neelin School, and I simply must finish it."

"Skip it," said Brad nonchalantly and meandered back to his table. His enthusiasm for communicating was gone, and he showed it in his lack of interest in the morning's activity.

Throughout the day Miss Blake kept remembering the good intentions she had at the beginning of the year to *listen* to a student when he had something important he wanted to discuss. It wasn't enough that she had determined to *teach* listening lessons. She had determined that she would *listen*. Yet too many demands were made upon her.

Several days later Brad repeated the behavior of the earlier morning and came to where Miss Blake was working, this time on her plans for the afternoon classes. He said, "Miss Blake, I bet you can't guess what happened on the way to school."

Miss Blake looked up, thinking, "Oh, no! Not Brad again!" But she smiled and said, "I am so anxious to hear all about it. I'll tell you what we'll do. Mr. Harris wants this list of people going on the field trip this afternoon. If you will take it to the office for me, it will save time and we can talk when you get back. Okay?"

"That's fine. Thanks!" replied Brad.

"For what?" asked Miss Blake.

"Don't you know? You always tell us to listen. Thanks for practicing what you preach. We like to be listened to also."

In a listening-centered environment, the quality of communication rapport is readily apparent. Interaction and rapport between child and child *and* teacher and child become extremely important in the development of the personality of the pre-adolescent. Both non-verbal and verbal behavior become signs that tell the student he is an important human being who has a right to be heard. The sensitive teacher recognizes the value not only of teaching listening skills, but also of demonstrating skill in listening.

Under the pressures of the crowded curriculum and classroom routines, teachers all too often fail to evaluate their listening program as an integral part of the curriculum. Periodic self-evaluation is the key to success in teaching. Self-evaluation is the key to a successful listening program.

1. Do I provide a classroom climate which fosters good listening habits?
2. Do I provide opportunity for the development of a wide variety of listening skills?
3. Do I provide a listening center where children may go to carry on listening activities that is comparable to the art center, music center, the arithmetic center, the library?
4. Do I arrange for the use of the language laboratory for practice in improving listening skills?
5. Do I record stories and programs for use in the listening center?
6. Do I use tapes of educational radio programs available?
7. Do I keep alert to the special needs of those children who need to replay the tape, record, or film?
8. Do I encourage children to carry on some of their listening activities in small groups at the listening center?
9. Do I plan as carefully to help children learn to listen for various purposes as I do to help them learn to read for various purposes?
10. Do I make use of listening activities for self-teaching and self-testing?
11. Do I listen to children as courteously as I should?
12. Do I initiate activities for various purposes for listening in terms of the interests, abilities, and needs of the children?
13. Do I get the attention of everyone before I start speaking?
14. Do I teach the children to be courteous listeners at all times?
15. Do I involve the children in setting standards for listening?

16. Do I guide the children in developing an appreciation and awareness of the sounds in our language?

17. Do I keep in mind that children spend more time in listening than in other communication skills?

18. Do I develop a balanced program in which listening skills are taught consistently and practiced through such specific activities as: listening to evaluate an idea or point of view, listening for directions, listening for main and subordinate ideas, listening for enjoyment, listening to appreciate poetry, prose, and music, listening courteously to communicate and engage in conversation, listening to learn to discriminate sounds?

19. Do I understand the factors that influence listening?

20. Do I keep a record of each child's listening progress based on a form such as the following?

Progress Chart for Listening

Name of Child ____________________
Grade ____________________
School ____________________
Name of teacher ____________________

Item	Comments	Date
1. He evidences a readiness for listening with a purpose.		
2. He disregards distractions in the environment.		
3. He comprehends what he hears.		
4. He listens courteously.		
5. He listens critically for evidence, logic, main ideas.		
6. He listens for enjoyment.		
7. He listens appreciatively.		
8. He follows the thread of the conversation.		
9. He makes good use of the differential in time between thought and speech.		
10. He reinforces the speaker by showing an interest in the topic.		

Pupil Self-assessment Chart

Name ______________________ Sex ______ Age ____ Date ______

Directions

Put an X in column 1 if you **almost always have to be told to listen.**
Put an X in column 2 if you **usually have to be told to listen.**
Put an X in column 3 if you **sometimes have to be told to listen.**
Put an X in column 4 if you **usually listen voluntarily.**
Put an X in column 5 if you **almost always listen voluntarily.**

	1	2	3	4	5
1. I listen to the teacher attentively.					
2. I listen to the ideas of others.					
3. I listen to follow directions.					
4. I listen for the main ideas of a speech.					
5. I listen to important announcements from the principal's office.					
6. I listen to enjoy a story the teacher reads to the class.					
7. I listen to the speaker's evidence before I make up my mind.					
8. I listen to appreciate poetry, stories, drama, music.					
9. I listen to music so I can show how it makes me feel by painting a picture, writing a poem, or creating a dance.					
10. I listen to my friends so I will know what to say when they are through talking.					

It is important for teachers to realize that if they expect children to listen, they must have something worthwhile to say. They must realize, too, that if they expect children to listen to directions and explanations, the directions and explanations must be clear and concise. They also must be aware that if children are to listen to stories and poetry with enjoyment and appreciation, the teacher must have developed skills in oral interpretation.

Self-evaluation for the Reader

Answer the following questions by checking the column Yes, No, Doubtful.

	Yes	*Doubtful*	*No*
1. Can you follow directions after hearing them only once?			
2. Do you listen primarily for ideas rather than facts?			
3. Do you try to differentiate facts from opinions when you hear people talking?			
4. Can you anticipate another person's next ideas when you listen?			
5. Can you summarize the remarks of another person to whom you listen?			
6. Do you easily remember ideas you try to carry in mind as you listen to others?			
7. Do you have a desire to ask questions of a speaker?			
8. Do you suspend judgment for a time on new arguments which you hear?			
9. Can you listen to an argument without becoming emotionally upset?			
10. Do you remember the idea that was illustrated by a story?			
11. Are you aware of things the speaker might have said but avoided saying?			
12. Do you recognize a speaker's transitions from one idea to another?			

	Yes	Doubtful	No
13. Do you notice any digression of a speaker from his main line of thought?			
14. After listening to someone, are you more inclined to discuss his ideas rather than his manner of speaking?			
15. Can you listen without being distracted by other sights and sounds?			
16. Can you listen to a speaker without thinking about other listeners?			
17. Can you notice violations of good speech without disliking the person speaking?			
18. In a conversation, do you hear the last comment of another before you speak?			
19. Can you receive value from a speaker to whom you are required to listen?			
20. Do you tend to change your attitude toward the speaker as you hear more from him?			
21. Can you listen well to a person whose racial or religious background is different from yours?			
22. Are you aware of why you do or do not listen to someone?			
23. Do you get new insights regarding yourself when you listen to others?			
24. Do you listen objectively to criticism of your efforts?			
25. Do your friends ask you to listen to their problems?[48]			

In checking your answers to these twenty-five questions, try to relate them to the *Guides to Effective Listening*, pages 50-52 of your text.

Concluding Statement

Listening to learn rather than merely learning to listen should be a goal of the creative communications program. The child does not automatically listen. He must be taught to listen for a variety of purposes. He should participate in a well planned, well articulated, well balanced, and well directed developmental listening program. This should begin in the kindergarten and continue throughout the elementary school. He must achieve ever increasing mastery of this tool for learning if he is to live successfully in a society that demands a citizen who can listen critically as well as appreciatively, who can listen with comprehension as well as with enjoyment, who can solve problems as well as follow directions, and who can listen to communicate as well as to discriminate sounds.

The imperative need for listening purposefully, effectively, and efficiently in a wide range of listening situations will be met only if the school assumes its responsibility in this area. This necessitates preparing teachers to carry out a well planned program of training in listening. In a classroom oriented to listening, the child develops the auditory sensitivity and the functional facility that ensures that he will be equal to purposeful listening and creative listening with a minimum expenditure of time and energy and a maximum of enjoyment, satisfaction, and reward.

"Through listening the student experiences satisfactions in hearing beautiful phrases and artistic expression; he enhances his appreciation of poetry, drama, and various forms of literature; he grows more discriminative in evaluating the language he hears and thereby extends and improves his own usage; he becomes better able to recall information and ideas; he learns to react critically and become selective as he learns."[49]

The teacher learns to listen perceptively to the student and understand him as a person. In the words of Carl Rogers, "Real communication occurs . . . when we listen with understanding. What does that mean? It means to see the expressed idea and attitude from the other person's point of view, to sense how it feels to him, to achieve his frame of reference to the thing he is talking about."[50]

Sweeny reinforces the importance of listening as a significant factor in relating to others as he states, "The effective adult will be a person who sincerely values and cares about other people. He will be a good listener, i.e., a person who can understand both the verbal and non-verbal communication of the other person. In addition to being a good listener, he is able to communicate that he has understood."[51]

"The momentous impact of listening competence in all our lives demands that we in education place a greater emphasis upon this most important language art skill."[52]

References

1. By permission of National Council of Teachers of English, *The English Language Arts*, Appleton-Century-Crofts, Inc., New York, 1952, pp. 273, 271.
2. Joseph Mersand, "Developing Competence in Listening in Secondary Schools," *The Speech Teacher*, 7:301, November, 1958.

3. Leland B. Jacobs, "Speaking and Listening," in Helen McCracken Carpenter (ed.), *Skill Development in Social Studies*, National Council for Social Studies, NEA, Washington, 1963, p. 141.
4. By permission from Thomas R. Lewis and Ralph Nichols, *Speaking and Listening*, William C. Brown Company, Publishers, Dubuque, Iowa, 1965, p. 6.
5. Dominic Barbara, "Listening with a Modest Ear," *Today's Speech*, 9:3, February, 1961.
6. Mark A. Neville, "Listening Is an Art: Practice It," *Elementary English*, 36:226, April, 1959.
7. John Irwin and Marjorie Rosenberger, *Modern Speech*, Holt, Rinehart, and Winston, Inc., New York, 1961, p. 42.
8. Thorrel B. Fest and Martin B. Cobin, *Speech and Theatre,* The Center for Applied Research in Education, Washington, 1964, p. 14.
9. Irwin and Rosenberger, *op. cit.*, p. 42.
10. *Ibid.*, p. 41.
11. Paul T. Rankin, "The Importance of Listening Ability," *English Journal* (College Edition), 17:623-630, 1928.
12. Harry Goldstein, "Reading and Listening Comprehension at Various Controlled Rates," *Contributions to Education,* No. 28, Teachers College, Columbia University, New York, 1940, p. 56.
13. By permission from Ralph G. Nichols, "Do We Know How to Listen?" *The Speech Teacher*, 10:119, March, 1961.
14. *Ibid.*
15. By permission from Miriam Wilt, "A Study of Teacher Awareness of Listening as a Factor in Elementary Education," *Journal of Educational Research*, 43: 626-636, April, 1950.
16. *Ibid.*, p. 635.
17. Ursala Hogan, "An Experiment in Improving Listening Skills of Fifth and Sixth Grade Pupils," masters thesis, University of California, Berkeley, 1953.
18. E. K. F. Edgar, "The Validation of Four Methods of Improving Listening Abilities," doctoral dissertation, University of Pittsburgh, Pittsburgh, 1961.
19. T. C. Devine, "The Development and Evaluation of a Series of Recordings for Teaching Certain Critical Listening Abilities," unpublished doctoral dissertation, Boston University, Boston, 1961.
20. Sara Lundsteen, "Teaching Abilities in Critical Listening in the Fifth and Sixth Grades," doctoral dissertation, University of California, Berkeley, 1963.
21. Sara Lundsteen, "Critical Listening: An Experiment," *The Elementary School Journal*, 66:315, March, 1966.
22. Sue E. Trivette, "The Effect of Training in Listening for Specific Purposes," *Journal of Educational Research*, 54:276-277, March, 1961.
23. Robert G. Canfield, "How Useful Are Lessons on Listening?" *Elementary School Journal*, 62:146-151, December, 1961.
24. Robert E. Kraner, "A Comparison of Two Methods of Listening Instruction in an Eighth Grade Language Arts Program," doctoral dissertation, University of Texas, Austin, 1963.
25. John L. Meyer and Frederick Williams, "Teaching Listening at the Secondary Level: Evaluations," *The Speech Teacher*, 14:304, November, 1965.
26. Charles M. Kelley, "Mental Ability and Personality Factors in Listening," *Quarterly Journal of Speech*, 49:152-156, April, 1963.
27. Ann E. Jackson, "An Investigation of the Relationship Between Listening and Selected Variables in Grades 4, 5, and 6," doctoral dissertation, Arizona State University, 1966, in *Dissertation Abstracts*, 27(1) 53A, July, 1966.
28. Ramon Ross, "A Look at Listeners," *Elementary School Journal*, 64:369-372, April, 1964.

29. Clotilda Winter, "Listening and Learning," *Elementary English*, 43:569-572, October, 1966.
30. Anthony L. Norwich, "A Career Development Program in the Chicago Public Schools," *The Elementary School Journal*, 71:391-399, April, 1971.
31. *Ibid.*, p. 393.
32. Keith Brooks and Sister J. Marie Wulftange, "Listener Response to Oral Interpretation," *Speech Monographs*, 31:73-79, March, 1964.
33. Albert L. Furbay, "The Influence of Scattered Versus Compact Seating on Audience Response," *Speech Monographs*, 32:144-148, June, 1965.
34. David B. Orr, Herbert Friedman, N. Cynthia Case, "Self-Facing Behavior in the Use of Time-Compressed Speech," *Journal of Educational Psychology*, 60:28-31, February, 1969.
35. C. David Wood, "Comprehension and Compressed Speech by Elementary School Children," doctoral dissertation, Indiana University, 1965, in *Dissertation Abstracts*, 28(2) 336A-37A, August, 1966.
36. Joseph M. Miller and John B. Voor, "Effects of Practice Upon the Comprehension of Time-Compressed Speech," *Speech Monographs*, 35:452-454, November, 1965.
37. Carole H. Ernest, "Listening Comprehension as a Function of Type Material and Rate of Presentation," *Speech Monographs*, 35:154-158, June, 1965.
38. Howard H. Spicker, "Listening Comprehension Retention of Intellectually Normal and Retarded Children as Functions of Speaking Rate and Passage Difficulty," doctoral dissertation, George Peabody College for Teachers, 1963, in *Dissertation Abstracts*, 24(5), November, 1963.
39. See also Harold G. Shane et al., *Interpreting Language Arts Research for the Teacher*, Association for Supervision and Curriculum Development, NEA, 1201 Sixteenth St., N.W., Washington, D.C. 20036, 1971.
40. Ralph G. Nichols, "Do We Know How to Listen? Practical Helps in a Modern Age," *The Speech Teacher*, 10:120-124, March, 1961.
41. *Ibid.*, p. 122.
42. *Ibid.*
43. *Ibid.*, p. 124.
44. Lillian M. Logan, *Teaching the Young Child*, Houghton Mifflin Company, Boston, 1960, p. 176.
45. Lewis and Nichols, *op. cit.*, pp. 56-8.
46. Virginia A. Woodward, "Young Children Initiate Their Own Listening Experiences," *Young Children*, National Association for the Education of Young Children, 31:10-11, October, 1965.
47. Adapted from Larry L. Barker, *Listening Behavior*, Prentice-Hall, Inc., Englewood Cliffs, N.J., 1971, pp. 142-4.
48. Adapted from Karl Robinson and Albert Becker, *Effective Speech for the Teacher*, McGraw-Hill Book Company, New York, 1970, pp. 52-53.
49. Lillian M. Logan and Virgil G. Logan, *Teaching the Elementary School Child*, Houghton Mifflin Company, Boston, 1961, p. 223.
50. Carl R. Rogers, "Barriers and Gateways to Communication," *Human Relations: Rare, Medium, or Well Done*, Harvard College, 1954.
51. Thomas J. Sweeny, "Adult Models for the Emerging Adolescent," paper prepared for the Council on the Emerging Adolescent Learner, Washington, D.C., 1971.
52. Rhoderick J. Elin, "Listening: Neglected and Forgotten in the Classroom," *Elementary English*, 49:231, February, 1972.

4

Freeing the Child for Effective Speaking

A controlled body gives a controlled voice.
Carrie Rasmussen

Bodily activity is the very basis of speech. Since words themselves are produced with muscles, the muscles of the body must be controlled to have effective speech. It takes a controlled body to produce a controlled voice.

Teaching children to speak effectively begins with attention to bodily movement and rhythmic activity. The relationship between bodily movement and speech has long been recognized by those of the world of the theater. It was also early recognized by Señorita Zapata, Chief of Preschool Education in Mexico for more than fifty years. It was her conviction that there was a close relationship between bodily action and speech. She stated, "When children say 'Buenos Dias' they should say it with their eyes, their voice, and their bodies. There must be a correlation among voice, language, ideas, and bodily action. This has been my belief and practice. [The three year preschool curriculum] offers numerous opportunities for speaking, listening, discussion, creative dramatics, rhythms, storytelling, puppetry, and other types of oral expression."[1] An excellent approach to speech in the elementary school is through a developmental program in which rhythmic activity, creative movement, pantomime, and dramatic play introduce the child gradually to the wonderful world of creative speech.

The child is enthralled with the discovery that the body is an instrument through which he can express without words his moods, emotions, and ideas. He soon finds, however, that he must add words to his actions to communicate better what he is thinking, feeling, and experiencing. Pantomime combines readily with activities in the dramatic play of the young child. Dramatic play leads naturally into creative dramatics, a perfect vehicle for creative expression.

Experience in rhythms and pantomime gives the child the expressive body so essential for expressive speech. Thus non-verbal communication forms the bridge for the later speech activities of dramatization, oral interpretation of literature, panel discussions, the planning and organization of speeches, and other related speech skills. When the teacher realizes the importance of freeing the child to use his body spontaneously, creatively, and joyously, he is paving the way for every child in his class to develop self-confidence, poise, and ease. Movement, rhythms, pantomime, and dramatic play afford opportunities for language and conceptual growth as well as creative expression.

Creative Movement

Creative movement is as natural to the child as breathing. He expresses his joy of living as he sways, bends, and dances; as he skips, runs, and prances. He moves to express his feelings, his ideas, and his aspirations. For him physical response is an integral part of the rhythm of life. "With the first breath and the first heartbeat, rhythm becomes an urge demanding response. . . . If no words are said and no songs sung, there are other ways of responding to the inner urge of rhythm."[2]

The ancient Greeks recognized this principle as they harmonized rhythm with the art of living. Man has always expressed his deepest feelings, his strongest emotions, his most significant moments in movement. In the rituals of the dance, in the processional, in the recessional, in the most solemn occasions, response to the measured beat is essential. Movement free or movement patterned in regular rhythmic sequence of recurring beat remains throughout life one of the greatest avenues for self-expression.

How to capitalize on this inner urge to rhythm is the challenge to the teacher who guides children's rhythmic response from tentative movements to bold communication of ideas. Observe the young child as he responds to the rhythm of the marching band, the ballet, or the ocean waves. His body is an instrument for expression. He does not need to be told to march, to fly like a bird, to lumber like an elephant, or to float like a cloud. He *is* the bird flying across the sky or hopping across the green to get a worm, or the elephant lumbering along in the circus parade or stampeding across the veldt. He *is* the cloud floating lazily across the sky. He identifies as readily with the elements of nature as he does with the creatures of nature. Through movement alone he can express his moods, feelings, and concepts about life.

Creating an Environment Conducive to Pre-Speech Activities

The teacher must create a receptive environment in which originality, spontaneity, and creativity can flourish. Children must be free to explore, to experiment, to create, to express ideas, and to invent patterns of movement, knowing that their contribution will be valued and that they will not be laughed at. They must recognize, too, that within the framework of freedom of expression many activities require specific techniques. A favorable attitude on the part of the teacher does much to encourage children to express themselves freely in movement.

The teacher must provide *space* in which to move freely. If space in the classroom is limited, he should find a time when the playground is free, the auditorium or activity room is unoccupied, or the gymnasium is empty. The gymnasium, however, may be too large to establish a feeling of rapport so evident when the space is right. Enough space for rhythmic activity may be found in the classroom if the furniture is rearranged. The resourceful teacher is alert to possibilities for providing space; he knows the importance of movement not only for creative expression and recreation, but also as an antidote to tension, fatigue, and negative behavior.

Through integrating activities the teacher can provide *time* for a balanced program in which children respond to rhythm, plan group activity in movement, create new forms and designs in rhythms and dance. Time is needed for planning, participating, and evaluating.

The teacher must have *skills* for guiding activities. Children need guidance in order to develop. They need a teacher who has the skills that will enable him to direct the various phases of the program in such a way that growth, not chaos, results. They need a teacher who has a creative imagination, a sense of rhythm, and ingenuity in providing an accompaniment. They need a teacher who enjoys movement.

Essential Skills for the Teacher

Creative imagination. More essential than the other requisites for guidance is a creative imagination. A teacher must be able to inspire children to create; and this is possible only if he himself is creative. He must know how to develop the child's imagination and encourage him to use his own ideas. He must remember what it is to be a child; he must keep alive the wonder and the awe of experiencing something new. The teacher should participate in creative experiences himself in order to understand their value. The creative teacher does not teach the same songs, the same dances, in the same way, at the same time. One non-creative teacher kept a record over a period of twenty-three years and prided herself on the fact that she never failed to teach the identical songs, games, and rhythms on the same day of the same week each year. Leap year was always a problem for her.

A sense of rhythm. Most people have a sense of rhythm. They respond spontaneously if they are asked to move on the beat or off-beat. They can keep time with the music and swing and sway, hop and skip, march and dance. Those who feel a lack in this area should avail themselves of the opportunity to develop their rhythmic skills through pre-service or in-service experiences in a class in rhythms or dancing.

Ingenuity in providing an accompaniment. Running, skipping, marching, walking, and other basic rhythmic activities may be accompanied not only by the piano but by the auto-harp, the drum, and other percussion instruments. Instrumental music is essential to accompaniment in folk dances and can be an invaluable aid in guiding rhythmic response. However, there are activities in which the beat of the drum or the tom-tom, the music of the tambourine or triangle, or the regular recurring beat of the rhythm sticks can serve to accompany the children in rhythmic activity.

Enjoyment of movement. Children are delighted when the teacher actually does a skip, a slide, a polka, or a folk dance step. Children like to watch him. Not only must he be willing to guide rhythmic expression, he must be enthusiastic about it. In addition to skills, he must also have a sense of enjoyment. Music and movement should offer the child an exciting adventure throughout the elementary school years. They should stir the creative impulse of the teacher as well as the children. They should add zest to living.

Among the rhythmic activities that children enjoy are: creative rhythms; fundamental movements (locomotor and non-locomotor); dramatizing nursery rhymes, poems, and songs; singing games; dancing (folk, creative, and social).

Creative movement offers an excellent avenue for creative expression. Many children are led to an appreciation of rhythm through the physical response to music, the beat of the tom-tom, or the rhythm of the sticks. With little motivation other than the sound of the music, many children will move out to the center of the floor and begin to dance. Those who are more timid respond to "acting out" songs. All, however, are eager to participate in such basic locomotor activities as walking, running, skipping—the primary rhythms. Secondary locomotor rhythms are hopping, jumping, leaping, galloping, sliding. Non-locomotor rhythms that they enjoy are swinging, bending, rocking, swaying, stretching, pulling-pushing, twisting-turning, reaching-stretching, rising-falling, bending-lifting.

As primary children grow into intermediate children, they create designs which become more precise and more complex. Throughout the elementary school, children need a balance of rhythmic activities that afford opportunity for individual and group creativity. In guiding rhythmic response, the teacher must keep in mind freedom of motion, originality of expression, spontaneity of movement, sensitivity of emotional response, and communication of ideas.

Helping children get started in creative movement. Helping children get started in creative movement is an important skill that encourages the teacher to use his own creativity as well as that of the children. There is no magic formula, no one sequence for introducing children to creativity through movement. The teacher could employ the strategy of inquiry to bring the children to the delight of discovery. Questions, cues, and experiences used to motivate a particular group must be based on the teacher's knowledge of that group. He might start with a simple question "How would you 'Hippety Hop to the Barber Shop'?" Further questioning could iead to more complex designs employing such basic locomotor activities such as jump, walk, hop, and so forth. Another way could be to question axial movements such as swinging or a combination of movements such as rocking horses (push and pull). "We discover many possibilities concerning the movement, how we do it, what we are doing, how we can do it better, what it reminds us of, how it feels and how it looks."[3]

It is important that the teacher know his group, that he be aware of various approaches he might use, and that he is willing to adapt the approach to the specific needs of a specific group at a specific time. Never should the approach become crystallized at the level of a technique. The ingenuity of the teacher and the creativity of the children should merge to make of every rhythmic experience a creative one.

Unlike the physical education teacher who teaches movement with emphasis on physical development, the teacher of speech emphasizes movement as it prepares the child for speech skills. An evaluation of the effectiveness of the program will focus on such questions as the following.

Does the child use free bodily movements in his activity? The child's body tells us much about his experiences. Does his body seem tense, his movements jerky or is he relaxed and able to use his body freely? Is there a sureness in his movements and muscular coordination? Does he move his arms and hands freely as a part of an integral whole body which moves rhythmically in any creative activity?

Does he verbalize during any phase of the creative expression? Does he talk, hum, sing, or use nonsense words? Does he giggle, laugh, shout? Is his voice shrill, tense, aggressive; soft, excited, enthusiastic, matter-of-fact? Does he try to communicate what the creative activity means to him? What specifically does he say in his own words? Does any relationship exist between what he says and what he is expressing with his body? What appears to be the purpose of his verbalization? Does the activity seem to require verbalization?

Questions such as these may serve to give the clue to the teachable moment when the child and/or the group is ready to move toward activities related to using more specifically planned movements to express ideas.

Rhythmic Activity

One of the most successful ways of getting children to express themselves creatively is through listening to music and interpreting it in free bodily activity. In creative rhythms the emphasis is on responding to the mood of the music. The music itself motivates each child to move in his individual way. The music should be highly rhythmic, strongly accented, and contrasting in mood. If children are expressing themselves to music that has variety, they will show greater originality.

In responding creatively to music, children should listen first, then move out on the floor spontaneously and, in a completely individual interpretation, express themselves to the music they hear. As they become aware of unity, balance, and climax in the music, they integrate these elements into a design that is a creative experience for them. Rhythmic activities of this type prepare the child for responding to the rhythms of poetry and the more subtle rhythms of prose. "Unless certain basic skills are mastered, later, more elaborated ones become increasingly out of reach."[4] Rhythm is basic to all the language arts.

In creative rhythms the emphasis is on originality of expression, not conformity. Teachers will find this a rewarding approach when they create a favorable environment, are enthusiastic about creative movement, understand the children they teach, and have the necessary skills to blend these elements in such a way that response is natural, spontaneous, and vital. Most young children have few inhibitions about expressing themselves through creative movement. When they are given ample opportunity for creative expression through this avenue, they grow in enjoyment. It is vital that this should continue to be an integral part of the education of all children, an aid in achieving their potential speech skills. Findley states, ". . . bodies should be as plastic, as responsive as their voices. . . . The actor who has a finely tuned rhythmic body will have a perfect instrument for the expression of his art."[5] This is as true for the speaker and reader as for the actor.

Fundamental Rhythms

The approach to rhythms may also be made through the basic locomotor skills. Children walk, march, run, skip, slide, gallop, jump, and hop. When the spirit is willing and the body is ripe, the moment comes when the child wants to express himself through these basic movements. Physical maturation as well as the willingness to try influence the child's success in such activities. Allowance should be made for individual differences in the fundamental rhythms. There are children who feel initially more at ease with fundamental movements such as walking, running, hopping, leaping, skipping, and galloping.

Some activities in fundamental rhythms are:

Walking
(1) Clap or tap out the beats.
(2) Walk to music.
(3) Dramatize different types of walk.
(4) March to music.

Running
(1) Begin by walking.
(2) Gradually increase the rate of the music or drum beat until the children are running.
(3) Combine running, marching, and walking movements.
(4) Have different children set the tempo and others follow their lead.

Hopping
(1) Suggest that the children be a favorite animal that hops around.
(2) Use such activities as skipping rope.
(3) Dramatize one of the nursery rhymes that requires a hop.
(4) Play hop-scotch or similar games that require a hop.
(5) Create a group pattern in which walking, running, and hopping are combined.

Leaping
(1) Develop from a long run.
(2) Jump as though jumping over a puddle.
(3) Create a ballet movement.
(4) Combine a leap with other movements.

Skipping
(1) Clap out the rhythm of a skip.
(2) Respond to the rhythm of a skip—long, short; long, short.
(3) Move with a long and short step, getting upon toes, and then off the floor.
(4) Dramatize nursery rhymes in which skipping is suggested.

Galloping
(1) Clap out the rhythm of long and short beat (heavy-light).
(2) Use coconut shells to create the sound of horses galloping.
(3) Dramatize horses galloping.
(4) Combine movements in a creative design.

Ideas

Ideas afford an excellent approach to rhythmic response. They form an important motivation for movement. Instead of initiating the activity by playing music that evokes the basic rhythms of walking, running, jumping, or hopping, the teacher might begin by asking the children how they would walk if "there are pebbles under your feet and you are barefooted" or if "the sidewalk is hot and there is a hole in the sole of one shoe"? Other leading questions could be:

Can you think of a musical instrument you would like to be and show with your body how you would make music? (The children might be a music box, a spinning top, an accordion, a trombone.)

Can you think of Christmas toys you could be? See if we can guess what the toys are? (Bouncing ball, train, robot, doll.)

Can you think of new ways to stretch and bend your body?

Can you demonstrate in movement some type of activity observed at the zoo?

Can you show me how the animals at the zoo move?

Lengthy discussion is not effective with young children. For the younger child, the urge is to respond immediately. Suggestions for improvement come better after the movement is under way.

However, as children grow in this type of response, they will be eager to suggest ways of improving. For example, Tommy might think of a variety of ways birds would fly to get to their nests. Jimmy might suggest a new way for flying a jet. Marilyn might try a new movement for the dancer on the top of the music box, and Lucille might suggest having some one dance a ballet while the others watch the music box as it is being wrapped up for a gift. Some of the children get their inspiration for creativity from a poem; others get it from music; still others seem to have it within them and respond to any approach to rhythm.

Older children may be motivated by such suggestions as:

Find an area where you can move without interfering with any one else and work out an idea using your arms, your legs, head, or torso.

What activities can you work out if you stay in one spot?

What activities can be integrated in a complex situation such as a circus, a carnival, a ball game, a railway station, or an airport?

Ideas for creative expression in movement may come at times when children are not even participating in rhythmic activities. They may originate in other curriculum areas. For example:

A group of fifth grade children were working with chalk, experimenting with ways of getting different degrees of intensity in color. David, while thinking about what to do next, yawned and stretched. Then with a sudden outburst he said, 'Say, I've got an idea—watch me.' As the children watched, he explained and demonstrated a stretch that could be intense, while the recoil could be just the opposite. 'Couldn't we put this on paper?' he asked. This idea led to an interesting combination of experimenting with movement, color, and line in which all the boys and girls became interested. In an informal way, some worked alone, first 'feeling', then 'drawing'. Others worked in twos, one child 'doing' and the other getting it down on paper. Some started with the 'drawing' and then translated it into movement. Soon, this particular group listened to some favorite music and then transferred what they felt 'inside' to movement and paper.[6]

Poetry

Bodily response to poetry offers the child essential activity correlated with the rhythm and rhyme. He responds to the moods in the poetry as he moves to the rhythm. Among the poems the authors have found effective are the following.

Galloping. "I Had a Little Pony", "Ride a Cock Horse", "The Huntsman" "To Market", "Little Boy Blue", "Lucy Locket", "I Saw a Ship a-Sailing".

Jumping and hopping. "Jack Be Nimble", "Diddle, Diddle, Dumpling", "Hoppity", "Once I Saw a Little Bird".

Marching. "The Brave Old Duke of York", "Yankee Doodle".

Running. "Wee Willie Winkle", "Hickory, Dickory, Dock", "Tom, Tom, the Piper's Son".

Clapping and tapping. "Pease Porridge Hot", "Mrs. Peck Pigeon", "Pat-a-Cake".

Rocking. "Rock-a-Bye Baby", "Hush-a-Bye Baby".

Flying. "Bless You, Bless You, Burnie-bee".

Skipping. "Little Miss Muffet", "Little Jack Horner", "Jack Sprat", "Peter, Peter, Pumpkin Eater", "Pop Goes the Weasel".

Swinging and swaying. "The Swing".

Walking. "One Misty, Moisty Morning", "Hot Cross Buns", "There Was an Old Woman Who Lived in a Shoe".[7]

There is a wealth of children's literature that can be used to motivate rhythmic response. Action and pantomime may be suggested by the words. The teacher should be sure that the children are familiar with the rhythm and have an opportunity to discuss it before dramatizing it. The highly creative child is not limited by the text, but spontaneously adds much in pantomime to the bare outline suggested by the words.

Pantomime

Long before a child communicates in words he communicates through movement; he uses his entire body to express himself. Thus pantomime is a natural avenue for creative expression. Children come by pantomime naturally. As an art form, however, pantomime requires concentrated effort and is not usually perfected at the elementary school level.

Strickland recognizes the close relationship between the actor's control of his body and the poet's choice of words. She states: "The poet's selection of specific words to express his thoughts and feelings is similar to the actor's selection of specific actions through which he, too, may reveal his thoughts and feelings. . . ."[8]

Pantomime involves action and/or gestures without words as a means of creative expression. It is one of the most effective modes of non-verbal communication. Children pantomime spontaneously in dramatic play. Pantomime is an outlet for the imagination. The child, like the poet, expresses himself in whatever media he chooses at a particular moment. In creative movement the child uses his entire body as an instrument of expression. This is particularly true in pantomime. As children develop skills in this medium they become increasingly adept in relating an experience or telling a simple or complex story wholly through action.

Pantomime affords children excellent opportunity for creative expression through doing, feeling, and reacting. The child, for instance, may use pantomime to depict what he is *doing*. Instead of using words to express his ideas, he demonstrates with his body.

Doing. Camping or picnicking.
Exploring a cave.
Searching for a lost article. After searching earnestly, finding it, and showing through pantomime what it is.
Receiving a birthday gift, unwrapping it, showing pleasure (or disappointment), and showing through pantomime what it is.
Showing favorite activities of the different seasons of the year.
Selecting a favorite toy and playing with it.
Participating in any sport.
Going to a circus, observing and/or being the various acts in the big tent, the side shows, the midway.
Passing a tray of food. Each child takes something, and portrays what it is by the way he holds and eats it.

Feeling. After initiatory experiences the teacher may introduce the next step in pantomime action—feeling. Each of the actions suggested above should show how a person feels while he is doing it. For example, the pantomime of eating should be extended to find out if the person likes or dislikes what he is eating. This opens up a variety of participation activities to stimulate the emotional state of mind and the physical response.

Reacting. Here the important factor is the ability to empathize and identify with the action from the *inside out*, to feel the part, to be aware of every possible detail which clothes the pantomime with reality. For example, if a child picks up a basket, one should be able to tell if it is filled or empty by the muscle tension employed. As children develop, the feeling and reaction steps usually precede the doing. They are ready to discuss and plan the characterizations in more detail. For the young child, "the play's the thing".

Refinement in this art does not come all at once. It is the result of much experience in developing powers of awareness, sense reactions, and characterizations, and playing out simple situations creatively.

Educators are no longer satisfied to leave the child alone in the mistaken belief that all that is needed is a climate of psychological safety which frees the child so that his emotional and psychic energy will fill the void and he will create. Without some specific techniques and skills, be it in dramatics, art, or writing, the growing child will be at a loss. Although it is true that the very young child in no way senses a need for technique or skill in expressing what he feels and experiences, as he matures he is no longer so confident about expressing his creativity. It is at this point that the child will feel the need for help in the skills. According to Eisner, "Creative ability is, to a significant degree, specific to the subject matter. . . . a person must be able to control the syntax and techniques of the discipline within which he is working if he is to use it creatively."[9]

Through pantomime and impersonation the child develops specifically in (1) imagination, (2) awareness, (3) sensitivity, and (4) communication of a non-verbal nature.

Developing imagination. Children naturally imagine and create. They are endowed by nature with the creative spirit. They need, however, opportunities for developing the aptitudes for creativity which they possess. As the imagination takes over, the child uses his imagination spontaneously; he transforms a sandpile, a few old pans and some well-worn blocks into a railroad terminal. The imagination, too, is developed as the child decides on a characterization he wishes to portray with bodily actions alone. Through insight, perception, and developing technique in the dramatic skills, he becomes increasingly adept at portraying imaginatively.

Swartz defines imagination as "the recall to consciousness of mental pictures produced through the senses, without the present stimulation of these senses in the original way".[10]

Some suggestions for developing the imagination follow.

Walk around the room like a giant.

Be a mouse scampering for food.

Be a giant who decides to go for a swim.

Change from a giant swimming to an insect allergic to water.

Developing powers of awareness. Pantomime offers the child a built-in avenue for developing his powers of awareness. He must in pantomime not only give the impression of walking up the stairs, he must show through the movements of his body, his muscles, the weight exerted by the body in going up the stairs. Developing awareness is a responsibility of every teacher. A good teacher makes children aware of their environment through sense training. For example, the teacher calls attention to such impressions as smelling rain and bonfires, feeling the touch of velvet and other fabrics, listening to voices, pleasant and unpleasant, tasting sweet and sour, enjoying beautiful cloud formations, snowflakes falling, and other such common experiences. In every possible way the child should be encouraged to cultivate awareness of detail, sensitivity, and the quality of perceptive reaction to stimuli. Awareness implies vigilance in observing or in drawing inferences from what one hears, smells, touches, and so on.

An experience such as a visit to the farm can provide many opportunities for developing awareness as well as stimulating the imagination as the experience is recreated. The children may recapture the impressions of holding the warm, soft, baby chicks, throwing corn to the chickens, cobs to the pigs, (showing that this requires greater strength and control as the cobs are heavier than the grain) squealing like baby pigs, neighing like horses, frolicking like baby lambs, and prancing like ponies.

Specific activities for developing sense awareness include:

sewing and sticking yourself with the needle

smelling several kinds of perfume and deciding on which to give mother for her birthday tasting a dish of jello and discovering that it is only egg white beaten without sugar added

coming upon the witch's house in *Hansel and Gretel*

crackling of twigs when you are walking in the woods while you are trying to observe a deer; when you are lost and it is getting late

arriving on earth if you are a creature from Mars

Developing sensitivity. Pantomime, to be effective, requires the individual to have a clear understanding of the situation to be portrayed. The individual, in order to portray a character, must search for clues to the inner motivations expressed in a person's overt actions. "He must gain insight into a character's inner life *if* he is to understand the turbulence beneath the facade of appearance."[11] To portray the character intuitively and with sensitivity, the child must *become* the character. There must be an interaction of doing and feeling as he works out the situation. Sensitivity implies the capacity to respond quickly and acutely to actions of others, to impressions and/or external stimuli.

Communication of a non-verbal nature. Pantomime offers excellent opportunities for communication of a non-verbal type. Action is not mere random activity. Pantomime must be purposeful, expressive, and significant. "The quality of the action reveals the dramatic intent. . . . Much of the significance of language results from the actor's delivery, which includes gesture, posture, facial expression, and movement".[12]

Non-verbal communication is intensified by pantomiming characterizations (always from the inside out), *feeling* the emotion, *reacting* to the emotion, and getting the audience to *respond empathically.*

Some suggestions are:

a child panicking in a stalled elevator

a miser counting his money

a witch stirring her brew

a peddler selling his wares

a beggar finding a purse

a mother receiving word of a son lost in battle

a villain plotting an evil deed

a person receiving a telegram—good news

a child in a department store realizing he is lost

Guidelines for the Teacher

Teachers frequently ask what they can do to help the child develop skills in pantomime. They are conversant with their responsibility for providing an environment in which children are free to express themselves creatively through many avenues. However, they are aware that for each creative medium there is a body of knowledge, a discipline, some specific skills and techniques which if understood can facilitate the quality of the creative expression.

The following brief suggestions will be helpful in guiding activities in pantomime. The child should be encouraged to:

Use spontaneous action, not planned action. Pay no attention to rules, elegance, or correctness, but act on impulse. (This is especially true in the early attempts. As skill is gained the pantomime will become more polished.)

Use abundant action. Avoid timid, stereotyped, restrained, or half-hearted movements.

Use the entire body as an instrument of expression.

Express genuine thought and feeling. Characterization requires a "from the inside out" approach.

Understand the difference between *covert and overt action.* Overt action involves the whole body in large movements like walking, nodding the head, curtseying, gesturing. Covert action is more subtle and oftentimes may go unnoticed as action. It consists of the muscle sets and tensions that reveal the inner feelings, the mood, the emotional state of the character.

Brigance gives an excellent example of covert action.

A child stands in front of a window filled with candy. He is standing stock still; and at first you might say 'He's not doing anything', or 'He's looking at the candy'. But a second look will tell you that his posture and face are saying, 'I want that candy', and you know his salivary glands are overworking, his stomach is contracting and expanding, his blood pressure is up, and his endocrine glands are pumping fluids into his blood. You don't see this terrific internal activity; you do see the hungry look in the boy's face and posture. What you see is *covert* action. Rather it is the outward sign of covert action; and when you see these outward signs you infer the inner action and react to it.[13]

And so it is in pantomime. It is not enough to catch the overt action. One must also capture and relate the covert action—the body set, tilt of the head, total muscular tension—to convey the intense feeling within. When the body catches and reveals the muscle sets and tensions the audience reacts with empathy.

As the child develops in the art of pantomime, he tries to recreate the feelings of the character in his imagination. Good pantomime requires a fine sensitiveness to a situation. Stanislavsky held the belief that to make the public aware of the fine shades of your feelings, you have to experience them intensely yourself.

For the teacher who would guide children's creativity through pantomime, an understanding of the importance of sensitivity to a situation is vital. To the child the important thing is that he can show exactly how he feels without saying a word.

Dramatic Play

Variously termed the "mirror of the child", "trying on life", "imitation of life", and "orientation to life", dramatic play *is* life for the child. Through instantaneous, spontaneous, unstructured free activity of "make-believe" the child utilizes his sense of the dramatic. The play life of the child is a mirror which reflects not only his relationships with the external world but also his inner self. He is unrestricted in the use of his imagination as he takes on the role of the person, phenomena, animal he wishes at a particular moment to identify with. There is no need for plot, audience, or external direction. The younger the child, the more able he is to identify, to shift from one role to another. In the space of a morning he may be a pilot, a captain, a passenger, a fireman, a tree, a mother, father, brother or baby sister, a bird, a jet, or an astronaut.

> One has merely to observe a group of children at play to realize the intensity and spontaneity with which they absorb the happenings of the day and react to the environment; the swiftness with which they respond to crises; the eagerness with which they absorb radio and television; the wholeheartedness with which they identify with the world of people, places, and things; the boundless energy which they bring to their activities. Listen to a group of five-year-olds as they drone out "ten, nine, eight, seven, six, five, four, three, two, one. BLAST OFF."
>
> "Wait," shouts Johnny. "I'm Glenn, the first orbiting astronaut, blasting off into outer space in Friendship VII."
>
> "No! You're not!" insists Glenn. "I'm Shephard and I'm going first."
>
> "You can be the countdown man. He's important."
>
> At that moment of indecision Nancy runs up and throws her arms around Johnny. That settles the argument. "I'm Mrs. Glenn. I'll be praying for you. Do be careful."
>
> And off John goes into space. Allen, content to remain with Nancy and be the countdown man *this* time, drones out, "Ten, nine, eight, seven, six, five, four, three, two, one. BLAST OFF!"
>
> Never mind that you're the countdown man this time. Next time you can be Glenn. In dramatic play you can be anything you want to be. If you're fat you can be thin; if you're short you can be tall; if you're homely you can be handsome; if you're as poor as a church mouse you can be rich as Croesus. You can be what you want to be.[14]

By dramatizing, by acting out his ideas, feelings, emotions, the child communicates his concept of the "world and I". Regardless of the role he is playing, he is working out some of his feelings and frustrations about this world. He is assimilating on his own level of understanding events which are happening all around him. In this way they take on meaning for him and extend his understanding about the complex world.

Essential to dramatic play is a creative teacher who encourages the children to use their imagination; provides exciting activities which stimulate the imagination; rewards original responses and ideas; gives children time to think, to imagine, to play with ideas; and equips them with needed tools of expression *when* and *if* they are ready for them. Critical thinking and evaluation of play activities are an essential part of dramatic play if it is not to deteriorate into chaos and confusion.

The usual patterns of dramatic play of young children include: (1) play centering around activities of the home, such as building, furnishing, cooking, eating, entertaining at parties, taking care of younger brothers and sisters, being fathers, mothers, and grandparents; (2) buying and selling at the supermarket or neighborhood store; (3) transportation: building and playing in boats, trains, airplanes, cars, busses; being captains, engineers, pilots, bus drivers; running gas stations; and assuming duties of employees at air terminals or railroad stations; (4) community helpers: policemen, firemen, postmen; (5) playing legendary persons: Santa Claus, Easter Bunny, St. Valentine; and (6) being animals, particularly pets such as cats, dogs, and birds.

"Playing house" is the universal favorite of the preschool years. The sophistication with which the child reproduces the conversation as well as the tone of voice and mannerisms of the person whose role he is taking on is revealed in the following scene.

> "This is a nail file to do your hands. I'll put it on the dresser. I bought it down town. You really call it an emery board, but filing nails is what it does. Why don't you sit down and do your nails before we go to the party with the Nelsons? O, just a minute. There's the telephone now. That's probably them calling. What time will you be ready? O.K."
>
> Jim smiles gaily at Ann as he answers the phone. "Yes, Mrs. Nelson. Ann is home, but she's busy doing her nails. I got her a new emery board. *Emery* board—you know, what you use to file your nails with. NOT ironing board. She likes it fine. Oh, just a moment, she'll be right here to talk to you. Then you two can get together on the time."
>
> Today Jim is the father, but yesterday he was the little boy.[15]

This is dramatic play, a forerunner of creative dramatics. In dramatic play verbal expression is incidental. The child becomes the individual he is characterizing—whether child, adult, animal, or tree.

A Developmental Approach to Speech

"The World and I" might well be the title of the spontaneous activities of the play life of the child regardless of the medium through which he expresses his ideas: blocks, toys, paints, tools, actions, words. He relives his family life in play; he dramatizes current events; he organizes the world of people and events on his own level by playing out the roles. He dramatizes his own emotions, fears, doubts, loves, hates, and anxieties.

A developmental approach frees the child for guided speaking activities. One of the most effective ways of guiding the child from tentative excursions in movement to creative communication is through successive experiences in dramatic play, rhythmic movement, pantomime, dramatization of simple verses, and finally dramatization of simple stories.

Dramatic Play and Rhythmic Movement

Dramatic play is a form of undirected self-expression which is spontaneous, original, and creative. In this play the child identifies with mother and household activities; with father and the world of occupations and business; with community workers—milkman, bus driver, grocer, postman, nurse, doctor. He identifies, too, with the world of nature—wind, rain, snow, trees, animals, birds, insects.

He is engaged not only in self-expression, but in self-discovery. As he experiments and explores movement, sensation, and relationships, he forms his own concepts of the world in which he lives. In dramatic play he can rapidly shift roles as he manipulates, organizes, and restructures his environment.

Movement is a natural expression of the young child, and it forms a basis for getting in tune with one's self. The teacher serves as a guide in creative living as he encourages self-expression through movement. Capitalizing on the interest of the children and utilizing movement based on those interests, the teacher may chant rhymes that have a strong rhythmic pulse to help children become free in creative movement.

Kalunk—kalunk—kalunk,
I'm an elephant swinging my trunk.

I love to skip alone
On the beach in moisty weather

Winifred Welles

Run on the rocks where seaweed lives,
Watch the waves and the beautiful ships.

Mary Britton Miller

Slowly ticks the big clock;
tick-tock, tick-tock!
But Cuckoo clock ticks double quick;
Tick-a-tock-a, Tick-a-tock-a,
Tick-a-tock-, tick!

Unknown

I climbed upon the merry-go-round,
And it went round and round.

Dorothy Baruch

Bring the comb and play upon it;
Marching, here we come!
Willie cocks his highland bonnet,
Johnnie beats the drum.

Robert Louis Stevenson

Spring is showery, flowery, bowery;
Summer; hoppy, croppy, poppy;
Autumn; wheezy, sneezy, freezy;
Winter: slippy, drippy, nippy.

Mother Goose Rhymes

Pantomimes Based on Real or Imaginary Situations

Wishes
Dreams
Camping
Painting

Circus
Occupations
Sports
Vacation

Going to the zoo
Going to the beach
Going on a picnic
Going to a movie

Pantomime with Music

The toyshop. Toys come to life in a toy shop. Each child decides what kind of toy he is. Some of the dolls may be old and rusty. They will move stiffly. Others will be new. They will move with ease. Create a movement in response to the theme and music. Move around the room. Some of the toys may run down, so the leader must wind them up. Some of the animals (teddy bears) might prefer to watch the other toys perform. The toy soldiers may want to march. Suggested music: Victor Herbert, "Toyland", or Tchaikovsky, "Nutcracker Suite".

A spring storm. Listen to the music of "Cloudburst" from Grofe's *Grand Canyon Suite*. Respond to the music of the wind and rain of a sudden storm. Pit your strength against the fierceness of the storm. Decide whether the storm subsides and you emerge victorious, or the storm destroys you before it subsides.

An autumn morning. Curl up like a seed buried deep within the earth. Decide what kind of flower you will be. Feel the warmth of the sun in the niche in the earth. Grow very slowly and unfold into a flower. You enjoy the summer days as the warm sun shines on you and the gentle showers give you a drink. But autumn comes on. The wind and the rain are more fierce. It may hail and your leaves are bruised. React to the music. Finally frost comes, and the flowers wither and die as the music fades away.

Winter wonderland. Create a fantasyland display as seen in a store window at Christmas time. Select appropriate movement, mood, and music which motivates a variety of situations.

Pantomime with Simple Poems[16]

The Wonderful Weaver

There's a wonderful weaver
  High up in the air.
He weaves a white mantel
  For cold earth to wear.
With the cold for his shuttle
  and clouds for his loom,
How he weaves, how he weaves
  In the light of the moon.

Excerpt from a poem by George Cooper

How would you fashion your snow flakes if you were the wonderful weaver?

If you could weave your snow flakes and drop them over the country, where would you drop them?

Where would you want your snow flakes to land? How would you feel when you had accomplished your mission?

The Secret

We have a secret, just we three,
  The robin, and I, and the sweet cherry tree;
The bird told the tree, and the tree told me,
  And nobody knows it but just we three.

How would *you* keep a secret?

But of course the robin knows it best,
Because he built the—I shan't tell the rest;
And laid the four little something in it—
I'm afraid I shall tell it any minute.

What could you find to build the nest?

But if the tree and the robin don't peep,
I'll try my best the secret to keep;
Though I know when the little birds fly about
Then the whole secret will be out.

How would you make sure the secret was kept?

Author unknown.

The Little Plant

In the heart of a seed
Buried deep so deep,
A dear little plant
Lay fast asleep.

How would you feel closed up so tight?

"Wake," said the Sun,
"And creep to the light."
"Wake," said the voice
Of the raindrops bright.

What might you see as you poked your head above the ground?

The little plant heard
And rose to see
What the wonderful outside
World might be.

How would you feel?

Excerpt from a poem by
Katie Brown

Imagine

Imagine a tiny red door that leads under a hill
Beneath roots and bright stones and a pebbly rill.
IMAGINE!

Where might *you* find *your* tiny red door?

A quaint little knocker and shoescraper too
A curious carved key waiting for you—
IMAGINE!

How would you feel when you first discovered it?

Now at the doorstep you're turning the key,
The red door will open and there you'll be.
IMAGINE!

Where would you find the key?

Shut the door tight so no one can see,
No one will know then where you will be!
IMAGINE!

What would you see on the other side? How would you feel about what you saw?

Dramatization of Poetry

On a wintry day a group of children were watching snowflakes outside the primary room. The teacher began, "Boys and girls, I know of a

Wonderful weaver high up in the air.
He weaves a white mantle

For cold earth to wear.
With the wind for his shuttle
And clouds for his loom,
How he weaves! How he weaves!
In the light of the moon.

The group discussed the power of the weaver, speculating about him.

Tim: Sometimes the weaver might just be mad because people had been hurt and he had to go without food because of too much snow just like people get hurt sometimes when others get mad and lose their tempers.
Martha: But there is more beauty all over the earth—if you just look for it. (Martha had really been wondering if the blizzard could be because the weaver was angry.)
Teacher: Let's all be the wonderful weaver fashioning snowflakes in our very own way and send them to some special spot on the earth below. Please close your eyes and think of the one spot which you can make beautiful. Let the music tell you when it's time to send your surprises on their way.

To the music of "Clair de Lune" by Debussey, each responded creatively and became intent upon sending the best he could fashion. Some sent one snowflake at a time, watching until it was out of sight. Some dumped containers full of flakes and watched with glee. Others grew weary of weaving.

Teacher: I'm sure some have painted a beautiful picture on the earth. Who will tell where theirs were sent?
Responses from the Children:
I waved my magic wand and sent all of mine to the top of a mountain.
I sent one at a time along a wire fence. But you can't see it now.
I sent mine in front of the manger where Baby Jesus was born.
I sent hundreds down to a pile of coal in a mine.
I had fun sending mine to a pond on a farm. You should have seen the ducks—they couldn't understand it.
I sent mine high on a window sill of a children's hospital.

When the children said, "Let's do it again," the teacher used a slightly different approach. She organized the children into four groups, with one child in each group to be the wonderful weaver who would send them down to earth as snowflakes with a special message for the earth. Each group took a corner of the room for planning.

Teacher: As we decide what our special message will be and how our snowflakes will be sent to earth, let's imagine we're on a special mission.
When the players were ready, each group shared its creation.
Group I: The wonderful weaver fashioned the snowflakes from the clouds, sending them down to a little church. The snowflakes were calling the people to come to church. The North Wind at first was in the way, but relented when he heard the church bell ringing.

Group II: This group chose a fairy princess to spin the flakes out of a fluffy cloud to be sent to little boys and girls. One child in a hospital pressed her nose against the window; another waited until there were enough to roll into a snowball; a puppy's nose was the target for one big flake.
Group III: This group cut snowflakes carefully with special scissors. The wind carried them to a pond below. Some children caught them and as they melted drank the "melt". The ducks on the pond were puzzled until they saw the message, "We will give you a drink."
Group IV. The last group sent snowflakes to be used as a protective blanket to cover the first blossoms which were ready too soon.
Evaluation—comments by the children:
The one walking to school in a blizzard might have been bent against the wind and snow showing how he feels in a blizzard.
We could add other characters such as birds in the trees and seeds to create a countryside scene.
Let's make the most beautiful snowfall of the year.[17]

Dramatization of Simple Stories

Pantomiming episodes from well known stories is an excellent way to lead into dramatizing a complete story by a group. The transition from dramatic play to creative dramatics is a natural one. Through feeling, thinking, creating, and improvising, the child moves from play to "the play". Dramatization will be discussed in a later chapter, because more emphasis is placed on the speech skills.

The Role of Bodily Action in Communication

Movement is vital in effective communication at all levels. Freedom of movement is essential if the speaker is to communicate his ideas and feelings effectively. In communicating with others it is the total response, the total interaction which determines the quality of understanding and communication. Not alone the words people speak, but the subtle, covert actions convey ideas and feelings. The non-verbal communication—the actions of the speaker—help or hinder his attempt to communicate effectively because the listener interprets the actions as well as the words. "As psychiatrists and psychologists remind us, one gets to know something of mental and organic states by noting the type, directions, and force of bodily activity. . . . In the absence of direct signs, we rely on evidence furnished by bodily action."[18]

A prerequisite to effective communication is control of bodily action in order to release the individual to speak more freely and fluently, think more efficiently, and move with greater ease and freedom. Achievement of motivated bodily action helps the individual gain poise, so essential in effective communication of ideas through verbal and non-verbal means. An absence of motivated bodily action in relation to speech often leads to sluggishness, lack of self-confidence, and random movements.

The teacher must keep in mind the need for the student at all educational levels to develop coordination and bodily poise as a prerequisite to effective speaking. Controlled and properly employed, bodily action clarifies meaning, provides emphasis, and permits the audience to empathize with the speaker. The lines of the popular song, "Every Little Movement Has a Meaning of Its Own" is a case in point.

In helping students reveal meaning through bodily action, the teacher might well emphasize pantomime and improvisation. In both pantomime and improvisation, posture gives the first clue to characterization. For instance, in "The Emperor's New Clothes" posture should immediately distinguish the Emperor from the weavers. In "Rumplestilskin" when the miller's daughter becomes the queen she immediately assumes the queenly bearing.

Exercises centering around posture, gestures, and movement should not be practiced in isolation but as an outgrowth of meaningful situations. When this is done, they will result in animation, spontaneity, co-ordination, and creativity. As the student gains in his control of bodily action, he will readily and easily integrate his movements and speech as he interprets feelings, emotions, and ideas creatively.

Suggested activities designed to free the body for effective speaking are:

A. Pantomime.

1. Individual pantomimes.
   a. A traffic policeman.
   b. A waiter taking an order.
   c. A person watching a hockey game.
2. Group pantomimes.
   a. Scenes from movies.
   b. A photographer taking a family picture.
   c. A club meeting.

B. Exercises for spontaneity and co-ordination.

1. You have a baseball in one hand. You see a window. You are tempted. Throw the ball.
2. You are a graceful dancer. You are trying to teach another person to dance.
3. You overhear a story that is false. You cry out, "That's a lie! Go!"

C. Exercises for the development of posture.

1. Walk to the front of the room, assume good standing position, ask a question, and return to your seat.
2. Walk to a chair at the front, pick up a book, be seated, open the book and read from it; close the book, rise, put it on the chair, and return to your seat.
3. Step forward to indicate, "therefore", "also", and "furthermore".
4. Walk to different parts of the room. Indicate a different mood as you change directions.
5. Say five short sentences, shifting weight on each sentence.

D. Exercises for the development of gestures (group exercises).

1. You, there in the front row, and you by the door, listen to this!
2. Hand me the book, please.
3. I shall have nothing to do with you.
4. All of you, stand up, sit down.
5. Look out of the window. What do you see?
6. The box was this long, and this high.
7. Don't speak to me!
8. I can give you three reasons.

E. Speech involving action.

1. Tell a story and act out the characters.
2. Explain how to do something; use visual aids if you wish.
3. Give a talk in which you handle an object or use materials in a demonstration.
4. Defend some person or cause.
5. Dramatize action in social situations (introductions, telephoning, etc.).[19]

The importance of bodily action for effective speaking cannot be over-emphasized. In the physical education classes, the training designed to help the individual develop the control, co-ordination and bodily poise so essential for success in games is equally vital for effective communication. It is necessary, however, for the classroom teacher to help children to make use of the bodily control gained in physical education classes for more effective communication. The activities suggested here provide the teacher with some idea of what should be accomplished in helping pupils gain the needed physical skills necessary to speech. In the chapter "Explorations in Literature" the topics of improvisations, dramatics, and drama will explore further the relationships between bodily activity and creative communication.

Concluding Statement

Through rhythmic response children express the creative urge as spontaneously as they breathe. For them movement provides a release for the imagination, sensitivity, feelings, and ideas. They move not because they are pressured, but because movement gives them a tremendous lift, a sense of freedom, exhilaration akin to flying high above the waters, above the clouds, above the earth, and into the sky.

The teacher creates the environmental conditions for such response; the child provides the expression. The teacher provides the propitious climate; the child brings with him the urge to move—and so it goes. For the child, the movement, the expression, the creative process is the important element of the rhythmic activity. For the teacher, providing the climate for the expression of ideas, giving guidance in the essential skills, and encouraging growth in creative expression are means to the all important end—creative communication.

Creative communication is fostered through varied activities: approaching free bodily movement through creative rhythmic response which impels a child to express his feelings, ideas, emotions; participating in locomotor movement of various types and modifications which the child originates; moving to the chanting of poems and ballads; creating new rhythmic designs; expressing emotions and moods through pantomime; and enjoying dramatic play. Just as the child crawls before he walks, so should he experience the creative expression of the rhythmic impulse as an aid to understanding the rhythmic nature of speech.

The teacher should capitalize on the inspiration of the moment whenever that is possible: the first snow fall which sends children scurrying to the window and leaves them breathless a moment before they dance out on the floor; the quiet rain as it patters on the roof; the music of the masters that evokes from the children the beautiful dance of the Sugar Plum Fairy; or the beat of the tom-tom which is the catalyst for the Indian dance. The creative teacher provides the climate, the inspiration, the guidance; the creative children do the rest. Nowhere more than in creative movement can children translate their dreams and use their imaginations which they have in such abundance—*if* they are encouraged to do so. Communication is a revelation of the inner self.

In guiding children toward effective communication, they must be freed to use their bodies as avenues for expression of their ideas. Whether the child expresses himself through pantomime or dramatic play, he communicates by the use of the entire body. When the child becomes adept at expressing in pantomime and dramatic play, he is ready to move confidently toward speech as an art. Before he can command his voice to speak as he wishes, his body must be free.

References

1. Virgil G. Logan, "Speech Education in Mexico," *The Speech Teacher*, 11:228, September, 1962.
2. Edna Johnson, Evelyn R. Sickles, and Frances Clarke Sayers, *Anthology of Children's Literature*, 3rd ed., Houghton Mifflin Company, Boston, 1959, p. 1001.
3. Gladys Andrews, *Creative Rhythmic Movement for Children*, Prentice-Hall, Inc., Englewood Cliffs, 1954, p. 55.
4. Jerome Bruner, "Education As Social Invention," *Saturday Review*, 49:72, February 19, 1966.
5. Elsie Findley, "Rhythmic Practice," *Theatre Arts*, September, 1927, p. 41, quoted in Loren E. Taylor, *Informal Dramatics for Young Children*, Burgess Publishing Company, Minneapolis, 1965, p. 61.
6. Gladys Andrews et al., *Physical Education for Today's Boys and Girls*, Allyn and Bacon, Inc., Boston, 1960, p. 50. Reprinted by permission of the publishers.
7. These poems are all available in Johnson et al., *op. cit.*, pp. 6-21.
8. F. Cowles Strickland, *The Technique of Acting*, McGraw-Hill Book Company, Inc., New York, 1956, pp. 22-3.
9. Elliot W. Eisner, "Fostering Creativity in the Classroom," *The Instructor*, 72:92, May, 1963.
10. D. Swartz, "Developing Creative Imagination," *High Points*. 14:43-46, 1932, in Morris I. Stein and Shirley J. Heinze, *Creativity and the Individual*, The Free Press of Glencoe, Glencoe, 1960, pp. 407-8.
11. Theodore W. Halten, *Orientation to the Theatre*, Appleton-Century-Crofts, New York, 1962, p. 24.
12. *Ibid.*, p. 23.
13. William N. Brigance, *Speech: Its Techniques and Disciplines in a Free World*, 2nd ed., Copyright, 1969, by Appleton-Century-Crofts, Inc., p. 334. Reprinted by permission of Appleton-Century-Crofts, Educational Division of Meredith Corporation.
14. Lillian M. Logan, "What Are Today's Children Like?" in William Crowder (ed.), *Social Education of Young Children*, rev. ed., National Council for the Social Studies, Washington.
15. Lillian M. Logan and Virgil G. Logan, *Teaching the Elementary School Child*, Houghton Mifflin Company, Boston, 1961, p. 519.
16. Winifred Ward, from workshop in Creative Dramatics, Owensboro, Kentucky. 1954.
17. Suggested by a workshop by Margaret S. Woods.

18. Horace G. Rashkopf, *Basic Speech Improvement,* Harper and Row, New York, 1965, p. 214.
19. Adapted from "Fundamentals of Speech: A Basic Course for High Schools," *The Speech Teacher*, 8:96, March, 1959.

5

Oral Communication

Speech is civilization itself. . . . It is silence that isolates.
Thomas Mann

Twenty-five hundred years ago, Confucius was asked how he would begin to govern his nation if he were placed in power. He answered, "I would begin by establishing correct use of speech." He went on to explain how destructive incorrect speech is to the social and political structure. He concluded by saying, "A gentleman never uses his speech indiscriminately."

Quintilian defined an orator as "a good man skilled in speaking". From the lips of a good man speech is a force for right. From the lips of a demagogue it is a force for evil. In a society in which group action is an integral part of the pattern of life, it is essential that all the members recognize the power of communication skill. They must recognize, too, that with power goes responsibility for using it to improve society.

George Orwell, in looking to the future in his *1984*, paints a picture of the final ruin of a free society by a totalitarian tyranny whose secret weapon is degrading society to the level of robots through a distorted, controlled, and ever shrinking vocabulary.

As the world shrinks, communication becomes ever more important. Ability to express ideas clearly and succinctly, to listen courteously but critically, and to evaluate introspectively yet objectively is imperative in a democratic society. It is to individuals who possess skills of communication, who work well with others that we look for leadership.

The best defense against the ever-present danger of misunderstanding is to speak in words which have the power to communicate clearly. Abstract language which fails to reach the listener is as empty as an unkept promise and as futile as a broken reed.

Speaking is the other side of the coin of listening. Both are essential for communication. How the teacher develops the experiences determines whether the emphasis is to be on listening or speaking in a given situation. In speaking, the child *gives* information; in listening, the child *gets* information. The good listening habits children are developing in the listening program will be reflected in better speaking habits, because children imitate the speech they hear. Thus the arts of language and the skills of communication complement one another. They overlap and cannot be, nor should they be, completely isolated one from another.

Activities which give children opportunity to share experiences, to converse, to interview, to give talks, to participate in formal and informal discussions, and/or to practice parliamentary procedure require both a listener and a speaker. Each child through such experiences communicates his needs, ideas, and feelings. Through speech he clarifies his thinking, shares his information and beliefs, and learns to control his environment.

Guiding children in the development of one of the most powerful instruments for both self-fulfillment and social utility requires that the teacher:

- understand the basic concepts in speaking to communicate
- organize a balanced speech program
- direct speech activities which implement the defined objectives
- be aware of the relationship between creative thought and speech
- develop and utilize instruments of evaluation of speech competency
- understand the sequence of learning experiences

Basic Concepts in Speaking to Communicate

Speaking and listening are reciprocal activities. The speaker and the listener engage in a reciprocal activity interchanging roles spontaneously and easily. The speaker is concerned with securing a response from the listener, and the listener, in order to respond effectively, must have sensory adequacy, interest, and experiental background in order to catch the conversational ball and bounce it back and forth in his mind before deciding whether to hold on to it or toss it back to the sender (speaker).

Speech is a process by which individuals communicate. A child uses speech to adapt to his social environment. He uses speech to influence and control others in his environment, and in turn is influenced by them. Speech is for every individual the most important tool for communication. It is through language that each of us can claim membership in the human family.

Speech is creative expression. Through creative speech man is doing more than expressing ideas. He is manifesting his unfolding personality. Not only does he use the magic of the spoken word to say what he wants to say, he says it with originality, fluency, sparkle, and spontaneiety. His growing perception and sensitivity coupled with increasing skill in communication stimulates him to achieve at the highest level of creative and intellectual expression. "Depending upon the capacity of the speaker, oral communication [speech] can be creative in the best sense of that term, or it can degenerate into banality."[1] Thus speech is more than a means of communicating ideas already conceptualized; it is our principal medium for creating and formulating new ideas.

Speech is behavior. "Part of what occurs [in speech] is expressive—a symbolization of the speaker's internal state; part is dynamic in the sense that it involves the speaker's purposes toward events around him—toward a listener, or an object."[2]

Speech is a learned behavior. Most children have acquired speech before they come to school. Although children express themselves orally before they are formally taught by a teacher, they need guidance in the development of skills in speaking. They learn to speak through frequent opportunities to speak in a variety of speech situations in a speech-oriented environment. Such skills include articulation, voice control, bodily control, pronunciation, word choice, appropriate usage, and organization of ideas.

Speech is stimulated by rich experiences. The child who has had rich and varied experiences is eager to talk about them. The child who has experienced little, who feels that what he has to say is unimportant is reticent. In one culturally deprived area, the kindergarten children had their sharing period at the close of the morning session. When asked why they waited until the end of the morning, the director replied, "The children have nothing to say when they come to school. After we have had some interesting experiences here they want to talk —all at one time, perhaps, but they want to talk!" Children need experiences before they talk, and time to think, discuss, and share ideas.

Speech is a means of extending horizons. Speech not only helps the child to express his ideas, feelings, and imagination, it helps him to extend his horizons and to increase his knowledge. How eagerly he asks questions before the adults around him have taught him to refrain from questioning. "What?" "Why?" "When?" "Where?" "How?" These are questions that call for answers; questions that lead to discovery; questions that help him think aloud. Through observing, through a growing awareness of the environment, through involvement in the world about him, the young child learns by asking, by searching, by discovery. Speech helps him to understand himself and the world in which he lives.

Linguistic skills and environment are interrelated. The child is a product of his environment. If he finds people who talk to him, who are concerned with the questions he asks, who provide an environment in which speaking, listening, reading, and writing are integral parts of the daily activity, the child will come to school with an eagerness to continue his excursions into the world of words and ideas. On the other hand, if he is in an environment in which linguistic activities are at a minimum, in which there is little if any dialogue between members of the family, and in which communication is forgotten or ignored, he will bear the mark of that sterile speech environment. Too, if he is surrounded by slovenly, illiterate speech, he will come to school bringing with him the habits formed in the preschool years.

Speech reflects personality. We reveal ourselves to others in many ways: through movement, speech, gestures. We indicate how we feel, think and perceive life through listening and speaking. Speech is an index to personality. Voice quality, tone, pitch, and rate are indicators of the emotional state of an individual. The high-pitched, shrill, unpleasant voice of the anxiety-ridden, neurotic adult has its counterpart in the child's voice in a fit of temper or a moment of tension. The child who is worried, tense, strained shows it in his voice. As the violin string is tightened to produce a higher tone, so the tightening of the throat muscles produces a high-pitched, unpleasant voice. A pleasing voice is one in which the qualities of pitch, rate, rhythm, and articulation reflect an integrated, self-reliant, alert personality.

Effective Guides to Teaching Speech

That teacher is most effective in teaching children to communicate who is adept at arranging an environment in which there is encouragement, time, stimulation, and guidance. The teacher who makes a difference in the lives of children is one who understands the importance of the process of speech as well as the content. For him the primary function of all language is communication. Because he realizes the significance of speech in the life of the individual, he utilizes this knowledge in establishing objectives for teaching speech effectively. Such a teacher demonstrates a knowledge of speech as an academic discipline as well as a process.

The Speech Association of America in 1963 prepared an official document entitled "The Field of Speech: It's Purposes and Scope in Education". In part the document states:

> The use of the term "speech" to identify an academic discipline emerged in the first two decades of this century. . . . Although its name is a coinage of this century, speech as a field of study grew from an academic tradition as old as the history of Western education. The study of the theory and practice of public discussion, under the name *rhetoric*, was a central concern of Greek, Roman, medieval, renaissance, and early modern education. Subjects allied to rhetoric also flourished in the Western educational tradition: argumentative dialogue and logical inquiry, usually called *dialectic*; literature which was inseparably linked to rhetoric; and speculative inquiry into the nature and function of language.
>
> Growing thus from a major educational tradition, the field of speech has shared in the unparalleled expansion of knowledge characteristic of this century, and in the specializations of research and instruction.
>
> . . . Despite their manifest specializations, teachers and scholars in the field of speech share these assumptions . . . :
>
> (a) Speech is man's most distinctive and significant behavior. Speech is learned, and it is learned from teachers. The "teachers" include all members of the social groups in which the child moves as well as the persons who give direct attention to speech instruction in formal educational settings. . . . Speaking is prerequisite to the child's development of a sense of identity. . . . No one can be said to be knowledgeable about himself and his environment unless he understands speech, its nature, structure, and functioning.
>
> (b) An educated person needs more than an understanding of speech behavior. He should be capable of transmitting his meanings with accuracy, correctness, and clarity. . . . In the education of such a man, knowledge and skill meld inextricably. . . .
>
> (c) Man cannot avoid being essentially and significantly a communicator. . . .
>
> (d) The acts and arts of communication in speech and language are humanistic. . . .
>
> The learning of speech begins before formal education, and the development of knowledge about speech behavior and the development of skill in speaking are necessarily continuous processes. At every level of education the speech and language skills of the student both limit and are limited by the kind and extent, the breadth and

depth, of the student's knoweldge. . . . Hence continuity of instruction in speech is of primary concern in formal education. . . .

. . .Despite massive evidence to the contrary, the assumption that speaking skill can be expected to develop as a by-product of instruction in reading and writing seems still to be prevalent. In too many schools, instruction in speech is represented only in extracurricular endeavor.

. . . Innumerable graduates of the common schools have practically no knowledge of speech behavior and of the arts of communication. . . . Such an attenuated and unbalanced treatment of the study of language and the development of language skills is a most serious problem in . . . education. Teachers of speech and English must recognize their related problems in the curriculum in the English language arts and confront them co-operatively.[3]

Organizing the Speech Program in the Elementary School

"The time has come, the walrus said,
to talk of many things:
Of shoes—and ships—and sealing wax—
of cabbages—and kings. . . ."
Lewis Carroll

Objectives of the Program

An understanding of the term speech is essential to the teacher in organizing a speech program. "For our purposes speech may be defined as the communication of thought and emotion by means of voice, language, and/or bodily action. By speech we can mean conversation, discussion, public speaking, reading aloud, or even booing, hissing, heckling, or sign language."[4]

Organization of a speech program must consider at the outset the objectives to be developed. Specific speech attitudes and skills to be developed through the speech program in the elementary school curriculum are:

1. a desire to express worthwhile ideas effectively
2. the skill to select and organize ideas efficiently
3. the ability to use words which express ideas clearly and accurately
4. the skill to use voice and articulation so that speech will be heard and understood
5. the skill to use appropriate bodily actions to reinforce the speaker's message
6. the ability to adapt speech behavior and speech organization to group situations such as conversations, discussions, etc.
7. the skill to communicate thought and mood of the author through oral reading, choral speaking, and dramatic activities
8. the ability to shift gears in terms of the social demands of the situation

Scope of the Program

Before organizing the speech activities, the teacher must have a clear understanding of the *scope* of the program. Simply defined, scope is the *what* of the curriculum. From preschool onward the child must be given opportunity to participate in a wide range of speech activities. This will involve a balanced program of activities, both in informal and formal situations.

> Nowhere in the elementary school is the guiding of language experiences more rewarding than in the kindergarten and primary grades. At this stage children develop rapidly in speech skills and vocabulary. The teacher should keep in mind objectives of oral communication [speech] as he organizes stimulating activities in meaningful situations.
>
> One of the most significant changes in speech education during the 20th century has been the new emphasis upon informal speaking. Since it is this form of communication which we employ largely throughout most of our waking hours, and by which we are most often judged, speech teachers should feel a challenge to help students to increase their skills in using the speech of everyday life.[5]

Informal Activities

Through informal speaking situations the child makes his first excursions into the social environment of the school. As he shares his personal experiences, follows directions, participates in the give and take of conversations and discussions, he learns to express his ideas. He soon discovers that if he wants to influence his peers he must speak clearly and accurately. The teacher sets the stage for informal speaking situations.

The teacher must provide guidance to help children develop the needed speech skills. He offers this guidance through such techniques as asking questions that elicit critical and creative thinking, giving a word of encouragement when needed, and providing motivation for exploration of concepts and ideas.

The school has a two-fold responsibility in organizing the informal speech activities—to create a need for interesting and effective communication through utilizing, enriching, and expanding those activities which involve oral communication, and to teach directly those speech skills essential to fulfill this need.

Among the early informal speech activities which should be an integral part of the curriculum are:

sharing experiences
conversing
telling the news
making announcements
making introductions
telephoning
giving directions, explanations, instructions

The teacher who is conscious of the significance of speech education will create an atmosphere in the classroom which stimulates informal speaking. For example, arranging a bulletin board to keep posted on the latest news events is an open door to informal discussion. Placing copies of children's books and magazines where they will be "discovered" motivates informal speaking. Displaying maps, dictionaries, supplementary materials where they can be explored and discussed is an open sesame to conversation. Motivating interest in a new unit through pictures, realia, art objects; planning excursions to the farm, the market, the railway station, the airport—all these stimulate discussion. Placing captions such as "Come and See," "Come and Discuss," "Come and Share Ideas" at strategic places is a catalyst for expression of ideas. A classroom that is speech-oriented is filled with many interesting activities which literally cry for expression.

Guiding Informal Speech Activities

Although the child's basic speech is established by the time he enters school, he must be provided with numerous opportunities and a variety of activities to improve his speech skills. Teachers have the responsibility for providing both informal and formal speech activities throughout the elementary school years to meet the child's need for developing skill in communication.

Specific suggestions for informal speech activities are presented as guides for the teacher.

Sharing Experiences

"Share and Tell" is an activity which should give the child an opportunity to use language creatively. This can become a significant part of the daily living and learning at school *if* the teacher uses some simple guide lines to motivate the experience. When the children understand that listening is as much a part of "sharing" as speaking, it helps to ease the frustrations and tensions that too often exist where there are large groups. Sharing interesting happenings which occur in the home, at school, and out of school offers opportunities for developing creative communication.

Sharing experiences, as any other type of speech situation, requires standards to be set if the performances are not to deteriorate into a waste of time. "Share and Tell" also stimulates observation and reporting needed in imaginative and expository writing, as well as in creative and critical thinking.

An effective sharing period is the result of careful planning, group evaluation, and standards in harmony with the developmental level of the children. However, the teacher should be careful lest the experience degenerate into a monologue in which the teacher does the sharing and the child the listening. The following is a verbatim account of one such experience.

> *Teacher*: Oh, Dorothy, you brought your new doll to show the class. Isn't that wonderful! Did your mother get her for you?
> *Dorothy*: Unh unh.
> *Teacher*: Did Santa bring her?
> *Dorothy*: Unh huh.
> *Teacher*: How do you like her? Does she close her eyes? Oh, my! She walks, too. Did everyone see Dorothy's doll? Thank you for sharing her with us and helping us get acquainted.
> *Dorothy*: Her name is Sarah.

Teacher: Oh, she has a name and I forget to ask what it is. I'm sorry. Next time we will not be so rushed and you can tell us more about her. (And Dorothy is pushed aside to make way for Tommy who is rushing up with his robot.)

In contrast, another group of children and their teacher facilitated the development of creative language and skill in communication as an outgrowth of their mutual discovery of the following standards for their "share and tell".

The Speaker

Wait to speak until everyone is ready.
Have something interesting to tell.
Think before you speak.
Show interest in the experience.
Use colorful words.
Organize the ideas in sequence.
Give interesting details.
Have an interesting conclusion.
Look at the audience.
Speak clearly and forcefully so everyone can hear you.
Be alive! Use expressive gestures.
Finish speaking before starting back to your seat.

The Listeners

Listen courteously.
Keep your mind on the speaker.
Respond to the enthusiasm of the speaker.
Do not interrupt.
Ask good questions when the speaker invites them.
Listen to the whole thing.
Avoid anything that might distract the speaker.
Watch for evidence of non-verbal communication through gestures and bodily movements.
Show genuine appreciation through such non-verbal means of communication as smiling, nodding, shaking the head, and having an attitude of listening carefully.

To the extent that the speaker succeeds in getting and holding the attention of the audience, his communication is effective. To the degree that the speaker finds increasing satisfaction in oral communication will it become a significant medium for creative self-expression.

Conversing

Unfortunately, the type of speech that individuals will engage in more than any other type is rarely provided for in the curriculum. Genuine sparkling conversation, which has been termed the poetry of the literate, needs both time and opportunity if it is to flourish as the child becomes an adult. Conversation is dialogue in discovery, for through such an experience one individual discovers another individual and engages in one of the most fascinating creative experiences possible. However, an entire class is too large for genuine discovery to take place. Artificiality results when groups are assigned to engage in conversation about a specific subject. Conversation is an art which develops best when a few individuals have genuine need to share experiences, ideas, and aspirations, serious or humorous. Opportunity should be provided for this phase of the language arts program throughout the elementary school years. It is not enough to provide time for children to talk with children. Most children on their own will find time for this. Time must also be planned for child-adult dialogue.

Conversation between children and adults is an avenue along which children travel toward self-understanding and maturity. Even a child is stimulated by the give and take of spirited conversation. Conversing should become an intellectual adventure to which children look forward eagerly.

Where children grow up without interchange of ideas they often develop a negative self-image that leaves the mark of cultural deprivation upon them.

The role of dialogue has achieved an even greater significance as travel is facilitated, boundaries are erased, and the population of nations is in a state of mobility. Political tensions will be increased or lessened in proportion to the ability of man to communicate effectively with man.

Helping Children Participate in Conversation

School does not always provide the child with opportunities for communication. According to a report on the study of the schools in a city, which could be duplicated across the North American continent, when a child enters school, "*his right to speak out freely is curtailed*. He is subject to countless restrictions about the days to attend, hours to fill, when to talk, where to sit, length of teaching periods, and countless other rules."[6]

Equally revealing, but in the words of the child, "Said a second grader to an entering first grader whom he was orienting, 'There's just one thing to remember and that is not to talk.' In many schools a tremendous value is placed on quietness. We teach children *not* to talk. We threaten them if they do talk and then we initiate elaborate lessons to stimulate them to speak."[7] Such inconsistencies do not go unrecognized by the school child; they should not go unrecognized by the teacher.

Why not capitalize on the child's natural inclination to talk? Some ways in which a teacher can help children participate effectively in conversation are: use every opportunity to motivate children to converse, involve individual children in conversational groups, help children develop skills in conversing with ease, and encourage them to evaluate their strengths and weaknesses.

Developing Skills in Conversation

A. Objectives.

1. To instruct pupils in conversational techniques.
2. To help pupils use conversational skills in their social contacts.
3. To help pupils identify and correct their weaknesses.

B. Techniques of the teacher.

1. Have children dramatize some situations requiring conversation.

C. Activities.

1. Dramatize specific situations.
2. Divide into pairs and select an interesting problem for the dialogue.
3. Have the students suggest appropriate topics for conversation.
4. Compose an imaginary conversation with an imaginary character of one's choice.
5. Have pupils listen to and evaluate tele-

B. Techniques of the teacher, cont.

2. Discuss the attributes of good conversation; spontaneity, fluency, respect for others' ideas, alert listening, pleasant voice.
3. Discuss conversation as an informal speech activity.
   a. Importance of conversation.
   b. Consideration of others in conversation.
   c. What to talk about.
   d. Keeping well informed about happenings.
   e. How to avoid awkward pauses.
   f. Learning from conversationalists in real life and in literature.

D. Evaluation.

Ask questions such as:

1. Did all of the children participate in the conversation?
2. How many times did each person participate?
3. Did anyone tend to monopolize the conversation?
4. Did the conversation capture and maintain interest?
5. Were the contributions worthwhile?
6. What effect did the conversation have on others in the group?
7. Did the contributions promote successful group living?
8. Were the participants thoughtful, courteous, and kind in their remarks?

C. Activities, cont.

vision programs involving conversations and/or dialogues on subjects of general interest.

6. Have each student bring to class, to be read aloud, the best conversation that he has found in his reading recently.
7. Have the class draw up a list of ways to become better class conversationalists.
8. Tape several of the best conversations. Have the class listen to them and evaluate them on the basis of the criteria set up.
9. Have the students report to the class on a conversation in which they took part.

Social Situations

Social situations offer excellent motivation for meaningful informal speech activities. When social forms are taught functionally, as they are needed in response to a real situation, the children learn them readily and eagerly. The kindergarten child is as anxious to learn correct forms of introducing his parents as is the intermediate child. The first grader is eager to learn how to be an effective host or hostess, how to extend invitations, and how to make and acknowledge introductions properly. Children should be taught in a functional setting how to accept thanks graciously or how to accept congratulations modestly after winning an award at the speech festival, athletic event, or music contest.

A. Objectives.

1. To help children improve their skills in human relations.
2. To instruct students in social situations in a functional setting.
3. To give students practical experience through dramatizing situations.

C. Activities.

1. Draw up a list of suggestions for making introductions.
2. Practice the procedure for making introductions by introducing the following people:
   a. A classmate to your mother.

B. Techniques of the teacher.

1. Point out to the students the social amenities.
2. View a film which demonstrates correct social behavior.
3. Discuss the need for knowing what to do in specific situations.
4. Use creative dramatics as a preparation for the "real" experience.
5. Have children introduce parents, relatives, visitors, friends.

D. Evaluation.

Have the class evaluate the correctness of the introductions.

C. Activities, cont.

b. A relative to your teacher.
c. Your mother to your teacher.
d. A boy to a girl.
e. Two girls to each other.
f. One group to another group.

3. Dramatize the following introductions:
   a. The Premier of the province or mayor of the town to the class.
   b. Judge Brown, senior resident, to your teacher.
   c. A friend to a member of your family.
4. View a film demonstrating correct procedure for making introductions and note how well the introductions were "cued in" to start a conversation, how well the cues were picked up, and so forth.
5. Dramatize: You are sitting at your desk and your mother comes to the door. You present your teacher to her.
6. Have students pair off and select types of introductions they wish to demonstrate for the class.

Order of Introduction

Manner of Introduction	Introduce first the person who because of age or sex is entitled to greater respect. A girl is introduced first when being introduced to a person of the opposite sex. "Mary, this is Dan Mabrey. Dan, this is my cousin, Mary Davis".
Correct Phrases	"May I present?" "This is my Mother".
Response	"How do you do?" *not* "I'm pleased to meetcha" or "Charmed".
When to Shake Hands	If a boy is introduced to a girl, he waits for her to initiate the action of shaking hands. Men always shake hands.
When to Rise	In the presence of an older or distinguished guest one always rises. A boy always rises in the presence of a girl or woman.
How to introduce a person to a group	Present the honored person to the entire group at once.
How to proceed easily from the introduction into conversation	Add a comment telling something about the individual you are introducing that will give a clue to or springboard for conversation. For example, "Miss Jenson, this is my friend Alice. She has just moved to Manitoba. She lived in Ohio before she came here." "How do you do, Ann? Do you find the climate here quite a contrast to that of Ohio?"

Telephoning

Telephoning is a special type of conversation which requires specific behavior. Instruction in the use of the telephone should emphasize the fact that other people may need to use the phone. Under any circumstances, prolonged conversation is thoughtless. When the telephone clicks showing someone needs the line, it is a mark of considerateness to hang up and release the line.

A. Objectives.

To teach children:

1. To speak with clarity and expressiveness.
2. To use correct form in answering the phone.
3. To use correct form in: calling home, calling a friend, calling the school.
4. To distinguish between correct forms used in business and social calls.
5. That courtesy in the use of the telephone is essential to developing good manners.

B. Techniques of the teacher.

Develop the following concepts through direct instruction to help children establish standards for telephone use:

1. Speak directly into the transmitter.
2. The use of the telephone for prolonged social conversation is seldom legitimate.
3. Certain formal procedures in answering the telephone will greatly increase the efficiency of conversations.
4. Telephone conversation requires more careful articulation than does face-to-face conversation.
5. The person initiating a telephone conversation should plan his remarks carefully before calling.
6. The use of "thank you" and "you're welcome" in telephone conversation is one way to smile.
7. It is always a mistake to shout.

D. Evaluation.

1. Have the class evaluate the performance using the code for telephoning drawn up by the class.

C. Activities.

1. View one or more films such as:
   Speech: Conversation, 11 min.
   Young America Films.
   Telephone Courtesy, 25 min.
   Thanks for Listening, 25 min.
   Bell Telephone Co.
2. Have the class draw up a "Code for Using the Telephone" which combines courtesy and efficiency.
3. Dramatize emergency situations.
   a. Calling in a fire-alarm.
   b. Calling an ambulance.
   c. Reporting to the proper city official the presence of the stray dog on the playground.
   d. Calling the family doctor.
   e. Reporting a fire.
4. Dramatize social situations.
   Set a timer, so that conversation is limited, in each case, to three minutes.
   a. Inviting a friend to a party.
   b. Asking a friend for a homework assignment.
   c. Calling mother to get permission to purchase a ticket to the play.
   d. Calling a friend to talk about a party, a movie, a new dress, a hockey game.

Giving Directions

In helping children become oriented to the world in which they live, it is essential that they understand relationships of space as well as time. For example, they must develop the ability to give precise directions for finding a specific address. The young child should be taught to recognize the familiar landmarks which tell him he is near home, near the school, etc. He should have the clues which enable him to direct a person to reach the desired destination.

In giving directions, instructions, and explanations effectively, children must learn to express themselves with precision, accuracy, terseness, and logic. Careful thinking, concise speaking, and a well ordered, clear picture in one's mind are essential if this informal speech activity is to be fruitful. Perhaps of all the informal types of speech situations and language activities, giving clear directions gives a true reflection of the child's ability to organize his thinking clearly, logically and concisely and offers opportunity for developing the thought processes of children.

A. Objectives.

1. To develop habits of logical thinking.
2. To develop ability to organize ideas in narrative sequence.
3. To give directions and explanations concisely and clearly.

B. Techniques of the teacher.

1. To make use of child's interest in his environment to teach him the skills of order, logic, sequence in relation to his world.
2. To provide a natural outlet for the child to explain, to give directions and instructions.
3. To provide activities that will enable the child to use knowledge about his physical environment and the people in his environment, and the desire to explore.

D. Evaluation.

Among the questions to be asked are:

1. Did we tell things in the right order?
2. Did we organize ideas in narrative sequence?
3. Did we learn to use spatial sequence organization?
4. Did we arrive at the correct destination by using the directions given?
5. Did we make use of diagrams and maps to make our directions clear?
6. Did we learn the difference between chronological, logical and spatial sequence?
7. Did our knowledge of logic, order, and sequence contribute to our enjoyment in going to and from school, in going to town, and/or taking trips?
8. Did we learn to listen more carefully in order to carry out the directions, explanations, or instructions given us?
9. Did we become more accurate, concise, and terse in our speaking as a result of experiences in this phase of speaking?

C. Activities.

1. Have children give directions for getting to their houses.
2. Take a walk to a home of a child within walking distance of the school following the directions given earlier.
3. Make a map showing the location of a park, store, post office or a public building within walking distance of the school.
4. Take a walk to the specified location using a commercially printed map as a guide.
5. Compare the map and the diagram made by the children.
6. Select a specified place for the class to visit and make a diagram of the bus route.
7. Have a child explain how to make a certain object.
8. Have a child explain a process and have the children carry out each step as he explains it—e.g. proper folding, cutting, solving an arithmetic problem, making a kite, assembling a model airplane, etc.
9. Give some clues about a hobby and have the children guess what it is.
10. Explain how to arrive at the answer to an arithmetic problem using the new math.

Formal Speech Activities

It is not enough to allow time for children to express ideas in informal situations only. Planned formal situations must also be provided. "The total oral communication skills must be taught well at all levels of instruction so that pupils may develop proficiency not only for adequate participation in society but also for self-fulfillment."[8]

This gives a mandate to the teacher to equip himself with the knowledge of the speech curriculum in order to teach effectively. The language behaviors of children are formed early, are formed solidly, and are formed regardless of whether there is an able teacher or not. Even if oral language or speech is included in the curriculum guide, in the final analysis what is taught is what the teacher knows and can teach well; what the teacher knows about what should be taught, when it should be taught, and how it should be taught.

Among the formal speech activities that should be organized developmentally are:

- giving talks
- planning and evaluating
- interviewing
- discussion
- parliamentary procedure
- storytelling

Giving Talks

As children develop interest in sharing experiences with the group, it soon becomes evident that their eagerness to talk sometimes exceeds their skills of expression. They enjoy telling what they did during the work period. They want the group to hear what happened over the weekend; they like to explain the process they used in building a boat, making a kite, constructing an airplane. They can tell how to get to the post office, the library, the playground, the recreation building. They develop standards for a particular activity. They can talk about trips, hobbies, and activities. They need help, however, in moving from tentative expression of ideas to carefully planned and organized talks. This involves guidance in selecting an interesting topic, collecting material for the talk, organizing the material, and presenting the material.

The extent to which the teacher gives such help in the primary grades will be dependent upon his knowledge of speech, his understanding of the needs of children, his ability to create situations in which children become aware of their needs for increased speech skills, and his ability to give direct instruction in the skills of oral communication through planned speech activities.

The young child is content to talk about topics such as pets, games, excursions, people, places, and things. He subconsciously chooses subjects with which he is familiar, is interested in, and has some enthusiasm for. As he grows in linguistic skills and experience, he learns to express ideas in a more colorful, imaginative, and vivid manner. He finds that his audience of children listens with greater interest. He learns, too, that if he is going to hold the interest of the group, he will need a plan of organization.

The teacher can give guidance by suggesting the child have a plan for the talk. Even kindergartners and first graders can readily work out simple plans for a talk. For example, they can relate in sequence what they saw on a trip; or they can indicate the steps to take in making jello in the school cafeteria. Third and fourth graders can make an outline and list the main points they intend to cover in the talk. Fifth and sixth graders are ready to make a more detailed outline showing the main points and the subpoints. By the time the children complete the elementary school, they should be able to use sentence outlines and plan carefully so that they can decide the particular type of organization they wish to use. At all educational levels the teacher should be alert to the child's need to include the necessary facts, omit unrelated details that detract from the talk, organize the ideas in a logical manner, and give the talk in an interesting, exciting fashion.

Planning and Evaluating

Participation in planning the activities throughout the day should begin early in the child's school experience. When the children are familiar with the timetable, when they know what comes the first thing in the morning, what happens after recess, what the afternoon session holds, they feel a sense of security. They can move readily from one activity to another without consulting the teacher at each turn. A daily schedule on the chalkboard goes a long way toward enabling each child to look ahead and plan his day's activities.

Before the day begins, there should be time for conscious planning with the children in order for them to understand the specific goals for the day and to share in long range planning. They should take part in decisions on some of the class activities such as presenting special programs for parents, giving a program for another group, taking a field trip, setting standards for behavior, drawing up plans to simplify routines, deciding on committee responsibility.

Evaluation, too, is an important daily oral activity for which time and guidance must be planned. The class should plan time to check their progress toward stated goals. They should be helped to formulate such questions as: "What do we hope to accomplish today in Social Studies?" "What do we need to do to get ready for the music festival?" "How can we improve our creative dramatics program before our mothers come to hear us?" "What needs to be done to help our class improve its record of behavior on the playground?" Evaluation of activities should be a continuous process. Teachers should keep in mind such dimensions of evaluation as the progress each child is making toward individual goals, the progress the child is making toward his group goals, and the progress the entire group is making toward defined goals.

Involving children in evaluation affords an excellent avenue for oral expression. One primary group set up a standard for evaluating their own progress in giving talks.

We speak in a conversational tone.

We speak so we can be heard.

We look at the audience when we talk.

We have worthwhile content.

We organize our talk clearly.

We make it interesting so people will want to listen.

When children have a part in setting standards, when they know what they are to be judged on, the desired behavior becomes the basis for evaluation. If children have a part in setting up goals, in working together to achieve them, and in evaluating progress, skills in speaking will improve *and* so will behavior.

Interviewing

Children learn in many ways. They observe, read, experiment, explore. Very early in life they discover that one way to find answers is to ask someone who knows. This is the simplest form of interviewing. Interviewing as a speech activity is the natural outgrowth of the child's quest for knowledge. He becomes more effective in his questioning when he learns what to do, what to say, how to say it, and how to terminate the interview. He discovers that a successful interview requires both a friendly manner and careful preparation. This means that he must have a specific purpose, a planned procedure, and criteria for the selection of the person to be interviewed.

If the children are studying the community, they might well choose to interview a public official. They may wish to interview a school inspector, a mayor, a chief of police, or a city manager. They should be aware that the person they choose to interview has no time to waste. Thus they will plan carefully to the last detail. Each interview entails a series of experiences in oral expression: opening the topic with the interviewee; formulating questions that elicit information desired; introducing new aspects of the subject as the interview proceeds; adapting the inquiries to new or unexpected turns in the developing interview; attentive listening; and tactful, courteous behavior throughout the interview. Since the reputation of the group is involved, they should select one of the most capable pupils to carry on the interview.

Role playing before the interview is an excellent practice for getting children to understand the challenge of the give-and-take situation inherent in the interview.

The following suggests four steps in the interviewing procedure.

1. Greet the interviewee politely and express your pleasure at his willingness to be interviewed. Look directly at him during the interview.

2. State the purpose of the interview clearly to refresh the interviewee's memory as soon as his cue allows you to do so.
"Mr. Blank, we are studying conservation and there is a difference of opinion as to the policy we should follow to conserve wild life in the province. What do you think should be our attitude?"

3. "I have a list of questions which our class prepared and I would appreciate your commenting on them." (The interviewee will be pleased that you have taken time to draw up questions, but you may not have to follow them rigidly.) It is possible that in discussing the first question he will have answered several others. Perhaps by the time he pauses for breath you will know his stand on the questions you have written down. If not, select those items that his answers have not clarified. Be flexible, but try to get a clear picture of the situation.

4. When you have the desired information, the interview should terminate. Follow the clue. If he gives no clue to end the interview, take

the initiative. This you may do by saying, "That should give me all the information we need. Thank you for your time and help. I know the members of the class will appreciate it."

Remember that each interview with a member of the community is an important means of public relations. It is well to remember that the courteous, intelligent behavior of the interviewer reflects positively in the school's interest.

Things to do in Interviewing Practice

1. Dramatize the following situations which entail an interview for information.

   (a) A person who has just returned from Europe; your class is studying Switzerland.

   (b) A person who has won a trip to the Capital.

   (c) A student who won the poetry writing contest.

   (d) A foreign student who has just enrolled in the school.

   (e) Tape an interview to use for evaluation.

   (f) A new principal has been appointed; you are asked to interview him about his hobbies, family, interests.

2. Evaluate the experience.

   Did the interviewer report the facts accurately?

   Did the interviewer seem to understand the interviewee's point-of-view?

   Did the attitudes of the interviewee come through in a clear and unbiased picture?

   Did the interviewee appear to be comfortable during the questioning?

   Did the interviewer remember to be courteous, friendly, and natural during the interview?

   Did the behavior of the interviewee prove helpful to the interviewer?

Discussion

Beginning in the kindergarten, discussion is a significant part of the language arts curriculum. Throughout the day children talk about questions of common interest. They make plans for their work. They make preparations for trips and then they discuss them afterwards. They decide to present a puppet show and make arrangements for the entire school to see it. In this way, they find answers to their own inquiries. A well organized program of discussion is an important facet of the elementary curriculum. The spirit of inquiry brought about by a willingness to talk things over freely accounts in many cases for the successful environment in a classroom as a setting for creative learning.

In the primary grades, discussion takes on the procedure of talking over problems such as how to get along, how to prepare for a specific event, how to plan a program for mothers, how to spend the money allocated for the class by the Home and School Association, etc. Here the teacher starts with group discussion as an informal opinion sharing experience on common topics or problems of interest to the class.

Primary grade children should be taught basic facts about discussion. Discussion involves two or more people, listening and speaking interchangeably, thinking interactively, and working cooperatively to solve a common problem or concern. It is not a debate in which children take sides—pro and con. Neither should it be a pooling of ignorance. Under the guidance of the teacher, the children can engage in problem-solving situations in which they solve the problem at hand using the best thinking of the group in terms of predetermined criteria and careful, critical thinking.

A Discussion in a Second Grade

An illustration of a second grade group who solved a problem cooperatively follows.

> The children in Miss Lang's group had planned a party for Valentine's Day. The problem was how to finance the party. They decided to make and sell valentines. This created many new problems. Among these were: how to announce the sale, how to make the valentines, where to get the needed materials, when to begin the sale, how to handle the money, how to plan the schedule for the children who would sell the valentines each day, and what to do if they ran out of time, materials and valentines before the announced sale ended.
>
> On the first day they seriously set about solving the problems they had previously listed. They started with the one that dealt with the announcement of their project—the sale of valentines. They came up with several ideas and then Nan said: "Why don't we have two of us dress up to look like the Queen of Hearts and go to each of the rooms and announce the valentine sale?" John chimed in, "I couldn't be the Queen of Hearts, but I could be the Knave of Hearts and go with you. I could hold up a poster for everyone to read." "Who would make the poster?" questioned the teacher. "I would," said Ralph, "and if I need help I'm sure Mother would help me." "I could be the Knave's servant." At this point Andy said, "Why don't we send a small group in to say 'The Queen of Hearts'—you know, choral speaking—like we did for the speech festival, last year. Remember our class did well."
>
> At that point Miss Lang summarized, "We have really had some excellent ideas. Let's write them down." This is what she wrote.
>
> A valentine sale in the second grade.
> Announcement by the Queen of Hearts.
> Poster carried by the Knave of Hearts.
> Poster made by John—the servant of the Knave of Hearts.
> Choral speaking—group to be selected to say "The Queen of Hearts".
>
> The following day the children attacked the problem of making the valentines. Jill suggested that they get help from Miss Jackson, the art teacher. Jack volunteered to bring some "boughten" ones from his father's store to use for ideas.
>
> Miss Lang suggested they turn to the next problem—when to begin the sale. Janice wisely questioned "Won't that depend on how

quickly we can have some ready?" It was decided that perhaps Miss Jackson could give some suggestions to Miss Lang so they could get started on the project. Because the agreement came readily it was possible to discuss another problem—what to do about the schedule for selling the valentines once they were finished. Ann suggested that the children who had the highest grades in arithmetic should sell the valentines so they would be able to make correct change. Jim suggested that they get permission to open the "store" each morning about fifteen minutes before school started and at noon, ten minutes before the tardy bell rang. This discussion took time because of the decision to get permission from the principal. It was suggested by Tony that the class write a letter to ask permission. However, Lester suggested a personal interview with the principal might expedite matters.

On the following day they were ready to grapple with another problem—what to do if they ran out of valentines *before* the sale was scheduled to close. Again Jack came to the rescue by offering to take out on consignment four dozen valentines from the store. "Because", as he said, "our sale at school will be over before Valentine's Day, so my dad can still sell the valentines—unless they are soiled." That brought up the problem of care of merchandise. "We'll choose people with clean hands to handle the merchandise." This from Nina, who was always careful about washing her hands.

Discussion of the final problem—what kind of a party to have—was postponed until the sale was over so they would know how much money they had to spend. The two weeks passed quickly as they were all busy working on the project in one capacity or another. What surprised them was the enthusiasm of the whole school in their project. Big brothers and sisters from the upper grades came to buy their wares and the children were delighted. Their project was highly successful, for they made $25.00. "Of course," said Jack, "my father donated the valentines he loaned us. He wanted us to have a good party." "Yes," said Miss Lang, "but the valentines that were sold first were the ones you people made yourselves."

The final discussion was concerned with the party to be held on Valentine's Day. They talked it over and finalized plans. (1) We will make the cookies ourselves. (2) We will invite our mothers. (3) We will have punch with the cookies. (4) We will serve the punch and cookies when the mothers come in. Each one will escort his mother to the punch table. (5) We will sing some valentine songs. (6) We will dramatize the "Queen of Hearts". (7) We will open the valentine box and choose a postman.

Obviously, the valentine project provided numerous opportunities for learning and using the techniques for successful discussion at their level of development. Teacher and children pooled their information to solve the problems involved.

Group discussion serves the elementary teacher and children in four ways: (1) it provides an opportunity for purposeful oral expression; (2) it encourages children to pool information; (3) it stimulates children to seek and find solutions to a problem; and (4) it motivates critical thinking.

Through group discussion children and the teacher cooperatively study the various aspects of a problem. In doing this they state the problem, analyze its various aspects, discover the possible solutions, decide which is the best, and recommend ways of carrying it out. Both in pooling information and in seeking a solution to a problem, children are stimulated to think critically as well as reflectively, creatively as well as analytically, cooperatively as well as individually.

Parliamentary Procedure

Parliamentary procedure is the term applied to those rules in accordance with which any organization attempts to carry on its business in an orderly and democratic manner. In a democratic society such as Canada and the U.S., the citizens are great "joiners". Logically, children follow the example set by the adults. In the primary grades this takes the form of class meetings, clubs, and organizations of various types. In order to be a contributory member, one must have an understanding of the simple basic procedure for conducting meetings and expediting business.

In a sense, parliamentary procedure simply provides one set of rules within which debate, discussion, or public speaking may take place. Including parliamentary procedure in the elementary curriculum rests on the premise that it is useful to the individual to have some knowledge of and skill in using the procedures which facilitate decision making.

Without knowledge of basic parliamentary procedure, groups are almost inevitably inefficient. With a knowledge of procedures for conducting meetings, however, even primary grade group organizations can be efficient and effective.

If children are taught the purpose of rules in conducting meetings, if they are guided to understand that in a democratic society there must be opportunity for free discussion of opinions, they will grow in appreciation of parliamentary techniques as well as in skill in using the techniques for worthy ends.

Such rules contribute to orderliness, efficiency, fairness, courteous behavior and organized thinking. Thus parliamentary procedure protects the rights of each individual to participate in a meeting; no one can monopolize a meeting in which rules and regulations are understood and obeyed.

Primary children frequently organize into a class organization or club. They write and adopt a constitution (rules to live by), elect officers, and propose action. This action may range from such simple behavior as wording a motion, amending a motion, and voting on the motion at the primary level to becoming skilled in the intricacies of main, subsidiary and privileged motions by the end of the elementary school.

Even first graders can be taught how to make a motion and amend a motion, and that only one person can have the floor at a time and only one item of business can be taken up at one time. No new business may be initiated until the motion at hand is disposed of.

The teacher helps children follow proper procedure and use correct terminology. For example, he may say:

Keep your remarks pertinent to the topic. Not—stick to the point.

Kindly keep personalities out. Not—don't be rude.

Amend the motion. Not—change the motion.

Delete the words. Not—take out the words.

A Third Grade Meeting

During the spring of the year, Mr. Tarnrushè's class decided to organize as a club. The teacher suggested that he be the parliamentarian in order to guide the group. Officers were elected, weekly meetings were scheduled, and plans for organizing the meetings were accepted. Soon the time came to have the second meeting of the club.

Meeting on March 3.

Chairman: Will the meeting come to order please? Will the secretary please read the minutes of the last meeting?

Secretary: (Reads minutes.)

Chairman: Are there any additions or corrections? If not, all in favor of approving the minutes raise your hand.
Children respond.

Chairman: Those opposed? (None.) The minutes are approved as read. May we hear treasurer's report?

Treasurer: (Reads report.)

Chairman: Are there any errors or ommissions? If not, all in favor of accepting the report please raise your hand?
Children respond.

Chairman: Those opposed? (Pause.) The report is accepted.
Are there any reports of standing committees? (Listens to reports on social events, supplies, monitors, etc.)
Is there any old business? (Pause.) Since there is no old business we can consider new business.

(Each speaker addresses the chair and waits to be recognized before he speaks.)

Child: Mr. Chairman, I think we should plan a Mother's Day Tea.

Child: I think we should too; the third grade always plans one.

Child: How much would it cost?

Child: When should we have it? On the Friday before Mother's Day?

Child: Should we have it in the morning or afternoon?

Teacher: Mr. Chairman, since there seem to be so many questions, I suggest that we appoint a committee to look into the idea for us. Perhaps they could contact Miss Jones who taught the third grade last year. Will someone move that we appoint a committee of five to get as much information about last year's Mother's Day Tea as possible and report at our next meeting?

Child: Mr. Chairman, I move that the executive appoint a committee of five to investigate last year's Mother's Day Tea and report back to the group.

Chairman: It has been moved and seconded that the executive appoint a committee of five to get as much information as possible from Miss Jones about last year's Mother's Day Tea.
Is there any discussion? (Pause.) Since there is no discussion, all in favor of the motion raise your hands. (Counts hands.)
Those opposed? (None.) The motion is passed.

Teacher: Mr. Chairman, I am afraid our time is up.

Chairman: Is there a motion to adjourn?

Child: I move that we adjourn.
Chairman: Is there a second?
Child: I second the motion.
Chairman: All in favor of the motion to adjourn, raise your hands. All opposed. The same. (Pause.) (No dissenting votes.)
Chairman: The meeting stands adjourned.

These children had many prior experiences in informal and problem-solving discussions before they were able to manage the formal business meeting. As can be noted, this class followed the traditional pattern of a meeting. The chairman called the meeting to order, followed by secretary's report, treasurer's report, committee reports, old business, and discussion of new business. Technically, discussion of new business should not be permitted until *after* a motion has been made. The teacher will have to use judgment in deciding when a group is ready for the more complicated procedures such as amending motions, referring to committees, etc. Participation in class or club meetings should be a right of the primary child; it is a way of becoming an effective member of a democratic society. This is possible if the teacher keeps in mind that previous participation in discussions is a prerequisite to participation in parliamentary procedure.

Storytelling

Storytelling is an activity that for many children is an avenue to effective communication as well as to creative expression with literature. Many a child enjoys telling a story he knows, sharing it with his classmates, and because he enjoys it so much, he is able to communicate more effectively than in other activities of oral expression. Watch him as he forgets himself in the telling of the tale, in the building up of the events leading to the exciting climax or the satisfying conclusion. Here he uses his body readily as a medium of communication. He talks with his hands, his eyes, his entire body. As he watches the interest of his audience, he is stimulated to so identify with the story that he and the characters become one as it were; and it is only when he is playing the role of the narrator that he assumes an objective attitude toward the story he is relating.

Although storytelling is a formal speech activity, it depends upon literature for its content and thus will be considered in detail in the chapter on literary appreciation.

Giving Oral Reports

The teacher who is really concerned about helping children express their ideas clearly and interestingly will begin in the kindergarten and primary grades to motivate children to give oral reports effectively. True, reports become a major responsibility of the intermediate grade teacher, but the intermediate grade teacher merely builds upon the foundation the primary teacher lays. A kindergarten child who had visited a filtering plant over the weekend reported on the experience with as much clarity and organization as any adult who had had a similar initial experience. He began by getting the interest of his audience by an anecdote that demanded and received attention. During the presentation, the listeners were entranced to follow his plan of organization, his selection and sequence of ideas, his discrimination in the choice of incidents and information that carried their interest as he literally took them with him from the moment he got into his father's red convertible, drove down the highway to the new filtering plant, and followed the guide as he took them through the plant. The child used effective gestures that told more clearly than mere words what he had seen and heard on the excursion.

If a kindergarten child can be taught the elements of presenting a vivid, exciting, stimulating, and informative report, it is certainly the responsibility of the primary teacher to equip children with skills which will change the report from a dull, lifeless, tedious, boring session to one that is vital, alive, and worthwhile.

This requires that the child:

1. is interested in the topic
2. is selective in the material he chooses
3. decides on the main ideas he wants to present
4. selects supporting material to implement and support his main idea
5. organizes the information in an interesting manner
6. presents the report making use of colorful language and visual aids

A good report is no accident; it is the result of careful, organized planning coupled with skill in communicating ideas to an interested group. An effective plan for presenting the report follows.

Get the attention. For example, begin with a startling statement or visual aids that arouse curiosity. Be sure that these are pertinent.

Create or point out a need in the audience for the report. Relate the speech to *their* interests or problems.

Present the report. Have the report organized in your own mind so you can develop it naturally, spontaneously, and vividly.

Keep the sequence in mind. Memorize the sequence. Use a key-word outline.

Conclude with a summary or recapitulation.

The student who develops to his highest potential in oral communication during his intermediate and upper school years has a distinct advantage over his peers throughout his lifetime. Our future leaders will be found among those who not only have something significant to say, but also have the ability to say it well. Such an attainment does not come automatically. It is the result of a clearly articulated, well organized, and well taught speech curriculum throughout the elementary school. It consists of more than a conglomeration of oral activities which are auxiliary tools in imparting and reinforcing learning experiences in "real" disciplines. It must go beyond the conversation hour, the book report, the occasional panel discussion in the social studies class, the six-weeks oral English unit, or the sporadic choral reading, creative dramatics, orations, and dramatic presentations to get ready for the Speech Festival. "When we sacrifice the development of critical and intellectual skills for practice in telephone talking and conversation, . . . when, for all our tools of communication we share so few ideas and materials capable of uplifting the quality of . . . speech education, *we* have failed."[9]

It is during the middle years that the skills initiated in the primary school demand a curriculum commensurate with the added maturity, increased skills, broadened interests, and greater needs for expression.

Planning and Organizing Speeches

It is essential that the teacher have a clear understanding of both the theory and practice of public speaking. This includes:

the purpose of speaking before a group
speeches for special occasions
types of organization of speeches
organizing a speech effectively
giving the talk
evaluating the talk

The Purpose of Speaking Before a Group

There are two kinds of speakers, those who "have something to say" and "those who have to say something". The first has a purpose in speaking, the second merely fulfills an obligation. Too many teachers fail to help the student distinguish between them. Selecting the specific purpose for the speech is an important factor in the effectiveness of the speech. The speaker must also be aware of the general purposes for which people make speeches: to entertain, to inform, to stimulate, to convince, and to actuate.

The speech to entertain. The sole purpose of the speech to entertain is to get and hold the attention of the audience. Any information that is given is purely incidental. The speech is characterized by humor, spontaneity, excitement, or adventure.

The speech to inform. The speech to inform is one of the most widely used purposes. Children spend much time in explaining or giving information which is not already known by the class. This speech is fundamentally one of explanation: how to do something, how to make something and how it works, clarifying plans, relating details of an experience. The speech to inform is basically the simplest for children. However, it requires that the information be given in such a way that it is clearly understood by the audience, that it is interesting as well as informative, and that it contains illustrative material as well as facts. Flavoring the facts with humor, vivid language, and visual aids lends a refreshing touch to this type of speech.

The speech to stimulate. Sometimes known as the speech to inspire, the speech to stimulate has as its goal arousing interest in doing what the listeners know they should do. The belief already exists, but the urge to do something about it is lacking. This type of speech is more complex than either the speech to entertain or the speech to inform. Without both interest and information, it fails to stimulate. The speech must be developed on the basis of the needs, wants, hopes, and aspirations of the audience in order to vitalize their behavior.

The speech to convince. The purpose of the speech to convince is the changing of the attitudes of the listeners who may be indifferent or opposed to the proposal. Not only must the speaker stimulate the listener, he must motivate him to change his attitude or to alter his opinions. He must present evidence to show the logic of his cause. He must give reasons that will help his listeners to change their minds.

The speech to actuate. The speech to actuate may be the outgrowth of either the speech to stimulate or the speech to convince. Here the group is stimulated to take action. They go out to support the campaign, to vote for the candidate, to sign the petition, to go to the game following the rally, or to participate in the Speech Festival.

Speeches for Special Occasions

In our society, numerous occasions arise in which one must be prepared to give brief speeches for special occasions both in and out of school. If one has developed the skills, one will enjoy these challenges.

The speech of presentation. Frequently awards or trophies are presented to or from a group, and someone is required to make a speech. Such an occasion should be prepared for ahead of time—just in case. It calls for dignity, clarity, and precision. Since there is an audience of some size, it is necessary that the audience be able to hear, understand and enjoy the remarks.

A three-part formula for a speech of presentation is:

1. State the occasion for the award and the reason for making it.
2. Tell the major reason or reasons for awarding it to this specific person or group.
3. Express the pleasure of the donors in making this award.

This formula is short, simple, and concise. It is possible to treat the three elements simultaneously, not necessarily in a consecutive order. For example, the following speech includes all the essentials.

"Each year the Imperial Order of the Daughters of the Empire presents a trophy to the group demonstrating the best performance of a dramatic portrayal of a literary classic. In keeping with the tradition, excellence is understood to involve two factors: creativity and effective communication. This year the award goes to the students in the fourth grade of the Earl Oxford School for their excellent portrayal of 'The Emperor's New Clothes.' Their performance showed creativity, effective communication, and total class involvement. It is with real pleasure that I present this trophy from the local chapter of the IODE to the fourth grade group in Miss——————'s room."

Should one wish to amplify the speech, it would be possible to stress the background or history of the award, the names of previous winners, and the honor which goes with it.

Displaying the award or gift is an added attraction. Describing the gift if it is uniquely appropriate, or if it is a radio presentation is also suggested. Be sure to congratulate the recipient as he steps up to accept the reward. A handshake is appropriate at this point.

The acceptance speech. A speech of acceptance should be short, particularly if the award is unexpected. In such a case a simple "Thank you" expressed clearly and sincerely is more appropriate than a polished, lengthy acceptance speech. If one is really surprised, it would seem awkward to give a major address in saying thank you. A simple "Thank you, Madam President, thank you very much" or "Thank you. I appreciate this very much" is sufficient. If, however, he were informed about the award beforehand, he might extend the speech.

"Thank you, Madam President. To me, the award from the Imperial Order of the Daughters of the Empire is the highest honor a student at——————————could aspire to achieve. It is my sincere hope that I will be worthy of the honor and will do my best to carry out the traditions of those who have won this award in previous years."

The speech of farewell. When a pupil who has been active in a class leaves the vicinity, he may be called upon to make a speech of farewell. Another occasion for a speech of this type may be giving up responsibility for some office—club or class president, for example. In either case, the speech should include the expression of:

1. appreciation for the gift or award, if one has been received
2. regret over leaving the vicinity or the office
3. pleasure in the associations of the past year or years
4. thanks for the cooperation given by classmates or club members
5. reminiscences of memorable occasions or episodes

The essence of a farewell speech is to express sincere appreciation for having been an integral part of the class, community, or club and to thank them for making it a memorable experience.

The after-dinner speech. Although less frequently needed by elementary school children, there are occasions in the upper elementary grades when an after-dinner speech is demanded. Speakers on such occasions are expected to give a speech that is at once humorous, amusing, provocative, filled with surprise, and delivered with élan.

"The best after-dinner speeches carry a message, communicate an idea, but build up to it gracefully and lightly. The light touch is evident in the very title of the after-dinner speech. . . . such topics as 'The Conquest of Space' or 'Adult Education' need rephrasing to 'Shooting the Moon' or 'Have Books, Will Travel'."[10]

The speech of introduction. The most common speech for special occasions is the speech to introduce. The purpose of a speech of introduction involves (1) setting the stage, (2) preparing the audience for what will be said by the speaker, and (3) establishing a spirit of rapport between the speaker and his audience. The formality, the length of the introduction, and the manner of the presentation are determined by the occasion, the type of program, and the known reputation of the speaker.

The following is a formula for an effective introduction.

Be brief. The introduction should not detract from the main speaker. Therefore, brevity is important. Give the name and office of the speaker clearly and distinctly.

Be relevant. Be sure that the introduction leads into the speech by mentioning the topic to be discussed. Mention also that background of the speaker which is relevant to the speech.

Be provocative. Arouse the interest of the audience in the speaker and/or the speech by giving pertinent and provocative information which:

1. *Gives prominence to the speaker by*:
   (a) telling briefly about the speaker's career
   (b) expressing the honor and pleasure of having him speak to the group
   (c) introducing him with the title of the talk

or

2. *Gives prominence to the subject by*:
   (a) emphasizing timeliness of the subject
   (b) describing the achievements of the speaker in this field
   (c) introducing him with the title of the talk

Be sincere in your praise. Your role as a good host is to make the speaker comfortable. Compliment, but don't flatter. Over-praise is obnoxious to an effective speaker.

Be conscious of the audience. Don't address your remarks to the speaker. Remember you are talking to the audience about the speaker. When you complete your introduction, turn to the speaker and mention his name.

Be alert to the situation. Remain standing where you are until the speaker acknowledges the introduction, comes forward to the microphone and nods, smiles or gives you a word of thanks. If there is applause, it is proper to join in with it. Then take your seat as quietly as possible.

The mood of the introduction should be appropriate to the occasion. Like all good speeches of introduction, it gets the attention of the audience, brings speaker and audience together, and leads directly into the subject. Funny stories are incongruous as a prelude to a serious speech. The reverse is also true.

The nomination. With the early interest in politics at all levels, especially in class organization, it is essential that children be taught early the correct form for making a nomination speech. The nominating speech is a specialized form of praise or eulogy, a eulogy with a specific, practical design, and an immediate purpose. It may vary in length from the short impromptu speech which is made on the spur of the moment to a distinctive oration, polished to the last pause. A formula for an effective nomination speech includes specific qualifications of the candidate for the office: (1) the character, personality, education, background, and experience which fit him for the office under consideration, (2) the need of the class, the community and/or the country for an individual of such accomplishments, personality, and spirit, (3) the willingness of the individual to be considered for such an auspicious position, (4) a positive statement attesting to the support of the candidate for the office.

Types of Organization of Speeches

Speeches in the elementary school may be organized on any of the following patterns: chronological (time sequence), spatial (space or location sequence), causal relations (effect and cause), need and plan, personal experience, order-of-importance sequence, string-of-beads, visual aids, and topical.

Chronological. The chronological pattern is one of the simplest for the elementary school child. He arranges ideas or events in the time order in which they happened. It is useful in describing a vacation trip by telling what happened every day. It is especially successful in topics focusing on history, biography, travel, and adventure. In a report on the founding and development of a province, the student would begin with the early explorers and follow through in sequential order with selected significant events. In planning a speech on the biography of an individual, one could organize it according to the early years, the middle years, and the sunset years.

Spatial. In the spatial organization, the child has several choices. Spatial refers to the division that can be made within any given area of space: from north to south, from left to right, from back to front, from bottom to top. Space sequence helps in describing a place, talking about geographical subjects, or locating objects. The child tells what he sees step-by-step. If he is describing his school, he will start with the view when he turns the corner and sees it, then the close-up description of the grounds, the entrance to the building, the hall leading to his room, and the sequence as he goes to his desk. He may wish to describe the school in terms of (bottom to top) first floor, second floor, third floor. Or he could use spatial order to describe only his classroom. He could begin at the left side of the room and proceed with all the items from left to right. The spatial pattern is an excellent way to organize a speech to inform.

Cause and effect (or logical order). In the cause and effect pattern, commonly used in persuasive speech, the student states the problem (the effect) and then goes on to tell the various causes that he has found leading up to it. In arguments from effect to cause, the conclusion shows an observed phenomenon was caused by certain other observed facts or events. An example of effect to cause: "The present difficulties of the party in power are due to unsuccessful attempts in the last campaign to purge the party of certain individuals who were opposed to policies to strengthen the federal government."

The need and plan. This speech is excellent for the elementary school child at every level. Children frequently give this type of speech without being conscious of making a speech. A classic example is the annual picnic. Here is a need —a felt need. The need is explained, a picnic. The class makes plans designed to make the picnic a success. Johnny has investigated the situation early. He remembers the last picnic when it rained. This time he wants it in the park close to the school. He uses the need (the picnic) and the plan (where to have it) as his type of organization. This development is used for the speech to inform, stimulate, or convince.

The personal experience. This speech forms an excellent basis for informal speeches. It is appropriate for the young child as he relates experiences he has had while at home, on trips, shopping, or sight-seeing in the community. To entertain or inform is the purpose of the speech which is used as a stepping stone to speeches of more complex organizational patterns appropriate for older children. However, for children in the intermediate grades transferring from schools where they have had little or no formal speech activities, the personal experience speech is a good one to help them get their bearings in a public-speaking situation.

Order-of-importance. The order-of-importance speech pattern is helpful to the student who chooses to speak about things in terms of priority. Progressing from the least important to the most important, or starting with the most important and going to the least is an interesting way to organize a speech. For example, in discussing favorite hobbies, if collecting rocks is the least important, a speaker should start here, go on to creative dramatics and playing the accordion, then finish with his favorite—building model trains. In discussing the cities in a province, one could take Manitoba and go from Greater Winnipeg, the largest, down through Brandon, Portage la Prairie, Flin Flon, Dauphin.

The "string-of-beads". This is a favorite with the new-comer to the speech program as well as with the younger child. It consists of a series of incidents or stories tied together or related to a single theme—the "string" on which the beads are strung. If the string (or theme) on which the beads are strung is thin, the speech will fail to be effective. If it is a strong one, however, it will make an excellent speech to entertain or interest an audience.

The visual aid or demonstration speech. This speech gives the child a perfect setting for demonstrating how the toy he received at Christmas works, whether a simple or complicated mechanism or principle operates it. He can show step-by-step how to make a puppet, a theater. He can point out on the map the route the family took to the Orient and relate details of the trip. He can demonstrate how to use a back-hand drive in tennis; how to stand for putting in golf, and how to block a goal in hockey. The demonstration speech, too, makes a good speech to inform or to entertain. Although the speech to demonstrate is a pattern within itself, it does not preclude the use of visual aids in the other speech patterns.

Topical. The topical organization is useful for the speech that does not seem to fit any of the other classifications. For instance, in explaining how a combustion engine works, the speaker would explain the functions of the various parts, carburetor, spark plugs, and so on. A home economics student might explain the principles involved in redecorating her room.

Organizing the Speech

The traditional method of organizing a speech is: introduction, body and conclusion. Monroe, however, has taken a different approach to this task in the development of a speech organization based on the "motivated sequence".

Whereas the traditional organization focuses on the speech itself, Monroe focuses on the reaction of the audience to the speech. It is his belief that the impact of a speech will be greater if the student plans in advance how to direct the audience's attention to the subject at the beginning and how to maintain that attention throughout the entire speech. States Monroe, ". . . the speech must be built with the specific audience always in mind, and the structure of the speech must conform to the thinking process of the listener. To do otherwise is as foolish as trying to make a man fit a suit."[11]

> **A speech structure to motivate audience response.** In daily conversation most of us speak to get a certain response from our hearer. We may shout 'Hey!' simply to get a friend's attention, we may tell him that he needs a haircut, or we may ask him to help us with our work. In each case we had an objective in mind, one that we tried to reach by speaking.
>
> The public speaker also seeks a definite response when he faces an audience. Because public speaking situations are generally more complex and formal than private conversations, however, he must organize and construct his speech beforehand so that it will have the best chance of achieving his purpose. The motivated sequence is a method to help him do this successfully.[12]

The popularity of this motivated sequence is attested to by thousands and thousands of students who have been introduced successfully to the experience of speaking to motivate audience response through this method.

The five steps which make up the complete motivated sequence form a basic plan which is applicable to almost all types of public speech and can be modified to fit the general purpose of a particular talk.

Step I	Attention
Step II	Need
Step III	Satisfaction
Step IV	Visualization
Step V	Action

In the elementary school a modified motivated sequence is sufficient to meet the requirements for most speeches; in the chart which follows the role of each step in getting an audience response is clearly evident.

The Motivated Sequence Applied to Entertaining Speeches[13]

Step	*Function*	*Audience Response*
1. Attention Step	Getting attention and retaining interest through entertainment	"I want to listen, and I'll continue listening because I'm enjoying myself."

The speech to entertain consists entirely of an expanded attention step. The other four steps are omitted.

The Motivated Sequence Applied to Informative Speeches[14]

Step	Function	Audience Response
1. Attention Step	Getting attention	"I want to listen."
2. Need Step	Demonstrating the need to know	"I need information on this subject."
3. Satisfaction Step	Presenting the information itself	"The information being presented helps me understand the subject more satisfactorily."

The speech to inform requires only the first three steps in order to achieve its purpose. In fact, only when the purpose of the speech is to *stimulate*, to *convince* or to *actuate* are all five steps used.

The Motivated Sequence Applied to Persuasive Speeches[15]
(. . . to stimulate, to convince, to actuate.)

Step	Function	Audience Response
1. Attention Step	Getting attention	"I want to listen."
2. Need Step	Showing the need: describing the problem	"Something needs to be done (decided, or felt)."
3. Satisfaction Step	Satisfying the need: presenting the solution	"This is what to do (believe, or feel) to satisfy the need."
4. Visualization Step	Visualizing the result	"I can see myself enjoying the satisfaction of doing (believing, or feeling) this."
5. Action Step	Requesting action or approval	"I will do (believe, or feel) this."

From the above charts it is evident that each step of the motivated sequence has a particular function to perform in stimulating audience response. The ideas and supporting material included in each step, therefore, must contribute to the achievement of the purpose of that step.

Planning the Speech

Once the student has decided upon the pattern of organization he wishes to use for his speech, he is ready to go about organizing the speech itself. Although the introduction of the speech is presented first, it should be planned last. The *body* of the speech should be planned first. He decides upon the main point or points of the speech and then finds supporting materials to reinforce these points. The purpose of supporting materials is to develop the main points by using explanations, illustrations, examples, statistics, and quotations.

11 12 13 14 15 *From Principles and Types of Speech*, Fifth Edition, by Allan Monroe. Copyright © Scott, Foresman and Company. Reprinted by permission.

The difference between dull, dry, disorganized speeches and sparkling, stimulating, sagacious speeches often lies in the development of the main ideas. It is not enough to simply state the main and subordinate points in a speech (a fault common to the novice). The speaker needs supporting materials —illustrations, examples, statistics, quotations. Supporting materials develop the main and subordinate points in the speech.

Supporting Materials

A speech with only main points is very much like a skeleton with no flesh. Although the skeleton is necessary, it lacks grace and beauty. The supporting materials give the clarity, the beauty, the logic that the main points need to make the speech acceptable. Among the most used types of supporting material are: explanation, illustration, examples, statistics, documentation, testimony, and comparison.

Explanation. Explanation as a type of supporting material consists chiefly in reiterating, discussing, and extending the main points, saying them in different words, going into greater detail, and amplifying the original concepts. By observing the audience closely, it is possible to tell when it gets the point and clearly understands what you are saying.

Illustrations. An illustration is an elaborated incident with enough detail to make it clear and interesting. Illustrations may be factual or hypothetical, which ever is needed to get the point across to the audience.

Examples. Examples are sometimes called specific instances. They differ from illustrations in that they are merely mentioned, not elaborated. The examples should be familiar to the listeners so that they may fill in the details. At times the speaker may prefer to give many examples rather than a few illustrations.

Statistics. It is true that statistics can be boring to an audience. They need not be. Used with discrimination, statistics aid greatly in supporting a point. The speaker should be accurate in his use of figures. If possible, they should be placed on a chalk board or projected with an overhead projector. If charts are used, they should be large enough to be easily read.

Documentation. Documentation is a vital form of supporting material in many speeches. Library facilities, journals, magazines, as well as encyclopedias and books are essential if students are to give evidence which is authoritative and authentic. Quoting from authorities in the field lends support and credence to the ideas presented. In quoting documentary evidence, it is necessary to give credit for the quotation. The source—book, journal, magazine, or other—should be cited with the correct date and page number if possible.

Testimony. Testimony is evidence based on an individual's reputation. Unfortunately, the reputation is often gained in a field far removed from the area of concern. Hockey players, for instance, are seldom nutritional experts. When the person whose testimony is quoted is noted in the field in which he gives testimony, the effect is usually convincing to the listening audience.

Comparison. Comparison points out the similarities between that which is already known or believed and that which is not. Sometimes the comparison is literal, but equally effective may be a figurative comparison. Comparisons are weak as proof because of the many factors which may be different in the items compared. They may show a high degree of probability, however.

Developing the Speech

In developing a speech and getting ideas organized, the following sequence will facilitate the task. Because speeches should in the early stages reflect the interests of the speaker:

Start with the knowledge the speaker already has.

Get information from people conversant with the topic.

Make use of personal observation.

Read widely to broaden knowledge.

In helping a child prepare a speech, it is very important that the child should begin with what he knows. This is the reason the speeches that deal with personal experiences are effective in helping beginners express their ideas vividly, interestingly, and effectively. The child should be encouraged to go back into his memory and try to recall experiences, bringing to mind examples, observations, and specific instances which will put life into the speech, which will clothe the skeletal frame with flesh and blood and make it come alive. This is only the first step.

The speaker must be helped to go beyond his limited knowledge. He should extend his knowledge by talking with others about the topic and getting other viewpoints. He may get this information through conversation, discussion, interviews, and critical listening.

In addition, the speaker makes use of personal observation to gain greater insight and understanding of the problem. Finally, he must read widely to verify the tentative conclusions he has reached based on previous knowledge, interviews, and observations. As he finds interesting, relevant material for developing his main ideas, he should take notes in such a manner that the material is readily accessible. This involves careful documentation in the notes so he can quote with authority, secure in the knowledge that he can give the source. He should plan to have more information than needed to give the speech. Then he will be able to organize the information in such a way that he can discard irrelevant material.

Robinson and Becker suggest the following basic steps in preparation of a speech which place emphasis on developing the extemporaneous method.

1. Select the subject.
2. Analyze the audience and the occasion.
3. Determine the purpose, adjusting it specifically to the analysis you have made.
4. Investigate and gather necessary material.
5. Organize the material into a usable outline with introduction, body, and conclusion.
6. Practice the speech aloud, wording it properly, with the outline as a guide.[16]

"Isn't it peculiar that the human brain begins to function from the moment you are born, improves as you grow older, then stops completely when you stand up to talk?" This oft-quoted saying, loved by after-dinner speakers, all too well expresses the feeling all of us have had in the first few moments of facing an audience.

Organization alone is not sufficient. Effective speaking is not automatic. Aristotle expressed this concept when he wrote, "It is not enough to know what to say, but it is necessary to know how to say it." Knowing how to say it, or giving the talk in a manner that the speaker communicates effectively and the audience responds favorably, can be facilitated through a three dimensional approach.

The oral dimension. The oral dimension is concerned with the voice. The inexperienced speaker tends to speak without expression. He needs to cultivate variety, not for the sake of variety, but to give meaning to his ideas. Variety is obtained by varying the force of the voice, the pitch of the voice, the quality of the voice, the rate of speaking, and the total design in which these elements are combined to give emphasis to words and conviction to the concepts.

The visual dimension. Every speaker gives two speeches simultaneously—one with his voice and one with his body. Nowhere is the truism "Actions speak louder than words" more self-evident than in the delivery of a speech. The listener may ignore the words and concentrate on the actions. Therefore, the speaker must be sure that the speech in action corresponds with the speech in word.

In terms of the visual dimension of the speech, the speaker must be aware of the importance of eye contact, facial expression, gestures, movement, and posture.

The psychological dimension. This is one of the most fascinating dimensions of giving a speech. It deals with the psychological elements within the speaker which determine the attitude of the audience toward what he has to say. During a speech, the audience is evaluating the person as much as the words he utters and the gestures he uses. As Irwin expresses it, "You must deliver *yourself* in an effective manner if you expect your ideas to arrive in perfect condition. How well you succeed depends upon your attitude."[17]

Some guidelines Irwin suggests for evoking responses are: (a) be sincere, (b) be poised, (c) be friendly, (d) be positive, and (e) be forceful. These are self-explanatory, yet how often do we see speakers who fail to get their ideas accepted, not because the ideas are worthless, but because they lack the personal qualities that combine to make the speaker effective.

If for no other reason than keeping the audience awake, the admonition to be forceful is worthwhile. At a Speech Festival, listen to the same oration delivered by different speakers. Who gets the attentive listening, the response, the thunderous applause? The person who is listless, disinterested, and dull? Delivering a speech in a dynamic manner requires energy, strength, and power.

Methods of Delivery

The question of what method of delivery should be used—the impromptu, the extemporaneous, the memorized, or reading from manuscript—frequently arises. The answer depends upon the occasion and the purpose of the speech. The four differ primarily in the manner of delivery.

The extemporaneous method. Most successful speakers use the extemporaneous method. The method calls for thorough research, completely outlined and rehearsed from the outline. At no two rehearsals is the attempt made to use exactly the same wording. The advantage of the extemporaneous method is that only the outline is memorized, allowing for spontaneity in delivery and flexibility in adapting to audience and to time limit. The outline is used to fix the sequence of ideas firmly in mind. Thus delivery has the advantage of being polished without being stilted or disorganized.

Speeches which lend themselves readily to this method include anecdotes, explanations using visual aids, informative talks, and, in fact, all except the most formal of speeches. The elementary school child is unlikely to have an occasion when the extemporaneous method is unsuitable.

Reading from manuscript. A second method is that of reading from a manuscript. The speech has been written out verbatim. The disadvantage of this method of delivery is that few students can communicate with the audience effectively. Concentrating on the reading usually blocks audience contact. The danger of a monotonous, dull, uninspiring delivery is ever present in this method. Only a skillful reader is likely to use sufficient emphasis and vocal variety to give life to his ideas. Most readers sound as though they are reading a speech (which they are) instead of communicating with the audience.

Only on occasions where a slip of the tongue could bring dire consequences or serious misunderstanding, or where time limits must be observed, such as in television or radio, is it wise to use this technique. Even then, the attempt should be made to adopt a conversational rather than a reading delivery.

The memorized speech. Here the speech is not only written out but committed to memory. The method of memorization is a risky one. If his memory fails, the speaker is embarrassed and builds up a block against speaking in public. Even where the memory is a servant rather than a master, the fear of forgetting places a strain on the speaker which detracts from the effectiveness of the delivery, and a strain on the audience as they empathize with the reciter. Too often the result is a stilted, inflexible, and artificial presentation. This is not an advisable method for the elementary or secondary school pupil.

The impromptu method. The impromptu method is characterized by lack of formal preparation; the student has to rely on his general knowledge and skill. The ability to speak impromptu has little value except in an emergency. Speaking on the spur of the moment, speaking "off the cuff", speaking from "the top of the head" is disastrous for all except the most experienced speakers, and even these did not acquire their skill from this method. The impromptu method has no place in an educational program.

Evaluation

Evaluation should include both teacher- and self-evaluation. Unless pupils understand the specific areas in which they are evaluated, it is difficult if not impossible for them to develop skill in self-evaluation. The ability to improve in any of the linguistic skills is influenced by a knowledge of the specific points which are to be evaluated.

A rating scale which is clear about the weaknesses pupils need to overcome in developing communication skills is helpful to both the teacher and the pupil. Such a scale enables the teacher to check frequently recurring weaknesses in student speaking. Detecting the specific weakness of the pupil is more difficult for the average individual than giving a generalized statement of approval or disapproval of the speech. With a minimum amount of effort the teacher can indicate to the student his weakness or weaknesses.

In the rating scale opposite, the scale from 1 - 5 makes rating simple. Space is given for brief comments which should emphasize the strong points of the speaker. Of special significance is the fact that the negative qualities listed in the rating scale have been found to distinguish good from poor speakers. Scales of this type are especially helpful to teachers who are trying to help every pupil develop at least minimal powers in oral communication. Simplicity, comprehensiveness, and utility are the characteristics which make such a device of inestimable value to the classroom or the special language arts teacher.

Teaching Group Discussion in the Elementary Classroom

"I was going to say something, but somebody else made another comment, then I was afraid my idea was too late."

"Ed Page and Mary Farmer and some of the other kids talk so easily that I don't feel I can keep up with them . . . so I don't try."

Comments such as these are less frequent when the teacher is aware of the values, the types, and the methods of teaching group discussion. With such a teacher, group discussion becomes a vital part of the school curriculum—not alone in language arts, but in other curriculum areas as well.

Types of Discussion

The classroom teacher should keep in mind that there are two purposes for discussion—one, an informal searching for information and pooling of ideas, and, the other, the more formal, structured problem-solving techniques. Both have their place and should be widely used in all classrooms.

Informal Discussion

Many of the problems that arise in day-by-day living in the classroom can find their solution through the group discussion process under the guidance of a teacher who is concerned with helping children develop skill in critical thinking, reasoning, and problem solving. The following account of an informal proce-

Rating Scale for Giving a Talk

Name Date

Subject of Talk Grade

Criteria for evaluation	*Rate 1—5*	*Comments*
Attitude of Speaker Indifferent Tense Flustered	*Rating* Apologetic Antagonistic Artificial	
Bodily Action Random movements Slovenly posture Exaggerated gestures	*Rating* Weak Monotonous Unmotivated	
Voice and Articulation Weak Monotonous Poor quality Non-rhythmic Poor pitch	*Rating* Loud Indistinct Poor articulation Dialect	
Language Usage Slang Incorrect usage Ambiguous	*Rating* Stilted Inexpressive Limited vocabulary	
Content Lacks clarity Insignificant Dull Limited material	*Rating* Inaccurate Lacks imagination Lacks unity Lacks coherence	
Organization Lacks purpose Poor introduction Central thought not clear	*Rating* Insufficient supporting material Weak transitions Sequence not clear Weak conclusion	
Projection to audience Lacks eye contact Little facial expression	*Rating* Inappropriate gestures Fails to communicate	
Audience Response Fails to get attention Fails to maintain interest Fails to consider audience	*Rating* Fails to get confidence Ignores audience Avoids audience analysis	
General Effectiveness	*Total Rating*	

dure shows how a group and teacher function in talking over common problems.

> Getting out "The Mission Star", the sixth grade classroom newspaper in a school in San Bernardino County, California, was the task at hand. In the left-hand column is an account of what was said and done when the group gathered to evaluate and plan after a 40-minute work session. In the column to the right are comments about the groups. Considerable restraint was exercised by the author when he refrained from comment in this column about the teacher's development of direct and concomitant learnings in skills and content. Since the intent of this piece is to study the teacher's utilization of group forces, comments are focused upon the group with special emphasis upon the teacher's leadership function.

Discussion	*Comments on Procedure*
Teacher: During our planning periods many important and special problems and plans were discussed. Perhaps others have arisen.	The class is a group and a combination of groups. Each individual is also a member of one or more subgroups.
Murray: I had some real help today. Brownie and Ricky met with the city editor and reporter of the primary page. Did everything work out okay, Brownie?	
Brownie: Fay can tell you about the meeting she had about the drawing on the primary page.	
Fay: Well, we had the meeting, but only three reporters came. Still, we decided on something.	Duties and responsibilities of members must be decided upon.
Teacher: Do you remember that Penny suggested that everyone should have an opportunity to come?	
Fay: No editors came!	
Teacher: Let's consider the matter briefly. Why, in your opinion, was it possible for the reporters to come and not for the editors?	The teacher helps the group to understand its members.
Rose: The reporters were interested.	
Judy: Well, we could come too, because we didn't have to go out on assignments.	
Penny: All the editors were very busy, and probably couldn't leave their work.	
Teacher: One of the reasons for the success of our paper has been the sharing of responsibility. Our policies may be determined by the large group but often a few can help make other decisions. Fay, what was the decision of your group?	To be successful, groups set policies by which they are guided.
Fay: We decided we had enough stories to fill up all but one-fourth of our primary page. We can put Larry's drawing in that space.	To achieve goals, channels of communication are left open.

George: That's still too much for a drawing.

Teacher: Why will we not be able to accept any more suggestions for this page?

John: The meeting for the suggestions is over.

Teacher: We shall say, then, that the editor of our primary page is reporting the final suggestions.

Ricky: Fay may be little, but she is sure stubborn.

Teacher: Is it necessary to be stubborn at times? When is it necessary?

Murray: In the city editor's case!

Penny: I'll say! He can't always let people do what they want or our paper wouldn't meet the deadline. Also, I think, Fay knows what little children would like about drawing for the primary page. She talked to the primary teachers.

Group activities foster cohesion. Difficulties can be dealt with as a problem for the group.

Teacher: Sometimes people think of stubborn behavior as bad behavior, but synonyms for the word are: determined, persistent, and tenacious, as well as holding firmly. If one believes in certain principles or ideas, it is often necessary to be determined or tenacious. Other times it is necessary to compromise, or adjust our ideas in order to work out plans together. Our evaluation and planning periods often require us to be persistent, or to compromise. Incidentally, how would you explain the meaning of evaluation?

The teacher leads the group towards an understanding of the deviate.

Carolyn: Our evaluation period usually involves a problem and how we worked it out, or sometimes we sum up our progress, and what we did.

The teacher guides the members of the group in an evaluation of their work.

George: We look over what else is needed.

Babs: We always talk over our work and how good it is, or how we could do better.

Teacher: Your understanding is excellent. Were there evidences that other things were needed in today's work period?

The teacher asks for, and gets, an additional problem.

Ricky: Mrs. Allyn's husband is being transferred to Pasadena. She's leaving; so is Mr. Aring (secretary and gardener).

Teacher: How we shall miss them! What is significant also about this in relation to "The Mission Star"?

Sue: Mrs. Allyn has always helped us

so much. She showed us how to type correctly.

Carolyn: And she's our librarian.

Carl: When I cut my forehead she fixed me up.

Some irrelevancies arise before attention is applied to the problem facing the group.

Margie: We couldn't list all the things she has done for us; it would take all day.

Murray: Couldn't we put something in the paper to show our appreciation?

Lynette: I think we could make a manuscript in appreciation. She'd like that. (This sixth grade had made illuminated manuscripts as an industrial arts activity related to their social studies experience—Modern Press and the History of Records. They were very proud of them and enjoyed decorating them in the style of the monks of the middle ages.)

Rose: Let's ask Larry to paint the one for Mrs. Allyn.

Babs: And Margie could do the manuscript printing.

Informal planning.

Group agreements without need for voting.

Teacher: How about writing a cooperative note of appreciation during the Language Arts period today—in addition to the manuscript? (The class approved this plan.) Carolyn, what was the outcome of the work period regarding the editorial page?

Carolyn: Babs, Judy and I got our ideas worked out for the second page. We can start typing the master copy pretty soon. On the overflow page we have our appreciation to the custodians and Miss Kims' third grade poetry. George also wants some of his sports news on this page.

Subgroups permit interaction not otherwise possible.

Teacher: Do you think the problem would have been solved in this way on a large city newspaper? Would a sports item be carried over to an editorial page?

Teacher helps group to clarify its problems.

Leroy: Well, big newspapers have several pages for sports.

Teacher: Can anyone define the biggest difference between a school newspaper and a city newspaper?

Danny: Most big papers have lots of pages.

Penny: That's because they use A.P., I.P., and U.P. news coverage.

Teacher writes on board:

School Newspaper
small
school news

City Newspaper
large, many pages
local news, and A.P., I.P.,
and U.P. coverage

An occasional summary helps the group to solve its problem.

Susan: The city paper is out for profit; we're a nonprofit paper.

Teacher: Would you amplify, or extend your statement, Susan? What is the meaning of non-profit?

Clarification of terms helps communication among group members.

Susan: Well, we're not making money with "The Mission Star" because we don't charge for it. (Teacher adds profit and non-profit to the list on the chalkboard.)

Teacher: There are many other differences between our school paper and a city paper. If you think of more later, we'll add to our list. Were any other problems solved?

LeRoy: When I was running the galley proof press, I noticed a word I thought was spelled wrong. I couldn't figure out what it was, but I just thought it was wrong. Connie helped me find out what was wrong.

Desire for group approval leads to high standards of workmanship. Cooperation among members strengthens the group. Teacher's praise encourages group members and helps set group standards.

Teacher: You're a fine printer, LeRoy, to recognize the need for a copyreader's help. Is it a good idea to think there may be need for improvement in one's work?

John: Yes, we should look into the matter.

Teacher: Margie, did you work out a solution to your story about the manuscripts?

Margie: I read over Ramona's story about the manuscripts, too. I think it is clearer than mine, so if we need any story to fill in, we might use hers.

The group learns to be task-centered in decision making.

Murray: Why not read both stories so we can decide, Margie? (Margie reads both stories.)

Penny: Both of the stories are very good, and they have excellent information. Perhaps we can use them both.

Carolyn: Margie tells about the decorating and writing, and Ramona tells about the making of inks and colors.

Teacher: Does anyone have an opinion on how both stories may be used in our paper? Connie, you read both stories carefully as a copyreader. What do you think?

Teacher helps group draw out and develop potentials of members.

Connie: Maybe they could be put together to make one article.

The group often helps its members attain

Joey: Then Margie and Ramona could both be the writers of the story.

Murray: Couldn't Alan put the stories together? He's our rewrite man.

Teacher: Alan, what is your opinion?

Alan: They'd make a very good article; I'll do the rewriting.

Teacher: Another reason for the success of the Star is your ability to accept suggestions and figure out, or analyze the situation. Sometimes 11- and 12-year-olds do this better than many adults. Are there any other questions and suggestions?

goals which they could not achieve otherwise.

Encouragement strengthens the group.

This session with the staff of "The Mission Star" obviously does not illustrate all the factors of group structure and function. Just as obviously, another teacher might have taught the lesson differently, but the fact remains that "The Mission Star" group did illustrate a few important ideas about how groups can function effectively. The manner in which the teacher encouraged, helped and challenged the group may be worth special attention. Without knowing the group better, it is difficult to know whether the teacher offered too many opinions or made too many judgements. Perhaps the leadership might have come more from group members in a group that had worked together successfully over a longer period. By the same token, a group with less experience in group work might have needed even more teacher direction than was given here. How would you have done it?[18]

Formal Discussion

Although all discussion occurs in face-to-face situations, the formal discussion is more highly structured, both in format and techniques. The formal discussion usually has a leader who has the responsibility of guiding the discussion toward predetermined goals.

Discussion seeks to accomplish any or all of the following purposes: locating and defining the problem, analyzing the problem, exploring possible solutions, and in some instances reaching a single or preferred solution.

Formal discussion normally has one of three purposes: to investigate facts, to analyze problems, or to formulate solutions.

Among the most commonly used types of formal discussion are the following.

The committee. The committee is a selected group of individuals appointed to carry out specific functions. The leader presents the problem and guides the group in seeking a solution. The secretary or recorder takes notes on what is said and later presents a summary to the group for their consideration. The committee has become an integral part of democratic living. Students who have learned to accept responsibility for the various committee functions will have a decided advantage throughout their educational and professional careers.

The panel. The panel is a situation in which four to eight *informed* individuals are chosen to represent various viewpoints of the group. They should be "specialists" in specific phases of the problem, and carry on a conversational discussion before an audience. After careful research (reading, interviewing, and studying), they discuss the problem under the leadership of a moderator. No one presents a set speech. A panel is a give-and-take situation in which no one monopolizes. If possible, the group meets ahead of time for a planning session in which they decide on the scope of the discussion, definition of terms, the points-of-view, and a time budget. Panels are frequently used in classrooms, for the culmination of units, in Home and School, and in school assemblies.

Dialogue. The dialogue as a term applied to discussion is fairly recent. It is a conversation between two people in the presence of an audience. One person, usually designated as the chairman, questions a second person, usually designated as the respondent, in order to seek information which an audience may need or want. It is essential to the success of this form of discussion that the respondent be an expert in the specific area under discussion. The responsibility of the chairman is to understand what the audience wants to know and to be able to phrase his questions effectively and appropriately to elicit this information.

The dialogue differs from the interview in that the dialogue takes place before an audience, making the information immediately accessible. Following the dialogue, the audience may direct questions to one or both of the participants.

The round table. The most commonly used type of discussion in the classroom is the round table. Children and teacher work together to solve a particular problem. Together they define, analyze, and attempt to reach conclusions. The round table discussion involves the entire classroom under the direction of a leader. In the early grades or in the initial experiences in the higher grades, the teacher should be the leader.

The symposium. In the symposium, three to six students give *prepared* talks on various aspects of a problem. Each speaker is an *expert* in his phase of the problem, is specifically prepared, and gives a set speech. The speaking time for each participant as well as the total time alloted for the symposium must be predetermined and strictly adhered to. The length of each speech should be planned in terms of the number participating. Ten to fifteen minutes is the customary length. Each person presents a different point-of-view or aspect of the problem. It should be determined in the preplanning that each speaker contributes to the clarification of the problem as a whole. The chairman makes the necessary transitions and correlations, and conducts the question and answer period.

The forum. The unique feature of the forum, whether presented alone or in combination with other discussion methods, is the role the audience plays. The forum may be combined with the panel, dialogue, symposium, lecture, or film as a means of involving the audience in participation.

The chairman or moderator presides; he directs the questions from the audience to the various members of the panel or symposium, or to the person being questioned in a dialogue. He makes transitional remarks. The functions of the chairman are to explain the specific procedure to the participants and audience, stimulate the audience to ask questions, rephrase the questions when necessary, repeat the questions so they can be heard by all the audience, close the meeting at the determined time. The duties of the audience are to ask pertinent questions, ask answerable questions, phrase questions well, allow various members to ask questions. The duties of the members being questioned are to answer the questions to the best of their abilities, be brief, avoid making a speech in answering the questions.

Problem Solving: The Process of Discussion

Every classroom teacher should be aware of the process of problem solving, from both the analytical and creative viewpoints. The analytical approach involves recognizing and defining the problem; clarifying the problem through defining the terms, distinguishing between facts and assumptions; collecting and organizing data; formulating possible solutions or hypotheses (explanations); selecting one or more promising hypotheses for testing and verification; and stating tentative solutions.

The classroom teacher should provide a variety of situations which require problem-solving techniques for their solutions.

The following outline for analytical problem-solving sequence has been successfully used by elementary teachers in many parts of the country.

1. Phrase the problem as a question.
   a. Question may concern a matter of fact. What method of teaching reading are we using?
   b. Question may concern a matter of value. What are the advantages of our present approach to the teaching of reading?
   c. Question may concern a matter of policy. How can we improve our present reading program?
2. Define the problem.
   a. Determine the objectives.
   b. Define the terms.
   c. Reach an agreement upon acceptable definitions.
3. Determine the extent of the problem.
   a. Explore the scope of the problem.
   b. Limit the scope to the ability of the group.
   c. Limit the scope to the time available.
4. Set up tentative solutions to the problem.
   a. Begin with known information.
   b. Locate the possible sources of information.
   c. Collect additional data needed.
   d. Organize the data into tentative solutions.
   e. Suggest the possible solutions.
5. Choose the best solutions.
   a. Analyze and interpret all solutions, checking each against the objectives.
   b. Choose the solutions which best meet the objectives.
6. Carry out or recommend the chosen solutions.

Participating in Discussion

As Miss Jonison, the language arts specialist, came into the teacher's lounge, she overheard Miss Simon say, "I don't know how I can teach discussion when the day is already crowded. I have to teach reading, writing, spelling, social studies, science, and mathematics." Mrs. Peters interrupted, "Don't forget art, music, literature, and physical education. If I take time to teach discussion, too, *when* will I teach the content subjects?" Miss Jonison took up the conversation where it had abruptly ended. "The question, simply put, is 'Why teach discussion techniques?' Is that it?" The next few minutes were spent in developing with the two teachers the values of discussion and the techniques in which the skills of group discussion using critical and creative thinking could be integrated into the curriculum.

Among the values Miss Jonison pointed out were: developing the ability to express one's ideas with increasing effectiveness, promoting critical and creative thinking on the part of the group, fostering interest in attacking problems, developing improved relationships among members of the group, learning to distinguish fact from fiction, learning to evaluate, making sure of data before coming to conclusions, and applying problem-solving techniques in their classes in science, social studies, mathematics and reading as well as in language arts.

"There are still a few wrinkles to iron out," admitted Miss Lamson, who had been very quiet up to this point. "I need a few ideas about selecting a good problem for discussion, being sure of the role of the leader in the discussion, and the role of the members. Once I get this straightened out I'll go into it with zest."

Selecting the Problem for Discussion

The place to start in selecting a problem or subject for discussion is the group itself. Not only must the group be interested in the question, they must have knowledge, opinions, and feelings about it. In addition, it must be within the capabilities of the group and have within its scope the need for critical thinking.

Finally, the problem should be significant enough to warrant research, study, and discussion. It should be either timely or timeless. It should have more than one point of view. Obviously a problem with a clearcut "yes" or "no" answer should be avoided. In a capsule form, the problem for discussion should:

1. be within the range of the experiences of the members of the group
2. be concerned with a problem of significance to the group
3. be controversial in nature, except where the purpose is merely to impart information
4. serve as a basis for planning and solving problems in the classroom
5. be a vehicle for critical and/or creative thinking

The Role of the Leader

Several qualifications are required for a successful discussion leader. The most important qualifications are personal. Among these are intelligence, pleasant personality, optimism, enthusiasm, tact, sense of timing, awareness of others, energy, effective speech, and experience in oral communication—particularly in discussion.

Specific responsibilities of the leader in a discussion group include the following.

1. Understanding the discussion process and the responsibilities of group leadership.

2. Knowledge of the subject matter of the discussion topic or problem.

3. Planning the discussion with the participants, following the general steps for the problem-solving sequence. The planning session may vary from a few ideas jotted down to a full-scale planning session, depending on the particular situation.

4. Introducing the speakers to each other and to the audience.

5. Opening the discussion by: (a) announcing the topic, (b) explaining its nature and importance, (c) informing the audience of anything necessary for an understanding of the problem.

6. Keeping the discussion moving.

7. Establishing and maintaining an atmosphere of informality and of pleasant relationship.

8. Exerting leadership through not dominating the meeting, but through encouraging and guiding the participants to contribute their ideas. It is the function of the leader not only to guide but also to be aware of the types of people in his group—the shy, the aggressive, the hostile, the monopolizer, etc.—and deal with them wisely.

9. Closing the discussion effectively. Summarizing the main points briefly, and stating the decision if one has been reached.

10. Making sure that the physical conditions, such as size of room, seating arrangements, ventilation, microphone, will be taken care of. If no one has been designated to do this, it may be necessary for the leader to assume the responsibility.

Evaluation

In teaching discussion, it is necessary to add two final steps—evaluation of the leader and evaluation of the participants.

The role of the leader. Did the leader:
- state the problem clearly?
- encourage the group to think critically?
- involve everyone in the discussion?
- elicit the needed information?
- handle conflict skillfully?
- summarize frequently?
- help the group to reach solutions to the problem?

The role of the participants. Did each participant show:
- familiarity with the problem-solving sequence?
- a desire to help other members of the group form ideas?
- a willingness to admit his own errors and to credit the contribution of the others?
- a willingness to answer the question of others directly?
- ability to present ideas conversationally, concisely, and in a friendly spirit?

a willingness to stick to the subject?
a willingness to avoid monopolizing by giving others their fair share of discussion time?
skill in using facts and pertinent information objectively?
ability to weigh critically the contributions made by himself and others?
a willingness to follow the leadership of the moderator or chairman?
a willingness to help the group to explore its chosen solution, even if opposed to it?
ability to differ without losing one's temper?

As the students participate, they will become skilled in using the process of critical thinking as a way of solving problems. They will find, too, that not only in the confines of the school, but in life outside the school, many of the problems can best be solved through creative thinking and creative communication.

Speech Activities for Stimulating Creative Thinking

The teachers who would guide children's learning in solving problems should be conversant with a wide variety of techniques for stimulating creative thinking. This requires specific training. Creative problem solving, perhaps more than any other single activity involving oral communication, presents the individual with an opportunity to break from the stereotyped, routinized ways of thinking and branch out in new and different directions in solving problems. In the creative process, the individual proceeds from *cognition*—the awareness of the need to solve a problem—through the phase of *conception* in which he is searching out many possible solutions. If successful at this stage, he has enough insight to move on to the phase of *combustion* when the plausible solution to which he is being drawn becomes conscious. Brainstorming, checklists, Phillips 66 (buzz session), and synectics are some of the techniques that have been developed to free the individual for creative thinking. He finalizes with *communication,* in which he shares his findings.

In order to help children develop creative thinking abilities, it is important to give them opportunity and training in creative problem solving as well as creative self-expression in the art forms of speech.

Brainstorming. Brainstorming is the term used to describe the novel and exciting problem-solving conference method originated and popularized by Osborn. The rapid-fire, spontaneous suggestions which come from a group participating in this activity is exciting to children as well as adults. Unlike reflective thinking where producing ideas and evaluating ideas take place concurrently, thereby slowing down the tempo at which ideas are generated and expressed, in brainstorming the two activities of producing and evaluating ideas are completely separated.

The momentum of rapid-fire conception of ideas carries those children along with the current who normally have little, if anything, to contribute to group discussion. The opportunity to participate in the spontaneous solution of specific problems, limited in scope, without receiving adverse criticism and having to defend one's ideas the moment they are given makes it a fun activity. It is important that the leader make sure that the rules are not disregarded and that the group does not break down into sub-groups. Later the list of suggestions is carefully scrutinized for fruitful ideas. If some five percent of the ideas are accepted, the session is considered a success and the participants are happy over the outcome.

Some basic rules for brainstorming are:

1. All ideas are accepted, impractical as they may seem.
2. Quantity rather than quality is emphasized.
3. All criticism of ideas is prohibited in the early stages.
4. Combination of ideas is encouraged.
5. Evaluation is deferred until after the idea-producing stage.

Among the obvious advantages of brainstorming are the elimination of criticism and all evaluation during the idea-producing stage, the encouragement of every idea—good or bad—to be heard, and the conservation of time because of the rapidity with which ideas are produced.

What brainstorming purports to do is to provide a psychological climate in which encouragement, respect for the ideas of others, and excitement of group success is fostered.

Checklist. A useful type of checklist is that developed by G. Polya of Stanford University for guidance in solving single-answer mathematical problems. With a creative teacher it can be modified to apply to multi-answer creative problems.

> **First.** *You have to understand the problem.*
>
> **Understanding the problem.** What is the unknown? What are data? What is the condition? Is it possible to satisfy the condition? Is the condition sufficient to determine the unknown? Or is it insufficient? Or redundant? Or contradictory? Draw a figure. Introduce suitable notation. Separate the various parts of the condition. Can you write them down?
>
> **Second.** *Find the connection between the data and the unknown.* You may be obliged to consider auxiliary problems if an immediate connection cannot be found. You should obtain eventually a plan of the solution.
>
> **Devising a plan.** Have you seen it before? Or have you seen the same problem in a slightly different form? Do you know a theorem that could be useful? Look at the unknown. Try to think of a familiar problem having the same or a similar unknown.
>
> Here is a problem related to yours and solved before. Could you use it? Could you use its results? Could you use its method? Should you introduce some auxiliary element in order to make its use possible? Could you restate the problem? Could you restate it still differently? Go back to definitions.
>
> If you cannot solve the proposed problem, try to solve first some related problem. Could you imagine a more accessible related problem? A more general problem? A more special problem? An analogous problem? Could you solve a part of the problem? Keep only a part of the condition, drop the other part; how far is the unknown then determined, how can it vary? Could you derive something useful from the data? Could you think of other data appropriate to determine the un-

known? Could you change the unknown or the data, or both, if necessary, so that the new unknown and the new data are nearer to each other? Did you use all the data? Did you use the whole condition? Have you taken into account all essential notions involved in the problem?

Third.

Carrying out the plan. Carrying out your plan of the solution, check each step. Can you see clearly that the step is correct? Can you prove that it is correct?

Fourth.

Examining the solution obtained. Can you check the result? Can you check the argument? Can you derive the result differently? Can you see it at a glance? Can you use the result or the method for some other problem?[19]

Phillips 66 (Buzz Session). Developed by J. Donald Phillips of Hillsdale College, this technique has been termed a "mass brainstorming session". It is so called because it is merely the application of the brainstorming technique as a way of facilitating problem solving within a large group. Following a lecture, panel, movie, or excursion, the audience is divided into as many groups of six persons as are required to give every individual a place within a group. A chairman is appointed from within each group. It is imperative that the chairman understands the technique of the buzz session.

Once the groups have been formed and the brainstorming technique explained fully, each group is on its own for the brainstorming session. The length of time is predetermined; six to ten minutes is usually adequate. At a signal from the leader, each group stops producing ideas and moves into the phase of evaluating and selecting the ideas which seem to have merit. If possible, within the time limit the one most meritorious idea is selected. When the evaluation phase is completed, the chairman of each group is called upon to present the ideas selected to the entire audience.

The success of this technique depends upon the ability of the leader to organize the whole group into buzz groups rapidly, and the briefing of the audience on the brainstorming technique effectively within the time alloted, and the willingness of the members to contribute.

Some Unusual Speech Activities

The speech teacher is frequently in search of different approaches to course objectives. This article presents some activities that are a little different and have been found to interest students and teachers alike.

The activities described are based upon the assumptions that variety in activities is desirable and can be highly motivating. The activities are not intended to serve as "a course of study," but, rather, are intended to provide speech teachers with some examples of activities that are little out of the ordinary.

What does the record say? Each student chooses a popular song which he feels (1) has a personally significant message, (2) expresses an idea representative of his generation, or (3) explains something important to society. The activity is then to develop a speech around the theme of the record and, within the speech, include an oral interpretation of the song.

To put it another way . . . Students are asked to compile lists of current "in" words. They are also asked to follow up on this by talking with their parents, neighbors, etc., and to work with them in compiling a list of "in" words from their era. From the lists turned in, groups of students can discuss the meanings of the words and the derivations of the words. Perhaps a dictionary of "in" words from various eras could also be compiled. The short life span of this kind of vocabulary could also be discussed.

"Tuning in" on traditional poetry. Each student goes through a collection of poetry with the expressed purpose of finding a poem which considers a contemporary problem. The student is then asked to prepare an oral explanation of the poem and how it relates to the contemporary problem. (The activity could be introduced through reference to Edwin Arlington Robinson's "Richard Cory," recently recorded by Simon and Garfunkel.)

Bringing up parents. In this activity, students are asked to take the part of their parents. From that role, they are to explain their philosophy of life, of bringing up children, etc. Following the speech, the students comment on where and why they disagree and agree with their parents. At the conclusion of the presentation, other class members question the speakers on their philosophies. (It would be interesting to have some of the parents attend these sessions.)

Let's organize a demonstration. The students are to locate a situation of concern to them, in or out of school, and decide what can be done to remedy the situation. Ideally, the problem selected will be one where there could be a solution forthcoming. Lobbying for a stop light on a dangerous corner or proposing a new method of electing student council representatives are two examples of situations potentially ripe for remedy. After the problem is defined, the students' job is to prepare a plan to solve the problem and to actually carry out this plan, examining what happens as they go. (Encourage them to start small and build. Science students in Pacific Grove, California, for example, launched a protest against pollution of Monterey Bay by designing and printing bumper stickers that called attention to the problem and read, "Monterey Bay—A Royal Flush.")

Such an assignment provides an ideal opportunity to discuss issues related to freedom of speech. In addition, questions regarding methods and means of dissent, the history of dissent, and so forth become important.

History often does repeat itself. The young are generally bombarded with expressions like "It wasn't like that in my day," "That wouldn't have happened in the good old days," and "Times have changed." Sometimes these reactions are worth investigating. The activity would be to probe and find comparisons and contrasts. Studying the Boston Tea Party, the woman's suffrage movement, repeal of prohibition, the Civil War, and so on, might lead to some interesting historical parallels. The activity would be to take a current problem and explore its historical roots and then present the findings to the class.

"Fearful earfull." Some of our students are not aware that we all have fears and that many of these fears are a bit irrational. In order to make students aware of this circumstance, try having students talk about their fears with other students. One outcome might be humorous speeches about fears.

Non-verbal behavior. The teacher begins by randomly passing out pieces of paper with numbers on them to the students. Students are told that they are not to utter a word because they are studying non-verbal behavior. Students are then instructed to find others with the same number on their slips of paper (all the "1's" form a group, all the "2's" form a group, etc.) and form a group. The assembled group is then instructed to build something that describes their group. After all projects have been completed the projects are presented to the entire class and inferences are made about what the group has non-verbally communicated about itself to others.

This assignment is an excellent way to lead into the study of small groups and non-verbal behavior. Considerations as to how leadership develops, roles, the need for language, and the nature of group interaction flow naturally from the activity.

Games people play. Students prepare for this activity by reading Eric Berne's *Games People Play*. They are then asked to talk about or act out games that they, their teachers, their parents, and their friends play.

Needless to say, not all of these activities would work for all teachers or with all groups of students. In many cases the teacher may believe that only a few class members would be interested in the activity. Fortunately there is a solution to this problem. Offer the students some "options." That is, tell them about some possible activities and let them select the one that most appeals to them. There is nothing sacred about everyone working on the same assignment at the same time. There may be students who are not interested in any alternative presented. Allow them to propose an acceptable alternative. Why not? Activities can become self-motivating when students have selected them or developed them. Experiment and see what happens.[20]

Conducting a Meeting

Which motions have the most success?
For which do persons yearn?
One is the motion to recess,
The other, to adjourn.

Richard Armour

"Mr. Chairman, I move that. . . ." "I rise to a point of order!" "I move to amend by. . . ." "I move to refer to a committee. . . ." "I favor this motion because. . . ." "I move to adjourn." A knowledge of parliamentary procedure is essential in a democratic society. The individual who understands and uses parliamentary procedure can present his views, protect his rights, and help secure wise decisions in any organization of which he is a part. It prepares him, too, to execute his duties of office effectively should he be elected.

The classroom teacher should be familiar with such elements of procedure as making motions, making amendments, organizing committees, voting, and the order of precedence of motions. Children in the elementary school become intrigued with the rules and regulations of parliamentary procedure and should be encouraged to use such procedures in their meetings with the help of the classroom or language arts teacher.

Key Concepts

The following are some key concepts that are useful both in the language arts and social studies classes.

Parliamentary procedure is an orderly, efficient, and impartial method of conducting the business of a class, organization, or club.

The rules of parliamentary procedure are established on the principles of fairness, order, the rights of the minority, and the rule of the majority.

The participation of every member is essential to democratic living.

Each individual is responsible for acting with the courage of his convictions, tolerating and respecting the opinions of others, and accepting and abiding by the decisions of the majority, although a member is entitled to give a minority report if he so chooses.

Each member is expected to carry to completion an assignment which he has accepted as part of a group.

Each individual has the duty of becoming a good citizen and an intelligent voter who becomes familiar with issues in order to make wise decisions.

Basic Principles of Parliamentary Procedure

The basic aim of parliamentary procedure is to enable a group to come to a decision in the simplest and most direct manner while providing for free debate, protecting the rights of the minority, and ensuring the rule of the majority. This aim is accomplished in several ways.

Only one proposal may be debated at a time.

Every subject is entitled to full debate.

Each member has an equal right to propose subjects for consideration, to speak on a subject, to vote as he pleases, and to have information supplied about the proper procedure.

Order is necessary in order to ensure that these procedures obtain.

Members must cooperate, must speak in proper sequence, one at a time, and must speak to the specific matter before the group.

Each member has an equal vote in reaching any decision.

Order of Business

Through the years a uniform procedure for conducting a meeting has evolved. The teacher may act as chairman until the president has been elected. The president then asks for nominations for the remaining officers. After nominations are closed, the members may vote by secret ballot or by raising hands. To facilitate business, the teacher should instruct the class in the rules of order and in the order of business. Such rules are best learned through participation, whether the class is in the lower or upper echelon of the school.

1. Call the meeting to order.
"The meeting of the ——— club will please come to order."
(The chairman is standing and raps his gavel as he calls the meeting to order.)

2. Read the minutes.
"Will the secretary please read the minutes of the last meeting?"

3. Approve or correct the minutes.
"Are there any corrections or additions?"

4. Announce the results.
"The minutes are approved as read (or corrected)."

5. Ask for reports of committees.
"We shall now have the reports of the standing committees."
(Standing committees report in the order listed in the by-laws. Special committees report in the order in which they were named. Each chairman presents his report and moves the acceptance.)

6. Approve reports of committees.
"Is there any discussion of the report?" Following discussion, if any, the chairman states, "If there is no objection, the report will be filed as read." If action is recommended, the chairman of the committee moves its adoption.

7. Ask for unfinished business (business arising out of the minutes).
"Is there any unfinished business?" Or "We will consider business arising out of the minutes."
(This refers to business uncompleted at the adjournment or business postponed to the next meeting.)

8. Ask about new business.
"Is there any new business to be brought up?"

9. Turn the meeting over to the program chairman (if a program is to follow).
"I shall now turn the meeting over to the chairman of the program committee."

10. Ask for motion to adjourn.
"Is there any further business to come before the club? If not, I will entertain a motion to adjourn."

11. Announce the adjournment.
"The meeting is adjourned until ———."

Obviously, if students are to learn the fundamentals of participation in meetings, clubs, and other organizations, if they are to learn such things as individual responsibility and social reciprocity, they must have opportunity to practice these behaviors in school situations which have meaning for them. These behaviors cannot be "lectured" into students. They must be a part of the guided activities of the students.

Some of the situations that may be a puzzle to teachers and pupils alike are related to such points as ways of calling for a vote, types of motions, postponement of motions, order of dealing with motions that are tabled, wording of motions, behavior in making a motion, and gaining recognition in order to state a motion.

The chairman may call for a vote in one of four ways: by a show of hands, by a standing vote, by a voice vote, and by a secret ballot. Normally the chairman has no vote except to make or break a tie. If the vote is by secret ballot, however, he must vote at the time the group votes.

Types of Motions

Motions are proposals submitted for decision by the group and may serve many different functions. A brief look at their functions will serve to clarify them. There are four types: main, subsidiary, incidental, and privileged.

Main motions. Main motions are initial proposals for action. They introduce a subject for the group to act upon. Any motion is treated as a main motion when there is no other business before the group.

Subsidiary motions. Subsidiary motions are those which act directly upon the main motion in some fashion; they change its content or dispose of it temporarily or permanently. The purposes of the subsidiary motions are: to change the debate on the main motion, as by amending it; to dispose of the question for that particular meeting, as by postponing the motion by laying it on the table, or by referring it to a committee; to postpone action until a definite time; to stop debate; to limit or extend debate. Subsidiary motions must be considered and disposed of in the order of their precedence before the main motion may be considered.

Incidental motions. Incidental motions are tools that provide a means for correcting or changing the procedure under which motions are handled. For example, a member may feel that the chairman has made a decision contrary to parliamentary law and may wish an appeal from his decision. Another member may wish additional information from the maker of a motion. Or he may wish to rise to point of order (to enforce rules), etc.

Privileged motions. The purpose of privileged motions is to protect the rights and comfort of members of the group. They involve such problems as taking a recess, adjourning, adjusting heating and lighting in the room, calling for the orders of the day. They require the direct and immediate attention of the group because of their importance. They have precedence over subsidiary motions and the main motion.

For all business meetings, the procedures should be as simple as possible. The machinery of parliamentary procedure should not get in the way of expediting business. The degree of formality with which a meeting is conducted depends largely on the group involved. The presiding officers should master the procedures in order to conduct business with dispatch in an orderly, organized, yet democratic manner.

Duties of Officers

When the officers have a clear understanding of their duties and responsibilities and are willing to fulfill them, the organization is fortunate. The by-laws will usually state the qualifications for and duties of the various offices. There are certain general duties commonly assigned to the chairman and secretary. The other officers' duties will vary with the organization.

The Chairman. If the president of an organization or the chairman of a committee has already been chosen, he automatically becomes the presiding officer. When no such officer has been selected, the first duty of the group is to nominate and elect by a majority vote a chairman from among the members.

The chief function of the chairman is to expedite business. To avoid confusion, speakers are required to address the chairman and be recognized by him before speaking. Only one person may speak at a time. It is the responsibility of the chairman to be familiar with the order of the business of the meeting and to understand the order of precedence of motions. In informal groups, the chairman may enter the discussion and vote on proposals which are presented. He may also remain seated during much of the meeting. It is proper for him to stand as he calls the meeting to order, as he puts questions to the vote, and as he gives decisions. In formal meetings, the chairman may stand much of the time. In informal meetings, he sits much of the time.

A good chairman should be able to speak well. He should help the group expedite business with the minimum amount of formality. For example, contrary to strict parliamentary procedure, he may permit the discussion and modification of business before a formal motion is placed before the group for voting. If, however, extraneous matters are introduced, the chairman must call for a main motion. Technically, nothing can be declared out of order if there is no motion before the group.

The Secretary. The secretary is responsible for keeping the minutes of each meeting. These should include the following.

1. Name of the organization
2. Kind of meeting (regular, special, etc.)
3. Date, time, and place of meeting
4. Name and title of presiding and recording officers
5. Fact that a quorum was present
6. Notation as to the reading and approval of the minutes
7. Record of the reports by officers and committees
8. Record of all main motions, except those withdrawn, and name of mover
9. Record of all other motions, including their order of disposition, and name of mover
10. Record of all votes taken
11. Time and type of adjournment
12. Signature of the secretary

The minutes should be written in ink or typed. A loose-leaf notebook, size 8½" by 11", is quite convenient. It is wise to allow wide margins so that any changes may be legibly entered in the margins. The secretary's book becomes part of the permanent records of an organization.

In addition to keeping the minutes, the secretary may handle the correspondence, prepare the agenda for meetings, coordinate committee work, and perform such other duties as prescribed by the constitution or bylaws.

Evaluation of Parliamentary Procedures

Teacher-pupil evaluation of growth in the development of social skills in parliamentary procedure will progress to a greater degree if cooperative formulation of criteria for evaluating club meetings is undertaken by children and teacher. An example of the results of such a group effort follows.

> Are we following the rules of parliamentary procedure in conducting our business?
>
> Are the meetings worthwhile? Does the knowledge of procedures help things move smoothly?
>
> Are members courteous to one another? Do they show respect for the officers?
>
> Do members speak convincingly? Do they formulate their motions and ideas effectively before presenting them as items of business?
>
> Do all members share in the club activities or does a minority "run" the club?

Sequence of Speech Activities in the Elementary Grades

In the placement of activities throughout the elementary grades, the authors have kept in mind the aims of oral communication, the language development of pupils, and the need for the refinement of linguistic skills for the expression of ideas and for the freeing of creative potential. They have also been cognizant of the individual differences of children at each developmental level and have suggested a variety of activities from which the teacher can choose in order to meet the needs, interests, and abilities of the group. Some of the children will be ready for the activities at an earlier time than others. Children grow differently; they react to their environment differently; they have different skills. It is the responsibility of the teacher to provide a speaking environment which will challenge all children and which will have for each child the particular activity that best meets his abilities and growing needs. Although children develop some speech skills through group activities, opportunities must also be provided for personalized speech activities for both individual growth and evaluation.

Concluding Statement

The child learns to speak before he comes to school, before his formal education begins. However, his skills in speaking are far from perfected. The development of skill in speaking is a continuous process. Throughout the child's educational experience, his speech and language skills both limit and are limited by his experiential background, native abilities, and instruction. "The growth, refinement, and permanence of communication habits parallel the development

Speech Development[21]

Aims in Teaching Communications	*Language Growth of Children Five to Nine Years Old*	*Speaking Activities*
	In the Kindergarten	
To talk fluently about experiences. To listen appreciatively to others.	Fives like to talk. Conversation is egocentered—pets, hobbies, and arguments. They like to tell what happened at home, on trips.	Conversation about items of interest to the child, such as home activities, family, birthdays, holidays, play activities, weather, pets, trips, visits, new clothes, new experiences.
To use speech as a tool to adjust to social situations. To take advantage of opportunities for developing language through a variety of experiences.	Fives greet friends, say "Please", "Thank you", "I beg your pardon", "Excuse me". They introduce mother or friend, acknowledge introductions, invite visitors to come in.	Greeting each other and strangers. Introducing parents or friends. Serving as hosts or hostesses to mothers or children from other grades. Saying "Thank you", "Please", and other forms of the social amenities. Dictating a letter to the parent who went with the children to the zoo, or to the firemen who showed them around the fire station, or to a child who is in the hospital.
To listen to stories appreciatively. To tell a short, simple story. To participate in choral speaking of favorite poems. To tell the story ending when the teacher asks them to do this.	Fives like to listen to stories. Some like to read. Children of five can narrate a complete occurrence and repeat a familiar story in sequence.	Listening to the teacher tell and read stories. Listening to the children tell stories. Creating stories and dictating to the teacher. "Reading" the stories from the chart. Repeating with the teacher favorite refrains of nursery rhymes or stories. Retelling a simple story to the group. Participating in choral speaking.
To contribute information to the class.	Fives seek information. They ask innumerable questions. Fives are interested in using new, large and colorful words.	Explaining the work accomplished during the work period. Explaining how to do a certain task or how to get to a particular place. Explaining standards of behavior on trips.

(Speech Development, continued)

Aims in Teaching Communications	*Language Growth of Children Five to Nine Years Old*	*Speaking Activities*
		Explaining and interpreting the picture painted during the work period. Telling why they did work as they did.
To begin to take part in group planning.	Fives like to make decisions. They exhibit increasing willingness to share and are beginning to be interested in the welfare of others.	Planning the work of the class. Planning the work of small groups. Planning the standards of the group. Planning activities for entertaining parents. Discussing the behavior of the group during the fire drill or trip.
To express one's self in dramatic play.	Children of five are highly dramatic. They like to imitate adults. Both girls and boys play in the doll house and take the roles of adults. Boys and girls choose the same activities in the kindergarten. Fives are highly imaginative, but some are beginning to distinguish fact from fancy.	Dramatic play in the doll house. Role playing of events such as going to the dentist. Dramatizing stories. Dramatizing nursery rhymes. Using hand or stick puppets to tell nursery rhymes and stories.
	In the Primary Grades	
To talk freely and easily about new experiences. To listen with increasing ability to get other's point of view. To increase fund of ideas through listening to literature, listening to music, looking at and "reading" pictures, taking trips, listening to people who come in to talk to the group.	Children of six, seven, and eight are interested in almost everything. Sixes use language aggressively. Sevens are more introspective. They like to talk about themselves. They are likely to use language to complain. Eights talk a great deal. They tell tales, boast, exaggerate. Some prefer to talk to adults and engage in real social conversation with adults. Nines talk things over with adults.	Conversation about topics of mutual interest or class activities. Relating personal experiences. Talking over the trip on returning from an excursion.

(Speech Development, continued)

Aims in Teaching Communications	*Language Growth of Children Five to Nine Years Old*	*Speaking Activities*
To use the telephone correctly.	Sixes use the telephone with ease. Sevens do considerable phoning. They call home to see about lunch money or after-school plans. They use the phone for helping mother with grocery list. They receive and send messages.	Using the telephone to give and receive invitations. Using the telephone to deliver simple messages. Ordering supplies. Taking simple messages.
To respond easily to simple social situations.	Sixes enjoy offering and receiving hospitality from their peers. Some sevens like to introduce their mothers to their friends. Eights use language fluently. Nines are more cooperative and make plans far in advance, without adult direction.	Giving and receiving invitations. Making introductions. Serving as host and hostess to visitors. Responding to introductions. Greeting guests. Showing visitors around the room. Carrying on an interesting conversation with visitors.
To tell stories for others. To listen appreciatively to stories.	Primary children respond to humor. Primary children can listen to stories for twenty minutes with courtesy and obvious enjoyment. Sixes like legends and fables as well as stories about themselves and the activities of other children. Sevens have wider interests; they are interested in stories about nature, animals, space ships and rockets, children of other countries. They like myths, legends, some fanciful tales, and stories about grown-up occupations. Eights show interest in primitive cultures. They also are turning to stories of adven-	Listening to stories read or told by the teacher. Telling stories to the group. Telling stories the children have created. Listening to a story the teacher reads and making up the ending.

Aims in Teaching Communications	Language Growth of Children Five to Nine Years Old	Speaking Activities
	ture and humor. They still enjoy stories of children, animals, and wee folk. Nines love adventure stories.	
To tell an experience. To report an event or activity in an orderly manner. To stick to the main point and develop the point by means of a simple sequence of ideas.	Sixes show a marked interest in construction, transportation, and science. Sevens want to acquire knowledge of natural and social sciences, through excursions, projects, and celebration of holidays. Eights show a greater interest in people of foreign lands and like to read about strange and distant places. They are extremely interested in nature and science and they have numerous hobbies.	Participating in a sharing period. Reporting materials read. Explaining pictures they have painted or colored. Explaining a game or process. Reporting on events, seen or heard. Reporting on individual or group activities.
To read aloud a simple poem or story and share it with the group.	Sixes, sevens, and eights like to read aloud to the group. Nines are getting to be avid readers. Some nines also like choral speaking.	Reading a story or poem aloud. Reading reports aloud. Choral speaking with children selecting the poem and deciding on the interpretation.
To select a topic for discussion. To share information by means of group discussion. To settle issues through group discussion.	Children cannot plan far in advance. Sixes need help in making choices. They should not be confronted with too many alternatives.	Planning activities (both of the class as a whole and sub-groups).
	Sevens find it easier to make up their minds but harder to change. They engage in genuine argument in which they put forth reasons in support of the assertions they make. Sevens are methodical and like to plan their day.	Planning and preparing for trips and excursions. Talking about the trips. Talking about the benefits gained from the trips. Discussing the work of the members of the class.

(Speech Development, continued)

Aims in Teaching Communications	*Language Growth of Children Five to Nine Years Old*	*Speaking Activities*
	Sevens are very critical. Eights make up their minds easily but they listen to reason and are willing to change their minds. Eights verbalize ideas and concerns. They begin to understand relationships of cause and effect. Eights take criticism if it is sincerely given. They want to improve in what they do. Nines listen to others.	Evaluating work. Settling an issue through group discussion.
To engage in dramatic play. To dramatize a story so that the listeners can follow it readily and enjoy it.	Children from six to nine enjoy dressing up and playing appropriate roles, which they not only play but live. Several children will make up a play, work on it by themselves, and present it to the group. Sixes increase in ability to tell fact from fantasy. They like spontaneous dramatic play and creative dramatics, not a formal play. They pretend to be a pony, an airplane or a space ship. For them, a block or piece of furniture can be anything they want it to be. They play school, house, library, grocery store, travelling by boat, train, bus, or plane. Outdoors they choose more active games. Sevens want realism in their play. They play transportation activities, community helpers such as postman, fireman, policeman, grocery man. Outdoor games are active. Girls tend to be dancers and prima	Dramatizing every-day occurrences. Pantomiming. Playing a story or poem with stick or hand puppets. Dramatic play in the room using doll house and later building post offices, florist shops, markets, stations, airports, in the room. Dramatizing puppet plays. Choral speaking.

(Speech Development, continued)

Aims in Teaching Communications	*Language Growth of Children Five to Nine Years Old*	*Speaking Activities*
	donnas; boys tend toward television stars and gun play. Sevens, eights, and nines all enjoy putting on a show or playing a dramatic role. Each age group participates in dramatizing events and activities. They impersonate things and people as well as animals. Nines enjoy dramatization and creative play.	

(Speech Development, continued)

Aims in Teaching Oral Communication in the Intermediate Grades	*Language Growth of Children Ten to Fourteen Years Old*	*Speaking Activities*
To converse intelligently. To have something to say. To say it well. To respond actively to another's conversation. To listen courteously and critically.	Children show definite interest in communicating with their peers. Are improving in speech skills. Are critical of their own and others speech. Are increasing vocabularies.	Conversation Participate in conversation. Choose subjects for conversation. Learn how to carry on conversation. Plan how to change the subject. Discuss how to be interesting listeners. Demonstrate this knowledge.
To speak courteously and effectively on the telephone. To know how to begin and end a telephone conversation.		Telephoning Take messages accurately. Ask for information. Carry on business over the telephone. Ask permission by means of the telephone to visit a market or institution.
To interview to gain specific information.	Recognize need for increased language facility.	Interviewing Plan an interview. Dramatize interviews. Conduct an interview in front of the class. Conduct an interview outside of the class and make a report to the class.
To participate in social situations with ease. To learn to be considerate of guests.	Children are ready to begin to learn and practice social amenities. Classmates set standards of manners. Children from nine to eleven are ready for widening social contacts.	Social Situations Serve as host or hostess in school functions. Welcome the guests. Express sympathy and congratulations.
To give speeches to entertain, to inform, to stimulate, convince, actuate. To collect and arrange material for a talk.	Base reasoning on direct observation. Begin to make assumptions, generalizations, deductions.	Giving Talks Give short talks to inform, entertain, stimulate, convince, actuate.

(Speech Development, continued)

Aims in Teaching Oral Communication in the Intermediate Grades	*Language Growth of Children Ten to Fourteen Years Old*	*Speaking Activities*
To provide supporting material. To organize ideas. To develop research techniques. To know where to look to find information.	Use research methods in collecting data.	Make and use simple outline for speech. Find specific facts for talks from magazines, books and journals. Evaluate own and peers' talks.
To cooperate in informal group discussion. To think critically about what others are saying. To be willing to change one's mind. To stick to a point. To participate constructively in formal group discussion. To experiment with creative ways of solving problems. To know which type of group discussion techniques will best serve a specific purpose. To serve as an effective discussion leader.	Children are eager for activities which require them to make decisions and cooperate in planning. They are eager to think independently and critically. The predolescent is quite willing to express his ideas. He has not yet become fixed in his ideas. In planning, children at this age can be guided to set up standards for discussion and follow through. Children enjoy contributing ideas without evaluating first as in brainstorming. The preadolescent likes to make guesses and state hunches. He is beginning to discriminate in types of discussions to meet a particular problem or question.	Discussion Participate in informal planning sessions of class routines. Plan activities of the class. Pool information. Participate in various forms of discussion: committee, round table, panel, symposium, forum. Participate in planning and carrying through different types of discussion in terms of the needs of the situation. Be a discussion leader. Follow the problem solving sequence in a discussion.
To conduct a meeting by means of simple parliamentary procedure.	The intermediate grade child is gregarious and enjoys organizing a club and being a vital part of it.	Organizing a Club Conduct club meetings following the correct order of business. Use the correct form for making the various motions.

(Speech Development, continued)

Aims in Teaching Oral Communication in the Upper Grades	*Language Growth of Children Ten to Fourteen Years Old*	*Speaking Activities*
To gain greater skill in conversing with peers and adults about a variety of topics.	Increased complexity in sentence structure and greater vocabulary development.	Conversation Converse with adults. Study the characteristics of a successful conversation. Select broad range of topics for conversation.
To use the telephone in a mature manner.	More concern with approved usage.	Telephoning Arrange interviews by telephone. Ask a favor. Invite a resource person to the school. Plan a class activity. Express sympathy over the telephone. Order materials. Make a business complaint. Plan to visit a telephone office.
To plan an interview, carry it through courteously and effectively.		Interviewing Study interview techniques. Participate in an interview. Dramatize an interview: as an interviewer, as an interviewee.
To be a cooperative, social member of the group, considering others and making them feel at ease.	Early adolescents are eager to learn correct vocabulary and usage required by the various social amenities.	Speaking in Social Situations Study what is required in different social situations in the way of speech. Role play social situations demonstrating effectively used correct form.
To participate with increasing effectiveness in discussion.	Early adolescents are anxious to have their ideas accepted in group planning.	Discussion Participate in pupil-teacher planning.

(Speech Development, continued)

Aims in Teaching Oral Communication in the Upper Grades	*Language Growth of Children Ten to Fourteen Years Old*	*Speaking Activities*
To listen critically and courteously. To participate in critical thinking. To participate in creative problem solving. To be a discussion leader. To participate in parliamentary procedure. To be a parliamentarian.	They see clearer cause and effect relationships. They can solve problems involving concrete situations. They enjoy role-playing situations, brainstorming, and buzz sessions as an aid to finding solutions. They analyze, "talk-out" problems, and clarify through group thinking. They tend to draw conclusions from limited data unless they are guided.	Plan the work of the class in units. Plan activities of the group. Use discussion technique in social studies, science and mathematics as well as in oral communication. Discuss problems of concern to the group, the community, the province, and the world. Follow the steps of problem solving. Participate in critical thinking and creative problem solving. Be a discussion leader. Conduct a meeting using approved procedures.

of knowledge built into the process. Hence continuity of instruction in speech is of primary concern in formal education."[22]

It is through speech that a child first expresses his ideas. It is through speech that he makes his wants known and develops a sense of identity. It is through speech that the quality of his thoughts, that the form and worthwhileness of his relationships with others are mirrored. In the elementary school the child has his first direct training in transmitting his ideas with accuracy, correctness, and clarity; he learns to speak in ways that help resolve misunderstanding and aid in bringing groups to worthwhile decisions. Here he is introduced to the study of speech processes and forms, and he develops speaking skills in functional, meaningful and creative situations. The elementary teacher must have the preparation which will enable him to guide children effectively in the skills and art of communication.

Opportunities for developing creativity through the medium of the spoken word abound in the classroom. However, the teacher must be aware of the need of the child to think, express, experiment, create, and communicate. He must also be able to guide him through the many types of communication such as sharing experiences, conversing, giving talks, discussing problems, and conducting meetings. The child, by the time he completes the elementary school years, has found in this area of the curriculum one of the most significant as well as effective means for developing and realizing his creative potential.

Through the spoken word, the child finds an effective answer to his need for releasing creativity, communicating with his peers, and developing his personality. He learns to confront problems with eagerness, born of confidence in using the techniques for critical thinking, group discussion and creative problem solving. As he learns to communicate his ideas effectively, he finds the bridge between him and other individuals is spanned and understanding ensues.

Speech is an essential part of the education of the elementary school child. Any curriculum which omits the development of the oral skills is like a car which has been artistically designed, carefully assembled, made up of the best materials available, but allowed to go on the market without an engine. Unless our development of creative potential is going in a direction which brings greater understanding of others and self, the individual does not benefit and society is the loser.

References

1. Robert G. Gunderson, "Teaching Critical Thinking," *The Speech Teacher*, 10:100, March, 1961.
2. Donald K. Smith, "What Are the Contemporary Trends in Teaching Speech?" *The Speech Teacher*, 10:89, March, 1961.
3. By permission from *The Field of Speech: Its Purpose and Scope in Education*, The Speech Association of America, Statler Hilton Hotel, New York (Pamphlet).
4. Milton Dickens, *Speech: Dynamic Communication*, 2nd ed., Harcourt Brace Jovanovich, Inc., New York, 1963, p. 5.
5. "Fundamentals of Speech: A Basic Course for High Schools," *The Speech Teacher*, 8:96, March, 1959.
6. *Living and Learning*, Report of the Provincial Committee on Aims and Objectives of

Education in the Schools of Toronto, Ontario, Department of Education, Toronto, Ontario, 1968, p. 54.
7. Lucile Lindberg, "Oral Language or Else," *Elementary English*, 42:760, December, 1965.
8. William E. Buys, "Speech Curricula for All American Youth," *The Speech Teacher*, 15:25, January, 1966.
9. Ronald R. Allen, "The New Speech Educator: Philosophy and Standards," *The Speech Teacher*, 15:18-9, January, 1966.
10. Reprinted by permission from *Speech for Today*, by Hibbs, Fessenden, Larson and Wagner. Copyright © 1965 by McGraw-Hill Inc., Manchester, 1965, p. 283.
11. From *Principles and Types of Speech,* Fifth Edition, by Allan Monroe. Copyright © 1962 by Scott, Foresman and Company. Reprinted by permission.
12. *Ibid.*, p. 285.
13. *Ibid.*, p. 290.
14. *Ibid.*, p. 289.
15. *Ibid.*, p. 287.
16. Karl F. Robinson and Albert B. Becker, *Effective Speech for the Teacher*, McGraw-Hill Book Company, New York, 1970, p. 65.
17. John Irwin and Marjorie Rosenberger, *Modern Speech*, Holt, Rinehart, and Winston, Inc., New York, 1961, p. 246.
18. Murray M. Horowitz, "The Teacher Utilizes Group Forces," *Learning and the Teacher*, 1959 Yearbook, Association for Supervision and Curriculum Development, Washington, D.C., 1959, pp. 119-24.
19. G. Polya, "How to Solve It," in Sidney Parnes and Harold Harding (eds.), *A Source Book for Creative Thinking*, Charles Scribner's Sons, New York, 1962, p. 253.
20. Carol Kohl and Roy Berko, "Some Unusual Speech Activities," *The Speech Teacher*, 19:320-2, November, 1970.
21. Lillian M. Logan, *Teaching the Young Child*, Houghton Mifflin Company, Boston, 1960, pp. 225-232.
22. Donald K. Smith, Andrew T. Weaver, and Karl R. Robinson, "The Field of Speech: Its Purposes and Scope in Education," Official Document of Speech Association of America by action of the Administrative Council in Denver, Colorado, August 18, 1963, Section 4.

6

Corrective Speech: What Every Classroom Teacher Should Know

It is so easy to think of words as words rather than as thoughts or messages; to view words only as sounds or coordinations rather than as carriers of communication.

Charles Van Riper

A student is identified as a speech handicapped person when his speech interferes with his communication. When this definition is understood, the teacher will approach the improvement of individual sounds and words with the objective of total communication. This implies an understanding of articulation and pronunciation in relation to language development. Articulation is concerned with the formulation of individual sounds of the language, pronunciation with the choice and combination of those sounds acceptable to the society in which he lives. Unless the child can form the individual sounds correctly, he will have difficulty in pronunciation of individual words. Expressive vocalization and articulation depends on the coordinated functioning of all speech organs working with the interpretive concepts of the mind.

Most children take this complex process in their stride. By the time they come to school, they are able to speak so they can make their needs known. For this reason, teachers too often fail to realize the needs of the children who are not so fortunate. To know when to help a child with his speech, what kind of help to give, and how to provide such help is essential for the teacher in the elementary school. Learning how to identify speech defects is essential for the prospective teacher.

In the average classroom, some five to ten percent of the children are unable to communicate effectively. They need special help. The teacher will begin by organizing activities based on the premise that what is good for the normal is good for the child with speech problems. Although some children may need individualized help from a speech therapist, they should not be excluded from group speech activities. The admonition of Van Riper, "Speech therapy cannot be carried out in a vacuum. The ebb and flow of communication, the give and take of messages, these are the opportunities for learning to speak as others do"[1] should be heeded.

In many schools, the development of each child to his maximum potential is interpreted to include speech development. In such schools, there is a team approach to helping the child with speech difficulties as well as the child with other handicaps and the child with need for speech improvement rather than speech correction. The team is concerned with the speech development of *all* children. Thus there is a concerted effort of speech and hearing therapists, classroom teachers, administrators, special teachers, and parents. The classroom teacher plays a distinct role in helping each child with his speech improvement. Specifically this requires a knowledge of: (1) defective speech, (2) types of speech disorders, (3) identification of speech and hearing defects, (4) ways to help the child with a speech handicap, (5) development of normal speech, (6) techniques of speech improvement in the classroom, and (7) a professional relationship between the classroom teacher and the speech therapist.

What Is Defective Speech?

"Speech is defective when it deviates so far from the speech of other people that it calls attention to itself, interferes with communication, or causes its possessor to be maladjusted."[2]

Such a definition is of significance to the classroom teacher as well as to the speech therapist. It brings to the fore the responsibility of the teacher to share in the improvement of the speech of every child in the classroom.

The speech handicapped represent the largest group of exceptional children. The main types of difficulties include: articulatory defects, stuttering, voice disorders, retarded speech development, organic disorders such as cleft palate and cerebral palsy, and the speech problems of the hard of hearing.

With such proportions of children requiring help in speaking effectively, the task of the classroom teacher in identifying the speech defective is facilitated if he is aware of the speech behavior that hinders effective communication: speech that is *conspicuous,* speech that has *poor intelligibility,* speech that is *unpleasant.*

Conspicuous Speech

Conspicuous speech calls attention to itself and is characterized by a speech pattern that varies from the norm to the extent that, for the developmental level of the child, it is inappropriate. It does not include the child of four who refers to the red wagon as "da wed waddon". The child of eight, however, who says the same thing would be considered defective in his speech. Also, if the speech differs radically from the cultural group of which one is a member, it is conspicuous and could be classified as defective speech.

Poor Intelligibility

Poor intelligibility interferes with communication. It may be the result of either organic or psychological problems. It is characterized by such speech patterns as dysphonia, cleft palate, excessive nasality, cluttering, stuttering, jargon, sound substitutions, sound omissions, lisping, and idioglossia (baby talk). In each of these cases, the speaker is unable to communicate effectively.

Unpleasant Speech

Unpleasant speech is characterized by vocal elements which are unpleasant to the listener or physical manifestations which are distasteful to the observer. Examples of the former would be gutteralness, extreme variations in pitch or monopitch, nasality, hoarseness, harshness, huskiness, breathiness. Physical characteristics would include secondary stuttering, excessive saliva, muscular contractions of spastics, fascial grimaces.

This type of speech may not be unintelligible, but it can contribute to emotional maladjustment and personality problems that in turn intensify the speech defect. If children are criticized for unintelligible speech, if they are laughed at for conspicuous speech, it is possible for them to become so concerned over the affective aspect of trying to speak that they feel rejected and become emotionally upset and disturbed.

The often frustrating and seemingly interminable task of aiding the speech handicapped child to reach *his* potential can be made enjoyable if the teacher is knowledgable and skillful in this vital area of the child's development.

Types of Speech Disorders

> Spasmophemia, rhotacism, uranoscolalia, lambdacism, rhinolalia, sigmatism, idioglossia, and bradylalia. Do not worry: we do not intend to inflict such a heavy burden of polysyllabic jaw-breakers upon your tender memory. Translated, in sequence, these terms refer to stuttering, defective *r* sounds, cleft-palate speech, defective *l* sounds, excessive nasality, lisping, delayed speech characterized by jargon, and speech which is uttered too slowly.[3]

This is not the complete list of speech disorders; it is simply cited to point up the necessity for becoming familiar with those which are common to the children enrolled in our schools in order that the teacher can: (1) learn to identify them, (2) recognize the symptoms which characterize the speech of children who need special help, (3) refer to the speech therapist or speech clinic those who require such help, and (4) plan a program of speech improvement for *all* children in the classroom. This should include both the children whose speech is developing normally and those whose speech is defective. In addition to the special help they receive, the latter should be included, when possible, in all the speech activities.

A helpful classification of speech disorders based on the behavior itself is that of Van Riper who divides the disorders into four major categories:

> *articulation*, *time* (or rhythm), *voice*, and *symbolization* (language). This fourfold classification, it should be understood, refers to the *outstanding* features of the behavior shown. Thus even though his stuttering causes certain sounds to be distorted, we place the stutterer in the second category because the major feature of his disorder is the broken timing of his utterance. The person with aphasia often shows articulation errors, broken rhythm, inability to produce voice, but the outstanding feature of aphasia is the inability to handle symbolic meanings and language. Therefore, we would place aphasia under disorders of symbolization or language.[4]

Articulation

Among articulation disorders are those characterized by substitution, omission, addition, and distortion of speech sounds. Baby talk or infantile perseverance is a disorder which also fits this category. The chief characteristics of articulatory disorders are distorted, substituted, omitted, or added speech sounds.

In the very young child, this all passes as a normal part of learning to speak. As he enters the elementary school, however, he is expected to make himself more clearly understood. When his language pattern develops into a "self-language" which is incomprehensible to all except his fond mother, he is in need of special help. The child flies into a temper tantrum at school because he is not understood when he says, "Taw uh Dwamma Doody toh tay me tow." It is the rare teacher who can translate the jargon into "Call up Grandma Coodry to take me home." In the situation of this type, the emotional scene which ensues wears out the teacher and frustrates the child. Although all teachers would consider this a serious articulatory problem, most feel that the problem of articulatory disorders in general are relatively unimportant. However, in the personality development of the child, the need to be understood is imperative. It is, therefore, essential to aid the child to overcome his difficulty. Articulation problems present a challenge to the classroom teacher. They are the most prevalent problems of the speech difficulties and the ones which the classroom teacher should be equipped to handle. Any articulatory problem which persists into the second grade should receive individualized attention—the more severe ones by the speech therapist if one is available. Kindergarten children and first graders benefit most from group speech activities in the regular classroom. Individualized help should usually be casual.

Disorders of Time and Rhythm

Children differ in their tempo in speaking, in their fluency, and in their pattern of speech. Good speech is characterized by fluency of speech without an undue amount of um's and uh's, ah's, hesitation, false starts and repetitions. When the timing of sounds and syllables is so far off the standard that speech is unintelligible, unpleasant, or conspicuous, there is a defect of rhythm. In stuttering and cluttering these deviations are serious enough to cause problems in communication.

Stuttering. Stuttering is a nonfluency which has become habitual and noticeable. Symptoms which give evidence of stuttering include: blocking on sounds, repetition or prolongation of words or syllables, repetition or prolongation of sounds, and spasms of the speaking mechanism in severe cases. Stutterers differ in the stimuli which motivate stuttering. At times they speak with comparative or complete fluency. The teacher should distinguish between the nonfluency which is common with all children and stuttering which becomes habitual nonfluency. The teacher and other adults should not demand such perfection in speaking that they change the normal child's pattern of nonfluency into a pattern of stuttering.

Cluttering. Cluttering is garbled speech. It is frequently confused with stuttering. Cluttering, nevertheless, has distinctive elements. The major features are: (a) excessive speed of speaking; (b) disorganized sentence structure; (c) omitted or slurred syllables and sounds. The clutterer speaks in a garbled manner without being aware of his problem. The speech of a clutterer has been described as a torrent of half-articulated words, following each other like peas running out of a spout. The flow of his speech is hard to listen to.

Voice Disorders (Dysphonias)

Voice disorders have to do with faults of pitch, quality, or intensity. In each of these elements of speech, abnormalities can be found, and there are individuals with voices which may be defective in all three.

Pitch disorders. Pitch disorders include: too-high pitch, too-low pitch, monotone, pitch breaks, and stereotyped inflections.

We all have recollections of individuals—children and adults—whose defects in pitch proved to be a handicap. For example, the high-pitched, strident voice of Joanne who made all the children turn to look at her; the low-pitched husky voice of Charles whose ability to simulate a fog horn in creative dramatics proved highly unpopular in other class situations. An extremely high-pitched voice in a man is definitely a handicap socially, communicatively, and economically. The expressionless voice of the teacher is often a cause of lack of success in the classroom.

Disorders of voice intensity. Defects of intensity are readily recognizable; the *too-loud* voice, the *too-weak* voice, no voice at all (aphonia), peculiar *stereotyped patterns* of emphasis, loudness or inflection. The extremely loud voice may be caused by a hearing problem or a personality problem. The extremely soft voice may be the result of a feeling of inadequacy, insecurity, or lack of confidence. When a beginning teacher or a student teacher is criticized for the very soft voice, it may be pointed out that success in the teaching experience may bring a more appropriate voice quality. The strident voice of the veteran teacher may turn the budding teacher against the profession, and a too-thin voice may change a room of confident young children into anxiety-prone youngsters who cry, whine, and have other problems caused by a lack of trust in the adult with a child-like voice. The strain of being in a classroom with a teacher whose voice is barely audible or harshly strident is evident in children who appear emotionally worn out by the end of the day. The teacher must set an example of appropriate intensity as well as appropriate usage.

Disorders of voice quality. There are as many different voices as there are different faces. If one listens carefully, he will learn that even where voices apparently sound the same, discriminating listening will distinguish differences, however subtle. The student who listens to a recording of his own voice for the first time is often shocked and is unable to believe that the voice is really his. Some students are so discouraged after listening that they are ready to seek help in voice improvement. Among the types of voices that cause discouragement because of their unpleasant quality are those characterized by hoarseness, raspiness, harshness, nasality, tenseness, denasality, breathiness, or throaty, guttural, and pectoral qualities.

Symbolization Disorders

Some children are able to perceive but are unable to translate into linguistic formulation. The general term for all disorders of symbolic formulation and expression is known as *dysphasia*.

Unfortunately, children with problems of this type are all too frequently classified as hard-of-hearing or mentally retarded. When the problem relates to failure in using or comprehending spoken symbols, it should be dealt with by a speech correctionist.

The problem of bright children who have been unable to learn to read and write because of Specific Dyslexia (specific language disability) which makes it impossible for them to perceive and/or record accurately the symbols of the printed page, has only recently been recognized by educators.

Delayed speech. Often children suffer from delayed speech or persevere in baby talk because parents learn the language of the child instead of teaching him to imitate adult language. Betsey was an example of this lack of parental teaching. At three and a half, Betsey was speaking a language which no one but Mother could understand. Instead of expecting Betsey to speak so she could be understood, her mother translated the language and Betsey enjoyed the power the little game gave her. Not until a new baby arrived and Mother was too busy to take the time to translate Betsey's every whim did she feel motivated to speak clearly enough to make her wants known. When she finally did, she discovered that the language everyone could understand was far more satisfactory than the limited communication of the past.

Wendell Johnson lists the following common factors in delayed speech development:

1. Mental subnormality.
2. Illness and physical impairment, such as brain injury or paralysis.
3. Lack of sufficient speech stimulation, as in homes where no one coos or babbles to the baby, or where the members of the family talk very little among themselves.
4. Impaired hearing.
5. Inadequate or disturbing or inconsistent rewards—even a certain amount of misplaced punishment—for the child's early attempts at speech.
6. A pattern of rewards and in general a relationship of such a nature that he gets along so well without speaking that he lacks sufficient motivation for attempting to learn to speak.
7. Intense shock, fright or shame, experienced over a sustained period or on one or more crucial occasions.[5]

Identifying Speech and Hearing Defects

Regardless of the type of speech and hearing program which operates within a given school system, the teacher's observations will continue to play an important role in identifying the children who need therapy. Although the more progressive school systems and teacher training institutions have assumed their responsibility in providing for the needs of speech handicapped children, the classroom teacher still has a vital role to play. It is essential, therefore, that every teacher should be sufficiently familiar with the observable symptoms of speech and hearing problems to be able to identify and refer such children to a speech and hearing therapist, or to other designated personnel. To help the classroom teacher determine which pupils have speech or hearing handicaps, the inventories that follow are presented.

Speech Inventory[6]

Pupil's Name ____

The speech difficulties checked below have been observed.

I. Articulation.

1. Can hardly understand him ________
2. Omits certain sounds ________
3. Uses "baby-talk" ________
4. Substitutes wrong sounds for right ones, such as "w" for "r" ________
5. Has a foreign accent ________
6. Has "sloppy" speech ________
7. Distorts certain sounds ________
8. Protrudes tongue for s-z sounds ________
9. Sounds which appear inaccurately made: p-b-m ________ wh-w ________
   t-d-n ________ h ________ y ________ k-g-ng ________ f-v ________
   th ________ l-r ________ s-z ________ ch-j ________
   vowels ________

II. Voice.

1. Usually has weak voice and can hardly be heard in class ________
2. Has a very monotonous voice ________
3. Is too breathy when talking ________
4. Is throaty and guttural ________
5. Has a husky, hoarse voice ________
6. Sounds too nasal ________
7. Is too high pitched ________
8. Speech lacks variety and life ________
9. Usually talks in a whisper ________
10. Usually talks too fast ________ too slowly ________

III. Fluency.

1. Repeats initial sounds, syllables, and phrases ________
2. Blocks sometimes and can't get words out ________
3. Speech is jerky ________

IV. Other problems.

1. Has cleft palate ________
2. Has cerebral palsy ________
3. Appears to be hard-of-hearing ________
4. Very poor oral reader ________
5. Avoids speaking in class ________
6. Appears tense and uncomfortable much of the time ________
7. Has symptoms of nervousness ________
8. Unusually shy ________
9. Frequently too aggressive ________
10. Does not co-operate well in the group ________

Hearing Inventory[7]

Pupil's Name ____

The hearing difficulties checked below have been observed.

I. Physical symptoms.

1. Frequent earaches ________
2. Running ears ________
3. Faulty equilibrium ________
4. Chronic colds ________

II. Speech and voice symptoms.

1. Omission and substitution of certain sounds of speech ________
2. Mispronouncing common words ________
3. Other speech defects ________
4. Voice lacking in intonation pattern ________

III. Behavior reactions in the classroom.

1. Request for repetition of words ________
2. Turns one side of head (better ear) toward speaker ________
3. Inattentive in class discussions ________
4. Watches teacher's lips ________
5. Shows strain in trying to hear ________
6. Unusual mistakes in taking dictation ________
7. More than normal use of hands to make wants known ________
8. Frequent mistakes in following directions ________
9. Low achievement for age ________

IV. Some signs that may indicate hearing impairment.

1. Irritability ________
2. Child appears more intelligent than work indicates ________
3. Temper tantrums ________
4. Inferiority complex ________
5. Child is tense ________
6. Child sometimes appears dull ________

Following the identification of the child with a speech and/or hearing problem, the teacher refers him to the speech therapist, or to the principal who contacts the designated personnel. More and more the cooperative efforts of teachers, parents, speech and hearing therapists, doctors, psychologists, and other personnel are utilized in diagnosing the problem and undertaking a program of therapy.

Helping the Speech Handicapped Child in the Classroom

Logan and Logan emphasize the need for understanding by the classroom teacher in dealing with the speech defective child.

> First of all, the teacher must understand that the child who has difficulty in his speech usually differs from the rest of the children in no other respect. The same range of intelligence, the same likes and dislikes will be found in those who speak easily and those who have problems in speaking. Differences in personality are usually the result not of any basic differences in the children but the frustrations and misunderstandings brought about by their speech problems. . . . If the problem he faces in communication difficulties could be understood there would be fewer extreme differences in his behavior pattern. Co-operation with the parents, speech therapists . . . and the child himself is essential to make sure that both the goal and the methods for reaching the goal are mutually understood.[8]

In making provisions for the speech handicapped child, the teacher should have some guidelines which will aid in helping a child with a specific handicap during the time he is in the regular classroom. Not only must the teacher arrange for the speech handicapped child to have special help, he must also include him in the regular speech program and encourage him to participate in the speech improvement activities.

Helping the Stutterer

The child who suffers from occasional or habitual nonfluency needs more than anything else to be in an environment in which he feels accepted, valued, and secure. It is especially important for him to be a part of the classroom activities, to be successful in endeavors he chooses, and to know that he is free to participate when he feels comfortable about speaking and is free to refrain when circumstances cause too great anxiety. The classroom teacher can best help the pupil who stutters by giving him opportunity for oral communication in an environment in which acceptance, warmth, empathy, and approval predominate, free from discrimination, fear, tension, and disapproval.

Helping the Hard-of-Hearing

The development of speech is normally dependent upon auditory impressions. Impaired hearing involves, potentially or actually, a degree of distortion of auditory perception. The hearing handicapped child in the classroom should be provided with the instruction in speaking and listening which has been discussed in the preceding chapters. It is essential that he be given opportunity to participate in speaking activities of all types plus activities in rhythms, dramatics, improvisation, and choral speaking. This child has the same physical, social, emotional and intellectual needs as other children.

The classroom teacher who is concerned with helping this child is alert to signals such as: earache complaints, running ears, stupid expression, poor speech, poor spelling, need for teacher to repeat questions, and watching the speaker with a special intentness.

The teacher should give consideration to the following responsibilities for helping the child.

1. Seat the child as near as possible to the instruction area.
2. Allow the child to move around the room when the instructional area shifts.
3. Make a special effort to be certain that the child hears what is said.
4. Help the other children in the class assume a positive attitude toward the problem.
5. Include the child in regular and extra-curricular activities of the class.

Delayed Speech Development

Here, especially, the child must be helped to develop language concepts and vocabulary through listening and speaking activities. Dramatic activities stressing bodily action and rhythmic movement are valuable in stimulating children's development of linguistic skills. Because the classroom teacher must work with the handicapped child for the larger part of the day, it is evident that the handicapped child must be encouraged to participate with other children in discussion, dramatic activities, and choral speaking.

Speech Improvement

From the first breath of life, beginning with the birth cry, the child continues to express through vocalization, feelings, wants, and ideas. He is not born with speech; he acquires it through the use of muscles and organs that have biological functions far removed from speech. The quality and purpose of human sounds undergo changes as the child responds to his environment and learns to control it through language.

The ability to think develops before the ability to express ideas. The ability to express ideas develops before the ability to read. For this reason, it is imperative that a planned program for the improvement of speech be instituted in the primary grades and continued throughout the elementary school. Experiments have shown that where children are having difficulty with articulation this sequence of learning the sounds has been successful—first the child is helped to distinguish and make the sound in isolation, then to use the sound in nonsense syllables, then in unfamiliar words, and finally he is guided to establish the habit of using the sound correctly in familiar words.

As an aid to adults in fostering speech development during the preschool and primary years, Hanson cites speech norms and suggests games for each age to stimulate the development of specific speech sounds. The chronological age norms represent the *outside* limits of consonant maturation; many children will have acquired these phonemes by earlier ages.[9]

> **Games: Soundscotch.** A hopscotch diagram should be drawn on paper, sidewalk or floor. Each square should be named for a sound in a word. The child hops from square to square saying each sound as he does so. He is not permitted to advance to the next square until he utters the sound in the preceding. If he is nonfluent, however, no penalties should be attached for a failure to comply. (Note: For older misarticulates or stutterers the sounds may be printed in the squares.)
> 3½—p, m, w, h, b
>
> **Sound Toss.** A funny picture of an animal or clown is required. Holes should be left or cut for the eyes, mouth, ears and nose and the spaces given names. The child should aim the chip or play coin toward a hole (different values may be assigned each target) and if his chip goes through one, he must say its sound name to get credit. (The holes, of course, have been captioned after difficult or feared sounds or words.)
> 4½—t, d, n, k, g, ng, y
>
> **Games: Fishing.** Vari-colored slips of paper, to which small clips have been fastened and representing the child's problem words or sounds (mispronounced or stuttered) should be prepared. If the children are older, the words or sounds should be printed on the slips. A dime store magnet is fastened to a line. The child is then instructed to drop his "line" (the magnet) by the "fishing pole" (pencil) into the "pond" (area containing the word or sound slips). If the paper and

clips are sufficiently light, they will adhere to the magnet, and constitute the child's "catch", which can serve many different purposes. In the ear training stage, he has "caught" a fish when he recognizes his sound in a word, or discriminates a good production or a poor production of it by his parent, or pronounces it correctly himself. Should he be nonfluent, then he is asked to say the word or sound in a phrase or sentence. However, in whatever manner the stutterer pronounces his "fish" he should not be directly corrected. The parent or teacher can improve any incorrect sounds of potential stutterers by example and simply saying the sound or word after him correctly. If the nonfluent child seems to be having particular difficulty with certain sounds or words, the pond can be filled with more of these; in this way there will be practice on the poor words or sounds but without making the child conscious of being "taught". Those extra "p" or "t" or "d" words simply happen to be his "haul".

Sound Ladder. The instructor should draw a ladder and name or print each rung with a sound or word difficult for the misarticulating child. To climb the ladder the child must identify or pronounce correctly, etc., each rung. If he is nonfluent he may simply be asked to name the rung to climb the ladder, and if he makes any speech attempt credit should be given. If he does not wish to climb it, he should not be forced.

5½—f

Games: Sound Hide and Seek. This game may be played several ways depending on the nature of the child's problem. If he is misarticulating sounds, and in the ear training stage, a picture or object may be hidden in the room, the child sent to look for it, and the correct version of the sound used by the teacher as he approaches its hiding place, the error production if he moves away. If the child sometimes mispronounces a sound, but has reached the stage of producing it with occasional success, he may hide the picture or object while the parent or teacher looks for it and he signals their nearness to it by producing it himself in the correct manner. If the assistant moves away he speaks it incorrectly. It should be pointed out quickly here that it does no harm, and actually helps, for the child consciously to produce the sound incorrectly at times. However, this technique, called negative practice, should be used only with his awareness that he is deliberately producing an error. Later, with the older stutterer, negative practice is used in therapy in a form called voluntary stuttering; it is not, however, commonly used with the nonfluent youngster. At this age, mere speaking of the word or sound is sufficient and helpful.

6½—v. th-(unvoiced), sh, l, zh

Games: Riddleree — I see something that begins with. This old favorite may be used for continued practice on particular sounds or words giving trouble to the child who misarticulates or stutters. The former should be corrected for errors in response but no comment should be made on the quality of the speech attempt of the stutterer or nonfluent child. With this game, as with others used with stutterers, elimination of the fear of speaking and increasing talking time are the primary objectives.

Sound Spinner. The teacher should construct a cardboard circle with a spinner and divide it into squares, named or printed after the child's difficult or feared sounds or words. The youngster spins and where the spinner stops he must say the sound or word in that square (or the parent or teacher may pronounce it if he is still at the ear training stage). The young stutterer, again, should not be forced to verbalize but encouraged to do so in the "spirit of the game" to comply with the "rules." In this and other exercises, the regulations calling for a spoken response (for points or a turn or a move, etc.) should be clearly outlined and reiterated before the game begins; they should be followed, too, as if part of a ritual, with the misarticulates. If her tone is kept light and gay, the teacher may even remind the stutterer at first of the "rules" but if he does not comply should not be insistent. It will help in securing compliance, however, if the "rules" of the game are printed, read and made to seem an *intrinsic* part of the activity from the start of the game.

Pin the Sound. This exercise is a version of the one above and similar to the old birthday favorite, *Pin the Tail on the Donkey.* In this case, a map or picture of some scene should be substituted. The different areas should be given the names of words or sounds produced incorrectly, whether misarticulated or stuttered. The child is given a tail, a shape of a state, a tree, or merely a slip of paper, blindfolded, and told to try to pin the tail on the donkey, or the state on the map in its proper location. Where he pins the form he must say the word or sound written in that area (or the name which the teacher has assigned it). Different areas may be given different values but pronouncing the word is a condition of earning points. The stutterer, if he forgets to say the word, may be gently, gaily reminded of the "rule" but not compelled to follow it.

7½—s, z, r, th- (voiced), ch, j, wh

Games: Banking. This is a popular game with many possible variations. Play money (coins or bills), colored slips or chips may be used as rewards. If a child identifies a sound or pronounces it correctly in isolation, nonsense syllable or word, or if a stutterer, simply speaks the word, he is "paid" with money or chips. Difficult words may earn bigger bills or coins or more slips. If he mispronounces a word or fails to identify sounds he forfeits his turn or pays the parent or teacher from his "roll" or "stack". (The only exception to this procedure is in the case of a stuttering child who is not to be corrected for any speech errors but only encouraged to talk. With a nonfluent youngster, it is sometimes helpful to deflect attention from the *speaking* act, to emphasize the thinking of a sentence in which the sound or word may be used.) In this, and preceding games, MAKE SPEECH FUN! This last suggestion, again, applies equally to the misarticulating child although the latter may be corrected directly and the former only very lightly and indirectly.

Additional games. The following will be effective at any age level, with the child who misarticulates or stutters.

Missing. Objects or pictures should be placed on a table. These should bear sounds or words which the child mispronounces or repeats or fears. He should then be requested to close his eyes, while parent or teacher removes one of the items. When he opens his eyes, he should try to guess what is "missing". (Through repetition of the "s" in missing, each round of the game, sufficient practice on this phoneme is afforded, that if it is the one defective, the items themselves need not also contain the sound.)

Tic-tac-toe. This is a convenient game for the busy parent or teacher. To place an X in his square (or preferably the letter or some symbol representing his sound, or the word itself), the child must perform some speech task, identifying or recognizing a sound, or if a stutterer, simply produces it or a problem word. A row of his sounds or words constitutes a win and he should say "bingo" or, perhaps, one of his defective sounds or words if this has been agreed upon earlier.

Sound Scavenger. Several pictures, some containing his error sounds or words, others not, are placed about the room. If he is misarticulating the child should be required to return with pictures containing his sound and perhaps pronounce same, if he is ready; if he is a stutterer he is asked to find a particular picture and then say the word to earn points in a game. Riddle-like directions as to the location of the pictures may be used to add interest.

Sound Authors. A series of flash cards using defective or anxiety-laden words or sounds should be prepared. The game is then played like the traditional Authors, only with four sounds or words of a kind comprising each "book". This pastime is always valuable in stuttering therapy but should be employed with misarticulates only when the child has passed the ear training phase and is pronouncing words.

Situational practice. The parent or teacher may send the stuttering child (and the misarticulate, too, when he has reached the stage of pronouncing words) on errands around home, school or store which will require use of the difficult sounds or words.

Any game. While the ideal speech activities are those in which the speech task is central almost any game can motivate practice. In order to take a turn or make a move, the youngster must perform some specified speaking or listening act, whether recognizing a sound in a series of nonsense syllables or in words, or pronouncing it correctly himself. The stutterer, of course, need merely use such in a phrase or sentence.

If the program for speech improvement is to be successful, it must go beyond the mechanics of speech drills into the area of meaningful language and exciting activities. It should have as its ultimate goal the objective of helping children improve their voice and speech. This goal is achieved through helping them to organize and verbalize their thoughts—to be able to think on their feet.

The Role of the Teacher

The key task of the classroom teacher in meeting the speech needs of children centers around organizing, planning, and directing activities which contribute specifically to speech improvement. Some elementary teachers are well prepared for this responsibility. Others, however, need help in developing activities which will meet the goals of speech improvement for *all* children. The following are suggested to facilitate the establishment and implementation of a successful speech improvement program: determine the specific needs of the pupils; plan purposeful activities consonant with the needs; develop procedures that will achieve the purposes; build an activities and materials file; and present an example of good speech.

Determining Specific Needs of Children

The average kindergarten child does not yet have mature speech. Although maturation will take care of many speech problems, some will persist. Therefore, throughout the elementary school years a short speech improvement period for all children several times a week is recommended. In the kindergarten and primary grades, emphasis should be placed on group games and rhymes. Children who are already proficient in speech will benefit from these games and those who have difficulties can participate without any feeling of being singled out or pressured.

The chart opposite will be useful for all grades in determining the specific defects children have and should be considered in working out a speech improvement program.

Planning Purposeful Activities

Meeting the needs of children in speech improvement requires planning purposeful activities. Once the teacher has determined the needs of the children (with the help of the speech therapist if one is available), a specific program for speech improvement can be drawn up relating needs and objectives.

The Major Goals in Speech Improvement

1. Improve the speech of all children. All children can improve in at least one area: volume, inflection, usage, articulation, etc.
2. Eliminate speech problems such as infantile speech, lisping, indistinct speech and careless use of voice such as too loud or too soft. This program also helps the child with a severe problem.
3. Develop a good phonic background. It helps to improve habits of listening, increases the attention span, and helps articulation.

Specific Goals

1. Develop the attitude that the speech improvement period is fun time. Remember the enthusiasm of the children is directly parallel to that of the teacher.
2. Develop the ability to relax.
3. Develop good coordination. Big muscle coordination must precede fine muscle coordination.
4. Improve the ability to listen.
   a. Gross sounds.
   b. Speech sounds in isolation, nonsense syllables, words, simple sentences, poems, games.
5. Develop the use of a pleasant and audible voice.
   a. Develop the recognition of gross differences in quality, volume, pitch and rate: the Big Billy Goat Gruff and the Little Billy Goat Gruff, the Big Bad Wolf and the Little Pig.
   b. Develop an awareness of the voice to use when speaking to one, a small group, or the entire class.

Phonatory Defects

A. Quality

1. Nasal (positive nasality) . . . . ______
2. De-nasal (negative nasality) . . . . ______
3. Breathy (aspirate) . . . . ______
4. Hoarse-husky . . . . ______
5. Strained and harsh (strident) . . . . ______
6. Throaty - guttural . . . . ______
7. Falsetto (juvenile voice) . . . . ______
8. Weak - thin . . . . ______
9. Tremorous . . . . ______

B. Pitch

1. General level high (above average) . . . . ______
2. General level low (below average) . . . . ______
3. Monopitch . . . . ______
4. Pitch spasmodic, uncontrolled . . . . ______

C. Intensity

1. Too weak . . . . ______
2. Too loud . . . . ______
3. Spasmodic, uncontrolled . . . . ______

Articulatory Defects

A. Speech Sounds

1. Omitted . . . . ______
2. Substituted . . . . ______
3. Added . . . . ______
4. Defective . . . . ______

B. Oral inactivity (indistinct articulation) . . . . ______
C. Slow, labored . . . . ______
D. Rapid, slurring . . . . ______
E. Articulation below age level . . . . ______
F. Foreign dialect . . . . ______
G. Regional dialect . . . . ______

Linguistic Defects

A. Speechlessness . . . . ______
B. Speech confusion, search for words . . . . ______
C. Cannot understand words . . . . ______
D. Cannot write words . . . . ______
E. Reading below grade or age level . . . . ______

Defects of Rhythm

A. Abnormal repetition of sounds . . . . ______
B. Abnormal repetition of words . . . . ______
C. Speech blocks . . . . ______
D. Abnormal hesitations . . . . ______
E. Cluttering, irregular rhythm . . . . ______

General Observations

A. Tics, facial grimaces . . . . ______
B. Excessive stage fright . . . . ______
C. Unusual posture or bodily movement . . . . ______
D. Abnormally shy, unresponsive . . . . ______
E. Belligerent, negativistic . . . . ______
F. Other problems . . . . ______

6. Develop the correct use of the speech sounds. One sound should be stressed at a time.

   a. Develop the use of the articulatory mechanism.
   b. Encourage the use of natural weak forms in all speaking activities.
   c. Endeavor to correct marked deviations.

Developing Procedures

Opportunity for children to participate in speech activities in a relaxed classroom atmosphere is the first step toward improving the child's speech.

In such an atmosphere and with the rapport between teacher and child developed through each child being an accepted member of the group, the speech handicapped child as well as the child with normal speech will benefit from a program of activities designed to improve speech.

The scope of the program in speech improvement is both comprehensive and balanced. It includes provision for activities increasing the agility of the tongue, lips, and jaw for both the consonants and vowels. Through games, jingles, stories, poems, dramatics, and exercises, children improve voice quality and speech ability.

Guidelines for Speech Improvement

1. Each lesson should start with RELAXATION. It is difficult to get all children to relax. Relaxation is the basis for good speech.

Suggestions:

a. Raggedy Doll. The teacher reads this rhyme aloud and then re-reads it (better to say it from memory) while the children interpret with arms, head and bodies. Parts of this may be used in emergencies to start lessons when for some reason the room has been under special tension.

> Let's play rag-doll
> Don't make a sound
> Fling your arms and bodies
> Loosely around
> Fling your arms! Fling your feet!
> Let your head go free!
> Be the raggest rag-doll
> You ever did see.

b. Playing Rag Doll. This requires the use of "play-magic", which the teacher makes by waving her arms. With one wave, the feet turn to rags; at the second wave, the knees, then the back, arms, elbows, hands, neck and head, in the order given. The teacher then goes on a tour of inspection, gently shaking arms, shoulders, head, and lifting knees to be sure all are relaxed. Some she will find "made of paper", some of "wood", and some of "rags"—but highly starched. Then with one magic wave the room must be awakened and the exercise repeated.

c. Playing Scarecrow. "Magic" is again utilized as in "Rag Doll"; this time, in order to turn the children into scarecrows as in the "Wizard of Oz". This exercise is done standing with arms at right angles, stiff and tense, the hands, head, chest are limp. At a signal, the wind blows and the scarecrows wave gently.

d. Floating. Have the children lie with their backs on the floor, face upward. Tell them to imagine that they are floating in the water. When given the command to "float", direct the children to lie with arms at right angles with the body, heels together and at rest. Go to each child and lift his arm or leg to see if it falls of its own weight. The speech of the teacher must be slow and quiet. Compliment each child when he is relaxing or improving. If children are seated at desks, direct them to stretch their arms forward, place their heads on the desks, and relax when given the command to "float". Go to each child to see if he feels relaxed.

e. Flowers. Let each child play that he is a flower. The kinds of flowers may be chosen according to the season of the year. Tell the children to imagine that the wind comes along and causes them to nod their heads very slowly, down around to the right shoulder, back to the left side and front. Let the jaw drop. The wind blows a little harder and the body gently sways in the direction the head is moving.

f. Let the children play elephant. They stand, bend from hips, allowing head and arms to drop limply, and sway loosely from the ankles.

2. Develop correct breathing. Encourage the children to close their lips and to breathe with a quiet rhythm. Develop deep breathing but do not encourage gasping in a great amount of air. Deep breathing means taking an adequate supply of air and expanding the lower region of the chest.

Suggestions:

a. Pretend you have a little candle for a birthday cake. Hold it up and blow it out.

Pretend you have a larger candle. Hold it farther away and blow it out.

Pretend you have a big candle. Hold it at arms length and blow.

Do not permit noisy blowing.

The breathing will be deeper each time. There will be more chest expansion.

b. Blow up a balloon. Each blow will require greater chest expansion.

c. Blow the candles on a birthday cake. Pretend they all go out except two and then one. The blowing will start with great chest expansion and end with little.

d. Provide the students with bright paper pin wheels. Who can keep his pin wheel spinning the longest? The fastest? Who can blow a "soft south wind" and make the wheel spin slowly for a long time? Give each student a turn to come before the class to show how steadily and long his wheel will go. By placing your hands gently on the student's ribs, you will be able to test his ability to expel air evenly. The muscles should contract evenly and gradually.

e. Have the student hold the wheel close to his lips and talk to it. "Where are you going, little wheel?" "Why do you whirl so fast, little pin wheel?"

f. Have the student place a two-inch square of light paper against the wall, mouth high, and try to keep it there by blowing a steady stream of air against it.

g. Have the student imitate the long, drawn out tooting of a distant train—(distance will require less volume) tu-u-u, tu-u-u.

h. Ask whether they have ever watched a dog breathe. Have them open their mouths and pant as a dog does on a very hot day while they put their hands on their stomachs and feel the rapid motion of their bodies.

i. Have the students inhale slowly, 1-2-3-4-5; exhale on whispered "choo, choo, choo", as an engine would leave the depot. (Teeth are closed, air is forced through.)

j. Inhale slowly and steadily, 1-2-3-4-5; cool burned fingers by blowing cooling breath on fingers through small lip opening, 1-2-3-4-5.

k. Repeat Exercise j, warming cold fingers through the open mouth.

l. Teach the students to hold a tone while your hand is raised and to stop the instant you lower your hand. Varied exercises may be used to develop breath control. The exercises should be graduated as the students develop. (For example, gradually increase the time of holding a steady tone or increase the number of short tones given at one breath.)

m. The game of laughing may be played during the dramatization of the Mother Goose rhyme "Hey Diddle Diddle". Show the students how the little dog laughed. Place one hand on your diaphragm while you give quickly and forcibly "Ho, ho, ho, ho". Be sure that your muscles go in and out vigorously. Have the children place their hands on their diaphragms and test each individually to see which is the best dog who "laughed to see such sport".

n. Have the students practice whispering several sentences. This will assist in securing deep, controlled breathing and will improve the enunciation as well.

o. Have the students place their hands on chest and diaphragm. Have them imitate a pricked balloon, the sound "puh".

3. Encourage greater flexibility of speech organs.

Suggestions:

a. Tongue

Have visual aid material: a clown, baby, cat, dog, pumpkin with an open mouth. Use a tongue blade painted red to encourage the children to look, follow, and imitate the movements you make with it.

Have the children make the watch sound (T) and use the tip of tongue, then make the coughing sound (K) and use the back of the tongue. Make the tongue rock both ways (T-K) and (K-T) several times.

Have the children say these with exaggerated tongue action. Following the drill work have the children repeat these poems with "normal" tongue action.

Jack in the Box

Jack jump out,
And Jack jump in!
Jack jump up,
And Jack jump down!

Shake your head!
Look out and in!
Go in and shut,
The cover down!

Lapping Milk

Little kitty laps her milk,
Lap, lap, lap!
Her tongue goes out,
Her tongue goes in,
Lap, lap, lap!

Little kitty likes her milk,
Lap, lap, lap!
Oh, see her tongue
Go out and in,
Lap, lap, lap!

Thomas A Tattamus

Thomas A Tattamus took two T's
To tie two tups to two tall trees,
To frighten the terrible
Thomas A Tattamus
Tell me how many T's there
are in all that.

Dotting the Roof

My tongue can dot
The roof of my mouth;
Dot—dot—dot.

It touches the front
And middle and back;
Dot—dot—dot.

Can your tongue dot
The roof of your mouth?
Dot—dot—dot.

Can it touch front,
And middle and back?
Dot—dot—dot.

b. Lips

Use visual aids material: clown, babies, cats, dogs, with lips in open spread or rounded positions.
Read the following poems with first exaggerated, then normal lip action.

Tu-whit'. Tu-whoo'.

The owl by day can't see, 'tis said!
OOoo, OOoo, OOoo!
He sits and blinks, turns his head,
OOoo, OOoo, OOoo!

But when the stars come out at night,
Tu-whit, tu-whoo, tu-whoo!
He calls his mate with all his might,
Tu-whit, tu-whoo, tu-whoo!

The Chee-choo Bird

A little green bird sat on a fence rail,
Chee-choo, chee-choo, chee!
Its song was the sweetest I ever have heard,
Chee-choo, chee-choo, chee!
I ran for some salt to put on its tail,
Chee-choo, chee-choo, chee!
But while I was gone, away flew the bird,
Chee-choo, chee-choo, chee!

Pitty Patty Polt

Pitty Patty Polt
Shoe the wild colt;
here a nail
and there a nail,
Pitty Patty Polt.

The Little Bird

Once I saw a little bird
Go hop, hop, hop,
I said, "Little birdie,
Will you stop, stop, stop?"
He looked me up and down
With a peep, peep, peep,
And across the grass he went
With a leap, leap, leap.

Bubble Bath

Bubble bath, bubble bath
    In a white tub
Hear the little bubbles go
    Bub, bub, bub.

c. Jaw

Use visual aids material: clowns, cats, dogs, etc., with closed and open mouth.

Read the following poems first with exaggerated, then normal jaw action.

John Cook's Grey Mare

John Cook had a little grey mare,
    Hee, haw, hum;
Her legs were long and her back was bare,
    Hee, haw, hum.
John Cook was riding up Shooter's Bank,
    Hee, haw, hum;
The mare she began to kick and to prank,
    Hee, haw, hum.
John Cook was riding up Shooter's Hill,
    Hee, haw, hum;
His mare fell down and made her will,
    Hee, haw, hum.
The bridle and saddle were laid on the shelf,
    Hee, haw, hum;
If you want any more, you may sing it yourself,
    Hee, haw, hum.

Examples of Speech Improvement Activities

Every speech improvement lesson should have a specific purpose related to the needs of the children in the group. It should be carefully planned so that the purpose, procedure, and development will be in harmony with good principles of teaching.

In the second grade class where there was a general tendency toward careless, slovenly speech, the teacher decided to teach a lesson emphasizing distinct enunciation.

Purpose: To develop distinct enunciation through awareness of movements of the jaw and lips for the vowel sounds.

Materials: Traditional song: "Old MacDonald Had a Farm".

Procedure: *Teacher:* Let's sing a song we all know, "Old MacDonald Had a Farm". Ready———

Teacher and Children: "Old MacDonald had a farm, E-I-E-I-O. And on this farm he had some ducks, E-I-E-I-O."

Teacher: Let's find out what we do with our lips and mouths when we say the vowels in the song. What do we do when we say "E"?

Child: We smile, our mouths are almost closed shut.

Teacher: Let's all say "E" and be sure we are smiling.

Children: "E"

Teacher: What do we do when we say "I"?

Child: We open our mouths wide.

Teacher: Let's open our mouths wide and say "I".

Children: "I"

Teacher: What do we do when we say "O"?

Child: We round our lips.

Teacher: Let's all pucker our lips and say "O".

Children: "O"

Teacher: Now let's all sing E-I-E-I-O again. Sing it distinctly.

Children: "E-I-E-I-O"

Teacher: Now let's sing it fast.

Children: "E-I-E-I-O"

Teacher: Now that we know the first part of the song and can sing it distinctly, let's list some of the animal noises we can include in the song. I will write the words "smile", "open" and "round" on the chalkboard. Give me as many animal noises as you can. Tell me which column to write them in.

Children:	*smile*	*open*	*round*
	chick-chick	quack-quack	moo-moo
	peep-peep	gobble-gobble	oink-oink
	neigh-neigh	baa-baa	caw-caw

Children: Meow-meow belongs in all three columns.

Teacher: Let's say the words in the "smile" column.

(Children repeat "smile" column.)

(They do the same with the "open" column and the "round" column.)

Teacher: This time let's make it harder. We'll do one word in the smile column, one in the open column and one in the round column. We'll do this for all the words and end with "meow-meow". (Children repeat sounds after the teacher. They then sing the entire song about Old MacDonald, using all the animal noises and singing distinctly.)

Evaluation: *Teacher:* Did we achieve our purpose?

Child: Yes, because we used our mouth and lips to form the vowel sounds correctly and, therefore, we learned to enunciate more clearly.

It is often effective to interchange activities involving music, oral reading, and choral speaking in teaching a lesson on enunciation to motivate interest in accurate articulation. Children enjoy singing their way to better speech.

This can apply to teaching of specific vowels, dipthongs or consonant sounds as well.

Correlating speech improvement with other areas of the curriculum enhances a child's enjoyment of speech and improves his skills in speaking. The following are among the areas that combine readily with voice improvement.

Rhythms—poems for skipping, galloping, clapping, rocking

Art—tell about pictures

Music—good articulation and rhythm

This should help to develop: poise, a favorable attitude toward speech, good habits of socialization, listening habits, big and fine muscle coordination, awareness for better voice, awareness of speech sounds, better articulatory patterns consistent with chronological and physical maturity, and use of sentence to express ideas.

Speech Improvement in the Intermediate and Upper Grades

Teachers who work with speech in the elementary schools sometimes find themselves confronted with sixth, seventh and eighth graders for whom speech improvement no longer has appeal. Motivations used with success and delight in the lower grades have lost their magic. They are confronted with vital needs which demand a fresh and broader approach.

An Experiment through Discovery

It requires ingenuity to impress upon upper grade students the significance of the fact that, even though we live in a democracy, our society does still recognize what Bernard Shaw dubbed "vocal class distinctions". Most students do not believe that careless, incorrect speech can be a real barrier to success, blocking one's career and one's fullest self-realization in his personal life. To counteract this attitude, Nurk turned to the story of *Pygmalion* and *My Fair Lady*. She found in them a dramatic medium for motivating children in these grades to consider speech improvement in its proper perspective.

Introduction. She introduced the unit on *Pygmalion* to the children by discussing the concept of the changes that stories undergo through the ages. As life and civilization change, each age leaves its imprint on its old favorites.

She approached the basic idea of change by relating an anecdote of a youngster who, when asked to choose a bedtime story, begged eagerly for "the cat and the fiddle and the cow that went into orbit around the moon". The appreciation of the sixth graders for the changes civilization wrought on the simple Mother Goose rhyme led readily into the discussion of a story which was older than the oldest Mother Goose rhyme. The story to be considered dated back to the time of the "Golden Age of Greece", some four thousand years ago.

Background. Discussion followed, centering around the knowledge the children had of Ancient Greece, the Greek's love of beauty and appreciation of the arts, and the architectural style of their buildings. They saw the role that sculpture played during that period. They learned that many of the great stories of that age logically centered around sculpture. This led into the story of Pygmalion, the King of Cyprus, who was a gifted sculptor. When his search for the perfect woman ended in repeated disappointments, he decided to create a perfect woman through his art. He worked several years, carving from rough, crude stone a beautiful woman. Pygmalion fell in love with her beauty, and prayed that the gods would bring her to life. His prayer was answered and she became his Queen.

The story of Pygmalion has been retold through the centuries. George Bernard Shaw, the English playwright, decided to write it into a modern play. Not being a Greek, nor living in a "Golden Age of Sculpture", he did not choose a sculptor as the hero. The questions the teacher asked to involve the children in the solution of the problem were: "Whom do you think he would make the hero of this modern story?" "What kind of an age is this?"

In the discussion that ensued, the children began by suggesting "atomic age", "space age"; following this they were asked the question, "What new development has permeated the private life of our whole society"? Further analysis lead to the conclusion that the basic and most fundamental things that radio and television give us is speech. Thus they agreed that this is the age of speech.

In answer to the question, "How do we know this?" the children answered, "Never in any age has speech been so important. There is no profession or field of endeavor in which speech is not important in this era. If one achieves in any area, be it architecture, biochemistry or politics, he must be ready to present his accomplishments and convictions through the medium of speech to millions at a time, as well as in person. This is, indeed, a speech age!"[10]

Having through analysis and problem solving arrived at the conclusion that the significance of speech in our age is of inescapable importance, a very real motivation for speech improvement was immediate.

Procedure for development. At this point, the class was ready to return to its original question, "Whom do you think Shaw would make the hero of his modern story? Who, in a radio and television age, would be searching for the perfect woman? The television producer, the radio announcer? No, the speech professor! And when he could not find her, how would he go about trying to create a perfect woman?"

The class concluded that he would accomplish his goal by giving her such perfect speech that she could travel in any society she chose. Although ideas of physical beauty have changed since the days of Greece, there is no way to camouflage incorrect and unpleasant speech. The perfect woman must have beautiful speech.

Activities. The class was introduced to Professor Higgins and Eliza Doolittle, and the plot of Shaw's play. They listened to the recordings of the musical *My*

Fair Lady. They listened for the distorted vowels heard in the early selections of the record. They listened critically for the following high points: (1) Professor Higgin's conviction that speech determines our class distinctions; (2) the contrast of the speech of the streets with the professor's speech; (3) the contrast in values held by Eliza and the professor; (4) Eliza's hatred of the professor for his relentless drill and correction; (5) the professor's joy and delight when Eliza began to "get it"; (6) Eliza's joy when her speech no longer condemned her to the gutter, when the professor could invite her to accompany him to social functions; (7) the changes that occurred in the speech of the characters as the story developed.

Evaluation. Evaluation followed after listening to one side of the record. This involved such questions as: "What voice qualities characterized the gutter girl (specifically voice, articulation, and vowel quality)?" "What characterized the speech of the professor as well educated, cultured person (voice, articulation, diction)?"

The class discussed the speculation among the guests that Eliza was really a Hungarian Countess, thus reinforcing the idea of the social importance of speech. "These basic truths, coupled with vivid examples of contrast in voice quality, range, articulation and diction make this story and the records of *My Fair Lady* a treasure chest for one working to inspire and challenge upper elementary and junior high pupils to appreciate and to strive for excellent speech."[11]

Activities and Materials File

A comprehensive collection of activities and materials for use in a speech improvement program is essential. Such a file will include not only those materials and activities which are specifically speech-oriented but also those which can be integrated with other curriculum areas.

The speech improvement program should be an integral part of the classroom activities; it requires a dual approach—direct and integrated. The direct teaching focuses on speech and voice improvement per se, while the integrated utilizes all curriculum areas for speech improvement. For example, ear training in relation to phonics offers an excellent activity in which source materials may come from the phonics in reading. A music period may stress vocalized rhythm and variations in pitch and volume. It may emphasize the use of distinct enunciation. Spelling gives the teacher an opportunity to introduce new words with emphasis on accurate articulation. Units in language arts and social studies may center around such communication skills as using the telephone, speaking over the radio, or appearing on television, actual or simulated. Creative art, too, can be integrated with speech improvement. Frequently children tell the class the story "behind the picture", or read the caption for the teacher. Creating rhythms and dramatizing stories stimulate speech improvement spontaneously. Stories for such activities should have strong action and strong sensory appeal. *The Three Bears, Angus and The Ducks, Millions of Cats, The Story About Ping, Curious George*, are some examples.

Speech improvement integrates readily with science. For example, children can begin a scientific study of the voice organs. Such a study involves the use of films, charts and models of the throat, mouth, and nose, to see how sounds are produced and resonated. This will help them understand what happens to the vocal organs when they yell at a hockey game.

A file of available recordings, films, and film-strips is useful in the speech improvement program.

Many business concerns make available free materials that are excellent for use in the program.

Materials from children's literature can make a great contribution to speech improvement and provide a readily available source for the teacher. Many of the poems and stories stimulate the child's flow of thought so that his speech patterns improve without his being too conscious of the response.

"At the right moment a child will yield his mind with ease to a story or poem which delights him. The focus is there without push or strain."[12] Children will enter into the experiences of the characters of the story and repeat with the teacher the repetitive phrases or repeated words which normally they might not attempt to articulate.

The right poem at the right time for the right group of children is the watchword of the effective teacher.

Especially conducive to speech improvement are the folk tales and rhymes handed down from one generation to another by word of mouth. The innate rhythm found in the "speaking them down" rather than "writing them down" from one person to another makes them ideal for speech practice.

Poetry is rich with immediate and direct fulfillment of most of the requirements for good speech practice. "Poetry goes directly to the crystal-clear imagery of an experience. A very essence which makes it poetry is the rhythm and often its verbal repetition."[13]

The Speech of the Classroom Teacher

The teacher has a great responsibility in speech improvement in setting an example of speech that provides children with a model which they can emulate. His voice should be pleasant, without harshness and strain. Articulation should be free from deviations, and enunciation should be clear and distinct. Needless to say, the teacher should use speech which is appropriate in usage and contains clear diction components. He should be conscious of the ingredients which go to make up good speech—quality, inflection, rhythm, and articulation. These are reflected in an integrated, wholesome, self-reliant, and alert personality. The well modulated, distinct, pleasant, rhythmic speech of the teacher reveals a well adjusted individual who inspires confidence in the boys and girls he teaches. If the teacher recognizes that the voice mechanism is an instrument which is both the medium for communicating ideas to the students in the class *and* a means of creating a climate in which speech is improved, it is likely that the goals of speech will be achieved.

A check list which has proved helpful to teachers in assessing their own speech follows.

		Self-evaluation
Voice	Volume	Is my voice loud enough to be heard?
	Pitch	Am I using my optimum pitch? (It may be high, low or medium.)
		Is the pitch flexible to denote change in meaning?
	Inflection	Does my voice glide from one pitch to another?
	Quality	Is my voice free from huskiness and nasality?
		Is my voice free from harshness and shrillness?
		Does my voice reveal fullness rather than breathiness of tone?
Rate	Tempo	Is my speech fast or slow?
		Does the rate vary with mood or emotions?
	Flowing	Is my speech normally uninterrupted?
		Is it free flowing?
	Smooth	Is my speech rhythmic?
		Is it free from repetition or undue prolongation?
Articulation	Formation of Sounds	Are my habits of good articulation so well established that I am not conscious of the mechanics of articulation?
		Do I produce the speech sounds accurately?

The Relationship Between the Classroom Teacher and the Speech Therapist

The roles of the classroom teacher and the speech therapist are mutually supporting. If there is a speech therapist in the school system, he shares with the teacher the responsibility for aiding those children whose handicap is of such a severe or specialized nature that it requires the help of a specialist. The presence of a therapist in the school system does not relieve the classroom teacher of the responsibility for the speech improvement of his children.

If there is a speech therapist, however, he works cooperatively in inaugurating, coordinating and implementing a speech improvement program.

The presence of the speech therapist serves to facilitate, enhance and enrich the speech improvement program. The activities suggested in this chapter do not require the services of a speech therapist. The procedures for motivating and directing activities for speech improvement can be satisfactorily handled by the classroom teacher as a phase of the three-part program in speech: development of speech skills, directed speech improvement lessons, and integrated activities.

Concluding Statement

Because most children speak easily when they enter school, good speech is taken as a matter of course. Some teachers, it is true, are concerned with the problem of impaired speech and hearing and their relation to the child's progress in other class activities. However, all too often, unless the teacher is aware of the significance of speech as a medium of communication and self-expression, the child with speech problems is neglected.

Unfortunately, neglect of speech problems blocks progress educationally as well as socially. Living in a society in which communication skills are so vital in meeting the social, educational, and vocational demands of today's world, the ability to communicate effectively and to express ideas clearly and distinctly within the limits of individual aptitudes and abilities is imperative.

Schools have a responsibility to bring every child to his maximum potential in speech as well as in other communication skills. A program for speech improvement provides ample opportunities for every child to develop good speaking and listening skills. In addition, there must be a program for helping the child with specific handicaps of speech and hearing. A planned, consistent course of speech improvement should be carried out in the regular classroom.

Every classroom teacher must have an understanding and knowledge of (a) defective speech, (b) types of speech disorders, (c) techniques for identifying speech and hearing defects, (d) ways of helping a child with a specific type of speech handicap, (e) the development of normal speech, (f) speech improvement procedures in the classroom, and (g) relationships between the classroom teacher and the speech therapist and/or other personnel responsible for meeting the needs of speech handicapped children in the elementary school.

The estimate of speech disorders in the elementary school population ranges from five to twenty-five percent. Some of these disorders require the services of a therapist. The remainder, however, can be helped by the classroom teacher. Early in the school year, an analysis of the speech and hearing of the children in the room should be made. Errors in articulation, ability to discriminate between speech sounds, quality of speaking voice, fluency in speech, delayed speech, and problems of a more serious nature are recorded. By early identification of those who need special help, the teacher can initiate the speech improvement program. The teacher who is knowledgeable about the various disorders in speech can cooperate and contribute to the work of the speech therapist if there is one. If there is no one to whom she can refer children with handicaps, it is the duty of the principal to take the responsibility for contacting the proper agencies.

In the primary grades, speech improvement is largely group oriented. Group learning provides spontaneous stimulation and motivation. The activities suggested in this chapter are effective in helping children improve their speech skills and attitudes. Through the use of good resource materials the teacher can integrate speech improvement with the language arts and other curriculum areas.

The importance of the teacher's voice cannot be overestimated in the total program. The teacher should set a model in voice and speech which is worthy of imitation and emulation. The teacher with a pleasant voice, an interesting and lively manner of speaking motivates children to effective speech.

The teacher who creates a relaxed, democratic atmosphere in which children are free to communicate, to exchange ideas, and to express them without fear of cutting criticism contributes to confidence in developing adequate speech skills.

References

1. Charles Van Riper, *Speech Correction: Principles and Methods*, 4th ed., © 1963, p. 2. Reprinted by permission of Prentice-Hall, Inc., Englewood Cliffs, New Jersey.
2. *Ibid.*, p. 16.
3. *Ibid.*, p. 14.
4. *Ibid.*, pp. 18-9.
5. Wendell Johnosn, *Children with Speech and Hearing Impairments*, U.S. Department of Health, Education and Welfare, Bulletin No. 5, Washington, D.C., 1959, p. 11.
6. Ruth Irwin, "How Can a Speech and Hearing Program be Initiated?" *Bulletin of the National Association of Secondary School Principals*, 34:173, November, 1950. Reprinted by permission of the National Association of Secondary School Principals, Washington, D.C.
7. *Ibid.*
8. Lillian M. Logan and Virgil G. Logan, *Teaching the Elementary School Child*, Houghton Mifflin Company, Boston, 1961, p. 772.
9. Jane Hanson, "Fostering Speech Development During Pre and Primary School Years: Norms and Speech Games," Special Educational Services, Evansville College, Evansville. (Mimeographed.)
10. Maude Nurk, "Motivating Speech Improvement in the Upper Grades," *The Speech Teacher*, 9:302, November, 1960.
11. *Ibid.*, p. 303.
12. Marjorie Carey, "Children's Literature - Creative Speech Practice," *Today's Speech*, 7:27, November, 1959.
13. *Ibid.*, p. 29.

PART THREE

The Curriculum—Written Communication

7

Painting Pictures with Words: Creative Writing

As imagination bodies forth
The form of things unknown, the poet's pen
Turns them to shapes and gives to airy nothing
A local habitation and a name.
Shakespeare

In creative writing, as in any creative activity, the crux of the experience lies in the degree to which it is the spontaneous outpouring of the child's imagination, experience, and/or idea. The child who expresses his creativity through writing is exhilarated by the experience. Having tasted the deep delight of creating with words, he rarely rests content, but repeats the experience again and again. His work tends to be spontaneous, sparkling, and scintillating. Because he is spurred on by the excitement of creating, his words dance as he stretches his imagination and follows where fancy leads. A flight of the imagination, a memory to be recorded, an experience to be recalled are the motivations that may spark the "creative itch" as Santayana terms it.

In creative writing it is possible to discern the working out of the creative process clearly. It is here that one observes both the effervescent power of the creative process as the words run over themselves and sparkle and glow, *and* the scrupulous polishing and perfecting of the expression. Fluency with words is not enough. The child must have something to say—something which he believes is important to express.

Although children create out of the imagination, the well must be replenished with fresh experiences and literature which exposes them to rhythm, rhyme, beauty, and sparkling, scintillating words. Children need to balance impression with expression, intake with output. Carlson recognizes this need for learning to use sparkling and spinning words. In creative listening to good literature, "the child listens to the beautiful and descriptive words and phrases of prose and poetry. He becomes alerted to the original, the different, the unexpected quality of expression as contrasted with trite, stereotyped clichés and hackneyed phrases."[1]

Akin to composing music, writing has its distinctive movement, rhythms, and cadences. It flows along merrily until it comes to a resting point. The movement that follows is in contrast to it in tempo, mood, and rhythmic devices. There must be contrast and balance in the design. It may spring forth full blown like the romantic songs of Schubert; it may take weeks, months, even years, or may never reach fruition like his "Unfinished Symphony".

Before They Write Creatively

If every child were sufficiently free to originate ideas spontaneously and sufficiently skilled to express himself fluently in this medium, the teacher would merely provide a stimulating environment, a climate of psychological safety free from external source of evaluation, and say to the child, "Create". However, even before the child has developed the manual dexterity necessary for writing, he has the desire and ability to express himself creatively with words. At this stage he needs someone to capture and record the creative moment. This poem by Klaus is an example.

> In the country where I lived, there was no Shopper's Fair.
> But there were woods and trees and flowers everywhere
> In the country where I lived, way over there.
> Would you like to go with me to that other land?
> There are no roses at the door, and all alone I stand
> Waiting for Rosemary and Lee—in the country where I lived.
> There were woods and trees to see—
> But only one of me.[2]

Klaus, a five-year-old kindergartner who had arrived from Germany a few weeks earlier, expressed his loneliness to an imaginery companion. The teacher's discerning ear caught the loveliness of the "creative moment". The creative teacher is sensitive to moments such as this and stands ready to give whatever help is needed. This he can do when he understands the obstacles which confront children in writing creatively. He recognizes that children have such specific needs for creating with words as: opportunity for broad experiences, development of perception and imagination, experience with literature, skill in using words, and skill in communication.

Children Need Experiences Out of Which to Create

Without experience the child has little to communicate. How can he write graphically of the trees, the hanging leaves, the bare bough shaking in the winter winds—the boughs that only shortly before harbored nests of singing birds—when he has never seen them? How can he write of the crowded tenements with only the pavement for his playground when he has never seen them? How can he write of the first flowers of spring if he has not observed them as they push their heads up out of the ground and turn to the light? How can he write vividly of ocean liners if he has never been near the ocean? How can he write of the way he feels when he flies above the clouds in a jet if his feet have never left *terra firma*? It is when he experiences first-hand or vicariously that he writes most vividly. Experiences form a reservoir from which the child can draw in expressing himself creatively—experiences which make an impression so deep, so vital that he is not content until he has shared them.

Children Need to Develop Perception and Imagination

By perception we mean the sharpened awareness of all that is around us. It goes beyond mere observation. By imagination we mean the ability to form mental images which correlate with the experiences of the senses.

Stephen Spender points out the relationship between imagination and memory. The poet should be able to think in images; he should have as great a mastery of language as a painter has over his pallet. "Imagination itself is an exercise of memory. There is nothing we imagine which we do not already know. And our ability to imagine is our ability to remember what we already once experienced and to apply it to some different situation. . . ."[3]

A child can develop his imaginative powers through experiences involving sense impressions. He should smell the rose, feel its velvety texture, experience the prick of its thorns. He needs to become aware of his kinesthetic sense to aid him in responding empathically to experiences involving muscular tensions. The child should develop an ever-increasing perception of and sensitivity to his environment.

Sensory experiences should not be limited to the traditional five senses. Lowrey and Johnson stress the value of others which are important in the development of the imaginative powers including the sensations of lightness or heaviness, temperature, equilibrium, emptiness or fulness.[4] In order to write imaginatively, one needs "to feel the dancing, the running, and the galloping; the tense quietude, the agony of immoble suspense; or the slow resistless movement of ponderous things. Depth and vividness of appreciation lie in this response, through intimate sense imagery, to the things about me."[5]

All too often the teacher is concerned only with expository writing. The richness of writing creatively demands the ability to write out of the imagination. It requires not only the ability to recreate what one has experienced, but also the power of portraying mental images which correspond to the experiences of the senses—conceptions, notions, and fanciful ideas. Words become wings to take the child on his flights of imagination. The young child does not distinguish between inner fantasy and outer reality as adults do. To him both are equally real and satisfying.

We like to think that children will write creatively if we give them rich experiences, teach them to perceive, help them to develop their imaginations, and utilize imaginative content. There still remains, however, the need to replenish the source of ideas. Literature which is characterized by imagination, spontaneity, brilliance, originality, rhythm, and clarity of style is one of the most effective means of accomplishing this end. Children can stretch the imagination and stand on tiptoe as it were to catch the stars as they twinkle in a world of words—words of color, fire, and imagination, words that fall trippingly from the tongue and find a haven in the mind and heart of the child until he calls them forth to embody an idea or to clothe an emotion.

Exposure to fine literature improves the child's acquaintance with words and thus increases his ability to express his own ideas. As he listens to and/or reads for himself from the treasury of literature he will not only develop understanding, insight, and vocabulary, but assimilate into his design for living what he reads. Thereby it becomes an integral part of his personality. From fiction, biography, hero tales and legends, from travel and adventure, mythology and archaeology, he will dip into the literary well and incorporate into his own thinking and creative expression the stuff from which dreams are born and writers are created. Stories about the enchanted world of elves, gnomes, and goblins; the exploits of space men and astronauts; the heroes of Greek and Roman mythology; or the feats of everyday men of the work-a-day world will replenish the reservoir of ideas and stimulate creativity. Through books we can put on the shoes of swiftness, sense the power of subduing the elements, discover the secret virtues of minerals, sail the seas, fly across the mountains on a magic carpet.

Children Need Skill in Using Words

Children love words. They love the rhyme and rhythm of words; they love their lilt and melody; they love their sparkle and spinningness. They love the feel of words as they roll off the tongue. They love their mouth-tickling quality as they dance with melody, mood, and movement. But words serve for more than to tickle the tongue or spark the imagination. They serve to communicate ideas. The child who sees in the right word the power to create a picture or portray an emotion has taken a big step forward in creating with words. The discovery of the feeling for the combinations of words that set the imagination soaring is one of the spurs to creativity. This, coupled with the ability to say something worthwhile, is the essence of true creative communication. "Words are the verbal means of taking our listeners or readers along with us to our destination in communication. If the other person cannot or does not 'ride along' with the words we are using, he will not cover the same territory and hence will not understand what we are trying to express in words to him. . . ."[6]

Children Need Skill in Communicating Feeling and Ideas

Mere facility with words will not ensure the effective communication of feelings and ideas children wish to express. If we really want a reader to share our emotion, there are two things we may do: "We may say 'I felt like a million dollars—I had that wonderful feeling you get when the pain of a terrible headache suddenly leaves—I felt like writing a poem.' Or we may set about describing all the circumstances of yesterday's moment—the things about us, the events, what she looked like, what she said, what we said. Or we may use both methods. What we are forced to do to communicate our feeling is what the poet is forced to do."[7]

The writer must recreate the experience in such a vivid manner that the reader will experience the emotion the author intended. Whatever the inspiration for the creative writing, the emotion that touched it off may come suddenly unawares. To satisfy the creator completely, the work must evoke a response from the listener. To the extent that the writer is able to reveal his emotion, his idea to another—to recreate an original experience in such a way that it expresses what he remembers of how he felt about the experience—is the creative process completed and the creator satisfied. The artist, whether he reveals his art through marble, music, dance, or words, must have guidance in handling the materials by which he expresses his concept and/or emotion. Added to this, he must have the techniques for handling the material he uses to express his creative idea and recreate the emotion or feeling he wishes to convey. Fortunate is the child who creates spontaneously with words. "Facility in the use of language and facility in thinking depend each upon the other. As thought is an essential in the use of language, imagination is the *sine qua non* of creative reading [and creative writing.]"[8]

Emotions, sensory awareness, and imagination are the ingredients which go into creating with words. Combining these elements with children, experience, and expression, the teacher becomes a catalytic agent who makes possible the process of creating.

In an experiment validating the idea that the development of sensitivity to environmental stimuli affects the quality of creative productions, Littwin reports three methods he used in developing imaginative writing with three matched groups of seventh and eighth grade pupils. "Over a ten-week period, one group practiced writing vivid descriptions of pictures which they had previously studied; the second studied literary models containing words of sound, color, and movement; and the third group practiced describing all the possible sensations, such as sight, smell, touch, and hearing, that they could experience in examining an object or situation. The group emphasizing perception through the various senses showed significantly greater gains on composition tests than did the other two groups."[9]

The Creative Process in Creative Writing

In creative writing the phases of the creative process can be clearly discerned. A reexamination of these from the viewpoint of creative writing will bring into focus the relationship of the teacher, the child, and the stimuli.

> Cognition—awareness of a problem which can best be solved through writing
>
> Conception—prelude to the moment of insight involving conscious and unconscious assimilation of ideas gained through observation, experience, memory, and/or the imagination
>
> Combustion—the ignition of the spark, the idea takes fire
>
> Consummation—perfection of the expression, the rewriting, and the polishing process
>
> Communication—the sharing of the product

Cognition. The child is aware of the wealth of ideas around him that are the source for adventuring in creative writing. As he explores the commonplace and the unusual, the sordid and the beautiful, the actual, the fanciful, the world of reality and the world of the imagination, he is moved by external stimuli or inner need to express. In a climate of psychological safety, rich experiencing, and effective guidance, he is propelled into the phase of conception.

Conception. The fruits of creative imagination do not always spring forth full-blown, nor do they function by the clock. To tell the child, "You have half an hour in which to write a story" is to ignore entirely the law of creativity. There

Formula for Guiding Creativity in Writing

PHASES OF CREATIVE PROCESS	THE CHILD	THE TEACHER
COGNITION	Becomes aware of the desire to write	Provides the stimulus for writing Creates climate for expression
CONCEPTION	Toys with ideas Considers several possibilities	Stands by to give help as needed
COMBUSTION	Discovers the ideas Starts to write	Provides encouragement
CONSUMATION	Completes the writing to his own satisfaction	Provides time, guidance, and encouragement
COMMUNICATION	Shares creative product if he chooses	Listens with interest, sensitivity, and courtesy Provides for publication of the writing Occasionally shares own creative product with group

must be time for thought to take shape, for ideas to be "toyed with", looked at, and examined for possible development—and perhaps be discarded. For children who do not work rapidly under the momentum of original inspiration, or whose stimulus was not originally strong enough to carry the idea forward, the teacher accepts the delay, the uncertainties, the false starts, and with quiet encouragement, patient, skillful questioning, or simple suggestions, gives the needed help and confidence that is prelude to the high moment of creating.

Combustion. When the spark is ignited and the flame is kindled, the child is catapulted into the "Eureka" phase by the sheer momentum of the idea. It is at this point that the previous experiences, the knowledge, the impressions, and the imaginings of the child merge. "Tinged with magic and flamboyant though it may sound, the concept of the creative flash is not a figment but is firmly rooted in experience."[10] Brief, satisfying, and swift is this creative moment. To be sensitive to such a moment is the mark of the creative teacher.

Communication. Communication is for some children the most exciting phase of the creative process. They are eager to share with others the product of their creative expression. The goal of their writing is the sharing. They are confident that their story or poem will be enjoyed, that their writing will be valued, and that their ideas will be respected. Because the ideas, the style, and the form are theirs, because they have said just what they wanted to say in the way they wished to say it, or just because, they are confident that a sympathetic audience is waiting for their written expression.

In this sharing period, there is a discussion in terms of the child's purpose for writing, his own interpretation of the extent to which he feels he fulfilled his purposes. Not unless a child asks should the teacher evaluate his writing. Nor is evaluation of creative writing a responsibility of his peers. He shares with them for enjoyment, for exchange of viewpoints, for communication of ideas, feelings, and imaginings. He is still trying his wings, feeling his way, exploring with words ideas, and form. Creating is sometimes a lonely job.

Children differ in abilities in writing as they do in other creative activities. For some, the mere opportunity to write is enough. They get astride their Pegasus and ride into the wind across the prairie, over the dunes, and follow hidden trails. They are aware of the sights, the smells, the sounds—both real and imaginary—around them. They may see the rustling wheat in the prairies, smell the salt of the ocean, or hear the flutes of Pan playing in the marshes. What these children need is time, time to listen, time to think, time to imagine, and time to express. They move rapidly from cognition to communication in the writing cycle, each child writing in his unique manner.

The Creative Product

In these examples, each child followed his creative muse in his own way. Some had a feeling for action, others for "painting" pictures of rare beauty, and still others for recreating half-remembered experiences.

April Wind

April wind, April wind
  Tossing kites so high
Whipping wash hung out to dry
  You go whizzing by

April wind, April wind
  I wonder if you care
If all the clothes are torn to shreds
  And field flowers are stripped bare

April wind, April wind
  Blow with all your might
I love to hear you, feel you, touch you
  This lovely springtime night.

Douglas—Kindergarten

In the wintertime I like to go out and play
  And make a great big snowman every single day.

Jonathon—Kindergarten[11]

In Winter

It was summer once,
  Then came fall.

But now comes what
  I like best of all.

I made a snowball big and round
  And rolled it softly on the ground,
I rolled it into a giant ball,
  Then I made another great big snowball.

I rolled it into a fat snowman.
  I got a carrot for a nose,
I got two cherries for the eyes.
  (He didn't even have a toe.)

But I got a curved stick for his mouth
  And I painted it fire-engine red.
And last of all, I put on his head—
  You're right—my father's stove-pipe hat.

John Carlin—Kindergarten

If I had a horse I'd feed him hay
  I'd sing him a song most every day—
If I had a horse.

And in the barn I'd stay far back
  Cause those hind feet can really whack!
If I *had* a horse.

Cheryl—First Grade

Oh the snow, the beautiful snow
  Filling the sky and the earth below;
Over the house tops—over the street
  Over the head of the people you meet.
    Dancing
      Flirting
        Skimming
Beautiful, beautiful, snow.

Pamela—Second Grade

The scent of apple blossoms in spring
  And burning leaves in autumn
The sound of footsteps in the snow
  And sand slithering through my hand—
    in summer

Greta—Third Grade[11]

The snow falls
      Softly
From heaven,
Cloaking the waiting earth
      With beauty.

Softly it comes down
Like fairies
          On fragile
Crystal wings.

Nancy—Fifth Grade[11]

It's a sign of the season when the crocus pokes through
   And covers the prairies with its dazzling hue,
And every little boy and girl
   Picks a bouquet for his Auntie Pearl.

It's a sign of the season when pussy willows bud
   And the streams well up and sometimes flood
And the frogs come back from underground
   To jump and play with a leap and a bound.

It's a sign of the season when each morning
   You are awakened without an alarm clock's warning
By the cheerful "Cheerup, cheerup, cheerup"
   Of a robin who sings in a nearby tree.

It's a sign of the season when the gentle rain
   Softly beats on the glistening window pane
To wash the winter's smog away
   And lift up the flowers that grow in May.

What season have I been singing of?
   The very best that life can bring.
It's the season that makes me laugh and sing.
   Of course you've guessed it—it's here.
It's Spring!

Rosemary—Fifth Grade

The Role of the Teacher in Guiding Creative Writing

Although these children expressed their creative urge spontaneously through the written word, others find this a difficult medium of expression. It is the responsibility of the teacher to give the needed guidance in each case. Most children need specific guidance as well as opportunity if they are to reach their potential. This is most effectively accomplished in an atmosphere in which each child can express his ideas freely, knowing that he will receive not only appreciative comment on writing which gives evidence of vivid expression, originality, awareness, imagination, and invention, but also recognition for his best efforts even when he falls short of the goal he has set for himself. Children need a teacher who understands each phase of the creative process and stands ready to give the needed help.

Such a teacher is cognizant that his role includes: (1) conscious awareness of the effect of the teacher's attitude toward creative writing, (2) an effective approach to guiding writing, (3) spurs to creative writing, and (4) evaluation procedures which foster creative writing.

The Attitude of the Teacher

A good teacher knows that the acquisition of skill in writing is a developmental process, interrelated with and dependent upon the process of physical, social, emotional, esthetic, and intellectual growth. A good teacher realizes that helping students write creatively is a day-by-day process that requires not so much instruction in the mechanics of writing, but sympathetic understanding and guidance. As the child develops confidence in writing, he will recognize his need for direct instruction in organization and other writing techniques.

A good teacher takes pleasure and shares in the delight and joy of discovery which comes to the student as he gains power in expression of ideas. He treats their works or creations as tenderly as if they were his own. He is constantly reminded of the value of creative expression because he too experiences the rewards of his own creative writing.

A good teacher recognizes that in guiding the truly creative child his chief function is to provide an atmosphere wherein creativity can flourish.[12] He allows time for writing, plans rich experiences which furnish a fund of ideas, stimulates their imaginations through reading good literature to them, and teaches them the needed skills of writing.

A good teacher guides creative writing in a way that enables children to set and achieve their own goals and attain self-realization through writing. This guidance is determined by his understanding of children, his knowledge of writing, his skill in knowing when to give direct instruction, and when to stand back and merely provide a place for creative expression to take place.[13]

An Effective Approach to Creative Writing

In creative writing, emphasis is on the expression of the ideas, feelings, and imagination of the writer. It is that kind of writing in which the child, in one way or another, expresses his feelings, ideas, or reactions to an experience, real or imaginary. Creative writing is concerned with artistic self-expression, whereas expository writing is concerned with functional communication. Creative writing appeals to the senses and emotions; expository writing to common sense and logic.

Guidelines for Creative Writing

Provide the motivation. To guide creative writing successfully, the teacher should be familiar with stimuli to creative writing. Prairies, weather, seasons, stars, night, birds, fish, streams, wheat fields, lakes, fire—any of these may stir a response in children. Any of the exciting experiences from real life, literature, or the imagination can serve to ignite the spark that results in creative writing.

Provide for exchange of ideas. Not all children are self-starters—some need to have a push. They need opportunities to get their ideas from others. They need time for the exchange of ideas, to talk, to think through before they are ready to write.

Help children express ideas. Children may have ideas, but they need words to express them. Through vocabulary development children will be stimulated to find the exact word or phrase that fits the expression. To help children increase the pool of words from which they draw in writing, the teacher may:

1. keep a list of colorful phrases and descriptive words in a file box
2. play word games in which children pantomime the meanings and shades of meanings of words.
3. keep a list of shining words, and trite words
4. list on a chart various categories of words such as colorful, gay, tranquil, sad, angry
5. describe common, every-day occurrences in interesting, exciting, and vivid ways

Encourage new ideas. When a child expresses an idea in a unique way, he should be commended for it and the expression added to a big book of "Unique Ideas".

Guide the writing. The teacher should circulate among the children and give them help and encouragement when they need it.

Provide for sharing the writing. Sharing or publishing creative work stimulates some children to write both more frequently and with greater discrimination. Publishing the work of children in a mimeographed or printed form is an incentive to further writing.

Evaluate the creative writing. The teacher does not mark up the child's creative writing with red pencil. This does not preclude, however, a discussion with the child which leads him to make suggestions for improvement. Among the questions such a discussion may bring forth are the following.

1. Did you enjoy writing it?
2. Does it say what you wanted it to say?
3. Is the content original?
4. Are you giving an old idea a new twist?
5. Has the writing imagery, comparison, rhythm?
6. What sensory appeals did you use?
7. Are there enough colorful and descriptive words?
8. Are there too many descriptive words so that the meaning is obscured?
9. Could you improve this if you wrote a second draft? (If the child is satisfied with the first draft in creative writing, he should be permitted to choose a new subject for his next creative writing experience.)

The following is an example of how one teacher applied these guidelines.

Provide the motivation. "Let's pretend that the whole class is suddenly transported to the pampas of the Argentine. You have seen the pictures of the pampas and the gauchos or cowboys in the books on the library shelves. You remember the films, pictures, and exhibits of Argentine artifacts.

Provide for exchange of ideas. "Now close your eyes, and when you have a picture that you see clearly in your mind's eye, will you exchange ideas? Who has a starter for a cowboy adventure? I'll write your ideas on the chalkboard."

John: A cowboy was hunting stolen cattle and came upon the rustlers unaware.

Susan: A cowboy was caught in a blizzard with his cattle and he rescued a baby calf from the wolves.

Tom: A cowboy - - - -

(As soon as the children finish sharing ideas, they choose the one they want and start writing.)

Help children express ideas and encourage new ideas. (Some children have difficulty in expressing the ideas, even when they get the basic thought for the story. When this happened, the teacher continued in the following manner.) "How would you describe the great plains of the Argentine?"

Tom: The rich stretches of the pampas.

Mary: Grass flowing in the wind like a sea.

Susan: The mahogany faces of the cowboys from living with the wind and the sun.

Isabel: The easy way the gaucho rides his horse and the long, easy lope of the steed.

Guide the writing. (During the writing, the teacher circulates among the students, giving a helpful word here, an encouraging smile there, helping the child observe, feel, imagine. She draws out *his* ideas, then helps him express them.)

"What a delightful sense of humor you have."

"You have a genius for invention."

"You are an artist with words."

"I like the way you are developing the story."

"Tell me what you want to say and maybe we can get it down on paper."

(The teacher continues to circulate among the children, encouraging, praising, suggesting.)

In the early grades, creative writing takes the form of group stories, poems, or short plays, first dictated to the teacher and then, as the child gains skill in handwriting, in the child's own writing.

Provide for sharing. When the children finish their writing, they drop it into the Treasure Chest in the writer's corner. Once a week it is opened and the stories are shared. At the end of a term, the children compile their own anthology of creative writing, each child choosing what *he* considers to be his best work. It is mimeographed. The children might even have an "Author's Tea" when another grade, or the parents, are invited and the authors autograph their work.

Spurs to Creative Writing

There are many spurs a teacher can use to stimulate creative writing. He should keep in mind the needs, abilities, interests, and experiential and developmental level of the children in his group: those whose creative spark has never been kindled, those whose flame is burning low and needs rekindling, and the talented whose flame would burn more brightly with guidance.

Many spurs can act as catalysts for creative expression. The expressive and descriptive language found in literature contributes to stimulation of creative writing. The stories children themselves write, although they may not be examples of literary excellence, are worthy of a hearing. They often carry the vigorous action children demand and act as a stimulus to the group. No matter how simple the stories may be from an adult standpoint, the wise teacher treats the children's stories with respect, as treasures to be shared if the author so desires. If the teacher can read the story expressively, lending it the appropriate dramatic interpretation, the child achieves the satisfaction that comes from being an author.

A serial story. Starting a story and sharing it episode-by-episode with the class is another spur to creative expression. The teacher can ask children for suggestions for the next episode, or invite designated children to carry on with the episode for the day. In this experience children frequently use puppets to present the day's adventure.

Tall tales. The natural outgrowth of the oral telling of tall tales is the written expression. Most children have a desire to exaggerate in a legitimate manner. In the lower grades children can take a cue from "And To Think I Saw It on Mulberry Street". Paul Bunyan and Chinook Tales are enjoyed by intermediate and upper grade students.

Sensory experiences. Sensory experiences are a good source for motivating creative writing.

1. *Auditory.* Sounds are mysterious. Children love to listen to and express the sounds they hear. A group of children who experimented with sounds listened to some thumb tacks falling into a pan. (They were unable to see the source of the sound.) This is the result as each wrote what he heard: popcorn popping, tiny rocks falling, beads breaking, tacks bouncing, marbles falling, buttons dropping, big hail balls, pumpkin seeds falling into a pan, money jingling, shotguns popping, pencils dropping, crayons drawing, chalk writing, electrons going all over.

Listening to music is another excellent auditory "spur" to creative writing. Many children have oral contributions to make about what they hear in music. Saint-Saëns' *Carnival of the Animals* was played after a statement that the music was written to remind us of different animals. The music was then replayed, and the children wrote as they listened. Most of the writing consisted of disconnected sentences. Some of the results follow.

> The ostrich with a beautiful tailfeather is dancing. A baby duck and a mother duck are lost. A butterfly flying in the air. A little blue bird. A mad tiger hunting food. A beautiful swan that is as white as snow. A little red squirrel jumping from tree to tree.

On another occasion Debussy's *Afternoon of a Faun* brought out the following story.

Once upon a time there was a husband and wife robin. Mother Robin was waiting impatiently for her eggs to hatch. One sunshiny day they did hatch, that is, all except one. Mother Robin worried and worried and waited and waited.

After about four days the last egg finally hatched. Now the family was really worried for the baby did not look like a robin at all. The more Mother Robin looked at him the madder she became. Finally she could stand it no longer and she kicked him right out of the nest.

Soon it was almost time for fall and the robin couldn't fly yet so he sadly watched the others fly by overhead. A solid red bird was up in the tree watching and when he saw how sad the little bird was he chirped a shrill "Hello!"

Little Robin was glad to find someone to talk to and when he told the bright red bird his story the other bird laughed harder and harder. Soon Little Robin was so bothered by the strange actions of his friend that he stopped talking and started crying.

"There is no need to cry," chirped the bright bird. "You are very lucky, really. I could have told you right away that you are not a robin at all but a cardinal, so there!"

The story spread and other cardinals came to help Ugly Robin learn to fly. He was so happy and he learned quickly. Before the really cold days came, he joined his kinfolks and flew quickly away.

The music that will inspire creativity is plentiful. The following is merely a suggestion.

Debussy	*The Afternoon of a Faun, The Submerged Cathedral*
Elgar	*Pomp and Circumstance*
Gershwin	*Rhapsody in Blue*
Gounod	*Funeral March of a Marionette*
Grieg	Ase's Death from *Peer Gynt* Suite
Grofé	*Grand Canyon* Suite
Haydn	*The 'Toy' Symphony,* Andante from *The 'Surprise' Symphony*
Herbert	*March of the Toys*
MacDowell	*Woodland Sketches*
Mendelssohn	*Spring Song*
Pierne	*March of the Little Lead Soldiers*
Poldini	*The Waltzing Doll*
Ponchielli	*Dance of the Hours*
Prokofief	*Peter and the Wolf*
Ravel	*Pavan for a Dead Infanta*
Rimsky-Korsakof	*Scheherazade*
Saint-Saëns	*Animals' Carnival, Danse Macabre*
Schumann	*Papillon, The Wild Horseman*
Smetana	*The Moldau*
Strauss	*Pizzicato Polka, Blue Danube Waltz*
Stravinsky	*Firebird* Suite
Tchaikovsky	*Nutcracker* Suite
Wagner	*Ride of the Valkyries*

2. *Kinesthetic.* Children are intrigued by the feel of objects. The teacher may have each child come to his desk, reach into a box, feel an object (one that has an unusual shape or texture), and then return to his seat to write his reactions to the experience, giving his sensations and description of the experience.

3. *Olfactory.* Have the children recall and write about their most pleasant odor, their most unfortunate experience with odors, and/or an exciting story about tracing an unusual and unknown odor to its source.

4. *Gustatory.* Have the children describe the taste of a favorite food without naming it. Have the other children guess what it is. Write the most vivid words and phrases on the chalkboard to use in the self-chosen writing activity.

5. *Visual.* Pictures offer excellent avenues for evoking creative expression. Children view a picture, discuss it, look at it again, and then write. Only fine examples of art should be used. The instructor can also have a file to which children may go to select a picture. Questions may be written at the bottom of the picture to stimulate writing. A vocabulary may be provided on the reverse side of the mounted picture. For example, if a child selected a picture showing a clown in a gay costume and a spirited pose, the questions might read: "What trick do you want me to do?" "What do I do with my time in the winter season?" "Do you suppose I am as happy as I look?" On the reverse side such words might appear as—clown, trick, tent, circus, joke, etc. The picture file should include pictures of animals, children, life in other countries, seasonal scenes, and others to provide motivation for writing.

6. *Word pictures and descriptive phrases.* Painting word pictures is an activity which children enjoy. For example, the teacher might give a word and the children respond with descriptive phrases or synonyms. These should be put on cards and placed in a file where children can refer to them when they are writing.

Examples:

snow:	soft and crisp and white drifting lazily through the air sailing along the boughs of the tree covering the country side with feather-light flakes
waves:	rolling endlessly toward the shore crashing thunderously against the grey rocks sending countless sprays of foam skyward galloping out into the lost horizon white caps rolling in for sleep
softness:	snow flakes floating softly by bits of dainty, frilly lace
whiteness:	new fallen snow a billowy white cloud a field of daisies
quietness:	a quiet lullaby a cooing dove a velvet glove

darkness: a gathering storm
a thundercloud
a sky at dusk
a gloomy cave

sharpness: a clap of thunder
a blue jay's cry
a crow's caw
an eagle's scream

As children develop their imagery and become aware of their ability to paint pictures with words, they can be guided to discover relationships between such categories as softness, darkness, freshness, sharpness, and to project the picture into a situation in which they might integrate the various elements. As one child said during an experience with this word-painting, "I don't know whether to get out my paints and paint a picture of a stormy beach or write a story describing a storm—not that I ever saw one like I'm going to describe—but I have the words that can paint the picture."

Frequently after a group experience of developing concepts, the individual children will be motivated to express their own unique creative work.

The two examples illustrate the group composition and an individual expression.[14]

Snow, snow everywhere,
Snow on the ground but we don't care.
Snow on the pond, snow on the hill,
So come and play with us if you will.

Snow, snow, soft and white
Falling, falling pretty and bright.
Snow, snow everywhere,
Snow in our hair,—but we don't care.

Third Grade—Harwood School, Evansville, Ind.

I looked into the valley
And almost like a dream
So clear so white so starry bright
So beautiful and clean

The sparkling snowflakes
Like fairies dancing on a knoll
Had clothed the valley with their light
The brightly, swirling, falling snow

Jane—Third Grade

Poetry: A Spur to Creative Writing

Another effective spur to creative writing is poetry. However, if poetry is to be used as a motivational factor, it must be read to the children by a teacher who loves poetry and who can read it well. Only after listening to a wide variety of poems read well and learning to read it themselves with skill and understanding are the children ready to create their own in the form demanded by the idea they wish to express. They also should be encouraged to experiment with various poetic forms, such as *Haiku,* couplets, and limericks.

Most children have a natural feel for the poetic. In the early grades they should be encouraged to follow this inherent sense. As they gain experience in using "their" poetic form, they should be encouraged to experiment with a wide variety of forms. In this way they will discover that the content determines form.

For example, a primary grade teacher read "If Only" by Rose Fyleman. It was not difficult for the children to think of what they would like to buy if only they had some money. This poem practically writes itself with any primary or intermediate group of boys and girls—especially at Christmas time.

A fourth grade teacher who had allowed complete freedom in choice of poetic form in an experiment to broaden the children's writing experience introduced the couplet by reading Rosetti's "What Is Pink?" After hearing and discussing the poem, the children tried their hand at writing questions about various colors and then supplying their own answers with descriptions in the couplet form.

What is white? Clouds are white
See them in the morning light.

What is blue? The sky is blue
It's the very loveliest hue.

What is red? Blood is red
See it running down your head.

What is pink? A rose is pink
Fresh and cool as a big, big drink.

What is green? The grass is green
Softest velvet ever seen.

What is black? The night is black
Dark, mysterious and black.

What is gray? A cat is gray
Lying on the soft mown hay.

The lyricism as well as the imagery is often the result of listening to poetry read aloud by the teacher or another adult. Children are able to immerse themselves in the content of the poetry and simultaneously are motivated to avail themselves consciously or unconsciously of the tools and literary devices of poetry. The older they are, if they have been writing happily, the more they incorporate the literary devices they find in the well loved poems.

I saw a broken moon go down,
In the slithery stillness of night
I watched it slowly disappear and
Finally drop from sight

I watched a broken dream slip by
In the willowy flight of dawn
And thought how surely one bright night
The moon would laugh once more.

Jean, age ten

Whenever teachers ask, "What motivates children to write?" one might well answer, "Whatever interests them deeply." They like to write about themselves, their pets, quiet lovely things, sensory experiences, biography, nature, people, their environment, make believe, the jet age.

Applegate suggests, "A child's poem is a talked-out feeling. . . . Fine poems only pop out when they have the push of emotion behind them. But so facile are children's imaginations that they have feelings on the strangest subjects."[15]

Such results in writing, using words to paint pictures, come not from a vacuum. They are the result of an environment rich in experiences, filled with poetry read aloud, poetry spoken in choral reading, creative movement, and rhythmic expression, coupled with time for discussion, development of ideas, experimenting and creating with words, and sharing writing with others.

Literature

There are books and stories a teacher reads to the class which somehow automatically spur children to creative expression. This expression may take the form of creative dramatics, a painting; at other times it emerges in creative writing. A group of third graders, after listening to the story of *The Little Red Lighthouse and the Great Gray Bridge,* discussed the possibility of finding an old landmark in their community that had outlived its usefulness. They found it without too much trouble: an old hitching post at "Five Points". The rings for the horse's reins were still attached. Such questions arose as, "How does the hitching post feel in this day of jets, planes, helicopters?" This was the stimulation for numerous stories about *Hiram, the Hitching Post*, with as many endings as there were authors in the class.

In the collection *Patchwork Plays*, Rachel Field points the way for creative writing using an Aesop fable as a starter. In "Miss Ant, Miss Grasshopper and Mr. Cricket", she presents a dramatization of the well known story of the ant and the grasshopper with a new character and a happy ending. However, a group of sixth graders were dissatisfied with this version of the story for their puppet play and rewrote the ending.

In *Children and Books*, May Hill Arbuthnot includes two poems written by upper grade pupils as a sequel to "Nancy Hanks" the poem by Rosemary Carr Benét. Nancy Hanks asks:

"What's happened to Abe?
What's he done?"

The children answered the questions in the poems they wrote. In order to answer the questions they tried to find information about Lincoln not included in the Benét poem.

Canadian writers offer a challenge to children's imagination. The book *Great Canadian Writing*, an anthology of Canadian writing edited by Claude Bissell, has a wealth of material that will challenge the intermediate and upper grade children.

Motivating Creative Writing of Poetry[16]

Motivating children to write poetry takes on many colors, styles and forms.

Humor. Writing poetry may be motivated through humor. The teacher first reads some humorous poems. Then he may write a humorous line on the chalkboard and suggest that the children think of a second line for the poem, ending with a rhyming word. This is copied off the board. The problem of the third and fourth lines is considered. They must follow the trend of the first two, and carry on the meaning. The last line is usually the "punch" line.

Limericks. After reading several limericks and discussing the form, the teacher writes a line suggested by a student, perhaps "There was a young man from Brandon." The procedure for finishing the limerick will be like that suggested above—the class suggesting and working out a class effort.

Figurative language. On a winter day when it is snowing, the teacher may read some snow poems, then ask, "How would you describe the snow?" The children listen to some poems again, listening especially for the figurative words. These are listed on the chalk board. Other figures are suggested that could describe snow. Then, with these words and phrases before them to help, they compose poems describing snow as it appears to each. This helps them realize the value of descriptive words and figurative language. Thus, they develop a feeling for the magic and power of words.

Personal feelings. "How did you feel when you were embarrassed?" "How did you feel when you were sad—happy?" "How did you feel when you were very angry?" Questions such as these bring a flood of descriptive words, metaphors, and similies which the teacher may then write on the chalkboard. When a child has an inspiration to write, he begins, in either prose or poetry, to describe the feelings he experienced at that particular time.

Wishes. "Did you ever wish for something, or for something to happen?" "Did you ever wish you could be someone else?" The teacher might read poems about wishing, discuss the poems with the class, and ask the children to express their greatest wish or deepest desire in any type of poetic form.

Visual stimuli. Pictures serve as an excellent stimulus for writing. The teacher might place several pictures on the bulletin board. These should suggest action. Various interpretations may be given through discussion. Each child starts to write his interpretation of the picture he chooses. One of the pictures is that of a large wishbone; another is an apple with one large bite taken from it. Others are pictures of circus animals, people, elements of nature.

Sense impressions. Poems about sensory elements—smells, tastes, sounds, sights, touch—motivate creative writing. The teacher might read a poem about smells and ask children to list the smells mentioned in the poem. "What smells do you like?" These may be listed on the chalkboard. "What smells do you dislike?" They are then invited to write individual poems describing or reacting to smells they liked or disliked. The other senses can be used in the same manner.

Inanimate objects. "Did you ever wish you were an inanimate object? A tree, a car, a stick, a stone, a magic wand?" These questions motivate children to respond with varied ideas. Following discussion, they are invited to pretend to be an inanimate object of their choice and put their thoughts into a poem.

Music. Recordings of different types of music provide excellent stimuli.

After listening to recordings children are asked, "What did you hear in the music? How did you feel when you heard this ——— passage? What impression did you get from the music?" They enjoy writing their impressions, feelings, responses, and interpretation of the music.

Vivid impressions. Experiences which are vivid to children, e.g., an accident, a fright, a loss of something valuable, form the basis of story poems. The story poem has a plot and can be developed from an entirely true experience or a fictitious one. The story is the child's own, so he should write it as he chooses.

Poems based on current interests. The daily interests of children form a basis for creative poetry. For example, if interest has been aroused because someone has a new pony, several poems about ponies or horses could be read to the class. "How do you think a horse feels when he is left alone in a large, strange pasture?" "How do you think the horse felt in Robert Frost's poem 'Stopping By Woods on a Snowy Evening' "?

A treasure hunt. A field trip may become a treasure hunt for children, the treasure being the poem inspired by the trip.

Elements of nature. Children are intrigued with elements of nature. As soon as they have command of literary devices such as personification, they may make cards to use as a basis for creating poems. On a rainy day—"Wind gossiping in the trees as though making friends with the rain." "What is the wind saying?" "How would you make friends with the rain?"

Such poems could be the beginning of an anthology of nature poems. Rainbows, storms, thunder, blizzards, lightning, snowfall, etc. all have possibilities for motivating poems for the anthology.

Take your choice. A picture of two children at the seaside, a poem describing a winter scene, the sound of a loud metallic crash, and the sight and touch of a large rusty key stimulate a variety of creative responses.

Experimenting with forms of poetry. *Haiku,* a seventeen-syllable, unrhymed verse of Japanese origin, is a form which may be used successfully. It is a three line poem, the first of which has five syllables the second seven, and the third five. The *Haiku* is basically a nature poem which implies the season and tells or suggests the writer's feelings.

Tanka is based on the *Haiku* with two additional lines each of seven syllables. It was originally a highly sophisticated form of entertainment among the Japanese intellectuals. One person would improvise a *Haiku* and another would immediately add the last two lines of the *Tanka.*

Cinquain, an unrhymed verse easily patterned, was developed by Adelaide Crapsey. It consists of five lines, with a syllable count of 2-4-6-8-3. It has since received many variations, the most popular of which is: line one—a noun, line two—two adjectives describing the noun, line three—three participles related to the noun, line four—four words making a statement about the noun, line five—one word summing up the mood, emotion, or experience.

Examples of Haiku. Students in the seventh grade room at Earl Haig Junior High School under the direction of the teacher, Mrs. Marion Pinta, experimented with *Haiku.* Some of the results follow.

Bells chiming clearly
Ribbons of joy surround us
Carols softly sung.
Patsy Daniels

Snow softy falling
Feathers floating forever
Silently downwards.
Susan Weibe

Korean Sijo. Although many schools have experimented with writing the Japanese *Haiku*, the form of oriental poetry known as Korean *Sijo* is not as well known. This form consists of three sentences divided into six lines with no rhyming scheme. Each sentence contains between 14 and 16 syllables. It is not as tightly structured as is *Haiku* and, especially in the early stages of creating poetry, children appreciate the additional freedom.

The most difficult things children find is to keep the language simple, yet effective enough to express their feelings. As they develop skill in this form, they begin to delve more and more into the abstract and symbolic, the essence of Oriental poetry. The more successful they become in expressing their feelings symbolically, the more they enjoy their products. Although *Sijo*, like *Haiku*, deals primarily with the emotions and nature, it is freer. It is this freedom that makes it an excellent avenue for motivating creativity in poetry. The following are examples of *Sijo* done by elementary school children.

A flashing mane and tail
Glistening in the golden sunlight.
Dainty hooves pound out a
Rhythmic beat upon a dusty path.
Oh the beauty and wonder of
These kingly, graceful beasts.

Somewhere in the shadows lurks
The sleek, black hunter of the night.
On padded feet he makes his way
Through brush and tangled vines.
With fangs bared, the panther
Springs upon his unwary foe.

Rhymed couplet. This is another form which students enjoy composing. Two lines are usually easier for them. Later, they may want to do a complex poem in the couplet form.

The more creative students often wish to experiment with longer stanza patterns—the sonnet, lyrics—and some may even want to try their hand at putting the lyrics to music after the manner of Gordon Lightfoot, or any of the popular writers of words and music.

These motivations for writing poetry serve equally as well for the writing of prose. Only the form is different.

Creative Writing of Stories

Ideas for writing of stories come from many sources—from half-remembered dreams, from bits of conversation, from stories heard or read, from experiences real or imagined. At times, ideas erupt spontaneously; at other times, they remain buried beneath the surface awaiting the stimulus that calls them forth into existence. If the child is ready to start writing, the teacher merely steps aside and lets him write. However, not all children are self-starters. Some need a gentle push. Some need a tow truck.

Among the techniques teachers have found successful are: The Idea Box, Let's Pretend, Exciting Phrases, Flash-back Technique, Sentence Starters, Unfinished Story, A Fish Pond of Titles, "Imagine you are . . .", "If you were . . ."

Possible ways to begin a story. Although the "Once upon a time" still holds enchantment for many listeners and readers, there are other possibilities which might well be explored by the embryo story teller. The following are some ways that have proved successful in getting a story started.

A conversation to set the stage for action

The flashback technique—start with the ending and proceed to the beginning

A description of the setting with emphasis on mood

A description of the main character or characters

A statement of setting—time, place, or situation

A question which holds the essence of the story

A summary paragraph—condensation giving the point of the story

A day in the life of an individual (real or imaginary)

A journal, diary, or personal writings of well known historical figures

Story Checklist. A story checklist will serve as a guide in the writing.

Setting. Tell where and when—the place and time. Describe the place. What does it look like? Tell time of day—of year—of history.

Characters. Animals? People? Name them. Describe them.

Plot. What happens that sets the characters against each other? What happens to make the problem *more complicated?*

Climax. What is the peak of the action—the high point?

Conclusion. How does the story end? Is the ending logical? Was it prepared for?

Title. Usually the title comes last. Reread the story carefully. Make up several striking, attention-getting titles. Select the one that best fits your story.

Rewrite. Read and reread the story, making improvements as you read. Read the story aloud to someone. Ask them if the plot is clear, the characters real, the climax believable. When the corrections are noted, rewrite the story in the best form possible. Be sure this time that you check spelling. Give it to the teacher to advise for further improvements, or place it in your creative writing folder until you are ready to share it with someone.

The Group Story

No great literature has been produced by a group. However, many children feel more secure in writing if they can participate in a cooperative venture.

Group composition can be used throughout the elementary school to improve as well as to stimulate written expression. It offers the opportunity to share ideas, to develop a colorful and descriptive vocabulary. It acquaints children with experiences of other children and opens the door to new interests.

The teacher who is committed to helping every child develop his potential in a variety of creative experiences will provide him with varied media of creative expression. Each child should have the opportunity to experience working with words as a way of self-expression.

He must, of course, discover the particular medium which suits his mode of expression and his need for expression at a particular time. Winged words can readily become the Pegasus for a child to adventure with words in a group situation, whereas he might well be too timid to venture in a solo flight. For such a child, particularly, the security of the group carries him along. In the group he is able to contribute ideas without being responsible for an entire composition. For such children, the cooperative story is both satisfying and rewarding.

Listening to a well loved story, planning an imaginary trip, taking an excursion on the ferry, a train, or a plane—any of these may be the spark that catapults a group into a cooperative writing venture. Children contribute their ideas rapidly, spontaneously, and generously as the teacher takes on the role of a scribe and writes on the chalkboard as the ideas come. As rapidly as the story unfolds, the teacher records it. Depending upon the impact of the experience, the background of the children, the skill in using words and ideas, the teacher directs attention to such elements as development of the plot, picturesque language, exciting climax, and originality of expression. Even preschool and kindergarten children enjoy the experience of being authors, as evidenced by the following writing.

The Little Train That Broke Down

by A B C Playschool

A little train was loaded with people, and it was broken down. The wheels wouldn't go around—they were stuck, and the engine wouldn't make the train go. The train was going to California with boys and girls who wanted to visit Disneyland. They thought the train was too full of people; that the load was too heavy. So, some of the people got off, but the wheels still wouldn't go around and the engine wouldn't make the train go. The engineer got off and walked around the train, and, what do you know, one of the wheels was missing.

Johnny, whose daddy rode in the caboose, was riding in the caboose with his daddy. Johnny thought he saw the wheel lying way down the track, so he asked his daddy if he could go see, and his daddy said he could. So Johnny ran down the track as fast as he could go, and sure enough, it was the wheel. Johnny tried to pick up the wheel, but it was too heavy to carry, so he rolled it down the track. Then they had to find a bolt to hold the wheel back in place.

Just then they heard another train coming. They were afraid it might hit them, but it was on the other track and it stopped to help them. The mechanic on the other train brought his tool box out and helped get the wheel back on.

When they got the wheel back in place, the engine went "chug-chug," the whistle blew, "toot! toot!" The conductor called, "All aboard for Disneyland!" The wheels went round, and they all got to Disneyland after all.

A group composition by four-year-olds in nursery school in co-operative group effort with their teacher Twila Hills, Findlay, Ohio.

Little Joe

Once upon a time there was a boy by the name of Little Joe. He lived on a farm with his mama and papa and his three pets, a dog, a kitten, and a parakeet.

One day Little Joe's papa bought him a new pop gun. He took his three pets out into the woods to see if his pop gun worked. As he walked through the woods, he met a cougar. The cougar said, "Gr-r-r-r! I'm going to eat you up, Little Joe."

Little Joe said, "Please don't eat me up, Mr. Cougar. I'll give you my dog and with him to follow you around, you will be the grandest cougar in the woods."

Said Mr. Cougar, "Of course I'll let you go on if you give me the dog." And he went off saying, "Now "*I'M* the grandest cougar in the woods."

As Little Joe went on, he met another cougar who wanted to eat him up. So Little Joe said, "Please do not eat me up, Mr. Cougar. I'll give you my kitten and with her to ride on your back, you will be the grandest cougar in the forest."

This cougar was not so sure he wanted the kitten. However, he decided to take her and off he went saying, "Now *I'M* the grandest cougar in the woods."

As Little Joe went on, he met another cougar who said, "Gr-r-r-r, I'm going to eat you up."

Little Joe said, "Please do not eat me up. I'll give you my parakeet."

Mr. Cougar said, "What would I do with a parakeet?"

"You could have him sing to you and be your friend," said Little Joe.

Why, of course," said Mr. Cougar, "and now *I'M* the grandest cougar in the woods."

Going deeper into the woods, Little Joe met another cougar. This fourth cougar said, "Gr-r-r-r! I'm going to eat you up, Little Joe."

"Please do not eat me up, Mr. Cougar," said Little Joe; "I'll give you my pop gun."

And so the fourth cougar went off with the pop gun tied to his tail. He was saying, "Now *I'M* the grandest cougar in the woods."

Walking further into the woods, Little Joe was very sad. Then he heard all this noise. He looked around to see the four cougars chasing one another around a rock. Little Joe said, "Don't you want my pets and pop gun any more?"

The cugars were so afraid that one might get away, they just held on to each other's tails saying, "Gr-r-r-r". They got so hot they turned to tar.

The pop gun got untangled and flew right into Little Joe's arms. He gathered up his pets and hurried to his farm.

Little Joe's papa was coming home from town with a pail on his head and he saw the tar the cougars had made. He said, "I could use this tar to mend our silo and walls." So he picked up the tar and carried it home.

There he plugged up all the holes in the silo. Now all the cows, horses, and pigs would have enough food for the long cold winter. There was plenty so the cows had fifteen bushels, the horses had twenty bushels, and the pigs had one hundred and five bushels of grain.

First Grade—Hahn School, Wayne, Nebraska.
Supervising Teacher—Vesta Wright.

Older children, too, find the cooperative story fun on a slightly more mature basis. They enjoy dividing into groups of three or more pupils to create an entire story or a sequence of episodes which can later be woven into a story. They work in groups of their own choosing, discuss the story or episode which they wish to take responsibility for writing, decide what form it should take and begin.

Through pooling ideas, dictating to a scribe selected by each group, taking turns at being scribe, children who might otherwise fail to experience this form of written expression find satisfaction in being authors.

In guiding such an endeavor, the teacher moves from writing group to writing group, discussing and giving encouragement and help where it is *really* needed, eliciting ideas from the group, and being a good listener when ideas are flowing spontaneously. At times he gives direct instruction to the combined groups by pointing up common problems, literary devices, and asking the class for solutions and suggestions. At other times giving direct instruction to small groups is more valuable.

While there are those who believe all writing should be of an individual nature in the intermediate and upper grades, there is merit in group activity in which children collaborate as authors. Cooperative effort can be a stepping stone to individual activity as well as a different way of expressing ideas.

Enjoying the Writing of Others

Children may be overwhelmed by the skill and perfection of the professional writer and become discouraged with their own efforts. The wise teacher provides examples of fine creative writing by children across the country.

The stories that follow are typical examples of what children write in the average classroom when they are given time, encouragement, and guidance.

Ready For Christmas

Once upon a time there was a little squirrel who didn't have any food to eat. He had eaten everything except one little hazelnut. That one last nut he must save for his Christmas dinner. So he put on his raincoat and went for a walk in the woods. He walked and he walked, but as the sun set in the west, he found he had no nuts to carry back to his home. All at once he looked up and who should he see but a little lady with a fairy wand. She didn't say a word, but led him straight to a little house that had a pleasant look. He followed her and peeked in at the window. Lo and behold a woman who looked very much like the lady in the woods was baking a Christmas cake. He could hardly believe his eyes when he saw the little lady had six beautiful pecans ready to put in to the batter. He made a squirrelly noise. The little lady, thinking it was the telephone ringing, left the kitchen to answer the phone. This was his chance. He grabbed the pecans and stole away.

The little lady came back to the kitchen to find the pecans gone. So the little lady sat down and cried. "There will be no fruitcake for Christmas!" Ever since little squirrels go hunting for nuts early, so they have enough to last all winter, and little ladies baking fruit cakes for Christmas use raisins when there aren't any nuts.

As for the little squirrel, merrily scampering up the hill with the nuts, he chuckled to himself, "I'm ready for Christmas. Are you?"

Phyllis Gass—5 years old. Henry Reiss Kindergarten, Evansville, Ind.

A Grumwuff

Once upon a time there was a grumwuff. Before I tell you the story you must know what a grumwuff is. A grumwuff, so I've been told, is a furry pink animal with no arms and legs. It sits on your shoulder all day, even when you're playing ball or brushing your teeth. Since it doesn't have any legs, a grumwuff just bounces from place to place.

That is, a proper grumwuff does. But this grumwuff wasn't happy bouncing from place to place, so he said: "I will ask the gods to teach me to fly." And that he did. And that they did. And on a summer's evening when the sun in sinking in the west you may see a streak of pink against the sky—a streak of fluff that wings across the sky. And you will hear the wind sigh: "Grumwuff-grumwuff-Grumwuff— . . . There he goes!"

Mary Becker—6 years old.

The Lost Pearl

Once upon a time there was a Queen who had a neclace with dimonds and one big pearl in the middle. One day she was looking over the pond to see her pretty reflection in the water, when suddenly her neclace broke, splash, splash, SPLASH! That was the big pearl. The Queen ordered some men to look for the dimonds. They brought out dimonds and dimonds and dimonds, but not the big pearl. A man was fishing one day and caught a big fish. That fish had ate the pearl. His wife sewed in on his jacket. There it is on the old man's jacket—to this very day. [Spelling and usage are Connie's.]

Connie—7 years old. School District No. 67, Duncan, B.C.

The Six-inch Monster[17]

Once there was a monster that was about six inches high. If you got a ruler and measured him you would find that he was exactly six inches high.

And you could measure him because he was very polite. That is, if you could ever find him. I know where he lives and I visit him sometimes. He has a lot of money that he has hid somewhere. He digs holes and puts it in. He has a lot of holes with money in it. Because he is so little and couldn't handle very much at a time. He told me where a pot of gold was but that little monster had just dug it up to give it to someone for helping him. That monster is really just an overgrown fairy. I've been calling him a six inch monster because he plays so many tricks.

Once I went to visit him to get some butter. When I knocked at the door I listened for a while. And all I heard was that little monster trying to teach his dishes how to sing. Then I knocked again and he opened the door and gave me some butter right in the face.

He said, "That is what you wanted, isn't it?" So I never tried to borrow anything from him again. And once I lost my purse and I told the little six inch monster about it and the next day I went to visit him. He came out with a big thing (anyway it was big to him) on his back.

I asked him what it was and he said, "It is your purse." I took it off his back and it was my purse. He said he took a long walk but it was just a few steps away. He said he had to cross an ocean, but it was really just a little puddle. He said it was too long to go around. But the funny thing about it was he had fun. [Spelling and usage is Phyllis'.]

Phyllis Ormand—8 years old. Third grade.

Lucky Dan

What strange and mysterious experiences I have been having. For months I have been cold and all shriveled up in the dark soil under the snow near my brothers and sisters. One day we began to feel warmer and we started to stretch upward as though we were being drawn. One day a wonderful thing happened. I became so large that my head popped up a little, my arms stretched way out and I had a first chance to look around. I was sitting on a beautiful soft green blanket and near me were many lovely yellow flowers. They all seemed so much taller and more beautiful than I. It was such a frightening experience. There were many giant feet that came close and sounded so much like thunder. They made me shake and I wished I could go back into the soil. One day a huge lady came with a basket and a sharp thing that hurt so badly when she cut as she tried to destroy all my family and friends. Somehow she didn't notice me and I was relieved to hear her go away and never come back. I was beginning to feel so much better when a machine which made a horrible noise and a man whose voice I had heard go by often, came close again and again to snip off our heads. I should be glad now that I never grew very tall, for again I was left. The beautiful warm sunshine and gentle breeze made me feel so wonderful. Many days went by, then one day my coat of gold seemed to become dry and I felt different than I had ever felt before. I became so light and I was white now and looked something like down. Not long after, a gentle breeze came by coaxing me to to come along. It coaxed and pushed and coaxed and finally I felt myself flying through the air like a fairy. I felt so light I wanted never, never to stop again.

Phyllis Reeder—10 years old. Findlay, Ohio.

Baby Shoes

My name is Baby Shoes and I am on the shelf. You see I am Tanna's best shoes. I am only for special occasions. I am yellow with white pom-poms on the laces. When Tanna's mother puts me on, Tanna's pink toes make me laugh. Her mother takes special care of me, but not to her other shoes. Tanna plays in mud puddles with her other shoes and in the garden and she also scuffs her other shoes on the sidewalk but not me. But, one day when they were going to church mommy went back to the house and she told Tanna to stay where she was, but Tanna didn't. She went over to her little pool and splash, she was in the water. Mother and Father came running and took her out of the water. I began to cry because I was all wet. After Tanna got her dry clothes on Mother said "Oh you are a very bad girl and I'm going to punish you, no candy for two weeks." Then Father said "And you have ruined your best shoes too!" They still have me sitting on this shelf.

Cathy Taylor—Fifth grade. Neepawa, Manitoba.

The Missing Tooth

Once there lived a very poor family. The family was made up of an old man and his young grandson, Punco. Punco had a little bull named Pekelo.

One morning Punco got up early for today Punco and Pekelo were going fishing. As Punco sat eating his food, Pekelo devoured his food . . . which was half Punco's that he was sharing.

When Punco returned home, his grandfather said to him, "Punco, we have no more food. We will have to sell Pekelo."

"No, I will never sell Pekelo," said Punko.

"But you must," replied the grandfather.

"Run, Pekelo, run!" shouted Punco.

Pekelo understood, but since he had been very young his eyesight has not been good. He ran right into a big tree. Punco ran over to the tree.

"Are you hurt, Pekelo? Are you hurt?"

Pekelo gave Punco a big smile. Punco saw that the bull had knocked one of his teeth out. Punco looked on the ground for Pekelo's tooth. He found it.

"Pekelo, I will put a hole in this tooth and put it on a string. I will put it around my neck and when grandfather takes you away I will always remember you."

About 17 years later when Punco was a full grown man he was going to fight a very mean bull. Punco sat in his room thinking about when he was a little boy. Then he heard his cue to go out. He walked in to the pen very straight. The pen door swung open and the biggest bull Punco had ever seen charged out. The bull hated the sight of the man with the red cape. The bull was going to attack Punco. Punco drew his sword. Then the bull stopped and gave Punco a big smile. Punco saw that one of his front teeth was missing. Punco pulled his tooth out from around his neck. Punco put his arms around his lost Pekelo.

Then Punco heard the crowd howling too, boo. Punco and Pekelo walked out of the pen together.

"Pekelo, if it hadn't been for your missing tooth, I might have killed you," said Punco.

Punco was a little sad because the people didn't like him as a bull fighter, but he did find Pekelo and he was very happy for a long time.

Zelma Anderson—11 years old. West Elementary School, Mt. Vernon, Indiana.

A Ring

The low clouds hung like ragged folds in a gray dress. Nowhere did the sun peek through with its warmth and comfort. The sunlit green had seeped out of the trees and they stood back, silhouetted against the sky. Beyond the trees a small bright flame rose and fell as the rain drizzled down.

Nestled in her coat, a young girl sat nearby, her face brightening and darkening with the fire. Between her fingers she carefully held a small ring. As her blue eyes looked lovingly at it, she smiled. The ring was old and the silver had tarnished. The stone was chipped and worn, but as the flames leapt against it was flecked with gold.

Although it was no longer beautiful, her feelings for the ring continued to shine in her eyes.

Susan Paxton—13 years old. Vancouver, B.C.

The Arsonist

Hunched under the lee of the towering building the man tried to keep himself warm against the squalling wind and rain, and the night which coated him in a black jacket. Suddenly a flashlight moved its beam to the man. His mask thrown off, he stabbed through the wind and night leaving the searching beam to dash itself among the spidery trees that covered the spot. From the spot a fire sprang its clawing hands into the wood. It soon brightly illuminated the fleeing trees and the human form that quickly was swallowed by the night.

David Poskitt—13 years old. Balmoral Junior Secondary School, North Vancouver, B.C.

Questions. Thought-provoking questions may also be used to develop the art of thinking, feeling and expressing. How would you feel standing in a room completely filled with your favorite color?

This question presented to a class of fifth grade boys and girls in a creative environment brought the following response.

Pink is the color I like the best,
If I were a bird I'd put pink in my nest.
Babies wear pink and so do you,
I'm not a baby but I like pink too.

Look out in the yard with spring in the air
And put a pink cherry blossom into your hair.
Roses are pink and so are carnations
Pink is the favourite all over the nation.[18]

Expressions follow closely on the heels of strong impressions when teachers are sensitive to the phenomena in the environment, to the child's innate urge for expression, and are skilled in asking questions which spur creative expression.

A question which always evokes creative expression is one dealing with weather. "What tells you that Jack Frost is just around the corner?" To the question "What does up mean to you?" numerous responses are possible.

Integrating the arts. Stimulation for creative writing is where you find it. A sixth grade teacher came up to a group of children who were manipulating the potter's wheel. As a child worked the treadle, others in the group responded to the rhythm by tapping, clapping or otherwise reacting to the rhythm. Someone began humming a few notes. The group joined in spontaneously. The teacher went to the chalkboard and wrote the melody on the board as the children created it. They added to the notes and melodic pattern until someone said, "That's it."

Each child wrote his *own* words to the melody on the basis of the rhythm of the potters wheel. Here was creativity—music and poetry intertwined. Here is one example.

> Hear my wheel turn round and round
>
> Listen to the humming sound whrrrrrrr, whrrrrrrr, whrrrrrrr,
>
> See my wheel spin round and round
>
> As if my foot never left the ground—whrrrrrr, whrrrrr, whrrr.

Children write because they have a desire to express their ideas, their feelings, their imaginations. The teacher is there to clear the track, to encourage each child, to stimulate his thinking, to help him develop the skills he has a need for, and to give the recognition that will make him eager to write, eager to improve, and eager to express through the medium of the written word.

Literary Devices

The young child plays with words for the joy he finds in the sound and rhythm. As he matures, however, he senses a need to develop techniques for expressing his creative ideas more effectively. It is at this point that the perceptive teacher will introduce him to various literary devices upon which he can draw. This implies that the teacher will himself be well versed in the various literary devices and will be at ease in pointing them out to children in their literature as well as helping them become skillful in their use. As the artist learns to use the whole spectrum of color, so the weaver of tales learns to use words to express precise meaning as he develops his unique writing style.

Techniques which add color to a writer's palette. Unless the child is in command of a variety of literary devices, his writing tends to be sterile and stereotyped. Robert Frost once said, "All the fun's in how you say a thing." The following devices can serve as tools for saying it in vibrant, rich, colorful language.

1. *Figures of speech.* Figurative language is a picturesque comparison designed to make vivid an idea or to illustrate a thought. The expressed likeness of the simile and the implied likeness of the metaphor intrigue children. "Old as Methuselah", "tall as a stringbean", "time's winged chariot", "starry vaults of the heaven", "jumping on the bandwagon", "sly as a fox", "eyes bigger than his stomach", "slow as molasses in January", "innocent as a dove" are some that come readily to mind. Good writing makes use of figurative language. "I saw him [Napoleon] in Russia, where the infantry of the snow and the cavalry of the wild beast scattered his legions like winter's withered leaves. I saw him

at Leipsic in defeat and disaster—driven by a million bayonets back upon Paris. . . ."[19] How do you see him?

Children enjoy completing such phrases as:

as soft as	The wind howled like a . . . .
as loud as	Jack was as restless as . . . .
as happy as	All day long I've been busy as . . . .
as sad as	This gadget is as useless as a . . . .
as stern as	She turned green with . . . .
as quiet as	The doctor was tied . . . .
as gentle as	He put his foot in . . . .
	He was a . . . . in the fight.

The simile is commonly used by children in their writing. The metaphor is seldom found. The use of the metaphor will make children's writing even more vivid. "Metaphor is the device by which we use words which signify objects in the physical world to imply a comparison and to express the unknown in terms of the known. It has been called the device by which we express the inexpressible."[20]

2. *The historical present.* Transporting the reader into the past by means of the present tense is an effective literary device commonly used in television, radio, and documentary films. It is especially liked by elementary school children, particularly when they can present some historical episode which has significance in their social studies or literature class.

3. *Inverted word order.* One of the most widely quoted phrases using this technique is that of John F. Kennedy. "Ask not what your country can do for you—ask what you can do for your country." Although all sentences contain parts of speech or classes of words, these need not necessarily always follow in the SVO (subject, verb, object) sequence. Experimenting with word order is a worthwhile activity for the embryo writer.

4. *Rhythm and rhyme.* Children should be encouraged to listen to the rhythm and flow of language. As teachers read aloud, children become aware of the singingness, the rhythm and the rhyme of poetry, and the flow of prose. They should be led to appreciate good literature by hearing it read by a teacher who reads it beautifully. They thus become aware of the elements of style. At times they should be encouraged to write in the style of a chosen author as a means of developing their own.

5. *Alliteration.* The repetition of the same initial sound in successive words is euphoneous. Witness the effect of "wild, woolly west", "let me languish in loneliness", "purple pansies preening in the picture window", "soft slumbering summer", "lonely leaf", "wide, wonderful world".

6. *Assonance.* Somewhat similar to alliteration is the repetition of the same sound in successive words although in different positions within the word. Whereas alliteration generally involves consonants, assonnance usually is related to vowel sounds. "Dennis the menace", "more bounce to the ounce", "molten-golden notes", "I like Ike".

7. *Imagery.* Images are an integral part of the writer's stock in trade. They may be classified in several different ways, but a useful way is

classifying them according to the kinds of sensations involved. The most important from the standpoint of the elementary and upper grades are: images of sight (visual), images of sound (auditory), images of movement (kinesthetic), images of touch (tactile), images of taste (gustatory), images of smell (olfactory).

8. *Antithesis.* A form of comparison that lends color to the written word is sometimes compressed, and a graphic statement in which ideas are set off one against the other and in which opposites are brought close together is often effective. "A man is never so tall as when he stoops to help a little child."

The wise teacher knows that developing skill in expressive writing does not come easily. It is a gradual process. The creative idea should be put on paper as quickly as possible. However, as the child matures he discovers that much refinement and rewriting are necessary before he is ready to share his work with others.

Writing Stories

Ideas for writing stories come from many sources—from half-remembered experiences, from bits of conversation, from stories heard or read, from experiences real or imaginary. At times ideas erupt spontaneously. At other times they remain beneath the surface and refuse to come until someone has provided the stimulus.

Getting the Story Started

If the child knows what he wants to write, the teacher should step aside and let him write. However, for the child who is having difficulty, the effective teacher will have at hand a number of useful techniques to help him get started.

The idea box. Children respond readily to the "idea box". The teacher may need to provide the initial supply of ideas. The children should be encouraged to replenish the "idea box" before the list is exhausted. Sometimes a committee of children is chosen to gather, screen, and catalogue the ideas. Titles that "strike oil" are:

The Lonely Stegosaurus
Witches Brew
Fire! Fire!
Lost in a Storm
The Hidden Valley
A Falling Star
The Little Lost Bunny
A Bear in the Camp
The Biggest Fish I Ever Caught
The Man with Balloons
The Time I Almost Drowned
A Horse for Henry
First Prize for . . . .
The Bear that Couldn't Hibernate
The Missing Link
A Lucky Fall
An Exciting Discovery
The Time I was Rescued
The Tall Tale to End All Tales
The Night of the Big Blizzard
The Rescue at Sea
A Plane Crash
The Mysterious Box

Let's pretend. Children enjoy pretending to be someone or something and then telling what would happen if they were—a football, a tea kettle, an eyebrow, a tooth, a turtle, an airplane, a shoe. For the older children this leads naturally to imaginative writing relating to the historical past. Such suggestions as—If I were:

Travelling across the mountains in a covered wagon a hundred years ago
A rider for the Pony Express
A member of the Hudson Bay exploring party
A pioneer in the province in which I live
An astronaut
A cowboy on a drive to market
A hockey star who has a bad season
A pair of baby shoes

Sentence starters. Children of all ages enjoy sentence starters. As with the idea box, they should be encouraged to contribute. Older children should develop a file of their own. These sentence starters have been contributed by children.

If my ruler were only a magic wand I ....
The day I went to the moon I ....
On my last visit to the circus the lion ....
If I could go to any place in the universe I would ....
I feel proud when ....
I was walking along the beach at Point-No-Point when suddenly .
My hair stood on end as ....
Our entire house seemed to explode as ....
If I could have one wish I ....
If I were in Never-Never Land I ....
We never thought a stray puppy could cause such a rumpus. ....
Teddy Bear sat at the table slurping his ....
The hinge creaked behind me! ....
The old woman and the girl walked slowly up the street. ....

Phrases. Sometimes a phrase is all that is needed to get the story under way. Sometimes a single phrase will be given. Sometimes two or three will be given to be included somewhere in the story. Several exciting stories were based on these three phrases: "a twisted old tree", "faint blue hills", "a tumbled down shack".

Phrases that suggest moods for the stories are often helpful. Try the following suggestions.

Write a story using some of these phrases that give you a lonely feeling.

faint toot of an engine	empty and quiet
longing for the sight of someone	aching heart
sad and anxious eyes	homeless
shut in by towering trees	surrounded by stillness
lengthening purple shadows	steady downpour of rain
mirrorlike surface of the sea	disappointed sighing
on the shelf	landing at the airport in deep fog

Write a story using some of these phrases that give you a gay feeling.

flowers turning to the sun	white cottages freshly painted
wishes coming true	a rainbow bridge in the sky
squirrels scampering	boys whistling while fishing
a shining blanket of white snow	birds singing in the trees

Write a story using some of these phrases that give you a spooky feeling.

shutters banging back and forth	dark mysterious shadows
sudden hooting of an owl	round and smiling moon
sighing, sobbing wind	branches bending and groaning
creeping closer and closer	black and scary night
anxiously listening	listening and shivering
high, terrifying scream	strange, unusual footprints

Complete the story. Some children need more than phrases and ideas. If the actual story is started, they may find it easier to complete it.

> One evening I was walking through the jungles. I was all alone. The night had many noises. All of a sudden I came to a bend in the road and there I saw....................
>
> The night was still, broken only by shrill screeches of the owl. The black, shabby house looked forbidding in the pale moonlight. The leaves on the trees made eerie rustling sounds as a faint breeze blew in the night air. Suddenly I thought I heard ....
>
> Into the dark, cold den he crawled for the third time, slowly and painfully. On he crawled to the end of the cave where the great wolf was lying very still. Was she really dead or was she just stunned? He wondered if he dared approach any nearer. Cautiously he held the torch nearer her nose....................
>
> The King lay stretched in the warm sun on the east side of the cabin. At times he moaned. His legs jerked as he dreamed of rabbits racing through the tall grass. The Princess eyed him from the corner, then hobbled over, squatted down, and playfully whacked the King on the nose with her wooden leg....................

Story based on a picture. All teachers should have a file of pictures. At times a single picture may be shown and all children write stories inspired by the one picture. They enjoy hearing how each reacted to the one scene. At other times the children should be encouraged to find pictures of their own and write a story using the picture to illustrate it. For the children who do not have a source of pictures, the teacher may have a table or cupboard with magazines and catalogues that the children may cut up.

Developing the Story

After children have had some experience in writing stories, they will recognize the need for specific guidance in developing a story line. First of all, a story must have a beginning. Traditionally "once upon a time" was all that was needed to get the writer off to an exciting start. Today's children use a wide variety of starting sentences. The opening sentences should lead into the statement of the conflict or problem that requires a solution. Specific and interesting details are introduced and developed as the story moves to its climax. The problem is solved as a result of the climax. The ending should be brief. The writer should be helped to keep his focus on the climax and to refrain from introducing extraneous and/or superfluous details and incidents.

Evaluating the Story

In the initial story writing experiences at any grade level, the attention should be centered on the structure of stories, including such elements as an interesting beginning, a sequential development of ideas, a high point or climax, and an effective ending. As these basic elements are mastered, the child's attention should be directed to the novel ideas, ingenuity, and other personal and imaginative qualities. It is only when teachers themselves understand these additional qualities can they help the child evaluate his own writing.

There are several scales for rating written compositions which are helpful to the teacher and pupil in discussing and evaluating written expression. Yamamoto at the University of Minnesota issued a scale and scoring manual for evaluating imaginative stories. The Yamamoto scale has six major divisions to evaluate organization, sensitivity, originality, imagination, psychological insight, and richness. The illustrative subdivisions under various categories are useful to the teacher in planning the writing conference.[21]

Originality	*Imagination*	*Richness*
choice of topics	richness of imagination	expression
ideas	fantasy	ideas
organization	abstraction	emotion
style of writing	identification	curiosity
sense of humor	reasoning	fluency

A widely used scale is that developed by Torrance in what he called "Supplementary Scoring Guide for the Evaluation of Originality and Interest". Part I evaluates originality. Part II assesses the interest of imaginative stories.[22]

One point is awarded for each interest item that appears in an original story. Samples of stories are given in the Torrance Scale.

Carlson prepared an analytical originality scale as a part of a doctoral dissertation, *Stimulating Children in Grades Four, Five and Six to Write Original Stories*. The Carlson Originality Scale has five divisions: Story Structure, Novelty, Emotion, Individuality, Style of Stories.[23]

The creative teacher will use this scale to bring into focus some of the characteristics of creative writing in an individual writing conference with a child, *not as an effort to evaluate the child's writing*. It can well serve to teach children the difference between clichés and fresh, vivid writing. As Carlson points out, "Teachers in elementary and secondary schools, concerned with the mechanical elements of written expression, may fail to recognize unusual qualities of thought, style, and form.[24]

Developing Style in Writing

Each individual's writing is the expression of his personality, experience, and ability. Phrasing, tempo, content, and form determine his style. Just as the artist combines the elements of color, form, and design to personalize his conception into a visual creation, so does the writer use his materials to create his own inimitable work of art in written expression. "Style," says Lee, "is the significant contribution of the individual artist, whether his tools be the power of the word, the brush, or the sculptor's knife. We recognize the personal touch in athlete and artist alike. It is what gives him his color, his particular conformation. . . . It is the means by which the artist achieves an end. . . ."[25]

What the writer does with the elements unique to the process of writing creatively, what he does with the materials—the vocabulary, the words, and the ideas—and how he manipulates and shapes these determines his style.

It is within the province of the teacher to help the child to develop his own style, to become cognizant of the worth of his own expression, to be confident of the importance of what he has to say, and to develop skills as he needs them. Not limiting oneself to imitation, nor copying the manner in which another expresses his ideas, but becoming confident through increasing skills in using words contributes to successful writing. The teacher's manner, as well as his words, tells the child, "You have something to say. Say it in your own words—don't look to anyone else. Follow your own inner impulse."

Children should be encouraged to play with ideas, to choose topics for writing which appeal to them, and to experiment in finding new ways of expressing ideas, new relationships between ideas, and connecting links among experience, imagination and creative communication.

A perceptive teacher is ready to motivate, nurture, and guide children in their written expression. He maintains a fine balance between standing back and allowing the child to express his ideas and helping him develop the needed skills.

A perceptive teacher realizes when a child is in need of learning skills which will enable him to see relationships between experience, communication and the nature of the subject. He will help the child become familiar with such styles as narrative, historical, or argumentative.

The elements of composition must be mastered. As an artist masters color and design, as a dancer masters body and movement, as a musician masters form, harmony and melody, so the writer masters words and their ways. As the writer writes expressing himself in his own way, style becomes the outer clothing for his inner thoughts.

Evaluation of Written Expression

In considering evaluation of written expression, it is necessary to focus on evaluation of creative writing separately from expository writing. Each must be evaluated in terms of the purpose of the writing. The purpose of creative writing is artistic self-expression. Thus the focus of evaluation is the child. Strickland supports the idea of self-evaluation on the part of the child in writing. "It would appear that the key to good work may lie not in the standards the teacher sets for the children's writing, but in standards each child is helped to set for himself. . . .[26]

The teacher who is concerned with helping children become confident writers will begin with writing experiences which focus on what the child wishes to say and his purpose for saying it. As the child matures, he will discover that form is determined by the content. The content should be emphasized above the form while children are trying their wings in written expression. "It is impossible to correct or improve a child's expression until he offers enough of it to work with. When it is flowing as freely as he is capable of at the time, he is ready for help with form and correctness."[27]

Self-evaluation and self-confidence go hand-in-hand. If self-evaluation is to be meaningful, every child should have a folder in which he can keep his writing. This will enable him to see his own growth. It will also enable him to evaluate his own writing.

Questions the Child Asks Himself

As the child is growing in self-expression through writing with a teacher who helps him lift his sights without causing him to lose confidence, he assumes a large share of responsibility for evaluation of his own work and will in time become his own best critic. Some of the questions the child asks as he evaluates his work are:

> Did I say what I wanted to say—not approximately but as precisely as possible?
>
> Did the words run trippingly along with rhythm, grace, and spontaneity?
>
> Were the words blended with artistry, strength and finesse?
>
> Were the words briskly alive?
>
> Will they ignite the imagination of the listener and thrust him forward on a journey of adventure, anticipation and enjoyment?
>
> Did the writing communicate my feelings as well as my ideas?
>
> Did the style express my personality, *my* ideas, and *my* feelings?
>
> Will the listener recognize the style as my own?
>
> Did I show improvement in the use of the tools and techniques of writing?

Did the experience of creating with words bring me a feeling of exhilaration?

Did anyone else enjoy what I had written?

Periodically each child should be invited to bring his folder of creative writing to a conference with the teacher. This will include all the writing he may have done. The following questions may be used.

Questions for the Child and Teacher to Discuss in Conference

Do you feel that you said what you wanted to say?

Did you really know enough about your subject—either real or imagined experiences—to write about it?

Did your choice of words express your ideas clearly, vividly, and precisely?

For your stories were your plot structures clear and plausible?

Did you use imaginative, vivid language and appropriate rhythms in your poems?

Did you use imaginative structure (optic patterns)?[28]

Siamese Cat

Boisterous monkey
black - faced
black - eared

elegant
long
tailed
yet
how
mischievous
playful, daring
yet how faithfully
canine, more like
a puppy with its need for adoration

Did you use variety in sentence structure in your prose?

Have you any suggestions or questions about the mechanics and form?

Do you enjoy writing?

What are your next writing plans?

There are important questions, too, which the teacher must ask himself if he is to carry out the objectives of a creative writing program in the language arts curriculum.

Questions the Teacher May Ask Himself

Do I provide a climate for creative expression?

Do I recognize each child's need for creative expression in writing?

Do I allow freedom to create while at the same time provide the needed tools and techniques when the child requests them?

Do I provide time, encouragement, and opportunity for children to experience, discuss, and create through written expression?

Do I help each child establish a purpose for writing?

Do I share the child's enthusiasm when he brings me some of his writing?

Do I understand the difference between guiding creative writing and teaching the techniques of composition?

Do I point the way toward improving the writer's craft without destroying his creativity?

Do I help each child develop his own style of writing?

Do I allow children to become their own critics?

Do I occasionally share some of my own creative writing with them?

Do I make provision for sharing and publishing the works of children who are ready for this experience?

Do I tread a fine line between giving needed encouragement, recognition, and praise for the child to continue his creative efforts, and offering subtle suggestions and techniques for improvement to enable him to raise his sights in harmony with his growing needs and abilities?

Although self-evaluation and teacher evaluation are vital for the success of a creative writing program, they are not in themselves adequate. The total staff should be involved in the evaluation of the program.

Questions for the Staff About the Creative Writing Program in the School

Has the school as a whole established objectives for a long range creative writing program?

Are the objectives consistent with the socio-economic level of the community?

To what extent are we as a staff achieving our objectives?

Are there occasional staff conferences for the improvement of teaching creative writing?

Are there opportunities for action research in this curriculum area?

Are the parents kept informed of the purposes as well as the products of the creative writing program?

If the objectives of the creative writing program are to be met, evaluation must be comprehensive and continuous; it must focus on the individual—his needs, abilities, and interests—and it must be a cooperative enterprise. The entire school staff as well as the parents and the community should be concerned with evaluation. Children can have a part in setting up goals, in working together to achieve them, and finally in evaluating progress. When the child knows where he is going, what he is expected to do when he gets there, and how to judge whether he has accomplished what he set out to do, he is well on the way.

Concluding Statement

What makes the difference between writing that is spontaneous, sparkling and scintillating, and writing that is dreary, drab, and dull? How the child expresses his creativity in writing is dependent upon such factors as native capacity, degree of perception, ability to absorb, aptness in seeing relationships, fluency with words, aptitude for the miracle of words, and skill in portraying through written expression the images he sees in his mind's eye.

How the child expresses his creativity in writing is dependent, too, upon the skill and insight of the perceptive teacher. Such a teacher creates an environment of psychological safety in which children are free to express ideas; provides stimulating experiences; allows time to explore, experiment and create; supports children during the creative activity; provides them with the needed skills and tools; helps them in making words come alive; motivates them to become more aware, more perceptive, and more sensitive to people and phenomena; plans opportunities to share the writing products; and guides children in evaluating their own writing in terms of the goals they set for themselves.

The teacher must be aware of the phases of the creative process through which the child progresses as he moves from cognition to communication, and he must be there to give the needed encouragement and help. Creative writing, the teacher knows, is personal, individual, and imaginative.

The locus of evaluation is the student. Since the purpose of creative writing is artistic self-expression, evaluation must be based on the extent to which the child grows in his own ability to express his ideas in a manner satisfactory to him at any given point in his development.

When the child has had sufficient time to experiment, to explore, to create with words, he is ready to consider seriously the discipline of the writer—form. He becomes concerned with organization, style, and convention as well as invention in writing. Until he reaches this point through writing frequently and confidently, he is not ready for external evaluation.

Children vary as widely in linguistic development as they do in other phases of development. The perceptive teacher recognizes this and plans his writing program to meet individual differences. The spiral curriculum facilitates planning. At every level it is important to provide each child with freedom to invent before he becomes concerned with the conventions of the discipline.

Children differ; so will their experiences in writing. There are those who move quickly from experience to expression; there are others who need stimulation plus encouragement; and there are some who need motivation and direct help. Not all children will find in writing their favorite mode of creative expression. *But* every child can know to a degree the delight, that begins with curiosity and ends in wonder, of putting into words how he felt on that afternoon in the first storm of summer when he watched a dark cloud come from out of the west, cover the sun and send peals of thunder, shafts of lightning, and torrents of rain, where moments before he heard birds singing, saw clouds floating lazily across the sky as he lay on the velvet green grass. Such a child, in the final phase of creating, finds the communicating of his idea to another the capstone of the experience.

References

1. Ruth Kearney Carlson, "Sparkling and Spinning Words," *Elementary English* 41:55, January, 1964.
2. Lillian M. Logan and Virgil G. Logan, *Teaching the Elementary School Child,* Houghton Mifflin Company, Boston, 1961, p. 335.
3. Stephen Spender, "The Making of a Poem," in Brewster Ghiselin (ed.), *The Creative Process,* The American Library, New York, 1955, p. 121.
4. Sara Lowrey and Gertrude E. Johnson, *Interpretative Reading,* revised edition, Appleton-Century-Crofts, Inc., New York, 1953, pp. 26-59.
5. Clarence T. Simon, "Appreciation in Reading," in Gertrude Johnson (ed.), *Studies in the Art of Interpretation,* Appleton-Century-Crofts, Inc., New York, 1940, p 26.
6. Leland Jacobs, "Teaching Children More About Words and Their Ways," *Elementary English,* 41:33, January, 1964.
7. Wright Thomas and Stuart Gerry Brown, *Reading Poems,* Oxford University Press, New York, 1941, p. 746.
8. Lowrey and Johnson, *op. cit.,* pp. 20-1.
9. By permission from E. Paul Torrance, "Creative Thinking Through School Experience," in Sidney J. Parnes and Harold F. Harding (eds.), *A Source Book for Creative Thinking,* Charles Scribner's Sons, New York, 1962, p. 34.
10. H. Herbert Fox, "A Critique of Creativity in Science," in Myron A. Coler (ed.), *Essays on Creativity in Science,* New York University Press, New York, 1963, p. 133.
11. Lillian M. Logan, *Teaching the Young Child,* Houghton, Mifflin Company, Boston, 1960, pp. 332-4.
12. Winifred E. Taylor and Kenneth C. Hoedt, "The Effect of Praise Upon the Quality and Quantity of Creative Writing," *Journal of Educational Research,* 60:80-3, October, 1966.
13. Richard Doyle Biberstine, "Fourth Graders Do Write About Their Problems." *Elementary English,* 45:731-5, October, 1968.
14. *Kreative Writing,* Evansville Public Schools, Evansville, Indiana.
15. Mauree Applegate, *Easy in English,* Harper and Row Publishers Inc., New York, 1960, p. 262.
16. Adapted from Lillian M. Logan and Virgil G. Logan, *Design for Creative Teaching,* McGraw-Hill Ryerson Limited, Toronto, 1971, pp. 169-73.
17. Logan and Logan, *Teaching the Elementary School Child,* pp. 335-6.
18. Margaret S. Woods, *Thinking, Feeling, Experiencing: Toward Realization of Full Potential,* Department of Elementary-Kindergarten-Nursery Education, Washington, 1964, pp. 20, 21, 22. Reprinted with permission of the Department of Elementary-Kindergarten-Nursery Education and the author.

19. Walter W. Stevens, "Attention Through Language," *Today's Speech,* 11:23, November, 1963. A quote from *The Liberty of Man, Woman and Child.*
20. Mary Elizabeth Fowler, *Teaching Language, Composition and Literature,* McCraw-Hill Book Company, New York, 1965, pp. 54-5.
21. Ruth Kearney Carlson, "An Originality Story Scale," *The Elementary School Journal,* 65:366-371, April, 1965.
22. *Ibid.*
23. *Ibid.,* pp. 368-371.
24. *Ibid.,* p. 373.
25. Sherman E. Lee, *Japanese Decorative Style,* The Museum of Art, University Circle, Cleveland, 1961, p. 2.
26. By permission from Ruth Strickland, "Evaluating Children's Composition," *Children's Writing: Research in Composition and Related Skills,* National Council of Teachers of English, Champaign, 1961, p. 64.
27. *Ibid.*
28. Brian Powell, *English Through Poetry Writing,* Heinemann, London, 1970, p. 129.

8

Linguistics, Usage, and Grammar

Language is a tapestry of culture representing the people who use it and have made it.

Priscilla Tyler

Language is a social phenomenon, as well as a social institution. It serves to integrate cultures, to bind people together in a common approach to living. Language as structure confronts the students, as does language as process. How one views language influences what one does with language and how one uses language. Moulton views language as an abstract structure that is connected with concrete reality at two external ends. "At one end it is connected with sound—all the noises the speakers of a language make when they talk. At the other end it is connected with human experience—all the things the speakers of a language talk about when they use language. And language itself is the correlation between the two external ends."[1]

The linguist is a student of language as a science. Linguistics is defined by Lamb as the scientific study of language which involves the sounds of the language (phonology), the origin and changing meaning of words (etymology and semantics) and the arrangement of words in meaningful context in different languages (word order—syntax—structural or transformational grammar).[2]

A more comprehensive definition views linguistics as the "study of human speech: the units, structure, and modification of language, languages, or a language including especially such factors as phonetics, phonology, morphology, accent, syntax, semantics, general or philosophical grammar, and the relation between writing and speech."[3]

Guth defines linguistics concisely as "the study, according to rigorously defined methods or principles, of *language as a system*."[4]

Postman and Weingartner define linguistics in behavioral terms. "Linguistics is a way of behaving while one attempts to discover information and to acquire knowledge about language."[5]

This definition meets the criteria for creative learning. It emphasizes the inductive, creative approach to learning, a spirit of discovery, rejection of authoritarianism, and the creative process of problem solving. Children in the elementary school may well study linguistics if it is carried on in the spirit of inquiry and discovery.

Closely allied to the study of linguistics *per se* is the recent extension into language behavior and learning (*Psycholinguistics*), society and language (*Sociolinguistics*), and the more totally inclusive "study of mutual relationships between language behavior and other modes of human behavior"[6] (*Metalinguistics*).

One of the most important decisions to make is that of the role of linguistics in the modern elementary classroom. In the view of Fries, leading American linguist, it is not the techniques and tools of linguistics which have a place in the classroom but rather the knowledge derived by the teacher from linguistic study which should be assimilated and used "to shed new light upon the problems that arise wherever language is concerned."[7]

The effective teacher digests the information about linguistics, integrates the findings with his own understanding of language and children, and utilizes this knowledge in bringing children and language together in a more creative, meaningful way. Among the insights that a knowledge of linguistics brings to the teacher of creative communication are the following.

Everyone speaks his native language, to a degree, in his unique way with his particular resources for language. This is his idiolect.

Language is a creative activity of each individual.

Language has a present, a past, and a future.

Language is continually changing.

Language patterns are learned by the time a child is five or six.

The young child usually knows and uses all the basic structures of language.

Speech is the language; writing reflects speech.

The writing system or code of English is alphabetic and has certain inadequacies.

Language habits, once learned, change slowly.

Language varies with the age, sex, socio-economic group, and geographical region of the speaker. This is his dialect.

The concept of appropriateness has replaced the concept of "correctness". Alternatives appropriate to the situation in pronounciation, word choice, phrasing, and construction make language a more creative activity.

Objectives for Teaching about Language (Linguistics)

Statements of objectives are useful in planning and implementing programs of language which are geared to the needs of children in today's schools. A language program developed under the direction of Robert C. Pooley has as its major objectives: (a) to increase curiosity about language in general and the English language in particular, and (b) to help students use the English language more effectively. Principles of the program which have relevance for teachers are: (a) the development of language proficiency through a spiraling and sequential program of activities from kindergarten through grade twelve; (b) an eclectic approach to the teaching of grammar, and (c) acquisition of experience with language based on individual needs and abilities.

In kindergarten through grade six, it is anticipated that children should become aware of language processes through games, through observing word order in oral and written discourse, from practicing verb forms in sentence patterns, and so on.

In grades seven through nine, various concepts and generalizations from structural and transformational grammar are to be taught to the end that students learn to create varied sentences, in addition to acquiring the ability to classify words as parts of speech.

In grades ten through twelve, transformational grammar is to be used as the basis of sentence development to "achieve greater sophistication in syntactical structuring and manipulation commensurate with the varying abilities of high school students and the different grade levels."[8]

Another statement of objectives designed to aid children to discover the exciting vagaries of English language is directed specifically toward:

1. Displaying to children that English is primarily a word-order language, that the structure of English syntax is often of utmost importance;
2. Giving children an understanding of the sound (phonology) of the language, its music;
3. Giving them an understanding of the language's historical dimensions (where our vocabulary came from, etc.) and of the evolution of its spelling system, understandings so important not only to spelling, but to reading; and
4. Giving them an understanding of the extent to which punctuation is a written representation of the suprasegmental features of spoken discourse.[9]

In planning activities in communication in the elementary school today, it is important to keep in mind such objectives of *creative* communication as the total development of the child, the role of language in helping the child attain his creative potential, and the extent to which a specific activity will contribute toward a greater appreciation of language.

The following chart identifies the respective roles of linguists and teachers.[10]

The Linguists:	*The Teachers:*
Describe how a language works by establishing its grammar. This is done through analysis.	Help children to use language to communicate ideas. Analysis is done to improve usage.
Study dialects and record unique expressions.	Help children to practice a dialect approved by the culture of a community.
Are concerned with the meanings of words and expressions.	Are concerned with the experiences of a child that give meaning to expression.
Are objective about words. "The word is not the thing." "The map is not the country."	Recognize the emotional tones of words and expressions in terms of the social forces of the community which determine their acceptance.

	The teacher is a social agent working to help children become participating members of society.
Are concerned with the means of decoding and encoding the language.	Are concerned with the appreciation and attitudes that poetry and stories will develop in the learner. The content of literature is the focus of interest.
Relate the problems of multilingual children in terms of language contrast.	Respect the individual background and needs of children, but accept a predetermined goal as the one to achieve.
Write dictionaries, create pronunciation keys, define words, and collect examples of usage.	Help children to use the dictionary to check standard spelling, pronunciation, and meaning of words.

The perceptive teacher recognizes linguistics as an integral part of creative communication. For example, as early as the primary level "creating with words" is exciting to children and provides legitimate opportunities to teach about speech sounds, pitch, intonation, and stress, as the need arises. At both primary and intermediate levels, attention can be given to rising and falling inflections in literature children read aloud. At every level children are interested in forms of words. They are quick to detect physical differences in written symbols, as well as meaning elements in word form changes, as in tall, taller, tallest, girl-girls, go-going.

The history of language is fascinating to all children. For example, in kindergarten children enjoy saying nursery rhymes and noting the words which are fun to say, but literally have no meaning in today's world. "Little Miss Muffet Sat on a Tuffet" is one such rhyme. Intermediate children naturally study the origin of words in greater depth. The study of dialects, too, has great appeal at all levels. Some of the more interesting stories for primary children involve characters having varied social dialects. Observing and comparing dialects in literature offers a challenge and a basis for identification.

In composition children enjoy rearranging sentences to clarify meaning, to eliminate unnecessary words, and just for fun.

Linguistics: Language Explorations in the Elementary Grades

Some activities for language explorations in the elementary grades follow.

The Nature of Language

Playing around with words—rhyming, onomatopoeia, trying out new words, creating new words—presents opportunities to teach distinctive speech sounds, pitch, and stress.

Practice creative reading in which emphasis is placed on expressive reading utilizing rising and falling inflections to provide a realistic interpretation.

Discover that words are added to a language as the need arises. Discover that there are patterns in the language, both in words and sentences. Discover that words have different meanings, and that the meaning is clear only when they appear with other words which express a thought.

Listen to stories which emphasize different dialects. Listen to the story "The Little Island" and discuss human and non-human communication, verbal and non-verbal communication.

Compare words such as Mother and Father as they appear in languages other than their own, i.e., *Madre, Mutter, Padre, Vater.*

Read the story "Mr. Popper's Penguins"; reread the parts which include the penguin sounds. Discuss the degree to which they are similar to human sounds.

Experiment with non-verbal signals—use gestures which other cultures used. Pantomime ways of communicating which would be understood in other parts of the world and in other times; for example, "Come here"—finger in beckoning motion, "Keep quiet"—finger on lips, "No good"—thumb pointed down from closed fist.

Discuss the priority of oral language.

Discover pairs of words and note the difference in spelling.

color	honor	airplane	recognize	(U.S.)
colour	honour	aeroplane	recognise	(British)

In each case, the words are pronounced alike, but the spelling is different.

Phonology[11]

Phonemes—alliteration. Listen to "How the Rhinoceros Got His Skin" or "The Elephant's Child". Think of a color. Then think of something that begins with the same sound. Next add an action word beginning with the same sound. Pantomime the action word; for example, red rabbit runs. Try the same idea using numbers; six soldiers sat.

Phonemes—minimal pairs. Listen to "The Town Mouse and the Country Mouse". Supply rhymes for key words.

mouse	*mice*	*cat*	*dog*	*town*
house	nice	rat	frog	clown
louse	rice	hat	hog	brown

Develop sentences using many words beginning with the same sound. *The cute clever country cat caught his cap.*

Make up rhymes containing riddles.

I rhyme with boy.
You play with me.
What am I? (toy)

I rhyme with now.
A dog says this.
What am I? (Bow-wow)

Intonation. Listen to "Millions of Cats". Identify the stress patterns as in "*Hun*dreds of cats, *thou*sands of cats, *mil*lions and *bil*lions and *tril*lions of cats." Create new refrains with similar patterns of strong stress.

Morphology

Look through a favorite story to discover ways to form plurals. Write a story in which both singular and plural forms of words are used. Find examples of inflected verbs ending with *-ed* from a favorite story. Discuss the words with suffixes as to (1) ways in which they are alike, and (2) the meaning of -ed.

tied to a leash

climbed up on his mother's lap

Jimmie was *worried*

Tom and Jim *looked* at each other . .

Discover variant ways of forming plurals in English.

man	men
horn	horns
cattle	cattle
ox	oxen

Analyze the formations of words such as the following.

word	*root*	*meaning*
inscribe	scribe	to write
scriptorium	script	room for writing

Discuss and illustrate the way words in our language are formed by the use of *affixes, prefixes,* and *suffixes.* Select examples from literature and from one's own writing. Practice use of singular and plural forms, verb tenses, and sentence patterns provided by the teacher. Create games in which specific word forms, etc., are required.

Syntax

Sentence openers. Complete sentences using the following words as the first word in the sentence. (Simple adverbs)

Later	Hastily	Again	Firmly	Swiftly
Jokingly	Earlier	Previously	Briskly	Quickly
Slowly	Simply	Surely	Sweetly	Sourly

Complete sentences using these phrases as the first words in the sentence. (Adverbial phrases)

On the moon	Above the earth	Back at the ranch
By the car	Beyond his reach	Under the saddle
Across the ravine	At the beach	Beneath the tomb

Complete sentences using double adverbial phrases as sentence openers.

Beneath the tomb behind the old house

In the tree on the topmost branch

On the beach by the water's edge

Compose a sentence opener selecting one of the above types of construction and write a story in which you develop an appropriate theme.

Practice four techniques in revising sentence structure: changing, shifting, cutting, and adding.

History of the English Language

Middle English. Notice the words that are obsolete.

Read *Robin Hood.*

Listen to nursery rhymes.

Discuss the changing nature of language which is apparent as it reflects the attempt at "Middle English" flavoring.

Discuss the way in which people received their names from their trades, the locale in which they lived, etc.

Discuss what children in modern times might have as names if they were named for the kind of work they might do, where they were born, etc.

Read *King Arthur and His Knights of the Round Table.*

Notice the way the English language is changing. Discover words in common use in the Middle English period which are no longer in use.

Discuss differences in vocabulary and morphology of Middle and Modern English.

Find the origin of the root words of communication and civilization.

Write the word used chiefly by the British to name a two-week period of time which comes from the phrase *fourteen nights.*

Spelling of Words

Compare the spelling of certain words in the King James Version of the Bible and in a modern translation.

Make a chart showing changes in spelling of certain words.

List words as they appeared in Middle English.

shewe	—	show	fayn	—	fain
certayn	—	certain	wolde	—	would
wryton	—	written	satisfye	—	satisfy
doo	—	do			

Trace origin of words which give trouble in spelling.

Look for use of words in advertising displaying creative spelling.

nite	—	night
thru	—	through
eze	—	easy
show biz	—	show business
kreme	—	cream

Dialect

Take a poll to discover if any one in the class has moved recently from another area of the country.

Mark out "home towns" with colored flags on a large map.

Listen to and write stories using various dialects.

Read stories containing dialect such as the Uncle Remus stories.

Prepare stories having dialect to share in oral reading or readers' theater.

Substitute other words (or other dialect words, if possible) for the dialect words in passages from *The Wind in the Willows.*

Locate social and geographical dialects in passages and practice reading them aloud.

Rewrite passages containing dialect in your own style.

Look up unfamiliar words to see if they are in a standard dictionary and still in common use.

What Research Says to the Teacher About Grammar and Usage

Grammar

Some confusion still exists in understanding the terms grammar, usage, and linguistics. A study of current literature indicates that what is usually termed *linguistics* by educators refers to *grammar* (the study of the structure and operations of language). Usage is thought of as inseparable from grammar by teachers of English. Quisenberry asserts, "This marriage of terms, a shotgun wedding at best, was annulled by linguistic science."[12]

Research has clarified the distinction between grammar and usage, Loban[13], Strickland[14], and Goba[15] concur that *grammar* pertains to the linguistic processes involved in human communication, while *usage* pertains to a given dialect in a given social setting. Pooley further clarifies the distinction as he states: "Grammar and usage are not synonymous. Every language has its own grammar. Usage is to grammar what etiquette is to behavior. Behavior simply notes what people do, etiquette sets a stamp of approval or disapproval upon actions, or sets up standards to guide actions."[16]

Sherwin[17] generalized that instruction in formal grammar results in little, if any, improvement in language skills (as measured in the writing produced).

Blake and Hammill[18] found no conclusive support for teaching grammar at the elementary level. Melon[19] found no valid research supporting formal grammar instruction.

Bateman and Zidonis, however, concluded that high school students at the tenth grade level were able to learn the principles of generative grammar fairly easily. Work with generative grammar enables the students to increase significantly the proportion of well formed sentences that are of greater than average structural complexity. A knowledge of generative grammar could enable students to reduce errors in writing.[20]

Usage

Marcus[21] reports on research carried out with children of non-standard dialects focusing on the communication problems arising between teacher and the child. In answer to two questions, "If a car ran over your pet, how would you feel?" and "If you could be a policeman or a fireman what would you choose?", all the speakers of "standard" English answered, "bad" and "policeman/fireman" respectively. But with the disadvantaged group children answered "good" and "gum" respectively. The preliminary analysis is that, although every child was familiar with all the words involved in these questions, the "if . . . how . . ." or "if . . . what . . ." type of grammatical structure was not shared by a great number of the children. Hence, they apparently salvaged "How do you *feel?*" and "What do you *chew?*" from the questions that were asked.

Baratz[22] reports on the value of the use of materials written in the dialect of black students in teaching reading. Labov[23] questions the idea that ghetto children are in any way "verbally deprived" and strikes hard at the position taken by Bereiter and Engelmann,[24] Jensen,[25] and others that these children are verbally inarticulate.

McDavid[26] takes a different route. From work done on *The Linguistic Atlas of the United States and Canada,* he draws pertinent samples of dialectual differences in expressions, pronunciation, and grammar, pointing out that, according to various sources of cultural history, regional and non-standard dialects , far from being "degenerate versions" of some ideal standard language, are rather one of "many varieties of standard American English".

Hernandez and Johnson[27] determined from their study of employer interviews that the most significant personal characteristic that limits a young person's chance for employment is the inability to communicate either orally or in writing.

Loban advises, "Whether we like it or not, children who speak a social class dialect need the opportunity to learn standard usage if they are ever to be free to choose whether or not they will use it."[28]

Implications of Research

Implications of research for the classroom teacher indicate that there must be pre-service practical training in linguistics for any teacher dealing with language and language problems, as well as in-service training for the teachers without such prior training. Teachers must proceed on the principle of adding standard English to the dialect of students whose speech reflects economic disadvantage. Teachers need not become dialectalogists. They should, however, be able to discern sounds independently of letters. For example there is a dʒh sound at the beginning of judge, and there is no /h/ sound in *this,* and the final sound in *missed* is /t/ not /d/.

It is not enough to teach the learner to respond automatically to predetermined stimuli; language instruction must lead to creative communication in new situations.

Language can be acquired by active listening (listening and doing) even more successfully than by listening and repeating.

Programmed language instruction not motivated by a meaningful goal will have limited results. Knowledge of the learner's native language or social dialect will help the teacher plan a meaningful program of instruction.

It is not enough to learn a language *per se*; one also needs to learn how to use it. Language use is closely allied to political, historical, religious, cultural, and economic factors.

Individuals tend to learn a language of high status rather than one of low status.

Presentation of material should encourage discovery and inquiry in the formulation of rules rather than memorization of specific items.

Teachers should become familiar with the terminology of usage, guidelines for teaching usage, and some promising practices in teaching usage effectively.

The way to teach usage is through the oral approach in a meaningful context.

The teacher should be open to innovation in teaching usage, and experiment in new ways of helping children use language.

Terms of Usage

In order to teach and use grammar, spoken and written, a knowledge of the terminology is essential.

Language. Language as used by the linguist refers to speech and its recorded forms. Written language is an attempt to record in a series of written symbols, the stream of sound shaped by the inhabitants of a specific culture.

Grammar. Grammar is the study of the structure and function of the sentence: parts of speech; subject, verb, object, etc.; case, gender, mood, voice, etc.; sentence, phrase, clause; and associated matters of consonance and agreement. Excluded are the mechanics of writing and problems of usage not related to structure. Terminology varies with different approaches to the teaching of English. Pooley distinguishes grammar as an inventory of the choices open to the user of the language.[29]

Standard English. Standard English is the dialect of educated speakers, those prominent in business and in public and cultural affairs of the community. Standard English is ". . . the English that with respect to spelling, grammar, pronunciation, and vocabulary is substantially uniform though not devoid of regional differences, that is well-established by usage in the formal and informal speech and writing of the educated, and that is widely recognized and acceptable wherever English is spoken and understood."[30]

Good English. "Good English is that form of speech which is appropriate to the purpose of the speaker, true to the language as it is, and comfortable to speaker and listener. It is the product of custom, neither cramped by rule nor freed from all restraint; it is never fixed, but changes with the organized life of the language."[31]

Usage. Usage is ". . . the term employed to cover the full range of choices and discrimination in the use of language. Usage makes choices, expresses preferences, takes sides, creates standards. The bases upon which choices are made, preferences are expressed, sides are taken, and standards are set up is the concern of usage."[32]

In a later publication Pooley reiterates,

> I am willing to stand upon this definition still. Usage is to grammar as etiquette is to behavior. Behavior simply notes what people do, etiquette sets a stamp of approval or disapproval upon actions, or sets up standards to guide actions. The specific business of usage, therefore, is to determine what choices and what discriminations are made in the use of English, and then to analyze the forces, social and psychological, which determine the choices. In practical terms, usage is the study which notes the variety of choices made in the use of English, observes the standards set up by such choices or created to influence such choices, and attempts to evaluate the validity of such standards.[33]

Usage is the way people use language. Correction thus becomes a matter of helping children become aware of and sensitive to social acceptability and appropriateness, much as one teaches a boy to remove his hat in church and a little child to say "Please" and "Thank you".

Colloquial usage. "Colloquial, properly interpreted, is a label indicating a functional variety, not a level of the language, nor was the term, as used by lexicographers, ever intended as a condemnation."[34]

That teachers too frequently interpret colloquial as substandard usage is evidenced in the following passage.

> Even teachers of English frequently misunderstand the application of the label *colloquial* in our best dictionaries. Some confuse it with *localism* and think of the words and constructions marked "colloquial" as characteristic of a particular locality. Others feel that some stigma attaches to the label "colloquial" and would strive to avoid as incorrect (or as of a low level) all words so marked.[35]

Nonstandard usage. Nonstandard usage is common in certain locales and socio-economic levels. English language varies in word choice from the "middle class" to the culturally disadvantaged group in the community where words such as "drownded" and "his-self" might be used. Nonstandard usage calls attention to the speaker's lack of education; for this reason it is the chief concern for the teacher in the program of improvement of usage.

Disputed usage. Disputed usage includes ". . . the items of language use which are widely current, which are often heard in public speech and frequently appear in print, yet are condemned by many textbooks and are disliked by conservative teachers, editors, and other language-conscious people."[36]

Guidelines for Teaching Usage

The teacher who is alert to the child's growing need of language and the grip habit has on his communication will appreciate the incident of the child who began eagerly to tell his mother, "Me and Jimmy went to the store to see if they had a pumpkin." "Jimmy and I," corrected his mother. Painfully he started again, "Me and Jimmy went to the store to. . . ." "Jimmy and I went to the store," interrupted his Mother again. This was too much for the child to bear, and he shouted in protest, "But Mother you weren't even there."

The pattern of language usage is deeply ingrained by the time the child enters school; and, unless the teacher is skillful in redirecting some of the most appalling errors, it is doubtful if much progress will be made. The teacher should keep in mind the statement by Labov that "despite the obvious surface differences between the standard and nonstandard, they are both based upon the same deep structures and are used to convey the same underlying logical propositions. From a linguistic point of view, this seems well established."[37] It is possible however, to guide children in language learning, which helps them succeed in communicating ideas under varied circumstances.

The purpose of language is effective communication. With that as the criterion, the following suggestions are pertinent in teaching usage.

Stimulate the student to explore the variety of ways in which one can express the same idea.

Find ways of expressing an idea in patterns of formal, colloquial, and nonstandard usage.

Lead the student to discover the various levels of expression used in literature to establish a *tone* or mood.

Help the student to become sensitive to the appropriate level of usage in specific situations.

Help the student develop appreciation of the shades of language usage. In society, the well mannered person is the one who is sensitive to all aspects of a society and behaves in a way that is appropriate to the specific situation: formal when it is appropriate, informal when it is desirable, and familiar when acceptable. English usage is exactly the same; "to say the right thing in the appropriate manner in a suitable tone of expression is the ideal for which we are striving."[38]

Teach the use of the dictionary and handbooks in mastering acceptable usage. Acceptable usage must be substituted for nonstandard usage as the child is motivated to change. Before a change occurs, the child must see a purpose for the change. He must be motivated *before* he will make the effort.

Set an example of socially acceptable usage, and gear the teaching to the needs, abilities, and linguistic level of the students. The method of ear training in usage is more effective than merely correcting the student's written work, for the errors in written usage are the reflection of unconsciously retained speech patterns.

Children bring to school a wide assortment of speech habits and patterns of usage. Those from homes where cultural speech is an integral part of the environment, where usage errors have been corrected since infancy, will need little direct teaching. Others, less fortunate in background, bring to school patterns which differ.

Utilize the native spirit of linguistic play in teaching children the skills of literacy. Capitalize on the tendency of children to learn the language freely and creatively, enjoying the game they make of mastering a complex language system.

Stimulate interest in words and phrases, apt expressions, and an appreciation of the fitness of words in a particular context.

Encourage self-evaluation of progress in usage as in other areas of the language arts program.

Usage should be an integral part of a broad program in creative communication. The teacher should provide opportunities for usage in a functional setting rather than in an artificial, isolated drill situation.

Aid the child whose dialect restricts his communication process to expand his linguistic skills so that he gains a larger measure of control over his social environment.

Refrain from instant correction and incessant criticism of every so-called mistake in usage in the child's speech, reading, and writing.

Remember to help children shift gears in language, to tailor the language to suit the occasion, and to use language to communicate effectively, expressively and creatively.

Persistent Problems in Teaching Usage

How Should Language be Classified?

Whether one attempts to classify language usage by *levels* (formal, standard, colloquial, nonstandard, disputed, and/or illiterate) or by *labels* (standard and nonstandard, good and bad, correct and incorrect), many of the same problems still persist. One cannot escape the fact that usage is associated with socio-economic groups. Children must be taught to see that there is a standard language used in formal public communication. The informal playground communication is acceptable for that occasion. But what is acceptable in an informal discussion in the classroom may be inappropriate in a formal presentation, either oral or written. In formal communication activities in the classroom, normally one expects standard English or what has been termed *prestigious* dialect of the educated people of the community. Even with standard English there is considerable latitude. Children have a right to know what is expected of them in the classroom setting.

What Usage Should be Taught?

Pooley has consistently held that current social acceptability is the criterion for standard usage. It is the teacher's responsibility to help each child to develop the ability to select the appropriate usage for the situation. This provides him with the power of choice to decide for himself what usage is appropriate on the basis of (1) the purpose of the communication, (2) the meaning he wishes to communicate, and (3) the effect he desires the communication to produce.

What Usage Items Should be Taught?

Each school should establish the minimum acceptable level of usage in each educational level. To aid the staff in deciding what usages may need direct instruction, the following list of problem items is suggested.[39]

ain't or *hain't*
yourn, hern, ourn
hisen, theys
youse
onct
hisself, theirselves
hair *are*
a orange
have *ate*
they *eats*
was *broke*
he *brung*
he *come*
clumb
had or have *did*
she or he *don't*
it *don't*
didn't ought
hadn't ought
he *give,* he *walk*
my brother. *he*
her and *me* went
there *is* four
there *was* four
they *knowed*
if they *growed*
haven't *no,* isn't *no*
leave for *let*
haven't *nothing*
that's *mines*
where *it at?*
where is she *at?*
he *run*
have *saw*
I *says*
he *seen*
them books
this here
that there
us boys went
we, you, they *was*
with *we* girls
have *went*
have *wrote*
the *mens*
learn me a song
me and Mary went
she *taken*
I *likes* him
I *drunk, drunks*
can't hardly
does we have

Obviously, it is important that the teachers within the school plan together on a minimum number of items from the list to be emphasized at a particular educational level. Decisions should be made on the basis of the need of the children to communicate effectively at their particular developmental level or stage. No teacher should deprive children of creative experiences in order to concentrate unduly on the usage aspect. Concentrated attention should be given to those items which are the most glaring errors in terms of the particular community, rather than in terms of the particular teacher!

What Should We Do About Slang?

"At its best, a slang expression can be vivid, racy, euphonious, and apt; when fresh and spontaneous, it can add sparkle and wit to a conversation or to a written article. At its worst, it is dull, lazy language, vague in meaning, repetitious, trite, pretentious—even offensive and rude."[40]

Slang is used as a symbol of belonging, a means of creating a language which only the "in-group" can interpret. It is popular among teenagers who are feeling the importance of the group to a marked degree, and make use of slang to shock, to hide insecurities, to provide feelings of intimacy and belonging.

However, even among teenagers, the creative speaker or writer tries to express his ideas in the most meaningful, the most creative, the most communicable language. He selects judiciously, as an artist selects from his palette, the precise, the concise, the vivid, the colorful words that serve best from all the resources the language has to offer.

Some valuable suggestions for the elementary grades come from Sybil Shack[41] as she suggests the children discuss the topic of slang.

> They read the following sentences and select the words and phrases which until recently have been categorized as slang, but now have become a part of the acceptable language.
>
> 1. The musicians played jazz far into the night.

2. The wild-cat well brought in millions of gallons of oil.
3. The tight-rope walker did many daring stunts under the big top.

Answers: 1. jazz, 2. wild-cat, 3. stunt and big top.

Children are invited to do the following.

1. React to the question "Do you think slang is interesting? Why or why not?"
2. Make a list of slang expressions you use, then tell why you use them.
3. Ask adults what slang terms they used when they were growing up. How do you regard these slang expressions?

One of the persistent problems middle-class teachers have in teaching the so-called culturally deprived child is the dilemma of teaching standard English to children whose dialect is discovered to be functioning as a primary language. The following illustration of a teacher in an elementary school in a disadvantaged area is a case in point.

> One day after class, as she was putting her hat on to leave for the day, one of her students approached her with the compliment, "That's sure a tough hat you got on."
>
> The teacher, who had heard enough "Hip" spoken among her charges, tried the time-honored approach to correcting the boy: "Don't say tough, say pretty or nice." The boy thought about that for a moment, then concluded: "Okay, but that pretty hat sure is tough."
>
> That might have been the end of this particular story except that this particular teacher also gave some thought to the exchange.
>
> First, she realized that she had come up against a case of linguistic inversion—a social situation in which a dialect was the primary language.
>
> Second, and most important, the teacher recognized that by attempting to correct her student's speech in the conventional way, she had confused him about the nature of the avowed teaching objective. Worse, she had antagonized him. To the student's mind, the teacher had been asking him, not so much to learn something, but to reject something—his primary language, the slang, the non-standard "Hip" spoken in his home, among his friends and neighbors. The result was hostility—determination by the student to *not* learn—expressed, with just the necessary touch of humor, in the put-down phrase, ". . . that pretty hat sure is tough."
>
> In short, this teacher had hit on a truth fundamental to the fact of language: One's primary language, because it is primary, is not to be denied lightly, for it is, in very basic ways, one's own self. Asking the disadvantaged child to suppress the language he brings to the learning situation is equivalent to demanding that he suppress his identity, and all the defenses that go with it. . . .[42]

Once this teacher was aware of the truth, she took a new approach to teaching standard English. She made a game of it, the *Dialect Game.* She asked the students to explain the meaning of a word heard frequently in their vocabulary—in *their* language. Then she proceeded to ask them how to explain "cool" in the language heard on TV.

Some of the answers she received were "calm", "casual", "collected", to which she added the more formal "nonchalant".

As a result of this new approach, the students who had previously gone to sleep during English classes became interested. They became aware that they were playing a game—"digging the teacher's jive".

As a consequence, they increased their vocabulary and found new ways of expression in a context which did not demand rejection of their own language. In short, they were learning standard English as they might learn a foreign language, a second language. As they continued this approach to language, they learned about language itself: its forms and the social role language plays. By approaching standard English as a foreign language, they became aware of the untranslatability of much of the language *per se*. They discovered the reason for incorporating foreign phrases intact, without translation, for example *esprit de corps, coup d'etat*. They discovered, too, that many of the "Hip" words and phrases that make up their primary language have been accepted for usage in standard English conversation. "Knowing this, they were in a position to equip themselves with a basic sense of linguistics style, which can be simply defined as the ability to choose among words and phrases according to their social appropriateness."[43]

Basic to such an approach to the student's primary language is the acceptance by the teacher of the student's nonstandard language. He utilizes it as an avenue to that other language which, in more formal circumstances, can produce more effective communication and gain for the student entrance into a wider society.

Thus the teacher takes the child *as* he is, *where* he is, and *builds* on what he brings to the classroom with him. He does not *take away from* the pupil. Under such an approach the student's sense of identity, his self-concept, and his sense of language—all language—grow. This is the beginning of a love of language and its literary form.

The problem of teaching culturally different youth in the English class is not different in kind from that of teaching other students; it is different in degree, and therefore more visible. Long before "disadvantaged", "culturally different", "deprived" youth came to be regarded as a special problem, Parker, a member of the Quincy, Massachussetts School Board, wrote this report in 1873. "The pupils could parse and construe sentences and point out the various parts of speech with great facility, repeating the rules of grammar applicable in each case, yet were utterly unable to put this theoretical knowledge to any practical use."[44]

Unless they are led to discover the need for expressing themselves in and through language, to fulfill a purpose which is meaningful to them, the culturally different are prone to reject help.

The Culturally Different Child

What the Teacher Should Know

The culturally different child equates rejection of his language with rejection of himself.

Regional dialect is closely tied to political, cultural, religious, and economic factors.

Every child should be given an opportunity to learn standard usage in order to be free to select the appropriate usage for the situation.

The teacher is responsible for helping each child see his need for extending his range of dialects.

Learning experiences should motivate inquiry, exploration, and discovery of generalizations.

Learning a second language or a new dialect usually involves a shift of allegiance from one's own group.

The culturally different child has difficulty in conceptualizing in the new dialect.

When talking with their children in the standard dialect, parents of culturally different children tend to use a "restricted" code, in contrast to the more extensive one used by middle-class parents. This limits the child's linguistic background to short, simple sentences, little use of subordinate clauses, limited use of adjectives and adverbs, and illogical statements containing few specific referrents, with the speaker taking for granted that the listener will "fill in" between the lines spoken.

Procedures Which Aid the Culturally Different

Act as an agent for social change in order to help the child discover that there are concepts and skills of communication which he must master in order to survive in a verbal world.

Select content which is relevant in terms of the locale in which he lives.

Utilize the principles of discovery and multi-sensory stimuli to motivate creativity in language. Make use of concrete objects, reinforced by media, and first hand experiences in a process-oriented curriculum.

Vary the learning experiences to provide the element of surprise, in place of routines which can be stultifying.

Utilize external rewards. The culturally different child is greatly encouraged by both intrinsic and extrinsic reinforcement and by immediate feedback. (This accounts for success in using programmed instruction with some of these pupils.)

Plan functional situations in which language learning is an integral part.

Provide the culturally different child with experiences in literature with which he can identify as well as literature which involves a dialect which is foreign to him.

Limit the number of usage items to be mastered in a given period.

Vary both the activities and the organization of the group.

Provide opportunities for communicating through non-verbal modes of expression: painting, drawing, sculpting, pantomiming, rhythm, dance and movement. Often children develop facility in creative verbal communication *after* they have experienced success in expression through non-verbal language. They are then more favorably inclined toward expanding the language skills they possess.

Approaches to Teaching Grammar

Although attitudes toward teaching formal grammar in the elementary school are changing, this does not relieve the teacher of the responsibility for extending his own knowledge of the various aspects of language. The more he knows about linguistics, grammar, and usage, the better equipped he is to help children use language purposefully. According to Marckwardt, "The impact of linguistics is likely to be greater in terms of the way the teacher and the textbook writer think about language than in any other specific body of procedural gimmickry."[45]

The teacher's language background is certain to be reflected in his every-day experiences in language with the children he teaches. He should keep abreast of what is happening in the field of linguistics. He should be knowledgeable about the concepts, methods, and teaching stategies involved in traditional, structural, and generative grammars, not because he is to teach them *per se,* but because they should be a part of his educational background and general knowledge. He should be familiar with effective ways of teaching usage. Emphasis will be on usage, which is the result of an understanding of the what, why, and how of language, not the memorization of rules found in the textbook.

Teachers who approach language with the spirit of exploration will discover that both they and their students find language exciting, exhilarating, and challenging. The teaching of language today requires the mastery of new terms, concepts, and methods.

Terms Used in the Study of Grammar

Grammar. Grammar is the study of the structure of the language. It involves the study of the sentence—what it consists of, how it patterns for clear communication, and what signals are necessary to convey intended meanings. Grammar is the behavior, not the etiquette, of the language. It includes three main branches: morphology, syntax, and phonology.

Morphology. Morphology is the study and description of the formation of words. It includes inflection, derivation, and compounding. For example, the addition of *s* to form the plural of most English nouns or the *ed* suffix showing past tense of verbs.

Morpheme. A morpheme is the smallest portion of an utterance that expresses meaning.

Syntax. Syntax is a study of word order in meaningful communication, and ways in which words are arranged to form sentences. This involves the study of the variety of sentence structure, modification and subordination of words and phrases, clauses and independent elements.

Phonology. Phonology is the study of the sound system of a language, of the stresses, pauses, intonations and the melody of speech.

Phonetics. Phonetics is the systematic study of the sounds of a language.

Phoneme. A phoneme is a group of similar sounds distinctively different from any other group of sounds. For example the "t" sound in *not, button,* and *tap* varies in each word, but is recognized as a "t" sound.

Allophone. The allophone is a submember of a phoneme. It is the term applied to the variations such as the variations in the utterance of the "t" sound in the example above.

Grapheme. A grapheme is a single letter or combination of letters that represent a phoneme, e.g., the grapheme "gh" of *hiccough* represents the phoneme (sound) "p". It could be the "d" in the word *day* or the"ay" which represents the phoneme (sound) "a".

The purpose of the study of grammar is improved communication by a careful consideration of the ways in which ideas may be structured within a sentence. Thus evaluation becomes the measurement for testing the ability to structure ideas into a sentence in a way which improves communication of ideas. To teach coordination, subordination, order, and modification requires some simple machinery—the basic sentence elements: subject, verb, modifier, connective, phrase, subordinate clause, and main clause.

Traditional grammar. The traditional grammar (often called formal grammar) is well known to English teachers. This grammar is an analysis of the language according to classifications and definitions based on Latin grammar and formulated in the Middle Ages and the Renaissance to meet the needs of scholars concerned with the study of classical languages rather than of the vernacular. Largely *prescriptive,* traditional grammar presents rules and regulations as to the correct way words should be used. The new grammars in contrast are descriptive; they formulate generalizations about language on the basis of its use and describe the way it works.

Structural grammar. Structural grammar analyzes the living spoken language to ascertain the basic structure of English sentences, the stress and intonation patterns which signal meaning, and the words which operate as signals to indicate parts of speech.

Transformational or generative grammar. Transformational or generative grammar, as it is often called, has been claimed to be the most significant development in linguistics in the past thirty years. Generative grammarians assert that if preschool children of limited intelligence can generate thousands of new sentences based on the early sentence structures they have learned, there must be an underlying process which can be explained and taught. Basically, transformational grammar makes clear those relationships that the native speaker of a language perceives intuitively.

Roberts identifies elements of transformational grammar thus: "*Kernal sentences* are the basic, elementary sentences of the language, the stuff from which all else is made. *Transforms* are the 'all else' structures drawn from the kernal to produce all the complications of English sentences."[46]

Methods in Teaching Grammar

In the past, grammar has too often been taught as a body of incomprehensible rules handed down with authority to be learned without question and often with a minimum of explanation. This is no longer adequate. Today's emphasis on inquiry should arouse the student's curiosity about his language and how it functions. However, this requires a change in the method of teaching grammar. At least two things can be done to achieve the change. *First,* the student should be introduced to the techniques by which grammatical formulations are arrived at, and shown how these statements are rooted in observations of language itself. This is most easily accomplished by what is known as *inductive teaching,* the method whereby students are led to discover principles for them selves. Since the data is readily available and generally familiar, grammar is a suitable subject for this method of learning. *Second,* students must be led to be not only critical about language, but equally critical about our understanding of language. At appropriate places they must see that there is more than one way to describe a significant point of structure, to analyze a particular group of sounds, and to explain a specific concept in verbal expression. By the time a student enters high school, he should be aware of the major approaches to syntax. The educated teacher should be conversant with linguistics. He should become familiar with such names as Bloomfield, Jespersen, Roberts, Fries, Chomsky, Scargill, Penner, and others who contribute to the ever-expanding understanding of language.

In teaching grammar, the dilemma of freedom of expression versus correct form may be solved by placing the emphasis in the elementary grades upon spontaneity of written expression, and introducing only those terms and concepts the child needs in order to be effective in oral and written communication. Children vary in their needs for formal instruction in the terminology of grammar and for practice in identifying, naming, and using the parts of speech or functions of the sentence. Terminology should be introduced as children ask questions involving the use of grammatical terms such as, "What is that word called?" "How is it used in this sentence?"

If the program is planned with a view to relating these learnings to significant experiences, most of the mechanics and tools of language can be learned effectively. Learning to speak and write well becomes synonymous with *wanting* to speak and write well.

A Formula for Teaching Grammar Effectively

The challenge of a functional approach to teaching grammar involves a change in method, emphasis, and attitude. It is imperative that grammar be reoriented toward analysis, the observation of data, and the framing of descriptions. That is, we must teach not only a body of facts and theories but also a technique by which the body of facts and theories can be augmented as needed. The content of the syllabus for the new grammar must include only the most general principles, particularly those rooted in the nature of the subject itself.

The inductive method. The inductive method has been applied in various ways ranging from the use of problem solving of a simple type to free-wheeling investigations of language, following whatever students suggest. The problem-solving techniques suggested in the chapter on speech will provide practice in genuine analytic process and thus train the students to observe language scientifically. Grammar presents many interesting and instructive problems of varying degrees of complexity which, rather than mere memorization of rules, can be the basis of discovery of principles.

Formal instruction should begin with principles antecedent to the definitions of parts of speech. Just as in modern mathematics the student is introduced to number concepts rather than beginning a study of addition as a manipulation of numbers and a set of "arithmetic facts", here the student is introduced to grammar as a part of the study of language as a whole.

Inductive teaching of grammatical concepts, although slower, less precise, and more demanding of patience and careful planning on the part of the teacher than deductive teaching, brings better results. This type of teaching leads to understanding and application much more readily than does mere memorization of rules. The following diagram illustrates inductive teaching in grammar.[47]

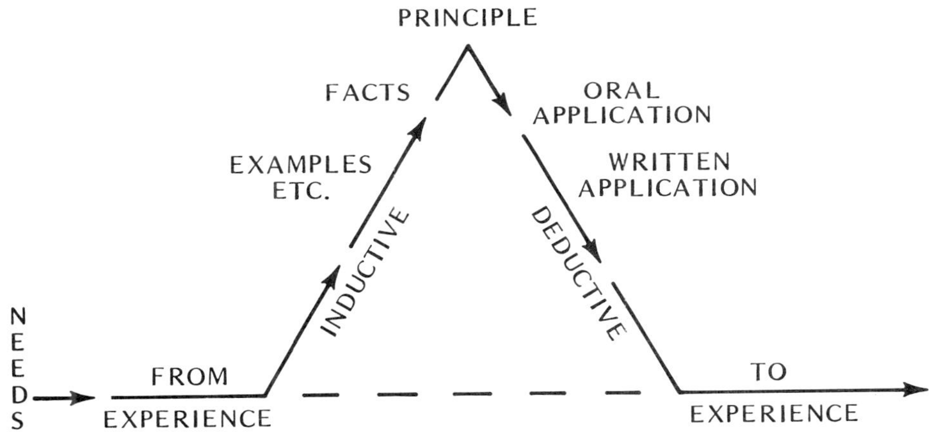

The following points should be noted.

1. Motivation should be from felt needs of pupils and should grow out of pupils' previous experience.

2. Teaching should be inductive. Pupils derive their own rules or principles from an examination of a number of carefully chosen examples. The teacher elicits rather than tells, guides rather than directs.

3. The first application of the principle should be oral so that re-teaching can readily be done when necessary. The first written attempts should be largely successful so that right patterns will become established.

4. The teacher should know in advance what transfer she expects from grammar to oral and written composition.

5. Drill lessons begin at the apex of the triangle with a review of work previously taught, and are largely deductive in nature.

In a Sixth Grade Classroom

Problem: Understanding Inverted Sentences

The teacher places four words on the board: *ball, window, desk, bird.* With the class divided into two sides, the first side creates a sentence in which something happens to one of the objects listed, as in "He pushed the desk close to the door." The opponent's task is to turn the sentence around, placing the thing acted on ("desk") at the beginning of the sentence (subject position) and change the verb to a "was" construction. Side 2 then creates a sentence, with Side 1 inverting the structure. Example—

Side 1: The centerfielder hit the ball over the fence.
Side 2: The ball was hit over the fence by the centerfielder.
Side 2: The hunter standing in a deep field of wheat shot the rabbit.
Side 1: The rabbit was shot by the hunter who was standing in a deep field of wheat.

In the first stages, it would be best to have three persons on a side. As long as the four words are listed on the board and the students know that the "object" must appear at the beginning of the inverted sentence, this exercise can be worked. From success in this simplified form, we can hope to build a sensitivity of ear to reverse-order or "inverted sentences".[48]

In addition the students can formulate the generalizations from which they will derive rules for further use.

Linguistics—a unifying force. Increased recognition must be given to the child's development of linguistic usage long before he has contact with that part of the curriculum labeled "grammar". The child in the preschool as well as in the primary school is dealing constantly with language. As he learns the skills of listening, speaking, reading, writing, spelling and new forms of oral language, he inevitably picks up unformulated ideas and feelings about language. By recognizing the importance of the role of oral language instruction *prior* to other language arts; by improving the teaching of phonics so that it will take advantage of our best phonetic and phonemic understanding; by seeing relationships between spelling, writing, reading, listening, and speaking; by giving increased attention to sentence structure in beginning reading; and finally by utilizing foreign language instruction in the elementary grades, improvement may be anticipated. The roots of effective communication are laid in the preschool and primary grades. Every element in the language arts curriculum must be reexamined in the light of its contribution to basic linguistic understanding as the foundation for creative communication.

> **Changed attitude toward grammar.** Traditionally, it (grammar) has been looked on largely as a tool useful in the teaching of correct speech and writing, but of no independent intellectual value. It has been a Cinderella consigned to scouring the grimiest pots in the composition classroom. . . . If prescriptive notions of correctness are abandoned and if language is approached inductively against the background of a broad set of fundamental principles, attitudes toward language will inevitably improve. There is one essential additional

step. We must also develop a critical attitude toward the tools with which language is investigated and the framework within which it is discussed. We must not simply replace naïvete about English with dogmatism about linguistics. A critical approach to language must turn back on itself and examine its own instruments. An educated person needs to understand not only the nature and function of language but equally the nature and function of grammars, for these also have their strength and limitations, and our understanding of language is inevitably colored in various ways by them. . . .

The contrast of one grammar with another can give us much insight into the nature and functioning of grammars.[49]

Utilizing the findings from research. As teachers become conversant with the findings of research and become open-minded about experimenting in the classroom, they will find new and effective ways of teaching grammar in much the same way that they utilize research from other curriculum areas. An example of research carried on in which the attempt was made to compare the results of traditional and structural approaches to grammar gives insight into some of the challenges as well as the problems of experimentation in the teaching of grammar.

An Experiment in Teaching Grammar

In a seven-month study comparing the structural and traditional approach to teaching grammar at the junior high level, the accepted definition of grammar agreed upon was "grammar is the study of the sentence—what it consists of, how it patterns for clear communication, and what signals are necessary to convey intended meaning." Grammar, in other words, was to be considered as the *behavior,* not the *etiquette,* of the language.

As the lessons were planned, the basic viewpoints, the basic differences between the approaches were under constant study. In the group taught by the traditional approach, the emphasis was on definition and classification of words and word groups. These were used as criteria for identification of the words and word groups. Meaning was used as guide to the structure of the English sentence. Prescription rather than description guided the pupils in their study of the language.

The students analyzed or diagrammed "ready-made" sentences. They were taught punctuation through a study of rules and of sentences which showed the application of these rules.

The method in the traditional approach was deductive as contrasted with the inductive method in the structural approach. In the structural classes the emphasis was on sentence "patterns". Sentences were classified according to their patterns—the position of words in sentences; phrases and clauses were identified by their structure and position. In short, the English language was *described.* Stress was placed upon what the language communicates through its structure.

Another difference between the two approaches was the opportunity the students in the structural group had in creating their own sentences according to suggested formulas rather than working with "ready-made" sentences.

Too, attention was given to the importance of various oral or sound signals in the language. As the students studied punctuation they were made aware of the part intonation plays upon sentence meaning.

Finally, the teaching methods of the two approaches were different. Instruction in the structural approach was inductive. The text books used were Roberts' *Patterns of English* for the experimental groups and *Building Better English* (Harper and Row) for the control group.

Significant results of the study as summarized by Klauser were:

1. On the basis of tests administered, the pupils in both groups at each of the three grade levels made significant gains in achievement. There were, however, no significant differences in the gains made by the groups being compared. We can say, therefore, that both approaches to the teaching of grammar were effective.
2. In the ninth and the seventh grades, the pupils studying grammar by a structural approach made more significant gains in understanding effective writing than did the groups studying grammar by the traditional approach. . . .
3. In the seventh grade the group studying grammar by a traditional approach made more significant gains in accuracy of writing than did the experimental group studying structural grammar. . . .
4. The eighth and ninth grade groups studying grammar by a structural approach seemed more enthusiastic and interested than did the groups at the same grade levels studying grammar by a traditional approach. This conclusion is based on the attitude—questionnaires, which required the checking of ten items under the two major headings of "I liked grammar because . . ." and "I did not like grammar because . . ." Pupils also had the opportunity to give reasons other than those stated; on the final questionnaire an additional part (C) asked for the following information:

   Grammar this year was
   1. More interesting than before.
   2. Just as interesting as before.
   3. Boring.
   4. Easier than before.
   5. Harder than before.
   6. Neither easier nor harder than before.

   Answers to part (C) of the final questionnaire indicated that twenty-three of the twenty-five ninth graders studying structural grammar found it *more interesting* than the traditional grammar previously studied, and none in this group found structural grammar *boring,* fourteen found it *harder,* whereas three found it easier. . . . Among the eighth graders, thirteen from the experimental group in contrast with seven from the control group found grammar *more interesting* than before; six of the experimental group found it *boring*; nine of the experimental group found it *harder*. . . .
5. Seventh graders in both groups had positive attitudes toward grammar. Those in the structural class asked to continue with structural grammar the next year.
6. The teachers of the three levels liked many of the features of the structural approach and expressed a desire to use this approach, perhaps with some modifications, again. . . .

7. There was no evidence that either the traditional or the structural approach which was used would be more appropriate for a particular grade in junior high school. Superior teachers can achieve good results regardless of what approach they use. . . .

The following conclusions seem valid: (1) Since pupils of the structural grammar indicated that it aroused their interest in the English language and taught them "new and exciting things" about it and since no such statements were made by those studying traditional grammar, we can feel that the study of structural grammar made an important contribution. (2) The teachers who taught both kinds of grammar felt that the structural emphasis on the studying of sentence patterns and the writing of original sentences resulted in better understanding of sentences than the traditional methods of diagramming, identification, and classification. (3) Since in a period of only seven months a new method (the structural) produced as good results as a conventional method (the traditional), continuation of a structural approach for a longer period seems feasible.[50]

On the basis of studies such as this, it would appear that the teacher should inform himself about the various approaches and experiment with them in the classroom. The emphasis upon functional and interesting features of the structural approach is a catalyst which stimulates teachers to try it in an effort to arouse enthusiasm for learning about language on the part of *both* student and teacher. Other teachers have found transformational grammar fully as challenging. A willingness to learn and an open mind about new methods characterize the creative teacher.

Evaluating the Program in Linguistics, Usage, and Grammar

The teacher helps students achieve the objective in language-creative communication by bringing children to the knowledge of the language options so that they are free as speakers and writers to choose their language mode of expression. As they progress they develop confidence in their power to use language effectively and to communicate creatively.

Some questions the teacher might ask follow.

1. Have I helped students to develop confidence in themselves while they were in the process of using language to communicate?
2. Have I allowed them frequent opportunities to express themselves both in speech and in writing?
3. Have I responded to their use of language as individuals expressing their uniqueness?
4. Have I continually rewarded each little step in the improvement of their communication skills?
5. Have I sent them on to the next educational level with greater confidence in themselves as masters over their own use of language?
6. Have I given them freedom to experiment with language and to choose from among its many options those language forms that

most closely match the purpose of their communication with a particular audience?

7. Have I made the individual—not the class—the central concern of my language teaching?

8. Have I utilized literature as an avenue through which the student will develop a more creative response to life, through sensing the many options open to him?

Concluding Statement

The responsibility of the school is to keep alive the interest in language that children have when they come to school and to build on that interest in such a way that they will be able to select their appropriate language for the specific occasion. No individual should be deprived of the opportunity of moving into a new social milieu because he has not been equipped linguistically to take his place in it. Language and the ways people use it opens doors; it also closes doors.

Regardless of the choice made in the approach to teaching grammar, students have a need to understand the nature and structure of the language they speak. Traditional grammar, with its innumerable rules, definitions, generalizations, and abstractions, poses almost insurmountable difficulties for a child of culturally disadvantaged socio-economic level, or a child of average or below average intelligence. Both structural and transformational grammar challenge the student to experiment with the parts of language to see how it works.[51]

Whether the approach is traditional, structural, or transformational, the mastery of the language involves an understanding of (1) the word classes (parts of speech); (2) basic sentence patterns; (3) operations of modification, coordination, and subordination; (4) the intonation patterns, pitch, pauses, stresses which act as signal systems in English; and (5) the mechanics involved in transcribing oral language into the written word: punctuation and spelling.

In one way or another, the teacher must come to grips with the idiosyncrasies of the English language while he deals with the structure of the language as it is, rather than as it would have been had it remained a highly inflected language. In other words, he will have to make explicit those grammatical devices which children subconsciously recognize and utilize from the time they first begin to speak in meaningful utterances. Somehow, he must find a way to help children discover grammar as an exciting vital part of the curriculum—a language in which, *if* one begins with an oral approach, one may sense the humor of the following verse.

We'll begin with box, the plural is boxes,
    But the plural of ox should be oxen, not oxes,
Yet the plural of mouse is never meese.
    You may find a lone mouse or a whole nest of mice,
But the plural of house is houses, not hice.
    If the plural of man is always men,

Why shouldn't the plural of pan be pen?
The cow in the plural may be called cows or kine,
But a bow if repeated is never called bine;
And the plural of vow is vows, not vine.
If I speak of a foot and you show me two feet
And I gave you a boot, would a pair be called beet?
If one is a tooth and a whole set is teeth,
Why shouldn't the plural of booth be called beeth?
If the singular's this and the plural is these,
Should the plural of kiss be written kese?
We speak of a brother, and also of brethren,
But though we say Mother, we never say mothren.
Then the masculine pronouns are he, his, and him,
But imagine the feminine: she, shis and shim!
So English, I think that you all will agree
Is the funniest language you ever did see.

Author Unknown

References

1. William G. Moulton. "Language and Human Communication," in Albert H. Marckwardt (ed.), *Linguistics in School Programs,* National Society for the Study of Education, The Sixty-Ninth Yearbook, Part II, University of Chicago Press, Chicago, 1970, p. 12.
2. Pose Lamb, *Linguistics in Proper Perspective,* Charles E. Merrill Publishing Company, Columbus, Ohio, 1967, p. 11.
3. The Nebraska Curriculum Development Center, *A Curriculum for English Language Explorations for the Elementary Grades,* University of Nebraska Press, Lincoln, 1966, p. 2.
4. Hans P. Guth, *English Today and Tomorrow,* Prentice-Hall, Inc., Englewood Cliffs, N.J., 1964. p. 4.
5. Neil Postman and Charles Weingartner, *Linguistics, A Revolution in Teaching,* Dell Publishing Company, New York, 1966, p. 4.
6. *Ibid.,* p. 197.
7. Charles C. Fries, "Advances in Linguistics," *Linguistics—Current Issues,* National Council of Teachers of English, Champaign, Ill., 1961, p. 37.
8. Wisconsin English-Language Arts Curriculum Project, *Teaching the English Language in Wisconsin,* Experimental Edition, Department of Public Instruction and the Cooperative Research Division of the U.S. Office of Education, Madison, Wisconsin, 1967.
9. *Nebraska Curriculum for English, op. cit.* p. xxii.
10. Adapted from Paul S. Anderson, *Linguistics in the Elementary Classroom,* The Macmillan Company, New York, 1971, p. ix.
11. See *Language Explorations for the Elementary Grades: A Curriculum for English,* University of Nebraska Press, Lincoln, Nebraska, 1966.
12. James D. Quisenberry, "Linguistics, Grammar, and Usage", in Harold G. Shane et al., *Interpreting Language Arts Research for the Teacher,* Association for Supervision and Curriculum Development, NEA, 1201 Sixteenth Street N.W., Washington, D.C. 20036, 1971, p. 106.
13. Walter Loban, "Teaching Children Who Speak Social Class Dialects," *Elementary* English, 45:592-99, May, 1968.
14. Ruth G. Strickland, "What Children Need to Know About Language," in Alexander

Frazier (ed.), *New Directions in Elementary English,* National Council of Teachers of English, Champaign, Ill., 1966.
15. Ronald J. Goba, "Grammar, Usage, Teachers of English, and Paul Roberts," *English Journal,* 58:886-91, September, 1969.
16. Robert C. Pooley, "A Perspective on Usage," *Language, Linguistics, and School Programs,* National Council of Teachers of English, Champaign, Ill., 1963, p. 66.
17. J. Stephen Sherwin, "Increasing Skill in Writing: Traditional Grammar, Linguistics, and Writing Practice," in J. Stephen Sherwin (ed.), *Four Problems in Teaching English: A Critique of Research,* International Textbook Company, Scranton, Pa., 1969, pp. 109-68.
18. Howard E. Blake and Donald D. Hammill, "Structural Linguistics and Children's Writing," *Elementary English,* 44:275-8, March, 1967.
19. John C. Mellon, *Transformational Sentence-Combining: A Method for Enhancing the Development of Syntactic Fluency in English Composition,* Harvard University Publishing Office, Cambridge, Mass., 1967.
20. Donald R. Bateman and Frank J. Zidonas, *"The Effect of a Study of Transformational Grammar on the Writing of Ninth and Tenth Graders,"* U.S. Office of Education Cooperative Research Project No. 1746, The Ohio State University, Columbus, 1966.
21. Marie Marcus, "What Would You Choose? Gum," *Elementary English,* 45:987-8, November, 1968.
22. Joan Baratz, "Teaching Reading in an Urban Negro School System," in Joan Baratz and Robert W. Shuy (eds.), *Teaching Black Children to Read,* Center for Applied Linguistics, Washington, D.C., 1969, pp. 92-116.
23. William Labov, "The Logic of Non-Standard English," Florida FL Reporter, 7:60-74, Spring/Summer, 1969.
24. Carl Bereiter and Siegfried Englemann, *Teaching Disadvantaged Children in the Pre-Schools,* Prentice-Hall, Inc., Englewood Cliffs, N.J., 1966.
25. Arthur R. Jensen, "Social Class and Verbal Learning," in Martin Deutsch et al. (eds.), *Social Class, Race, and Psychological Development,* Holt Rinehart and Winston, Inc., New York, 1968.
26. Raven I. McDavid, "Variations in Standard American English," *Elementary English* 55:561-4, May, 1968.
27. L. F. Hernandez and K. R. Johnson, "Teaching Standard Oral English to Mexican American and Negro Students for Better Vocational Opportunities," *Journal of Secondary Education,* 42:151-5, April, 1967.
28. Walter Loban, "Teaching Children Who Speak Social Class Dialects," *Elementary English,* 45:592-9, May, 1968.
29. Robert C. Pooley, *Teaching English Grammar,* Appleton-Century-Crofts, Inc., New York, 1957, p. 49.
30. *Webster's New Third International Dictionary,* G. & C. Merriam Co., Springfield, 1961.
31. Robert C. Pooley, "A Perspective on Usage—Standard vs. Substandard," in *Language, Linguistics and School Programs,* National Council of Teachers of English, 1963, pp. 65-6. Reprinted by permission of the National Council of Teachers of English and the author.
32. Robert C. Pooley, *Teaching English Grammar.* Copyright 1957 by Appleton-Century-Crofts, Inc. Reprinted by permission of Appleton-Century-Crofts, Educational Division of Meredith Corporation.
33. Pooley, "A Perspective on Usage—Standard vs. Substandard," p. 64.
34. College Entrance Examination Board, New York, *Freedom and Discipline in English: Report of the Commission on English of the College Entrance Board,* 1965, p. 33.
35. *The American College Dictionary,* Random House, Inc., New York, 1964, p. 19a.
36. Pooley, "A Perspective on Usage—Standard vs. Substandard," p. 69.

37. William Labov, *The Study of Nonstandard English,* National Council of Teachers of English, Champaign, Ill., 1970, pp. 46-7.
38. Pooley, "A Perspective on Usage—Standard vs. Substandard," p. 70.
39. Pooley, *Teaching English Grammar, op. cit.* Robert C. Pooley, "Dare Schools Set a Standard in English Usage?" *English Journal,* 49: 176-81, March, 1960.
40. Ruth E. McConnell and P. G. Penner, "Words on the Run: Fugitive Language," in M. H. Scargill and P. G. Penner, (eds.), *Looking at Language,* W. J. Gage, Ltd., Toronto, 1966, pp. 158-9.
41. Adapted from Sybil Shack, *Communication 2,* The Macmillan Language Program, Macmillan of Canada, Toronto, 1971, p. 155.
42. By permission from Frank Riessman, "Digging the Man's Language," *Saturday Review,* 49:80, September 17, 1966.
43. *Ibid,* p. 81.
44. *Francis Wayland Parker: His Life and Education Reform Work,* E. L. Kellog and Company, New York, 1900, p. 8. Quoted in Percival M. Symonds, *What Education Has to Learn from Psychology,* Bureau of Publications, Teachers College, Columbia University, 1961, p. 42.
45. Marckwardt, *op. cit.,* p. 325.
46. Paul Roberts, *English Syntax: An Introduction to Transformational Grammar,* Harcourt Brace Jovanovich, Incorporated, New York, 1964, p. 1.
47. By permission from E. B. Brooms, "The Teaching of Grammar," *Macmillan Bulletin for Teachers,* March, 1956.
48. By permission from John Maxwell, "Creative Language Teaching: Grammar and Usage," in Verna Anderson et al., (eds.), *Readings in the Language Arts,* The Macmillan Co., New York,1964, p. 276.
49. Reproduced by arrangement with Holt, Rinehart and Winston, Inc., New York, from *Linguistics and English Grammar,* by H. A. Gleason, Jr., copyright © 1965.
50. Adapted from Lucile Klauser, "Structural or Traditional Grammar?" *Delta Kappa Gamma,* 31:42-44, Summer, 1965. By permission of the Delta Kappa Gamma Society and the author.
51. See William W. West, "Written Composition," *Review of Educational Research,* 37:165, April, 1967. See also Hugh Agee, "Zonking in the Classroom (or Language Lessons from the Marketplace)," *Elementary English,* 49:780-4, May, 1972.

9

Expository Writing: Writing for Others to Read

Every piece of writing produced by a child . . . is a reflection of the oral work that goes on.

Ruth Strickland

The child is fortunate to be in an environment where he is challenged to express his ideas, thoughts, and feelings creatively and to begin his writing as a means of creative self-expression. He has been encouraged to explore his world through his senses, to formulate his impressions, and to express them through language—first oral and then written. In an environment which is challenging, nurturing, receptive to ideas, and under the guidance of a sympathetic, creative teacher, he takes great pleasure in communicating his ideas. **The wise teacher recognizes the need to allow the freedom of creative expression, both oral and written, as a prelude for the more strict discipline and conventions involved in expository writing.**

The child who through oral language has developed many of the skills he needs in communicating ideas and experiences with coherence, organization, and confidence is ready to apply these skills to expository writing.

If the teacher sees writing as a dynamic, developmental process that takes time, practice, encouragement, motivation, and direct teaching of skills in terms of each child's developmental pattern, the child will grow in power in written expression. As children grow in the arts and skills involved, they learn to organize their ideas, choose the precise word which conveys a specific meaning, select the form they wish for the content, and shift gears as readily and easily in writing for various purposes and functions as they do in oral expression.

Expository writing is that writing which the child employs to fulfill a practical or utilitarian need—to report, to record, to review a book, to write a letter, to transmit specific information or beliefs. He learns to observe the conventions and skills of handwriting, spelling, usage, punctuation, and capitalization. He concerns himself with form as well as content from the initial experiences in expository writing. Organization of ideas, clarity of expression, development of style, proofreading, and rewriting are integral parts of expository writing. Evaluation is based on these factors and proceeds from three sources—the child, the teacher, and the group.

The teacher must create a climate by providing experiences which give children a springboard for writing. These will include such things as trips, films, recordings, discussions, and debates as well as broad literary experiences which give children insights and broaden horizons. Through literature they become aware of the style of the various authors, the world of words and of ideas. In a linguistically-oriented environment, the child has opportunity for oral language activities as a prelude to writing. There is time for expression of ideas and direct teaching of needed skills, opportunity for evaluating and sharing the writing products. Expository writing provides the opportunity to teach children writing techniques and to develop the essential skills. **Writing is both a creative art and a communicative skill.**

Expository Writing: A Developmental Process

Expository writing, unlike creative writing, is *factual, functional* and *utilitarian.* It is writing for the purpose of communicating information, ideas, or facts. The child knows that when he talks his words are quickly forgotten; when he writes his ideas are recorded.

Children need an environment in which writing is valued. They need a classroom organized on the premise that children need time to grow, to experience, and to develop. They also need time to write. They cannot write in an environment in which they are hurried, harassed, or pressured. Tension and good writing are antagonistic.

A developmental approach to writing will facilitate the realization of the broad objectives of writing with accuracy, truth, logic, organization, and correct mechanics as well as exploiting the expressive possibilities of the language.

Objectives in Expository Writing

Instructional objectives emphasizing form in expository writing are:

to provide experiences which will stimulate children to express ideas, record facts, and compose reports;

to establish a purpose for each writing assignment;

to provide opportunity to write on a variety of topics and to use a variety of forms of literary expression;

to provide direct teaching of form, organization, mechanics, and correct usage in a functional setting;

to set standards of evaluation that motivate each child to become increasingly competent in improving his writing;

to help children form the habits of the writer: proofreading, rewriting, and analysis of one's own writing.

Instructional objectives in expository writing emphasizing content are:

to reveal to the student how common experience is a vast and often unrealized source of material;

to reveal to the student that reason, imagination, awareness, and sensitivity are crucial to good writing and to develop the habitual use of those faculties when writing;

to encourage the student to state and test specific principles and prejudices of his philosophy of life, to be conscious and confident of his own point of view and open to that of others;

to sharpen the student's sense perceptions as a basis for developing figurative imagery in his writing;

to develop language and composition skills with which the student can express personal experience and observation in an informal style.[1]

A good writing program takes into consideration both form and content.

Developmental Steps in Teaching Expository Writing

Children do not enter the primary school as full-blown writers. They develop ability first to express their ideas orally. Developing skill in expository writing progresses through several steps, each of which requires motivation, guidance, and evaluation from the teacher.

1. Composing and dictating experience charts or stories to the teacher who acts as a scribe.
2. Dictating and copying messages.
3. Learning skills needed in writing through directed practice.
4. Developing independence in writing to communicate facts, ideas, and happenings.

Composing and Dictating Experience Charts or Stories

Children are eager to talk about exciting group experiences and many times wish to keep a record of the happenings. Wise teachers use this built-in motivation and plan such activities as excursions both on and off the school grounds to stimulate a writing experience. Acting as a scribe, the teacher elicits from the children a group composition which includes the main points of interest, the exciting adventure, and the culminating point of the experience.

Children learn to organize ideas, develop interest, and record their impressions. The teacher encourages them by accepting their statements, approving their expression of ideas instead of putting words into their mouths. He asks thought-provoking questions, as well as questions which elicit recall. Thus he stimulates thinking, encourages recall, and motivates expression of children's ideas.

Dictating and Copying

As soon as the children have the necessary handwriting skills for copying from the script on the chalkboard or newsprint, the teacher can begin helping them in written expressions by eliciting from them expressions such as "Happy Birthday", "No School Thursday", "Home and School Wednesday", "To Mother".

Until their handwriting skills approach their linguistic skills, the teacher continues to be the scribe. He helps them organize their ideas which he writes on the chalkboard for them to copy. Thus, in a functional, meaningful setting, children learn to organize ideas and express them clearly, logically, and fluently.

Directed Practice

As the children participate in writing messages, they begin to see the need to learn the mechanics of composition. When this need becomes evident, the teacher calls attention to such items as placement and capitalization of the title, capitalization at beginning of sentences and proper names, punctuation, margins, and spelling of difficult words.

Mechanics are important in factual writing, for this type of writing is written primarily for someone else to read. Some children pick up the needed skills earlier than others because of their developmental readiness, interest, and special concerns. Practice must be geared to the needs of the children as well as the abilities of individual children to benefit from direct teaching and directed practice.

Independence in Writing

Children vary, too, in the time required to become independent in writing. Some teachers respond to the child's desire to move ahead in writing independently by using such techniques as the following.

The unfinished story. The unfinished story is developed cooperatively by the group, following a group experience such as a trip to the fire station or a farm. It is written on the chalkboard by the teacher. The end of the story is left for each child to write in terms of his own reaction to the experience.

An unfinished letter. A letter is started by the class and written on the chalkboard by the teacher. The last part is left unfinished for the individual response of each child.

Writing captions. Children enjoy writing titles for pictures on the bulletin boards and for movies that they create from their favorite stories. Experience in writing captions teaches children to be brief, provocative, and relevant.

Illustrating a process. (A series of pictures which describes a process). The teacher asks the children to fold a large sheet of paper into six or eight sections, which becomes the frame for each picture the children create. They write captions and the description of the process at the bottom of each picture. Experience in awareness of the need of the exact sequence in a particular process is gained through this technique.

Activities for Expository Writing

Many meaningful activities for purposeful, factual writing, as well as for developing skill in written usage based on correct oral usage, must be provided if the children are to be motivated to sharpen the tools for writing. The following activities challenge children to communicate effectively through written expression, and at the same time encourage development of the mechanics of writing and the level of language usage.

Group Activities

Composing experience charts and cumulative stories

Writing captions for movies and illustrated stories

Writing letters, invitations, and thank you notes

Keeping a record of daily plans, weather, etc.

Formulating problems for a unit of work in social studies

Planning and listing questions to be answered during an excursion

Listing names of characters and scenes in dramatizations

Listing room duties, committee assignments, books read

Outlining plans for a party, games to be played, rules for the games

Composing new articles, summaries, and book reports

Individual Activities

Writing captions and labels

Writing messages on gift cards

Observing and recording daily temperatures

Writing daily news items

Keeping records of library reading

Explaining arithmetic games

Framing questions for interviewing people: the nurse, custodian, policeman, fireman, fire chief, librarian, postman, the inspector, student teacher

Keeping a personal spelling list

Making a picture dictionary

Writing descriptions based on incidents in the social studies or other reading materials

Writing experiments in science

Appropriate Usage

The school must take responsibility for helping a child understand levels of usage. Appropriateness is the criterion.

Providing the child with a model of good English, reading literature of high quality, taking an oral approach to usage, and helping children use language appropriate to the situation will go far in improving a child's sense of fitness in written expression.

In expository writing the basic conventions of written expression are taught and practiced in terms of a functional setting, a purposeful activity, and individual readiness for the activity.

Letter Writing

Letter writing can be a challenging adventure or a dull routine chore. If children are taught that letter writing is a natural mode of expression which involves such elements as writing in a conversational style, planning the organizational pattern, using vivid description and imagery, including news which will interest the reader, and observing conventional forms, they find it exciting.

Since letter writing is an activity that will continue throughout the life of the average individual, learning to write them in such a way that they give pleasure to the reader as well as the writer is an achievement worthy of time and space in the language arts curriculum. Artistry in letter writing goes beyond stating the facts; it recreates in words, pictures, and actions what the writer experienced.

A couplet which wisely suggests how to start a letter contains more truth than poetry.

> Don't begin your letter with an apology—
> It will do no good, and it's bad psychology.

In letter writing the student should understand the conventional forms of a letter and the function each serves. Social letters are written in an informal conversational style about things of mutual interest to the writer and reader. Business letters are more formal. Precise information should be given. The letter should be concise, legible, and brief. The value of learning to write, and the importance of writing such letters as thank you notes, congratulations, and invitations should be impressed upon all students. The written word of appreciation is even more rare than the spoken word, and valued more because of its rarity.

Writing letters to pen pals in other parts of the world has become an integral part of the social studies as well as the language arts program in many schools, and has led to greater understanding of other cultures and people.

Reporting Information

The student has many demands for reporting information. Among these are: writing summaries of books, speeches, articles, motion pictures, television, or radio programs; summarizing discussions carried on in student councils, class or club meetings; writing research reports based on interviews, wider reading on specific topics, personal experiences. The student should follow the suggestions for organizing such information in much the same manner he would organize it to report orally to the group.

News Writing

News writing is one of the most challenging activities which motivate writing in the elementary school. Children become so intrigued with collecting and reporting news in the school newspaper that they have been known to publish a weekly newspaper in the summer holiday to "keep their hand in", as it were, until school opens again.

From the child's point of view, publishing a newspaper is fun. From the teacher's point of view, it is work. However, it is an excellent motivating device for language arts, and an effective way of helping children learn to work together, to set standards, to take responsibility, and to write for a purpose.

The student editor of one elementary school paper gave this list of suggestions to each staff writer.

> News is where you find it.
>
> News is anything that interests the reader.
>
> News should contain answers to questions. *What? Where? Why? When? How? Who?*
>
> Any rare happening is news.
>
> Facts must be accurate, relevant, and unbiased.
>
> A news story must have a *lead* line.
>
> A feature story is a newspaper highlight, and must be unique as well as interesting.
>
> An editorial states the opinions of the writer on a timely issue in an effort to persuade the readers to his point of view.
>
> All copy must be on time.
>
> Publishing a newspaper may be work, but it is fun.

The daily newspaper is one of the very best sources for ideas about writing because it makes use of expository writing: the news report, the feature story, and the editorial. In addition, it molds public opinion and forms the basis of critical analysis and evaluation of writing in the upper elementary grades. A unit on newspapers and magazines is an excellent motivation for expository writing. The teacher can organize this unit around such topics and activities as: getting acquainted with newspapers, writing captions and headlines, writing a news report, writing classified advertisements, learning to write an editorial, and organizing a newspaper.

Getting acquainted with newspapers. Students should study the format of a newspaper to discover the many sections that go to make up a daily and/or weekend newspaper. Ask the students to examine the newspaper for its daily features, the variety of topics included and the type of news which appears on page one. Provide the students with a formula for studying the questions answered by each news item: When? Who? What? How? Where? What happened? and Why? This is another way of stating the usual time, name, event, manner, place, result and cause items.

During the period of study and analysis, students should have access to local newspapers as well as some of the more illustrious examples of newswriting in order to look for such characteristics as simplicity, clarity, vividness and conciseness in the writing. The students should be encouraged to study the writer's style which distinguishes his writing from that of another individual.

As soon as students are ready to move into the next unit, they should be encouraged to try their hand at giving evidence of their ability to report a good news story within their realm of experience. It might be a sports event, a party, a debate, a play, a school party, or any news event of interest to the readers.

Writing a news story. A news story is a report that gives accurate and objective information about a specific event. Personal bias and personal reaction to the news story interfere with effective reporting. In all good news stories there are three main divisions to consider: a headline, a lead, and a body. The headline printed in large black type is a title meant to be eye-catching. It also gives the leader a brief summary of the content of the article. Writing headlines can be exciting. Emphasis should be on clear, precise, concise, economical writing. The students should study the style used by good writers and become aware of the almost telegraphic style they adopt. Evaluation should be a part of each writing assignment whether one is engaged in writing captions, headlines, news reports or other types of news writing.

Related to news reporting are activities such as personal interviews with well known personalities in the community, visiting celebrities or government officials. The same principles apply for effective interviews which are to be printed in the newspapers as apply to carrying on successful interviews as a speech activity. The student who has learned in a speech class the type of questions to ask, the behavior appropriate for the situation, and the organization of material will bring such knowledge to the writing assignment for the school paper.

In the discussions which follow the news reports, the student has an opportunity to report an event from his viewpoint. No two students who observe the same event will have the identical experience. No two students will write it up in exactly the same manner. This is to be expected. However, the importance of accurate, objective and reliable reporting is emphasized throughout the newspaper activity. Again, emphasis is placed on the importance of answering correctly such questions of the happening as who, what, when, where, why and how. Guidelines for writing a news story include: (1) choosing a subject of general and personal interest, (2) presenting the most important information in the heading, (3) writing the story impartially, and (4) reporting the events accurately. That names are spelled correctly and dates and statistics are accurate goes without saying.

Classified advertisements. Classified advertisements, too, furnish motivation for expository writing. The study of advertisements in the daily paper, magazines, and weeklies will furnish the reader with a format based on psychological motivations. As the student listens to advertisements over the television and studies the examples in the classified ad section in the papers, he should become aware of the need for logical thinking as well as clear, concise and honest writing.

Writing an editorial. Editorial writing requires more sophisticated skills than the other types of writing discussed. Here the student is expected to make full use of his powers of critical thinking, reasoning, and logic in presenting his point of view on an issue of significance to the readers. Although the editorial page is not always read first, it is one of the most important parts of a newspaper and should be studied carefully by novice newspaper writers. Most editorials are written with one or more of the following purposes in mind: (1) to present certain facts and to comment on them, (2) to put forth arguments for and/or against a particular course of action, and (3) to influence public opinion. This necessitates that the writer be aware of his facts when he makes assertions. It is not simply a vehicle for "getting things off one's chest". Indeed, any opinions expressed should be based on fact. Documented evidence is important in writing an effective editorial.

Before starting out to write an editorial, the students should study the format used and look for such elements in the construction of editorials as: the introduction; the body of fact, opinion, and reason which motivated the writer to address himself to the topic at hand; and a summary of the facts of the case.

In planning an assignment on editorial writing, it is important to give consideration to the topic. Subjects which have vital interest to the students as well as to the community at large will evoke better writing than subjects in which students are only mildly interested. The following illustrates topics which can stimulate effective editorial writing.

1. Announcing tryouts for the spring play
2. Reading good books
3. Good behavior in the auditorium
4. Friendliness to the new student
5. The teams in next week's hockey game
6. Honesty is the best policy
7. Consideration for minority groups
8. Integrity to stand up for one's convictions
9. Ecology
10. Second-rate citizenship
11. Our town needs an athletic field
12. Truancy and petty crimes are the result of lack of discipline in the home
13. Protest movements

Using the local newspaper to discover topics of vital concern to the citizenry is an avenue for bringing the composition assignment and a functional situation together in a meaningful fashion.

Before students write on topics of vital concern, they should carry on research, interviews, and discussion in order to produce an editorial that is characterized by the behavior of the newspaper writer—careful thinking, accurate information, and skillful presentation of the facts and a specific point of view on an important issue.

Organizing a newspaper. When students are becoming skillful in various types of writing which a good newspaper provides, they enjoy the experience of organizing a real newspaper. It can be set in any period of history the class decides. In conjunction with a social studies unit it might well become a newspaper of the past, thus involving much research into past history; it might, on the other hand, be set in the present scene.

Whatever the decision for the period of time, the newspaper gives excellent motivation for expository writing and research. It also provides the embryo author, historian, or social scientist with motivation for perfecting the craftsmanship so essential in good newspaper writing.

The extent to which schools go into the publishing business varies with the situation. If the project is to be an extensive one, it will be important to select an editorial committee, a production committee, a publicity committee, and a financial committee.

As each set of sheets is rolled off the press, there must be room for them, there must be a place where they can be assembled, and finally there must be a plan for distribution of the finished product. Teachers may motivate newspaper writing with a minimum of expenditure of finanical means; however, they cannot motivate it without a maximum expenditure of time and energy. Those who have tried it are convinced that it is worth both the time and energy involved.

Getting acquainted with magazines. In addition to making use of newspapers as a motivation for good writing, teachers are finding magazines stimulate interest in writing as well.

Students can make use of magazines in preparing research on specific topics, and will find that in gathering statistics and other supporting material for an essay, technical, scientific, business and consumer magazines are helpful.

Other assignments related to magazine activities are the assembling of an ideal magazine from poems, articles, features and stories of high literary quality. Another could be to select the contents of a magazine from the writings of the members of the class. There should be variety in content, quality in style, and unity within diversity.

Written Book Reports

A book report should be interesting. One purpose of a book report is to create the desire on the part of other students to read the book. The following are some suggestions for successful book reports.

1. Organize the report on the development of plot.
2. Organize the report on the development of characters.
3. Organize the report on the use of descriptions.
4. Analyze the central theme.
5. Compare the protagonists.
6. Write the report in the form of a letter to the author giving what was liked and what was a disappointment.
7. Select the most exciting episode and tell why it was chosen.
8. Find recurring words that are especially significant to the story. Show how they were effective in creating mood, developing characterization or moving the story along.
9. Analyze the story in terms of cause and effect.
10. Compare this story to one in a similar theme by a different author.

As a guide to the writing of the book report, the pupils may develop a brief form which they may use as an outline in working out the report or review.

My Book Report

Title ....

Author .... Illustrator ....

Characters essential to the development of the plot ....

....

....

The most exciting episode ....

The conflict ....

The resolution ....

The epilogue ....

My reaction to the story ....

It is the responsibility of the teacher to motivate each child to achieve loftier aims and more satisfying experiences in writing. In the section on speech many types of activities which stimulate oral expression were presented. These are also effective in stimulating written expression. Activities which have their origin in social situations, or situations with social implications, serve to motivate children to write.

As they develop the habits of rhetorical and mechanical skills needed in expository writing, they automatically use these competencies in their creative writing without losing the spontaneity which characterizes creative expression.

Sequence in Teaching Composition

Sequence in composition should introduce children to problems of expressing ideas in various forms. From the beginning the child must be taught to relate his ideas to the appropriate organization in terms of the purpose of writing. It is the teacher's responsibility to provide direct teaching and guided practice in writing so that the child may grow in the efficiency with which he manipulates the form of the sentence, the paragraph and the longer composition. This is frequently planned in the course of study for the entire school.

Sequence in writing should also consider and make plans for a balance of all important aspects of writing. This is to say that attention should be centered on ideas, organization, diction, style, and usage. Avoid an *overabundance* of time given to the mechanical problems of handwriting, spelling, and punctuation—important though these are.

If teachers are to vitalize the area of expository writing, it is essential that each school agree on sharply limited areas of emphasis at each instruction level and hold students responsible for minimum essentials necessary before they are ready to attack the next level of skills.

Agreement on the scope and sequence of activities by an entire school staff assumes teachers who are knowledgable about the growth and development of children, the organization of activities, the development of needed skills, and the methods of teaching which are effective at each educational level.

Not only must there be an understanding of the broadening scope of the activities; there is also a need to plan for the sequence in these writing activities. There are a number of ways in which the sequence is organized to help children develop essential skills in written composition. In the plans illustrated below, scope and sequence of activities in various writing experiences common to pupils in the elementary school have been successfully used: (1) levels, (2) grades, (3) junior high.

Levels in Teaching Composition

If the program is arranged by levels rather than by specific grades, it enables pupils to attack the assignments and to experience suggested learning activities on the basis of their readiness for the task rather than on the basis of their grade level. Some pupils may never progress beyond the third or fourth level; others, however, will be ready for the kinds of writing suggested for levels five or six before they complete the elementary school. Teachers will select materials and/or assignments from the levels on the basis of needs, abilities, experiential background of the children in the class.

The sequence or "horizontal" arrangement of the program provides for development over the period of years the child spends in the elementary school. The scope or "vertical" arrangement of the program suggests the kind of writing activities which the pupils might reasonably be expected to deal with during a specific year.

In the following chart, the sequence of writing activities proceeds from simple to complex, from easy to difficult, from brief papers to longer ones, and from assignments focusing on the child's world of experience to increasingly challenging topics demanding research, critical thinking, and creative interpretation. Such a sequence of learning experiences takes into account current research in child development and language learning. It takes into consideration the child's progression from the stage of exploration and freedom during his early years, into the stage of precision in his middle years of childhood, and finally into stages of generalization as he moves into adolescence. The chart should serve as a guide, not as a prescription, for planning.

In planning a sequence for such organization, the staff as a whole meets to clarify its philosophy, define its goals, and plan activities which will be appropriate for each level.

The Role of the Teacher

The most important factor in a successful writing program is the teacher. To the extent that the teacher assumes the responsibility for implementing the goals of writing in terms of the children he teaches will they develop power in written expression. Teaching practical, functional, and utilitarian writing involves: setting the stage, putting the program into practice, providing for individual differences, and designing an effective evaluation program.

Setting the Stage

Writing does not come naturally to the child. He must be *taught* to write clearly, concisely, and accurately by a teacher who is knowledgeable about the characteristics of good writing and the literary heritage of expository as well as

Levels in Teaching Composition[2]

Kinds of Writing	Level One	Level Two	Level Three	Level Four	Level Five	Level Six
Simple Exposition Skills: using clear, concise, specific language; following logical order; writing directions or accounts of processes; writing clear definitions	Giving directions for a simple act or process: tying a shoe, starting an outboard motor . . .	Writing definitions of everyday words (*door, chair, pencil*) and comparing with the dictionary definition. Writing personal definitions of abstract words: *happiness, friendship, beauty* ("What —— means to me")	Same, with more complicated topics: directions for going from a known location to an unknown; processes such as developing a film, changing a tire	Explaining the organization and work of a club or group: Boy Scouts, PAL, Boys' Clubs, etc.	Describing and explaining the function of a well-known activity to someone who has not had experience with it: a pep rally, a square dance, a religious festival or ceremony	Clarifying the meaning of complex abstractions (*democracy, liberalism, prejudice, integrity*) by giving many specific illustrations and exploring the diverse meanings of these terms
Narration Skills: handling of different kinds of order; selection of detail to develop one central theme	Accounts of family or school incidents, of family trips or celebrations; narratives of personal experience or incident			Describing an incident from a particular point of view; selecting details for vivid narration; selecting details about complex event to convey a single theme		
Reporting Skills: using the language of fact with clarity and precision	Factual reporting of simple incidents, school trips, accounts of firsthand observations, family or school incidents. Writing reports of class meetings, keeping notes on class discussion and assignments			Reporting discussions of controversial issues in student council or committee meetings, town meetings, community groups. Factual reporting of speeches and events. Note-taking on lecures, assignments, and readings		
Description Skills: use of concrete words, selection of detail to support a single impression; accurate use of language	Brief papers describing familiar scenes, places, or persons	Descriptions emphasizing sensory impressions with concrete detail	Descriptions of place or scene to evoke mood; character sketch to emphasize a dominant trait	Longer papers of more complex descriptions: a holiday celebration, a person, a group of people in action	Description of something minutely observed: an animal, bird, flower, anthill. Technical descriptions, as of laboratory equipment, mechanisms, etc. Description of the dramatic, the violent, the unusual: an accident, a storm, a street fight, a group in a moment of crisis	
Library Reports Skills: learning the techniques of sum-	Brief reports on the history and de-	Report on the history of a custom,	Investigation of topics suggested by	Report on an aspect of the history	Using reference materials to gather	Biographical report on a person

(Levels, continued)

Kinds of Writing	Level One	Level Two	Level Three	Level Four	Level Five	Level Six
marizing, paraphrasing, and interpreting reference materials for reports; learning the differences between honest borrowing and plagiarizing; gaining skill in documenting sources and mastering conventional form in footnoting and bibliography	rivation of one word	a superstition, place names, or similar language investigations	assignments in the study of language and literature; report on a mythological, Biblical, historical, or other reference in literature	of the language or of a point in changing usage	and organize a report on an investigation related to work in language: the invention of the printing press, the development of the alphabet, manuscript writing, code systems, Biblical analysis, problems in translation from a foreign language	who made significant contribution to a development of language: Braille, Caxton, Gallaudet, Helen Keller; teachers, writers, inventors. Biographical paper on the works of a single writer or group of writers: the Bronte sisters, Frost, Dickens, Emily Dickinson
Writing about Books						
Skills: dealing with literature from the critical and analytical point of view rather than the retelling of plot; writing honest reactions to literature; searching for author's purpose and theme; examining dominant tone, mood, symbolism	Personal reactions to characters and situations in books; agreement or disagreement with the choices or decisions characters make	Observing the steps through which a character changes or develops	Comments on the relationships between characters; observing the writer's description of place and character	Observing the conflict between forces in the piece of literature; analyzing the author's purpose; discussing the relation of the endings to the development of character and action	Discerning the writer's theme and how it is illustrated in the book; observing and analyzing stylistic characteristics	Analyzing the writer's central symbols in the book; developing thematic statements made by the author; commenting on books which illustrate a universal human plight or illuminate a major literary theme. Analysis of a literary theme developed in several readings, both fiction and non-fiction (for instance, the theme of racial injustice)

(Levels, continued)

Kinds of Writing	Level One	Level Two	Level Three	Level Four	Level Five	Level Six
Argument and Opinion Skills: practice in supporting opinion and argument by adequate evidence, in logical thinking and writing. The audience for the early years may be the writer's classmates; later, receptive adults; lastly, he may address an unknown audience: contemporaries outside his own school, unknown adults	Papers on such topics as "I believe my parents (teachers, etc.) are wrong about . . ."; pro or con arguments on problems of allowances, dating, chores, homework, school responsibilities or rules; letters to editors of school paper on school or teen-age problems	Arguments pro or con school requirements, policies, punishments, rules	Pros and cons of cheating, school and civic issues. Matters of school policy, changes needed, etc.	Pros and cons of personal standards and values	Argument and opinion about national or international issues; political, social, ethical, or moral issues; questions of human rights, educational goals, questions of values and beliefs. Papers should offer specific illustrations and deal with specific situations	
Critical Writing and Analysis Skills: exercise in critical thinking and writing about problems increasing in complexity; analysis of literary and mass-media sources to develop awareness of logical fallacies, semantic traps, propaganda techniques, and of stylistic features of literature	Practice in critical analysis of advertising appeals, TV stereotypes in family and western programs	Analysis of commonly used abstractions: *success, integrity, school spirit*	Analysis of the reality of characters in literature, credibility of motivation and dialogue, consistency of endings of fiction or drama	Analysis of newspaper editorials and mass-media materials for balance of fact and judgment; examination of such materials for validity of evidence. Analysis of a prejudice, a deeply held belief, an important value	Interpretation of a passage from literature, an aphorism, a parable, a folk saying, a well-known quotation, or a general truth. Interpretation of a poem or a short story. Critical review of a TV program, a play made from a book, or the film version of a classic	Critical analyses of some difficult poems, short stories, plays, and novels, with emphasis on theme, symbolism, structure, and style

(Levels, continued)

Kinds of Writing	Level One	Level Two	Level Three	Level Four	Level Five	Level Six
Exercises in Style Skills: developing sensitivity to a variety of styles in literature through "trying them on" in practice. Although the student's major problem in writing is to develop a style and voice of his own, occasional attempts to write paragraphs or brief bits modeled after well known stylists may help him develop an ear for style, and perhaps increase his own command of language. The writing of paragraphs modeled on the sentence patterns of a prose passage from literature may develop sensitivity to word order, syntactical patterns, and choice of words	Writing brief paragraphs in Madison Avenue English, sportswriters, or TV commercial language, or *Mad* magazine satire	Writing dialogue in the style of movie or TV romances, westerns, or mysteries; teenage fiction or popular magazine romance; trying *New Yorker* or *Time style.*	Writing a well known piece (a fairy tale, fable, or parable) in several styles	Attempting pieces of character description, dialogue, or action, modeled on the prose of Hemingway, Salinger, Lardner, Conrad	Attempting writing closely modeled on paragraphs from 18th, 19th, or 20th century prose masters: Johnson, Lamb, Stevenson, E. B. White, Mencken, and others (the teacher can find a wealth of examples for models)	

creative writing, and who is skilled in methods of teaching writing. Such a teacher combines knowledge of children and of motivation of children in setting the stage for the writing program.

The teacher creates an environment which is linguistically-oriented, in which there is time for the discussion and exploration of ideas. The children are secure in the knowledge that their best efforts are appreciated. They are motivated to master the technical skills necessary for clear writing.

Providing firsthand experiences. The more firsthand experiences available to a child the more likely he is to use these as a springboard for written expression. He uses these experiences as a basis for his expository writing.

Developing background for writing through literature. In the initial experiences the children provide the content and the teacher provides the form. Children's firsthand experiences are limited. Providing them with vivid, well written literature gives them a backlog of ideas out of which to write.

Establishing purposes for expository writing. If a child is aware of the purpose for which he is writing and the audience with whom he is communicating, there is a greater incentive to write with clarity, correctness, and with logical organization. In a linguistically-oriented classroom, there are numerous opportunities to write notices, invitations, thank you notes, daily news reports, business and social letters. It is well that the child as well as the teacher be conversant with the objectives of the program.

Providing time and encouragement. Teachers frequently ask children to write a paper, a paragraph, an essay, or a story without giving them time to proceed logically through the steps in writing. It is better to give fewer assignments, to make fewer writing demands and to give the child *time* for ideas to ripen, for thoughts to jell, for sequence to develop than to force the children into inferior work because of lack of time for preparation. Children need more than time, however. They need encouragement. Writing is a lonely job, and a word of encouragement is worth much in providing incentive for continued writing.

Putting the Program into Practice

A design for the composition process. There is a need for a practical, basic, effective plan for the teacher. One such plan involves six phases: (1) thinking, discussing, and reading; (2) planning the writing; (3) writing the first draft; (4) proofreading, evaluating, and revising; (5) direct teaching of the needed language skills; (6) sharing the final copy.

This process is basic to all forms of expository writing since it involves gaining ideas through thinking, discussing, and reading; organizing ideas in a manner appropriate to the material; writing the first draft; evaluating and rewriting; and finally sharing.

The following account of a series of lessons using this design involves all aspects of the language arts program.

Phase I Thinking, Discussing, and Reading

The teacher introduced the children to the assignment: "Select your favorite fictional character such as Tom Sawyer, Caddie Woodlawn, Cinderella, Alice in Wonderland, Casey at the Bat or one of the characters from *Aesop's Fables* and write a description of the locale of the story." A brief discussion of favorite characters followed. The characteristics of fictional characters and the impact of environment on character were discussed prior to the reading of the story.

Phase II Planning and Writing

Characteristis of the characters were reviewed. The elements of the descriptive paragraph were pointed out. Punctuation was reviewed and proper page form and literary style were stressed. A number of characters that were discussed were placed on the chalkboard. Each student chose one about which to write.

Phase III Writing the First Draft

Writing was not new to these children. In their creative writing they had worked with both characterization and description as a part of the story. Now they brought this background to the expository writing assignment which stressed the *elements* of both characterization and description rather than the creative aspects. The teacher was not surprised to see each child go directly into the writing of the first draft.

Phase IV Proofreading, Evaluating, and Revising

The children proofread their essays, and those who were satisfied with the result read them to the class. After each was read, the boys and girls told what they liked about it and where they thought improvements could be made. Revision was the next step. This consisted of revision of content, sequence, expression, etc. Next, they made corrections dealing with mechanics through the use of a directed, step-by-step look at the proofreading chart. They used symbols to indicate mechanical errors to be dealt with. The final draft was written from the corrected draft and turned in to the teacher. She had an opportunity to give help to eight students during this one writing period. More conferences were scheduled with other students at a later date.

Phase V Direct Teaching of Needed Language Skills

This phase of the composition process involves teaching thoroughly, some of the essential language skills. These were selected from those which the pupils were having difficulty with in their compositions. This lesson emphasized the use of descriptive, colorful adjectives. The children were shown the importance of adjectives in effective writing. An essay involving description was read to the class and the children were asked to identify adjectives. Children discussed colorful adjectives in relation to the five senses. They suggested words in describing nouns the teacher had written on the board. Then they wrote sentences using colorful language. Several children read what they wrote.

the crisp salad on the table
freshly washed air
the glowing pallet of Pinnochio's master
thunderous pounding of the surf
glossy-smooth sunset color of grapefruit
pigeon-toed woman
virgin eyes of the morning sun
unseasoned potatoes

Other children were asked to portray in pantomime the adjective modifying the noun being discussed. The remainder of the class attempted to guess what was being "described" in pantomime.

Phase VI Sharing the Final Copy

When the children had completed the final rewrite incorporating the language skills they accumulated during the direct teaching and the writing conferences, they were given a period in which to share. Sometimes the author read his own, sometimes the teacher read it for him. The compositions were filed in individual pupil folders and the class was ready to begin another basic, six-phase composition process.

Making assignments. In an effective writing program, making assignments is a challenging, creative task—not a dull, dreary chore. Too many teachers rely on prepared lists of topics without consideration of the interests, abilities, and needs of the students. When the children are involved in selecting their own topics, the literary quality of the writing improves.

Children will write about almost everything under the sun, and one of the stimulating techniques in planning topics for writing assignments is that of having them think up possible topics for each letter of the alphabet. The following list resulted from a brainstorming session.

Allowances: How do you spend your allowance?

Books: Write about a character from a book you have recently read.

Brainstorming: Define brainstorming and tell how you could demonstate it to your classmates.

Colors: What is your favorite color? Why?

Dinosaurs: Write an essay about the types of dinosaurs and their demise.

Enemies: Whom do you regard as the enemies of man?

Friends: Describe your best friend.

Games: Explain the rules of your favorite game.

Heroes: Describe your hero.

Island: Write a paragraph about the island you would like to visit.

Jobs: What jobs do you do around the house? What do you like best about them? Least?

Knowledge: Which subject do you like best? Why?

Lost and Found: Relate your experience with a treasure you lost and found.

Music: What is your favorite type of music? Why?

Nature: What outdoor sport do you most enjoy?

Opera: Describe a night at the opera.

People: Do you believe people are funny? If so, why?

Quotations: Select a favorite quotation and write a paragraph explaining what it means to you.

Radio: Write a script for a radio sports announcer announcing the most exciting play in a hockey tournament.

Sentence: "As the sentence was pronounced the prisoner fainted." Use this as a sentence starter.

Titles: My First Day in a New School, Halloween, A Bout with the Measles, It Happened Only Yesterday, The Day at the Circus, The Hardest Problem I Have.

Universe: If you could go anywhere in the universe, where would you go, how would you travel, and whom would you take along?

Vacation: The most exciting incident in my vacation.

Winter: Describe the most memorable scene on a winter's day.

X-Ray: Write a science fiction story about an X-Ray that can see into the minds of people.

Yarn: Tell the biggest yarn you have heard.

Zoo: Tell about your most interesting day at the zoo.

Guiding Principles in Expository Writing Assignments

The assignments must be difficult enough to make the student reach higher than he thought he could and stimulating enough to make him *want* to write. Haphazard assignments, flung out as the bell rings, are an invitation to false and superficial response. Making good assignments in writing is an art.

A good assignment evokes the best from the writer and gives the teacher the best chance to be helpful.

A good assignment aids learning and requires a response that is the product of discovery.

A good assignment furnishes data to start from.

A good assignment may take the form of, or be constructable into, a proposition.

A good assignment limits either form or content or both.

A good assignment will stipulate the audience to be addressed.

Assignments should vary in kind.

Developing an assignment. All good writing starts with an idea. Although words are the units of the idea, one seldom thinks in terms of individual words or sentences. These are merely the media through which ideas are expressed. The thought unit of the basic idea (the paragraph) is the key to good writing. Once the idea is down on paper, it may be necessary to search for a more precise word, a more expressive sentence, or a more coherent or dynamic structure. Getting the idea down is imperative. If, however, the teacher's first concern is with words and structure, the idea may never take shape.

One profitable way to approach the teaching of expository writing is to consider the component structure of prose—the essay, the paragraph, the sentence, the word—as these are shaped and controlled by the varying demands of the four elements of the writer, subject, purpose, and audience. Such an approach might conceivably "take off" with reading and analyzing selections of expository prose—usually complete essays rather than isolated passages.

Such analysis will point up the fact that good writing does not come from the mechanical application of rules but rather as a result of a series of choices involving the demands of the writer, subject, purpose, and audience. As the student experiences the writing of others, he is required to pay particular attention to the ways in which organization is determined by the writer's purpose, his acquaintance with his subject, and his awareness of the audience for whom he is writing.

The student who has a background in composing speeches throughout the elementary grades finds the problem of organization in writing to be negligible. If he has had practice in organizing his thoughts into logical oral expression, he will discover that the principles of rhetoric are equally applicable to written expression.

Techniques for teaching students to write paragraphs effectively include *analysis of paragraphs* written by professional authors of the daily papers and weekly journals in addition to those by great writers of the past. Through this inductive method the topic sentence is introduced; and, again, by studying the paragraphs of successful writers, students can see clearly the role of the topic sentence in the development of paragraph organization. They will see that the content determines the form as it does in creative writing. *Content and form cannot be separated.* What a writer says is not really separable from the way he says it.

Among the organizational patterns for developing a paragraph are: (1) definition, (2) specific instances, illustrations, anecdotes, (3) description, (4) comparison and contrast, (5) cause and effect, (6) need—plan (7) analogy, (8) restatement, and various combinations of these patterns.

At times it may be helpful to suggest topic sentences which will spark the idea and at the same time suggest the organizational pattern.

The following suggestions illustrate organizational design.

1. No one should have been surprised by the recent election results. (Cause and effect. Why not surprised? I was.)

2. Trying out for a school play is a grueling experience. (Specific instances, illustrations. Is it? Show me.)

3. Though on the surface they might seem to have much in common, the soldier and the sailor have vastly different responsibilities. (Comparison and/or contrast. How are their duties different or alike?)

4. The term "abstract painting" has been subjected to many nonobjective misinterpretations. (Definition. What do *you* say it is?)

5. "The quality of mercy is not strained." (Analogy. Remember how Shakespeare did it: "It droppeth as the gentle rain from heaven.")

6. Does today's student need more or less education than his parents received? (Cause and effect. Give reasons for your position.)

7. Courage and wisdom often go hand in hand. (Analogy. Definition, illustration or comparison and contrast. Get these concepts out into the open where you can deal with them.)

Providing for Individual Differences

The teacher's guidance is perhaps the most essential part of the actual writing process if each child is to develop power in expressing interesting, worthwhile ideas. A child does not learn to write by being told to write. The teacher must be there to suggest as well as to encourage, to help the child try out his sentences orally, to help him discover omissions in content as well as in form, and to demonstrate acceptable punctuation, mechanics, spelling, grammar, and usage.

An analysis of children's writing reveals a wide divergence in the expression of an idea, in organization, interest value, sentence structure, style, spelling, handwriting, capitalization, punctuation and usage. Some have already learned to write thoughtfully, clearly, concisely, critically, interestingly, legibly and creatively as well as with honesty, simplicity, and confidence. For these the process of composition is such that they can concentrate on content and the expression of ideas. It is important that the teacher recognizes the importance of supervision and guidance when children write. The responsibility of giving needed help makes it imperative that the teacher be there during the writing period to help individual children as well as groups with form, punctuation, construction, correct usage, and spelling. Children will require varying degrees and kinds of help. Some pupils will be ready almost immediately after an assignment is given to proceed, others will need more specific motivation. Some will be finishing their work while others are just getting under way. Some will be proofreading and others rewriting or recopying.

If the teacher observes that several children are having difficulty with the same problem—punctuation or capitalization, spelling or usage—he may give direct teaching to these pupils as a group in terms of their specific needs. At other times the teacher may use the writing conference as a means of individual guidance in writing.

The individualized reading conference is well known. Teachers are less familiar with the individualized writing conference. In such a conference the teacher assumes the role of the interested reader and comments upon the worth of the writing. He follows this by assuming the role of an editor. In this role he elicits from the child—he does not tell him—ways in which he could say better what he wanted to say.

It is during the writing conference that a teacher often discovers a child's specific needs and is then able to plan direct teaching of needed skills.

Evaluation

Expository writing is concerned with functional communication. It is utilitarian and practical. It is a service-type writing which grows out of individual and group needs. Therefore, it must be evaluated on the extent to which the writer meets certain standards of skills and abilities.

Self-evaluation

In becoming a writer the student must take more and more responsibility for evaluating his own work *before* he presents it to be evaluated by the teacher or group. Among the specific points to be evaluated are organization, content, mechanics, and style. In helping the child gain in skill in self-evaluation, the teacher should establish certain ground rules for learning to proofread and rewrite before turning in a written assignment. One practical plan for this activity follows.

1. After the material for the paper is assembled, the child writes a rough draft, keeping in mind the *organization* of the paper. He may use chronological order (sequence of events), cause and effect, need and plan, and so forth.

2. The child then assesses the paper for the development of the *content*.

3. He checks it for the *mechanics* (spelling, handwriting, punctuation, grammar, usage.)

4. He rereads it to see if the *style* is appropriate for the purpose.

5. Following this, the final draft is written and presented to the teacher or the group for evaluation. This last draft is carefully written in terms of organization, content, mechanics, and style.

Children gain skill in writing not only through self-evaluation, but also through group evaluation. The teacher selects papers which illustrate common problems as well as successful handling of the specific points which have been under consideration. By using an overhead projector, it is possible for the teacher to analyze for the class content, good points, faults, ambiguity, incompleteness, and improvement.

As the child progresses through the elementary school, the objectives of writing are broadened and, in turn, the expectations of the quality of the writing are heightened. Children who have been schooled in the importance of being precise with the use of facts, logical in drawing conclusions, and skilled in organization of ideas in both speech and written language will follow the tradition of good writers: clarity, brevity, simplicity, care in the use of writing techniques and conventions.

To paraphrase Cicero, the purpose of expository writing is to prove what we maintain to be true, conciliate those who read, and to produce in their minds whatever feeling our cause may require.

Group Evaluation

British educationists have devised a plan to relieve the English teacher's load while enhancing students' critical faculties. Responsible teachers have wholeheartedly embraced the plan, which makes use of what is called "writing workshops".

This program places more responsibility on the pupil for self-criticism and evaluation. Several times a year, the teacher allows each student to choose the composition he regards as his best up to that time. This composition is then evaluated in conference with the teacher.

In the meantime, the other compositions he has been writing have all been read and appraised in the various writing workshops. Organizing these workshops involves writing partners, a board of editors and teacher involvement.

Writing partners. Each student is provided with a writing partner chosen by the student or assigned by the teacher. Each student, then, has a writing partner to proofread his or her rough draft of a composition. Each writing partner checks his partner's composition for: (1) logic, (2) punctuation, (3) paragraphing, and (4) choice of words. Other points are added as the student's knowledge of writing techniques develop.

When the first draft has been written, the writing partner suggests changes, deletions or both, and the revised copy of the composition is written. His final copy is collected and read by the class's board of editors.

Board of editors. It is essential in guiding the board of editors in their function to select a small group who can work well together. Some teachers choose four students and set up with them standards for evaluating the compositions written by their peers. They use the criteria established in the class for each type of writing assigned. For example, in writing news reports they watch for organization and logic in writing; how, when, where, who, etc., must be answered in the article.

In working with the editors, it is essential that the elements of good writing be understood by the editors. Such elements as clarity, critical thinking, diction, vivid words, specificity in choice of known, etc., should be checked.

It is important, too, that the editors be prepared to defend their evaluation of a composition in terms of the compositions they evaluate as best and "runner-up". As they read, they should make notes which they can use in defending the choices they made. These notes include such phrases as: good diction, good sentence structure, good lead topic sentence, excellent imagery, etc. The editors should make suggestions for improving the writing, but they should select the most important point for improvement in a particular manuscript.

It is important that the editors read well orally since they will read the selections they chose to the entire class. They should be ready to defend their choice to the members of the class in the period following the oral presentation.

A final point for improving the writing through a workshop writing project is the importance of the teacher's own writing. If the teacher writes a composition on the chalkboard while the children are writing at their desks, he can provide the children with examples of the use of punctuation, vocabulary and style in his own writing. Creative teachers inspire creative writing in children.

Self-evaluation for the Teacher

The responsibility of the teacher for helping children to express themselves fluently and accurately in writing cannot be overemphasized. This he does by helping children develop their powers of observation. He guides them in selecting and organizing material wisely. He teaches them to compose clear and effective sentences, paragraphs, and essays. He motivates them to work toward accuracy in spelling, punctuation, capitalization, usage, and handwriting in harmony with their level of maturity. The teacher might use the following criteria for self-evaluation. *Do I implement the goals of written expression by stimulating in children:*

a desire to write and recognize the value of writing for clarifying one's own ideas, for sharing news with distant friends and relatives, for carrying on business or making plans at long range, for sharing, recording, and preserving facts, ideas, and experiences, and for exchanging messages and social courtesies?

careful observation, alert listening, sincere feeling, and clear thinking as essential elements in good writing?

skill in preplanning and critical thinking as means to selecting and ordering ideas, information, or experiences in logical or chronological order or in storytelling for the sake of suspense and interest?

skill in letter writing for practical purposes with attention to content, form, and manner of expression appropriate for the intended purpose, recipient, or occasion?

power to think clearly and logically, differentiating main from subordinate ideas, and mastery of the skills needed to make them clear to others?

a sense of personal integrity in writing and a willingness to stand by what they have said?

curiosity about words, their origins, their multiple meanings, their varied forms, and their relation to reality as a means of avoiding mere verbalism or semantic misinterpretations?

an interest in the use of fresh, concrete, and pictorial words to convey ideas?

mastery of sentence sense and a feeling for variety in sentence order together with an understanding of the capitalization and punctuation related to the sentence?

understanding of the paragraph as an organized unit of thought and ability to use it effectively?

facility in handwriting and accuracy in spelling, capitalization, and punctuation for making their ideas clear to others?

appreciation of the qualities of successful writing through attention to the improvement of a few elements at a time?

a sense of responsibility for self-evaluation and proofreading organization and form before submitting it for group or teacher evaluation?

Concluding Statement

Expository writing is that writing which the student does for a practical, utilitarian purpose. He has to write to keep a record, to transmit needed information, to communicate ideas to another person. This type of writing, then, demands that the writer write with clarity, organization, correct form and mechanics and that he develop a style which is appropriate to the writing task and in harmony with his own growing needs for expression.

The child seldom writes better than he speaks. Therefore, it is essential that he have much opportunity for oral language expression before he is faced with the task of putting his ideas down on paper. Writing is a process which requires the blending of the language arts of speaking as well as the mental act of logical thinking and the motor act of handwriting. The pupil who is effective in expository writing must be well versed in expressing his ideas logically, succinctly, and interestingly. He must have the spontaneity which comes as a result of much opportunity for creative oral expression in which his ideas flow freely and spontaneously.

The problem of organizing ideas, selecting a topic, developing the topic, researching the topic, and using the knowledge of composition he has learned in composing a speech will be of inestimable value to the child in expressing his ideas in written form.

The knowledge of the objectives to be attained, direct teaching by the teacher of specific skills needed in using various forms, encouragement to develop individualistic style, and the responsibility for evaluating his own writing will tend to help the elementary school child find in expository writing an outlet for expression throughout the educational years and into adult life.

Writing, like speaking and the other language arts, is a developmental process. It takes experience, time, opportunity, practice, specific skills, and direct teaching to become a writer. It takes ideas, logically organized, clearly expressed, and interestingly composed. It takes thoughtful research, accurate observation, precise discrimination in choice of topic, form and style. It takes writing, proofreading, rewriting and polishing to develop from an embryo writer to a satisfied author.

Writing Is for Reading

Unlike creative writing which may be read only by the author, expository writing is meant to be read by someone else. The purpose of mastering the form as well as the content of writing is clear to the child when he knows that what he is writing is meant to be read by an audience—his class, his friends, his family, as well as his teacher.

Writing Is Based on Experience

In expository or factual writing, what the child has experienced plays an important role. Motivation for writing is higher if the child realizes that what he is writing is related to some experience he has had or some experience he will encounter in which written expression is necessary. In all of the expository writing, the child's experience will become a valuable asset as he writes.

Writing Improves Through Guided Practice

Practice in writing is essential if the writer expects to develop fluency, skill, style and control over ideas he wishes to express. Children who feel insecure about writing frequently have not had sufficient opportunity to express ideas orally and lack encouragement in creative writing. The child who begins his written composition experiences via the creative writing avenue has little fear when he is asked to write something of a practical or functional nature. The empty page is a challenge!

Meaning Supersedes Form

The child must first be concerned with saying something he has to say before he is concerned about form in writing. The primary objective in expository writing in the elementary and upper intermediate grades is the communication of ideas. In a developmental program in which the child has a purpose for writing, he will first determine what to say and *then* give his attention to the form in which it will be meaningful to the reader. Thus, the need for organization, accuracy, clarity, and economy of words will serve the purpose of communicating one's ideas to another in such a way that the little black marks the writer puts on paper will have meaning for the reader.

Oral Language Activities Should Precede Writing

Written communication is enhanced when preceded by a rich background of oral activities. Opportunity to talk about what they are going to write about is essential. Few children write better than they talk. Children at all educational levels, especially the less verbal children, need many speech experiences before they write. The quality of children's writing can be little different from the quality of the oral language they use. Children who are more proficient in oral language development are significantly more successful in writing.

Researchers including Strickland, Burrows, Reid, Golub[3] and Loban recognize the significance of oral language as a prelude to written expression.

Composition in oral and written expression are closely related. The techniques of preparing a talk can be successfully used in organizing written expression. The student will discover that learning to compose using the written word is akin to composing a speech. The elements of organization, the ability to select, organize and compose using written symbols of communication are similar to the skills he is already familiar with through his experiences in speech or oral language activities.

References

1. Project Apex, Trenton Public Schools, 2601 Charlton Road, Trenton, Michigan 48183, rev. ed., 1970, p. 83. United States Office of Education, Project Number 66-1691, 67-3121.

2. From *Teaching Language, Composition, and Literature* by Mary Elizabeth Fowler, pp. 159-61. Copyright © 1965 by McGraw-Hill, Inc. Used by permission of McGraw-Hill Book Company.

3. Lester S. Golub, "Stimulating and Receiving Children's Writing: Implications for an Elementary Writing Curriculum," *Elementary English*, 48:33-49, January, 1971.

10

The Ancillary Tools of Written Expression

One may not move a mountain, but one may preserve a state
By cultivating commas. . . . And tomorrow is too late!
Anon.

Be gentle to the comma with its curly little tail:
Though dainty and diminutive, its power turns one pale!
It causes much confusion when neglected or misplaced,
So slur it not in ignorance, nor hobble it through haste!
Expressions parenthetical (*however* or *said he*),
All nominatives of address, appositives *aussi*,
Inverted-order clauses, which come before the main,
The members of a series (Lizzie, Annabel, and Jane),
Long phrases introductory containing verbal parts,
All nonrestrictive elements ("His hobby, which *is arts*—"),
Dates, addresses, in detail (10 Broadway, Hartford, Conn.,
Or Saturday, June 1, '36), and, last to ponder on,
The parts of compound sentences ("Ike hops, but Willie flies")
All these require commas tucked in their interstices,
One may not move a mountain, but one *may* preserve a state
By cultivating commas. . . . And tomorrow is too late![1]

Much of the drudgery associated with punctuation and spelling can be minimized if the program is planned in such a way that the student sees the purpose for learning. The staff should organize a sequential program in which the child develops skill through functional, meaningful situations and motivated practice in a classroom in which the language arts program is based on both integrated experiences and specific teaching of needed skills.

In the teaching of punctuation, as in the teaching of usage and grammar, handwriting, and spelling, every effort should be made from the very beginning to link punctuation with the expression of ideas, to make pupils feel that the presence or absence of a comma may change the meaning of a sentence. The student should especially be made aware of the distinction between restrictive and non-restrictive modifiers. As children grow in awareness of language and its subtleties, they should learn the use of the semi-colon as the mark of logical relationship in thought between independent elements.

An awareness of the function the mechanics of expression serve in communicating ideas acts as a catalyst for mastering them.

To a degree punctuation symbolizes the pauses we make in our speech, but only to a degree. In transferring the oral communication to the written expression, the natural pauses of speech can be a guide to punctuation. With practice, it is possible to hear those pauses in the inner ear. Correct punctuation reflects not only the grammatical structures of sentences, but also the particular conventions of the times.

The conventions of punctuation, like the conventions of etiquette, have to be learned. Punctuation, however, is not merely a series of rules; it is an additional means of clarifying expression. The prose style of the writer is very largely controlled by his use of punctuation marks where no rule clearly applies. Two rules of thumb which have helped experienced writers are: "When in doubt, don't." "When in doubt use common sense."

Dos and Don'ts in Punctuation

Do recognize that writing is recorded speech. Since the intonation, stress, and pause patterns of the human voice in speech are the original source of our system of punctuation, realize that awareness of intonation assists remarkably in punctuation.

Do learn the basic syntactic structures and sentence patterns of English. Once the basic structures are known, the task of gaining a command of punctuation is relatively simple.

Do observe current usage in punctuation. Much can be learned by reading textbooks, daily newspapers, magazines, stories, and so on.

Don't overpunctuate. When in doubt leave it out. There is more truth than poetry in that statement. Of the numerous rules for the comma in some composition handbooks, only five or six are commonly used in good contemporary writing and publishing. Learn those first.

Don't try to learn all the rules of punctuation individually. As in spelling, a large percentage of errors can be dealt with by using a basic group of concepts and guiding rules.

A Dimensional Approach to the Conventions of Written Expression

Sequence: The When of Mechanics to be Taught

The primary school. The conventions of written expression are best learned in conjunction with other language skills in a functional setting. Textbooks and curriculum guides offer well worked out sequences for teaching the skills of written expression. If these are incorporated into the writing program, most children will have developed some competency and many will have mastered the minimal requirements by the time they leave the elementary school.

In the primary grades the child is introduced to the need for these conventions as a part of his written expression. The following outline presents a guide for minimum objectives for Levels I, II, and III.

Writing in Level I

A. Use correct manuscript form.
   1. Head paper in correct form.
   2. Leave prescribed margin.

B. Use capitalization correctly.
    1. Distinguish between capitals and small letters.
    2. Capitalize the first word in a sentence.
    3. Capitalize greeting and complementary closing of letter.
    4. Capitalize names of people and places.
    5. Capitalize Mr., Mrs., Miss, Dr., Rev., Msgr.
    6. Capitalize the word "I".
    7. Capitalize the first word of each line of a poem.
    8. Capitalize the name of a day, the name of a month.
C. Use correct punctuation.
    1. Use a period at end of sentence.
    2. Use a question mark at end of sentence.
    3. Use exclamation marks.
    4. Use a period after Mr. or Mrs. and other abbreviations.

Writing in Level II

A. Use correct manuscript form.
    1. Head papers correctly.
    2. Leave prescribed margins.
    3. Write neatly.
B. Use capital letters correctly.
    1. Review items for first level.
    2. Capitalize titles of books, stories, poems, songs.
C. Use correct punctuation.
    1. Use a period after initials in proper names: H. A. Smith.
    2. Use a question mark after a direct question within the sentence: "Will you be ready?" the man asked.
    3. Use a comma after the greeting in a letter.
    4. Use a comma after the closing in a letter.
D. Spell correctly with the teacher's help

Writing in Level III

A. Use correct manuscript and correct cursive form.
    1. Review skills for second level.
    2. Use correct form in writing social notes and letters.
B. Use capital letters correctly.
    1. Review rules learned in first and second levels.
    2. Use capitals for such abbreviations as CBC, RCMP, UNESCO, BBC.
    3. Capitalize each word in the name of a street.
    4. Capitalize each word in the name of a town or city.
    5. Capitalize each word in the name of a province or state.
    6. Capitalize the titles of plays.
    7. Capitalize the titles of rulers.
    8. Capitalize the name of a pet.
C. Use correct punctuation.
    1. Review items listed for earlier levels.
    2. Use a comma to separate the name of a town or city from the name of a province or state.
    3. Use a comma to separate the number of a day of the month from the number of a year (July 1, 1972).
    4. Learn the skills in using the apostrophe: contraction, possessive singular.
    5. Use a comma to set off short direct quotations: "We are ready," called the girls.
    6. Use a comma to separate words in a series: John, Jack, Jim, and Jerry are cousins.

7. Use a colon:
   a. Before a long series: Mother bought: meat, vegetables, milk, jello and cake.
   b. To separate the hour from the minutes (2:30 A.M.).
   c. To denote examples (A proper noun should be capitalized: Martha).
8. Use quotation marks:
   a. In a quotation with the descriptive element preceding the quotation. (He cried, "Get a new player on third base!")
   b. In a quotation when the descriptive element follows the quotation. ("Get a new player on third!" he cried.)
9. Use a semicolon to replace the conjunction in coordinate clauses. (Mary was sad; Jim was happy.)

D. Spell correctly with the aids provided by the teacher.
   1. Develop the dictionary habit.
   2. Use other aids, such as a personal list, a spelling text list, a class list.
   3. Progress in mastering homonyms.

E. Expanded vocabulary.
   1. Add new words to writing vocabulary.
   2. Use descriptive words.
   3. Recognize literary and rhyming quality of words.
   4. Use writing terms as sentence, capitalization, period, question mark, comma, apostrophe, greeting, closing, margin, heading, indent, paragraph, contraction, imperative, expanding sentence, hyphen.

The above outline is merely a skeleton which comes alive only as a group of children and their teachers discover the excitement of making language live. When challenging activities are geared to the needs, abilities, and interests of the children, the mechanics and conventions of written expression become the tools for effective communication.

The middle school. It is important for the teacher to keep in mind that the mastery of the tools of written expression is a developmental process. Understanding the developmental progress expected of the average children in the elementary grades is important if the teacher is to assume responsibility for guiding this phase of the language arts program.

Writing in the Middle School: Levels IV, V, VI

A. Use the approved form for written work.
   1. Use manuscript lettering for charts, maps, posters, etc.
   2. Use approved heading for papers.
   3. Use required indentation of paragraphs, margins.
   4. Demonstrate habitually legible handwriting.
   5. Proofread before handing in written work.

B. Review and maintain skills learned in the primary school in the use of capitals: address, heading, salutation, complimentary closing of letters; first line of poetry, first word of a sentence; the word I, names of persons, pets; days of the week, holidays, months; names of cities and towns, states, provinces, streets and avenues; titles of stories, songs, plays, books, persons; abbreviations such as Mr., Mrs., Dr., CBC; names of rivers, a country, a school.

C. Learn new capitalization.
   1. Introduce in Level IV: First word in direct quotations, first word in exclamations, first word of topics in outlines, initials, names of characters, words referring to people of a country.
   2. Introduce in Level V: Geographical names, names of clubs, names of companies, names of programs, proper nouns, rural routes, sacred names, divided quotations consisting of more than one sentence.
   3. Introduce in Level VI: The names of newspapers, names in headlines, names in bibliographies, direction words in addresses, first word of details in outlines, proper adjectives, the departments of government, and historical events.

D. Use correct punctuation.
   1. Maintain skills learned in the primary school in the use of punctuation: comma in dates; comma after greeting and closing of letter; period after abbreviations and after numbers in listing; apostrophe for contraction and possession; quotation marks; exclamation point.
   2. Introduce in Level IV: A colon after greeting in a business letter.
   3. Introduce in Level V: Extension of the use of apostrophe for possession; comma in direct address; hyphen in separating word at end of line; dash between page numbers in an index.
   4. Introduce in Level VI: Comma to set off words in apposition; comma between last name and first name or initials of a person when last name is given first; question mark following any interrogative sentence being quoted in direct quotation; exclamation point following any exclamatory sentence being quoted in direct quotation.

E. Maintain the habit of checking spelling in writing and skill in finding how to spell a word needed in writing. Extend throughout the middle school: a study of homonyms; use of contractions and possessives; spelling of plurals ending in *s* and *es*; words changing final *y* to *i* before *e, es*; words dropping final e in adding *ing, er, ed,* or *y*.
   1. Introduce in Level IV: Plurals changing *f* to *v*; doubling the final consonant in adding suffixes like *ing, ed, est* (to keep short vowel sound).
   2. Introduce in Level V: Plural of words ending in *o*; words keeping the final e in adding suffixes like *ness, ment*; plural possessives; words with *ie* and *ei*.
   3. Introduce in Level VI: Adding prefixes like *un, im, dis*; capitalizing pronouns and adjectives formed from proper nouns.

When children write, they should be encouraged to make use of the dictionaries, to utilize the vocabulary lists readily accessible, to see clearly the models of legible handwriting before them, and to have within view examples illustrating the form required in their writing. When children have clear concepts of the goals to be achieved, when they are given direct teaching and time to write, they will master the needed skills.

A dimensional approach to the conventions of written expression offers a broad base for evaluating pupil progress. An inventory or check list whereby the student can keep a record of his own strengths and weaknesses enables him to identify readily areas in which he needs help. The following plan has been used successfully with students for self-evaluation. Each pupil is provided with mimeographed sheets like the one below which he keeps in his writing folder.

Name .... Grade .... Date ....

Mistakes I Make in Writing

Write your error on the blank line and your correction immediately below.

Sentences

Fragments ....

....

Comma splices ....

....

Run-on Sentences ....

....

Verbs ....

....

Pronouns ....

....

Word division ....

....

Capital letters ....

....

Punctuation

Commas ....

....

Semicolons ....

....

Colons ....

....

Quotation marks ....

....

Apostrophes ....

....

Spelling ....

....

Other mistakes ....

....

Teaching the Conventions of Writing

Teaching the conventions of writing involves more than providing the motivation and opportunity. It requires that the teacher: (1) plan carefully meaningful situations that will involve the specific skill; (2) provide for application and self-evaluation; (3) encourage and supply special practice on the basis of individual needs and abilities; and (4) integrate the learning of the specific skill, item, or convention with other learning activities in the language arts and in other curriculum areas.

A student must see a reason for and have opportunity to apply his newly acquired skill in a functional, real situation. He should evaluate the extent to which he is successful in that application. For example, if he is to use his new knowledge in writing letters effectively, he must have time to examine his performances to discover things he needs to do in order to improve in his communication skills.

Because children differ in their ability to learn and apply new skills, it is necessary for some to have special practice exercises in using those items which they find difficult to master easily. This special practice should be planned on the basis of individual needs. The particular items on which special practice is needed are those which are matters of habit formation and which are essential for practically all writing activities. Specifically, this involves writing good sentences, using capital letters and punctuation marks, using words effectively, and organizing paragraphs clearly.

To help children understand the interrelationships of the language arts and the need for effective communication of ideas in all schoolwork, as well as to provide further practice in a variety of situations, there should be opportunity for using skills learned in the language arts in other areas of the curriculum such as social studies, science, and so on. For example, in writing a report or in writing a letter in connection with social studies, the child must use correct mechanics in his written communication. In such an application of a specific written or oral activity, the child should be expected to apply the skills he has learned and to adhere to the standards which have been set out for him not only in the language arts class, but in other curriculum areas. In the following illustrations the principles suggested above are clearly seen.

Using Capital Letters and Punctuation Marks: A Third Grade

Plan. The children had been learning the purpose for using capital letters and punctuation marks. In the course of their study they received a letter from a pen pal who had written without using such clarifying marks. They were perturbed by the letter in which every word started with a capital and a number of the punctuation marks had been omitted. The teacher used the letter as a starting point for an assignment in using capital letters and punctuation marks. "Which words should begin with capital letters?" "Where should punctuation marks be placed in the letter from John?"

603 Elmwood Avenue
Victoria B C
January 6 19—

Dear Third Grade

What Do You Think I Got For Christmas My Dad Gave Me A

Puppy Called Rover I Am Going To Enter Him In A Pet Show Next Monday At Woodmere Park. My Mother Gave Me A New Bicycle My Sister Gave Me A Pïñata. What Did You Get For Christmas Please Write

Your Friend
John

Apply. *Directions:* Copy John's letter on a sheet of paper. Use capital letters *only* where they are needed. Put in the punctuation marks which have been omitted.

Evaluate. Use the rules on the bulletin board to help you check your paper. Correct any mistakes you find. Hand your paper in.

Practice. Write a letter centering around one of the following situations.

1. Your uncle sent you a present for Christmas. Write him a thank you letter.
2. Your best friend has moved. Write telling him the news of his friends and their activities.
3. Write an invitation to a party you are having for your birthday.
4. Write a letter to one of your friends about the things you are seeing on your holiday trip.

Integrate. Write a report of a trip (real or imaginary) you took to a neighboring province. Such a report should enhance the study of the neighboring province in your social studies class. Other suggestions for teaching capitalization and punctuation in meaningful situations include: rewrite the following paragraph using 6 sentences, 10 capital letters, 5 commas, 4 quotation marks.

mary reached into the large bag and pulled out a santa claus suit and held it up it was bright red with black fur trim billy could see that there was a set of whiskers and a cap and shiny boot made of black leather isn't it lovely she said to billy the minute i saw it i thought of you im sure it will be a perfect fit she said laughingly.

In teaching punctuation and capitalization, it is well to keep in mind that the important thing is the communication of an idea or a feeling to be aroused in the reader. Punctuation marks are there to help the words evoke that response.

As we begin to relate punctuation to oral expression, it will become clearer to the child that there is *no one* way of punctuating, that a knowledge of several approaches is extremely useful, and that the concept of creating with language can apply to clarifying ideas through punctuation.

As children progress in the elementary school, they need a change of pace and more complex activities to challenge their interest in this phase of the writing program.

T.V. and punctuation. A television program in which each punctuation mark appears and is questioned concerning its function and activities can be adapted to the format of the program "What's My Line?". Each punctuation mark appears as a guest. The Master of Ceremonies commences by a remark: "Our first guest does four things [or ten if it's the comma]. Let's name them all in order to identify him completely."

Punctuate trick sentences. Punctuate sentences such as the following.

The fight over the boys came home.

This is the story of walter who has not heard the story through it walter gained lasting fame a beautiful girl and a glorious name he also gained one autumn day on the muddy field in gridiron play the team was losing the clock moved fast any play could be the last of the game injured walter then called his own signal explaining men ill take the blame if we dont score he ran a full ninety yards or more

Dictation. To make sure the punctuation habits of students are deep-seated and automatic, teachers find frequent dictation a motivating device and excellent means for practice. Farrell suggests dictating to students while they copy it *verbatim* at their desks or at the blackboard. The students insert all punctuation marks and all capital letters; they decide when a sentence ends and when to start a new one; in longer passages they make their own decisions about spelling as well. This is the procedure.

Mr. McCorkell reads the passage aloud three times; once so that the students may learn the length and gist of it; a second time very, very slowly so that they may write it; a third time fairly quickly so that the students may check their writing.

Mr. McCorkell's methods of correction vary. (1) Each student corrects his own work. (2) The students correct each other's work. (3) Mr. McCorkell corrects all the passages. (4) Two or three careful students, chosen by Mr. McCorkell, form a committee to check the passages. A numerical mark is given to each paper. The procedure is simple.

Mr. McCorkell counts the number of words in the passage, say 100. He then divides by 5. This gives him the total mark possible for the passage. If there are 100 words, the possible mark is 20; if there are 25 words, the possible mark is 5.[2]

Dictation can be used in a number of ways to improve the mechanics of writing: spelling dictation, anecdote dictation, homonym dictation, poetry dictation.

Abbreviations. Have students answer questions such as the following.

1. What do the abbreviations stand for in the following sentences?
   a. The U.S.S.R. does not look with favor on the DEW line of MLF.
   b. Danny Kaye has done a great deal of work for UNICEF, a branch of UNESCO, which in turn is a specialized agency of the UN.
   c. I found a kitten riding under the hood of my GM truck and I took it to the SPCA.
2. Write the abbreviations for: Alberta, Florida, Prince Edward Island, Quebec, Alabama, Maine, Manitoba.
3. What are the abbreviations for: company, limited, association, pages, Doctor of Philosophy, postscript, manager, pound (money), pound (weight), ounces, prescription symbol (as used by doctors and druggists), parallel, triangle?
4. Give the abbreviations for the days of the week.

5. Give the abbreviations for the months of the year.[3]

6. Have students investigate abbreviations in current newspapers and magazines. Compare them with newspapers and magazines of earlier times.

If the teacher is concerned about helping children master the mechanics of writing, he will keep in mind the importance of: (1) knowing why punctuation is necessary, (2) understanding what must be taught at each educational level, (3) teaching in harmony with principles of effective motivation, (4) organizing learning activities with imagination, (5) using a functional approach in teaching, and (6) utilizing knowledge from research in linguistics and English which have implications for teaching.

Major ideas emanating from research and educational theory stress the significance of creating an environment which motivates and develops the oral and written expressive abilities of the students. The goals of the teacher, the teaching style he adopts, and the objectives to be achieved by the students must be clear not only to the teacher but to the student who comes to recognize the mastery of the skills as a vehicle for creative communication of ideas. It is a tragedy as well as a truism that many men and women with significant ideas, yes, even with sublime ideas, have failed to develop skill essential to communicate them to others.

Scope: The What of the Mechanics to be Taught

An overview of the *sequence* of items to be studied in developing the conventions of writing points to the dimensional nature of the curriculum as well as to the continuity, the sequential and cumulative nature of growth in this phase of language arts. The program may well be viewed also from the standpoint of *scope*. It is important in accepting the concept of a dimensional program which is cumulative in every step of the process of learning to use the tools of writing with clarity as well as creativity. It is essential, too, to realize that if one teacher along the educational ladder neglects his part, the growth of the child will not *necessarily* be irretrievably retarded. An understanding of scope enables the teacher to deal with the child's needs at a particular point in time and on the basis of the totality of skills he needs as an educated individual.

Conventions of Written Expression

The following outline will illustrate items in the conventions of writing which will form the basis for selecting priorities appropriate for a given group of children in a particular educational setting. Stress placed on them depends on how they fit into the goals of the school and the needs of the children at a particular stage of language development.

An Outline of Specific Items Useful in Teaching the Conventions of Writing[4]

Abbreviations.

A.D.	Anno Domini (in the year of our Lord)
Alta.	Alberta

A.M.	ante meridiem (before noon)
A.S.T.	Atlantic Standard Time
B.A.	Bachelor of Arts
B.C.	Before Christ
B.C.	British Columbia
Blvd.	Boulevard
C.N.	Canadian National (Railways)
C.O.D.	Cash On Delivery
C.P.R.	Canadian Pacific Railway
D.D.S.	Doctor of Dental Surgery
D.S.T.	Daylight Saving Time
e.g.	exempli gratia (for example)
E.S.T.	Eastern Standard Time
etc.	et cetera (and the rest)
i.e.	id est (that is)
M.A.	Master of Arts
Man.	Manitoba
M.D.	Doctor of Medicine
Messrs.	Messieurs (plural of Monsieur or Mister)
M.L.A.	Member of the Legislative Assembly
Mlle.	Mademoiselle
Mme.	Madame
M.P.	Member of Parliament
M.P.P.	Member of Provincial Parliament
N.B.	New Brunswick
N.B.	nota bene (note well)
Nfld.	Newfoundland
N.S.	Nova Scotia
Ont.	Ontario
P.E.I.	Prince Edward Island
Phm.B.	Bachelor of Pharmacy
P.M.	post meridiem (after noon)
P.Q.	Province Québec
P.S.	postscript
P.S.T.	Pacific Standard Time
Rev.	Reverend
R.I.P.	Requiescat in pace (May he rest in peace)
R.N.	Registered Nurse
R.S.V.P.	Répondez s'il vous plaît (Reply if you please)
Sask.	Saskatchewan
U.K.	United Kingdom
U.N.	United Nations

Apostrophes.

1. To form the plurals of figures, letters, and words: You need practice in writing your 4's, q's, and too's.
2. To show missing letters in contractions:

can't—can not	won't—will not
it's—it is	who's—who is
they're—they are	you're—you are

3. To form the possessive:

the boy's bike	the boys' bikes
the girl's shoes	the girls' shoes
the man's car	men's cars
the woman's house	women's houses

the child's toy	the children's toys
the lady's tea	the ladies' tea
the fox's den	the foxes' den
the bus's tires	the buses' tires
the Jones's house	the Joneses' houses

Parentheses.

To show a change or break from the normal structure of the sentence:

It was (as you already know) a hard test.

He said that he (John) agreed to mow the lawn tomorrow (Saturday).

He wolfed the food (for he was starving) and asked for more.

Capital Letters.

1. The first word of this and other sentences begins with a capital.
2. Number 1 is also true for written conversation:
   The teacher said, "We should leave now. Is anyone not ready?"
   "I'm not," groaned John, "because I can't find my lunch."
3. For proper nouns and their abbreviations:
   Buildings: The City Hall, the Parliament Buildings
   Churches: the United Church, the Roman Catholic Church, the Buddhist Temple
   Days, Months, Holidays: Monday, January, New Year's Day
   Historical Events and Documents: the Riel Rebellion, the B.N.A. Act
   Organizations: the Home and School Association, the Boy Scouts
   People: Sir John A. Macdonald, Bobby Hull
   Places: Winnipeg, Timbuctoo, Shangri La
   Political Parties, Languages and Races: Liberal, German, Negro
   Religious Words: Bible, the Holy Ghost, the Virgin Mary, He, Him
4. Proper adjectives made from proper nouns:

India—Indian	Canada—Canadian
France—French	Italy—Italian
England—English	Ukraine—Ukrainian

5. The first and important words of titles. In writing underline titles:
   Gone With the Wind
   The Wonderful Wizard of Oz
   30 Days to a More Powerful Vocabulary
6. Nouns showing occupation when part of the name:
   Call Doctor Brown! Is the doctor in?
   Here's Professor Smith. He is a professor.
   Have you seen Captain Kangaroo? A kangaroo that's a captain?
7. Nouns showing relationships when part of the name:
   Uncle Sam wants you! Did you write your uncle?
8. For particular places:
   the Saskatchewan River
   Main Street
   Snow Mountain
   Sir John A. Macdonald School
9. For the beginning of each line in poetry—unless the poet wrote it otherwise.

Colon.

1. In writing time:
   School is over at 3:15.
2. In listing a number of items:
   Each person will bring the following: two sandwiches, some pickles, a desert, a beverage, fifty cents.

3. After the salutation of a business letter:
   Dear Sir:

Comma.

1. In dates:
   July 1, 1867.
2. After the salutation and closing of a letter:
   Dear George, Your friend,
3. In the heading of a letter:
   187 Main Street,
   Winnipeg, Manitoba,
   July 1, 1970.
4. To set off the words yes and no:
   Yes, you may come; no, you may not.
5. To set off the name of the person spoken to:
   Mary, here I am.
   For the last time, Mortimer, be quiet.
   Where are you, Joan?
6. For words and phrases in a series:
   I like apples, oranges, pears, and bananas.
   They came from the north, from the south, from the east, from the west, and from everywhere.
7. To set off words of explanation:
   Mr. Bass, our new neighbour, raises tropical fish.
8. To set off such expressions as well, however, for example, indeed, maybe, nevertheless, too, OK, etc.
   OK, you go first. Nevertheless, I go second.
9. In quotations:
   "I found the money," he said, "so it's mine."

Contractions.

See Apostrophes, Number 2.

Dash.

A sort of strong comma or a type of brackets:

> You can do it—if you work hard.
> That boy—the one I told you about before—is the best hockey player in the school.

Direct and Indirect Speech.

Direct

"Oh, that's OK," George replied cheerfully. "Let me try it. I don't care if I can't do it."

Indirect

George replied cheerfully that it was OK. He asked to try it. He said he wouldn't complain if he couldn't do it.

Dots.

To show a change or shift in thought, a lapse in time, an incomplete thought. Often called "ellipsis".

> We had a lot of fun at the picnic . . . but it wasn't all fun.
> Today it's popular . . . next year it may be dead.
> But if I do that it may result in . . .

Exclamation Mark.

1. After exclamatory words:
   Oh! Look! No!
2. After exclamatory sentences:
   That's really great!

Hyphen.

1. To divide words into syllables at the end of a line:
   govern-ment hock-ey report-ed
2. To join parts of compound words.
   new-fangled old-fashioned protest-prone
3. To unify a phrase.
   He had that yeah-but-what's-in-it-for-me kind of attitude.

Indentation.

1. To indicate a new paragraph. (See any page of prose.)
2. To indicate a quotation of more than two sentences or more than four lines from some outside source.

Italics.

Italicised print is used for emphasis or to indicate a title. In handwriting, italics may be indicated by underlining.

Period.

To end assertive and imperative sentences.

Happiness is a warm puppy.
Please shut the door.

Person.

. . . "Person" is the *who* of narrative.

1. *First Person:* I or we. Traditionally used in monologues, diaries, and autobiographies:
   I would like to tell the class how I became interested in stamp collecting.
   Dear Diary, I feel very happy tonight because . . .
   My first real memory was at the age of three when I . . .
2. *Second Person:* You. It is *rarely* used in written language:
   You thought you were smart that morning, Charlie Brown, when you decided to get rid of Snoopy.
3. *Third Person:* He, she, it, or they. The most common person of written narrative:
   He captivated the class's interest in stamp collecting.
   She wrote in her diary that night that she felt very happy because . . .
   Her first real memory in life was at the age of three when she . . .

Possessives.

(See Apostrophes, Number 3.)

Question Mark.

To complete an interrogative sentence:

And where are you off to, Little Red Riding Hood?

Quotation Marks.

To enclose the words of the speaker:

Mary said, "I've got a new record."
"What's it called?" asked Sue.
"Hey, a groovy cover!" added Lois.
"This record," continued Mary, "is Gordon Lightfoot's latest."

Semicolon.

1. In compound sentences:
   Canada is part of North America; Chile, part of South America.
2. To avoid comma confusion:
   For breakfast we had: juice, bacon and eggs, and coffee; for lunch

just soup, sandwich, and milk; for supper, roast beef, mashed potatoes, green peas and ice cream.

Tense.

The tense of your writing will largely be determined by . . . [the demands of the assignment]. But don't shift from tense to tense except for special effects.

Writing.

Handwriting should be legible and neat. The characteristics of 'good handwriting' are: *spacing, slant, size* and *formation.* Here's a checklist for *your* writing.

Spacing

Are words too close or too far apart? Usually, an imaginary "o" between words is a good guide.

Slant

It doesn't matter if you use a forward *letter*, vertical *letter*, or backhand *letter* slant, but are you *consistent*—that's what is important.

Formation

Letter formation is individual but does your "a" look like an "a", rather than a "u" or a "ci" or an "ei"? The same holds true for other letters. Form them so they won't be mistaken for something else.

Teaching Spelling Creatively

"Who does not remember the enlivening effects of the spelling matches of his boyhood? So intensely was their attention concentrated upon the subject in hand, that grown men remember distinctly the very words missed by themselves and others in some remarkable contests."[5]

Methods of spelling have changed since the days when our forefathers "spelled down" in the little country school house. But have we in our emphasis on spelling simply as a tool lost something of the emotional involvement that was once an integral part of the experience of learning to spell? Can we in our technological age recapture some of the excitement, some of the challenge, and some of the competitive spirit that pervaded the spelling program? Can we blend it with what we are learning from research in making use of the clues we have gained about the interrelationships of the language arts, and what we are discovering from linguistics and creative learning to revitalize the teaching of spelling?

Insight into the relationship between a child's affective response to a learning situation, his joy in discovery, and his need to have a purpose for learning makes it possible for today's teacher to teach spelling even better than the teacher of yesteryear. Cannot spelling be retrieved from the dull, plodding routine of the daily utilitarian task to the enriched, creative conquest of new words and through them new ideas?

How well a pupil learns to spell depends largely upon his interest and attitude. His interest in and attitude toward spelling determine what he will do in attempting to learn, how hard he will try, and how persistent he will be in his learning effort. Today's teacher has the benefit of research to guide him. In an effective program the child's interest will be captured. His attitude toward learning to spell will be a positive one. He will have a motivation for learning to spell. Words which have meaning and value for the student will be selected. The practice of words will be limited to those he cannot spell and he really needs. He will be helped to develop individualized study habits. He will be guided in using self-evaluation techniques. Materials which have inherent appeal for the pupil develop not merely an effective spelling method but facilitate a creative approach to teaching spelling. A teacher must take the responsibility for discovering the key to unlock each child's interest in learning what he needs to know. Spelling is one of these needs.

What Research Says to the Teacher

The superior teacher always makes use of research findings to improve and vitalize his teaching.

Russell[6] reported that poor spelling ability in grades five and six is closely related to poor auditory discrimination and visual differences, although high spelling ability is not necessarily related to superior discrimination. Furness[7] emphasized the importance of correct pronunciation—including articulation, enunciation, and syllabication.

Russell[8] later reported that auditory abilities and spelling achievement appear to be related.

Damgaard[9] in studying auditory acuity and discrimination differences in spelling concluded that the pitch, loudness, and rhythm with which spelling words were presented influenced the results. Timbre of the teacher's voice did not influence results.

Rea[10] studied oral-aural training with 207 second graders and found that the teaching of principles in regard to the application of phonemes in contextual writing did produce greater transfer of learning to similar tasks than was evidenced by training which emphasized either the visual or the haptical approach (based on or relating to the sense of touch). Four abilities apparently essential to effective spellers are sound-symbol association, seeing and analyzing a word structurally, seeing a word and writing it, and coping with spelling demons.

Psychological Factors Are Involved in Learning to Spell

There is an emotional factor in learning to spell as well as a motivational factor. Among the points Furness[11] cited concerning psychological determinants of spelling success were the following.

> Ability to spell seems to be contingent upon two processes—recognition and reproduction.
>
> The older the child, the more difficulties and discouragements were encountered, but these old attitudes can be replaced with new ones.
>
> Indifference, carelessness, and distaste for intellectual drudgery are major factors in poor spelling, especially for the student with a high IQ.

> The skillful management of incentives is unquestionably more important than techniques of instruction.

There is a Close Relationship Between Spelling and Reading

The relationship between spelling performance and reading ability has significant implications, particularly in dealing with the poor reader. Plessas and Petty[12] found that the poor reader had a special problem in learning to spell. They point out that although good spellers are usually good readers and poor spellers are often poor readers, not all poor spellers are poor readers. Implications for the teacher of spelling in dealing with the poor reader are: (1) children should not be expected to learn to spell words they cannot recognize; (2) persistent failure in spelling can only reinforce undesirable attitudes toward spelling; and (3) there is little evidence to suggest that spelling instruction promotes growth in reading.

Many skills and abilities are common to reading and spelling. Reading and spelling are two facets of the language arts, not discrete fields. Each is based on oral language skill. Stauffer[13] found that:

> The correlations between reading and spelling are relatively high.
>
> The best single measure of a child's readiness for reading is how well he talks.
>
> Spelling rules, like phonetics, should never be taught in isolation.
>
> Self-study skills are important in spelling and reading.
>
> For best results, spelling instruction should be integrated with instruction in the other language arts and correlated with the different curriculum areas.
>
> As a rule of thumb, avoid asking a child to spell a word he cannot read, regardless of the curriculum area in which it occurs.

Teaching spelling through reading should be avoided. Russell[14] maintains that teaching spelling through reading interferes with the thought-getting process in reading. There is no basis for emphasis upon learning to spell through reading; in fact, certain techniques in learning to spell may interfere with reading comprehension. Gilbert and Gilbert[15] photographed eye movements of students while they were reading materials containing key spelling words. They concluded that many fixations during the eye movements in reading may indicate spelling reactions, thus affecting comprehension of printed matter. Emphasis on spelling can create a problem if a reader consistently focuses attention on the letters in words rather than on the meanings of these words during the reading process.

The Role of Phonic Skill Development

Aaron[16] found that ability in the spelling of phonic syllables seems to be predictive of spelling achievement. Newton[17] concluded that of the abilities and skills investigated, the ability to spell phonic syllables was the greatest contributor in learning to spell.

The controversy over the value of phonics in teaching spelling is a continuing one, with extensive claims being reported concerning the "regular" representation of *phonemes*.[18]

Some studies indicate that phonetic rules do not apply to a substantial percentage of *words* pupils are called upon to spell. The position of many is that some teaching of sound-to-letter and letter-to-sound relationship may prove of real value.[19]

Cues from Linguistics for Teaching Spelling

By far the most exciting cues for vitalizing spelling come from the linguists. "Typically, the teaching of spelling has been predicated on the assumption that there is little relationship between the way words are said and how they are spelled so that each word requires a separate act of learning. Consequently, lists of spelling words for class study have been selected largely on the basis of the utility of these words in children's and adult writings."[20]

Statistical analysis of phoneme-grapheme correspondences, on the other hand, suggests a considerably different rationale for spelling instruction. Research initiated by Hanna[21] in 1950 undertook to test the spelling consistency of the 3,000 most frequently used words in children's writing. It was discovered that phonemes (sounds) of the 3,000 words are regularly represented by certain graphemes (letters) approximately eighty percent of the time.

Later, with the use of computer technology, the Stanford (University) spelling research project attempted to analyze the orthography using linguistic techniques. These studies corroborate the findings. A study of more than 17,000 words reveals a relatively consistent phoneme-grapheme (sound to letter) relationship. By relying on phonological cues alone more than 8,300 words can be spelled correctly from the spelling list of 17,000 words. The basic question concerning the Stanford Study is the extent to which the findings will have utility in spelling methods. ". . . One evidently can hypothesize that even a limited knowledge of the phonological relationships between sounds and letters of the orthography can provide the power to spell literally thousands of words and that other abilities relating to morphology and syntax may give pupils the ability to spell the vast majority of the words in their oral vocabularies."[22]

The cues from linguistics still require the student to memorize certain of the words which depart markedly from the basic alphabetical nature of the orthography. More consideration must be given to the problem of determining which words should be selected to help the pupil arrive inductively at the generalizations that will guide him in translating oral cues into writing. The extent to which the child is able to make use of the most efficient method of learning to use spelling as a tool for writing more effectively is the measure of the good spelling program. The answer may well be found in a linguistically-oriented language arts program.

Suggestions for Improving the Spelling Instruction

Emphasis since 1963 has been on improving instruction in spelling. Among the suggestions made which are useful in teaching spelling are the researches of

Ediger[23], who restated the need for providing for individual differences, and Brown[24], who suggested the time-worn tactic of having each child make his own spelling list in terms of his daily writing needs. Ham[25] and Veto[26] concur with the need for an individualized approach.

Furness[27] presented basic principles of a sensory approach to spelling, noted factors which affect learning, and suggested teaching procedures. Sceats[28] recommended the i/t/a, the initial teaching alphabet, because of the ease of expressing one's idea in this alphabet.

Yee[29] supported phonics as an aid in spelling, but not as a substitute for a more comprehensive program. Cramer[30], in contrast, concluded that studies of the relationship of phonics instruction and spelling achievement yielded inconclusive evidence. Groff[31] edited the research critiques of the Hanna-Moore study, which brought to light that the 3,000 words in the basic vocabulary of the elementary school child were represented by regular spelling patterns eighty percent of the time. Venezky[32] proposed a spelling system based on linguistic principles as the key to later reading success; and Edwards[33] concluded that learning to spell through usage is more effective than learning thirty isolated words a week.

Ernest Horn[34] suggested that spelling should be integrated with other language activities and should be scheduled for about seventy-five minutes weekly, while Thomas Horn[35] suggested that greater application of research findings be applied to spelling instruction. Sherwin[36] compiled research, including spelling, in a volume that included a useful bibliography covering some ninety years. Sherwin[37] pointed out, among other things, some of the persistent problems which still face teachers in the spelling curriculum.

Problems Teachers Face

While researchers continue to explore, teachers continue to be faced with three basic problems: determining readiness for spelling instruction, selecting words that should be taught at various grade or educational levels, and utilizing effective methods of teaching and vitalizing the spelling program.

Readiness for Spelling

When is a child ready to learn to spell? Some children can spell a few words before they come to kindergarten. At home they have scribbled on writing paper and sent a letter to Grandma. When they get to kindergarten, they want to put their names on their work, write messages to Mother, and spell out their names and the names of their best friends. Many of them learn to print during the year. A number of them become interested in spelling games: "How do you spell ————?" "I see a little girl whose name is M-a-r-y." "Will J-o-h-n go to the desk and bring me a b-o-o-k?"

This informal experience with sound and letter in no way suggests that every child in the kindergarten is ready to learn to spell. The child is ready when he evidences certain abilities which are related to spelling—auditory discrimination, visual discrimination, muscular coordination, perceptual readiness, social and emotional control, intellectual curiosity, and mental maturity.

Beginning spelling instruction implies a readiness to integrate the skills of listening, handwriting, perception, and visualization for the purpose of communicating something through the written word.

Not until a child is able to discriminate sounds, associate sounds and letters, coordinate eye and hand, demonstrate muscular control of the instrument for writing, and has something important to say which motivates him to written expression does he give evidence of readiness. When a child associates the sounds he hears in words with letters he recognizes, when he reads words with comprehension, when he writes legibly, formal instruction in spelling can begin.

With the emphasis on the oral approach to written expression, it is obvious that the teacher must make sure that the child "hears" the sounds in the words he is learning to spell. A basic program of instruction in spelling should help the child: (1) hear, speak, and think these sounds clearly so that he is able to distinguish between them; (2) recognize that words he uses in communication are made up of sequences of individual single speech sounds (phonemes) blended together; (3) recognize that in the written form of our language each sound is represented by one or more letters of the alphabet; (4) develop an automatic association of a written letter with each of those sounds which is very commonly represented by a single letter; and (5) develop skill in manuscript writing in order to form letters legibly in a reasonable amount of time without undue pressure or stress.

Initial experiences in spelling should be based largely on words that are familiar to children in their speaking and listening vocabulary and are spelled in a phonetically regular manner. Words of high utility value that are not spelled phonetically should be introduced as needed but kept to a reasonable minimum.

In the linguistic environment the child learns to spell in the same manner in which he learned to speak. He listens and imitates. When his eyes are filled with print, his ears conscious of sound, his muscles able to form letters, and his ideas crying out to be recorded in permanent form, the child is ready to learn to spell.

Selecting Words to be Studied

As children progress in their linguistic development and do more writing, there will be some basic words which they will need to learn. Three widely used practices for selecting spelling words in the primary grades are: (1) selecting the words all children need to learn as they progress through the grades; these are found in the best of current spelling textbooks; (2) developing a list of spelling words which the class needs in its current activities; and (3) choosing the words that are important for individual children to learn for specific purposes. These words include family names, place names such as address, and words that are required in personal and expository writing. Children need these individual lists to fit individual needs. Each child also develops and keeps his own list of basic words that are difficult for him.

In the primary spelling program many common words are mastered. The child is also encouraged to use unfamiliar words and spell them to the best of his ability. As he writes, phonetic skills developed in the basic reading and spelling program help him to some extent in spelling these new words. The teacher should be prepared for "creative spelling" in creative writing since the child's speaking vocabulary outreaches his spelling vocabulary. The new words that he uses in creative writing become a part of his personal spelling list.

In the intermediate grades words to be studied will come from several sources: (1) a prepared spelling list taken from the textbook series being used in the school, (2) the list of words compiled by the teacher who foresees in a particular assignment words the children will be using, (3) a list of "spelling demons", (4) frequently misspelled words from the children's day-to-day writing and from words misspelled in special subject areas, and (5) a combination of a prepared list and an individual list for each child. However the words to be studied are selected, it is the responsibility of the teacher to provide for individual differences among children and to make the study of spelling interesting, challenging, and exciting.

Once the list is determined, it is important for the teacher to help children in the intermediate grades develop the ability to analyze spelling words phonetically and structurally. Children should associate the sounds of letters with the visual forms, and become skillful at adding prefixes and suffixes to root words and at hearing and seeing parts or syllables in words. They should have direct teaching and practice in forming plurals, possessives, and contractions; they should become familiar with homonyms and with compound and hyphenated words. Spelling power grows with direct instruction, regular practice, and application in meaningful writing activities.

In grades seven through nine lists in spelling continue to be made up of (1) basic lists from the spelling series, (2) "demon" lists, (3) special subject matter lists, (4) vocabulary development lists, (5) an individual list of words each student frequently misspells, and (6) a personal writing list.

Methods of Teaching Spelling

Spelling power cannot develop in a vacuum; it develops together with language power as children are motivated to express their own ideas clearly and fluently in speaking and writing. Learning to spell is a developmental process; it is a complicated process. If children were to delay writing until they were competent in spelling the words they need to use in their written compositions much of the motivation for writing would have disappeared. Children should not be forced to wait until they have learned to spell the words in a selected spelling list before they are free to use them in their writing.

The responsibility of the teacher is two-fold: to motivate children to develop spelling power *and* to teach children to become independent in their study of words. In order to accomplish these aims the teacher must have a clear understanding of what is involved in learning to spell. Learning to spell depends upon how accurately a child hears and says the sounds in a word, how clearly he visualizes the written form, the extent to which he has muscular control, and his personal involvement in learning to spell. Because of individual differences in children, a method of study that combines aural-oral, visual, and kinesthetic imagery with an inductive approach, and an understanding of psychological factors is necessary.

A brief examination of methods of teaching spelling will be important in solving the persistent problem of how to teach spelling effectively, efficiently, and creatively.

The textbook approach. The spelling textbook has traditionally formed the basis of the spelling program. In this method the textbook dominates the program. It determines the content, the scope and sequence, and, to a great extent, the procedure. Its main advantage is that it gives both the teacher and the pupils a well articulated, over-all plan for developing spelling skills throughout the elementary grades. Its chief disadvantage is that it may devitalize the spelling program into routinized, sterile, and rote learning.

In using the textbook method a plan similar to the following is generally used. The teacher must keep in mind both the teaching and learning process in planning the procedure.

A. For the Teacher.

1. *Introduce the word* (recognition and meaning).
Teacher says the word.
Teacher writes the word on the chalkboard.
Children point to the word in their books.
Children use the word orally in meaningful sentences.
2. *Identify the letters* (visual and auditory imagery).
"What letters are needed to write the word?"
"Do you see any new letter in this word?"
(If children answer yes, the teacher writes the new letter on the board demonstrating the proper formation of the letter.)
Children practice the letter. (Teacher gives help where needed.)
Teacher repeats, "What letters are needed to write the word?"
"Jane, Jim, all the boys, all the girls, row two, row five, etc., say the letters with me, fingers pointed to the word and eyes taking a photo of the word."
"Who can name the letters without glancing at the book?" (Spell the word.)
3. *Write the word* (visual and motor imagery).
Teacher writes the word on the board calling attention to the details of letter formation. (Using ruled lines sets example of letter formation and size of letters.)
Teacher writes the word again and a third time if needed to strengthen visual imagery and "reinforce" the learning. Children write the word once. (Compare with the teacher's example.)
Repeat until the word has been written several times.
Teacher gives help where needed.
4. *Use the same procedure* for teaching the next word.
5. *Review.*
Have children spell orally words learned during the previous spelling lesson.
Children recall and spell orally words learned on any previous day.
6. *Check Test.*
If time permits, children may take a written trial of words learned thus far (in a given week).

B. For the Child.

The child in learning to spell follows this sequence of six steps.

1. *Look* at the word. Look at it from left to right. Notice anything in the word you did not expect to be there.
2. *Pronounce* the word. Be sure to pronounce it slowly and distinctly. Say the letters to yourself.
3. *Visualize* the word. Close your eyes and visualize the word. Look at it again. Do you see it in your mind's eye?
4. *Write* the word. Write the word without looking at it.
5. *Check* the spelling. Did you get it right? Check with the word on the chalkboard or with your word list. If misspelled, write the word correctly.
6. *Use* the word. Write a sentence using the word. Check the spelling in a sentence.[38]

With the advent of linguistics on the spelling scene, a new formula which emphasizes the aural-oral approach is used. The child is told to:

Listen to the word
Pronounce the word
Visualize the word
Discover the word patterns
Spell the word
Write the word
Check the word
Use the word

The teacher who uses a linguistically-oriented spelling series develops a lesson through a sequence of aural-oral activities, sounds and patterns, structure and meaning, check-point, word knowledge, and word challenge.

1. *Aural-oral Activities*
Ask pupils to pronounce words after you. Help pupils discover the specific item that you plan to teach. Write words on chalkboard and let volunteers identify the item that has been introduced.

2. *Sounds and Patterns*
Have pupils turn to their books and follow the written exercise and identify the sounds and patterns in the spelling words.

3. *Structure and Meaning*
Have pupils do the exercise centering around the structure and meaning of the words. Use the dictionary as suggested in the spelling text.

4. *Word Knowledge*
Have pupils write sentences using the news words.

5. *Word Challenge*
Provide enrichment activities in using the words learned.

6. *Post Test*
Subsequent to enrichment activities, children are tested by dictation of sentences containing the word list.

An integrated spelling-writing approach. Obviously, spelling instruction, when integrated with fictional and creative writing, demands a technique different from that used in a textbook-centered spelling program. It is fostered in an environment in which each child is secure as he writes and is assured that, in his writing, misspelled words are temporarily acceptable and that he will have time to make the necessary additions or corrections *after* the writing is completed.

Suggestions for techniques and prepared materials which are helpful in allowing each child to do his best creative writing, in encouraging personal responsibility for correct spelling, and in developing ingenuity in locating and using information, follow.

> **Techniques.**
>
> Permit a child to write only the first letter of a word which he cannot spell, leaving a space for the word to be completed after the writing has been finished.
>
> List on the chalkboard a group of class-dictated words to be used as needed.
>
> Place topic words on a chart for copying as needed. Attractive and appropriate pictures drawn or pasted on the chart make it a joy to use.
>
> The chart may be stored for use at a future date when the same topic is being explored in greater depth. Additional words may be added at that time.
>
> Direct the child to find the word in a book where he remembers having read it.
>
> Help him personally if other avenues of self-help fail.
>
> **Materials.**
>
> The "Writer's Corner" contains a number of picture dictionaries, writing paper, pictures of interest to children, previously used charts, and books pertaining to topics currently being discussed. Word charts related to areas of interest to the children are prepared and filed in appropriately labeled envelopes. The children will use these as spelling helps when engaged in independent writing.
>
> The children construct individual dictionaries with several pages reserved for each letter of the alphabet. Under the direction of the teacher, they enter words which are important enough to be mastered. . . .
>
> [In such a setting, spelling,] as incorporated in a dynamic writing program, is carefully planned to promote continuous progress in writing proficiency and in the development of an expanding vocabulary. The word lists for mastery, when kept within the maturation level of the child, increase writing power and lead to satisfactory learning experience. The use of functional materials develops desirable work habits and self-reliance.[39]

Obviously, in this program it devolves upon the teacher to determine content and skills in accordance with the needs and interests of the children and the demands of the total curriculum. Skills are developed as they are called for by specific projects. Children are free to explore writing opportunities and to broaden their vocabularies beyond a ready-made list of words.

Care must be taken not to leave gaps in children's mastery of words within their maturational level. This program, when used by an effective teacher, fosters a high degree of interest in and quality of writing.

Individualized spelling. In the individualized spelling program, each child selects words from the authorized grade list which children are supposed to know by the end of the year. The words are alphabetized and graded 1 through 10 according to difficulty. Each week each child selects as many words from the list as he feels he can successfully learn in that week. This is his individual weekly list. Any words missed on the final weekly test are added to the following week's work. When he learns to spell the words on one graded level correctly, he is allowed to go on to the next graded level.

A weekly program illustrating this method follows.

> *First day:* Each child prepares his list. (This is done by the child selecting from the complete list those words he wishes to study according to the level he is on. In addition, his individual list includes words misspelled from the previous week and words that he may have needed to have spelled in Social Studies, Creative Writing, etc.)
>
> *Second day:* Each child practices his words (using the accepted method—look at the word, look away, write the word, *etc.*). In addition, the teacher gives help with spelling rules, associations, *etc.*
>
> *Third day:* Each child has a partner to whom he gives a practice test and from whom he receives a practice test; the test is corrected by the tester by comparing it with the list in the notebook.
>
> *Fourth day:* Same as the second day except the child is expected to pay particular attention to the words missed on the Practice Test.
>
> *Fifth day:* Final test.[40]

In summarizing the effectiveness of such a program, Eisman points out that the children in the individualized program were working on the average from .8 to 1.5 grades higher in spelling than children in the group program. The advantage of this program is that the student may work at his own rate and learn to spell by the method most effective for him.

Word mastery: the spelling-vocabulary partnership. Certain specific skills are introduced, reviewed and expanded in the junior high school. As a guide to help teachers in developing a word mastery program in grades seven through nine, the following list is presented.

> **Word analysis.** Heavy stress is placed on word attack skills and understandings in the junior high school. Study of suffixes, prefixes, and root words is fundamental to teaching spelling and vocabulary.
>
> **Pronunciation.** Although the lack of consistency in the spelling conventions of English is misleading, a valuable means of improving spelling is the study of pronunciation, including a review of phonics and syllabication. Pronunciation merits special emphasis in the junior high school, for this is a time when student exuberance often leads to careless speaking habits.
>
> **Demon lists.** A list of commonly used, frequently misspelled words has an important place in the junior high school program. In addition,

each student can be encouraged to develop a list of words he frequently misspells.

Dictionary. A continued, day-by-day emphasis on independent use of the dictionary is essential. Acceptance of the individual responsibility for learning correct spelling is fundamental to a growth program in this area.

Proofreading. Continued practice in proofreading can pay real dividends in the word mastery program. There is little doubt that students can spell correctly many of the words they misspell. There is also little doubt that students can recognize many misspellings of words which they have not yet learned to spell. These words can be learned with the help of the dictionary.

Spelling rules. A few carefully selected spelling rules can be helpful to students; however, the limitations of this deductive approach are apparent to the skilled teacher. A number of handbooks give rules suitable for inclusion in a word mastery program. Hook's *Guide to Good Writing* is one excellent source.

Homonyms. The study of homonyms is an important, although not major part of the word mastery program. In addition to the study of homonyms, attention will be given to words of similar sound and structure. Errors in writing related to similarities of words are often a result of inattentiveness and spontaneity, characteristics of many junior high students.

The preceding list is not complete, but it includes many methods of teaching and studying word mastery skills in the junior high school. It indicates that perhaps the most common cause of problems is lack of attention to detail. It suggests that word mastery is most effectively developed through understanding word meaning and the techniques of word analysis, but it also suggests other methods to be used in a successful program of word mastery.[41]

A discovery approach. The discovery approach is particularly effective in a program emphasizing independent study. A master list of possible questions is provided to guide the student in the problem of "looking at a word" in such a way that it will give practice in phonetic, structural, and meaning analysis as well as in usage practice. ". . . Under the teacher's guidance, a pupil will discover those questions which provide for more efficient independent study of words of the type habitually missed. With guidance, a pupil will discover those questions which he must apply to every word week after week. . . ."[42]

Teaching spelling creatively. While the various methods of teaching spelling are successful with some children, others are leaving the elementary school and the high school without the mastery of the tool of spelling. Although it would seem that the findings of research should enable every child to learn to spell, it is a fact that some children who spell words correctly on spelling tests cannot apply this knowledge in their writing.

An ally to teaching spelling effectively which but few teachers have recognized is combining the findings of research in the dynamics of communication, linguistics, and learning with a creative approach to teaching spelling. "Through a creative approach to teaching spelling," asserts Margaret Woods, "learning seems to be a highly personal matter. To a great degree, desire to learn is facilitated when feelings are brought into full play.

"Boys and girls can tell us much about effective ways of learning. They continue to show us that the imaginative process inherent in one method of teaching spelling causes children to feel compelled to communicate and to arrive at understandings which prove a potent source of new ideas, clear-cut actions, new understanding and new powers. The potential lies within, silently, but hopefully waiting to be enticed."[43]

In the description of the creative approach to teaching spelling, the author reinforces the answer the artist Cizek gave when asked—

> "How do you do it?" we asked at last,
> "But I don't do it", he protested. . . .
> "I take off the lid, and other art masters
> Clap the lid on—that is the difference."

The Creative Approach in a Sixth Grade Classroom

Motivation.

"Just suppose you were among the first to land on the moon. A sign on the post nearest the point of landing contained bold letters spelling out one word:

SUPERCALIFRAGILISTICEXPIALIDOCIOUS.

What meaning might that sign have for you?"

Challenged by an avid curiosity, a keen desire to discover a clue, children conjectured the following:

"It might mean quarantine."
"It might be a special moon plant."
"It might say, 'Parking lot full, go home'!"
"Well, it might say, 'Welcome'."
"When I use my imagination, it could be most anything . . . danger . . . surprise . . . adventure . . . This is really having fun while you're learning!"

Environment.

In this room the environment is such that the learner feels impelled to satisfy an avid curiosity and in doing so, responds with improved learning. Sincerity in expression, enthusiasm for learning, depth in thinking flourish in such an environment which tends to build in academic learning as well as ethical character.

Natural but successful ways of learning rely upon hidden sources of power occasionally belittled and ignored by baffled adults. . . . boys and girls consider imagination as a patent source of courage and confidence to achieve success. . . . One effective means of helping children achieve success in spelling relies heavily on use of the imagination. . . .

Presentation.

"How many experienced difficulty in getting a clear picture of the word chosen? Alright, take a second look. Close your eyes again." For some, need for double-checking is necessary since power to grasp meaning and arrangement of letters varies with intellectual abilities and background of experiences. "There are a number of ways we could let the class know which word has been selected. How? . . . Yes, through written expression; through verbal expression. . . . Yes, through drawing a picture. But this time, let's try a different approach. . . . Let's think about how we might "show" the word chosen through expression of movement and feeling. If you remember our imaginary trips and how real they seemed to us you will have an idea. . . . Without making a single sound, let's communicate to the class in such a way that they will be able to recognize the word you have selected."

"When you have a good audience, begin." Cliff begins when he has had eye contact with every member of the class. Sometimes when a check is made by the teacher, understanding of a good audience means "folding one's hands in one's lap", "sitting still", "paying attention", "being quiet while someone's talking". Now, however, understanding is shared by the total group. Good listening habits begin to develop to the point that a hush spreads over the room when someone steps up in front of the class to speak, for there exists a self-commitment to listening carefully and critically. Should it be difficult to achieve the quiet hushed mood prior to presentation, constant praise for those ready to listen encourages the reluctant to cooperate. "I like the way so many of you are ready to listen."

Sylvia attempts to show the word "scale" by stepping on an imaginary scale and appearing quite surprised and pleased at what she observed.

"Which word do you think Sylvia chose to show? . . . Why? What actions were convincing?"

"Because she lifted her foot and then the other and put them both down at a time on something small. Then she looked down and waited and watched. I think she was pleased with what she saw. The word was *scale*." . . . Since the word possesses added meanings, the teacher asked, "Who can think of a way to show this word, possibly as another part of speech?"

Fred proceeded to prepare bait for a hook and managed to catch a large fish. The group watched as he proceeded to *scale* the fish, careful to move the knife away from him as he removed the scales. Interest was high as the word, *scale* was shown. Used in this manner it was labeled a verb. . . . Pamela imagined she was a concert pianist in the midst of putting forth great effort in her daily routine of practicing. . . . Daryl carefully demonstrated safety measures on an imaginary crevasse prior to an attempt to reach the top of a mountain. Each interpretation of the word, *scale,* was identified as a specific part of speech.

With clear-cut movements, Ron communicated a feeling of danger ahead as he moved stealthily from tree to tree, constantly on the watch for the enemy. "I think that the word is 'danger' because of the way Ron moved."

"It might have been, but it doesn't happen to be the word Ron chose to show." Encouragement by discussing the "why" enables the hesitant one to look further and to see why his choice was justified.

"Cliff? Yes, why did you think the word was stealthily?"

"Well, the way Ron's eyes moved quickly and stopped . . .then he was all ears. When he took another step, he looked first to see if there was anything that might crack under the weight of his foot. . . . It's more than cautious." "Can anyone think of a time when you had to move stealthily?"

Brenda's reply, "I did when I heard somebody on the front porch when I was home alone. I tried to get to the window to peer out without being heard. It was such a relief when I discovered that the wind had blown over an umbrella."

Judy added, "I had to move very stealthily once when I had to kill a big rattlesnake. I didn't want to let him see my movements."

The time seems right for spelling of the word *stealthily*. "Now, will all of you please write the word, stealthily, at your desks? I like the way some of you are tempted to look at the word on the chalkboard but I can see that you are not doing so." Encouragement for quality action tends to promote higher standards of responding.

When the class has written the word at their desks, Judy is encouraged to spell her word. Class members check her spelling against theirs. Occasionally moved by excitement of learning through such natural and normal processes, a child encounters difficulty in the actual spelling of the word. Sometimes a second chance to spell is necessary. Even a third.

The teacher's encouraging remark, "That is a difficult word to spell. . . . I can remember when I used to miss that word. Class, what do you think we can do to be helpful?"

Members of the class automatically sound out the word which is the beginning of success, particularly for a reluctant speller. "This way you learn how to spell because you can do the best you know how to do and nobody grumbles. Besides, you're given a second chance."[44]

To better understand the lesson presented, the rationale for this method of teaching is presented below with an evaluation by children and teachers who have used it.

Method.

The process of teaching spelling creatively utilizes a method which:

1. Cultivates a readiness for spelling [at every level]
2. Fosters in the child a desire to spell correctly
3. Respects the wide span of spelling abilities within a given class
4. Challenges the quick to spell and brings success to the reluctant speller
5. Provides for the expression of the word first through non-verbal communication—then through written communication
6. Selects words in terms of needs, interest and subject matter

Procedure.

1. Listing of words on the chalkboard
2. Choice and discussion of a number of the words listed
3. Picturing the word in the "mind's eye"
4. Doublechecking the word by taking a second look at the word on the board
5. Showing the word through action and feeling (non-verbal communication)
6. Recognition of word and reason for recognition
7. Praise for clearcut actions and reactions (dramatization)
8. Written spelling of a word by children at their desks
9. Checking of spelling by children as contributor spells

Evaluation by Children.

Children who have experienced spelling sessions taught creatively state:

"When you spell this way you can see the word in your mind's eye. It's easy then."

"This way of spelling, the word becomes a real person or thing, and then it means something to you."

"When I spell this way it gives me courage to get up in front of the room."

"This way, you can spell with smart kids and not feel like a heel when you spell."

"When you learn to spell this way it seems like magic and magic makes you work."

"This way of spelling, the word gets inside of you and you get inside the word, then you understand."

"This way you really learn to spell because your whole self gets mixed up into the learning before it settles in your head for good."

Evaluation by Teachers.

Evaluation of this approach to teaching spelling has consisted of pointing to such advantages as the following:

Increased self-confidence among the reluctant-to-spell.

Equal benefits in the form of challenges activate keen interest on the part of the quick to spell.

Excellent means of vocabulary building.

Use of oral expression as motivation for written expression which follows serves to make spelling "come alive".

Provides new motivation and at the same time helps students gain insight into hitherto unknown and even abstract words.

Puts children at ease prior to the spelling experience.

On the debit side teachers who were quick to point up advantages of the creative approach felt that spelling with this approach was time consuming, but worth a try.

Intuitive appraisal of children and teachers along with records kept of children's progress in the mastery of spelling taught creatively, spells SUCCESS for children with a wide span of spelling abilities.[45]

Not until children are stimulated to take pride in words correctly spelled and legibly written, not until they become aware of the significance of accuracy in all written work, not until they sense the "magic" in spelling will the aims of instruction be accomplished. Each teacher must find ways of challenging the children he teaches. From the methods of teaching spelling presented, it is evident that there is no one way guaranteed to meet the needs of each child in learning to spell. The wise teacher makes use of the findings of research that facilitate the process of learning to spell; uses methods that take into consideration individual differences of children; motivates children through purposeful written work to improve ability to spell and write correctly; uses games, dramatization, competitions and spelling matches to stimulate interest in spelling accurately; impresses upon children the social as well as the utilitarian aspects of spelling; supplements basic texts and graded word lists with individual lists and written work geared to the child's individual needs and interests; and concentrates on teaching efficient techniques of word study.

Once a child learns that spelling can be mastered, that spelling a new word involves finding clues, discovering relationships, and figuring out generalizations, he will look upon spelling as an ingredient in written expression that not only helps him to write more fluently, but also brings a touch of magic into the program of written expression.[46]

Teaching Handwriting Developmentally

"The printing press, tape recorder, telephone, photocopier, and computer probably have tended to reduce relatively the amount of handwritten material circulated in our society. . . . Until microminiversions of these communication tools are produced, however, handwriting promises to remain a necessary and important part of the school curriculum."[47]

Handwriting is all too often the most neglected, the least understood, and the poorest taught subject in the elementary school. "Evidence has been presented that as high as 30 per cent of all school systems have no handwriting program and as many as 50 per cent of all schools have no separate handwriting period."[48]

Enstrom deplores that "handwriting has hit an all-time low. The problem is one that our schools can ill afford to ignore, for poor handwriting creates a host of difficulties."[49]

Although most teachers admit the importance of good handwriting, the common complaint is, "There is no time to teach it." But can teachers ignore it? How can they afford the tedium and the waste of time involved in trying to decipher poorly written papers? Surely the time and effort involved in helping children write legibly pays dividends for the teacher in time saved and for the child in the personal satisfaction in the quality of the handwriting. This may well give the child the needed impetus for creative and/or expository writing.

Creative expression and skill in handwriting are, in a sense, intimately related. Long before the child has developed the muscular coordination necessary for writing down his ideas, he is expressing his thoughts creatively. In order to enable him to record his own ideas as they come to him, it is necessary for him to develop the mechanical skills of handwriting. Two aspects of written expression—the skill involved in the mechanics of handwriting and the creative elements in the expression of ideas—must be developed if the child is to achieve his potential in written communication.

The teacher who keeps before him the goal of creative written expression will not be satisfied until he has taught the child the skills he needs in writing down his own thoughts. This responsibility on the part of the teacher makes it essential that he understand the developmental nature of the process of handwriting, key concepts about handwriting, issues in teaching handwriting, procedures which are indicated by research in the field of handwriting, and the persistent problems.

The Nature of Handwriting

Handwriting is a developmental process. It is actually one of the graphic arts, but because it is used as a tool for communication, it is usually taught in the language arts curriculum. It requires time, time to develop the necessary maturation, muscular coordination, and experiential background to understand its use in the expression of ideas.

Each child has his own design for development. This is as true of fine-muscle coordination, a prerequisite of handwriting skill, as it is in other phases of physical development. The small-muscle coordination of some first graders is so well developed that they have little difficulty in reproducing a sample of the teacher's manuscript writing or from the practice books. Others, however, whose small muscle development is progressing at a much slower rate, have difficulty in reproducing even the simplest straight lines, curves, and circles. Writing expectations of children in the primary grades must be realistic in terms of the developmental nature of growth in the process of writing. The child should not be pushed into writing too soon.

Before children are given writing instruction, they should participate in activities that involve the large muscles—work with easels, finger paint, clay, scissors and other materials which aid in developing coordination. When the child shows readiness for writing with chalk, pencil, or crayon, he is taught on an individual or small group basis.

In the intermediate grades the child gains greater control over both large- and small-muscle activities, and eye-hand coordination. His handwriting tends to become smaller. The teacher must be alert to individual needs of boys and girls as they work to achieve legibility and reasonable speed.

The urge to write well comes spontaneously if the child has a motivation for the drill and practice which are an integral part of learning the skill of handwriting. He will not, however, write well by merely being told to write well. Motivation, plus a readiness for the mechanical problems involved, provision for individual differences, an appropriate attitude, effective writing materials, direct instruction, and a continuous analysis of the writing are essential to success.

Key Concepts

An examination of the studies of handwriting and the recommendations for developing the skills involved reveals some key concepts that are invaluable to the teacher.

The child is the focus for making decisions about the most effective methods of teaching handwriting. It is the responsibility of the teacher to tailor the system to the individual needs of each learner.

Handwriting is more a graphic art than a language art. Where possible it is best taught in cooperation with the art teacher. Handwriting is a complex sensory-motor skill involving interrelationships of motor coordination, letter formation, words, symbols, and ideas in effective language patterns.

Handwriting skill comes from direct teaching and correct practice.

Handwriting is developmental. The process must be presented sequentially, with ample practice.

The goal in handwriting is legibility. Simplicity of letter formation, economy of time, and ease in writing contribute to this goal.

Provision should be made for the left-handed child.

Copying to learn the formation of letters is preferable to tracing.

Handwriting is an expression of individuality. No two individuals have the same walk, the same posture, the same handwriting. Individuality in handwriting should be encouraged within the framework of legibility.

Evaluation should be based on the child's developmental level, measuring the child's ability to adapt writing techniques to a variety of writing assignments, a variety of speed requirements, and a variety of qualities of excellence as he progresses up the educational ladder.

The teacher's own handwriting, his understanding of the developmental nature of handwriting, and his skill in handwriting procedures are important factors in the successful teaching of handwriting.

Quality of handwriting is not related significantly to intelligence. Improvement in handwriting quality comes as children are motivated to diagnose their own writing needs, to evaluate their own progress, and to receive direct help with their handwriting problems.

Issues in Teaching Handwriting

Some of the issues in the teaching of handwriting that concern the teacher are: (1) When should instruction in handwriting begin? (2) Should both manuscript and cursive writing be taught? (3) Should practice on letter forms and handwriting movements occur in isolation? (4) How should handwriting be evaluated? and (5) How can instruction be individualized to meet individual differences?

Readiness for Instruction

The young child is interested in scribbling, painting, drawing, modeling, constructing, and other similar activities without being aware that they are prewriting activities. It matters little to him that these activities develop muscular coordination of his fingers, hands, and arms. For him these are media for self-expression and for communication of ideas.

The teacher capitalizes on such manipulative experiences. It is through such activities that the child gains the needed development and control over the tools used in writing.

Another type of readiness experience is that designed to develop the child's ability in the use of oral language. There is little point in trying to teach the child to write before he can express his ideas orally. In the preceding chapters emphasis has been placed on the importance of providing varied and challenging activities which motivate the desire for communication and creative self-expression. Listening to stories, chanting rhymes, dictating stories and letters, writing the daily news, composing songs—these are experiences which lead to a readiness for writing. As children watch the teacher act as a scribe and write down their story, poem, letter, or invitation, the chalk becomes a magic wand. Out of this experience grows the desire to take the place of the teacher as the scribe.

Some children now are ready for those experiences which are specific pre-writing activities. During this stage children are introduced to the rudiments of manuscript through circles and sticks. They are encouraged to experiment at the chalkboard with drawing all the things they can think of that can be made from circles and lines. Among the responses are clocks, doughnuts, balls, bubbles, jack-o-lanterns, cats, Christmas trees, ornaments, and place settings of plates, knives, forks, and spoons. Children soon combine circles and lines and draw wagons, stick figures, animals, geometric designs, etc. As the teacher observes a child or group of children who appear to give evidence of interest in going beyond these preliminary steps, he can safely introduce manuscript writing if the following conditions of readiness obtain.

1. Facility in the use of crayons, scissors, paint brush, and pencils in a variety of self-chosen activities.
2. A persistent interest in learning to print his own name.
3. Ability to copy simple geometric or letter characters.
4. The establishment of hand dominance.
5. Interest in group or individual written expression.
6. A sense of personal need to learn to write.

Teachers have found simple, informal devices helpful in reinforcing their judgement as to which children are ready to gain from handwriting instruction. One such device consists of a sheet of paper, on one side of which is printed or mimeographed a series of geometric forms such as:

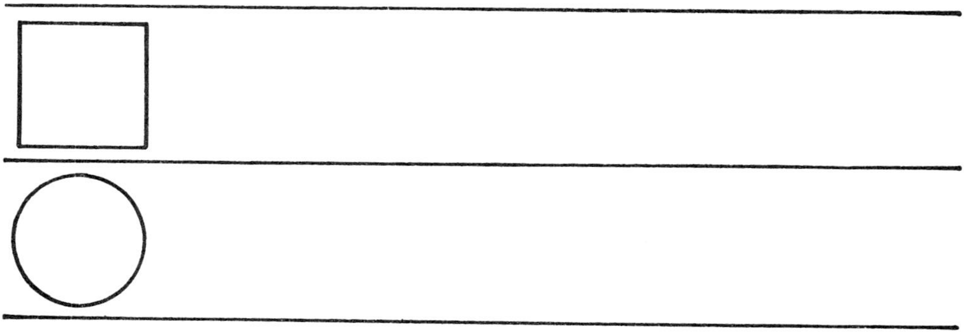

The teacher provides the children with pencils and asks them to copy each figure four times on the blank portion of the sheet. The copying is freehand with no time limit set. If the child can copy most of the characters successfully, with reasonably correct proportions and steady lines, he is giving evidence of motor readiness for handwriting. If he loses interest in the project, or finds it difficult to copy the figures, he is giving evidence that he is not at this point ready for handwriting instruction.

The teacher will find that as children give these signs of readiness and are ready to write their names, copy dictation from the chalkboard, progress from left to right on writing paper or newsprint, and write captions on the pictures they draw, writing instruction can begin. The teacher must expect individual differences in readiness for writing, in interest in writing, and in the amount of supervision needed. Some children are ready for formal instruction in writing in the first grade, while others should not be given formal instruction until later.

Manuscript and Cursive Writing

Manuscript writing has a distinct advantage for children who are learning to write. This form is relatively easy because it is made up of circles, straight lines, and combinations of lines and circles. Each stroke of a letter is formed separately and there is no need to join letters to form the word. Then, too, manuscript writing resembles the print children are accustomed to in their books.

More than ninety percent of the schools begin handwriting instruction with the manuscript form. Most schools teach both forms so this issue is largely one of evaluating the consideration which should be given to custom in the continuance of teaching cursive writing. There is a growing trend toward the maintenance of skill in manuscript form throughout the elementary school years. Schools that teach either manuscript or cursive style exclusively are in the decided minority. Upper grade teachers approve the change-over to cursive because they are not familiar with instructional procedures in manuscript and have no copy books for the pupils.

The evidence concerning the merits of manuscript versus cursive writing is inconclusive. Cursive writing tends to deteriorate with speed. Manuscript writing deteriorates less under pressure. However, cursive writing is considered the socially accepted form. Therefore, it continues to be taught.

Research has yet to determine that cursive writing is superior to manuscript. It is essential that greater guidance be given during the transition from manuscript to cursive, for it is at this time that many of the handwriting cripples are developed. Instead of laxity during this important step, greater attention should be given to this phase of the program.

A child will need practice and guidance as well as direct teaching in making the transition to cursive writing and continued practice and direct teaching in mastering cursive writing. There is evidence that the transition, if it is to come, should be postponed beyond grade two and be a gradual process rather than abrupt.

In the majority of public schools the transition to cursive is made in grade three.

The transition to cursive writing should not be dictated by the curriculum guide, the course of study, or the handwriting series. The dangers of teaching cursive writing to children before they have mastered manuscript are apparent. For slow learners or immature sensitive children, the changeover may be painful indeed.

Readiness for the Transition is Indicated by the Child's Behavior

Among indications of readiness for cursive writing are: (1) adequate physical development so there is coordination of muscles of the arm, hand, and fingers, (2) ability to write all the letters of the manuscript alphabet from memory, (3) ability to read simple passages written in cursive style of writing, (4) ability to copy a selection in manuscript maintaining quality and reasonable rate of speed, and (5) a desire to write in cursive style.

Transition from Manuscript to Cursive

There is a growing tendency for children to continue manuscript writing while they are making the transition to cursive. Thus, in their written composition they may be using the manuscript form for ease and fluency in writing, while learning to form the letters of the cursive alphabet.

Teachers who take into consideration the emotional, mental, and muscular elements involved in the transition to cursive writing as well as the visual ability needed to discriminate between minute differences in letters and letter formations make the decision to change to cursive on the basis of the best interests of the individual child. The program must be flexible to allow for individual differences in muscular coordination, desire to change, and willingness to apply oneself to the task.

It should be remembered that for the child learning the new system of writing there is an abrupt shift in motor skills. It is not simply a matter of joining the letters but of learning new letter strokes, new proportions, and slant. Some letters differ considerably from the manuscript style. The pen is not lifted from the paper until the end of the word, and there are connecting strokes linking the letters within the words. Too, letters that the child is accustomed to write beginning at the top in manuscript writing begin at the baseline in cursive writing, or there are reversals in letter formation. Examples can be seen in such letters as b and d, f and h, l, k, r, s.

Cursive writing is not a spontaneous development from unjoined manuscript. Joining must be taught and practiced. Unless there is direct instruction in the transition process, unless that teaching is persistent and thorough, some children become confused and never fully recover their original legibility and speed.

A growing number of schools are questioning the validity of making the changeover. They are asking: "Is this changeover necessary?" One proponent of retaining manuscript throughout the elementary school gives an answer to this question.

> 1. Manuscript style writing is a practical serviceable hand for all mature writing needs.
>
> 2. Changing over involves lost motion and in some cases actual distaste for writing.
>
> 3. The time and effort needed for mastering the new cursive style can be devoted to written expression and composition work.[50]

Should Practice on Letter Forms and Handwriting Movements Occur in Isolation?

In essence this issue revolves around the question of a functional approach versus learning the letter forms in isolation in large group sessions. It may become an issue in those schools which have no time set aside for handwriting, and thus give little if any formal handwriting instruction. In the functional approach the direct instruction in handwriting skills is incidental and grows out of the child's felt need to form specific letters. There are those who favor the functional approach, who believe that group practice should be supplanted by individual instruction governed by a diagnosis of handwriting deficiencies and related to the individual pupil's instructional needs.

On the other hand, Cole asserts: "The main thing to grasp is that handwriting is purely a muscular tool, without content or end in itself, and without any fixed relation to intellectual development."[51]

If writing practice is identified only with penmanship drills, push-and-pull exercises, with mechanical aspects that have no relation to linguistic experience, efforts to improve the child's writing will be dimmed. On the other hand, if instruction is left to chance and the child's "needs", he may be seriously limited in his ability to use handwriting as a tool. The recommendation is to provide the child with motivation for writing through making writing a functional skill, serving his purposes of communication from the beginning. Unless the child masters handwriting through direct teaching, motivation to express ideas will be of little avail. A judicious planning of the handwriting program as an aid to written expression is the answer to the dilemma. In other words, the functional approach to writing must be strengthened through directed practice.

How Should Handwriting Be Evaluated?

Many schools evaluate children's writing on an informal basis rather than through the use of commercial handwriting scales. One reason for this, of course, is the emphasis currently on individuality of handwriting. Handwriting scales should provide for self-diagnosis and should reflect current trends toward the cultivation of a natural, comfortable, personalized style of handwriting.

An examination of commercial handwriting materials reveals that there is a growing tendency toward providing for individual differences. Some, unfortunately, continue to neglect the individualized instructional procedure. This is particularly true with respect to the emphasis given rhythmic count in forming letters.

A perceptive teacher will allow variance, however, even if the school system is making use of a handwriting series which fails to consider adequately individual needs. If the teacher builds into the program diagnosis and self-evaluation as an integral part, provision will be made for individual differences. Adjusting instructional procedures requires taking into consideration: (1) the objective of legibility, ease, and simplicity of writing, (2) comfort, (3) economy of time, (4) differences in abilities of the pupils, and (5) awareness that pupils should develop "personalized" style of writing. It is imperative to develop programs which provide for individuality.

In evaluating growth in handwriting, the following basic principles should obtain: (1) evaluation should be based on objectives which are clearly understood by the child; (2) evaluation should be continuous and interrelated; (3) evaluation should be a cooperative enterprise—involving both the child and the teacher; (4) evaluation should involve self-appraisal of progress in achieving defined objectives.

In evaluating handwriting growth, it is of utmost importance that the child know the specific objectives and the criteria upon which his writing is judged. He should know whether he is trying to improve a specific skill in handwriting or writing to express ideas. Each purpose is legitimate. If the purpose is to improve his handwriting skill, he concentrates on that specific objective. He needs to have an individualized check list or progress chart which he can use in evaluating his own progress. As he improves through directed teaching, through planned exercises in handwriting, he enjoys charting his own improvement. Procedures such as the following are useful in initially motivating self-evaluation and pride in improvement.

An Evaluation Procedure: First Grade

Circulate around the room when children are writing. Check with them points such as the following. (In time they can learn to ask and answer these questions themselves.)

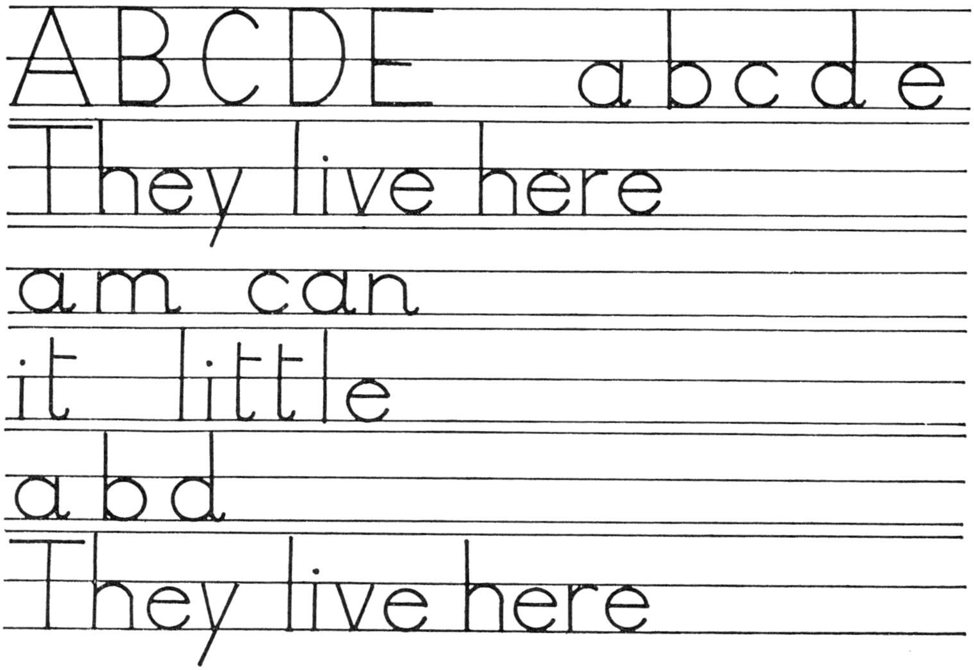

1. **Height and size of letters.**
   a) Are capital letters all the same size?
   Are they twice the size of small letters?
   b) Are small letters the ratio of 2 to 1?
   Are tall letters twice the size of small letters? *b, h, k, l, f*?
   c)Is the small *t* one and a half times the size of small letters?
   Are extensions below the line the length of a short letter?
   e.g. *g, p, j, y*.
   When first graders write they make the capitals and tall letters two spaces high.
2. **Alignment.**
   Do all letters rest on the base line?

3. **Spacing.**
   a) Is the space between two fat letters narrow?
   b) Is the space between two thin letters wider?
4. **Circular Letters.**
   Are the circular letters like circles?
5. **Parallel Strokes.**
   Are all down strokes straight and parallel?
6. **Vertical Down Strokes.**
   Are *k, v, w, y,* and *z* the only letters that do not have vertical and straight down strokes?

It is evident that, under such procedure, self-evaluation can become an integral part of the program. When the teacher and children both know what the goals and expectations are, the teacher can help children evaluate their own progress. A progress chart such as the one opposite can be inaugurated and used throughout the elementary grades.

Procedures for Teaching Handwriting

Handwriting is important to the child to the extent that it helps him do something that *he* considers worthwhile. For this reason, each handwriting lesson should involve a purpose—a situation which requires writing. This motivation is the focus of instruction. However, the child and the teacher who recognize writing as a tool also are aware that in order to be useful tools must be kept sharpened. A child is motivated to learn to write when he has something to say which he wants recorded.

Introducing Manuscript

Many children first become interested in writing manuscript as they watch the teacher writing on the chalkboard. Seeing the teacher act as a scribe when they have a story to tell, news to report, or questions to formulate furnishes the needed motivation. They enjoy going to the chalkboard and imitating the teacher's behavior. There is a similarity in the movements of writing and easel painting. The chalkboard provides for the use of the large muscles; another advantage is the ease with which the teacher can demonstrate and supervise activity in writing. The music staff liner, with chalk inserted in the first, third, and fifth holders, provides guidelines for the writing. As a group of children give evidence of readiness for writing, the teacher can invite them to the chalkboard. As new groups begin their writing experiences at the chalkboard, the others will work at their tables. A carefully planned handwriting experience will include the following elements: (1) visualization, (2) analysis, (3) practice, (4) evaluation, (5) correction, and (6) application. These components so essential in an effective teaching-learning experience are illustrated in the following example from a primary grade.

> The children in Miss Meredith's room were interested in sending out invitations for "Open House" at their school. Miss Meredith had prepared the invitations to parents but had left a blank line for the

MY PROGRESS REPORT

NAME ____________________

GRADE ____________________

	OCT.	NOV.	DEC.	JAN.	FEB.	MAR.	APR.	MAY	JUNE
Letter formation and size	NI*	S*							
Spacing within words									
Spacing between words									
Spacing between sentences									
Alignment									
Slant									
Line quality									
Letter joinings									
Letter endings									
Margins and arrangement									
Rate of Writing									
Neatness									
Position and Movement									
Key: NI = Needs Improvement S = Satisfactory									

children to write their own signatures. She had prepared a 3 × 5 card with each child's name in manuscript.

Visualization. "I wonder how many of you can read your own name? How many can read each other's name? Good. As I hold up the card, the person whose name appears on the card will come up and call on another child who is ready to read it. After all the cards have been read, you may each have your own name card."

Analysis. "How many of you have a name that begins with the letter 'A'? Allen, show us at the chalkboard how you make the capital letter 'A'. That's right, you started at the top. That is exactly the way I write it. Thank you, Allen.

Do any of you have a small 'o' in your name? Flora, will you come up and show us how to make a small 'o' and then write your whole name. Remember, the letter 'o' is the letter that is a complete circle. That's right, it starts at the two o'clock position, doesn't it? Thank you, Flora."

"George, will you come up and write your name? What letter does George have in his name that he writes in two ways? That's right, a 'G'. Will you underscore the capital 'G' as you write it? Let's watch as he forms each letter. Can you see the difference between the capital 'G' and the small 'g'? For the rest of the time each of you will write his name at his table except those in Mary's group. Remember, it's their turn to work at the chalkboard today."

Practice. "Be sure to look at your name card before you start to write. Those at the chalkboard be sure to use your guide lines. Remember, your capital letter is twice as tall as your small letters. When you have finished, be sure and check with your name card to see if you made each letter correctly. Those at your tables may practice in your writing book."

Evaluation. "How many of you made all the letters right? How many have all the letters resting on the base line? How many left space between letters? How many need to correct your writing?"

Correction. "Write your name again, making the corrections that are needed. Use your name card as a model while you correct it."

Application. "As soon as you have copied your name correctly, write it on the line in your invitation that I put on your table. Remember, when we write for someone to read, we write the very best we can, don't we?"

In teaching handwriting lessons, it is essential to have a clear idea of the elements of visualization, analysis, practice, evaluation *and* application in order to make the writing task as interesting, efficient, and effective as possible. Skills a child uses, he remembers.

As children progress in their work in beginning manuscript writing, they should be led to formulate guidelines which form the basis of their self-evaluation. One group of primary children developed the following guides.

1. We begin at the top of the letter when we write.
2. We make all our letters with straight lines and circles.
3. We move from the left to right in making letters, e.g., in making

small *d* we make the circle first, then the straight line. In making the letter *b* we make the straight line first, then the circle.

4. We make all capital letters two spaces high and all small letters one space high.

5. We space circle letters close together, circle and straight letters farther apart, and straight letters farthest apart.

6. We space words four fingers apart for chalkboard work, two fingers apart for newsprint, one finger apart on our writing paper, and the space of the letter O when we write on ruled paper with smaller spaces.

7. We write so our writing can be read.

Handwriting series vary not only in the way the letters are formed and in the sequence in which the letters are introduced, but also in their approach. When there is no specific system required by the school, the staff will need to develop a sequence and system based on the needs of the children. Two systems using different approaches are shown on the pages 341 to 344.

The Transition to Cursive Writing

The shift from manuscript to cursive writing is generally made in the third grade, when most children have developed muscular coordination, visualization, and eye-hand coordination required to maintain a smooth flow of movement from letter to letter. In making the transition, the teacher must plan specifically in terms of the readiness for the change and the need for direct teaching of the steps in the transition. Demonstrating at the chalkboard, the teacher can simplify the change-over by using the following steps.

1. Write the word in manuscript.

2. Use dotted lines to indicate the joining strokes.

3. Retrace the dotted lines.

4. Slant the letters and join the letters without lifting the chalk.

As children imitate the teacher in writing the cursive form, they will shortly be able to eliminate step 3 and use only three steps in changing from manuscript to cursive writing.

The Manuscript Alphabet

Introduction—Research proves that children are interested in writing something. However, they must first be taught how each letter is formed. Practicing the letters, themselves, should be kept at a minimum, with most of the writing period devoted to practicing words, phrases and sentences. To establish readiness, simple exercises, related drills and fundamental exercises should be practiced at the beginning of each writing period.

Descriptive Count—Rhythm plays an important role in teaching writing. While a numerical count cannot be given in print writing, describing each stroke as the pupils write it aids in the formation of the letter. Such teacher direction helps develop smooth, rhythmic strokes. The following analysis lists the sequence of strokes and the descriptive count for each letter in alphabetical order for easy reference.

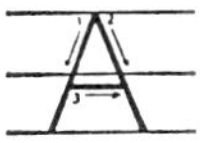
1. Touch, slant;
2. touch, slant;
3. touch, over.

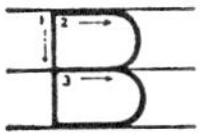
1. Touch down;
2. touch, over around, over;
3. touch, over, around, over.

1. Touch, around, down, up.

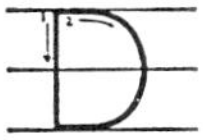
1. Touch, down;
2. touch, over, around, over.

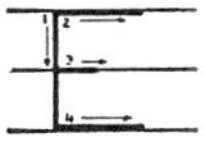
1. Touch, down;
2. touch, over;
3. touch, over;
4. touch, over.

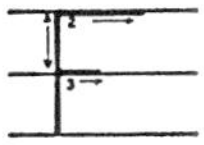
1. Touch, down;
2. touch, over;
3. touch, over.

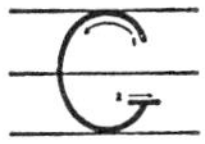
1. Touch, around, down, up;
2. touch, over.

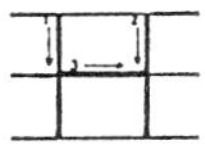
1. Touch, down;
2. touch, down;
3. touch, over.

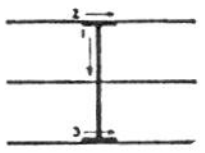
1. Touch, down;
2. touch, over;
3. touch, over.

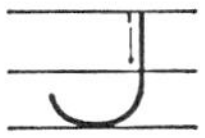
1. Touch, down, around, up.

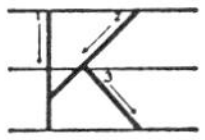
1. Touch, down;
2. touch, slant;
3. touch, slant.

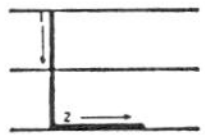
1. Touch, down;
2. touch, over.

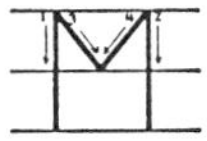
1. Touch, down;
2. touch, down;
3. touch, slant;
4. touch, slant.

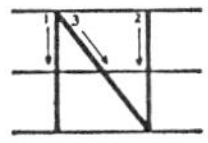
1. Touch, down;
2. touch, down;
3. touch, slant.

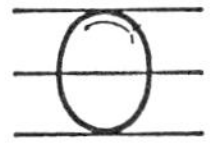
1. Touch, around, down, up, close.

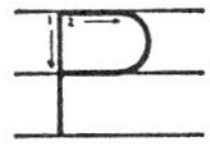
1. Touch, down;
2. touch, over, around, over.

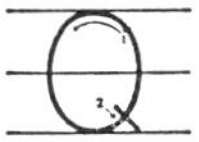
1. Touch, around, down, up, close;
2. touch, slant.

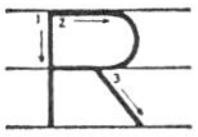
1. Touch, down;
2. touch, over, around, over;
3. touch, slant.

1. Touch, around, over, around, up.

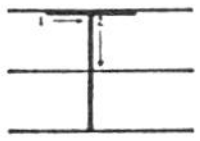
1. Touch, over;
2. touch, down.

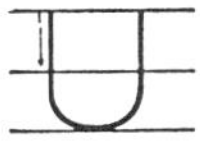
1. Touch, down, around, up.

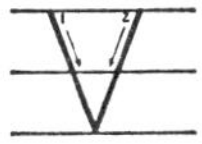
1. Touch, slant;
2. touch, slant.

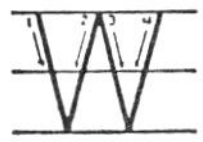
1. Touch, slant;
2. touch, slant;
3. touch, slant;
4. touch, slant.

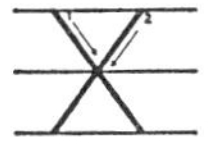
1. Touch, slant;
2. touch, slant.

By permission from *Peterson Directed Handwriting,* The Peterson System, Inc., Greensburg, Pa., 1963.

Y
1. Touch, slant;
2. touch, slant;
3. touch, down.

Z
1. Touch, over;
2. touch, over;
3. touch, slant.

a
1. Touch, around, down, up;
2. touch, down.

b
1. Touch, down;
2. touch, around, down, up.

c
1. Touch, around, down, up.

d
1. Touch, around, down, up;
2. touch, down.

e
1. Touch, around, down, up;
2. touch, over.

f
1. Touch, around, down;
2. touch, over.

g
1. Touch, around, down, up;
2. touch, down, around.

h
1. Touch, down;
2. touch, around, down.

i
1. Touch, down;
2. dot.

j
1. Touch, down, around;
2. dot.

k
1. Touch, down;
2. touch, slant;
3. touch, slant.

l
1. Touch, down.

m
1. Touch, down;
2. touch, around, down;
3. touch, around, down.

n
1. Touch, down;
2. touch, around, down.

o
1. Touch, around, down, up, close.

p
1. Touch, down;
2. touch, around, down, up.

q
1. Touch, around, down, up;
2. touch, down, around.

r
1. Touch, down;
2. touch, around.

s
1. Touch, around, over, around, up.

t
1. Touch, down, around;
2. touch, over.

u
1. Touch, down, around, up;
2. touch, down.

v
1. Touch, slant;
2. touch, slant.

w
1. Touch, slant;
2. touch, slant;
3. touch, slant;
4. touch, slant.

x
1. Touch, slant;
2. touch, slant.

y
1. Touch, slant;
2. touch, slant.

z
1. Touch, over;
2. touch, over;
3. touch, slant.

1 2 3 4 5 6 7 8 9 0

Descriptive Count 1—Touch, down. 2—Touch, around, slant, over. 3—Touch, around; touch, around. 4—Touch, down; touch, over; touch, down. 5—Touch, down, around; touch, over. 6—Touch, down, around, loop. 7—Touch, over, slant. 8—Touch, down, around, over. 9—Touch, around, up, down. 0—Touch, around, down, up, close.

4

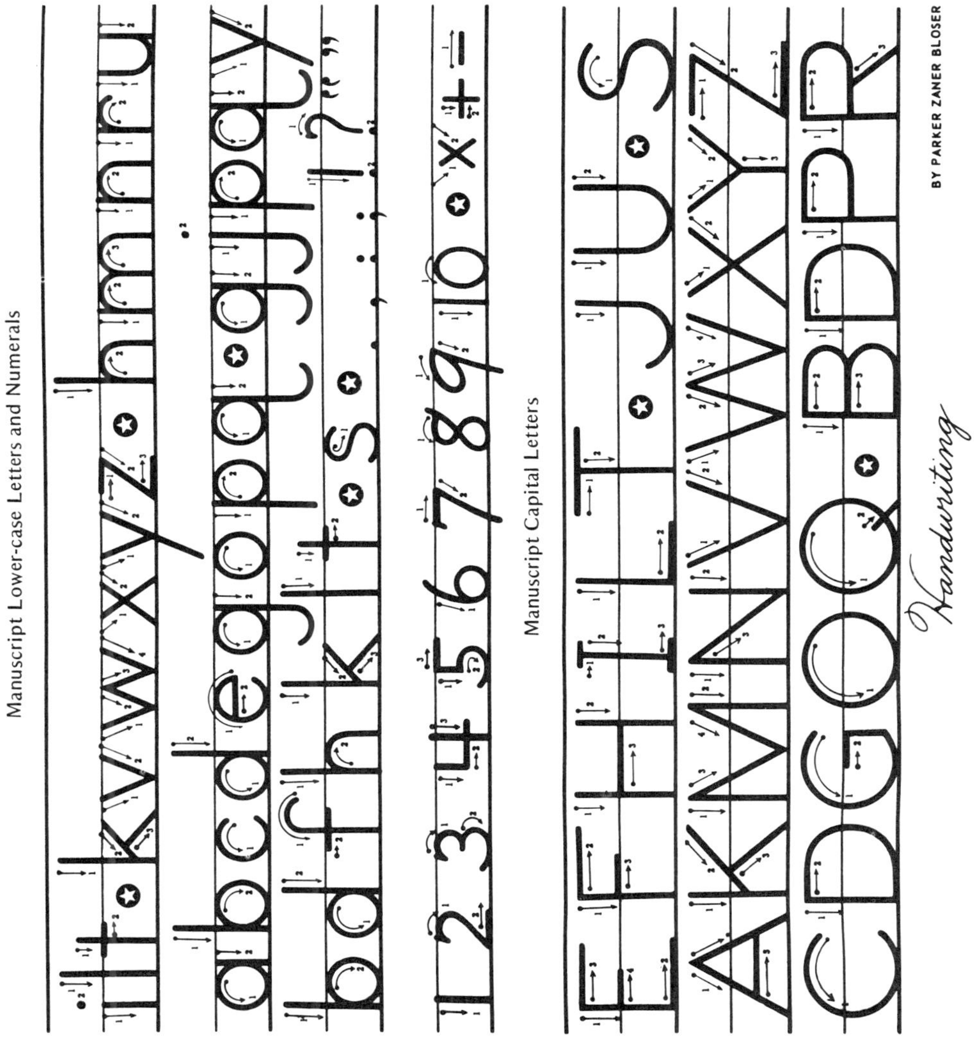

By permission from *Expressional Growth Through Handwriting,* The Zaner-Bloser Company, Columbus, Ohio, 1969.

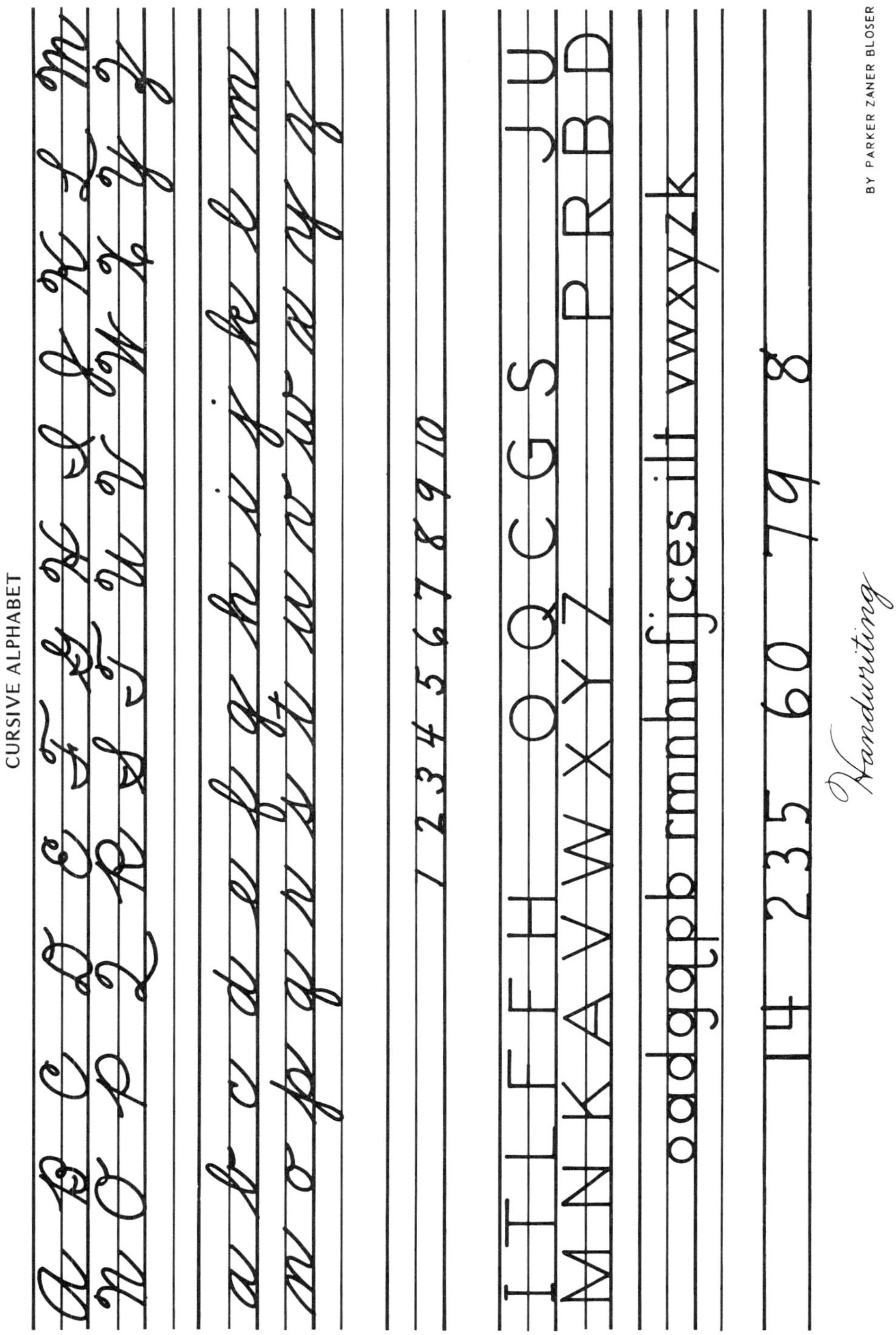

By permission from *Expressional Growth Through Handwriting,* The Zaner-Bloser Company, Columbus, Ohio, 1969.

1. Write the word in manuscript.

2. Use dotted lines to indicate the joining strokes.

3. Slant the letters and join without lifting the chalk (or pencil).

In this method, the procedure is characterized by moving first from manuscript forms to joined manuscript writing, then to vertical cursive, and finally to slanted cursive.

In teaching the child to make the transition, it is helpful if both teacher and children recognize differences between manuscript and cursive forms and their implications. Some letters in cursive are formed differently from manuscript—the child will need help in learning how to form these letters. The pencil is not lifted after each letter in cursive writing as it is in manuscript—the child will need help in joining the letters in a word. Cursive writing is characterized by a slant—the child needs help in changing from vertical writing to the proper slant of cursive writing. Cursive writing looks different from manuscript writing—some children may have to learn to read cursive writing.

Most teachers have found that periods of fifteen to twenty minutes per day over a period of four to six weeks are sufficient to help third and fourth graders make the transition from manuscript to cursive writing. [52]

Teaching Cursive Writing

Among the problems that children have in forming cursive letters are the following.

Failure to keep loop letters open: b,e,f,g,h,k,l,q,y,z.

Failure to use strokes instead of loops on letters: d,i,p,t.

Failure to close letters: a,o,d,s.

Failure to cross the t; dot the i and the j.

Failure to round the tops of m,n, and h so they are not mistaken for other letters.

While it is important for the teacher to develop a positive attitude toward handwriting and to be aware of the elements that make for legibility, it is also important to know the errors which block progress for many children. Among the most troublesome and frequent offenders are: (1) faulty endings; (2) incorrectly made undercurves; (3) mixed slant; (4) failure to give letters proper slant; (5) incorrect formation of the initial stroke of such letters as the capitals W,H,K; (6) incorrect endings in final h,m,n; and (7) failure to retrace the downstroke of t, d, and p.

The transition to cursive writing demands visualization of the new form of such letters as b,e,h,f,r, and s. These differ appreciably from the manuscript form. The teacher should begin instruction with cursive letters which more nearly resemble their manuscript counterpart. Writing in cursive style involves the ability to see the image of the letter forms in the mind's eye, to analyze the strokes involved, to feel the muscular movement in writing them, and then to make the necessary relationships. Until this process becomes automatic, handwriting is not an efficient tool for expression.

The use of commercially prepared material facilitates instruction of a specific drill type and allows the teacher to use the language arts time for applying the skill learned in a brief fifteen minute handwriting lesson.

Group instruction might well begin at any level with a self-evaluation lesson which emphasizes the objectives of the handwriting program.

The most important goal of handwriting is legibility. The intermediate grade teacher should begin the instructional program with a writing lesson which gives evidence of the child's handwriting ability. Each of the elements of good handwriting is analyzed by teacher and student and the self-evaluation form remains in his notebook throughout the succeeding lessons.

How Well Do I Write?[53]

A. Here is how I write when I am in a hurry:
(Write: "this is a sample of my writing")

. . . .

B. Here is how I write when I do my best writing:
("Write: "this is a sample of my best writing")

. . . .

C. I would grade my hurried writing: (Circle one grade) — Excellent Good Fair Poor

I would grade my best writing: (Circle one grade) — Excellent Good Fair Poor

D. Here is my analysis of my handwriting:

	Excellent	Good	Fair	Poor
1. Slant Do all the letters have the same slant?	______	______	______	______
2. Spacing . . . . Are the spaces between words uniform?	______	______	______	______
3. Size . . . . Are all small letters approximately 1/3 space tall?	______	______	______	______
Are all tall letters almost a space tall?	______	______	______	______

4. Alignment . . . .
Do all the letters touch the base line? ______ ______ ______ ______

5. Loops . . . .
Are l, f, h, k, b, well formed? ______ ______ ______ ______
Are g, y, z, j (lower loops) well formed? ______ ______ ______ ______

6. Closing . . . .
Are a, d, g, o, p, s closed? ______ ______ ______ ______

7. Roundness . . . .
Are m, n, h, u, v, w, y well rounded on top? ______ ______ ______ ______

8. Stems . . . .
Are all the downstrokes straight in the stem letters p, b, r ______ ______ ______ ______

9. Retraces . . . .
Are t, i, d, m, n retraced? ______ ______ ______ ______

10. Endings . . . .
Are all my words ended with good finishing strokes? ______ ______ ______ ______

Commercial handwriting scales also may be used to help children appraise their progress. Jill may compare her handwriting with the model and with the writing she did last month. She can note her progress and also what specific item she needs to improve, with help from the teacher. For example, the teacher might ask, "Will it help if you change the slant of the b?"

Teachers should be familiar with the standardized handwriting scales. Among the widely used scales are:

> *Ayers Measuring Scale for Handwriting*, Princeton, N.J., Educational Testing Bureau Service, grades 2-8.
>
> *Evaluation Scales for Guiding Growth in Handwriting,* Columbus, Ohio, Zaner-Bloser Company, Grades 1-9.

Other suggestions for vitalizing handwriting instruction which experienced teachers have found challenging include the following.

Have a writing clinic in which the best writers act as consultants for forming specific letters and for diagnosing writing problems.

Plan a writing exchange program with other schools in the city, region, or another country.

Collaborate with the art department in lettering for making posters.

Organize a Frank Laubach Week—"Each One Teach One"—where each child teaches another child or the group how to make one letter.

Encourage children to write the titles of their poems and creative stories in their best handwriting.

Put poems, jingles, and rhymes having unusual combinations of letters on the chalkboard for children to copy.

Make an Animal ABC alphabet for the first grade writing corner.

Make a chart grouping letters for cursive writing lessons.

Upper loop letters

Lower loop letters

Intermediate letters

Vary the procedure of the handwriting lesson so the element of surprise is an integral part of learning.

Self-evaluation is conducive to handwriting growth. A checklist such as the one below aids self-analysis and self-evaluation.

My Handwriting Chart[54]

Date	Sept.	Nov.	Jan.	Mar.	May
1. Capitals should be at least twice as large as small letters.					
2. The difference between o's, c's and a's should be clear.					
3. The round parts of m's, n's, and u's should be clear.					
4. The loops on f's, j's, g's, and y's should be clearly drawn below the line					
5. Loops should not intercept writing on lines above and below.					
6. T's should be crossed and i's dotted (not with a circle).					
7. Letters should not be crowded together.					
8. Letters should all slant in the same direction.					
9. Words should be separated by clearly defined spaces.					
10. A page of manuscript should have pleasing margins.					

Left-handedness. Since some five to ten percent of the population fall into the left-handed category, most teachers will eventually have to face it. The teacher should assure the child that left-handedness is not an uncommon occurrence.

If he is to be of help to the child, the teacher must know why the child gradually brings his hand around to the upside-down position. This is because the natural way to draw a horizontal line is from the middle of the body outward. A right-handed person naturally draws a line from left to right. The left-handed person draws the line naturally from right to left. Also, the natural way to draw a circle is counterclockwise for the right-handed child, clockwise for the left-handed. Since our language is written with left-to-right progression and since most ovals in cursive writing are made counterclockwise, it is unnatural for the left-handed child to write in the same manner as the right-handed child. Also, the right-handed child can more easily read what he is writing than can the left-handed child. The left-handed child tends to smear what he has written unless he gets his hand out of the way. Only as he twists his wrist around and writes upside-down can he see what he writes.

Drummond gives the following suggestions to help the "leftie" keep his wrist straight instead of crooked.

> Provide lots of writing on the chalkboard. It is practically impossible to use the upside-down style at the board.
>
> Make sure the paper is properly placed on the desk. For manuscript, paper should be square with the desk. For cursive, the bottom right corner should be pointed at the body. . . .
>
> Permit lefties to continue manuscript writing indefinitely. Their writing is almost always more legible before they learn to write cursive than afterward. As the left-handed children change to cursive, though, watch like a hawk the placement of paper.
>
> Encourage children to hold pencils or pens so that the top of the writing instrument is pointing over the shoulder of the same arm.
>
> Encourage lefties to develop a writing slant which feels natural and good. The slant will, undoubtedly, be a bit backhand compared to generally accepted handwriting styles because it's natural that way. . . .
>
> Furnish lefties with pencils which have slightly harder lead than that used by right-handers. Harder lead will not smear as easily. . . .
>
> When ink is used, be sure that all lefties have a good nonskip ballpoint pen which has a high-quality nonsmear cartridge.
>
> Encourage lefties to learn to type. Most classrooms should have type-writers to encourage children to write creatively. With lefties, the need for typewriters is even greater.[55]

If primary teachers will take responsibility for giving the left-handed child a good start, teachers in higher grades could give help in improvement of writing and using writing as a tool for communication.[56]

The Teacher Evaluates His Teaching Practices

If there is to be improvement in handwriting instruction, self-evaluation by the child is not sufficient. It is equally if not more important for the teacher to evaluate his teaching of handwriting. This he can do by asking such questions as the following.

Are my expectations of children's writing based on individual ability and development?

Do I help pupils set individual and realistic goals?

Do I plan the handwriting lesson in such a way that enthusiasm for *writing* is maintained?

Do the pupils see real purposes for writing legibly and with reasonable speed?

Does my own handwriting exemplify high standards?

Do I put increasing emphasis on pupil evaluation of individual handwriting needs and motivation toward self-improvement?

Do I value individuality in handwriting as an avenue of self-expression and encourage it?

Do I see the need for integrating handwriting with the other curriculum areas as well as teaching handwriting as a specific skill?

Do I enjoy teaching handwriting as a tool, not as an end in itself?

Do I enjoy teaching handwriting?

Self-evaluation. The student-teacher evaluates his experiences.

Do I know how to use teacher-prepared or commercially designed work sheets efficiently for instruction in handwriting?

Am I successful in teaching handwriting to a small group with similar needs?

Am I able to teach handwriting at the chalkboard (primary grades)?

Have I learned how to guide children in the transition from manuscript to cursive writing?

Have I skill in teaching drill lessons using the handwriting text?

Can I direct self-evaluation through tests, handwriting scales, overhead projector examples, the handwriting text, and examples of the child's own handwriting?

Am I competent in teaching remedial lessons to children with poor handwriting abilities?

Am I convinced that mastery of handwriting as a tool is essential for the elementary school child?

Among the factors which are essential to a handwriting program in the elementary school are an understanding of: the developmental nature of the process of writing, key concepts about handwriting, issues concerning handwriting, procedures for teaching handwriting, and a dimensional approach to the persistent problems.

Handwriting is a developmental as well as a personal skill, and a child's ability will depend largely on his muscular coordination, his attitude toward writing, and the quality of the instruction. Well planned practice periods throughout the elementary school with review of previously acquired skills to ascertain which children need reteaching and specific teaching will aid in strengthening the child's control and encouraging his efforts. Handwriting, to be an effective tool, must become so spontaneous that the writer's attention will focus upon the ideas to be expressed, not upon formation of letters. As practice continues, the pupil learns to become increasingly self-sufficient in evaluating his own writing with respect to letter formation and slant, spacing alignment, size and line quality. This means that teachers must strive continually to find better ways of teaching handwriting that combine legibility with speed[57], motor skill with social purpose, and basic principles with individual variation.

Concluding Statement

The need for mastering the mechanics of writing (punctuation, capitalization, spelling, and handwriting) is based on the premise that the mechanics of writing must be developed in a sequential order. Ability to express one's self effectively through the written word does not develop automatically. It grows gradually; it needs nurture, guidance, *and* direct teaching. Recognition of the interrelatedness of the arts of language, although it serves as a motivating force for writing, does not preclude the direct teaching of the mechanics and skills essential to the effective expression of ideas.

The complexity of written expression makes it desirable to focus on basic principles which contribute to growth in written expression.

Writing is an art, an art concerned with the creation of ideas, not merely with the structure of ideas. Writing is a craft and as such requires knowledge of form, modes of expression, and understanding of rhetorical principles. Writing is a skill and as such demands mastery of the mechanics, the conventions, and the tools. Writing is for communication. As a tool for communication it requires the habit of craftsmanship.

References

1. By permission from Herbert R. Mayes, "Trade Winds," *Saturday Review,* 49:12, October 15, 1966.
2. By permission from John Farrell, *The Creative Teacher of Language,* McGraw-Hill Ryerson Limited, Toronto, 1965, pp. 266-7.
3. Adapted from *Ibid.*, p. 274.
4. Gerald D. Bryars and George R. Hall. *This Book is About Communication,* Book I, McGraw-Hill Ryerson Limited, Toronto, 1971, pp. 266-72.
5. Lillian M. Logan, *Teaching the Young Child,* Houghton Mifflin Company, Boston, 1960, p. 202.
6. David Russell, "Second Study of the Characteristics of Good and Poor Spellers," *Journal of Educational Psychology,* 46:126-41, March, 1955.
7. Edna Furness, "Mispronunciations, Mistakes, and Methods in Spelling," *Elementary English,* 33:508-11, December, 1956.
8. David Russell, "Auditory Abilities and Achievement in Spelling in the Primary Grades," *Journal of Educational Psychology,* 49:315-9, December, 1958.
9. Thelma L. Damgaard, "Auditory Acuity and Discrimination Differences as Factors in Spelling Competence," unpublished doctoral thesis, Stanford University, Stanford, 1956.
10. Thelma Rea, "Disciplines in Oral-Aural Discrimination as a Factor in Developing Power in Spelling," unpublished doctoral thesis, Stanford University, Stanford, 1958.

11. See Edna Furness, "Psychological Determinants of Spelling Success," *Education,* 79:234-9, December, 1958.
12. Gus Plessas and Walter T. Petty, "The Spelling Plight of the Poor Reader," *Elementary English,* 39:463-6, May, 1962.
13. Adapted from Russell G. Stauffer, "Relationships Between Spelling and Reading," *Education,* 79:206-10, December, 1958.
14. David Russell, "Spelling Ability in Relation to Reading and Vocabulary Achievement," *Elementary English Review,* 23:32-7, January, 1946.
15. Luther C. Gilbert and Doris Wilcox Gilbert, "The Improvement of Spelling Through Reading," *Journal of Educational Research,* 37:13-23, February, 1944.
16. Ira E. Aaron, "The Relationship of Selected Measures at the Fourth and Eighth Grade Levels," *Journal of Educational Research,* 53:138-43, December, 1959.
17. Bertha Newton, "A Study of Certain Factors Related to Achievement in Spelling," *Dissertations in Education,* University of Missouri Bulletin, Columbia, Study 41, 1960, pp. 134-6.
18. Paul R. Hanna and James T. Moore, Jr., "Spelling: From Spoken Word to Written Symbol," *Elementary School Journal,* 53:329-37, February, 1953.
19. Ernest Horn, "Spelling," in Chester W. Harris (ed.), *Encyclopedia of Educational Research,* The Macmillan Company, New York, 1960.
20. By permission from Richard E. Hodges and E. Hugh Rudorf, "Searching Linguistics for Cues for the Teaching of Spelling," *Elementary English,* 42:527, May, 1965.
21. James T. Moore, Jr., "Phonic Elements Appearing in a Three Thousand Word Spelling Vocabulary," unpublished doctoral dissertation, Stanford University, Stanford, 1951.
22. Hodges and Rudorf, *op. cit.,* p. 532.
23. M. Ediger, "Teaching Spelling in the Elementary School," *Peabody Journal of Education,* 45:103-6, September, 1967.
24. L. Brown, "Let's Put an I in Spelling," *English Journal,* 54:644-5, October, 1965.
25. J. F. Ham, "Success Story: Individualized Spelling," *Instructor,* 75:145ff, September, 1965.
26. J. M. Veto, "Understanding and Meeting Individual Needs in Spelling," *Elementary English,* 41:753-4, November, 1964.
27. E. L. Furness, "Pupils, Teachers, and Sensory Approaches to Spelling," *Education,* 88:267-73, February, 1968.
28. J. Sceats, "Middle Way in Spelling," *Times Educational Supplement,* 2779:319, London, August 23, 1968.
29. Albert H. Yee, "The Generalization Controversy on Spelling Instruction," *Elementary English,* 43:154-61, February, 1966.
30. R. L. Cramer, "Influence of Phonics Instruction on Spelling Achievement," *The Reading Teacher,* 22:499-503, March, 1969.
31. Patrick J. Groff, "Research Critiques: Spelling from Spoken Word to Written Symbol," *Elementary English* 42: 582-7, May, 1965.
32. R. L. Venezky, "Reading: Grapheme-Phoneme Relationships," *Education* 87:519-24, May, 1967.
33. P. O. Edwards, "How to Build Spelling Power," *Grade Teacher,* 80:17, April, 1963.
34. Ernest Horn, *Teaching Spelling: What Research Says to the Teacher,* no. 3. Department of Classroom Teachers, NEA, Washington, D.C., 1967.
35. Thomas D. Horn, "Spelling," *Encyclopedia of Educational Research,* The Macmillan Co., New York, 1969.
36. J. Stephen Sherwin (ed.), *Four Problems in Teaching English: A Critique of Research,* International Textbook Company, Scranton, Pa., 1969.
37. J. Stephen Sherwin, "Increasing Skill in Writing: Traditional Grammar, Linguistics, and Writing Practice," in Sherwin, *op cit.*

38. See Maria Montessori, *The Montessori Method,* tr. by Anne George, Frederick Stokes Co., New York, 1912.
39. Wisconsin Dept. of Public Instruction, *Teaching Speaking and Writing in Wisconsin,* Wisconsin English Language Arts Curriculum Project, Department of Public Instruction, Madison, 1966, pp. 15-6.
40. Edward Eisman, "Individualized Spelling: Second Report," *Elementary English,* 40:529-30, May, 1963.
41. Wisconsin Dept. of Public Instruction, *op. cit.*, p. 70.
42. Howard Blake, "Studying Spelling Independently," in Robert E. Chasnof (ed.), *Elementary Curriculum: A Book of Readings,* Pitman Publishing Company, New York, 1964, p. 318.
43. By permission from Margaret Woods, "Success in Spelling: A Creative Approach," *Resources for Teaching and Learning,* The Official WDAVI Journal, April, 1965, p. 17.
44. *Ibid.*, pp. 16-7.
45. *Ibid.*, p. 17. (Adapted.)
46. See also Jeanne Tellier Leeson, "The Homonym Game," *Elementary English*, 49:784, May, 1972, and Lillie Smith Davis, "The Applicability of Phonic Generalizations to Selected Spelling Programs," *Elementary English,* 49:706-13, May, 1972.
47. Charles R. Culp, "Handwriting," in Harold G. Shane et al., *Interpreting Language Arts Research For the Teacher,* Association for Supervision and Curriculum Development, NEA, 1201 Sixteenth Street, Washington, D.C. 20036, 1971, p. 59.
48. Fred M. King, "Handwriting Practices in Our Schools Today," *Elementary English,* 38:483-6, November, 1961.
49. E. A. Enstrom, "The Decline of Handwriting," *The Elementary School Journal,* 66:22, October, 1965.
50. Gertrude Hildreth, "Manuscript Writing After Sixty Years," *Elementary English,* January, 1960. Quoted in Verna D. Anderson et al., *Readings in the Language Arts,* The Macmillan Co., New York, 1964, p. 165.
51. By permission from Luella Cole, "Reflections on the Teaching of Handwriting," in Anderson et al., *op. cit.,* p. 201.
52. Virgil E. Herrick, "Manuscript and Cursive Writing," in Robert Chasnoff (ed.), *Elementary Curriculum: A Book of Readings,* Pitman Publishing Co., New York, 1964, pp. 314-5.
53. Nathan Naiman, "Handwriting Blitz," in Anderson et al., *op. cit.*, pp. 176-7.
54. By permission from *Some Evaluation Techniques in Language Arts for Teachers and Pupils,* Portland Public Schools, Curriculum Publication LA-38, Portland, n.d., p. 6.
55. Harold D. Drummond, "Suggestions for 'Lefties'," from *The National Elementary Principal,* 38:15, February, 1959. Copyright 1959, National Association of Elementary School Principals, National Education Association. All rights reserved.
56. A complete set of writing Exercises for the left-handed child learning cursive writing can be procured from Dr. Warren Gardner, Interstate Press, 19 North Jackson Street, Danville, Illinois. See also: E. A. Enstrom, "The Little Turn That Makes a Big Difference," *Elementary English,* 43:865-8, December, 1966.
57. Lowell W. Horton, "Illegibilities in the Cursive Handwriting of Sixth-Graders," *Elementary School Journal,* 70:446-9, May, 1970.

PART FOUR
Reading and Literature

11

Developing Skills in Reading: Prelude to Interpretation

As children talk, so shall they read.
Helen Hickock

"The basis for reading is spoken language; if a child can understand and use spoken words well, he has demonstrated the capacity for dealing in symbols. In a society highly dependent on spoken and written words, early education must be concerned with the development of language skills, including preparation for success in beginning reading."[1]

Before the child can extract meaning from the printed page, he must be able to bring meaning to the printed page. This demands richness of experience and development of communication skills. The interaction between experience and language is constant. Spoken language is an index to the child's understanding of the world about him—the world of people, places, and phenomena. Spoken language is one of the communication skills essential for successful living in today's complex world. Systematic instruction in oral language is the responsibility of the elementary school.

Children must be equipped to deal critically, intelligently, and creatively with an enormous amount of printed material. Learning to read is a complex process. Pupils are led step-by-step to develop inquiring attitudes along with the mechanical skills of reading. They learn to understand ideas, examine them, and decide whether or not they are valid. They learn, too, to think of reading as a way of communicating with great minds of all ages, a way of expanding horizons, increasing understanding, and developing insights.

Every child should bring to reading a rich and varied experiential background, a fluency in oral language, a degree of emotional, social, physical, and mental maturity *plus* a desire to read. The eager pupil and the skilled teacher are the best combination for teaching reading.

"The skillful and perceptive teacher knows how to light a fire in a child's mind. She knows the kindling points of interest. Her own behavior initiates those activities which, when nurtured in refinement, can carry the child well beyond 'where he is'."[2]

Most children come to school with the belief that learning to read is an exciting adventure. The effective teacher capitalizes on their interest, curiosity, and desire to learn and provides a program geared to their needs. The teacher must: (1) be aware of the interrelatedness of the language arts, (2) utilize linguistic factors in teaching reading, (3) understand the nature of the

understand reading development, (5) be familiar with cur-
eading instruction, (6) organize a reading program, (7) help
ing skills, (8) provide for individual differences, (9) evaluate

'atedness of the Language Arts

Children enter school with widely varying language experiences. Some come with a vast fund of "capital stock" for the teacher to tap in initiating the reading process. They have already made a significant growth in speaking and listening. Others come from impoverished backgrounds and have limited skills in the language arts. Each teacher must build on whatever background of language skills the child has and on the basis of the child's individual needs.

Research findings give evidence of the significance of the interrelatedness of the language arts and the sequence in which the language skills develop. Loban's[3] study of the language development of 338 children from kindergarten through high school contains evidence of the extremely close relationship existing among the language arts: listening, speaking, reading, and writing. He reports that the group of pupils who were high in general language ability were also high in reading ability, while those who were low in general language ability were also low in reading ability.

Burrows has shown that when writing is preceded by oral language activities, all forms of written communication are appreciably improved. All children need a great deal of experience in oral language activities before they can be expected to write. Research makes it clear that "the quality of children's writing can be little different from the quality of oral language they use."[4]

Reading vocabulary requires two important factors: the ability to identify the word and the knowledge of its meaning. Robinson shows the relationship between reading and other language arts. "Reading vocabulary is built on listening and speaking vocabularies, with word identification added."[5]

Strickland concurs with this evidence since she found that pupils who ranked high in silent reading comprehension skills tended to use longer sentences or "utterances" when speaking and also used more "moveables" and elements of subordination.[6]

Armstrong asserts: "A total language approach is the key to better reading. The concept of the unity of the language arts has been well supported in theory if not in classroom practice, and the evidence that language competence is the single, most important factor in reading success is overwhelming. Language is the essence of reading readiness."[7]

Thus, an effective program in the language arts is based on the concept of interrelatedness. Activities should include both integrated experiences and separate teaching of the skills of communication. The strands of the language arts are so closely interwoven that development in one leads to greater skill in each of the others.

The interrelatedness and the commonalities of the language arts form a logical basis for planning the learning experiences. For example, each of the language arts depends upon the process of thinking and the expression of ideas for success. Growth in each depends upon experience with language and conceptualizing in an environment that is both stimulating and supporting.

As a prelude to success in reading, the child must have fluency with words. The foundation for reading is laid by providing the child with experiences in his physical and social environment which stimulate and give meaning to the symbols of language. As he develops meaning through experiencing, he is building a speaking and thinking vocabulary; as he learns to express ideas through oral language, he is developing the tools he will use to master the symbols of written language—reading and writing.

Experience, ideas, and the mastery of tools of communication—these are essential to each of the language arts. These are the threads which form the design for creative expression of ideas. The formula for weaving the threads of the language arts into a design for creative expression is:

$$E + W + T + C = CE$$

E Experiences—stimulate children to think

W Words—convey ideas, experiences and ideas take flight

T Tools—clarify meaning

C Creativity—expresses individuality

CE Creative Expression—the individual expresses his thoughts imaginatively, spontaneously, and with originality.

Linguistic Factors in Early Reading Instruction

"It is doubtful whether a child can become a fluent reader, comprehending fully what he reads, without a good oral language foundation and continued attention to oral language improvement."[8]

When the child comes to school he has already developed some skill in the use of oral language. If the first experiences in reading lead him to see the relationships between oral language and printed symbols, reading becomes meaningful. Consequently, success is more likely to follow. The child who is learning to read succeeds more readily if he is taught to relate the speech patterns he already knows to the symbols in the written language which he is trying to decode.

Learning to read, as every teacher knows, does not take place in a linguistic vacuum. It cannot take place outside the context of language. The fact that beginning readers already have gained a modicum of control over the spoken language does not negate the teacher's responsibility for continued experiences in developing the spoken language skills throughout the process of learning to read.

All too frequently teachers fail to provide time in the daily program for the activities designed to improve speech skills. They fail to realize the significant role oral language plays in learning to read. To skimp on time for speech activities in the belief that "reading is more important" is self-defeating. Time given for oral language is time given for reading since oral language experience is actually an integral part of learning to read. A good rule for the teacher is—Do not begin reading instruction without first taking into account

; status in speech. Develop oral language skills prior to and along with xperiences if you want your children to read effectively.

The study of linguistics has implications for instruction in reading. It reveals that "when a child is ready to learn to read, the *only* new skill he must master is the skill generally referred to as word perception—the ability to respond to written symbols with the appropriate sound . . . reading comprehension, interpretation, vocabulary development . . . are largely developed by children in the process of listening to language rather than in reading."[9]

The teacher should make use of the linguistic skills children already possess—skills of oral usage and listening. He should relate them to the new skills to be acquired in writing and spelling along with reading instruction. Composing sentences for the experience charts helps children develop "sentence sense". Writing (composing stories) reinforces the general linguistic skills related to reading with meaning.

Thus, teaching reading in a language-oriented, linguistic-centered program is more rewarding to the teacher than relying upon mechanical word drills, and motivates children to develop the essential reading skills of extracting meaning from a variety of syntactical patterns.

Reading is more than word-calling. It is an experience in which sounds are associated with meaning. Meaning is expressed not only by single words but by units of phrases and sentences. This is the language-centred approach to reading.

"The more extensive the child's experience in the language of speech, therefore, the better equipped he is likely to be in getting an author's meaning."[10]

As the oral aspects of the language provide the basis for achieving success in learning to read, so too does a growing mastery of the written symbols of language help the child develop interest in and sensitivity to the many facets of language: structure and form, rhythm of the language, translation of sounds and concepts into symbols that hold meaning for the reader, as well as for the writer. As the child gains in the command of oral and written language, he finds an open door to adventure. He develops an understanding of man and his universe, and gains greater insight into his dreams and aspirations.

The Nature of Reading

Never in educational history has there been such a great interest by such a variety of individuals and groups in the problem of reading. There was a time when primary teachers were lone voices crying in the wilderness about the importance of teaching children to read. Now they are no longer alone. Today teachers at all educational levels, the lay public, and governmental agencies are uniting in their efforts to improve reading instruction.

In order to cope with the demands of our technological age, new methods, new approaches, new materials for reading instruction are being tested. This concern for reading has resulted in incorporating principles and practices as well as theories and concepts from other disciplines.

An understanding of the key concepts concerning the nature of reading is a prerequisite for teaching reading successfully. The psychological, sociological, physiological, neurological, and pedagogical aspects of the reading process must be considered in developing a program whereby children can be successfully taught to read.

Key Concepts in the Nature of Reading

Reading is rooted in experience. The more you bring to a book, the more you will take from it. The initial focus must be on experience. The child extracts meaning from the printed page in proportion to the meaning he brings to it. Broad experiences and reading are mutually reinforcing. The teachers and parents have a responsibility to provide the experiences children need—both first hand and vicarious. Time spent in teaching word recognition and comprehension skills is wasted if the child has not had a broad enough range of experiences.

Reading as responding. "Reading is something we do, not so much with our eyes as such, as with our knowledge, our interests and enthusiasms, our hatreds and fondnesses and fears, our evaluations in all their forms and aspects."[11] Children respond to the printed page at three levels—word-calling, comprehension, and the creative level. The effective teacher endeavours to bring all children to the creative level.

Reading is reaction. Reading is reaction to the graphic representation of sound symbols in terms of *recognition* and *understanding*. Whether oral or silent, reading involves reaction to the abstractions of symbols that represent sound. Even at the most elementary level in teaching reading, two fundametnal skills must be developed. They are *recognizing words* and *getting meanings from them*. In the earliest stages of reading instruction, children learn to recognize the symbols that represent things and ideas. "The act of reading is a matter of using the stimulus of the marks on the page to recreate speech."[12]

The teacher should provide ample experiences with the oral language before he attempts to teach children to react to the written symbols. The average child by the time he enters the elementary school is no stranger to oral language. Experience in speech is intimately related to the process of learning to read.

Reading is a native language process. If reading instruction is tied closely to speech, the child will be more successful in reading. If the teacher begins with familiar materials from the child's spoken language, the more familiar the better, the child senses the relationship between his native language expression and the reading process. Thus, he sees that the way he talks, which requires the use of oral symbols, is related to the way he must translate the written symbols in order to make the meaning clear. "The teacher should talk out in normal speech patterns what is on the page and encourage the children to do so also. No reading singsongs should be permitted to develop."[13]

If children are encouraged to read as they speak with appropriate inflections, the word-droning—the bane of the primary reading class—will be held at a minimum.

Reading is complex. Reading is such a complex activity that any assertion that there is just one approach to teaching is as ridiculous as it is dangerous. A realization of the complexity is the foundation for progress. Anyone who has taught reading realizes that it involves physical, psychological, intellectual, and emotional responses. In the physical realm there are sensation and perception; in the psychological, abstract symbols are clothed with meanings; in the intellectual, critical thinking is a major goal; and in the emotional there is the nature and intensity of the reaction to the material presented by the writer.

The reading process involves perception (perceiving the words clearly), recognition (recognizing each word and its meaning), comprehension (understanding the meaning of words, sentences, and paragraphs and sensing relationships among the ideas), interpretation (making an accurate analysis of the meaning of the material read), evaluation (determining the adequacy of the ideas in the light of predetermined criteria), and utilization (using the ideas for a purpose). Research and empirical evidence attest to the complexity of reading. It is not a unitary skill. Rather, it has components of word-recognition skills, comprehension abilities, interpretative skills, and attitudes involving critical thinking and evaluation. The simple ability to recognize words will not meet the demands of modern life.

Reading is a tool for communication. Through reading the child communicates with great minds of the past as well as the present. Through reading he enters into experiences which otherwise would be closed to him. Words merely serve to convey the ideas set forth in a book. They come to life only as the reader brings meaning and experience to them. To the degree that he can unlock the printed symbol and associate it with meaning, is the recognition process effective in communicating ideas.

Reading is creativity. The creative reader brings to the reading material the skills of comparison and synthesis, the ability to see new relationships and to arrive at conclusions based on an "educated hunch". He anticipates outcomes, projects beyond the obvious, and "reads between the lines". The creative reader gains new insights, new understandings, and new appreciations of the ideas revealed in the printed page.

Reading is a developmental task. Society expects every child to learn to read during the first grade. It is one of the development tasks. This implies that at the time the task is presented the child will have sufficient maturity to achieve success when the opportunity to learn is provided. Unfortunately, however, this assumption is not consistent with our knowledge of individual differences. The teacher of beginning reading must reconcile the expectations of society with his own understanding of child development and learning. Each child learns at his own rate of growth, and in terms of his own needs, abilities, aptitudes, interests, and ways of learning. Unless a child recognizes that reading will meet his immediate needs, he will not be motivated to learn to read.

Reading is for specific purposes. People read for specific purposes. Reading serves at least four purposes in the life of an individual: reading for information, reading for enjoyment, reading to solve problems, and reading to evaluate. Reading stimulates thinking, creates broadened interests, and contributes to personal and social adjustment.

Reading is developmental in nature. Reading is a continuing process. It takes years to become what is known as a "mature" reader. Characteristics of a mature reader are cited by Gray and Rogers. "The mature reader has enthusiasm; reads widely and intensively; comprehends and interprets words, ideas, moods, and feelings; makes use of ideas gained in reading; reads critically and evaluates the material; integrates ideas gained in reading with previous experiences; adjusts pace to the occasion and the demands of interpretation; and discriminates in the selection of material and interpretation of the selection."[14]

Reading development progresses year by year, not in a series of separate steps but in patterns which emerge almost imperceptibly as one moves from stage to stage. The lack which college students show in attempting to meet the demands of the curriculum is in part the result of a lack of understanding of the importance of reading as developmental in nature *throughout* the individual's life.

Stages in Reading Development

Reading ability must be developed gradually and systematically. One ability is built upon another; one skill is interrelated with another; each phase merges into another. Each skill must be introduced at the time it is needed, related to skills already acquired, and reintroduced at a higher degree of competence at succeeding levels of development. As the child progresses through the elementary school, he needs to refine, perfect, and master abilities and skills introduced earlier. He develops news skills as they are needed.

The conscious planning in the school program to provide for continued emphasis on this important linguistic skill at an ever-deepening and broadening level truly makes it an element of organization helping to tie together the language arts curriculum. Reading serves usually both as an element of vertical organization and as an element of horizontal organization, since reading is commonly emphasized in the content areas of the curriculum as well as in the language arts.

Continuity in reading development is concerned with what happens to the learner as he moves from level to level, from phase to phase, from stage to stage in the reading program as he engages in an expanding variety of reading activities.

Research and empirical evidence indicate that children normally go through a sequence of stages in their development of reading abilities. However, it is important to point out that the general categories of stages presented are merely descriptions giving a general idea of a child's reading progress. These stages are not discrete but merge into one another. Furthermore, children vary widely in their rate of progress through the various stages. At any one educational level or at any one grade level children will be at several different stages of reading progress or in combinations of two or more. Continuity in reading development is facilitated if an entire school system plans for the reading program from kindergarten through the secondary years.

In a desire to delineate the concept of stages, some school systems have made specific designations and spelled out specific skills to be mastered at each step in reading development. For example, they have spelled out children's achievement in reading and study skills in the primary grades, not in the typical stages of readiness, initial reading, and the transition stage in fundamental skills but in eight to twelve "reading levels" or "growth levels". This system is used both in graded or ungraded primary and intermediate units. Frequently the "reading levels" are related to corresponding texts in the basal reading systems. An understanding of the stages of development in reading will give the teacher a bird's eye view of the developmental reading program: readiness stage, beginning-reading stage, initial stage of independent reading, the transition stage, the intermediate stage, and the advanced stages.

The Readiness Stage

In the pre-reading stage the child has his first association with phenomena in his social and physical environment. He learns that there is a relationship between language expression and the responses of others. He learns, too, that there is a relationship between sound and social responses. Then the sounds are linked to others, and the speech of adults, representing his first cultural contact, becomes important in setting sound patterns. He learns to associate the meaning of words with things; words become for him symbols of objects. He continues to associate words with objects and later with actions. Eventually he learns to use words and expressions he hears. Words become important to him in controlling his social environment as well as in self-development. He develops a number of abilities and skills in auditory perception and visual discrimination. In nursery school and kindergarten he is given continuous opportunity to develop language and conceptual skills. The teacher plans situations in which listening, storytelling, interpreting pictures, conversation, "talking time", dramatization, discussion, and evaluation are integral parts of the daily program.

A premium is placed on oral activity and the child is encouraged to express his ideas. He tries his prowess at interpreting pictures, observing sequence in telling about events, following simple directions, identifying colors, and coordinating muscular activities. Through written communication in the use of captions on pictures, invitations to "Come and read", "Come and look", etc., children will have a desire to learn to read. Too, they are interested in composing stories of their own. On the basis of interest in the language skills, it would seem that the early aspects of reading and writing should be included in the preschool experiences of some children. While there is an objection to insisting that every child be exposed to specific reading-readiness activities, there is no reason to deprive the child of language activities which are in harmony with his abilities, needs, interests, and desire to experiment. It is assumed that a good teacher will plan activities which will develop readiness for reading in a manner that does not destroy the child's enjoyment of reading when he is ready for the actual experience. On the other hand, it is equally undesirable to exclude instruction in reading and writing for those children who show the necessary maturity *and* a desire to read.

Specific pre-reading training in skills required before the child is ready to read include: (1) training in auditory discrimination, (2) experience in visual discrimination, (3) establishing left-to-right sequence in reading, (4) training in listening, (5) developing vocabulary and clarifying concepts to be used in beginning reading material, (6) observing the relationships between letter form and the sound of the letter, (7) seeing the relationship between visual and auditory elements of words and phrases.

Beginning Reading

Most children are introduced to reading during this stage. True, there are children who begin reading in kindergarten, or at home, but the majority have their initial experiences here. During this period they learn to use various techniques of word recognition—context clues, word-form clues, and phonetic clues. They acquire skills of deriving information from printed symbols, discriminating between letter and word forms, distinguishing between initial sounds of spoken words, transcribing oral language patterns, using an initial sound together with oral context to supply an unknown word, listening for specific purposes, and reading from left to right. From the beginning, children should learn to analyze new words flexibly, using various techniques for unlocking new words. Emphasis should be on reading for meaning—not on word recognition alone—if reading is to achieve its purpose. From the first, they should be challenged to react critically to what they read, and to interpret motives, behavior and actions of characters in the stories. The greatest weakness during this stage is the tendency for teachers to allow children to become enmeshed in plodding along instead of reading for meaning.

Initial Independent Reading

With this stage should come an increased desire to read, an interest in a variety of materials, and greater independence in word recognition, comprehension, and interpretation. Independence in reading thrives in an atmosphere in which the language arts are integrated, ongoing activities are provided which require mastery of skill in reading, creative activity is valued, and opportunities for language expressions are numerous. The interweaving of purposeful experiences in speaking, listening, reading, and writing is facilitated in a program which makes use of units of work and teacher-pupil planning. Independence in reading grows as time is allocated for instruction in reading skills, reading for a variety of purposes, learning to locate materials, and adapting reading techniques to the particular reading assignment.

Transition

The independence gained during the preceding stage merges into the greater independence and consequently increasing enjoyment in reading which characterizes the transition stage. Children now take more responsibility for reading on their own and for reading longer stories which demand increasingly complex skills of word attack, comprehension, critical thinking, and interpretation. Emphasis shifts from reading comparatively short units to reading longer and more complex materials, demanding a shift in purpose and variety of material in the content fields. The school librarian makes an especially fine contribution at this level in finding just the right books for the right child at the right time. The challenge to the teacher is to provide materials for a wide range in reading abilities, reading interests, and individual projects. A good reading program demands books, books, and more books, if the child's desire to read is to be met.

Intermediate

There are children who evidence their greatest spurt in reading during this stage: comprehension; reading for a variety of purposes; reading at appropriate speeds; reading fluently in the content fields; shifting method according to the demands of the material; reading for retention, enjoyment, interpretation, evaluation. Study skills such as skimming, summarizing, outlining, analyzing, giving critiques become increasingly important. Specifically, the teacher should expect to provide help needed in the following general areas: further training in phonetic analysis; development in structural analysis of words; emphasis on prefixes, suffixes, and roots through an inductive method; training in using verbal context to increase comprehension skills; training in the more mature use of study skills; more sophisticated use of the dictionary for word meaning and extension of vocabulary as well as pronunciation; increased development of critical and creative reading skills (analysis, comparison, interpretation, and synthesis).

Advanced — The Stage of Expansion

The more mature student affords opportunities for continued growth in a wide variety of reading skills and abilities. Greater development in word study, comprehension abilities, critical thinking, and creative reading are demanded in understanding satire, tragedy, comedy, and irony. Greater attention should be paid to semantics as well as vocabulary development, word recognition, phonetic and structural analysis of words. Emphasis is placed on refining the study skills, fluency and rate of reading, and adapting reading to specific purposes.

The student should concentrate on the ability to organize logically, comprehend realistically, evaluate critically, appreciate esthetically, and interpret what is read.

Knowledge of the developmental sequence in reading will enable a school staff to organize a program in terms of the needs of the children enrolled in a particular school situation. Further, knowledge of the process of development in reading implies an understanding of the objectives of reading, of the sequential development of skills in the reading process, and ways of providing for the individual differences to be found in every school, in every educational level, and in every class. In the elementary school the teacher will find children at all stages of development as they progress toward maturity in reading. It is only as teachers, individually and together with other teachers and educators on a school staff, recognize landmarks on the road toward maturity in reading that they are able to plan and carry out a program of reading activities and linguistic experiences that will guide each child toward his highest potential, not only *in* reading but *through* reading. With such a knowledge it is possible to organize a sequence of reading experiences commensurate with the needs, abilities, interests, and aptitudes of children, whether the administrative organization is based on grade levels, reading levels, or growth gradients.

Developing Basic Reading Skills

"What are the basic reading skills?" "What other skills are essential in learning to read and reading to learn?" "What skills does an individual need if he is to be successful in reading in the content fields, reading for a variety of purposes, and reading with comprehension, critical evaluation, and creative interpretation?" Question such as these are inevitable in a discussion of guiding children's development in and through reading.

Unless the teacher has a clear-cut notion of what the reading skills are, he will fail miserably in guiding children in the development of these skills as they progress toward maturity in reading. If child is to be successful in reading literature, science, social studies, mathematics, or any curriculum area where reading is an essential tool, if he is to successfully translate the graphic symbols on the printed page, he must be guided in the sequential development of the major skills demanded in the reading process. There are several broad categories of skills. Each category is further divided into sub-skills, each of which has its unique and special characteristics and each of which is dependent upon and related psychologically or logically to intellectual and conceptual processes involved in reading. Thus, to achieve competency in reading the child must master a number of different but complementary reading skills. The responsibility of the teacher is to guide the child step-by-step as he develops the necessary skills.

Regardless of the method of instruction, it is absolutely essential that the child have a comprehensive grasp of reading skills. In each approach, a carefully planned skill development program must be inherent in the instructional program. It is the teacher's task to be perceptive in sensing the specific needs of each child, and to be resourceful in helping children meet these needs.

The major areas in reading skills which must be developed include: (1) word recognition, (2) getting meanings from symbols, (3) study skills, (4) fluency and speed. These areas are the foundation upon which subsidiary skills are based and are the the nuclei around which these skills cluster.

What makes the teaching of reading so challenging is the complexity of the reading process, the varying rates at which children develop needed skills, and the intricacy of the design in which reading skills are interwoven, interlaced, and interrelated. An examination of the reading skills will provide the teacher with a better understanding of the unique characteristics of each, help him to differentiate between them and to utilize suggestions for helping pupils develop them effectively.

Word Recognition Skills

An effective reading program must provide for specific instruction in word recognition. Word recognition skills include: a sight vocabulary in which the child recognizes a familiar word, just as he identifies a familiar friend, by the way it looks; use of context clues—inferring meaning from context; use of word-form clues; phonetic analysis; structural analysis; and use of a dictionary.

In helping children develop skill in unlocking new words, flexibility and suitability are watchwords. To limit a child by insisting upon one method of attacking an unknown word is to deprive him of the tools he needs in learning to read. Further, it is depriving him of the success that is so essential in beginning experiences with the printed word.

The techniques in the diagram below are the principal ones by which children learn to develop independence in word recognition. Techniques that have lasting value to children in unlocking unfamiliar words independently are shown on the right side of the diagram.

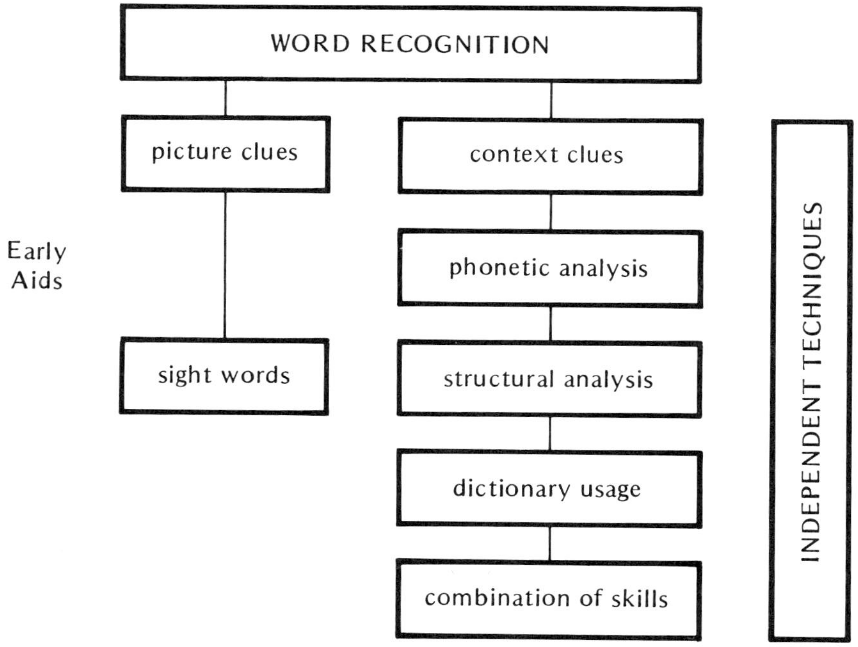

In order to pronounce a word, a child sees he must be able to transfer the word symbol into sound. Good readers accomplish this through attending to a variety of skills almost simultaneously.

Picture clues and sight words. Picture clues and sight words are temporary aids in the recognition of unfamiliar words. Independence in reading becomes a reality only as the child begins to develop skill in other clues such as contextual, phonetic analysis, structural analysis, dictionary usage and a combination of skills. Sight words are those words the child recognizes by sight without the aid of any other word-recognition techniques. Adults use sight recognition combined with all other techniques they have learned in their progress toward maturity in reading.

The early stages in the reading program give the child opportunity to make use of picture clues and sight words. At this time he brings to the process of word identification his past experiences and makes use of a clue in the pictures. Sight words are best learned when they are used in meaningful sentences and when contextual clues are also considered. The child who has learned to read before he comes to school has made use of the whole word method of learning. This natural way of recognizing words is in harmony with the Gestalt concept of learning, in contrast to concentrating in the beginning on memorization of small phonic elements. This is perhaps the most important function sight words serve in early stages of learning to read.

Sight recognition also serves the function of learning words that do not lend themselves to phonic analysis or structural analysis. Words such as *the, that, come, could, you, what, where, was, would,* etc. often frustrate the child, particularly if teachers insist (as some do) that every word be attacked from a phonic approach. If these words are learned as sight words, the child can move readily into reading for meaning.

Context clues. Context clues help identify an unfamiliar word in a sentence. Using context clues can be as exciting as using clues in solving a mystery. If the child is taught to read for meaning *from the beginning,* he will be conscious of the meaning implied in a sentence and bring this insight, hunch, or educated guess to the task. This type of skill is definitely one which marks a growing independence in reading power. Several types of clues which help the child get the meaning through context are experience, comparison or contrast, familiar expression or cliché, and definition. The key point to remember is that the word has to make sense in the context in which it is used. Mature readers make much use of this clue in encountering new words.

Phonetic analysis. An adequate understanding of the science of sounds is essential for the teacher and child. Phonetic analysis is primarily a process of associating the appropriate sounds with the printed word forms. Relating the phonetic analysis to the reading lesson, not spending time in isolated drill, makes this method meaningful. In a phonetic analysis the child perceives sound elements within the word—beginning letters, phonograms, consonant blends.

> The child who makes use of this skill can more readily figure out the pronunciation of many printed words the first time he sees them. Then he associates with the printed symbol the meaning or meanings that he has heretofore associated with the sounds of the spoken word. In order to use phonetic analysis successfully as an aid to word recognition, the child must identify the sounds that are used in our language and associate these sounds with the letter symbols that represent the sounds. Some forty-three separate and distinct phonemes, or sound units, are used in general American speech. Each of these is either a consonant or a vowel sound. The twenty-six letters of the alphabet are the written symbols that represent them. The difficulty lies in the fact that we have more sounds in our language than we have symbols. Therefore certain symbols are used to represent more than one sound. Each of the vowel symbols represents several vowel sounds. For example, the letter *a* represents a different vowel sound in *age, all, after, ago, bar.*

Word identification. As a background for helping children identify the printed symbols, the teacher should be familiar with the methods commonly used for word identification—synthetic, analytic, and analytic-synthetic.

Synthetic. The synthetic method starts with one of the word elements, letters (alphabet method), sounds (phonic method), or syllables (syllable method).

This method gets its name because the letters, sounds, and syllables must be combined or *synthesized* to form words.

Analytic. Historically, the analytic methods of reading include the word method, the phrase method, and the sentence method. These methods get their names because they begin by teaching the word, the phrase, or the sentences. The larger units are broken down into their "basic" elements.

Analytic-synthetic or synthetic-analytic. The analytic-synthetic method begins by teaching the total word and then *more or less* simultaneously breaking it down into its phonemic or sound elements. The synthetic-analytic method, on the other hand, begins with the phonemes (sounds) and then combines these to form meaningful words.

Most teachers favor a combination or eclectic method of teaching word identification and recognition. Research and good practice demonstrate that most children learn more effectively through a multi-sensory approach to independence in attacking words. The good reader unconsciously interrelates, intertwines, and integrates the analytic-synthetic methods.

Structural Analysis

Structural analysis clues are concerned with the units that make up the structure of a word, e.g., root, prefix, and suffix. These clues help children recognize: (1) the large number of words composed of basic roots to which endings such as s, ed, ing and various prefixes and suffixes have been added, (2) compound words and contractions, and (3) words of more than one syllable which must be divided into pronunciation units before "sounding out" is possible.

The effective use of structural analysis in unlocking new words demands several sub-skills. The child must recognize words formed by the addition of inflectional endings to root words, and associate varied meanings with these endings. He must recognize words formed by the addition of prefixes and/or suffixes to root forms, and associate varied meanings with these structural elements. He must recognize syllables in words and use them as aids in pronunciation. He should be able to compound words he already knows to create a new word. Most children enjoy combining simple known words to form compound words, and to reverse the procedure.

Reading involves the ability to keep in mind the totality of a word, phrase, or sentence to perceive the larger relationships. "Perceiving in a general way the whole, but not discriminating clearly among its component elements (letters, words, phrases) may cause as much difficulty in reading as does concentrated attention on word-analysis and word-calling."[15]

The Dictionary

The classical joke about using dictionary skills in identification and recognition is the one in which the child points out that if he knew how to spell it he wouldn't have to look it up. Dictionary skills become increasingly useful to the student as he has need for locating words in the dictionary, working out the pronunciation of words, and getting shades of meanings from words. These skills must be developed in such a way that the child sees the relationship among them; and, having learned the location skills, the meaning skills, and the pronunciation skills, he must learn to integrate them as quickly as possible. Later he will become familiar with syllabication and the understanding of diacritical markings.

Combination of Skills

No single method of word attack is effective in becoming a proficient reader.

What is important is the need for an economical method of word attack, one that helps both to identify the word with which the child is concerned and to use this present learning in the identification and recognition of other words. "The method should provide the maximum possibilities for transfer. It should help him to formulate inductively generalizations and rules that further aid word identification and recognition."[16]

It is interesting to note that the average and slow child gains more from concentrated training than the accelerated or bright pupil. The latter acquires his word attack skills through his everyday reading experience.

Getting Meanings from Reading

Until teachers understand the significance of the development of comprehension skills, there will be no reading in the real sense of the word. Pronouncing words is fruitless unless one brings to and gets from the printed symbols meanings and understanding.

There was a time in the primary grades when children were expected to learn to read; in the intermediate grades they were expected to read to learn; in junior high they were expected to read to evaluate; and, finally, in senior high they were expected to read creatively. Today, however, in order to equip children for life in a complex technological society we must teach them from the beginning the skills needed to read for meaning. Reading for meaning requires a child to master a cluster of distinctive skills, with experience in each of the skills at every level of reading, broadening and expanding his power to get meaning and interpret meaning in the books he reads.

"Reading is something we do, not so much with our eyes as such, as with our knowledge, our interests, and enthusiasms, our hatreds and fondnesses and fears, our evaluations in all their forms and aspects."[17]

We need to recognize the different categories of meaning-getting processes in reading. To do this we must break down the blanket term of comprehension. There are different kinds of comprehension which in turn call for the use of different mental processes. In the diagram on page 372 are graphically portrayed the specific meaning-getting processes which must be developed throughout the levels of reading growth if children are to read for meaning.

Reading involves the use of materials that are challenging and thought-provoking, so that each child will learn to use books to enrich his experiences, extend his horizons, broaden his understandings, and develop his insights. Growth in reading is a complex, continuous process. Reading for meaning is the door to that process. An understanding of the elements involved in reading for meaning is the key that unlocks the door.

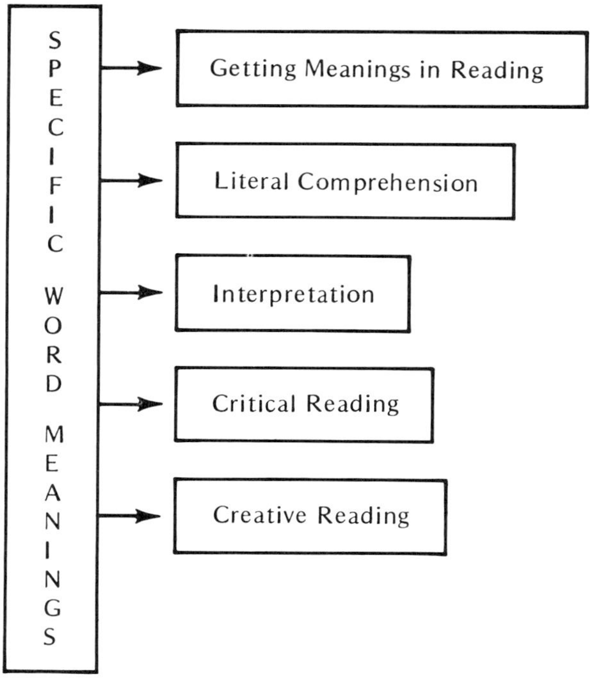

Comprehension Skills

Literal comprehension. Literal comprehension involves the skill of getting the literal meaning of a word, idea, or sentence in context. It is the level of comprehension which requires mere recall. There is no depth in this kind of reading, yet, all too frequently, practice in literal comprehension dominates the comprehension skills because teachers are content to use only the following techniques of meaning-getting.

1. Questions based directly on the text to elicit mere recall
2. True-false statements
3. Completion sentences
4. Multiple-choice responses

Among the types of questions which should be used in teaching literal comprehension are those which involve:

1. Getting the main idea
2. Recalling or recognizing details
3. Determining the sequence of events
4. Identifying things mentioned most frequently
5. Checking to understand the appropriate meaning

Interpretation. Interpretation goes beyond literal comprehension to supply meanings not directly stated in the text. It compels the reader to infer meanings which are not apparent in the words presented. The thinking skills involved are:

1. Drawing inferences
2. Making generalizations
3. Reasoning cause and effect
4. Anticipating outcomes
5. Making comparisons
6. Sensing motives
7. Discovering new relationships

Interpretation gives the child an opportunity to transcend the boundaries of a situation and, at the same time, recognize the limitations imposed by the author.

Critical reading. Critical reading requires the reader to go beyond interpretation of what the author says and to give his personal reaction. It involves the reader in evaluating and making personal judgments as to the quality, accuracy, and plausibility of what is read. It requires that the reader make intelligent observations. Greater awareness in children can be encouraged through questions which elicit comparison with the child's own experiences, ask the author's purpose, or ask the child to react critically to the style of the author.

Creative reading. Creative reading goes beyond critical reading. It involves more than the ability to judge what one reads, both in terms of content and manner of presentation. Creative reading calls into play a child's imagination, his flow of ideas, his ability to project himself beyond the limitations of the situation. The child enters into the author's experience and makes it his own. "Creative reading is concerned with the production of new ideas, the development of new insights, fresh approaches, and original constructs."[18]

The child can interpret in creative reading. "He can reorganize the ideas he receives into a pattern that is unique and personal. He can express his reorganized learning through various media—word and song, gestures and action, materials and composition, through the very make-up of his personality."[19]

Specific Word Meanings

The skills of developing specific word meanings permeate all levels. For many years we have concerned ourselves with helping students to obtain word meanings from sentences and paragraphs. We have come to realize that lack of a single word may interfere with a student's ability to get the meaning of all or part of a selection. The following activities will be effective in helping a child to develop skills in specific word meanings.

Methods of Developing Word Meaning

Through experience. Firsthand experience ranks highest as a technique in developing word meanings. Experiences build up a fund of clear, definite images which children use to relate the known to the unknown. The school can provide many experiences: direct experiences, with classroom activities and field trips, and vicarious experiences, through the various visual aids and sharing periods. Sharing of out-of-school experiences can be of specific benefit to our purpose when unfamiliar words are lifted from the conversation, presented on the board, and defined. The symbol should be associated with the experience to assure the child's knowing what he needs to know to interpret the symbol.

Through pictures. Collect pictures to illustrate meanings of nouns, verbs, adjectives. Use all levels of picture reading: naming the objects in a picture, telling what is happening, interpreting the artist's idea.

Insert a picture in a sentence to replace a word; follow with a sentence containing the corresponding word.

Through literature. Enrich the vocabulary through stories read or told by teacher and pupils. Have pupils retell a story told by the teacher using new words meaningfully. Read poetry containing sensory images.

Through creative expression. Motivating situations for creative expression may include:

1. Asking pupils to create similes for the sound of crushing leaves, splashing waves
2. Making lists of favorite sounds, sights, odors, foods
3. Having pupils think of "the quietest thing you can imagine"
4. Setting up a "Touch and Feel" table where children handle various objects and volunteer words that tell how each object feels in their hands
5. Asking such questions as "What does it look like?" or "How did you feel?" to start children searching for *precise* descriptive terms that make word pictures for others to listen to or to read
6. Writing group experience stories, incorporating new words gained through the class experience
7. Writing original stories, with each child building up his own dictionary or card file of necessary words

Through comparions and contrast. (1) Help pupils discover the comparative forms of adjectives and draw illustrations, e.g. tall, taller, tallest. (2) Collect or match pictures illustrating synonyms, antonyms, homonyms. (3) Discuss the multiple meanings of a given word, e.g. ball, bar, run, iron, mine.

Through supplementary reading. Create an atmosphere that will encourage free recreational reading among pupils by:

1. Being familiar with many books so that the right book may be made available at the right time
2. Having an ample supply of books at various interest and ability levels on the library table
3. Encouraging children to bring their favorite books to school to be shared with class

4. Following children's interests in selecting books from the library and in choosing stories to be read

5. *Reading some prose and poetry each day*

6. Binding experience charts and original stories into book form and making them accessible;

7. Providing definite times for recreational reading

8. Stimulating desire to read by providing for reporting, illustrating, or some other type of motivation

Through classification. List words under appropriate headings.

Things We Need in Art

Things We Take Home Today

People, Animals, Plants

Provide games based on this principle for children's free time.

Through dramatization. Action words (verbs) may be presented on word cards. Phrases may be used for the same purpose.

Through the use of proper terms. As children learn to read, they should be taught to use appropriate names for the concepts they encounter.

title	question mark	vowel
sentence	compound word	syllable
paragraph	consonant	prefix
period		etc.

This principle should be applied to other subjects in the curriculum, as well as to daily life in and out of school.

Through context clues. An unknown word may be defined in context. "First he *nibbled* on some *lettuce*." Then he took a bite of *parsley*." "The little rabbit liked *(vegetables)*."

Meaning as an Aid to Word Recognition

The meaningful word is the one most easily recognized and longest remembered. That is why nouns present little difficulty to children, compared with articles and adverbs, for instance. By developing word meanings in a variety of ways, we can increase their chances of being recognized on second meeting.

Through context clues. Several types of specific activities may be employed to promote skill in the use of context clues. These may involve group or individual work.

Completion sentences are useful in helping to develop the ability to anticipate words.

The rabbit has a short . . . .

Apples grow on . . . .

In a similar exercise the child selects from a group the correct word to complete the sentence. The entire sentence should be read before the selection is made.

Bill laughed at the . . . . snowman.

(cat, cold, funny)

To give practice in using a context clue to choose the appropriate word from two or three with similar configuration, sentences such as this may be used.

Tom . . . . to the store.

(went, want)

Completion sentences in which there is more than one possible answer may be used, first as seen below, then with the first letter of the missing word supplied, showing that visual clues may be used to check meaning clues.

Mother called Joe to come and eat his . . . .

Through relation to objects and pictures. The device of labeling furniture, pictures and drawings, science and nature displays, number symbols, supplies, etc., brings meaning that aids recognition.

Those words with abstract meanings should receive special emphasis upon presentation and considerable repetition thereafter. Devices to give meaning can sometimes be worked out.

The word card showing *here* may be placed on a ledge while *there* is placed at the opposite end of the room

Through comparison and contrasts. Exercises fixing the meaning of antonyms, synonyms, and homonyms also help to fix recognition patterns. Countless practice exercises can be devised to further both understanding and recognition.

The words can be matched with each other.

They can be matched with pictures.

They can be illustrated by pupils.

They can be used in sentences.

Through classifying. Familiarity with the meaning of words helps children recognize them in doing such exercises as these.

Finding and listing names of children, animals, toys, food, etc.

Classifying words under certain headings, such as things that come in pairs, things we ride, etc.

Separating words and classifying them under two headings, as wild animals or farm animals, things we see or things we do.

Through the use of the chalkboard. The chalkboard is helpful in the linking of word meaning with word recognition. The symbol should be associated with the experience to assure the child's knowing what he needs to know to interpret the symbol.

Lists should often be made for reference over a short period of time, even if there is to be no direct effort at teaching the words. What to take on our trip, words we use in arithmetic, workers we know are some possible classifications. (An especially troublesome word may have an honored place on the board for a while.)

Study Skills

There was a time when concern for techniques and skills related to reading in the content areas was considered to be the province of the intermediate grades. From recent research, from observation, and from evidence gained in working with children, three categories of study skills emerge. These enable a child to read effectively and to study successfully in the different curriculum areas and academic disciplines. The study skills are defined as: (1) common reading skills, (2) common study skills, and (3) specialized techniques, including vocabulary and skills specifically required for reading in a particular subject area.

It would be realistic to refer to these study skills in relation to an educational task assignment. As a matter of fact, the mature reader makes use

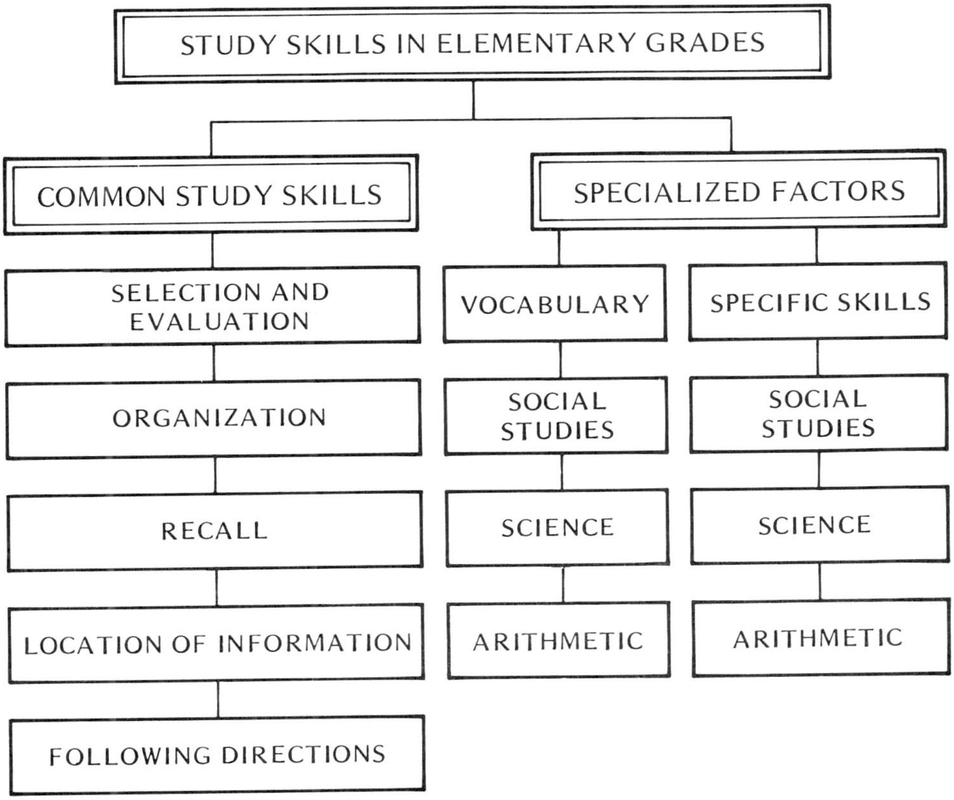

of these study skills in reading for purposes outside the school as well as in educationally-oriented tasks. Reading is a developmental process; it takes a lifetime to achieve the goals of reading. Study skills continue to be important throughout the life of the individual. Whenever the reader reads in the content areas he *needs* to use the study skills in both categories of common study skills and specialized techniques.

Common Study Skills

Selection and evaluation. Selection and evaluation are concerned with the process students use when they select from the printed passage the sentence, word, or idea that is most pertinent to a specific purpose expressed in a question eliciting reasoning, critical thinking, or creative thinking. Children should be taught from the very beginning to develop skills which call for thinking at a higher level than mere recall. They should learn to find in the written material documentary evidence to support a conclusion or a generalization, to prove a point, or to make a judgment leading to a decision.

Organization. Organization is essential if ideas are to be presented in a logical, concise, and comprehensive manner. Children should learn early to classify, to arrange ideas and sentences in logical sequence, to put objects in correct order, and to place phenomena in appropriate categories. Outlining, summarizing, organizing data, taking notes, and learning to evaluate their appropriateness are all part of developing skills needed in proficient reading in the academic disciplines.

Other common study skills such as recalling information read, locating information, and learning to follow directions should be taught in a developmental design. These skills should be an integral part of the language arts program.

Recalling information. Recalling information, fixing clearly in mind what one has read, is a skill which is important not alone for the child, but also for the adult. Information needed at a later time can be recalled by the child if the teacher utilizes the principles of learning and provides the motivation, the need, and the purpose for the activity. However, expecting the child to memorize without a clear purpose is fruitless for the teacher and frustrating to the child.

Locating information. Helping the child to learn how to locate facts and find information as he needs it is an essential task for today's teacher. The child should be taught to make use of the table of contents, index, and glossary of individual books as well as the resources in the library.

Following directions. Following directions has been discussed as a skill in listening for information in an earlier chapter. It is the responsibility of the teacher to *make sure* that children understand the written directions *before* they begin to work. Reading the directions orally, writing the directions on the chalkboard, asking a child to tell what the directions say, discussing the directions—these and other techniques can be used to ensure that *every child* knows what the directions say.

Specialized Factors

A knowledge of the cluster of techniques known as study skills is invaluable in teaching reading. It is equally important to have a knowledge of the specialized factors affecting reading in the content fields. Children need instruction and careful guidance in this area.

The content subjects require a different approach from the easier reading of graded stories and material found in the basal and supplementary reading series. The content fields require intensive study rather than a more casual approach and demand much more time for reflection, discussion, and comprehension. The development of concepts which is vital for creative learning is facilitated by the use of visual aids.

Each of the content areas has its own specialized vocabulary and a learning process unique to its discipline.

Reading in the field of science. The area of science poses a problem for many students. The New York City Metropolitan School Study Council recommends that to read science material successfully the pupils must apply the basic reading skills of (1) locating pertinent detail, (2) distinguishing between main ideas and supporting details, (3) visualizing, (4) following directions, and (5) drawing inferences. When children have perfected these skills, they can use them successfully for reading in social studies, in word problems in mathematics, and in literature as well.

Reading in the social studies. If social studies is to be more than memorization of facts which may already be obsolete, the reader must identify central issues, make judgements on the basis of evidence from a variety of sources, and generalize from evidence in the content read. He needs to be familiar with the special vocabulary and to adjust his reading rate to the material as well as to the purpose. He must develop skill in thinking critically.

Children must be taught all the reading skills: (1) those which are *shared* responsibility, such as locating information, organizing information, evaluating information, acquiring information through reading, interpreting pictures, charts, graphs and tables, and (2) those which are a *major* responsibility of the social studies, such as reading social studies materials, applying problem-solving and critical-thinking skills to social issues, interpreting maps and globes and understanding time and chronology.[20]

Reading in mathematics. Special training in teaching children to read in mathematics includes, in the words of Spache, instruction in "(1) organizing details into working ideas, (2) recognizing relationships, (3) organizing processes to find solutions, (4) adjusting rate . . . to secure a high degree of comprehension, (5) understanding technical vocabulary and symbols, (6) understanding common words with mathematical connotations, or more precise mathematical usage, (7) locating and selecting related readings, (8) evolving procedures for problem solving."[21]

As children progress through the elementary grades, an increasing amount of instructional time is, as a general rule, devoted to developing reading skills and vocabulary in the content areas. This is indicated in the results of the *Harvard Report on Reading in Elementary Schools* by Austin and Morrison.

Fluency and Speed

Another most important skill in reading is that of shifting gears on the basis of content, purpose, and difficulty.[22] Unless the child learns early that reading must be adjusted to the purpose for which he reads and to the difficulty of the reading content, as well as to the type of reading he is doing, he is in grave danger of developing a surface reading pattern, wasting valuable time, or reading too rapidly to savor the flavor of the story and the atmosphere of the narrative. Some material is meant to be read thoughtfully and reflectively; some material is meant to be read studiously; other material is meant to be skimmed lightly; and still other to be digested thoroughly.

Teachers should help children develop the ability to read for various purposes and approach the reading task in terms of the purpose. For example, they can give the students mimeographed excerpts from various sources to illustrate the need for different approaches in reading. A few paragraphs from narrative material can be written on a simple reading level and then on successively more difficult reading levels, until the material to be read challenges the pupil to go beyond the usual level of difficulty, to stretch his mind as well as his skill.

Excerpts can be selected, too, from various subject fields, content areas, or academic disciplines, written on the level of difficulty children can manage. Children can be asked to read these materials, shifting gears in reading to meet the specific purpose for reading and nature of the material. They will discover that narrative reading requires a different speed and attitude as well as a unique approach. The same is true of scientific and/or mathematical material and the social studies. They will grasp the concept that some materials can be understood through a rapid, single reading; other materials require reflective, thoughtful reading before they are comprehended by the reader.

To read material in the subject areas, a student must set a purpose for reading so that he knows which facts to select and which to reject as unimportant for *his* purpose. Pupils must learn to vary the reading speed to achieve the comprehension demanded for the purpose for which they are reading at a given time.

Current Approaches to Teaching Reading

Among approaches to beginning reading are: language experience, basal reader, individualized, phonic, linguistic, initial alphabet, multi-level reading, words in color, and programmed instruction. Some of the approaches are relatively new; others have been developed over fifty years or more. Some have been in continuous use; others represent older methods in new apparel; and still others have only recently appeared and have not been tested sufficiently under controlled situations to form conclusive judgment. A longitudinal approach to research studies of reading allows for inter- and intra-comparisons of approaches, methods, and evaluation techniques.

In becoming familiar with the basic ingredients of each approach, the reader is in a better position to evaluate its effectiveness in the light of the needs of children in a given situation, the availability of materials, and the willingness of the administration to cooperate.

Language Experience Approach

The language experience approach emphasizes the oral language background of the child as a basic ingredient in word recognition throughout the elementary grades. It is based on the premise that what a child thinks he can say, what he can say he can "write", what he can write he can "read". Here, more than in any other approach to reading, there is a developmental integration of the communication skills of listening, speaking, reading and writing. From the very first the child is encouraged to express his thoughts, ideas, and feelings. This approach to reading allows teachers to integrate and develop skills in all facets of language experience simultaneously and with equal emphasis instead of giving undue attention to any specific language skill.

Language experiences serve as the core of the program, thus contributing to balanced development of communication skills and attitudes. Van Allen and his co-researchers identified twenty language experiences which form the framework of the program. These comprise three major phases: (1) extending experiences; (2) studying the English language; and (3) relating author's ideas to personal experiences.

Vital to the program is the creative expression of ideas. The child's own expression is encouraged through the use of a variety of media such as painting, speaking, and writing. The child is given opportunity to work individually with the teacher, in small groups, and in the total class group. In each situation he is encouraged to express and record his own thoughts, ideas, and aspirations, as well as to read and understand the thinking of others.

Language Experience Approach to Reading[23]

An overview

Throughout the child's school experiences there is opportunity and need to help him improve his language power through listening, speaking, reading, and writing. To do this, the child goes through a sequence of language experiences which are designed to enrich his experiences and improve his skills. Some of the most important skills which must be developed in children who are expected to live effectively in a democratic society are:

1. *Sharing Experiences*—The ability to tell, write, or illustrate something on a purely personal basis.

2. *Discussion Experiences*—The ability to interact with what other people say and write.

3. *Listening to Stories*—The ability to hear what others have to say and relate it to their own experiences.

4. *Telling Stories*—The ability to organize one's thinking so that it can be shared orally or in writing in a clear and interesting manner.

5. *Dictating*—The ability to choose from all that might be said, the *most important* part for someone else to write and read.

6. *Developing Word Recognition Skills*—The ability to attach sound and meaning to the words in our written language.

7. *Making and Reading Books*—The ability to organize one's ideas into a form that others can use. Also, the ability to use the ideas which others have shared through books.

8. *Developing Basic Sight Vocabulary*—The ability to recognize at sight, to spell, and to write automatically the words of highest frequency in our language.

9. *Expanding Vocabulary*—The ability to expand one's vocabulary—listening, speaking, reading, writing.

10. *Writing Independently*—The ability to write their own ideas and present them in a form for others to read.

11. *Improving Style and Form*—The ability to profit from listening to and reading well-written materials.

12. *Using a Variety of Resources*—The ability to recognize and use many resources in expanding vocabulary, improving oral and written expression, and sharing ideas.

13. *Reading Whole Books*—The ability to read books for information, recreation, and improvement of reading skills on an individualized basis.

14. *Reading a Variety of Symbols*—The ability to read in their total environment—clock, calendar, radio, dial, thermometer.

15. *Studying Words*—The ability to find the correct pronunciation and meaning of words and to spell the words in writing activities.

16. *Improving Comprehension*—The ability, through oral and written activities, to gain skill in following directions, understanding words in the context of sentences and paragraphs, reproducing the thought in a passage, reading for detail, and reading for general significance.

17. *Outlining*—The ability to use various methods of briefly restating ideas in the order in which they were written or spoken.

18. *Summarizing*—The ability to get the main impression, outstanding idea, or the details of what has been read or heard.

19. *Integrating and Assimilating Ideas*—The ability to use reading and listening for specific purposes of a personal nature.

20. *Reading Critically*—The ability to determine the validity and reliability of statements.

The goals of broad language experience as stated above cannot be separated in an effective, efficient instructional program. To attempt to do so is to ask the child to do at an early age the most difficult tasks of the scholar—to integrate learnings into meaningful behavior. *To take reading out of its rightful place in the total language-experience program is to ask children to do what is impossible for many of them.* Or it requires the teacher to use valuable time to put back together what did not need to be separated out in the first place.

Teachers can achieve their goals of reading instruction in many ways. Some of them require that reading be brought out for special attention to the neglect of the other facets of language development. Other teachers are able to leave reading in its natural place and work to develop skills in all facets of language experience at the same time and with equal emphasis.

In this approach children are introduced to reading as a developmental communication art related to the other arts of language. They are exposed to oral and written symbols through several avenues. There is external stimulation and inner motivation to learn to read the products of their own thinking and writing.

Basal Reader Approach

The basal reader approach, in its most definitive sense, provides children with experiences which will help them learn *how* to translate printed symbols effectively and efficiently. This approach is used by well over ninety percent of the elementary schools as the major instructional tool in teaching reading. It provides a program whereby fundamental reading skills form the central focus of the program. These skills are those of analyzing, locating, interpreting, and comprehending written or printed symbols from the page. The objective of developing the basic skills involves direct, systematic instruction, usually on a daily basis. When properly used the basal readers serve as a spring-board from a skills development program to reading for information and enjoyment. Their usefulness lies in the carefully developed sequential organization for the development of reading skills and a controlled vocabulary. As the child progresses from one book to another, the number and complexity of skills are gradually increased. To provide for differences in abilities, three groups are usually utilized. Pupils may advance through this sequential program at different speeds but all must follow the predetermined sequence.

In addition to the readers, basal programs also provide a corresponding number of ancillary materials—manuals, workbooks, phrase cards, filmstrips, parallel story books, etc. However, when school boards do not supply the required materials they limit the effectiveness of the program.

Although the instructional design of these basal series varies, the reading skills introduced in the first grade generally include those designed to build reading vocabulary; increase interest and appreciation of books; develop word recognition, comprehension, and critical reading; and develop oral and silent reading skills.

The teacher's manual gives directions and suggestions for direct teaching with appropriate related and/or enrichment activities. These suggestions are directed toward major phases of the reading lesson: (1) *preparation* for reading—setting the stage and establishing a background for the story, discussing new concepts, and introducing new vocabulary, (2) *reading and discussion*—guided silent reading of increasingly larger units (sentences, paragraphs, stories) to answer specific questions, (3) *oral reading*—for interpretation, (4) *word analysis and comprehension building*—exercises in word analysis, phonetic analysis, and word meaning, (5) *enrichment activities*—the related creative arts of music, drama, art.

Basal readers serve as a spring-board for a logical skills development program to reading books for pleasure and information. The basal reading approach has its greatest value for the novice teacher who needs the security of following the carefully planned sequence of skills and content presented. Experienced teachers who use the basal series call upon their ingenuity and creativity in order to make reading more interesting for the pupil and more challenging for the teacher.

The Individualized Approach

Self-selection is the basis for the individualized approach to reading. The emphasis on the dynamic concepts of seeking, self-selection, and pacing produces results which delight children and amaze adults. The individualized methods are natural outgrowths of the result of child developmental studies. Individualized reading instruction is based on what is known about the differing rates at which children develop, sequence of development, and motivation for learning.

When children come to school, some already read, some would like to read, and others have little interest in learning to read. These differences become more marked as the child progresses in school. The child before he comes to school has assimilated some of the language patterns of the culture in which he lives. He has learned to speak and may have learned to read. The individualized reading approach "takes" the child from where he is.

In individualized reading the teacher employs a cultural approach. Appropriate books for browsing are available from the beginning. There is conversation, storytelling, and reading aloud. Simple labels and sentences help to identify things or experiences. The teacher provides in the classroom a supply of books varied in range of difficulty and interest.

Success and satisfaction for the learner are the motivating forces in this approach. The loss of face in being assigned to a slow group, being demoted from a higher group, or failing to please a teacher or admired adult is absent. The teacher does not set a standard for each child to achieve. He believes that each child is unique; each child will succeed in his own way, at his own rate, and in his own good time.

Hunt[24] suggests six identifiable steps in the individualized reading program which he believes if successfully developed by the teacher result in four values basic to productive reading. The six steps he cites are: (1) classroom environment, (2) quiet reading time, (3) instructional guidance, (4) conferences, (5) uninterrupted sustained silent reading for skill development, and (6) records and evaluation.

A brief examination of these steps indicates the interrelationships operating among the steps indicated.

Creating the reading atmosphere. This step requires not alone endurance and endeavor on the part of the teacher. It also enlists the key factors of the concept of quiet reading and skillful use of instructional guidance.

Quiet reading time. The perfect situation here requires that every child is so engaged in silent reading (or working on responses to such reading) that the teacher is free to work with students in a variety of ways, individually or in groups. Suggestions to students for their behavior in this period are placed on a chart similar to the following.

1. Select a book or other printed material.
2. Read quietly (see how much you can get done).
3. Have a conference (be prepared—know what to say).
4. Record your results—write about reading—chart your progress.
5. Study vocabulary.

Success in this phase of the program means that the child is able to (1) make wise selections of reading materials; (2) spend large blocks of time in independent silent reading; (3) prepare for the conference which will follow; and (4) prepare reports, keep records, and be ready to share his learning from books with others. It is important to note that at this stage there are many children who need instructional guidance more than they need conferences.

Instructional guidance. The principle which must be held inviolate during the reading period is that no one may act so as to interfere with the productive reading of another. While legitimate interaction may occur among various readers, it is necessary for the teacher to exercise his prerogative of admonishing an offender to "Sit down, keep quiet and start reading." Instructional guidance is crucial to the success of individualized reading programs.

Conferences. Just as the silent reading time with its atmosphere of productive reading is the heart of IRP, the conference time with book talks is the heart of the silent reading time. The prime purpose of conference time is not to question each and every child about each and every reader. Rather, it is to enable the reader to convey the meaning of what he has read. The key to the conference is in the degree of perceptive, penetrating questions which are asked. It is at this point that the teacher elicits various levels of thinking (critical and creative) as well as recall and reasoning.

USSR: the pinnacle of reading skills. What ever approach the teacher uses during this phase of the program, it is essential to keep in mind that for the child success means "learning to sustain himself with print for longer and longer stretches of time". Among approaches teachers use to help children accomplish this goal are: (1) using instructional devices such as charts to help children keep track of the amount of silent reading accomplished during the reading period, (2) sitting with groups in the reading circle and supervising or governing silent reading. There is no oral reading around the circle; the teacher is there to support and assist each child as he attempts to get as far as he can with his printed material during the time he is in the reading circle. The teacher helps with words, assists in interpreting sentences and above all establishes the setting so that maximum amounts of silent reading can be completed by each child. The teacher helps each child to extend his own previous limits through day-to-day practice.

Records and evaluation. If keeping records, keeping track of books, answering questions or writing resumés on books read takes more time than is spent by readers reading, then the teacher has become lost in nonessentials. Realistically, teachers, like youngsters, will behave in this activity as in all others—true to type. The object is not neat notepads filled with records; the object is productive reading.

In evaluating progress the teacher must seek to discover the extent to which each child is becoming an independent, self-sufficient and self-sustaining reader. Among the questions the teacher must keep in mind to evaluate growth are the following.

1. Can the reader find the sources important to him, and then find the truly significant ideas within them?

2. Once he has selected the proper reading material, does the reader have the staying power to follow through on long, intricate passages?

3. Is the reader able to be on his own in a world of print or does he need to follow the teacher's directions? Independence and self-direction are marks of the maturing reader.

4. Is he developing a love of books? A passion for reading? This deep love for books is one of the important qualities of an individualized reading program.

Not only do children have an opportunity to read the books they want to read, they also gain deep satisfaction from their opportunities to share their books with others since they are not all reading the same texts.

Obviously, however, such a program requires understanding of the interests and motivations of the children, knowledge of evaluation skills, a large number of books varied in interests and difficulty range, and the ability to organize reading in a classroom in a new and somewhat unorthodox manner.

Phonic Approach

Reading with phonics is a system which aims to develop efficiency in word recognition by employing a multi-sensory approach and a sequential introduction of speech sounds of the English language.

All approaches fall into two general categories: (1) those that start the beginner directly in learning the sounds of letters of the alphabet and letter combinations, and (2) those in which the child is taught to recognize whole words for a short time as a preliminary to teaching phonics.

In the first method, "phonics first", the initial emphasis is on learning the sounds of the language. One method based on this concept provides a manual and three books for first grade and a manual and two books for second and third grades. The program includes the development of audio-visual perception, the application of phonetic analysis, the mastery of other word-analysis techniques, and the use of reading for meaning. The development of audio-readiness precedes the application of the sounds of letters and of principles governing their sounds. The program for the first grade is organized in the following sequence: (1) eight weeks of readiness work, emphasizing listening to sounds within words, (2) two weeks of instruction with the phonics primer, followed by six weeks of reading other primers, and (3) five weeks with the phonic first reader, concluding with seven weeks of reading other first grade level texts and supplementary materials. The readiness materials start with long vowels, then short vowels, then initial consonants; pre-primer reading is delayed until *all single* letters have been introduced.

Other phonic systems include the extreme in which the twenty-six letters of the alphabet are introduced on the first day. Drill on letter sounds in isolation follows. Some seventy phonograms, thirteen phonics rules, and twenty-six spelling rules are included, most of which are taught in the first grade. Approximately two to four weeks are used in learning the letter sounds, about six weeks is given to spelling of words, and then reading is started with regular primer material, while intensive work in spelling continues as new phonograms are introduced.

In the second method the child is taught to recognize whole words as a preliminary to teaching phonics. Instead of giving only isolated drill on phonics, phonics is taught in connection with words that give children difficulty. This practice removes phonics from the category of the much criticized method in which children eager to read are dismayed to find that "reading" consists simply of memorizing phonic elements as an exercise in itself.

Research and modern educational psychology and philosophy make it clear that the concentrated phonics approach to teaching reading is diametrically opposed to what we know about learning. Teaching the child the sounds of the letters of the alphabet, then putting sounds together to make words, and finally putting words together to make sentences is in direct contrast to what we know about children's use of language when they come to school.

Recent studies and observation indicate that effective teachers reinforce phonics by teaching children other methods of "figuring out" how a new word is pronounced. Phonics is not fool-proof as a tool to use in ascertaining pronunciation. The method needs to be supplemented and checked by other word attack skills, using context clues, word analysis, and dictionary skills. Most teachers use phonics as *one* method of unlocking new words.

The preferred method is an eclectic approach in which the teacher keeps the objective of teaching reading (e.g., to develop a love for reading) clearly in mind. Thus, the teacher is concerned with developing interest in reading, developing an attitude that reading is an exciting process of getting meaning from the printed page by bringing meaning to it and that reading deals with ideas, not words, and sentences, not letters and syllables.

Linguistics in Beginning Reading

Linguistics is opening new doors to the teachers of reading. Educators generally agree that the child when he goes to school is in full command of the system of his oral language as presented to him by his family and his community and that it is so thoroughly a part of him that he uses it without conscious thought.

Lefevre emphasizes interrelatedness of the language processes in order to achieve maximum reinforcement of skills, and major emphasis on the larger segment of language approach to reading. "In teaching children to read, we should analytically slice larger language segments into smaller ones only to the extent that the learning process requires it. This is the heart of the approach: moving as needed from larger to smaller wholes."[25]

In contrast to the use of larger speech patterns in the teaching of reading, other linguists recommend the small unit approach. Fries describes current thinking on linguistics and reading in a summary indicating four essential features of an approach to beginning reading that applies linguistic knowledge.

> 1. The six-year-old school child understands spoken sentences in which the basic sentence patterns have, for their content, words that he knows. For the beginning reading material this child must recognize the written words in the sentence structures as those he already knows when he hears them spoken.

2. As the basic readiness requirement for beginning reading, the child must know the alphabet. He must be able to identify, by name, rapidly and accurately, the individual letters. He must also be able to determine immediately whether two sequences of two or three letters are alike or different in respect to both the individual letters that constitute each sequence and their order within each sequence.

3. English spelling, in its representation of English words, drastically shifted its basic principles from 1450 to 1600. It moved away from a representation that could be grasped in terms of correspondence between individual letters and individual sounds to a representation through spelling patterns. It made possible the "silent" letters of our etymological spelling as well as the differentiation, by spelling, of words having the same pronunciation.

These developments in English spelling provide a basis for a very different approach to the teaching of beginning reading. It features specifically, even from the very early steps, the making of independent extensions of the matrices to build the pupil's ability to read hundreds of words he has never seen written before.

4. Reading for meaning requires the building of *situation* meanings out of the words and sentences read. Beginning books without pictures compel the pupils to read for meanings rather than guess at words after looking at pictures.[26]

There is little emphasis on developing comprehension skills at early stages of instruction in this approach because of the definition of reading which the authors suggest. Initial reading involves only the decoding of printed symbols, according to this method. For this reason, the program does not include a systematic approach to the development of comprehension skills.

Such an approach limits the initial reading experiences of children. It is well known that children relish opportunities to use words and to read words that do not fit into this program of reading. Reading is more than decoding. The approach to reading should be broad, interesting, and challenging to children in the initial experiences. Since children's language patterns at the time of school entrance are far more sophisticated and interesting than the material they encounter in the early reading, it would appear that they need to work with ideas which extend their abilities and horizons to develop effective reading and writing skills.

Multilevel Reading Instruction

The basis for multilevel reading instruction, according to Parker, is founded on studies of reading process, children, and learning. Studies of *reading process* indicate the existence of specific reading skills essential for each child if he is to progress through the various stages of reading efficiency in a developmental sequence. These reading skills are on a continuum from easy to difficult, simple to complex. Studies of *children* indicate the unique design of development of each child. Thus, there must be a tailormade program in reading instruction to meet each child's specific needs in acquiring necessary skills in terms of *his* experiential background, cultural patterns, learning potential, and individual rate of learning. Studies of *learning* indicate certain cognitive processes.

The question to be answered is, "How can reading instruction for twenty-five to thirty pupils best be provided to meet their individual needs?" Parker's answer is "Use multilevel materials and instruction." This program is widely known as the SRA approach or the Developmental Reading Program.

In this approach the teacher introduces the materials of the learning laboratory to the class and gives individual guidance. Following a placement test, each child starts on the skill track at a point where he can achieve success with effort. Continuous testing provides the pupil feedback, reinforcement, or redirection of his learning efforts. Self-programming enables the teacher to give individual help as needed.

The program requires that the child learn the names and sounds of the English alphabet, its phonic and structural sight-sound combinations, and linguistic word patterning as units of thought. From there he proceeds to decoding meanings from more complex (symbolic) units (paragraphs, stories, chapters).[27]

From this multilevel instructional approach, and paralleling the development of skills, each pupil moves readily into an individualized reading program, selecting books he can read, as a balance between acquiring skills essential in reading and applying these skills in reading for his personal and assigned purposes.

Initial Teaching Alphabet (Augmented Roman Alphabet Approach)

The Initial Teaching Alphabet, or ITA as it is known, was developed in England. It consists of forty-four characters which provide each major phoneme of the English language with its own symbol. This eliminates the inconsistencies in the phoneme to symbol relationship in the English alphabet which consists of only twenty-six letters. It differs from other phonemic alphabets in that both ITA and its spellings were designed to simplify the transition to the regular alphabet *after* reading and language fluency are achieved. Sir James Pitman of London, England, the author of the ITA, asserts that since it is a *medium,* not a *method,* it can be used with any method of reading instruction. However, proponents of the system regard it as a distinct and unique *method* requiring special methodology as well as special materials.

The Augmented Roman Alphabet[28]

Number	*Character*	*Name*	*Example*	*Traditional spelling*
1	æ	ae	ræt	rate
2	b	bee	big	big
3	c	kee	cat	cat
4	d	dee	dog	dog
5	ɛɛ	ee	mɛɛt	meet
6	f	ef	fill	fill

7	g	gae	gun	gun
8	h	hae	hat	hat
9	ie	ie	tie	tie
10	j	jae	jelly	jelly
11	k	kae	kit	kit
12	l	el	lamp	lamp
13	m	em	man	man
14	n	en	net	net
15	œ	oe	tœ	toe
16	p	pee	pig	pig
17	r	rae	run	run
18	s	ess	sad	sad
19	t	tee	tap	tap
20	ue	ue	due	due
21	v	vee	van	van
22	w	wae	will	will
23	y	i-ae	yell	yell
24	z	zed or zee	fizz	fizz
25	ꙅ	zess	houꙅeꙅ	houses
26	wh	whae	when	when
27	ch	chae	chick	chick
28	th	ith	thaut	thought
29	th	thee	the	the
30	ʃh	ish	ʃhip	ship
31	ʒ	zhee	meʒuer	measure
32	ŋ	ing	siŋ	sing
33	ɑ	ah	fɑr	far
34	au	au	autum	autumn
35	a	at	appl	apple
36	e	et	egg	egg
37	i	it	dip	dip
38	o	ot	hot	hot

39	u	ut	ugly	ugly
40	ω	oot	bωk	book
41	ꙍ	oo	mꙍn	moon
42	σu	ow	bσu	bough
43	σi	oi	tσi	toy

Words in Color

Contrary to its name, color is far less important than the trade name indicates, since all books and written materials are in black and white. Only the wall charts use color. The use of color is purported to solve quickly and easily the problems created by the grapheme-phoneme relationship in the English language without affecting the usual spelling of the words. Thus, on the wall charts color provides a clue and word imagery is said to be more vivid. "The many spellings of each sound occur in the same color, and the many sounds of one spelling occur each in a different color (each of the 47 sounds of English identified has its own color). Examples: late, way, they, *ei*ght, stra*igh*t, veil, great, pa*i*l (same sound so in same color); pat, was, village, any, fatal, swamp, all, ate, care (different sounds, so in different colors).[29]

Originated by educator Caleb Gattegno as an experiment in Ethiopia for UNESCO, this approach reduced the learning time in Amharic, Spanish, Hindi, and English.

Basic to the approach is the full and rapid extension of the linguistic skills already possessed by the learner. The cognitive processes involved in speaking are extended to include operations in related symbols (written language) or talk written down. This makes use of a unified or integrated approach to learning to read *plus* a new set of materials used in solving the problem of phoneme-grapheme differential in the English language. The approach claims that the techniques and materials allow the teacher to initiate challenging and enjoyable intellectual games which provide practice, without creating boredom through drill or strain through memorization, and to generate self-direction and creativity in the development and use of written language. This claim is not unique. It is equally applicable to a number of approaches used today by effective teachers. For children who have difficulty in distinguishing color, this approach merely adds one more obstacle to learning to read for meaning.

The Programmed Approach

In a technological age it is not surprising to discover the use of the teaching machine in improving reading instruction. Programmed instruction in reading, as in other areas of the curriculum, concerns itself with the individual learning of the student through the use of carefully, sequentially organized materials which break subject matter or skills into small learning units. Responses are called for in connection with each unit and answers are provided to which the student can refer immediately *after* he has made a response. Programmed material takes the form of separate worksheets, cards, tablets, workbooks, or textbooks.

Whatever form it takes, the "teaching machine" is the instrument or workbook which presents the individual student the program of questions and answers, problems to solve, or exercises to be performed, together with a feedback of answers so that he may know immediately if he has been correct in his responses. Thus, he has the opportunity to correct his errors immediately after he makes them. It is the preprogrammed set of exercises or questions that determines the learning the student does. The effectiveness with which the information or skill to be learned is organized, developed, and presented is the test of the program that utilizes programmed instruction.

An approach to reading based on programmed instruction is that developed by Sullivan. Goss gives a description of this approach.

> Recently, a new reading program, *Programmed Reading,* was introduced which promises to solve many of the problems. . . . Under this program, first grade pupils learn the alphabet. They then learn certain associated sound symbols, such as "a" as in ant, "m" as in mat, "n" as in man, "t" as in tan.
>
> After a prescribed number of these sounds are mastered the children progress to a primer workbook. When the child has finished the first three parts of this primer, he takes a Reading Readiness Test. If he scores 80 percent or above in this test, he starts Book I of *Programmed Reading.* If not, he takes a supplementary section of the Primer and is retested.
>
> There are fourteen workbooks in the Programmed Reading Series, seven in Series I and seven in Series II. The two series correspond roughly to first and second grade levels. The children may read and work in these books as rapidly as their developing ability permits. Most of our children ask to take their books home so they may read and work in them during the evening.
>
> Each volume features pages of self-contained response requirements under which a pupil verifies his own understanding of the material. After every fifty such responses, there is an in-book, diagnostic test. The teacher can check the results at a glance, verify the child's progress, and correct any misconceptions. The teacher also has the opportunity, at this point, of hearing each child read his test to her. This provides an excellent time to work on a one-to-one relationship with the child, praising his progress and thereby encouraging even better work in the future.
>
> Some of the advantages of the *Sullivan Programmed Reading* are:
>
> 1. Each child may progress at his own ability level.
> 2. Since the children are all engaged in reading, the teacher has the time to help individual students.
> 3. The children are able to have a longer reading period since the three reading groups are eliminated.
> 4. The vocabulary is so controlled (the long vowels are not introduced until Book 8) that the children are able to sound out each new word they meet in their workbooks.
> 5. Punctuation is taught as a part of the reading program.
> 6. The pupils are able to write, spell and sound out each word they are able to read.

7. The child assumes more responsibility since he checks his own work, with the exception of the tests.

8. In a half-hour reading period, the average child makes between fifty and one hundred correct, written responses.

9. The material presented is interesting and challenging to the children. As the books progress, more factual material is presented in longer stories calling for greater comprehension.[30]

Programmed instruction cannot duplicate the role of the classroom teacher. It cannot carry on a good class discussion, nor can it discuss the pupils reaction to the reading. It cannot analyze the problems that the pupil is having. Handling discussion and questions, encouraging individual inquiry and discovery, motivating critical and creative reading—these are the areas which are neglected in a reading program that is centered too exclusively on programmed learning. Centering efforts on the individual student's learning is good. However, such efforts are more fruitful under the guidance of a knowledgeable, effective teacher.

Current Approaches to Reading in the Upper Elementary School

Teachers frequently ask, "What skills should the child master before he leaves the upper elementary grades if he is to be successful in his senior high school years?'

At every reading level it is desirable that the child read widely, ranging from books that he reads for specific purposes in school to books that he reads because he likes to read. Such wide reading, if encouraged, will develop vocabulary, increase fluency, broaden understandings, provide opportunity for utilizing skills, and open doors to adventure, knowledge, and the esthetics.

Specific objectives in reading skills and corresponding activities designed to achieve these skills during this developmental stage follow.

Reading Abilities	*Learning Activities*
Locating information	Solving real problems Giving oral reports Writing reports
Word-recognition skills Context clues Word analysis skills Phonetic clues Dictionary skills	Using appropriate method for dealing with unfamiliar words in meaningful situations
Vocabulary development Precise and vivid words Semantic interpretation	Coordinating word study with selections read Collecting synonyms, homonyms, antonyms Studying word structure, origin of words Interpreting symbols

Organization and utilization of ideas gained in reading	Discussing significant ideas Preparing oral and written outlines Giving reports, talks
Interpreting and evaluating Critical reading Generalizing Evaluating	Problem solving Discussing material read Evaluating style of author Finding clues to characters, plot, situations
Creative reading	Empathizing with the characters Making judgments concerning people and events Forming vivid images Ascertaining truth and error Projecting one's experience into the situation
Broadening interests	Individual reading projects Conferences with teacher Sharing books with others Reading widely for information, enjoyment, and problem solving
Developing taste	Establishing criteria Comparing books Discussing books Evaluating books read
Increasing fluency Adjusting rate to purpose and motive	Setting time limits Exercises in reading for different purposes Reading different types of material
Shifting gears	Demonstrating ability to shift gears in terms of content and type of assignment.
Utilizing content	Exercises in applying information gained in reading to: solve problems, relate information, share a creative interpretation, participate in a project, apply information read.

Guidelines in Evaluation of Reading Methods

There is no royal road to reading. Children learn to read via many approaches. Many methods have been and are being used by effective teachers to bring children and reading together in a life-long relationship. Whatever methods are used, it is essential that the teacher take responsibility for evaluating the method based on the specific needs of the children in each situation. It is essential, too, to keep in mind that objectives and evaluation are so closely related that in order to evaluate the effectiveness of any one method the teacher must keep in mind the primary objective of reading instruction: to develop the love of reading. Thus evaluation must take into consideration more than reading achievement. It must involve such considerations as the child's attitude toward reading, the choice of a wide variety of reading materials, and the demonstrated success in utilizing his reading materials purposefully and effectively.

The Teacher: Key to Success in Learning to Read

There is a growing evidence from recent research of the significance of the teacher as the key to effective reading instruction. Obviously, a method which capitalizes on a child's native abilities, interests, and linguistic development as well as experiences is important in motivating a child to learn to read. However, even more essential to success is a teacher who has the personal qualities as well as the necessary skill and behavior controls.

Teachers who tend to make reading come alive are individuals who motivate students to go beyond the ordinary in their effort to achieve objectives which are meaningful and rewarding. Such teachers have several important characteristics in common, although there are many individual characteristics which might be observed. Among these characteristics held in common by the creative teachers of reading and which are observable are the following.

Imagination. Imagination is one of the elements that leads to zest, vitality, innovation, and enthusiasm in teaching. The teacher who is able to find new ways of aiding children in learning to read is one who has developed an imaginative spirit in his teaching. It was Einstein who said, "Imagination is more important than knowledge."

Imagination implies not alone using imagination in teaching methods and procedures, but also in stimulating the imagination of the children. For example, stories and books can help us develop the creative imagination of our students with such questions as "What do you think happened before the story started?" or "Where does the butterfly go when it rains?" "The little boy in the story knows where the cows go, where the horses go, and where the pigs go, but where does the butterfly go when it rains?"

Knowledge. Some writers place knowledge as the first element in the list of special characteristics of effective teachers. It was Joseph Addison who wrote many years ago, "Man without education is like marble in the quarry, which reveals none of its inherent beauty until the skill of the polisher makes the surface shine, fetches out all the colors, and reveals every ornamental spot and cloud that runs through the body of knowledge."

It takes more than a slight acquaintance with the children we teach, the process by which learning proceeds, the reading process, and the interrelationships of the language arts and the art of teaching to fulfill our obligations to the children who sit in our classrooms. It devolves upon the teacher to use his knowledge in such a way that each child comes to the reading class or reading experience with anticipation and joy. Reading should be an avenue through which a child comes to know the wonder and delight of living.

In the *Art of Teaching,* Gilbert Highet compares teaching to painting a picture, creating a piece of sculpture, writing a musical composition, planting a garden, or writing a letter to a friend. Each requires knowledge *plus* imagination and skill.

Humor. Humor is that wonderful ingredient that oils the machinery of life, takes the friction out of work-a-day world, and releases tensions. Humor in the classroom is an essential. Humor in books and stories to read is a bonus. Books for children which capitalize on this ingredient include: *Stuart Little* by E. B. White, *Millions of Cats* by Wanda Gag, and *More Riddles* by Bennett Cerf.

Vision. Vision implies going beyond the given in a situation. "Where there is no vision the people perish". This is as true today as when the prophet first spoke and recorded it. The creative teacher has an understanding of the experiences each child has had before he enters her classroom, insight into the present status of his experiences, and interest and vision of what teacher and child together can plan in terms of objectives, experiences, and evaluation upon which to base the learning experiences which will ultimately lead to a successful future, not alone in learning to read, but in reading to learn about life and to participate in its exciting adventures.

Sensitivity. Sensitivity goes beyond understanding. It is more of the quality of empathy, a "feeling in" with people. It implies withholding judgment until all the facts are known. It involves not judging an individual until "one has walked in his mocassins." It means remembering what it is to be a child.

Sensitivity implies the ability not merely to diagnose a child's problems in reading, but to understand the root of the problems and to be able to deal with them. Dealing with them in this sense implies the ability to convey the conviction that the teacher believes in the child and expects him to be able to learn with help.

The key, of course, to effective reading instruction is the teacher.

Research on methods of teaching reading—particularly beginning reading—is extremely popular and prevalent today. New approaches, new ideas, new methods need to be explored if we are to improve the teaching of reading to all children. However, reading programs should be based on reliable evidence that improvement will result. Both administrators and teachers have the right to expect reliable evidence of the advantages of any program, however enthusiastically it may be endorsed by other schools or teachers. Also they have the right to know the limitations and weaknesses as well.

Every teacher needs to be aware that there is not just *a* method of teaching reading, but that there are many approaches which have been successful. In short, a method which capitalizes on a child's native abilities, interests, and linguistic development as well as experiential background will be more successful in motivating a child to learn to read.

Persistent Problems in Reading

The important objective is to develop a child's love for reading. In the struggle to develop basic skills, this objective is often overlooked. Many teachers who are successful in teaching the basic skills have difficulty in achieving objectives dealing with the broad aims of reading.

Some of the persistent problems which, when solved, contribute to the broad objectives of reading are: reading orally, reading critically and creatively, developing broad interests, providing for individual differences, and developing evaluation procedures.

Oral Reading in the Elementary School

It is essential to recognize that the significance of oral reading lies not in reading aloud as a diagnostic tool, but rather as a creative medium through which the child shares his appreciation of a selection of which he is especially fond.

With the increased emphasis on linguistics, the understanding of intonation patterns makes it easier to help the child learn to read with the same expressiveness with which he speaks. For years, teachers of reading have asked children to "read with expression" without giving them the techniques for doing so and without understanding the relationship between spoken and written expressions. As teachers become increasingly sensitive to intonations, stresses, and junctures, and help children become aware of these elements in sentence structure, oral reading will begin to improve and to gain a place of significance again as an expressive art. Hatfield states, "Pupils may well be asked to prepare oral readings by first reading silently with attention to the expression the authors intended. . . . This greater awareness of the speech values on the printed page may be invoked to increase enjoyment of literature, especially of poetry."[31]

Oral reading activities if properly guided contribute to the total development of the child, to his creative expression, and to his reading progress. It should be included in a well balanced reading program. Educators concerned with creative development of the child are convinced of its role in helping children develop creative potential.

The use of the "barber shop" style of reading aloud (the "line a child") has brought a blight upon the practice of oral reading, as has the practice of using oral reading for evaluating the basic reading skills of word identification and comprehension. However, if used to develop the art of communication and an appreciation for the spoken word, it can become an effective and enriching creative experience in the elementary classroom.

In oral reading the reader shares the content with the audience. He and his audience are together looking at the material. As a result it is put within the realm of the audience. It must give the effect of the first time and of being shared. It is necessary for the student to know the material thoroughly. In the best sense it is necessary for him to "think the thought". He must know it so completely that it has become a part of his thinking. For this reason the greatest emphasis is placed on getting the meaning, absorbing the meaning, and then giving the meaning. In interpretation the reader, as an individual, recedes into the background. Once the student realizes this fully, it releases many inhibitions. The conception finally gained that *he* is not important, but that the material is all important opens a new vista of freedom and creative expression.

Critical and Creative Reading Skills

If children are to become mature readers, they must become critical and creative readers.

The effective teacher will use all available means of challenging children through questions which elicit more than acquisition of mere factual material. Instead, they can be motivated to reason, to discover, to project beyond the printed page, and to evaluate. It is the responsibility of the teacher to teach the critical and creative reading skills at levels appropriate for the child's development, and to find ways of stimulating thinking beyond the literal meaning of passages read.

Critical reading involves the processes of problem solving and evaluation. If children are taught from the beginning to evaluate and react to ideas in the light of the author's purpose, the development of these skills will be an integral part of the reading program. Asking such questions as "How does the author know this?" "Is this information as true today as when the book was written?" "Why are these facts important?" "Do other authorities take the same viewpoint?" "Do the biases of this author color his presentation?" will help develop critical thinking.

For true creative reading to take place, the reader must recreate the material he is reading. He becomes a co-author and a re-creator of whatever he reads. Through his own experiences, imagination, and projection, he enhances and interprets the writer's meaning. Again, the teacher, through skillfull questioning, through development of imagination, and through a creative approach to literature will help children develop such skills.

Developing Broad Interests in Reading

How does one help a child develop broad interests in reading? There is an old saying that developing broad interests in reading is much like catching the measles—from one who has them. There is also another old adage which says:

Read
    Read some more
Read some things you yourself enjoy
    Read and talk about it
Read very carefully some things
    Read on the run most things
Don't thing *about* reading, but—
    Read!

Curiosity and the printed page are the warp and the woof in the design that leads to broad interests in reading. Through books we can put on the shoes of swiftness, sense the power of subduing the elements, discover the secret virtues of minerals, sail the seas, fly across the mountains on a magic carpet.

If we are to help children develop broad interests in reading, we must help them experience literature in ways that begin with curiosity and end in enjoyment. If children are to enjoy reading, they must understand what they read. To understand they must have broad experiences—real and vicarious.

If reading is to be a broad as well as an exciting adventure, the teacher must know the children in his group, their interests and needs. He must know literature, so that he can make available the right book, for the right child, at the right time. In this way he opens the world of the imagination, the world of yesterday, of today, and of tomorrow.

Providing for Individual Differences in Reading Achievement

The wide range in reading achievement in the average classroom emphasizes the importance of making adjustments to meet individual differences. This calls for varied grouping practices, provision of materials on many levels of readability, individualized instruction, and other techniques which take into account the differences which exist within a class.

Plans for organization for the reading program to facilitate learning are many and varied. Through the years many plans have evolved as teachers attempted to operate on the premise that there is an inverse relationship between the number of children in the class and the amount of individual assistance each student can receive. In other words, the fewer pupils the teacher must teach, the more individualized the instruction can be.

Many plans to meet the needs of individual children with unrelated rates of learning, independent experiential backgrounds, and individual capabilities and interests have been used. These attempt to individualize instruction, curriculum, and learning materials. Some of these plans focus on the organization of the instructional units, others focus on organization of curriculum, and still others offer a combination of method and materials.

Divided-day plan. One such plan, coming into favor after a forty year evolution, is becoming increasingly popular. Variously labelled as a divided-day, split-day, extended-day, and staggered-day, it is designed to give the teacher more time per pupil to strengthen instruction.

Organized primarily for use in the primary grades, it provides a reading period of one hour in the morning with half of the class, while the other half of the class arrives later and remains in school to receive instruction in reading after the first group has gone home. With a reduced teacher-pupil ratio, a more individualized reading program can be carried on. With split-day scheduling, there are four reading groups, two in the morning and two in the afternoon. The program can then be further individualized by providing appropriate books at the reading level of each child. The additional time spent with the teacher in the early stages of beginning reading contributes to an environment with less distraction as well as increased instructional time. Only half of the class is present at one time.

Nongraded organization. In this type of organization, sequential levels of reading growth are defined and presented as an aid to teachers in: (1) indicating the sequential development from one growth level to the next of the many skills, concepts, and activities a child must master in the course of learning to read, and (2) in functioning as a yardstick to determine the reading growth stage of a child in order to define the point at which his reading instruction should begin.

Continuous progress in which pupils may proceed through the first, second, and third years at their own rate characterizes the nongraded primary school. Grade lines are eliminated, and pupils are identified as primary. Slow learners may need a fourth year to complete the primary levels of achievement.

Since reading is a developmental process, reading instructional levels lend themselves to sequential and increasingly complex units. All pupils except kindergartners are grouped according to reading instructional levels determined by designed instruments of measurement. In the grouping the principal takes into consideration social relationships, emotional maturity, personality problems, and instructional needs. The result of this procedure is the formulation of groups. As the groups in different classrooms advance in reading, the picture changes. Further changes are made as pupils are promoted from one room to another at various times throughout the year. Evaluation is continuous and children are permitted to move ahead at their own rate and ability. Individualization of instruction is thus accomplished by removing the restrictiveness of gradedness.

Joplin plan. This plan is basically a method of grouping children for reading instruction homogeneously on an interclass basis. The plan involves the following successive steps: (1) measuring the achievement and needs of children in a reading program; (2) organizing the children into relatively homogeneous groups independent of their grade classification; (3) scheduling reading classes at the same period during the day throughout the school; and (4) dispersing pupils to reading classes where the instruction is geared to their reading level, not their grade level. Such a program emphasizes physical grouping arrangements in an effort to provide each child with the opportunity to read at his level of achievement.

Reading levels. Children differ widely in reading achievement as they do in other abilities and characteristics. As they progress in the elementary school the reading level of the poorest and the best reader in grade four may vary from that of an average second grader to that of an average eighth grader. This means that plans must be made to provide for the differences in ability at any given grade level. One of the effective ways of managing this problem is to provide reading materials for the various levels of reading ability without designating the grade level as such. Reading series which avoid the use of grade distinctions are a boon to children who are sensitive about reading below "grade" level. Teachers plan together to determine the specific skills, concepts, and competencies which are appropriate for a child at a given reading level and through the necessary remedial and motivational techniques help each child to master the needed skills.

Organizing combined programs. Teachers who sense the need for both individualized and basic reading periods combine the best features of each type of program. The individualized reading proceeds continuously whenever children are not working on the basic assignments. While the teacher is working with one group, the others will complete workbook requirements and then spend the remaining time on free or independent reading.

In some classrooms the basal readers are used in the morning and the self-selected books are used in the afternoon. Basic and individualized work can be readily combined by scheduling the sequential skills activity in the morning and the self-selected individualized reading during the afternoon period. This has been found by many teachers to make an effective first attempt to the individualized reading. By incorporating extensive free reading and personal conferences into a sound basic reading program, these teachers have the security of knowing they are not neglecting the developmental reading program while at the same time they are capitalizing on the child's interests and need for individual attention in learning to read.

A suggested *Week's Program,* combining basic and individualized reading follows on the next page.

Regardless of the administrative organization which the school employs to solve the problem of individual differences, the teacher's responsi-

Suggested Week's Program, Three-group Plan

Day	Min.	Group I (High)	Group II (Average)	Group III (Low)
Monday	20	Direct teacher guidance; new material	Work on individual problems, solo-team	Free reading; individual interests
	20	Committee work; planning of book reports	Direct teacher guidance: reading from text	
	20	Free reading	Reaction to story in art, drama, or writing	Direct teacher guidance: new story, guided reading
Tuesday	20	Free reading; individual interests	Direct teacher guidance: discuss story or answer specific questions	Independent activities, work-study, games
	30	Direct teacher guidance: presentation of oral reports, drama	Committee work; individual work	Free reading; work on skills
	10	All-group activity: choral reading, story, dramatizations, etc.		
Wednes-day	25	Reading related to unit of work	Work on individual needs: team, solo reading related to unit of work	Direct teacher guidance: silent-oral reading, work on skills
	25	Direct guidance: new story	Reading related to unit of work	Reading related to unit of work
	10	Help the children from different groups who have a common need to practice a specific skill; others continue their activity		
Thurs-day	20	Silent reading and reaction to story	Direct teacher guidance: discussion related to stories, planning of activities	Reading related to stories: help by pupil assistants
	20	Direct teacher guidance: discussion, oral-silent reading, work on skills	Developing activities related to readings (committee work, etc.)	Reading related to stories: help by pupil assistants
	20	Individual guidance on book selection for free reading, for unit reports, etc.; use of library aids		
Friday	40	Free reading	Work on individual needs: team, solo; committee work; reading related to unit, etc.	Direct teacher guidance: discussion; plans for sharing with class
	20	All-group activity: library, dramatizations, storytelling, etc.		

bility for individual instruction remains. There must be enough flexibility in grouping to allow children to experience success and satisfaction in reading if the child is to develop competency in one of the most important tools of communication. Among the special types of grouping that can be organized to motivate children to read are: self-chosen groups, interest groups, invitational grouping, skill grouping, recreational grouping.[32]

Finally, in providing for individual differences in reading among a group of children at any given developmental stage or chronological age the teacher may well consider the following suggestions.

1. Carry on a continuous program of evaluation of reading achievement.
2. Keep a complete and accurate account of each child's progress as he moves from grade to grade or level to level.
3. Provide a program of reading which utilizes a variety of required materials so each child will have material geared to his ability.
4. Use unit-type instruction for part of the reading program.
5. Develop a variety of supplementary reading, art, and construction activities related to children's reading interests.
6. Utilize audio-visual and programmed teaching materials to free the teacher for giving help as needed.
7. Plan exhibits, book collections, scrapbooks, friezes, dramatizations, choral speaking, role-playing activities centering around books they have read.
8. Differentiate assignments based on the ability to achieve.
9. Keep the groups flexible to allow for mobility.
10. Encourage varied types of grouping to supplement regularly organized groups.
11. Make use of team grouping and team teaching to facilitate learning.
12. Keep parents informed of the objectives, procedures, and outcomes of the reading program.
13. Read to the children to motivate their interest in self-selection and reading for enjoyment.

The extent to which innovations in organizational patterns, approaches, or materials will bring about the desired goals in reading is dependent on such factors as: the extent to which a school staff plans cooperatively a developmental reading program based on an agreed-upon philosophy, defined objectives; the provision for the gradual development of needed skills for achieving the objectives, learning experiences, and instructional provisions for children of varying abilities and interests, providing for the academically talented child, the slow learning child, and the child who needs special help; instruments of evaluation of pupil progress; and a broad program of evaluation. It depends, too, on the opportunity a school staff has for creative teaching, for cooperative or team approach to some teaching areas, and for an in-service program planned and endorsed by the teachers and supervisors cooperatively.

Such a program takes into account the children, the teachers, the administrative staff, the parents, and the community.

Evaluation Procedures in Reading

The nature of the evaluation process and the procedures used to gain evidence of growth vary with the accepted concept of reading. If reading is conceived as the sounding out of words with little concern for their meaning and application in meaningful situations, evaluation is simple. However, if reading is to involve thinking and feeling, the use of the cognitive, affective and perceptual powers, and self-confidence in attacking new tasks with persistence, then evaluation must be based on these concepts.

A broad evaluation program includes consideration of the child's comprehension, study skills, word-analysis and identification skills, appreciation of literary style, critical and creative reading skills, application of reading skills, reading interests, reading habits, shifting gears in reading, skills in reading in content fields, and self-appraisal. A variety of techniques of evaluation including observations of development, anecdotal records, work samples, analysis of student's oral and written responses to reading and related assignments, informal teacher-made tests and questionnaires, programmed reading materials, standardized tests of intelligence and reading achievement, and evaluative reports by teachers and pupils should be used. Not only should the teacher obtain evidence of the child's growth in reading, but he should be equally concerned with the more subtle aspects of development of the individual personality *through* reading.

Self-evaluation on the part of both the pupil and the teacher should be an integral part of the appraisal program. If the child early helps to set his own goals and assists in measuring his progress toward these goals, if he is a partner in gathering such evidence and clearly understands the purposes for reading and the reading experiences provided, it is understandable that he will move toward those goals with greater self-confidence and success.[33]

Concluding Statement

The main task of the educator is to organize a learning environment in which each child can develop to his maximum potential. This implies an educational setting and curriculum organization in which children are provided with experiences which motivate them to develop creatively, to solve problems, and to think critically. Such an objective implies, too, that every child must develop his powers to use reading as a tool for gaining information, solving problems, evaluating critically, and expressing creatively.

A program of this type offers a reading curriculum characterized by such factors as the following.

1. Understanding the interrelatedness of the language arts of listening, speaking, reading, and writing.
2. Utilizing the knowledge of the development of the linguistic skills and the role of oral language in reading. Competence in the spoken language is a necessary base for reading *and* writing.

3. Broadening the concepts of readiness for reading to include readiness for each new reading skill introduced in the elementary school.

4. Introducing the child early in the primary grades to the skills involved in critical and creative reading.

5. Providing for individual differences on a broader base of method, materials, and media. If every child is to achieve power in reading, it is essential to adjust the reading program to individual needs, abilities, and interests.

6. Knowing a variety of approaches and methods in teaching reading. Knowledge of and experience with a variety of approaches in reading instruction enables a teacher to meet the needs of a particular group of children more effectively.

7. Developing skills in reading is an objective in every reading program. Whatever method is used, the following skills must be developed if a child is to become a proficient reader: (1) word identification in reading through context clues, word-form clues, phonetic analysis, structural analysis, and dictionary usage; (2) comprehension skills—literal comprehension, interpretative skills, critical reading, creative reading, and word meaning; (3) study skills including research skills, technical vocabulary, and specific skills related to content subjects; (4) fluency and speed—dealing with abilities to shift gears according to purpose and materials read.

8. Developing broad interests in reading. Through providing books to meet varied needs and interests, assigning reading for a variety of purposes, encouraging individual reading, library projects, and free reading, the child is motivated to read widely with the result that his understanding of people, places, and phenomena develops simultaneously with his understanding of self.

9. Conceiving of evaluation as a shared responsibility. Today's teacher takes a dimensional approach to evaluation. (1) The child evaluates his own progress. (2) The teacher evaluates the extent to which he is helping children achieve individual and group goals in reading. (3) The teacher and staff evaluate the extent to which the reading program is contributing to the goals of the language arts in meeting the needs of the children in communicating creatively.

Today's teacher must provide effective instruction and challenging materials in thought-provoking situations which challenge each child to read to enrich his experiences, extend his horizons, broaden his understanding, develop his insights, and unlock the door to learning.

References

1. Donald Durrell and Alice Nicholson, "Preschool and Kindergarten Experience," in Nelson B. Henry (ed.), *Development in and Through Reading,* The Sixtieth Yearbook of the National Society for the Study of Education, Part I, University of Chicago Press, Chicago, 1961, p. 257.

2. Arthur I. Gates and Frank G. Jennings, "The Role of Motivation," in Henry, *op. cit.,* p. 122.

3. Walter D. Loban, *The Language of Elementary School Children,* Research Report No. 1, National Council of Teachers of English, Champaign, Ill., 1963, p. 87.

4. Alvina Burrows, "Helping Children to Listen and Speak", in Helen K. Mackintosh (ed.), *Children and the Language Arts,* Joint Publication of ACEI, ASCD, IRA, and NCTE, 1964, p. 17.
5. Helen M. Robinson, "Vocabulary: Speaking, Listening, Reading and Writing," in H. Alan Robinson (ed.), *Reading and the Language Arts,* University of Chicago Press, Chicago, 1963, p. 169.
6. Ruth G. Strickland, *The Language of Elementary School Children: Its Relationship to the Language of Reading Textbooks and the Quality of Reading of Selected Children,* Bulletin of The School of Education, Vol. 38, No. 4, Bloomington, 1962.
7. By permission from R. D. Armstrong and W. J. Gage Limited, from *Education 6.* Published by W. J. Gage Limited, reprinted by permission of Gage Educational Publishing Limited.
8. By permission from Gertrude Hildreth, "Linguistic Factors in Early Reading Instruction," *The Reading Teacher,* 18:176, December, 1964.
9. By permission from Thomas J. Creswell, "Linguistics and Reading: Remarks on B. Robert Tabachink's Paper," in Robinson, *op. cit.,* p. 109.
10. Gertrude Hildreth, *loc. cit.*
11. Wendell Johnson, *Your Most Enchanted Listener,* Harper and Brothers, New York, 1956, p. 123.
12. Ruth G. Strickland, "Implications of Research in Linguistics for Elementary Teaching," *Elementary English Journal,* 40:169, February, 1963.
13. By permission from Donald J. Lloyd, "Sub-cultural Patterns which Affect Language and Reading Development," in Bernard J. Weiss (ed.), *Language, Linguistics, and School Programs,* Proceedings of the Spring Institutes, National Council of Teachers of English, Champaign, Ill., 1963, p. 51.
14. William Gray and Bernice Rogers, *Maturity in Reading,* University of Chicago Press, Chicago, 1956. p. 56.
15. Jean Turner Goins, "Relation of Visual Perception to Reading," *Education Digest,* 24:44, September, 1958.
16. Emerald V. Dechant, *Improving the Teaching of Reading,* © 1964. Reprinted by permission of Prentice-Hall, Inc., Englewood Cliffs, N.J., p. 193.
17. Johnson, *op. cit.*
18. David Russell, *Children's Thinking,* Ginn and Company, Boston, 1956, p. 283.
19. Helen Huus, "Critical and Creating Reading," in J. Allen Figurel (ed.), *Reading and Inquiry,* Proceedings of the Annual IRA Convention, vol. 10, International Reading Association, Newark, 1965, p. 117.
20. Lillian M. Logan and Gerald T. Rimmington, *Social Studies: A Critical Direction,* McGraw-Hill Ryerson Limited, Toronto, 1969, p. 195.
21. By permission from George Spache, *Toward Better Reading,* Garrard Publishing Company, Champaign, 1963, p. 287. See also Edwin H. Smith, Billie M. Guice, and Martha C. Cheek, "Informal Reading Inventories for the Content Areas: Science and Mathematics, *Elementary English,* 49:659-66, May, 1972.
22. See Edward G. Summers, "Reading in the Secondary Schools," *Review of Educational Research,* 37:140. April, 1967.
23. By permission from R. Van Allen, *Language—Experience Approach to Reading,* Department of Education, San Diego, 1963. (Mimeographed.)
24. Lyman Hunt, "Six Steps to the Individualized Reading Program," *Elementary English,* 48:27-32, January, 1971.
25. By permission from Carl A. Lefevre, *Linguistics and the Teaching of Reading,* McGraw-Hill Book Company, New York, 1964, p. 7.
26. Charles C. Fries, "Linguistics in Beginning Reading," in Helen Mackintosh (ed.), *Current Approaches to Teaching Reading,* American Association of Elementary-Kindergarten-Nursery Educators, NEA, Washington, D.C., 1965, p. 3.

27. Don. H. Parker, *Schooling for Individual Excellence,* Thomas Nelson and Sons, New York, 1964.
28. Albert Mazurkiewicz, "Initial Teaching Alphabet (Augmented Roman) for Teaching Reading," in Albert J. Mazurkiewicz, (ed.), *New Perspectives in Reading Instruction,* Pitman Publishing Corporation, New York, 1964, pp. 543-4.
29. Dorothea E. Hinman, "Words in Color," in Mackintosh, *Current Approaches to Teaching Reading, op. cit.,* p. 5.
30. Reprinted from "A New Approach to Reading" by Janet Goss in *Journal of Programmed Reading* with permission of the Webster Division, McGraw-Hill, Inc.
31. By permission from Wilbur W. Hatfield, "Will Structural Grammar Help?" *The English Journal,* 48:570-75, December, 1958.
32. See Paul McKee, *Reading: A Program of Instruction for the Elementary School,* Houghton Mifflin Co., Boston, 1966, pp. 245-51.
33. David Allen, "Cue Systems Available During the Reading Process," *The Elementary School Journal,* 72:258-64, February, 1972.

12

Explorations in Literature

For sooth, he cometh to you with a tale, which holdeth children from play, and old men from the chimney corner.
Sir Philip Sidney

In our anxiety to teach children to read, to prepare them for living in a technological, computer-oriented society, is it possible that we fail to cultivate in them an appreciation for good literature? Are the schools yielding to external pressures to emphasize reading primarily as a utilitarian tool and neglecting reading as a means of developing moral and ethical values through literary experiences? The teacher of literature must be dedicated to a consuming interest in ideas and in the esthetic and moral values of the literature he is to teach. If he is to communicate the riches of the literary heritage—past and present—he must be a person who makes literature live.

Literature is a means by which children widen horizons, heighten awareness, develop the imagination, stimulate thinking, discover meanings, expand vocabulary, develop sensitivity to words, and grow in understanding of both other people and themselves. As children come in contact with the cultural heritage of the past and present through literature, they are guided to appreciate the gifts of past generations and of other peoples, and so understand better the cultural milieu in which they live. Familiarity with the classics and their well loved characters and plots aids children in understanding the many allusions to literature in everyday speech.

Children enjoy listening to stories and poems long before they are able to read for themselves. The wise adult fills their lives with books and provides numerous opportunities to experience literature. Discussing the characters, the plot, the events, times and places; participating in choral reading, reader's theater and dramatization are avenues through which children grow into appreciation of the best in literature. A teacher skilled in interpretation and sensitive to the needs and interests of the children is able to bring life to literature.

Effective teachers recognize the significance of literature to the child and the role it plays in a well planned language arts curriculum. They take the long view and plan learning experiences in such a way that by the time the child leaves the elementary school he has experienced literature which is balanced in scope. They include the best of poetry and prose both past and modern, fictional and factual, imaginative and realistic, informative and nonsensical. When children and literature are brought together by a teacher who has knowledge, appreciation, and enjoyment of literature; knowledge, understanding, and interest in children; *plus* perception, skill, and competence in teaching, children develop a life-long interest in reading.

Teachers need to remember, too, that the quality of their teaching will be determined ultimately by their qualities as human beings. The task of the teacher in literature is to select the poems, novels, plays, paintings, music, philosophies and ideas which can affect the student and make an adjustment between his present values and those of the writers, artists and thinkers.

What Is Literature?

Literature Is Experience

Literature is life as seen by the author. It is interpreted by the reader who brings to the printed page his own experiences, rich or limited. Literature is a way of looking at life, of questioning life, of structuring the components of life in such a way that what might seem ordinary, mundane, or menial may become suddenly extraordinary, exciting, and/or elevating.

Literature Is Both Creative and Recreative

The writer paints a picture, portrays a scene, and develops a concept with words as clearly as an artist does with paint and brush. The skilled reader, as interpreter, recreates first in his mind's eye images and ideas as vivid, as real, and as urgent as they were for the writer himself. As he reads, the words construct for the listener the time, the place, the scene, or the situation. To the extent that mood, situation, character, place, or time are made vivid, arresting and exciting, the listener as well as the reader can find adventure, mystery, nonsense, fancy. He can live in times and places he has never known except through books. "The writer has seen one or another part of life in a certain way. With the talent he can command, he writes about it, discovering a literary form which will convey his total meaning."[1]

Literature Is a Medium of Creative Communication

Literature, as such, is related to other media: radio, television, films, magazines, newspapers. Literature can be translated into a form for greater communication audience appeal, through films, radio, and/or television.

Literature Is Art

Art is the distillation or abstraction of an experience, real or imaginary, portrayed through a chosen medium, and restricted or enhanced by the experience, perception, and skill of the artist. Literature, like the other arts, is such an experience. A literary experience evokes response through identification. Creative teachers use many and varied methods for aiding the child in identification.

Through literature as an art form the child experiences, he identifies, he becomes a part of the content, a part of the world of ideas. By bringing to the student literature as art, the meaning of art is discovered through his own experiences.

Literature Is a Key

Literature is a key that unlocks doors, that opens windows, that helps a child understand people and phenomena he encounters. He identifies with the characters and "becomes" and grows as he lives with the heroes of yesterday and of today. Through biography, hero tales, and legends, as well as through stories of modern times, the child develops an affinity with people, a sensitivity to their joys and sorrows, an understanding of situations and periods of history. The world becomes more meaningful through folk tales, picture books, regional stories, stories of other lands, the world of nature and of machines.

A child will grow in an environment in which there is much creative experience with literature. He will grow in stature as a person, he will grow in competence as a reader, he will develop taste for good literature through many contacts with writers who use words with imagination, discrimination, and taste. The world of books broadens the child's horizons, gives him understanding and empathy, provides him with insight into human relationships. Good books provide him with clear standards of right and wrong, show him conflict and ethics of human behavior.

Teachers have two major responsibilities to the child in literature: first, to become keen judges of what distinguishes good literature from second rate; and second, to discover what literature appeals to different children at various age levels.

What Are Good Books for Children?

Good literature for children, like good literature for adults, mirrors the minds of men and the ever swifter pace of change in the universe. Books reach across the years and make the past come alive and real. They make the future seem as near and real as the present. Children respond to books on the basis of the experience and background they bring to the reading.

Children are pastmasters at rejecting books which they do not like, as countless well intentioned parents, grandparents, librarians and teachers have discovered. A book may be considered a juvenile classic by the experts, but if it does not touch the child, if it is beyond his understanding, if it is too far removed from his interests, he will be indifferent to it.

In deciding what is a good book for children in the elementary school, the following characteristics will serve the teacher as broad guidelines.

In a good book the child can identify with the main character. Admiring a hero of one of the great sagas a child might well say, "If I had lived in those times, woe to the evildoers!"

If, on the other hand, the main character lives in the present time, the reader might think, "I know how he felt. If my parents were to go to Pakistan, I would venture forth just as he did. I, too, would save the village from terror and destruction."

A good book is true to life. Being true to life involves such elements as realism, honesty, and integrity in developing the plot and the characters. It is at this point that many stories of adventure and mystery fail because of their falsity, shallowness, sentimentalism and/or sleaziness.

A good book is true to facts. If it is an informative book, it is important that the facts are accurate. Even science fiction should be based on what is now known and the potentialities of technology. If the author writes about a section of the country, a specific vocation or avocation, he must have the necessary background to make the characters plausible, the setting true to life, and the action logical in terms of the mores of the region.

A good book is true to type. Fictionalized biography and biographical fiction have their place, but they should not make the pretense of being biography. Modern writers of juvenile biographies of the childhood of the hero are careful to examine the facts before committing them to the printed page. Biography based on inaccurate, slight or nonexistent facts should not be included among the books recommended for children.

A good book has literary style. If children are to develop taste in literature, they must be provided with books that embody the elements of good writing. In poetry there should be rhythm; in fairy tales there should be cadence, the building up to the climax. In good fiction there is understanding, communication, and dialogue that rings true. Visual imagery, colorful language, choice words and phrases are important if a book is to live for children.

A good book has a dominant theme. There must be an underlying theme which motivates every episode and action. The theme may be simple, but it should have sufficient backbone to stand up firmly and support the whole structure.

A good book has richness of detail. A good book is more than a series of statements of facts. It recounts the events and episodes that lead up to the main event. It gives detailed and needed background of information to aid the reader in understanding and interpreting the actions of the characters. A book should give the reader the feeling of moving through the story in step with the character, empathizing with him all the way.

A good book, in short, offers identification, is true to life, sticks to the facts so far as they are known, is honest, and is true to its type. A good book is written in a style worthy of its content; it has choice language and vivid imagery, a dominant theme, and richness of detail. Whether fact or fiction, imaginative or realistic, a good book speaks to the child. It may tickle his funny bone, set him to chuckling, move him to pity, motivate him to achieve, thrill him with hope and courage, inspire him to be like the hero, and keep him hanging in mid-air of suspense. It should enrich his life and help him to understand better both life and his own actions. It should catapult a student out of the world of things into the world of imagination and bring him back better able to understand himself and the world in which he lives.

What Are Children's Interests?

Adults have made attempts to discover the reading interests of children in order to try to make available to them books which will meet their interests and needs at particular developmental levels. From 1893, when M.B.C. True reported "What My Pupils Read", to the present time there have been more than two hundred studies made to determine the amount and nature of voluntary reading preferences and activities. In 1925 Terman and Lima concluded that there are certain well defined tendencies in reading interests that change as the child's experience grows and as his imagination and reasoning powers develop. They identified a number of factors which contribute to the development of reading interests: age, health and physical development, school environment, home training, mental ability, and sex. Both boys and girls were found to enjoy animal stories, but boys preferred adventure and vigorous action while girls liked fairy tales, poetry, and "sentimental" fiction. Boys read more nonfiction than girls. The amount of reading increased from age six to twelve or thirteen and showed a gradual decrease from that point on. Sex differences in reading choice were increasingly apparent after age nine.[2]

Norvell[3] in 1958 investigated the reading interests of more than 24,000 children in grades three to six. He found the following elements in the books favored by boys: animals, humor, courage and heroism, and patriotism. They regarded as unfavorable elements: description, didacticism, fairies, romantic love, sentiment, girls or women as leading characters, and physical weakness in male characters.

Elements favored by girls were: lively adventure, home and school life, human characters, domestic animals and pets, romantic love, sentiment, mystery, the supernatural, and patriotism. Disapproved elements included violent action, description, didacticism, boys and girls younger than the reader (except babies), and fierce animals.

It was found that many selections classified as juvenile literature increased in appeal to a high point and then declined. Many Mother Goose Rhymes were enjoyed as late as grade six, others were rejected as early as grade three. *Aesop's Fables* and fairy tales were particularly popular in grades five through seven, myths, legends, and hero and folk tales were most popular in grades five through seven. Sex differences in children's choices in reading appeared early, and although girls seemed to enjoy many boy's books, boys rejected almost all girls' books. Some adult magazines were popular with both boys and girls.[3]

A later study of reading interests indicated that the first grade children's preference in reading ranked as follows: (1) make-believe, (2) happiness, (3) humor, (4) adventure, (5) history, (6) family, (7) anxiety, and (8) today's world. Adventure and history ranked highest for boys, while humor and family ranked second and fourth for girls.[4]

Nelson[5] ascertained that, at the primary level, best liked poems involved action, a story line, near nonsense humor, and little description. Pittman[6] identified rhythmic animal poems as favorites of third graders. Shaffer and Wilson[7] decided that children seeking information preferred textbook sources to other sources. McCloskey[8] concluded that early interest in books declined among 170 ghetto lads by the time they reached grade six. "Too hard" was the most frequent response. Simpson and Soares[9] in a study of 4,250 junior high school students found that action, conflict, suspense, and clarity of language were among the characteristics of popular books. Later research[10] added animal characters, teen-age heroes, and a bravery theme.

In May, 1970, *The New York Times Book Review* cited the ten best juvenile sellers since the first of the year, based on reports from stores throughout the country. In order they were:

White's *Charlottes's Web* (Harper, 1952)

Scarry's *Richard Scarry's Best Word Book Ever* (Golden, 1963)

Saint-Exupery's *The Little Prince* (Harcourt, 1943)

Steig's *Sylvester and the Magic Pebble* (Simon and Schuster, 1969)

Milne's *Winnie-the-Pooh* (Dutton, 1926, 1961)

William's *The Velveteen Rabbit* (Doubleday, 1926, 1958)

Dahl's *Charlie and the Chocolate Factory* (Knopf, 1964)

Scarry's *Richard Scarry's Best Story Book Ever* (Golden, 1968)

Seuss's *I Can Lick Thirty Tigers* (Random House, 1969)

McCloskey's *Make Way for Ducklings* (Viking, 1941)

A list is significant primarily in that it reveals the breadth of children's interest in literature. Included are fantasy, fairy tales, and a dictionary.

In November, 1971, from Sheffield, England, came the result of a survey by Yorkshire students of children's favorite books. More than 9,000 children were questioned. Enid Blyton is still at the top of the list after thirty years of popularity. The survey demonstrates that few books written in recent years have gained such a wide following as the classics. Runners-up were Charles Dickens, Agatha Christie, and Robert Louis Stevenson.

Children read all types of material. Some is poor writing, some is reasonably good and the rest is literature. Teachers have the responsibility of guiding children into broader interests and to raise the level of their enjoyment *if* they are to help them develop taste and appreciation.

Both boys and girls choose selections that are biographical, that deal with animals and nature, that relate adventure, and that contain humor and nonsense. Girls often read selections intended primarily for boys, but boys rarely read those obviously intended for girls.

Children read juvenile magazines and as they mature they read some adult magazines. Boys show a preference for sports and mechanics, and girls for home life, movies, and early romance. Comic books are popular and are read extensively, chiefly because they are easy to read, are readily available, relate humor and adventure, and are light and entertaining.

Prose is much more popular than poetry, fiction is more popular than non-fiction. However, children enjoy poetry read aloud *if* the teacher reads expressively. They enjoy particularly poems of a narrative type. Ballads are high on the preference list.

To aid the teacher in learning more about children's preferences, Squire[11] summarizes studies of reading interests. He found some general clues.

1. *Intelligence* is not a factor in determining reading interests.
2. *Sex difference* is quite significant.
3. *Age* is a more important factor in elementary grades than it is later.
4. *Socio-economic* backgrounds affect reading interests.
5. *Scientific themes, action, surprise,* and *humor* appeal to most young readers.

Television and other informational-recreational communication media have served to broaden the scope of reading interests of today's elementary school child. To meet these interests, many new and different types of books are being made available to children to hear and read.

Books about the world of space, other cultures, fictionalized and documented biographies of world leaders, books about developing nations, realistic books dealing with controversial themes are beginning to find a place in approved and/or recommended reading lists. Books dealing with narcotics, alcoholism, drugs, and delinquency make it imperative to know the school policies and parental biases in regard to the reading of controversial books in the elementary school.[12]

Because of the large number of books being published for children (Some 400 titles were published in 1920, compared to some 1,600 in 1960. Since 1960 the rate has increased so that in 1968, 2,318 titles were added to the publishers' lists.) It is increasingly difficult to be aware of the best that are being published.

In the 1970's, although the competition from television and other perhaps unknown media will be claiming the attention of the children, they must be motivated to catch a vision of the exciting adventures they can have only with books, old and new. This excitement for reading cannot be taught; it can, however, be caught from a teacher who shares some of the excitement, suspense, wonder, beauty, and satisfaction that comes from bringing the right child and the right book together.

The teacher should endeavor to keep up with the ever growing body of new offerings in children's literature, both prose and poetry. Fortunately, there are excellent sources of information and evaluation of new children's books. Among these are the review sections of books in the *Horn Book, Elementary English, The Reading Teacher, Saturday Review, School Library Journal, Association for Childhood Education, International, Educational Leadership,* and the book review sections of such metropolitan newspapers as *The London Times, The New York Times,* Vancouver *Sun,* Toronto *Globe and Mail,* Montreal *Gazette.*

Other basic sources are:

Children's Books Too Good to Miss, Western Reserve University Press.

Children's Catalogue, H. W. Wilson.

Notable Children's Books, American Library Association.

Reading Ladders for Human Relations, American Council on Education.

We Read, American Library Association.

Of interest, too, are the many award winning books for children, in particular the Caldecott Medal and Newberry Medal winners, recognized since 1938 and 1922 respectively.

How Shall We Select and Teach Children's Literature?

Anyone who has been on a committee to evaluate and select the best books for children is well aware that this is not a simple task. True, there are certain criteria one can draw up. Books selected must be written in good literary style, ethically sound, true to life, universal in appeal, attractive in format, give evidence of knowledge of children's interests and needs, and satisfy the innate curiosity of the reader. Having drawn up a list of criteria, the task remains to find books that will meet it. However, in spite of the help such criteria give, there still remains the unpredictable variable—the individual child.

Every teacher would profit from looking at the lists which indicate the best judgment of a group of specialists—librarians and teachers working with children and children's books over a number of years deciding which books should be salvaged from the old well-known and much loved ones and which of the new books should be included because of their rich significance for today's child.

Dora Smith compiled a list which may serve as a guide to elementary schools aiming to develop a well rounded literature program.[13] Even a cursory glance through this list of books reveals a broad scope of children's literature. The prospective teacher will find many of his favorites here and a challenge to new reading. It is in the interest of the children that he be able to select wisely books and stories on the basis of the particular experiential background of interests, needs, and temperament of his group.

The Heritage of Prose

Prose is the language of everyday conversation. Because of this, many teachers find the reading of prose more natural. "Once upon a time . . . " immediately gains the attention of the listeners. It is out of words that the reader creates those pictures that captivate the listeners. Teachers should familiarize themselves with representative prose selections from each of the categories.

There are often occasions for reading fables. Best known are *Aesops Fables*. These vary in difficulty of reading and in demands of maturity of the reader thereby meeting the growing and varied abilities and interests of children throughout the elementary school. These stories which invest animals with human traits to point a moral came to be called fables. With the passing of time they have found a place in children's literature.

Folklore is an integral part of every nation's heritage. McNeer and Ward's *The Canadian Story* contains anecdotes and legends built around the lives of colorful and diverse peoples who played important roles in Canadian history. These absorbing stories of human interest tales concerning Hiawatha, Evangeline, Count Frontenac, the "Mounties", and countless less-known characters, in conjunction with the exceptionally fine illustrations, stimulate genuine interest in the study of life in a rigorous era.

American folklore is characterized by the braggadocio of such heroes as Paul Bunyan and Pecos Bill. The stories grew with the telling and the fine line between the legendary and real is often a thin one. The folk tale, however, remains an avenue through which man voices his achievements, ambitions, dreams and protests.

In its truest sense, a fairy tale is the product of an individual in contrast with the tale which evolved from the "folk" and was handed down from mouth to mouth and generation to generation.

Some of the best loved tales of imagination were created by Hans Christian Anderson. Although the endings are not always happy and a sense of sadness pervades many of the Anderson stories, there is the feeling throughout that life is good and that in the end everything will be all right, that good will triumph over evil. There is even a sense of humor in the ending of "The Emperor's New Clothes." Among the well known collections, Eva La Gallienne's for young readers and Paul Leyssac's and Signe Toksvig's for intermediate and upper grades are exceptional for fluency in translations and appropriateness of their illustrations.

The Arabian Night Tales have long fascinated children with their magic, touch of mystery, and enchantment of the East. In Andrew Lang's version of *The Arabian Nights,* the stories of "Sinbad the Sailor", "Ali Baba and the Forty Thieves", "Aladdin and the Wonderful Lamp", and others provide much enjoyment for intermediate grades. "The Flying Carpet" in Marcia Brown's arresting edition has strong pictures in absorbing Oriental designs which in an age of supersonic aircraft and flying saucers hold a perculiar fascination for children.

From the English come some of the best known of all folk and fairy tales. *The Golden Goose Book* of Leslie Brooks with its charming pictures of "The Three Pigs" and "The Three Bears" continues to enchant children in today's kindergarten and primary grades. The atmosphere of the English rural scenes makes these tales excellent ones with which to introduce the fairy tales. There are numerous picture books of individual stories which are very popular with children in the beginning reading stages.

We have come to know Cinderella through the French fairy tales. Among the perennial favorites of Perrault are "Cinderella", "Little Red Riding Hood", and "Beauty and the Beast". These stories, however, are best when read or told to the children. The difficulty of the language of some of the tales makes it all but impossible for weak readers to enjoy them at a time when the stories are psychologically suitable for them.

"The Glass Slipper", Eleanor Farjeon's long version of "Cinderella," is almost a novel. A favorite with intermediate and upper grade children, "Cinderella" is excellent for dramatizing.

If it hadn't been for the scholarly German brothers Grimm, Jakob and Wilhelm, the world's most enchanting fairy tales might have disappeared forever. Their *Household Tales* were adapted from old folk tales rather than created like those of Anderson. Such favorites as "The Bremen Town Musicians", "The Elves and the Shoemaker", "Hansel and Gretel", "Rapunzel", "Tom Thumb", "The Frog Prince", and "Sleeping Beauty" are told in a way that appeals to children. The rewarding of virtue, the confounding of vice is handled with dispatch and with assurance.

Wanda Gag's retelling of "Snow White and the Seven Dwarfs" is enchanting with the diminutive dwarfs, the musical, rhythmical telling, and the childlike quality which is utterly devoid of the sophisticated treatment given by other artists.

From Scandinavia comes the folk literature of the ogres, giants, trolls, the charming ladies and devoted lovers. "The Three Billy Goats Gruff" has long been a favorite with primary children, as has "East o' the Sun and West o' the Moon".

Gudrun Thorne-Thomson, the famous Norwegian story teller of the Carnegie Library School, captures in her retelling of the stories from "East o' the Sun and West o' the Moon" the spirit of the Norwegian folk heritage. Correlating the music of Grieg with the literature gives children further insight into the cultural heritage of these people. The "Peer Gynt Suite" is exceptionally valuable in this connection.

The eight volumes of *Folk Tales from Many Lands* is typical of the numerous collections which have in recent years enriched the field of children's literature. As the world shrinks it is important to understand other cultures and other peoples. The teacher should be concerned with helping children appreciate not merely literature but also cultures of other lands.

Gods and heroes have long been a subject for writers. The great hero stories of the Bible, such as Moses and the Promised Land, David and Goliath, Daniel in the Lion's Den, Joseph and His Brethren, have laid the foundation for the Judea-Christian ethic, with its emphasis on moral heroism and the worth of the individual.

An early encounter with the Petershams' *The Christ Child,* selected passages from the Christmas story, illumined in gold, blue, and rose, provides children with a great literary experience.

The Myths of the Greek gods—Zeus, Poseidin, Apollo, Athena, and many others—have survived in all their grandeur. Children enjoy them in the upper intermediate grades and junior high school. Their acquaintance with the gods of Olympus and their intervention in the affairs of men introduce them to concepts and allusions they will meet in much of their later literature.

Kingsley's "The Heroes" and Sally Benson's *Stories of the Gods and Heroes* are helpful in understanding the epics. Individual children will vary in their readiness for such reading. The responsibility of the teacher is to plan a program in which the individual interests of children are broadened.

Myths and legends about great human heroes, hero tales and epics evolved in the days of man's greatest wondering about himself and his origin. Religion, magic, and explanation of life were intermingled. Out of this came great epics and stories. *The Illiad* and *The Odyssey,* of which Church's version has been a standard for many years, challenge able readers in the intermediate grades. Padriac Colum's *The Adventures of Odysseus* and his *Tale of Troy* are well paced and related with vigor. The teacher could well read them aloud to a class. Some individual children select such literature if it is available.

A favorite hero of English-speaking children is Robin Hood. Howard Pyle has an excellent way of telling the story, enabling pupils to relive the old days of Sherwood Forest and Nottingham Castle. His illustrations, too, are delightful. Some pupils, however, will enjoy reading the less demanding Carol Oman version, and leave the Pyle version to be read by the teacher during the story hour.

Other heroes are Beowulf, the Finnish heroes of the Kalevala, Roland of France, the Cid, and Don Quixote of Spain. Not to be missed is the story of Christian in Paul Bunyan's *Pilgrim's Progress.* Although written for adults it is relished by young students.

The Heritage of Poetry

Introducing children to poetry can be both challenging and exciting. Poetry is readily appreciated by a child because the poet and the child are kin in the sense that the child, like the poet, sees with the imagination, hears with the ear of the musician, and shares what he sees and hears. For every occasion there is a poem. The teacher who makes poetry an integral part of the day's activities will teach children that what we call the music of the words in poetry is actually what we hear through our thoughts and feelings. In a classroom in which a sensitive teacher has guided children into the wonder of words, poetry begins in awe and ends with delight.

For those who have the responsibility of bringing poetry and children together in a life-long union, to open the door to yet another avenue for creative communication, the directive might well be: keep alive your own enjoyment of poetry; read it aloud to children; and remember that there are many doors into the nonsense rhymes, humor, narrative poems, songs, ballads, and even poems whose meaning can hardly be fathomed, but whose beauty can be appreciated.

Fortunate is the child who is given a glimpse of the world larger than his own through an introduction to a poem from across the waters or from the other side of the earth. To a child who is reveling in the sound and magic of words, listening to the music, poetry brings a new experience. The music, the melody, the variety of rhyme and meter, the imagery and narrative of a make-believe and real world of people, places, and things are the child's birthright. From infancy he responds to the magic of poetry. Asserts Larrick, "I have become convinced that poetry is closer to the child—his language, his imagination, his sense of rhythm, his urge to create—than any other form of literature."[14]

Children should explore all types of poetry—poetry that fills them with laughter and delight, poetry that leaves them wondering and speculating, poetry that seeks answers, and poetry that brings solutions. From the jingles of the nursery rhymes and the established names of Walter de la Mare, A. A. Milne, Dorothy Aldis, Rachel Field, Eleanor Farjeon, Rose Fyleman, Elizabeth Coates, Harry Behn, David McCord, to mention only a few, the teacher can find poems that speak to children.

Recent years have seen the publication of anthologies which provide a wealth of poems for the children's repertoire and facilitate the selection of the appropriate poem.

For the teacher who is lighting the spark of interest in poetry some useful suggestions follow.

Capture for yourself the magic of poetry.

Read it aloud and listen to your own reading.

Stretch your imagination to see, feel, and experience the poem.

Respond to the imagery and mood of the poem.

Interpret the poem as a creative experience each time you read it.

Be satisfied if children enjoy the poem.

"If pupils have enjoyed a poem, the experience in itself is sufficient, and it is not necessary that they should be asked to talk or write about it. On occasion, however, they will welcome the opportunity to make a drawing, or painting to illustrate a poem or to dramatize its content."[15]

How Shall We Teach Children's Literature?

Individuals interested in the teaching of children's literature have long held that such instruction can extend the pupil's experience, develop his taste for literature, stimulate him to acquire high ideals and moral or spiritual values, develop an understanding of other peoples, and broaden the scope of his reading interests. Whether such goals are achieved depends on the selection of the material and on meaningful learning experiences. In all too many elementary schools, pupils' experiences in literature are limited to memorizing facts. Word study, rhythm, sentence structure, style, names of figures of speech, and other structural elements can be made important in aiding the students to understand and appreciate literature. It is the conviction of the authors that in developing appreciation of literature every aspect of the program should focus on the child's experience with the literature itself. The teacher utilizes the content as an avenue to deepening, broadening, and enriching children's experiences. By careful planning the teacher leads the child to project himself imaginatively into various times, places, and situations. This may be accomplished in various ways.

Guiding Principles

Fostering delight and hearty enjoyment of literary selections through experiences is the basis for developing appreciation and taste in literature.

1. Literature should be approached in such a way that the pupil comes to the experience anticipating that here is something to be enjoyed.
2. The approach to literature should be both creative and analytical.
3. The teacher must provide for a wide selection of books in order to help children broaden their interests in reading.
4. The reading of good literature to children and by children should be an integral part of the curriculum.
5. The teacher himself should have both an understanding of and appreciation for the literature he teaches.
6. Creative activities of many kinds should evolve directly from the child's experience with literature.
7. The best basis for developing taste and appreciation is the exposure to good literature over a long period of time.

What Are Some Creative Experiences With Literature?

Creative teachers are using many and varied experiences to vitalize the literature program in the elementary classroom. Here the teacher is not concerned primarily with reading ability but with guiding children to appreciate and enjoy literature through varied experiences. In developmental reading the teacher is concerned with the question. "What is Johnny doing in reading?" In literature he is concerned with the question, "What is reading doing for Johnny?" The teacher must ask himself, "Can I teach so enthusiastically, so effectively, so creatively that Johnny will under my guidance:

1. Share the real and imaginary experiences of the author?
2. Extend and enrich his own experiences?
3. Broaden the scope of his interests by bringing him in contact with a wide range of literature in a wide variety of situations?
4. Develop insight into his own personality and problems?
5. Develop discriminating taste and a permanent love for good literature?
6. Express creatively through literature?"

Oral Interpretation

Reading aloud is the most fundamental method of bringing children and literature together. The child's first introduction to literature of necessity is an oral one. Yet how often we hear teachers say, "There isn't time enough to read aloud to children."

Post emphasizes the importance of reading aloud at all levels of learning, from kindergarten into graduate school, as a way of advancing the appreciation of literature. "Reading aloud, more than silent reading, can make clear to young readers such literary elements as the role of the narrator and characters in short stories and the sound structure in verse."[16]

When one examines the importance of a regular "read-aloud period", one may well ask if he can afford not to take the time. If literature is an interpretation of life, and creative reading is an interpretation of literature, it follows that the creative reader is really an interpreter of life through the medium of literature. The teacher sets the standards for reading aloud. Even in the child's beginning experiences with reading, he should be encouraged to read interpretatively as he reads aloud to the group.

If the teacher is to make literature live for children, he must understand the fundamentals of oral interpretation both for himself and for the children he teaches.

It is through the interrelationship of the writer who creates the work of art, the oral interpreter who recreates the work, and the work of art itself that the creative process is set in motion again and again. It is when the oral interpreter recreates what the writer has set down in print that the listener shares in the creative process. The creative process is not completed until the product (the writing) is shared with another human being. In oral interpretation the interpreter becomes a creator in his own right.

When the young child who has faith in his own powers of creating reads aloud, he has such a vivid imagination that all he has to do when he is moved by literature which stirs within him concrete imagery is merely to recreate it. It is not necessary for him to have experienced everything he reads in order to appreciate it. He brings to literature a rich imagination which makes him capable of enjoying much he cannot comprehend or much of what he has never experienced except vicariously. This is particularly true in poetry and accounts for his enjoyment of poems which many times adults are sure he cannot understand. It accounts, too, for his affinity with nonsense poems.

To enjoy poetry one must read with the imagination as well as with the experience, and a child has the imagination.

Intermediate and upper grade teachers are familiar with the re-reaction of the child who brings to his reading the excitement and enjoyment that comes from having first-hand experience with a place, a phenomenon, a person. As the child grows and learns the meaning of specific words, he brings to the reading a more mature power of interpretation. He becomes aware of the power of a word to create a picture or portray an emotion. As he brings to each new experience with literature an explorer's attitude of discovery, new realms of enjoyment and creativity will constantly be opening to him.

To bring to the literature a freshness, a spontaneity, a recreation of the author's inspiration requires understanding, preparation, and skills which create "the illusion of the first time". This is achieved through a combination of understanding the meaning of the work, feeling the emotion, and sharing with another the ideas, emotions, and feelings which originated in the mind of the author and are communicated through the oral interpreter.

The effective oral reader understands the meaning of the literature he is interpreting, is sensitive to characterization, and is willing to experiment until he discovers the interpretation that is "right" for him. When he integrates body, voice, and feelings into an organic whole, he recreates for the listener the ideas, feelings, and emotions of the writer shaded by his own personality.

It is only when the oral interpreter understands the poem through his own background and imagination and recreates it in relation to his own experiences through an interrelation of voice, body, and inner voice that he achieves true creativity.

The intellectual and emotional experiences are joined in oral interpretation of literature. The teacher or child who reads interpretatively is actually interpreting life itself.

Storytelling

Storytelling is one of the best avenues for the development of the imagination and the manifestation of creativity. It is in storytelling that the art of communication receives its greatest challenge. It is here that the good oral communicator is in his element. He senses the need to put his listeners at ease as he invites them to share his inner world of delight, excitement, and suspense. Whether the child participates in this experience as a listener or as a teller of tales is immaterial. In either case he requires the full powers of an awakened imagination coupled with his skill of communication in order to express his creative urge. "Words used by the tale-teller are as colors used by the painter. Forms grow out of the materials of the tale and the teller's reaction to them." Sherwood Anderson proved this statement repeatedly in the tales he told.

There are those in the elementary classroom whose imaginations are so well developed and whose skills in communication so effective that they have within them the ability to hold the group of listeners as they proceed to transport boys and girls to the magic land of make-believe. Through the imagination, the development of the senses, the skill in using words, the ability to paint imagery pictures, the teller spins his tales to the enchanted listeners.

It is in storytelling that the teller who has perfected the requisite skills invites the listeners to come with him and share his inner world, his delight in the story, his excitement at the development, and the mystery of what is about to unfold. He conveys the feeling that there is something here that demands every ounce of the listener's attention and every ounce of the teller's energy, skill, and imagination in the telling. It is here that he can transmit to the listeners a feeling, too, of security and safety as they empathize with the teller.

Encouragement of the child as he tells stories he has heard or weaves new ones out of the figment of his imagination will help him develop confidence in his ability to share with others his joy in storytelling, whether as a weaver of tales, a teller of tales, or as a listener of tales.

In order to develop the ability to tell stories creatively there are certain guidelines.

1. Develop powers of awareness of the world in which you live; use your imagination and improve your ability to communicate what you see, feel, think, and imagine.

2. Select a story which appeals to the basic motivations of the audience. They like stories that deal with other human beings, their triumphs, joys, difficulties, struggles, sorrows, and final victories. They like stories that touch their heart strings, tickle their funny bones, and bring a tear to the eye, a smile to their lips, or a hearty laugh to all the listeners.

3. Always have the story clearly in mind before you try to tell it. Develop the ability to see with your inner eye in order that the audience shares with you your interest, excitement, and pleasure in the story as it unfolds.

4. Organize the story in logical sequence. If it is long, be sure the points are interesting and each leads logically to the next. Build to the climax. Plan the ending.

5. Get the attention of the audience from the beginning by making it interesting right at the start.

6. Don't retrace your steps obviously if you have forgotten some important point. Improvise and bring it in logically, or add it as an "aside" to the audience.

7. Increase your vocabulary so you are never at a loss for words. Don't break the continuity of your story as you search for a word that should be on the tip of your tongue.

8. Enjoy telling the story and work toward improving your ability to hold your audience.

9. Make the characters come alive. Differentiate between the characters by voice and action.

10. Remember that the storyteller is an interpreter, not an actor.

Storytelling can become a motivation for developing the powers of awareness, extending the imagination, improving the skills of communication, and understanding the needs, feelings, and viewpoints of other people, places, and times. It can become, too, a powerful means for revealing social and emotional problems as children identify with characters they discover, create, or recreate. For some the magic of storytelling becomes the avenue for expressing creativity and, thus, for moving toward self-realization.

Preparing a story. The teller of tales does not memorize the story in detail. Rather he learns the sequence of the important events, memorizes specific lines essential to the style, and fills in the details afresh each time he tells the tale.

A story well told is as a series of pictures unfolding. Here is an example of learning a story by pictures. "The Bremen Town Musicians" from the Brothers Grimm is a great favorite with children. Here are the pictures as they develop naturally in the mind's eye of the storyteller.

> An old donkey is the first character to be introduced. He has worked hard all his life. Now that he is too old to work his master has turned him out.
>
> He takes the road to Bremen. He will become a town musician. On the road he falls in with Growler, the old dog, who has fallen on bad times.
>
> Together they travel and meet up with Whiskers, the old cat. No longer able to catch mice, the cat overhears his mistress saying she will drown him.
>
> They come to a barnyard. They hear the old cock on a post bemoaning his fate. He failed to crow "fair weather" for Lady's Day, so he is to be served up for the holiday dinner.
>
> The donkey persuades all of them to come with him to Bremen and organize a band. Their spirits rise. They are no longer outcasts, abandoned by their masters.
>
> That night they take shelter in the woods. The cat and cock go up a tree, the dog and donkey lie down under it. Aloft the cock spies a light. It may offer better shelter.
>
> Making their way cautiously through the woods the four find a barn where robbers are hiding. They are feasting around a table.
>
> "Good fare for us" announces the donkey. It is high time to start trying out their prowess as musicians. On the donkey in turn mount dog, cat, and cock. Together they bark, caterwaul, and crow.
>
> Terrified, the robbers flee. The four take over the barn. They feast, then settle down for the night each in his accustomed spot.
>
> The robbers return. One of them attempts to discover what has happened. As he tries to find his way in the dark he is scratched by the cat, bitten by the dog, clawed by the cock, and kicked by the donkey. Terrified he tells the others that the place is bewitched. That is the last they see of the robbers.
>
> The four, left in peace, end their days in comfort and plenty.

"The Bremen Town Musicians" illustrates every point in a good story; it is brief; it is colorful; language is simple; introduction is brief; it develops logically; it ends quietly after the climax; and it satisfies. The story has a single central theme, and lends itself well to telling and later to dramatizing. Easy to learn and delightful to tell, it is a favorite with children.

When to read and when to tell a story. Picture stories should usually be read from the books because the illustrations are an integral part of the story. Illustrations should be large enough so that the children grouped closely around can see as the teacher holds the book open, faces children at their eye level, and turns the pages as the story unfolds. The teacher should know the story well enough so that he can share it with the children while holding the book for them to see. He should avoid constantly shifting the book from reader to audience. If the illustrations are small, the story should be read first; the pictures can be shown later as the book is passed around or placed on the library table.

Stories which depend upon exact wording of the author, as do some of the fairy tales, should be read rather than told. For example, "The Fisherman and His Wife" is most enjoyed when the verse repeated throughout the tale is given in exact wording.

The teacher should make a point of adding several folk tales each year to his repertoire. Telling stories creates an atmosphere of direct communication with the listeners that cannot be achieved in reading aloud except by the most experienced student of oral interpretation.

Storytelling can be a many-faceted activity in the elementary school. Children who hear a teacher tell stories are often inspired to try storytelling. Various techniques for motivating this type of activity can be used. Children can tell the stories during the story hour to the class or to their group. In individualized reading programs, children frequently tell parts of stories they have read to whet the taste of the listener to read the entire story. Children in the intermediate and upper grades gain valuable experince in storytelling to primary grade children during story hour in the school or public library. Children often write their own stories with a great deal of dialogue as tales to be told rather than read.

Through storytelling children become acquainted with a great variety of literature. In the process of choosing a story to tell they will read many. They should learn to tell them in the storyteller's style. The storyteller tells the tale as if it were happening *now*. Such telling involves the ability to keep in mind the setting, happenings in sequence, problem, characters, climax, and ending.

Experience with Poetry

Poetry is meant to be spoken and heard. Poetry is for enjoyment, not for dissection. Through listening to poetry children become aware of the sounds and symbols, the movement and moods, the rhythm and rhymes. The child, instead of viewing the literature parade from the traditional Mother Goose Rhymes to the stanzas of Auden with boredom, will experience poetry with delight.

If poetry is to become an integral part of the literary heritage, it must be planned as carefully as any other phase of the literature program. It is highly unlikely that a group will casually develop a liking for poetry. Enjoyment is more likely to occur in a classroom in which the teacher himself is enthusiastic about poetry and has a genuine liking for it. He has a wealth of poems at hand that fit the occasion or the mood of the moment. Poetry for young children should be for fun-filled experiences, entertainment and enjoyment, not for teaching rhyme schemes, figurative language, or metrical arrangements. Rather, the teacher pre-plans to recreate the sensory impressions, the word pictures, the mood, and the characterizations.

Reading poetry to the children makes it a pleasurable experience. In an atmosphere in which the teacher creates a mood *before* he introduces the poem, the readiness for listening is there. The teacher may simply talk about a familiar experience related to the poem; he may ask the children to react to the central idea of the poem; he may interest the children with the tongue-tickling words and phrases of the poem; he may have the children predict the content from the title; or he may simply begin to read the poem without a single introductory remark. He creates the mood for listening by setting the tone in the spirit of the poem: light and gay, or pensive; boldly adventurous, or timidly withdrawing; strong and vigorous, or playfully fanciful. It is through the invitation to listen that the child's attitude is shaped. For the teacher the invitation to listen to the poem is in itself a creative act which he should perhaps plan even more carefully than the introduction to other literary experiences.

Children should be encouraged to read poems in the classroom. Young children often learn their poems through repeated saying of their favorites, not through required memorization. Intermediate and upper grade children usually memorize the poems they have in choral speaking simply from the repetition during practice. Children memorize the poems they truly want to remember. Many are committed to memory from the sheer joy of saying them again and again. Pressure to memorize assigned poems has been a contributory factor to the dislike many children have for poetry.

Dramatizing poetry is another way of experiencing poetry. Since poetry is filled with numerous sensory images and rhythm, it is a natural avenue for creative expression. As children act out the poem they gain greater insight into its meaning.

Choral speaking enhances children's enjoyment and appreciation of literature through group experiences with poetry. Like group singing, it builds *esprit de corps,* releases creativity through a group enterprise, and develops children's taste in literature.

Choral Speaking: An Art Form

The chief value of choral reading lies in the process, not in the product. There is joy in feeling, in interpreting, in recreating the mood and meaning of the poet as a part of a group. Choral speaking is again taking its rightful place in the language arts program. It was an integral part of early Greek drama. With the decline in popularity of Greek drama, choral speaking as an art form nearly vanished. Its modern revival came about at the Glasgow Music Festival in 1922 through the work of Marjorie Gullan of London. Its popularity soon spread to Canada and the United States as Miss Gullan lectured and trained verse choirs in both countries.

Many of the basic concepts held by Miss Gullan influence our approach to choral speaking today. New ideas have been added, greater flexibility in method has evolved, but the definition and spirit of Miss Gullan remain with us. Miss Gullan often stated that choric or choral speech is the speaking of various verses or prose by a group of voices. It serves as a medium for creating appreciation of prose and verse as well as a means of teaching good vocal practices without the counter attraction of stage fright. Choral speaking is a means, not an end in itself. As a means it is invaluable; as an end it defeats its purpose.

Informal, incidental choral speaking is universal. The sports cheering section, mass chants in political rallies, congregational prayers, responses to the Mass, responsive readings, pledge of allegiance, toast to the Queen are all examples of choral speaking.

Choral speaking as a creative experience knows no age limit. It is enjoyed by the preschool child and the senior citizen alike.

Interpretation is a group product rather than an individual dictum.

Material should be of excellent literary quality, be within the perceptual understanding and interest of the group, and be objective rather than subjective in nature for the listeners.

The poem, not the director, should be the focus of attention.

Values of choral speaking. Choral speaking has both educational and psychological values. Among the education values are that it develops literary appreciation; stimulates imagination; improves oral reading and comprehension; develops a sense of rhythm; helps in analyzing ideas and abstract concepts; increases vocabulary and perception of meanings; improves speech skills; develops listening ability; and provides a treasure-trove of poems.

Among the psychological values are that it develops poise, enthusiasm, tolerance; provides avenue for achievement; provides outlet for emotional expression in an acceptable form; helps the aggressive child to blend his ideas with others; aids the timid child to build a positive image of self; provides for the individual's need for recognition; builds awareness of value of cooperative enterprise; and develops desirable teacher-pupil rapport.

Division of voices for choral speaking. There are several ways of dividing the voices for choral speaking. An understanding of the effects that may be gained by a creative use of these divisions will enhance the choral speaking experience.

The main divisions or types of choral speaking widely used in the elementary schools are: refrain, antiphonal, unison, sequential (line-a-child or line-a-choir), and dramatized choral speaking.

The *refrain* with solo and group arrangement is one of the most popular types of choral speaking. In the refrain an individual recites the narrative and the group responds with the refrain. At first the teacher may take the solo part and the class responds with the refrain. Later different children read the solo lines.

Antiphonal choral speaking capitalizes on contrasting voices. The most common division is into high and low voices. When the group gains experience, a third division may be added—the medium voices. In the upper grades separate grouping of the boys and the girls utilizes the natural contrasts in their voices. Antiphonal choral speaking is recommended when the poems contain considerable contrast.

Probably the most difficult form of choral speaking is *unison*. Exactness and precision are required in the rate of speaking, phrasing, pausing, emphasis, inflection, and pronunciation. There is little attempt to direct the voice pitch of the group except in the matter of interpretation. Each member of the chorus speaks in his own normal key or pitch, allowing his voice to move up and down the scale in response to the ideas or moods to be expressed. Harmony results from the blend of voices and unity is gained by the group interpretation.

In the *sequential* or line-a-child division each child reads a separate line. Each child should be well acquainted with the whole composition in order to achieve the proper mood and timing. It is essential for the child to respond at the precise and proper time.

Dramatized choral speaking provides an added interest for children to enjoy and experience literature. This form calls for the verse choir to speak while the action is being pantomimed by members of the drama and/or dance group. Dramatized choral speaking integrates the rhythmical movement of modern dance, portrayal of characters of drama, and reading by the speech choir. An understanding of each of these arts enables the teacher to blend them into a worthwhile experience for the children.

In developing such an experience, the entire class plans the arrangement of the material for the verse choir and the choreography for the performers. The procedure is somewhat similar to that of creative dramatics, but has the added dimension of choral speaking. Poems which are highly rhythmical or have an unusual beat that stimulate creative dance movements, ballads, and poems that suggest definite actions are most effective for this activity.

Introducing Choral Speaking in the Classroom

To introduce choral reading into the classroom, a teacher needs sincere enjoyment of poetry, an awareness of the instructional purposes, a knowledge of procedures and materials for choral speaking.

I. PROCEDURES

A. Preparation Before Reading

1. Careful reading of the selection
   a) Enjoy the thought of the poem
   b) Feel the rhythm without falling into sing-song
   c) Watch pronunciation of difficult words
   d) Note where enunciation must be especially clear
2. Noting tempo and tones called for
   a) Reflect the mood of the poem
   b) Plan variety of tempo, tone, and arrangements, emphasis
   c) Note words to be emphasized
3. Marking the lines of the poem to indicate readers
   a) A for all in unison
   b) BC, GC, for Boys' or Girls' Chorus
   c) BS1, BS2, etc., for Solo parts for boys

B. Reading the Poem

1. Start together on the first syllable at a sign from the teacher
2. Speak in natural voice
3. Subdue physical motions and emphasize the vocal inflection

II. MATERIALS

A. Selection According to Purpose

1. For *young* children, an activity rhyme and antiphonal reading

B: Jennie come tie my
Jennie come tie my (tying motion)
Jennie come tie my bonnie cravat

G: I've tied it behind
I've tied it before (tying motion)
I've tied it so often I'll tie it no more (finger shaking)

B: "Where are you going, my pretty maid?" (bowing)
G: "I'm going a-milking sir," she said. (curtsying)

B: "May I go with you, my pretty maid?"
G: "You're kindly welcome, sir," she said.

B: "What is your father, my pretty maid?"
G: "My father's a farmer, sir," she said.

B: "What is your fortune, my pretty maid?"
G: "My face is my fortune, sir," she said.

B: "Then I can't marry you, my pretty maid."
G: "Nobody asked you, sir," she said.

2. For shy children needing individual effort, a poem requiring sequential speaking, sometimes called line-a-child—

S1: Monday's child is fair of face,
S2: Tuesday's child is full of grace,
S3: Wednesday's child is full of woe,
S4: Thursday's child has far to go,
S5: Friday's child is loving and giving,
S6: Saturday's child works hard for a living;
A: But the child that is born on the Sabbath Day
Is fair, and wise, and good, and gay.

3. For most children in elementary grades, a poem with narrative interest, vivid imagery, and strong rhythm

The Pied Piper (selection)

BC: Rats!
They fought the *dogs* and *killed* the cats,
And bit the *babies* in the cradles, (build up)
And ate the cheese out of the vats,
And licked the *soup* from the cooks' own ladles;
Split *open* the kegs of salted sprats, (horror)
Made *nests* inside men's Sunday hats
And even spoiled the women's chats (climax)
By drowning their speaking
With shrieking and squeaking
In *fifty* different sharps and flats.

GC: At last the people in a body
To the Town Hall came flocking:
A: "Tis clear," cried they, "our Mayor's a noddy;
And as for our Corporation—shocking

To think we buy gowns lined with ermine
For dolts that can't or won't determine (anger of mob)
What's best to rid us of our vermin!"

Browning

4. For maturing children, a poem calling for appreciation of imagery and interpretation of thought

The Throstle

GC: "Summer is coming, summer is coming
I know it, I know it, I know it.
Light again, leaf again, life again, love again."

BC: Yes, my wild little Poet
Sing the new year in under the blue.
Last year you sang it as gladly.

GC: "New, new, new new!"

BC: Is it then *so* new
That you should carol so madly?

GC: "Love again, song again, nest again, young man,"

BC: Never a prophet so crazy!
And hardly a daisy as yet, little friend.
See, there is hardly a daisy.

GC: "Here again, here, here, happy year!"
BC: O warble unchidden, unbidden!
Summer is coming, is coming, my dear,
And all the winters are hidden.

Tennyson

5. For children experienced in group reading, a poem that challenges their skill

The Musical Trust

Group 1: There once was a man who could execute
Old Zip Coon on a yellow flute,
And several other tunes to boot,
But he couldn't make a penny with his tootle-ti-too.
One day he met a singular quaint old man
With a great big tuba, who solemnly said,

Group 2: 'I've travelled wide and I've travelled far,
But I never made a penny with my oom-pah-pah."

Groups 1 & 2: Then they met two men who were travelling
With a big bass drum and a cymbal thing
Group 3: Who said, "We've played since early Spring,
But we haven't made a penny with our boom-zing-zing."

Group 1: So the man with flute went tootle-ti-toot,
Group 2: And the other went oom-pah!
Group 3: While the men with drum and the cymbal thing
Went Boom-boom-boom, zing, zing!

All: And they travelled wide and they travelled far
Together they made the welkin ring
With their

Group 1: Tootle-ootle,
Group 2: Ooom-pah!
Group 3: Boom, zing-zing!
All: And oh, the pennies the people fling,
When they hear the
Group 1: Tootle-ootle, ootle-ootle, ootle-ootle, oo
Group 2: Oom-pah, oom-pah, oom-pah, oom
Group 3: Boom, zing-zing, zing-zing!

Author Unknown

Teachers approach choral speaking with a group in various ways. Miss Hart's fourth graders planned to use "Roads" by Rachel Field for choral speaking. The motivation for selecting this poem was their keen interest in the new highway being built past their school.

Introduction: Miss Hart asked the children if they knew any poems about roads. Children responded by recalling poems about roads. Finally Miss Hart said, "The author of 'Roads',* Rachel Field, has some interesting ideas about them. Will you open your books and read the poem?

Discussion: After reading the poem, the children volunteered their impressions. Miss Hart then asked for someone to read the poem aloud. They discussed the mood of the poem, the specific meaning of new words such as quays, bristly, foal. She asked such questions as, "What else can you name that is bristly?" "Where is the mountain?" "How does the poet picture the mountain?" "How does the punctuation help us classify meaning?" Various children then each read a couplet, discussing the couplet after each reading.

"A road might lead to anywhere—
To harbours, towns and quays,"

Children recalled trips they had made to Montreal, Halifax, San Francisco, New Orleans.

"Or to a witches pointed house,
Hidden by bristly trees."

This couplet started discussion of the witch's house in "Hansel and Gretel".

"It might lead past the tailor's door
Where he sews with needle and thread,"

This aroused a discussion about experiences of sewing, and one child contributed the fact that his father had his clothes tailor made. The discussion continued throughout the remaining couplets, concluding with the idea that after adventuring most people wish themselves back home again.

The children were ready now to suggest and demonstrate interpretations for various lines. The group selected the best interpretation and read it together. The children decided on an antiphonal arrangement of the poems by couplets. One child who read very well suggested that there be at least one solo couplet. The group agreed to try it.

The teacher directed the group in their chosen arrangement. They

*From Rachel Field, *The Pointed People.*

then evaluated their performance by responding to such questions as, "Did John's voice express fear of the witch?" "Did our voices show the excitement of searching and finding the treasure?" "Are we satisfied with our arrangement of the poem?" "Did we give the best possible interpretation?

The class decided that on the next day we would try a sequence arrangement in which seven pupils would have solo parts—first, lines 1 and 2, second, lines 3 and 4, third, lines 5 and 6, and so on—with the entire group coming in on a unison arrangement of the concluding couplet. The strength of Miss Hart's lesson lay in the fact that all the children were motivated to participate in the discussion, the interpretation, the reading, and the evaluation.

Children should be given the opportunity to determine the arrangement and the interpretation of poems for choral speaking. They will develop in perception and discrimination under a teacher who allows—even encourages—them to experiment.

Materials

In selecting materials for choral speaking, an acquaintance with a wide range of poems, a knowledge of the interests and needs of children in the group, and an awareness of the special qualities that make a poem adaptable for choral speaking are essential.

Specifically, the material should: be within the emotional and intellectual understanding, and the interest range of the group; have literary value; have a wide appeal; be in a form which is adaptable to choral speaking; be objective rather than subjective in nature.

All of the materials suggested below have been enjoyed by children and teachers in the elementary grades. The arrangements are merely suggestive. An imaginative teacher and his children can modify them for their own group. They are arranged broadly in sequence of difficulty and developmental level of elementary school children. However, specific grade levels are not cited as children vary in background of experience as well as literary appreciation.

Nursery Rhymes provide an excellent means for introducing young children to choral speaking. Take, for example, the well-known rhyme "Hickory, Dickory, Dock". Divide the group into two divisions; one group repeats the "tick-tock", "tick-tock" throughout the poem, while the other group recites the poem in unison.

Hickory, Dickory, Dock

Hickory, dickory, dock
The mouse ran up the clock.
The clock struck one,
The mouse ran down,
Hickory, dickory, dock.

An adventurous group enjoys experimenting with this poem.

Poor Old Woman

1 There was an old woman who swallowed a fly
All Oh, my! Swallowed a fly!
Poor old woman, I think she'll die.

2 There was an old woman who swallowed a spider;
Right down inside her she swallowed a spider;
1 She swallowed the spider to kill the fly
All Oh, my! Swallowed a fly!
Poor old woman, I think she'll die.

3 There was an old woman who swallowed a bird
How absurd to swallow a bird.
2 She swallowed the bird to kill the spider,
1 She swallowed the spider to kill the fly
All Oh, my! Swallowed a fly!
Poor old woman, I think she'll die.

4 There was an old woman who swallowed a cat,
Fancy that! She swallowed a cat!
3 She swallowed the cat to kill the bird,
2 She swallowed the bird to kill the spider,
1 She swallowed the spider to kill the fly
All Oh, my! Swallowed a fly!
Poor old woman, I think she'll die.

5 There was an old woman who swallowed a dog.
She went whole hog! She swallowed a dog!
4 She swallowed the dog to kill the cat,
3 She swallowed the cat to kill the bird,
2 She swallowed the bird to kill the spider,
1 She swallowed the spider to kill the fly
All Oh, my! Swallowed a fly!
Poor old woman, I think she'll die.

6 There was an old woman who swallowed a cow
I don't know how but she swallowed a cow,
5 She swallowed the cow to kill the dog,
4 She swallowed the dog to kill the cat,
3 She swallowed the cat to kill the bird,
2 She swallowed the bird to kill the spider,
1 She swallowed the spider to kill the fly.
All Oh, my! Swallowed a fly!
Poor old woman, I think she'll die.

7 There was an old woman who swallowed a horse!
All She died, of course.

This selection is an excellent example of sequential or line-a-child division.

A modification of the line-a-child division is the cumulative division. Timing is particularly important in this arrangement, as is building up to a climax. An additional person or group is added to each succeeding line of the poem. The entire group will be reading by the last line. An effective example of this type of division is "This Is the House that Jack Built".

In a classroom of thirty pupils, for example, there could be three children added to each line as the poem progresses.

This Is the House that Jack Built

This is the farmer sowing his corn,
That kept the cock that crowed in the morn,
That waked the priest all shaven and shorn,
That married the man all tattered and torn,
That kissed the maiden all forlorn,
That milked the cow with the crumpled horn,
That tossed the dog
That worried the cat
That killed the rat
That ate the malt
That lay in the house that Jack built.

Whistle, Whistle

Boys Whistle, whistle, old wife, and you'll get a hen.
Girls I wouldn't whistle, said the wife, if you could give me ten!

Boys Whistle, whistle, old wife, and you'll get a cock.
Girls I would'nt whistle, said the wife, if you give me a flock!

Boys Whistle, whistle, old wife, and you'll get a coo.
Girls I wouldn't whistle, said the wife, if you could give me two!

Boys Whistle, whistle, old wife, and you'll get a gown.
Girls I wouldn't whistle, said the wife, for the best one in town!

Boys Whistle, whistle, old wife, and you'll get a man.
Girls Wheeple, whauple, said the wife, I'll whistle if I can!

The Psalms are ideally suited for verse choirs. Psalm 24 offers many possibilities for arrangements, antiphonal being of the simplest and most effective.

Psalm 24

Solo-a The earth is the Lord's and the fulness thereof;
the world, and they that dwell therein. For he
hath founded it upon the seas, and established it
upon the floods.

B-2 Who shall ascend into the hill of the Lord?
Or who shall stand in His holy place?
3 He that hath clean hands, and a pure heart; who
hath not lifted up his soul unto vanity, nor
sworn deceitfully.

Solo-b	He shall receive the blessing from the Lord, and righteousness from the God of his salvation.
B-2	This is the generation of them that seek Him, that seek thy face, O Jacob. Selah.
G	Lift up your heads, O ye gates,
B	And be ye lifted up, ye everlasting doors
4	And the King of glory shall come in.
1	Who is this King of glory?
2	The Lord strong and mighty
3	The Lord mighty in battle.
G	Lift up your heads, O ye gates;
B	Even lift them up, ye everlasting doors
4	And the King of glory shall come in.
1	Who is this King of glory?
4	The Lord of hosts, He is the King of Glory. Selah.

The following ballad has possibilities for dramatized choral speaking for intermediate grade children.

Robbers:	See the Robbers passing by, passing by, See the Robbers passing by, my fair lady.
Neighbors:	What have the Robbers done to you, done to you, done to you, What have the Robbers done to you, my fair lady.
House:	Broke the lock and stole the key, stole the key, stole the key. Broke the lock and stole the key, my fair lady.
Neighbors:	How many pounds will set you free, set you free, set you free, How many pounds will set you free, my fair lady.
Robbers:	Twenty pounds will set her free, set her free, set her free, Twenty pounds will set her free, my fair lady.
Lady:	So much money I have not got, have not got, have not got So much money I have not got, my fair lady.
Robbers:	Then off to prison you must go, you must go, you must go, Off to prison you must go, my fair lady.[18]

The teacher and the children read the ballad to decide how to interpret the meaning, mood, and rhythm of the selection. Next they decide about the characterization and discuss the possibilities for dramatizing the ballad. The group first responds with bodily movement and creative interpretation. The teacher or leader may guide the discussion by asking such questions as: "What characters are there in the story?" "What type of people were the robbers?" "How would they stand, walk, move, behave?"

The children "try on" the characters: the Robbers, Neighbors, House, and Lady. The characters who have been selected portray the action while the verse choirs speak the lines.

Upper grade children will find a challenge in the following selection for dramatized choral speaking.

Sir Patrick Spens[19]

The king sits in Dumferling toune,
Drinking the blue-reid wine:
"O Whar will I get guid sailor,
To sail this schip of mine?"

Up and spak an eldern knicht,
Sat at the kings richt kne:
"Sir Patrick Spens is the best sailor,
That sails up the se."

The king has written a braid letter,
And signed it wi his hand,
And sent it to Sir Patrick Spens
Was walking on the sand.

The first line that Sir Patrick red,
A loud lauch lauchèd he;
The next line that Sir Patrick red,
The teir blinded his ee.

"O wha is this has don this deid,
This ill deid don to me.
To send me out this time o' the yeir,
To sail upon the se!

"Mak haste, mak haste, my mirry men all,
Our guid schip sails the morne."
"O say to sae, my master deir,
For I feir a deadlie storme.

"Late, late yestreen I saw the new moone,
Wi the auld moone in hir arme,
And I feir, I feir, my deir master,
That we will cum to harme."

O our Scots nobles were richit laith
To weet their cork-heild schoone;
Bot lang owre a' the play wer playd
Thair hats they swam aboone.

O lang, lang may their ladies sit,
Wi thar fans into their hand,
Or eir they se Sir Patrick Spens
Cum sailing to the land.

O lang, lang may the ladies stand
Wi thar gold kems in their hair,
Waiting for thair ain deir lords,
For they'll se thame na mair.

Haf, owre, haf owre to Aberdour,
It's fiftie fadom deip,
And thair lies guid Sir Patrick Spens,
Wi the Scots lords at his feit.

A more ambitious project for children experienced in choral speaking in which dramatization can be an important element is "The Circus".

The Circus[20]

2 Red and yellow posters on a fence and vacant wall
2 Little green leaflets fluttering in the breeze
2 Boys cry and girls cry from every gate and hall:
G The Circus
B   The Circus
4   The Circus comes to town!
1 Run and get your savings bank;
1 Shake the pennies down!
G Oh Mother!
B Daddy!
3 Please!
2 Please!
1 Please!
B I'll be a good boy, I won't go catching fishes;
G I'll be a good girl, I will wash the dishes!
4 Oh, but we'll be good—Better than your wishes!
G Please Mother!
B Please Daddy!
3 Please!
2   Please!
3   Please!
2 Red and yellow posters, can they all be true?
4 SEE THE GREATEST SHOW ON EARTH
3 See the hip-hip-hippopotamus and the gangaroo
3 (I know—kangaroo!)
2 There is to be a cage of monkeys,
2 And a big gorilla,
1 (That's the way your mouth looked
1 When you took sarsaparilla)
3 And a bunch of diving seals
3 Like a submarine flotilla!
4 GIGANTIC, STUPENDOUS, THE GREATEST SHOW ON EARTH!
G See the daring ladies On the high trapeze,
G1 This one hanging by her hands!
G2 This one by her knees!
G1 There's one hanging by her chin!
G2 (Golly, 'spose she'd sneeze!)
4 EPOCH MAKING, MARVELLOUS! THE GREATEST SHOW ON EARTH

(Calliope effect during this stanza to the tune of "Beautiful Ohio".) *Group 1*—TOOTLE TOOTLE; *Group 2*—Sh- Sh- Sh- Sh; *Group 3—OOM-PAH OOM-PAH OOM-PAH.* (Verse carried by small group of girls with solo boys and girls voice for two characters—Calliope off during their remarks)

I hear the Calliope—that's the big parade.
Off the street, boy! Down in front!
a Wow! Hear the Lion roar! Rats, I'm not afraid!
b Aw, shucks, who's afraid? afraid? afraid?
c I am. I'm afraid!
abc Never mind the wagons. There's nothing there to see
But here comes the horses,
abc Oh gee! Oh gee! Oh Gee!
White horses, white horses, white horses!
a I counted twenty-seven!
b I counted thirty-three!
Solo B "MARTHY 'TAINT SO GOOD A CIRCUS AS WE USED TO SEE"
Solo G "NO HENRY: YOU'RE RIGHT: 'TAINT SO GOOD AS IT USED TO BE
a Here comes the open cages; Hear the Hippo grunt—
b See the tigers! Oh, the lions!
b Watch 'em lash their tails in rage.
c There's a leopard, slinky leopard,
c Pacing up and down his cage.
a Look, there's the monkeys, doing tricks
a On a cunning little stage!
Solo B "MARTHY, THE CRITTERS AIN'T SO WILD AS THE ONE WE USED TO KNOW"
Solo G "NO, HENRY: THAT THEY'RE NOT. WHAT YOU SAY IS SO"
2 Clear the streets there boys! Then put'em down in front!
2 Red and yellow wagons croaking round the turn!
2 Boom tata rat-at-tat-boom!
2 Red and yellow banners in the sunshine burn!

(During this stanza—*Group 3* imitates a band with BOOM-BOOM-BOOM to tune of "Stars and Stripes Forever" until end of the two solo voices.)

2 Red and yellow uniforms—
1 Boom tata—rat-a-tat! Boom tata-rat-tat!
2 Boom! Boom!
1 & 2 Boom tata rat-atat- Boom tata rat-atat!
Tootle tootle tootle tootle
Tootle tootle tootle toot!
Tootle tootle toot!
Boom tata-rat-atat! Boom tat-a-rat-tat!
Boom!
Solo B WELL MARTHY, THAT 'AIRE BAND AIN'T BAD, BUT THEN I'VE SEEN IT BEAT!
Solo G YES, YOU CAN PLAY THE BIG HORN BETTER'N THAT. AIN'T IT MOST TIME TO EAT!
Babble *1* Boom tata-rat-a-tat Boom!
of voices *2* Red and yellow banners waving in the sun!

but each distinct *a* I see the clowns
b I saw them first!
c Oh, golly, see his nose.
d   Keep your eye on the shortest one!
e I wish he'd grin at me!
f   Hey, there, you, look this way!
g Isn't he the cutest thing!
h I'm going to be a clown someday!
i Didn't I?—
j   I say I—
k   No, I saw them first!
2 Red and yellow banners flapping down the street
3 Elephants go plodding plod-plodding in the dust.
2 Boom tata rat tat. Boom tata-rat-tat-
1 tweetle-tee   tweet!
1 Monkeys in the yellow wagons,
3   Tigers in the red,
2 A fat clown, a lean clown,
2   Standing on his head.
2 Show begins in half an hour. Never mind the dust.
1 Zip-yip- yip- yipp-i-oodle
2 & 3 Umph-a-umph-a-umph-a-umph-a-umph!
4 Circus! Circus!
2 Red and yellow tents—get your fifty cents!
3 Boom tata-rata-tat! Boom tata-rat-tat! Boom!

BOOM- TATA-RAT-TAT (1)
BOOM- TATA-RAT-TAT (2)
BOOM (3)
  BOOM (1)
    BOOM (2)
      BOOM (3)
        BOOM (4)

Solo B—MARTHY? I AIN'T SO YOUNG AS I WAS. I AIN'T HALF SO SPRY!
Solo G—HENRY, THE CIRCUS AIN'T TO BLAME. THE CIRCUS IS THE SAME:
B & G THE FAULT IS, YOU AND I
WE AIN'T HALF SO SPRY
YOU HAVE TO SEE A
CIRCUS WITH A
YOUNGSTER'S EYE

4 (loud) Ya-ay-ay! THE CIRCUS.

Choral speaking under the guidance of an enthusiastic teacher becomes one of the most effective ways of helping children develop skills and confidence in oral interpretation while at the same time providing an enjoyable avenue for appreciation of literature. Through choral speaking poetry moves from the inanimate page to become a living force on the tongues of the children who speak it.

Through the verse choir the members of the group will discover and express the essence of meaning and feeling in the subject matter. They all express the kernel which strikes the common responsive chord. They express only what all have recognized and can freely experience.

Experiencing Literature Through Dramatization

Readers' Theater

Readers' theater is a new approach to a conventional custom. We have been "reading plays" for years. What, then, is so new about readers' theater? The challenge in readers' theater is to create the dramatic impact of the theater through the medium of oral interpretation. Nelson defines readers' theater: ". . . [It] involves oral interpretation of a carefully cut script, usually by three to five readers, without memorization, special costume, lighting, props, or sound effects, portraying their roles by means of vocal and facial expression alone, a narrator possibly providing transitional expository lines for clarification . . . ."[21] The reader must enter into the script as spontaneously and enthusiastically as a young child enters into dramatic play. The readers must not leave the audience with the impression that three to five people have been sitting holding scripts, each declaiming his own lines.

The advantages of readers' theater become clear as one experiments with it. Without attention to set, costumes, or special effects, any number of worthwhile, readable plays and stories can come to life in the classroom in a most satisfying manner. The entire class may work concurrently and experimentally within the confines of the ordinary classroom. No special theater or auditorium is needed. For example, a class of thirty-five can readily be divided into seven working groups, each member actively engaged in the reading-interpreting assignment. Children too shy or withdrawn, or lacking in dramatic ability, find readers' theater within their powers, since the holding of the book and the group situation gives psychological support.

Readers' theater is a challenge to the imagination. Since it cannot depend upon the stage embellishments of drama it demands of the readers the ability to paint pictures so vivid that the listeners have the feeling of knowing the characters as real people. As for the listener, it develops his imagination as he visualizes the setting, the characters, and the action.

Readers' theater motivates excellence in reading skill. While there is no demand for acting ability as such, there is a great stress on effective oral interpretation, the use of the voice, and the accompanying facial gestures which make the reading come alive. Plays and stories of quality are much easier to read effectively and are more satisfying to both the reader and the audience. Although the teacher may use stories and plays from the children's reading series, it is important that the script be carefully edited. Which scenes to use, which characters to include, and what kind of narration is best suited to this medium must be guided by such factors as: (1) time allotment for the reading, (2) theme of the play, (3) significant scenes and lines, (4) clarity of plot and characters, (5) variety of mood, (6) balance in the use of readers, and (7) climactic arrangement.

Narration for transitional bridges should be in keeping with the style of the play and should be kept at a minimum. The narrator is an important part of the production, and he must be selected on the basis of his ability to communicate clearly with the audience, catch and hold attention of the audience and clarify and intensify each scene. This implies a sensitive, alert reader with a clear, flexible, and colorful voice.

For readers' theater the intermediate grade teacher will find useful *Thirty Plays for Classroom Reading* by Donald D. Durrell and Alice B. Crossley (Plays, Inc., Boston, 1968). These are tested plays adapted for readers' theater with clear instructions for the teacher and pupils. The teachers for grades five through eight will find equally effective for readers' theater the same authors' book *Favorite Plays for Classroom Reading* (Plays, Inc., Boston, 1965). Each of these books includes a wide variety of adaptations from the classics, comedies, mysteries, historical plays, legends, and holiday material. In content and spirit the plays offer enrichment of ideas, aesthetics, and literary values.

The mechanics of presenting a readers' theater performance are fairly simple. Readers may be seated on high stools behind lecterns, rising or facing front for each entrance and turning around on their stools when they are "off stage". If a platform is being used, readers may be seated in a semi-circle on chairs, turning when offstage, and facing when onstage. Readers may be seated at tables and remain in their places for the entire reading. Readers may stand in a semi-circle arrangement throughout the performance, with or without lecterns. If the cast is large, they may all be seated on the platform, and come forward when they are "on stage".

Upper grade children prefer sitting on tall stools and reading from manuscript placed on music stands.

Readers' theater affords still another avenue for making good literature come alive. It offers training in creative communication and appreciation of theater. It has a powerful appeal to those who enjoy dramatizing literature in any form.

Dramatizing Literature

For many children creative dramatics is the most exciting avenue for experiencing literature—both poetry and prose. "The World and I" might well be the title of a child's creative activity in drama. Play is natural for a child. It is through play that he "tries on life". He moves, he dramatizes his ideas, his feelings, and his imaginings long before he is able to verbalize. Through feeling, thinking, and verbalization he moves from play to "the play".

The child who discovers creative dramatics as an avenue for expression early in life often continues fulfilling his need for creative expression through active participation in little theater groups or solely as a spectator who understands and empathizes with the actors.

One has only to observe a group of children participating in creative dramatics to discover how much it contributes to the total development of the child—mentally, socially, emotionally, and physically.

The child develops his imagination as he thinks out solutions to problems presented in the dramatic situation. He tries on characters, improvises dialogue, decides how a scene should be played, determines the design for the stage setting and evaluates objectively *after* the play is ended.

Because there is no written script, the child is forced to use his imagination. It is as important for him to exercise his creative abilities as it is to exercise his muscles. Creative dramatics offers excellent opportunity for creativity in action.

The child develops socially through working effectively with others in the group, understanding the character he is portraying, appreciating cultural differences, and becoming increasingly aware of and sensitive to the feelings and needs of others. He soon learns that it is not enough to "walk through" the role. He must relate it to seeing and feeling if he is to be truly creative. He learns, too, that each member of the group has a responsibility to support and enhance the contributions of others and not to "steal the scene".

The child grows emotionally as he expresses his feelings, releases his tensions, and develops psychological stability through identifying with the characters he portrays. This is one avenue which permits him legitimately to release tensions and express negative emotions. He tries on new roles, identifies with desirable characters, and cooperates in group activities which are fun, exciting, and/or demanding.

For some, creative dramatics provides the first esthetic impact. They discover that beauty lies within them, waiting to be released. Here the child—the potential philosopher, artist, or poet—discovers the miracle of beauty, not alone in the unusual but in the commonplace.

The child gains in poise, muscular coordination, and bodily skills through participating in creative dramatics. As he portrays various characters, he must show that he feels the tensions, understands and depicts the characteristics of the strength of the evil giant, the power of the king of beasts, the fury of the hurricane, the agility of Robin Hood or Tarzan, and the weakness of the lame beggar treking along the country road. He develops command of his entire body as he creates a variety of characters and/or phenomena.

Through dramatizing literature a child becomes aware of the conflicts that confront others as well as himself. He grows in appreciation of drama as a means of self-expression.

Key Concepts in Creative Dramatics

Involvement is the essence of creative expression. In expressing creativity through any medium total involvement is important. In creative dramatics it is essential. The individual needs to feel, think, imagine, and enter into the experience completely. A total synchronization of thought, feeling, motion, and voice is required if he is to *become* the character he chooses to portray.

The creative process, not the product, is important. In creative dramatics it is the *experience* that is important, not the finished product. The creative process is concerned with ideas, the awareness of a situation, the development and the communication of feelings, attitudes and truths. Children proceed through the phases of the creative process from that moment of awareness to the final phase of communication to the group. Originality is rewarded, ideas are welcomed, thinking is stimulated as children are motivated to enter into the feelings as well as to think the thoughts of the characters with whom they are identifying as they express themselves creatively.

Creative dramatics develops understanding and empathy. Before one can portray a character, he must understand the character, emotion, and cause-and-effect relationships of actions. He must concern himself with the motivations of the character. Understanding and empathy come as a result of projecting one's self into the thoughts and feelings of others. It is through this increased insight into emotions which are common to all people that empathy grows. Children readily, through their power to imagine, *become* the character they portray.

Originality, not imitation, is the heart of creative dramatics. All children are creative. If this creativity is recognized and valued, children will be challenged to express original ideas growing out of their unique pattern of development. Originality may manifest itself in sequence of events, bodily movement, creative design of dance or rhythm, original turn of a phrase, stage design, or costuming. As the child develops confidence in *his* ability to think, feel, express, and communicate creatively, the inhibitions with which he may begin are shed.

The classroom climate contributes to the creative process. The optimum classroom climate is one of psychological safety which says, "We create conditions in which each child may succeed, but we also give him freedom to fail." In a climate of security children are quick to try out ideas, to respond, to experiment, to discover. Where originality is welcomed, children are valued, ideas are treasured, the shackles of conformity are released and children will create.

Creative dramatics is a vehicle for developing pupil-teacher rapport. In an encouraging environment in which children and teacher express themselves creatively, there is a minimum of misunderstanding, conflict, and negative behavior. As the teacher participates in the creative process, a bond of understanding and mutual respect is forged.

Ways to Dramatize Literature

Dramatic play. Dramatic play is the make-believe play of the young child. Spontaneous free activity, it boasts no plot, needs no audience, has no sequence. The child *is*, for that moment, the person, animal, or thing with which he has an impulse to identify. He shifts instantaneously from person, to animal, to thing.

Pantomime. Pantomime may be defined as the expression of thoughts, feelings, and emotions through bodily action. It is non-verbal communication. It is used alike by the uneducated and the literate.

Creative dramatics. Creative dramatics is an experience in which a group of children enact a situation based on life or fiction through creatively projecting themselves into the lives of the characters. It is distinguished from dramatic play by having a plot that builds to a climax. Since it is improvised it is never played the same twice.

Playmaking. The term playmaking is often used interchangeably with creative dramatics. It includes all forms of improvisation in drama such as dramatic play, pantomime, puppetry, and story dramatization. Impromptu, informal, and creative, it may be based on literature, history or it may be original in idea, plot, and character.

Puppetry. Puppetry, a form of creative dramatics, is especially valuable for the shy child who shrinks from performing in front of an audience. Here he can express his ideas and emotions through the voice and actions of the puppets. There are many types of puppets from the very simple stick puppets to the elaborate marionettes. One of the oldest forms of puppetry is the shadow play. "In the East it usually takes the form of a performance in which flat cutouts, made of leather, tin, or cardboard, are held between a light and a cotton sheet."[22] The shadow play spread throughout the East. In Java actors took the place of the marionettes in the shadow plays. From this developed the dance-drama of the Orient. Teachers and children have unlimited possibilities for creativity through the use of puppets and shadow plays.

Children's drama. Children's drama differs from creative dramatics in form, purpose, and character. It involves a prepared script, a formal presentation, and memorization of set lines. The story is written by children or by adults for children. The actors are selected on the basis of ability to portray the characters. The settings and costumes should be authentic. The audience is entitled to a finished performance.

Children's theater. Children's theater is primarily for child audiences whereas creative dramatics is primarily for the child who participates. It provides dramatic productions with adult actors. Through the medium of drama, children gain an understanding of life values drawn from the human experiences they see on the stage. The chief value of children's theater is the vicarious enjoyment each child experiences as a member of an audience viewing a finished performance.

Guiding Children in Dramatizing Literature

He who would guide children to create drama must above all remember what it is to be a child. "It is to be so little that the elves can reach to whisper in your ear; it is to turn pumpkins into coaches, and mice to horses, lowness into loftiness, and nothing into everything, for each child has its fairy godmother in its own soul."[23]

The teacher's ability to recapture this make-believe of childhood is essential if he would be truly successful in guiding children in dramatizing literature. In addition, the teacher needs to know the procedures he can use. Although no two experiences are ever the same, in each creative dramatic experience there is a basic procedure. It involves creating a mood, developing an idea, planning the action, playing the story, and evaluating the experience. The creative process in drama, as in other avenues of expression, begins with cognition and ends with communication.

Creating the mood. The teacher may create the mood by capitalizing on the season, a holiday, a current interest, a recent experience, a favorite story or poem, and so forth. Teachers frequently use a picture, music, a question, or an experience to arouse immediate interest. If an eerie mood is demanded, for instance, a slightly darkened room will contribute indirectly toward this feeling as will music of a mysterious nature.

Developing an idea. Once the mood is created, the children are ready to develop the idea, discuss the situation, and/or share the story. Given freedom of expression and time to develop ideas, children often reach unexpected heights in creativity. The successful teacher contributes by presenting the material with such enthusiasm that it reaches inside the children.

Planning the action. Before children can dramatize, they should plan the characters they deem essential to the play. Through pantomime and/or dialogue, they try out their ideas singly or in groups trying to *feel* the characters they portray. The cast is chosen from among the children who have tried on the characters spontaneously, joyously, and with understanding. Whether the poem or story requires one scene or several, the group will find the playing proceeds more smoothly if they determine ahead of time the number of scenes, the characters who appear in each scene, and the tone of conversation which will move the story along to the climax.

Playing the story. For children the moment for playing the story is the most exciting. Once these initiatory steps are decided, the play should begin and move along without interruption to the finale. Each player is responsible for staying in character; each member of the audience is responsible for being a good listener. When the play is finished the audience should show appreciation in relation to the effectiveness of the performance.

Evaluating the experience. Evaluation which begins with words of commendation and recognition leads to greater enjoyment and satisfaction on the part of the players and to greater appreciation on the part of the audience. "That was really good for the first playing." "I was very frightened when the ogre appeared." "What a pompous character the king was!" "You were certainly having fun creating the story." Such comments can precede more specific evaluation. There is *always* something good that can be found in a creative experience.

Specific elements to evaluate include characterization, pantomime, rhythmic movement, dialogue, teamwork, audience reaction, pacing, use of space, and time spent in preparing for the play. Praise for individual contributions is important, too. Such remarks may be, "Diane, you have given us excellent ideas today." "Genevieve, I'm glad you are thinking things through so well today." "Billy is the most imaginative person today. I am always surprised to hear the new ideas he comes up with." "John was such a pompous King. He used his own ideas in walking as he did." "I like the way Mary is original in her ideas. She was different from any godmother that we've had."

The following is one good scheme for evaluation.

General.

1. What did you think made our play interesting?
2. What did you think was particularly good about the way we played it?
3. How might we improve it?

Characterization.

1. Were the characters in our play thinking and feeling like the characters in our story?
2. Were they convincing?
3. How did they make you feel they were real?
4. Did everyone stay in character throughout the entire scene?
5. Did the characters interact with each other?

Action.

1. Was the play interesting to watch?
2. If you did not know the story, could you tell what was happening?
3. Did we keep the story moving?
4. How do you think we might have helped it to move along a little faster?

5. Did we crowd the characters into too small a space or did we use the entire space?

Story.

1. Was the story exciting and interesting, or did it seem ordinary?
2. Did our play tell the story?
3. Did we have a good climax?
4. Did you like the way it ended?

Dialogue.

1. Did the dialogue help to move the story along, or did the characters talk about things not needed in the play?
2. How did the characters help each other to keep the dialogue moving?
3. Did the dialogue seem to stop sometimes?
4. Did the dialogue seem real?

Cooperation.

1. Did we all work together to create the scene?
2. How did the audience help?
3. How did the characters who were off stage part of the time cooperate for the good of the play?
4. Did any character call attention to himself rather than help to make the play important?
5. Was there a good spirit among the cast?
6. How did the players help each other?

Pacing.

1. Did the play move along or did it drag?
2. If it dragged, what was the reason?
3. How might we improve it next time?

Voices of Players.

1. Did the players project their voices so that the audience could hear without straining?
2. How might the players improve their voices next time?

Audience Participation.

1. Did the audience take the responsibility of being good listeners?
2. Did they help us do our best work?
3. Did they laugh in the "right" places?

Time in Preparation.

1. Did we spend enough time in planning the play?[24]

The test of a creative dramatics experience is the eagerness with which the children want to engage in such an activity again and again. Given a teacher who understands the creative process and who is willing to experiment with techniques for releasing children's creativity through creative dramatics, children's imagination will be fired. When children are filled with the desire to create, when they have something they want to say, and when they have a teacher who is eager to accept their expression, creative dramatics is a natural outlet for developing appreciation of literature.

Guiding Creative Dramatics Experiences

Creating the mood. As Halloween approached a group of primary children began bringing in pumpkins, masks, and other objects symbolic of the coming holiday. Miss Penney capitalized on their interest by reading a number of Halloween poems and stories. One day she darkened the room and played the recording of "Hall of the Mountain King" from the *Peer Gynt Suite* by Grieg. Jimmy commented, "This number makes me feel spooky."

Developing the idea. Ann said, "It makes me think about the poem of the goblin who became an elf." "That's 'The Goblinade[25]'," said George. "I know that poem. Let's play it." The children eagerly agreed and asked Miss Penney to read it again.

The Goblinade

A green hobgoblin
Small but quick,
Went out walking
With a black thorn stick.

He was full of mischief,
Full of glee,
He frightened all
That he could see.

He met a little maiden
In the wood;
He looked as fierce
As a goblin should.

He crept by the hedgerow,
He said "boo".
"Boo," said the little maid,
"Where are you?"

"What," said the goblin,
"Aren't you afraid?"
"I think you're funny,"
Said the little maid.

"Ha!" said the goblin,
Sitting down flat.
"You think I'm funny?
I don't like that."

"I'm very frightening,
You should flee."
"You're cunning," she said
"As you can be."

Then she laughed again,
and
Went away.
But the goblin stood
there
All that day.

A beetle came by, and
"Well?" it said:

But the goblin only
Shook his head.

"For I am funny,"
He said to it.
"I thought I was alarming,
And I'm not a bit."

"If I'm amusing,"
He said to himself,
"I won't be a goblin,
I'll be an elf."

"For a goblin must be a goblin
All the day,
But an elf need only
Dance and play."

So the little green goblin
Became an elf,
And he dances all day
And likes himself!

Florence Page Jaques

Planning the action. Immediately following the reading Miss Penney said, "Now we're ready to plan the action. Have you been thinking about what goblins are like? How is this goblin different from other goblins? What could he do that shows he is different from other goblins? Do you remember what clues the poem gave us about the goblin?"

The children were vociferous in their responses. Among the suggestions were: goblins are mischievous; they could all be goblins; they could pretend they were carrying little black sticks; they could look for creatures to frighten. At first everyone was a goblin. Each had a different sized stick and tried in different ways to frighten the various creatures. Soon Ralph suggested that some could be the different kinds of creatures that live in the woods and that they could act out ALL the poem. Mary suggested that they needed a little girl and said, "Please, can I play that part?" Charles volunteered to be the beetle. The children suggested that Tony should be the goblin as he was the most frightening goblin in the group.

Miss Penney at this point interjected, "How many scenes should we have to make the action complete?" Obviously the children were "old hands" at creating a setting and immediately suggested four scenes. Scene one: The goblin meets the creatures in the woods. Scene two: Goblin meets maiden. Scene three: Goblin meets beetle. Scene four: Goblin becomes an elf. Peter volunteered to be the stage manager.

Playing the poem. "Characters in your places," said Peter in a stentorian voice. "Curtain ready!" Miss Penney motioned to Mabel and June who had not yet developed enough courage to play roles, but who liked to be the "curtain", to take their places at the center of the stage. "Curtain!" cried Peter. A hush fell on the audience as Mabel and Jane parted the "curtain" by each walking to her side of the room. The play was on! The children applauded spontaeously when the play was over and the "curtain" was again drawn. The children were now ready to evaluate their work.

Evaluating the experience. "Did we create a spooky mood?" "How well did we communicate our ideas?" "Did the characters feel their parts?" "What did you like best about the action?" were some of the questions that Miss Penney asked. Many details of action were commented on. The goblin received special praise. Miss Penney discouraged negative criticism. However, positive suggestions for ways in which the play could be improved by the next group to play it were encouraged. Among the responses were: "The little girl could have been doing something in the woods like picking flowers or gathering nuts." "The various creatures could have let us know who they were by the way they moved about." "The dialogue could have carried the story along better." "The beetle could have said 'Well' so the goblin knew he wasn't scared." "The goblin could have gone to see the fairy queen and request her to change him to an elf."

Playing the story. A story can also be the basis for a creative dramatics experience, as illustrated in this excerpt from *Creative Drama and Improvised Movement for Children* by Janet Goodridge.*

> An adaptation of the story 'The Magic Pot' provides a good example of the kind of story to use with this age group. It has a well defined, easily understood structure, it has humour, it has contrasting characters, and a variety of group activity. It is a drama-story easy for the teachers to organize and develop unobtrusively by being the narrator. With older or more experienced classes one or more of the children could be the narrator. Or, of course, the narration can be omitted altogether.
>
> Briefly, a drama version of the story could be this:
>
> A man finds a dirty old pot in his yard. Much to his surprise it begins to speak: 'Clean me and polish me and put me on the fire!' The old man is mystified and takes the pot in to his old woman who decides of course the dirty pot must be cleaned. As soon as the pot has been cleaned it speaks again: 'I skip, I skip!' The old folk ask, 'Where do you skip?' The pot replies: 'I skip to the house of the Rich Man, where all his cooks are making puddings!'
>
> And off goes the pot on his journey to the Rich Man's house. When he arrives there he makes his way to the kitchen and says: 'I'm cleaned and I'm polished and I want to be filled!' and because the Pot is Magic all the Rich Man's cooks put their puddings into the pot.
>
> Back goes the pot to the Old Man and the Old Woman who are very pleased to see all the tasty puddings. After they have eaten as much as they are able and have put the rest in the larder, the Pot speaks again: 'Clean me and polish me and put me on the fire!' The Old Woman does so. Then: 'I skip. I skip!' 'Where do you skip?' 'I skip to the house of the Rich Man where he's picking his apples!' And off goes the pot on his journey to the Rich Man's house. When he arrives

*Reprinted from *Creative Drama and Improvised Movement for Children* by Janet Goodridge, Plays, Inc., Publishers, Boston, Mass, U.S.A. 02116. Copyright © 1970 by Janet Goodridge. Published in Britain under the title *Drama in the Primary School* by Heinemann Education Books Ltd., London.

there he makes his way to the orchard and he says: 'I'm cleaned and I'm polished and I want to be filled!'

So all the Rich Man's apple pickers put their apples into the Pot. Back goes the Pot to the Old Man and the Old Woman, who are very pleased to see all the juicy fruit. After they have eaten as much as they can and stored the rest, the Pot speaks again: 'Clean me and polish me and put me on the fire!' The Old Woman does so. Then: 'I skip, I skip!' 'Where do you skip?' 'I skip to the house of the Rich Man, where he's counting his money!' And off goes the Pot again, on his journey to the Rich Man's house. When he arrives there he makes his way to the counting house where the Rich Man is himself and says: 'I'm cleaned and I'm polished and I want to be filled!'

So the Rich Man and all his servants in the counting house pour as many golden pieces into the pot as it can hold. When it is full, the Pot goes off again back to the Old Man and the Old Woman who are overjoyed to have the money.

The next day, the Pot says again: 'Clean me and polish me and put me on the fire!' The Old Woman does so, wondering where the Pot will be off to this time.

'I skip, I skip!'

'Where do you skip?'

'I skip. . . . OVER THE HILLS AND FAR AWAY!' and off goes the Pot. When the old people see the Pot going away, they follow, but he goes too fast for them. The cooks and the apple pickers, the servants and the Rich Man himself all try to catch the Pot, but he goes too fast for them too. So they return home so tired that they fall asleep.

An alternative beginning is: 'An old man and his wife are so poor that all they have left is one cow.' The old man goes out to sell it. Leading the animal along the lane, he meets a man with a pot who suggests he makes an exchange with the cow. At first the old man is reluctant, but then the Pot speaks: 'Buy me! Buy me!' So although feeling rather awkward, the Old Man agrees to part with his cow. Afraid of what his wife might say he ties the Pot to the cow post in the byre for the night.

In the morning his wife is very upset, but she is just in the middle of scolding her husband when much to their surprise the Pot speaks: 'Wash me and scour me and put me on the fire!' etc. etc.

Also, any alternatives can be used for the Rich Man's servants' occupations. For instance, the Pot could visit the barns where corn is being shovelled and stored, or the cellar where wine is being stamped out of the grapes, etc. etc., according to the movement experience which the teacher feels his class would enjoy and benefit from.

A theme which can run through the play is that of the cruel Rich Man: he has caused the poverty of the old couple and at the end the Pot either goes after him and chases him away, or he is so annoyed with the Pot taking so much of his goods, that he grabs at the Pot and, getting hold of it, is lifted up into the air. The Pot flies away with the Rich Man who is never seen again. This ending is more interesting but more dfficult for the children and teacher to organize.

The procedure with a story such as this is:

1. Tell the story, arousing interest and imagination.
2. (Preferably after some time has elapsed, e.g. the next day) in the movement lesson introduce movements needed in the story (with opportunities in (a)-(c) and (e) for partner work for children ready for this), e.g. (a) busy pudding baking: the use of imaginary large sized

basins which need several people to lift them and pour from them, carrying large boxes or bags of sugar and currants and tipping them into the pudding mixture; large scale stirring movements; stoking the oven; getting fuel for the oven; rolling out the pastry, etc.
(b) Climbing, stretching and picking fruit, carrying baskets, loading baskets
(c) Precise money counting, heaving sacks of gold along the ground; pouring coins into containers
(d) Washing, scrubbing, scouring, polishing a pot
(e) Pulling along an unwilling cow to market
(f) Being the Pot and going on journeys as the Pot
(g) Being the Rich Man
(h) Being the Old Man or Woman
3. Encourage the development of spontaneity.

The whole class should be given an opportunity for movement experience as indicated above which can have appropriate sound accompaniment. Then, with teacher as narrator, the story can be acted, bringing more life and action to it than in the original story. The children can at first all be everything as mentioned (the teacher giving plenty of time for the movement to happen) and then if they are ready for this development, they can choose which group to be in. In the latter case the structure of a play will emerge, and the groups can be placed around the floor of the hall—cottage, kitchen, orchard, counting house—allowing for plenty of journey space between each group. Each time the Pot is filled the servants concerned are in its power and realize too late what they have done—they can try to catch the Pot, but in vain and return to their work.

The Rich Man could come at the last moments of Pot filling and try to stop them and/or the Pot—also in vain. However, the final climax must be felt strongly so each time the servants and/or Rich Man could get nearer to catching the Pot. (If several children would like to be Pots, Rich Man, or Old Men/Women, there is no reason why they should not be.) Incidentally, the Pot(s) will have to be encouraged to take a circuitous route from cottage to Rich Man's house, rather than direct steps across the room. The children can be helped to follow the departure of the Pot into the air, focusing round the room and up and away until they imagine the Pot a dot in the distance. (If the teacher thinks the word 'skip' for the Pot's travelling might lead to stilted movement, of course he could change it to 'hop', 'run', or even 'hop-skip-jump' might be preferred.)

Children's own plays could evolve from discussion in answer to 'Where did the Pot come from?' 'Why?' 'When?' Also the children could speak during the action or make up words for the various scenes, e.g. dialogue between the Old Man and Woman, servants calling after the Pot or a chant for the counting house scene—'We count the money, count the money, clinkety, clinkety, clink', was one refrain made up for a chant, with accompanying percussion noises of money clinking, by a group of seven-year-olds, when they worked on this play with me.

Suggestions for the Teacher

Capitalize on the imagination of the children. As the children *feel* the mood of the story, situation, or poem they are dramatizing, encourage them to express their ideas. Stir their imaginations to see more in the situation or story than appears on the surface. Use skillful questions to draw out *their* ideas. Instead of suggesting what to do, ask questions which will motivate *them* to think. As children express themselves in creative dramatics ideas will flow freely.

Give children freedom in playing. Every player should have a feeling of success each time he makes a sincere effort. Try to choose some children in each cast who are uninhibited, free, and imaginative together with some who are shy, withdrawn, and less imaginative. Such questions as, "Who would like to be the__________?" "What role would *you* like to play?" often motivate even the shy child to volunteer. Try to involve as many children as possible in each playing. Once the child has selected his role, let him develop it in his own way. The teacher may have to give some suggestions to the timid child, but the characterization should finally be the child's own.

Children's Drama

Children's drama, too, can be a creative experience. It is also possible to be creative even though the child is involved with a written script. The child becomes familiar with the role through putting himself in the character's place and seeing the world through the character's eyes. Such complete identification aids in understanding the meaning of the lines. Thus he is able to speak the lines so that they flow naturally and spontaneously. When children's drama is a truly creative process the child puts himself in the place of the character, experiences the world of the play, and integrates actions and speech—thereby communicating the author's intent to the audience.

Suggestions for the Teacher

Selecting the play. In selecting a play (1) the script, (2) limitations of the stage, (3) the players, and (4) the audience must be considered. The *script* may be written by a professional playwright or by the children themselves. It should have literary merit; students should not be forced to memorize lines that have no literary value. It should hold the interest through rehearsal; it should have universal appeal. It should be chosen by the teacher and group on the basis of a predetermined criterion.

Staging limitation. The size of the stage, the lighting equipment, and the resources for designing and building scenery must be taken into consideration. With the interest in circle theater little attention need be given to staging or scenery and yet an effective performance may be presented. If children are talented in art and there is time to build scenes, fairly elaborate settings can be designed which enhance certain plays—for example, *Heidi* and *The Emperor's New Clothes.*

An extremely important consideration is the talent, number, and availability of the *players*. There are plays that hinge upon the talent of a single player—a ballet dancer, a singer, or an emotional actress. If there is no such individual available, it is well to select another play. Ideally, all rehearsals should be during school time. If there are few children who can rehearse after school, and that is the only time possible, it will be necessary to choose a play with a small cast. If only one or two boys can stay after school, the play chosen will have to have a predominantly feminine cast.

The final factor to consider is the *audience*. The director should select plays that the viewers will find interesting.

Children can be brought into the play selection group and given an opportunity to read, evaluate, and vote on the play to be selected—under the guidance of the teacher.

Organization. The creative director knows what he wants the play to say; but through discussion, he guides the children into understanding the roles they interpret. He does not *show* them how to interpret. Directing is not telling. It is getting the player to understand and interpret the role as he "lives" it. He *is* the character.

If the play is complicated the director needs an assistant. He also needs committees to take care of business, staging, lighting, prompting, costuming, properties, ushering, and scenery. The director organizes and coordinates the functions of these committees.

Casting. The director, or the director and committee, casts the players. Usually the time for tryouts is posted and those interested come at the prescribed time and read lines from the play. Players are chosen on the basis of ability for the part, reliability, cooperation, and willingness to work hard, take criticism, and work with the other members of the cast for the success of the play.

Rehearsals. Everyone must know what is expected of him, what is to be accomplished by the group, and how the director hopes to accomplish it. The director must be thoroughly familiar with the play before rehearsals start. He studies the setting, the historical and geographical background, the meaning of the lines, the life of the author, and the subtleties and allusions in the play. He discusses the characterizations with the pupils. Then they read through the lines to get an idea of the voices they will use. At a later rehearsal they will "walk through" the lines holding their scripts, and block out the action. The characters mark the general action on their scripts so that they can memorize action and lines together.

Guides for acting.

1. The actor should stay in character at all times.
2. The actor should not move on someone else's lines unless the move is a definite part of the action.
3. The actors must react to each speaker.
4. The actors should not turn their backs to the audience unless the action demands their doing so.
5. The actors should project to the back row of the auditorium but sound as if they were talking to someone on stage.
6. Exit lines should be delivered usually as the actor reaches the door exit.
7. The actor should remember that the stage is a picture and try to keep the "picture" in balance at all times.

Both informal and formal drama have value for the child. Informal drama emphasizes the process not the product, the expression rather than the impression, the journey rather than the destination. Formal drama stresses the product, the performance, and the destination. Children can be creative in both. The teacher who would guide these activities must understand the developmental nature of creative dramatics and relate it to the needs of the individual.[26] [27]

Concluding Statement

Enjoyment of literature through meaningful creative experiences should lead into a deepening appreciation of literature. Appreciation requires more complex skills and greater knowledge than mere enjoyment. It depends upon our conscious effort to deepen our understanding by discovering all we can about the specific literary work—its form, style, structure, development. As involvement is combined with knowledge, appreciation is deepened. Appreciation does not "happen". It must be developed.

The teacher always keeps in mind that the most important objective of the program is the child's experience with literature itself.

The program in children's literature in the elementary school is concerned with helping pupils read widely, develop taste, and grow in appreciation of the best in literature. The teacher must be familiar with the literary heritage and know how to capitalize on children's interests to bring children and books together. The attitude of the teacher should motivate interest in reading for enjoyment and growing in appreciation. An accumulation of knowledge will not burst into flame. The teacher must do something with the knowledge and that is what experiencing literature is all about.

Among the meaningful creative experiences with literature are: oral reading by the teacher and pupils, storytelling by teacher and individual children, choral speaking, readers' theater, creative dramatics, and children's drama. Using these creative experiences as a basis, the teacher may proceed through units organized around basic types of literature, to develop skill in critical analysis which leads to appreciation of a constantly widening scope of literature and the language in which it is communicated.

A good literature program will provide children with a rich and lasting experience with the world's best literature, develop a permanent interest in reading a wide variety of materials for enjoyment and appreciation, help children experience literature in such a way that contributes to creative growth and personal enrichment, and offer opportunities for the development of discrimination and taste in literature. To achieve such objectives, the teacher must make literature an integral part of creative communication and creative communication an integral part of the total school curriculum.

References

1. Harold Taylor, "The Aims of Education," *College English,* 18:249-50, February, 1957. By permission of the National Council of Teachers of English.
2. Lewis M. Terman and Margaret Lima, *Children's Reading: A Guide for Parents and Teachers,* rev. ed., Appleton & Co., New York, 1931.
3. George W. Norvell, *What Boys and Girls Like to Read,* Silver Burdett Co., Morriston, 1958.
4. Helen Rogers and H. Allen Robinson, "Reading Interests of First Graders," *Elementary English,* 40:707-11, November, 1963.

5. Richard C. Nelson, "Children's Poetry Preferences," *Elementary English*, 43:247-51, March, 1966.
6. Grace Pittman, "Young Children Enjoy Poetry," *Elementary English*, 43:56-9, January, 1966.
7. Edward J. Shaffer and Richard C. Wilson, "Reading Comics to Learn," *Elementary School Journal*, 66:81, November, 1965.
8. Elinor McCloskey, "A Study of the Free Reading Interests of Sixth Grade Negro Boys," unpublished doctoral dissertation, Columbia University, New York, 1966.
9. Ray H. Simpson and Anthony T. Soares, "Best-and-Least-Liked Short Stories in Junior High School," *English Journal*, 54:108-11, February, 1965.
10. Ray H. Simpson and Anthony T. Soares, "Interest in Recreational Reading of Junior High School Students," *Journal of Reading*, 11:14-21, October, 1967.
11. James R. Squire "English Literature," *Encyclopedia of Educational Research*, The Macmillan Company, New York, 1969, pp. 461-73.
12. See Zena Sutherland, "Sense of Sensibility," *Saturday Review*, 29:42, July 19, 1969.
13. Dora V. Smith, "The Children's Literary Heritage," *Elementary English*, 228-35, 1964.
14. Nancy Larrick, "Children and Poetry," in Mary Columbo (ed.), *State Supervision of English and Reading Instruction*, National Council of Teachers of English, 508 South Street, Champaign, Illinois, 1967, p. 65.
15. *Primary Education in Scotland*, Her Majesty's Stationery Office, 1966, p. 118.
16. Robert M. Post, "An Oral Interpreter's Approach to the Teaching of Elementary School Literature," *The Speech Teacher*, 20:167, September, 1971.
17. From *Introducing Choral Speaking*, Portland Public Schools, Portland, Oregon.
18. By permission from Loren E. Taylor, *Choral Drama*, Burgess Publishing Co., Minneapolis, 1965, pp. 25-6.
19. A modern translation may be found in Arbuthnot's *Anthology of Children's Literature*, 1961, p. 19.
20. Pearl William Walton from *Southern California Journal of Speech*, October, 1932, pp. 32-5.
21. Margaret Nielson, "Have You Tried Reader's Theatre?" in Leslie Irene Coger and Melvin R. White (eds.), *Studies in Reader's Theatre*, S and F Press, Vanderveer Station, Brooklyn, 1963, p. 9.
22. Kenneth Macgowan and William Melnitz, *The Living Stage*, Prentice-Hall, Inc., Englewood Cliffs, 1955, p. 299.
23. Sir Francis Meynell, *The Works of Francis Thompson*, Vol. III, Burns, Oates and Washburn, Ltd., 1913.
24. Lillian M. Logan, *Teaching the Young Child*, Houghton Mifflin Co., Boston, 1960, pp. 344-345.
25. Florence Page Jaques, "The Goblinade" in Winnifred Ward, *Stories to Dramatize*, Children's Theatre Press, Anchorage.
26. Geraldine Siks, *Children's Literature for Dramatization*, Harper and Row, Publishers, Inc., New York, 1964.
27. See Grace Layman (ed.), *Educational Drama: Classroom Activities*, Part I *Perception*, Part II *Relaxation*, Part III *Movement*, Part IV *Improvisation*, The Committee on Publications, Faculty of Education, Memorial University of Newfoundland, 1971.

Index

Index